Strategic Warfare in Cyberspace

Strategic Warfare in Cyberspace

Greg Rattray

The MIT Press
Cambridge, Massachusetts
London, England

This book was set in ITC Garamond by Best-set Typesetter Ltd., Hong Kong.

Printed and bound in the United States of America.

Library of Congress Cataloging-in-Publication Data

Rattray, Gregory J., 1962–
    Strategic warfare in cyberspace / Greg Rattray.
       p. cm.
    Includes bibliographical references and index.
    ISBN 0-262-18209-2 (hc.: alk. paper)
    1. Information warfare. 2. Strategy. 3. United States—Military policy. I. Title.
  U163 .R29 2001
   355.3′43—dc21   00-046061

Contents

I am an unlikely "digital warrior." When I entered the Air Force Academy in 1984, I was determined to become a fighter pilot after getting my degree in aeronautical engineering. As it turned out, I quickly realized that understanding the interaction of technology, national security policy, and military power held a much greater fascination for me, and I majored in political science and history. I subsequently spent much of the first portion of my military career as an intelligence officer dealing with problems of nuclear deterrence, arms control, and the challenges presented by the proliferation of weapons of mass destruction.

As the Soviet threat waned and the United States remained engaged on the world stage, I became aware that the nature of conflict and the role of the U.S. military was likely to shift dramatically in the coming years. After returning to Colorado Springs to teach at the Air Force Academy, I happened upon the Tofflers' *War and Anti-War* in a local bookstore. I was captured by their depiction of the forces that were beginning to reshape aspects of our profession and felt compelled to teach cadets and myself more about this transformation. I soon realized that grasping the subject required a greater breadth of knowledge than provided by my past academic and military background.

When the Air Force allowed me to return to graduate school to pursue a doctoral degree, I decided to deepen my exploration of "information warfare." Study and research provided me insight into the fundamental import of the subject while increasing my concern about how we understand this emerging form of conflict. Working on the Headquarters Air Force staff for two years only reinforced my conviction that we must ground our policy decisions, military reorganization, and resource investment in historical context and detailed analysis. These interests and experiences afforded me the opportunity and motivation to write this book. I hope it helps others comprehend the complexities, opportunities, and challenges presented for waging strategic warfare in cyberspace as we enter the twenty-first century.

I am deeply indebted to a great number of people for their accumulated learning, insight, and support. While a Ph.D. student, the committee that supervised my work provided an invaluable mix of wisdom and support. Professor Anthony G. Oettinger, Director of the Program on Information Resources Policy at Harvard University, offered a continual source of stimulating ideas, challenging feedback, and a deep well of reassurance about the value of my work. Professors Robert L. Pfaltzgraff, Jr., and Richard H. Shultz, Jr., at the Fletcher School of Law and Diplomacy at Tufts University were unflagging in their encouragement, patience, and guidance. I also received a great deal of support from others who gave their time to improve this work. The following individuals provided feedback on significant portions of this book: Dr. Dan Kuehl, School of Information Warfare and Strategy at National Defense University; Larry Rothenberg, Institute for Foreign Policy Analysis; Capt. Jason Healey (USAF) of the Joint Task Force—Computer Network Defense; and my parents, John and Virginia Rattray. Captain Richard P. O'Neill (USN ret.) was willing to engage me in a series of discussions that greatly improved my focus on the most important issues for the nation's future security and insight into how the defense bureaucracy was coping with these challenges. It would be impossible to thank everyone else whose insights and challenges improved my work. Those not mentioned here know who they are and have my thanks.

I also need to thank the editorial staff at MIT Press and, in particular, Michael Harrup. His eye for detail and sense of clear exposition have strengthened the argument presented in this book while the easing the reader's task of trying to understand a complex subject.

I must also thank two institutions for their support in my midcareer sojourn. The Department of Political Science at the Air Force Academy sponsored my Ph.D. program. The U.S. Air Force Institute for National Security Studies provided generous financial support to conduct research trips and interviews instrumental to the analysis and factual support in this work.

Finally my wife, Francesca, has my greatest thanks and love. She dealt graciously with countless inconveniences and frustrations. Even more, she unstintingly provided a daily sounding board for my ideas, an eloquent pen to improve my prose, and a partner who made the experience greatly more worthwhile.

Of course, no matter how much help and guidance others provided, errors of fact or interpretation are my sole responsibility. The reader must also remember that the views expressed in this work are the personal opinions of the author and do not represent the official positions of the Air Force, the Department of Defense, or the government of the United States.

Introduction

An Emerging Challenge

The United States is leading the world into an era often called "the information age." Developments such as the cellular phone, satellite TV, and personal computers with modems, faxes, the Internet, and the World Wide Web have made the world a much more interconnected place. The growing convergence of computer and communications technologies utilizing digital means for processing, transmitting, and storing information has revolutionized activities across society. The media have jumped on the bandwagon with almost daily features about the new world of "cyberspace." The business pages are filled with news about telecommunications and information technology deals and mergers. The U.S. government is endeavoring to create national and global "information infrastructures" while trying to decide on its role in regulating an explosion of activities in new areas. Many commentators have focused on how "information highways" will be paved with gold and good intentions. However, as the international environment adjusts to the end of the Cold War, a realization has dawned that this information age will also have a dramatic impact on security affairs.

As the Soviet empire fell into decline, a number of events highlighted the growing influence of information technology on national security. Successful integration of information systems in a sophisticated conventional force capability proved decisive during the spectacular U.S. military successes in the Gulf War. U.S. military involvement in Somalia and the Balkans has demonstrated the influence of increasingly global media coverage. At home, activities of hackers and systems failures affecting crucial institutions, such as the air traffic control system, the banking system, and the Department of Defense, have increased worries that a whole new type of national security threat may be emerging. Information systems may now serve as both weapons and targets.

Increasingly, these emerging national security concerns receive attention under the rubric of "information warfare." Futurists have outlined how a transition to a "third wave" information-based society has crucial implications for waging both war and peace. As the millennium ended, the Department of Defense and the military services were working vigorously on incorporating the impact of the information age into doctrine, operations, and organizations. At the same time, potential adversaries face a huge challenge in confronting the U.S. on the conventional battlefield and may pursue new approaches for waging conflict with the world's sole superpower.

Adversaries might choose to disrupt information infrastructures as a means of achieving political influence vis-à-vis the United States. Warnings of an impending "electronic Pearl Harbor" have been sounded. By 1996, the U.S. National Security Strategy stated that "the threat of intrusions to our military and commercial information systems poses a significant risk to national security."[1] Congress has focused attention on possible threats from digital attack and called for presidential action. Efforts by the Justice Department and FBI to deal with terrorism also now stress the "cyber" threat. Growing concern about this threat resulted in a Presidential Decision Directive addressing critical infrastructure protection. U.S. national security institutions enter the twenty-first century adapting to the challenges posed by potential threats arising from growing reliance on information infrastructures. The significance of commercial ownership and cooperation for developing an effective U.S. national strategy to protect such infrastructures has been recognized. However, the establishment of adequate mechanisms to bridge public and private interests has confronted difficult trade-offs such as that involved in establishing a national policy on the control of encryption technology.

Yet in all this flurry of interest and activity, frameworks for evaluating the capabilities of international actors to conduct conflicts based on attacking information infrastructures remain underdeveloped. Treatments of information warfare are overly broad. The "information warfare" rubric includes concepts ranging from straightforward destruction of communications between commanders and fielded military forces to "simula-warfare," positing that computer simulations could prove to an enemy that it would lose a real war. Most discussions make little distinction between activities traditionally segregated by categories of peace and war.

Discussions of information warfare also make little reference to the history of strategic warfare. Numerous studies detail the ease of attacking information infrastructures and the widespread availability of digital means for attacks. These studies, however, pay little heed to the relationship between ends sought and the utility of information warfare as a means of achieving these ends. Moreover, those who address information warfare generally gloss over the hurdles presented in adapting organizations and policies to deal with new technologies. The challenges of understanding fast-changing information infrastructures developed and operated outside the control of military institutions receive little attention. Academic treatments of, and government efforts to deal with, information warfare inadequately address trade-offs involved between commercial competitiveness, personal rights, and security concerns. The advent of an information age clearly has pervasive effects on security issues and its impact on warfare must be analyzed in a holistic fashion.

Overview of Contents

This work represents an effort to grapple with strategic information warfare as a distinct concern for the United States and other actors in the international system at the dawn of the twenty-first century. The analysis endeavors to provide frameworks to enable a deeper understanding of an emerging national security concern.

Chapter 1 delineates the possibility of "strategic" information warfare as a new means by which international actors may wage war by directly attacking an adversary's information infrastructures. My work focuses on the use of remote digital attacks as a new type of micro force for adversaries engaged in conflicts that can be analyzed with constructs used to address conventional and nuclear force. Distinctions are drawn between strategic information warfare and other types of information-based competition, such as financial crime and economic espionage. This chapter also provides a baseline regarding the nature of information infrastructures and their significance for the United States as potential centers of gravity for strategic attack. The analysis identifies implications of salient features of advanced information infrastructures—complexity of interconnection; civilian-sector technological leadership; dynamic change; and global interconnection, operation, and production—for the conduct of strategic information warfare. The chapter concludes by identifying how the distinct nature of the cyberspace operating environment will potentially affect warfare in this realm.

Chapter 2 extends past conceptualizations of the use of force and strategic warfare. A review and critique of the theoretical development and historical record provides an understanding of the beguiling aspects of strategic warfare and the difficult challenges involved in achieving desired effects. This analysis serves as a basis for establishing a framework of four enabling conditions for the successful conduct of strategic warfare:

1. Offensive freedom of action
2. Significant vulnerability to attack
3. Minimal prospects for retaliation and escalation
4. Ability to identify and target an adversary's centers of gravity

The second half of the chapter details potential strategic information warfare technologies and approaches. The analysis highlights factors such as the dual-edged nature of strategic information warfare tools, the speed of interaction, ambiguities involved in characterizing digital attacks, and the crucial role of intelligence. The chapter concludes with a framework for evaluating the utility of strategic information warfare.

Chapter 3 addresses the requirements for creating organizational technological capability to wage strategic information warfare. The nature of technology and technological mastery are analyzed to provide a baseline for delineating these requirements. Five facilitating factors for the establishment of organizational technological capability are identified:

1. Supportive institutional environment
2. Demand-pull motivation
3. Management initiative
4. Technological expertise
5. Learning ability

Using this framework the chapter analyzes a set of challenges previously overlooked for establishing strategic information warfare capabilities. Tools for digital warfare may be easy to acquire and unleash, but establishing offensive capabilities requires developing the requisite expertise to target attacks and assess the political consequences of information infrastructure disruption. Defensively, difficult challenges face the coordination of activities normally considered outside the national security realm. The political character of an actor will heavily influence its information infrastructure development and vulnerability to strategic information warfare. Crucial policy trade-offs for the United States will involve economic competitiveness and individual rights. Nonstate actors have significant advantages in minimizing their vulnerabilities to digital attack.

Chapter 4 steps back in time to analyze U.S. efforts in the period between World War I and World War II to develop strategic thinking, military organizations, and the technological capability to conduct long-range bombing as a means for prosecuting strategic attacks against industrial infrastructures. The facilitating factors developed in chapter 3 help explain why, despite strong doctrinal advocacy and the rapid emergence of technological tools, the overall adaptation of the U.S. military establishment to leverage strategic bombing capabilities occurred slowly. The halting process of organizational change and struggles for resources necessitated that the Army Air Corps sharpen its ideas about the possibilities and requirements for U.S. airpower. The analysis details how a convergence of doctrine, organizational structure, and technological conditions in the mid-1930s resulted in a strong commitment to strategic air warfare based on unescorted, daylight precision bombing by U.S. airmen. This commitment largely blinded U.S. air leaders to experiential lessons in China, Spain, and England, as well as to technological developments such as radar and capable interceptors. Doctrinal "lock-in" initially proved very detrimental during U.S. strategic bombing campaign against Germany in World War II.

Chapter 4 also describes how effective defenses and early failures faced by the United States were eventually overcome through a combination of good fortune, material superiority, and effective adaptation. Utilizing the framework of the four enabling conditions developed in chapter 2, underlying problems are identified as lessons that should inform those who would consider waging strategic information warfare attacks. Lessons include the great difficulty the United States had in identifying German centers of gravity and understanding the adaptability of German infrastructures to air attack.

Chapter 5 provides a detailed analysis of U.S. efforts in the period between 1991 and 1999 to develop the necessary doctrine, organizations, and technological capability to conduct strategic information warfare, focusing on the defensive concerns. Important similarities to the previous development of air bombardment capabilities are pointed out. The possibility of strategic information warfare has severely stressed military institutions to fit new missions into organizational constructs and reallocate limited resources. Continuing inquiries about the new form of warfare, such as those conducted by the Defense Science Board, Congress, and the President's Commission on Critical Infrastructure Protection have increased understanding of U.S. vulnerabilities to digital attacks. The forces driving commercial technological leadership, ownership, and control of the cyberspace environment have hampered efforts to reach a consensus regarding the proper balance of national security, commercial competitiveness, and privacy concerns. The analysis in chapter 5 delves into the role played by commercial technology producers in pouring weak technological foundations for U.S. infrastructure protection and the importance of properly managing limited human resources in dealing with decentralized defensive tasks.

The concluding chapter endeavors to bring together the principal threads of theoretical analysis and experiential lessons. The book concludes with recommendations for strengthening U.S. strategic information warfare defenses.

Note

1. White House, *National Security Strategy* (Washington, DC: Government Printing Office, 1996), 13.

ONE
Delineating Strategic Information Warfare: Key Concepts, Boundaries, and Operating Environment

War is a matter of vital importance to the State; the province of life or death; the road to survival or ruin. It is mandatory that it be thoroughly studied.

—Sun Tzu, opening statement of *The Art of War*

The global security environment has undergone a massive transformation. At the beginning of the 1990s, the United States emerged as the clear winner from decades of military competition with its major rival, the Soviet Union. The defeat of Iraq in the Gulf War cemented its position as the world's sole military superpower and reluctant manager of the global balance of power. Yet hopes of establishing a new international order have gone largely unrealized. Conflicts internal to states have emerged in places such as Somalia and the former Yugoslavia, less directly related to United States interests as well as less tractable to the employment of traditional military forces. The spread of weapons of mass destruction and the incidence of terrorism have raised serious concerns regarding the defense of the homeland that for the better part of two centuries was a strategic sanctuary.

The confluence of the information age with the ascendancy of the United States in global security affairs has also captured the attention of many. Similar to their response to the emergence the airplane and the tank during World War I, national security strategists and military planners now wrestle with the impact of new information technologies. The use of information technology to enhance traditional forms of warfare has become integrated into military thinking. United

States dominance in the Gulf War sprang in large measure from its ability to leverage sophisticated information-based systems. Discussions of a "revolution in military affairs" highlight the decisive nature of "dominant battlefield knowledge" and "information superiority" on the battlefield. Others warn of the loose control and fast diffusion of these technologies.

Cyberspace has become a new realm for the exchange of digital information to conduct commerce, provide entertainment, pursue education, and a wide range of other activities. Simultaneously, the last decade of the twentieth century has seen the rising concern over a new form of conflict, usually referred to as information warfare. Defense establishments must adapt to the new environment. Information systems now serve as both weapons and targets of warfare. The prospect of warfare in cyberspace presents military opportunities but also involves significant new national security risks. As the world's leading military power and the society most reliant on its information systems and infrastructures, the United States may well face adversaries searching to find new weaknesses.

Conceptualizing Strategic Information Warfare

Efforts to understand national security concerns in the post–Cold War period have grappled with the significance of the information age for military operations. The Persian Gulf War was quickly labeled the first "information war."[1] For U.S. commanders in that war, providing timely, precise information to military forces posed as much of a challenge as executing operations once targets were identified. Strikes against Iraqi information infrastructures blurred previously clear boundaries between activities categorized as "tactical" and those conceived of as "strategic." The United States attacked Iraqi command, intelligence, and communication networks to blind its opponents on the battlefield and disconnect the population from its leadership. After the war, discussions of a "strategic" level of information warfare emerged as the United States became concerned about its own vulnerabilities. Yet we do not yet adequately understand the objectives, actors, and types of activities that constitute this new form of warfare. My approach to analyzing information warfare begins with a clear delineation of the phenomenon we will examine in this book.

The scope of activities that constitute information warfare has provided a source of widespread disagreement. Definitions of information warfare range from those narrowly focusing on the improved use of electronic means to achieve advantage on conventional battlefields to very broad definitions conceptualizing information warfare as any effort to affect information systems in peacetime and wartime. The tendency since the 1990s both outside and inside the U.S. government has been to use overarching definitions that capture a wide range of activities.

Academic treatments of the subject usually begin with a broad construct. George Stein proposes a typical approach in stating that "information warfare, in its largest sense, is simply the use of information to achieve our national objectives."[2] John Alger, former dean of the National Defense University's School of Information Warfare and Strategy, has suggested a definition of information warfare drawn broadly enough to include financial crime, intelligence gathering, and terrorist- and state-based threats.[3] Georgetown University computer security expert Dorothy Denning has attempted to deepen the definition of information warfare to encompass "information in any form and transmitted over any media, from people and their physical environments to print to telephones to radio and TV to computers and computer networks."[4]

The national security community has also wrestled with capturing the essence of this emerging concern. The Air Force initially defined information warfare in 1995 as "any action to deny, exploit, corrupt or destroy the enemy's information and its functions; protecting ourselves against those actions; and exploiting our own military information functions."[5] During the late 1990s, efforts within the larger U.S. military establishment also expanded the concept under the rubric of "information operations." According to authoritative Joint Staff doctrine published in late 1998, the term "information operations" refers to "[a]ctions taken to affect adversary information or information systems while defending one's own information and information systems. Information Operations (IO) apply across all phases of an operation and the range of military operations and at every level of warfare. Information Warfare is IO conducted during times of crisis and conflict to achieve or promote specific objectives over a specific adversary or adversaries."[6]

Yet the U.S. intelligence community continues to use the label "information warfare" to characterize foreign programs and capabilities in this realm.[7] The Justice Department and FBI understand "information warfare" in terms of protecting critical infrastructures from cyberattack.[8] RAND Corporation analyst Martin Libicki has identified seven separate categories represented in the myriad discussions of information warfare: command and control warfare, intelligence-based warfare, electronic warfare, psychological warfare, hacker warfare, economic information warfare, and cyberwarfare. Libicki concludes that "slicing, dicing, and boiling the various manifestations of information warfare produces a lumpy stew."[9]

In trying to capture the essence of a new phenomenon, analytic constructs are crafted to avoid excluding any relevant pieces. Definitional breadth, however, inhibits the creation of boundaries to guide analysis. General usage of the term "information warfare" in the late 1990s rarely draws distinctions between categories of peace and war, often even suggesting that such categories no longer exist. The term has been used to describe hostile activity involving information ranging from acts by individual hackers against NASA's computers to the potential for a massive, coordinated attack by one state against another to accomplish significant political objectives similar to the nuclear Single Integrated Operation Plan.[10] This work focuses, within much more limited boundaries, on how the emergence of cyberspace and its significance across public- and private-sector activities in the United States and elsewhere may create a new form of strategic warfare.

As concern about information warfare grew in the 1990s, analysts began to examine how adversaries could strike directly at the U.S. homeland using digital means. One major locus of concern has been the potential of states and transnational corporations to wage economic competition through attacking and exploiting an opponent's information systems. Alvin and Heidi Toffler have described the possibility of transnational corporations emerging as global gladiators willing to use disruptive information attacks against competing firms. Winn Schwartau also raises similar concerns under the label "global information warfare," which he says may be "waged against industries, political spheres of influence, global economic forces, or even against entire countries."[11] Others within the U.S. government have picked up on this theme. The President's Commission on Critical Infrastructure Protection reported in spring 1997: "Threats from unscrupulous economic competitors are of concern throughout the U.S. business community. Industrial or economic espionage—targeted against proprietary information—is a major concern. Design, pricing, marketing, bid strategy and similar data have already been compromised using cyber tools. Resulting damage to companies and global competitiveness can be significant."[12]

At the extreme, such conceptualizations argue that economic competition is replacing warfare as governments' primary concern. Vicious—but bloodless—information wars in which corporate databases are savagely raided, manipulated, or destroyed for advantage in the global marketplace are held up as the wave of the future. Concern in this area often includes the use of information exploitation by state intelligence agencies in support of private corporations. Nations accused of waging such "strategic information warfare" against the United States include France, Japan, and Israel as well as other more traditional foes such as China and Russia. Numerous efforts to review the roles and missions of the U.S. intelligence community in the mid-1990s explicitly raised the question of whether U.S. intelligence agencies should also proactively engage in information warfare activities. Although the United States seems to have rejected such an offensive mission for its intelligence agencies, concerns remain about adversaries' use of the techniques associated with information warfare for the purposes of economic competition.[13]

Economic competition waged through information warfare could have strategic significance because of its potential effect on large numbers of people and the ability of states and others actors to conduct activities globally. Yet actions to achieve economic impact without direct, physical coercion such as embargoes are not generally considered warfare. Those analyses detailing the use of information attacks for economic advantage generally ignore the negative fallout resulting from clear identification of the perpetrators. Such discussions also leave fallow the potential to turn economic disruption into political influence rather than financial gain.

This book will not directly address activities intended solely as tools of economic competition as strategic information warfare. Use of economic espionage sponsored by states or commercial enterprises has a long history predating the emergence of the digital information age. Although recent advances in information technology have significantly changed espionage and commercial competition, these activities can continue to be distinguished from those categories of competition classified as warfare. Large-scale efforts to disrupt, damage, or destroy a competitor's information systems or resources would quickly begin to fall outside the accepted boundaries of economic competition in the marketplace. A tightly concealed form of disruptive economic guerrilla warfare may yet prove possible, but the risks seem very high, and the competitive advantage to be gained seems self-limiting.

More relevant to traditional approaches to understanding strategic warfare, analyses have also recognized that efforts to disrupt the underlying information systems and networks that underpin a country's military operations may allow its adversaries to affect other crucial sectors of societal activity. A 1994 Defense Science Board (DSB) Task Force study, "Information Architecture for the

Battlefield," went beyond a narrow look at military operations to articulate two types of information-based conflict. The DSB used the terms "information in war" to discuss enhancing battlefield operations through improved use of information resources and "information warfare" to refer to the potential use of information attacks against an opponent's computer-controlled telecommunications networks, databases, enabling software, and computers, which underpin both modern commerce and military operations. The following year, the Department of Defense commissioned the RAND Corporation to study strategic information warfare. The resulting report found that "[t]he United States has substantial information-based resources, including complex management systems and infrastructures involving the control of electronic power, money flow, air traffic, oil and gas. . . . Conceptually, if and when potential adversaries attempt to damage these systems using information warfare techniques, information warfare inevitably takes on a strategic aspect." RAND concluded that information warfare techniques "render geographic distance irrelevant; targets in the continental United States are just as vulnerable as in-theater targets."[14] In describing their concept "InfoWar," Daniel and Julie Ryan specifically set out boundaries for analyzing strategic information warfare. They state:

> Information warfare is, first and foremost, warfare. It is not information terrorism, computer crime, hacking or commercial or state-sponsored espionage using networks for access to desirable information. These are all interesting and dangerous phenomena that individuals, corporations and governments face in today's connected on-line world, but they are not InfoWar. InfoWar is the application of destructive force on a large scale against information assets and systems, against the computers and networks which support the air traffic control systems, stock transactions, financial records, currency exchanges, Internet communications, telephone switching, credit records, credit card transactions, the space program, the railroad system, the hospital systems that monitor patients and dispense drugs, manufacturing process control systems, newspapers and publishing, the insurance industry, power distribution and utilities, all of which rely heavily on computers.[15]

The national security community continues to try to characterize a strategic level of information warfare. Two major defense think tanks published studies in 1998 that focused on cyberspace as a new realm for conflict. The RAND study *Strategic Information Warfare Rising* built on its earlier work with an eye to identifying key policy issues for guiding how the United States manages the opportunities and challenges presented by this new form of warfare. The study distinguishes between two generations of strategic information warfare:[16]

> First-Generation SIW: SIW as one of several components of future stragegic warfare, broadly conceptualized as being orchestrated through a number of warfare instruments.

> Second-Generation SIW: SIW as a freestanding, fundamentally new type of warfare spawned by the Information Revolution, possibly being carried out in newly prominent strategic warfare arenas (for example, economic) and on time lines far longer (years versus days, weeks or months) than those generally or at least recently, ascribed to strategic warfare.

The Center for Strategic and International Studies also issued a task force report entitled *Cybercrime . . . Cyberterrorism . . . Cyberwarfare.*[17] The report spans a vast range of concerns posed by digital attacks, with one chapter specifically on the issues of strategic information warfare. The report stresses the need to understand and address concerted digital attacks by sophisticated opponents requires development of national policies and intelligence capabilities that did not currently exist. Analysis of information warfare and its strategic dimensions have become a growth industry within certain national security and academic circles.

What can we glean from the existing conceptions of strategic information warfare? First, these discussions have usefully moved beyond the common usage in the United States of the term "strategic" during the Cold War, when the term dealt solely with the use of nuclear weapons with intercontinental range. Discussion of strategic information warfare has since moved appropriately away from a single class of weapons delivered at a specific range; instead, usage now recognizes that a variety of means (including digital techniques designed to disrupt information infrastructures) can create "strategic" effects, independent of considerations of distance and range. The increasingly important role of communications and computer systems in conducting a broad range of significant activities across the public and private sector has been stressed.

These discussions, however, only implicitly address how attacking information infrastructures will accomplish war aims for state or nonstate actors in a conflict. Additionally, those grappling with the concept of strategic information warfare generally ignore past frameworks for analyzing warfare. Indeed, those addressing the topic often assume that cyberspace constitutes a wholly different environment in which the rules have all changed. Past conceptions of what constitutes warfare and its strategic dimensions need to be analyzed to determine how existing frameworks can usefully be applied or modified to understand the development of new means for waging such conflicts.

This book addresses strategic information warfare as a means for state and nonstate actors to achieve objectives through digital attacks on an adversary's centers of gravity. Additionally, the analysis herein focuses on how information infrastructures as centers of gravity require those who wage strategic information warfare to understand the specific offensive and defensive challenges of the cyberspace operating environment. I ground this work on the assumption that mining the intellectual capital of the past can improve our understanding of present challenges.

Using the Past to Understand the Future

German theorist Carl von Clausewitz's thesis that the political objective to be attained is the essential factor that determines the military objective pursued and the amount of effort required serves as a point of departure for the discussion in the book. "War," he states, "is politics by other means, never something autonomous." Though often misconstrued to be an advocate of total war, Clausewitz clearly establishes that the nature of a conflict varies with motives and political context. The notion and long history of waging wars through limited military means for limited political objectives has been a constant thread throughout strategic thinking, carrying forward to the modern day. As Clausewitz notes, "We see then that if one side cannot completely disarm the other, the desire for peace will rise and fall with the probability of further successes and the amount of effort these would require."[18] In analyzing the utility of force for states in the nuclear age, Thomas Schelling asserts that "most situations, even wars, are some combination of mixed incentives for cooperation and competition, not all out efforts to annihilate."[19] The measured relationship between political objectives and the use of military means must thus be kept in the forefront of analysis regarding the development of thinking about strategic information warfare.

However, this exhortation does beg two important questions: "Whose objectives?" and "What is meant by 'political' objectives?" In answering the first question, most past strategic thinking concentrates on the interaction between sovereign states. Theorists such as Clausewitz focused exclusively on military force as a tool of state power wielded only by governments to achieve the ends of the state in clearly defined "wars." However, the type and numbers of actors that can develop and use significant military force have changed. More recent efforts to analyze the nature of actors in the international system refer to "soft-edged" states as the scope of the sovereignty of states declines. Many have high-lighted the rise of a variety of nonstate actors with both the coherence and capability to act on the international stage.[20] The advancement and global dif-fusion of transportation and communications technologies has been a principal enabling factor in this development. Specifically, the increasing utilization of information technologies by state and nonstate actors makes both potential users and targets of strategic information warfare.

We must also address the question posed about "political objectives" to analyze the behavior of actors within an anarchic system. Traditional interna-tional relations theorists have focused on political objectives related to the self-interested goals of individual states, such as securing territory, establishing freedom of commerce, accessing resources, or pursuing the less tangible goal of national power. Similarly, strategists such as Clausewitz viewed conflict through a lens that saw wars as being fought by strongly established political entities with clear borders. More recent work by historians Martin van Creveld and John Keegan has analyzed the nature of objectives pursued by force in past political systems not necessarily dominated by states.[21] Both argue that a number of other interests, including justice, religion, and group survival also explain the use of force by organized groups. These analyses highlight how the pursuit of differ-ent objectives can result in dramatic asymmetries in motivation. Actors trying to ensure group survival may take a completely different approach to the selection of military means than actors pursuing limited political objectives. Also, such actors may seek to create damage and pain for adversaries without expecting changes in near-term political behavior of the targets. Certain actors, such as reli-giously motivated terrorist groups, may be willing to conduct a conflict over a very prolonged period of time. My analysis in this book acknowledges that actors may have a wide range of motivations in choosing to use force, including strate-gic information warfare. Rather than separating political from other categories of motivations, this work generically refers to political objectives as the wide range of motivations and desired end states of actors considering the use of force.

Differentiating Infrastructure Attacks and
Perception Management

This book also distinguishes between information warfare attacks intended to disrupt and destroy information infrastructures and efforts focused on manipulating the media and target audience perceptions. The latter category is sometimes referred to as "perception management." The use of information to influence an opponent's political decisions, undermine national will, and disrupt economic activity has a long history dating at least back to the ancient Greeks. In the twentieth century, Adolf Hitler's use of propaganda and fifth-column techniques contributed to his early, unopposed successes in Austria and Czechoslovakia. During the Cold War, the Soviet Union pursued an active disinformation campaign to undermine domestic support for U.S. defense spending and the cohesion of the NATO alliance. The United States has also engaged in such activity under the labels "public diplomacy" and "covert action." Benjamin Franklin is known to have forged documents discrediting the British during the Revolutionary War.[22] More recent U.S. efforts in this realm include Radio Liberty broadcasts to undermine communist regimes as well as support for democratic parties in western Europe during the 1940s through payment to journalists to publish articles fed to them by the CIA.[23]

The information age has created, through the increasing intrusiveness and speed of media reporting, new tools for practicing perception management. The rise of television and technologies enabling global reporting have made perception management a crucial dimension of conflicts in the second half of the twentieth century, beginning with Vietnam and continuing through the withdrawal of the U.S. combat forces from Somalia and combat operations in the former Yugoslavia.[24] The growing ease of receiving outside information through audio and video cassettes and fax machines played a major role in such tumultuous events as the fall of the Shah of Iran, the decline of communist rule in the former Soviet Union and the uprisings in Beijing's Tiananmen Square. In the late 1990s, China and Singapore endeavored to manage Internet access by their citizens to limit the intrusion of ideas perceived as corrosive to their societies.

The perception management aspect of information warfare is receiving an increasing level of attention within information warfare discussions. The possibility of real-time "hijacking" of television broadcasts and use of the Internet by political rebels and activists raises important issues regarding the conduct of conflict in the late twentieth century.[25] The United States could use its sophisticated knowledge of such tools as "soft power" to influence other actors.[26] As such, the information age presents new challenges to understanding the role of public diplomacy, media regulation, and propaganda. This book, however, focuses on efforts to achieve influence in a conflict through disrupting and destroying an opponent's information infrastructures.

Digital Warfare

I reject the assumption that strategic information warfare should be treated as a completely new phenomenon because of the "virtual" or nonphysical nature of operating in the cyberspace environment. The term "cyberspace," coined in 1984 by William Gibson in the science fiction novel *Neuromancer*, came into heavy usage during the early 1990s. Many commentators on the world of cyberspace stress that it is a fundamentally different place from the normal physical world of interactions. Nicholas Negroponte of the MIT Media Lab has asserted that the fundamental particle is no longer the atom but the binary digit, or bit, a unit of data usually represented as a 0 or a 1. *Time* described cyberspace as being "like Plato's plane of ideal forms, a metaphorical space, a virtual reality."[27]

Cyberspace, however, is actually a *physical domain* resulting from the creation of information systems and networks that enable electronic interactions to take place. The 1s and 0s of bits have physical manifestations in the state of electrons in a semiconductor gate or the waveforms of light passing through a fiber-optic cable. Human activity in this environment requires conscious direction and employment of energy. The transmission of computer images through the Internet requires only a small amount of energy compared to flying a plane to a given destination. However, both require the creation of a package of material to undertake the journey: an understanding of how to travel through the environment, of the protocols and regulations established for such travel, and of how to interact with other systems upon arrival. Those conducting information warfare must rely on knowledge of the physical principles and systems governing the information environment, just as traditional soldiers, sailors, and airmen require an understanding of the environments in which they conduct warfare.

Three Types of Information Infrastructure Attacks

Potential adversaries can conduct strategic attacks on information infrastructures using a variety of mechanical, electromagnetic, and digital means as follows:

• *Mechanical attacks.* Information systems and networks have long been targeted by mechanical methods of disruption and destruction during war and peace. Command and control systems can be bombed, fiber-optic cables cut, microwave antennas broken, and computers smashed or simply turned off. The physical interception of couriers has had major impacts on the outcomes of battles dating back to antiquity. In the Civil War, electronic telecommunications were subject to mechanical disruption as cavalry forces cut telegraph lines. Mechanical attacks require the adversary to attain direct physical access to the target. The results of such attacks are generally more observable than the results of those conducted by electronic means.

• *Electromagnetic attacks.* The electronic components and transmissions of information systems and networks are also vulnerable to disruption and damage from electromagnetic energy directed at them. In the military realm, efforts to jam electronic transmissions have occurred since radios began to be used in World War I. During the Cold War, efforts to protect U.S. nuclear command and control communications under an attack devoted considerable attention to solving the problem of the electromagnetic pulse (EMP) generated by nuclear detonations. A nuclear explosion causes a large flux in the electromagnetic field that sets up a current within any conducting material, resulting in the disruption or destruction of many types of communications and information systems. During the 1990s, analysts have highlighted the possibility of generating EMP-like effects in a much more localized and directed form.[28] To the extent that adversaries can gain and maintain sufficient proximity to key information systems, they may be able to use directed energy as part of their attack plan.

• *Digital attacks.* Most of the attention surrounding strategic information attacks deals with possible threats from intrusion and disruption of computer systems and networks that underpin advanced information infrastructures. The tools and techniques for conducting digital warfare will be developed in more depth in chapter 2. The desired effect of such attacks can range from total paralysis of targeted information systems and networks to intermittent shutdown, random data errors, theft of information, theft of services, illicit systems monitoring and assuming systems control, access to data, and injection of false information. Additionally, attackers could endeavor to insert corrupted system components into an adversary's information infrastructure, allowing the attacker access to monitor, disrupt, or destroy an adversary's systems and networks.

Although all three types of attack can be utilized in strategic information warfare, this book focuses on digital attacks. The possibility of employing all three means synergistically must, however, be kept in mind.

Digital attacks on information systems occur in the physical world. The bytes of information and instructions for running programs in computer systems are stored on physical pieces of equipment and carried over communication circuits when transmitted. Changing bytes within a program or deleting information in a computer involves very precise actions and very small amounts of energy but still constitutes physical activity. Gaining control of a computer system through transmission of a message over the Internet constitutes an attack through physical space that can be detected, traced back to its source of origin, and monitored. The levels of physical effort required, speed of transit involved, and paths of transmission pursued are much different for digital attacks than in traditional warfare. However, such attacks are just as much intended to cause disruptive and/or destructive effects as those through mechanical and electromagnetic means.

Strategic information warfare can be conducted in either a physically violent or nonviolent way. When a bombing attack destroys a telecommunications switching facility or an electromagnetic attack disables the signaling mechanisms in a subway system resulting in a train crash, these attacks clearly have violent effects. Digital attacks could have similar effects, such as causing a nuclear power plant to melt down by withdrawing the control rods in a reactor or blanking the screen of air traffic controllers so that airliners crash. Digital attacks could also achieve less observable physical effects, such as causing disease through corruption of water treatment control facilities. Although attacks that wreak this kind of havoc are not often termed "violent" because of a lack of immediacy of their effects, the pain and suffering they cause could quite possibly constitute an act of war. There is also significant potential for digital warfare to have major impacts on opponents without the use of violence.[29] Changing the information in control systems for a country's defense satellites or causing disruptions that undermine faith in its stock market may not directly result in death and destruction but may nonetheless threaten the viability of critical national security operations and financial institutions.

The question has been raised as to whether such attacks constitute a use of force in the traditional sense based on the notion expressed by Clausewitz and echoed by others that "violence is the essence of war." But the classics on warfare also recognize that violence need not necessarily play a central role in achieving the objectives for which wars are fought. Clausewitz acknowledges that "since war is not an act of senseless passion but is controlled by its political object, the value of this object must determine the sacrifices to be made for it in magnitude and also in duration."[30] Sun Tzu consistently advocates conducting war with the lowest possible expenditure of human life and economic resources, stating that "to subdue the enemy without fighting is the acme of skill."[31] If one conceives of warfare only as events involving violence, then by definition nonviolent military means will not be useful in war. In the broader context of understanding the utility of force, however, the achievement of political objectives may not require the actual use of violent means. The use of nonviolent digital attacks to achieve political objectives must be understood as part of a new form of warfare.

Compared to other types of military force, digital warfare represents a type of microforce. The distinction is analogous to the difference drawn between conventional military forces employing chemical explosives or kinetic energy as their primary means of achieving effect versus the megaforce unleashed by nuclear weapons based on the fission or fusion of atoms. At issue here is the amount of energy unleashed by a given weapon at the time of attack. Weapons across the micro–conventional–mega force spectrum can all cause very significant impacts. Chemical or biological weapons are referred to as weapons of mass destruction, not because of the amount of destructive energy released when they are deployed but because of the number of deaths they can cause. Large-scale conventional use of force, such as the bombings of Tokyo and Dresden in World War II, has caused massive damage. Despite the microforce nature of information attacks, disruption of the digital control systems of a nuclear power plant could cause similarly large-scale effects.

Examining the nature of digital warfare as microforce parallels efforts in the 1990s to reconceptualize the role of conventionally armed aircraft and missiles as such means have become more precise and difficult to detect. The challenge of learning how to utilize such microforce may evidence similarities to the doctrinal debates and organizational adaptations necessary to incorporate nuclear and advanced conventional weapons into existing military forces.

Clear differences in the effects caused by employing conventional military force and the potential devastation wrought by nuclear force resulted in debates over the political utility of nuclear weapons after Hiroshima and Nagasaki. As different states gained a nuclear weapons capability, each developed different approaches to its use. The United States initially treated nuclear weapons as an enhancement of its strategic bombing capabilities, which had been heavily emphasized in World War II. Nuclear weapons were believed capable of threatening an adversary with decisive defeat, negating the need to fight conventional wars. The Soviets, who were much less committed to strategic bombing, initially considered nuclear capabilities a superpowerful extension of artillery capabilities used to wage conflicts on land and at sea. Over time, both superpowers came to recognize qualitative differences in these forces but made different technological choices in creating capabilities and operating the forces. Although U.S. and Soviet leaders arguably came to a mutual acknowledgment that the existence of these weapons established new boundaries and levels of war, significant doctrinal differences existed regarding their political utility. Unexpected events played key roles in shaping the thinking regarding nuclear forces. The Cuban Missile Crisis in 1962 engendered cooperation between both sides regarding the need for caution when subsequent crises occurred. This crisis also reinforced a growing belief in the United States about the inevitability of a situation of mutually assured destruction. The Soviet Union, on the other hand, became acutely aware of the significance of its nuclear inferiority and the need to surpass the United States in the nuclear realm.

The nuclear strategies of the superpowers had to adjust over time to other states' joining the nuclear weapons club. During the first two decades of the Cold War, the United Kingdom, China, and France all developed nuclear forces. With these new weapons, distinct nuclear concepts such as the *force de frappe* emerged. Debates on the political significance of nuclear weapons have been renewed since the end of the Cold War. The nuclear doctrines of the undeclared or recently declared nuclear powers—Israel, India, and Pakistan—have become the focus of much attention. Concern about nuclear proliferation, even to nonstate actors, and about nuclear terrorism has risen dramatically. (The evolution of nuclear doctrines during the Cold War and the rising concern with nuclear proliferation will be addressed more fully in chapter 2.) The quantitatively and qualitatively unique nature of nuclear forces has meant that thinking about them has had to differ from thinking about conventional forces. However, thinking about the utility of nuclear weapons also had to be integrated with consideration of the capabilities of more conventional military forces.

Changes in the technological features of advanced conventional forces have also caused significant reconceptualization of their use. In particular, the relationship between information and energy used in applying force has been highlighted. The development of precision-guided munitions (PGMs) and stealth technologies leverages one's own information sources and reduces information available to an adversary, allowing one's forces to deliver maximum damage against targets with the minimum expenditure of effort. Increased efficacy in applying airpower to attack target sets provides a useful illustration. In World War II, it took nine thousand 500 lb. bombs dropped by 1,500 B-17 sorties to destroy a 60' × 100' target. In 1970, a similar effort during the Vietnam War required only 176 such bombs and 88 F-4 sorties.[32] During the Persian Gulf War, however, destroying such a target only took one or two laser-guided bombs in a single F-117 sortie. The result has been a significant rethinking of the role of airpower on the battlefield. According to the Joint Staff, "precision engagement" provides an operational concept to enable future U.S. dominance across the full spectrum of conflict. The next step in maximizing the use of one's own information about targets, limiting the enemy's ability to develop information about the attacking forces and minimizing physical effort expended, may be to wage digital warfare as a microapplication of force. In fact, former CIA Director John Deutch has already referred to the electron as the "ultimate precision weapon."[33]

Strategic information warfare's potential presents a challenge similar to that of the advent of nuclear weapons or PGMs. The microforce potential of digital information warfare is as yet unclear, but its utility for achieving political ends can best be analyzed within existing frameworks that have helped to guide thinking about conventional and nuclear force. The challenge is to properly discern what we can utilize from past thinking and how these frameworks must also be changed.

Boundaries for Analyzing Strategic Information Warfare

Generally, strategic warfare is assumed to describe efforts to defeat opponents through attacks on centers of gravity without fighting fielded military forces. In delineating the actors capable of waging strategic information warfare, the concept of a strategic entity developed by John Warden provides useful guidance. Warden states:

> A strategic entity is any organization that can operate autonomously; that is self-directing and self-sustaining. A state is a strategic entity as is a criminal organization like the Mafia or business organizations like General Motors. Conversely, neither an army or an air force is a strategic entity because they are neither self-sustaining or self-directing. . . . Of most importance here, however, is that our discussion of strategic centers and strategic warfare is as applicable to a guerrilla organization as to a modern industrial state.[34]

Potentially, nonstate as well as state actors must be considered as potential adversaries capable of waging strategic warfare. To conduct strategic warfare, however, an actor must possess the ability to set coherent objectives and to control its use of force in conducting offensive and defensive operations.

The possibility also exists for a significant information warfare capacity to be developed by groups within a country such as insurgent movements or militia groups that desire a political regime change. The potential for such internal information warfare is important, but my analysis here is limited to transgressions involving substantial international activity. An important gray area exists to the extent domestic groups could conduct strategic information warfare in conjunction with the objectives of outside actors. Such a confluence of activity could range from an explicit alliance and coordination, with assistance by an outside actor for the disruptive activities of groups internal to its adversaries, to simply a coincidence of objectives between external and internal actors.[35] This analysis includes activities of an internal group to the extent they are considered part of an international actor's ability to achieve its political objectives through waging strategic information warfare.

As with other forms of warfare, the presence and legitimacy of legal strictures and religious and cultural factors regarding activities classified as strategic information warfare could also influence the behavior of actors involved. What types of strategic information attacks would constitute acts of war or aggression, allowing states to invoke the right of self-defense? When would the effect of such attacks constitute transgressions against the rights of noncombatants? What obligations do neutrals have regarding the use of their telecommunications systems to transmit strategic information attacks? When can the President invoke the responsibility of a state to defend information infrastructures as part of national emergency or war effort? How will potentially significant information attacks by nonstate actors be treated? How will cultural and religious considerations shape the perceptions of the utility and moral nature of information warfare? The answers to such questions would have a major impact on decisions of all actors regarding the conduct of both offensive and defensive aspects of strategic information warfare.

Events of the late 1990s outlined the difficulties of arriving at clear legal boundaries regarding the malicious use of cyberspace. An emerging legal discipline deals with cyberspace laws and rights in the areas of intellectual property protection, privacy, and electronic commerce.[36] For a nation such as the United States, founded on the rule of law, legal questions surrounding the conduct of strategic information warfare will prove central to decisions regarding preparation and execution for conflicts involving such means. To deal with the potential for playful hacking, intentional crime, and unfair corporate competition, legal structures have begun to establish what constitutes criminal activity, the permissible monitoring techniques for law enforcement, and penalties for prohibited behavior in the United States and elsewhere. Yet the ability of transgressors in cyberspace to cross national boundaries and disguise their identities makes balancing of public and private interests extremely difficult, and progress of the law in this area has been tentative.[37] Within the United States, whether digital attacks are characterized as malicious international acts or domestic crime has crucial implications for the search and seizure constraints governing law enforcement and counterintelligence efforts as well as the role of the President and Congress in determining whether attacks constitute a national security threat.

Characterizing digital attacks as international conflicts between states and other actors also presents difficult issues.[38] Efforts to define acts of war or aggression have had a difficult time coming to grips with actions short of direct use of armed force and violence. The prohibitions in the UN Charter forbidding the use of force as well as subsequent efforts to arrive at definitions of aggression or intervention do not clearly apply to nondestructive uses of digital attacks. Moreover, international law has great difficulty in dealing with legitimate state responses to transgressions by nonstate actors. Existing international telecommunications law deals primarily with interoperability and noninterference, but its provisions are not applicable to actions between belligerents in wartime. Space law prevents the use of space for weapons of mass destruction but has no provisions to deal with disruptions due to digital attacks that do not create observable physical effects. Past state practice seems to condone much of what would constitute strategic information warfare in a declared conflict between states. Securing international cooperation in determining responsibility for attack may prove difficult, and efforts to unilaterally investigate the source of attacks may violate the sovereignty of neutrals involved.

The topic of what constitutes an act of war in cyberspace has received increasing scrutiny. According to a 1997 study published by the Center for International Security and Arms Control at Stanford University, "International law has not yet resolved ambiguities over the characterization of information warfare activities, and must face a conflict between the international system of sovereign states and the realities of global networks."[39] These ambiguities were a core focus of an assessment issued by the Department of Defense general counsel's office in mid-1999. This authoritative assessment finds:

It is far from clear the extent to which the world community will regard computer network attacks as "armed attacks" or "uses of force" and how doctrines of self-defense and countermeasures will be applied to computer network attacks. The outcome will probably depend more on the consequences of such attacks than on their mechanisms. The most likely result is an acceptance that a nation subjected to a state-sponsored computer network attack can lawfully respond in kind, and that in some cases it may be justified in using traditional military means of self-defense.[40]

Strategic information warfare waged to achieve significant political influence may involve such clear transgressions that legal ambiguities resolve themselves. Attacks on information systems that either involve direct violence (bombing a telecommunications switching center) or create violent effects (causing train or plane crashes) would clearly constitute acts of aggression. Actions with physical effects, such as the aerial dropping of carbon circlets to disrupt power lines (as done by the United States over Iraq in 1991) or naval blockades that inflict economic damage also fit comfortably within the existing definitions of war, force, and aggression. The level of direct disruptive effect and potential impact on confidence in institutions perceived as fundamental to the smooth operation of economic life will also influence leaders making decisions regarding whether particular actions are treated as acts of war. In 1980, President Jimmy Carter declared that "any attempt by an outside force to gain control of the Persian Gulf region will be regarded as an assault on the vital interests of the United States of America and such an assault will be repelled by any means necessary, including the use of force."[41] For two decades, the United States has stood ready to employ military force even if no Americans were killed and no direct destruction of U.S. property was likely. According to many commentators, the U.S. decision to wage war against Iraq in 1991 was motivated by this exact situation. Political concerns over the effect on the U.S. economy of the conflict between Iraq and Kuwait and international perceptions of the United States as a world leader made inaction an unacceptable choice. U.S. leaders may similarly treat information attacks that threaten the viability of critical U.S. governmental or commercial operations.

Ambiguity concerning legal treatment of information warfare would clearly arise in determining the legal status of digital warfare with nonlethal, nondestructive results, such as attacks on a banking system or a Social Security Administration database. Understanding whether an action or actor has crossed a legal threshold into the realm of strategic information warfare will likely remain an imprecise, largely political determination. However, the same challenges are involved in determining the legal status of use of other types of force as well. Debate raged in the early 1990s between Western states, Libya, and the International Court of Justice regarding whether the bombing of a Pan Am flight over Lockerbie, Scotland, constituted a general threat to "international peace and security." Did this bombing justify UN Security Council action or was the bombing simply a criminal act punishable under the Montreal Convention? Ambiguities may also arise based on the type of infrastructure attacked. Given both public and international legal ambivalence regarding espionage activities, would an attack on an intelligence agency's information infrastructure be an act of war or simply part of the "dirty game"?

As with more violent uses of force, some actors will want to operate in gray areas to avoid justifying retaliation but still cause significant pain. Yet if digital attacks inflict significant damage and disruption, the conduct of strategic information warfare may well cross clearly into a realm that most actors regard as international acts of aggression or war. Actors may well disagree about the substance or even the relevance of international law to information warfare. However, to the extent this law is regarded as operative, its general principles may influence the behavior of actors engaged in strategic information warfare.

Other contextual factors may play a role in determining what different actors may perceive as constituting strategic information warfare and its boundaries. Other countries and nonstate actors may pay little attention to Western notions of law, focusing to a much greater degree on religious and cultural considerations. Within Islamic nations, the tenets of the Koran may play a more significant role than precepts of international law in determining whether information attacks constitute a legitimate means of warfare and the appropriate response to such transgressions. The approaches of Asian state and nonstate actors regarding intellectual property, the legitimacy of government control of information, and what constitutes aggression may diverge significantly from those in the West. For example, a Chinese author has depicted information warfare as a new form of "people's war," involving "hundreds of millions of people using open-type modern information systems . . . the chance of people taking the initiative and randomly participating in the war has increased."[42] Such differences may figure prominently in how such actors decide what constitutes strategic information warfare and legitimate responses to it.

Separating the legal, cultural, and political influences of different actors may prove difficult in determining the legitimacy of conducting strategic information warfare. Understanding the interaction of these factors will prove a critical aspect of dealing with the challenge of this new form of war. Thoughtful consideration of what types of transgressions constitute politically motivated attacks against U.S. national interest necessitating response by force, whether through nuclear, conventional, or digital warfare, is necessary. Setting such boundaries will prove crucial to establishing policy to deter strategic information attacks or to authorize the use of digital attacks as coercive means against other actors. In all cases, contextual factors will play a crucial role in how strategic information warfare may eventually be waged.

The Operating Environment for Strategic Information Warfare

This section describes the operating environment within which strategic information warfare takes place: the information systems, networks, and infrastructures that create the medium and provide the targets that are the focus of digital warfare. The reliance on information infrastructures by nation-states, corporations, and other organizations as the new millennium begins provides the "centers of gravity" that make strategic information warfare a theoretical possibility. Analysis of the emergence of information infrastructures as a new center of gravity for strategic warfare must remain grounded in an understanding of the past while retaining the intellectual flexibility to recognize the different challenges presented by the future.

As civilizations have made increasing use of technology, complex systems have evolved to support a wide range of societal activities. These basic facilities, equipment, services, and installations needed for the growth and functioning of a country, community, or organization are called "infrastructures." The smooth functioning of these underlying infrastructures has become increasingly important to all sectors of societies as they have become progressively more technologically advanced. The Presidential Commission on Critical Infrastructure Protection describes infrastructures as "the framework of interdependent networks and systems comprising identifiable industries, institutions and distribution capabilities that provide a continuous flow of goods and services essential to the defense and economic security of the United States, the smooth functioning of government at all levels, and of society as a whole."[43] We will focus in this section specifically on "information infrastructures" as a category of infrastructure particularly significant at the beginning of the twenty-first century.

The Emergence of the U.S. Information Infrastructure

What constitutes the information infrastructure has become the subject of much discussion in the United States and elsewhere. Infrastructure systems for handling information have existed since the dawn of civilization, as the transmission and handling of information has always been essential to the creation and maintenance of organized human activity. Ancient societies around the world used couriers on foot, on horseback, or on waterborne vessels to carry messages between geographically separated groups. In the third century B.C., Hannibal's Carthaginian forces kept track of Roman forces by stationing observers on hilltops with mirrors for signaling, contributing to Hannibal's ability to win battles over a period of sixteen years.[44] As political entities and boundaries emerged, postal systems were created to ensure the delivery of messages within, and eventually among, entities. Such systems relied for centuries on land- and sea-based means to transport messages in a variety of material formats. In the late eighteenth and early nineteenth centuries, government semaphore systems were developed throughout Europe to permit visual transmission of information using a system of towers and signal formats.[45]

The establishment of commercially viable telegraph and telephone designs in the 1840s and 1870s respectively created new ways to transmit information based on electronic means. Significant quantities of information could now travel great distances quickly, but massive physical infrastructures in terms of wires, amplifiers, and switching centers had to be set up. These technologies, particularly the telegraph, were quickly put to use by military organizations in the United States and elsewhere during conflicts in the latter half of the nineteenth century. Control of the operations of far-flung military operations as early as the Civil War relied heavily on the use of telegraph technology.

Civilian institutions were eventually established to create and manage new communications infrastructures for use during peacetime. By the close of the nineteenth century, most Western nations had well-established postal, telegraph, and telephone services, known generically as post, telegraph, and telephone (PTT) organizations, either heavily regulated or directly operated by national governments. Similar models emerged in other areas of the world through colonial domination as well as reliance on the West for the underlying technology and international interconnection. In the United States, the American Telephone and Telegraph Corporation (AT&T) had become the dominant player by the early twentieth century. AT&T established a cooperative relationship with government regulatory agencies with the common goal of establishing a technologically advanced public telephone network providing universal service at a reasonable cost.

Technological advances eventually broadened the available electronic means by which information was transmitted and disseminated beyond telephone and telegraph. Pushed along by military applications in World War I, radio broadcast became a major source of information and entertainment for large numbers of people by the 1930s. In large part through military research and development (R&D) efforts during World War II, new means for carrying telecommunications such as microwave transmission rapidly emerged in the second half of the century. By the 1950s, television had supplanted radio as the dominant broadcast medium in the United States. In the 1960s, the first commercial telecommunications satellites were launched, initially under the auspices of international governmental organizations such as the International Telecommunications Satellite Consortium (INTELSAT) and the International Marine Satellite Consortium (INMARSAT).

During the 1960s, computers also became increasingly central to the operation of telecommunications networks. As businesses increasingly used computers to manage their operations, the exchange of digital data became an increasingly important role of telecommunications networks. Disenchantment with AT&T's monopoly in this area eventually led to the establishment of other private telecommunications carriers. In the early 1980s, the U.S. government decided to end AT&T's regulated monopoly on most major telecommunications and information network services. Competition in an increasingly open market was viewed as the best means to meet the objectives of rapidly incorporating new technologies to improve the performance of communications and information networks at the lowest possible cost. In moving toward deregulation of the communications industry, the federal courts decided to emphasize competition and customer costs despite objections from the Department of Defense about national security concerns and by the Department of Commerce about U.S. global competitiveness.[46]

As computing power and performance continued to increase exponentially during the 1970s and 1980s, new possibilities emerged to digitize and communicate almost all types of information. The ability to transmit information as data, voice, or images over digital networks is often referred to as the phenomenon of convergence. Digital convergence has created an information age in which "all kinds of [information] substance can be put in electronic digital formats, processed by computers in huge quantities at great speed, and sent around the universe riding on electrons or photons at per-unit costs that keep going down compared to costs of nearly everything else."[47]

As a result of this digital convergence, the term "information infrastructure" emerged as a broader concept than "telecommunications network," referring to the wide variety of means and organizations responsible for the formatting, transmission, and processing of information resources. During the 1980s, information infrastructures around the globe rapidly adopted increasingly capable and diverse means of transmission such as co-axial and fiber-optic cables. New cellular telephone and personal communications services networks also emerged. Convergence also highlighted the importance of developing common digital standards allowing interoperability across a range of different information formats, carried on infrastructures such as the transmission control protocol/Internet protocol (TCP/IP) and integrated services digital networks (ISDN) standards.[48]

Discussions of information infrastructures during the 1990s have paid great attention to the Internet. Development of what eventually became the Internet was largely initiated by the Defense Advanced Research Project Agency (DARPA) in the late 1960s as a way of allowing computer scientists and engineers working on defense research to share expensive computing resources.[49] Over the past three decades, organizations involved in broader academic research, then entertainment, and later commerce recognized the potential of the Internet to serve their needs to communicate over long distances via e-mail and transfer large amounts of data in a variety of formats. While employing the same means as other digital telecommunications transmissions, the Internet's use of TCP/IP allowed development of a network of networks emphasizing the ease of interconnection. The significance of the Internet received a dramatic boost in the mid-1990s through the widespread adoption by Internet content providers and users of the hypertext markup language (html) as the basis for the World Wide Web. This application language allows users to access and make use of a wide range of information resources through simple graphical interfaces. New technologies for using networked computers, such as Java "applets," which allow piecemeal development and use of software applications, and "pointcasting" to push tailored information to specific end-users, are being implemented at an ever more rapid pace as we begin the new millennium.

The extremely rapid transformation in the means, standards, and patterns of use of information infrastructures in the second half of the last century has created a situation of uncertainty and complexity for all types of organizations that rely on their use and for governmental organizations at various levels responsible for their regulation. Those considering the conduct of strategic information warfare are faced not only with rapid technological change but lack of clear governmental authority over the basic operating environment for such warfare.

Understanding Information Infrastructures

The information networks in the early twenty-first century are composed of many interoperating entities and systems beholden to no single overarching authority or design. Information infrastructures develop in an evolutionary fashion. Unanticipated capabilities, opportunities, and problems often emerge from this evolution. Understanding the underlying technologies, distribution means, operating organizations, and governing institutions involved in orchestrating the development and operations of information infrastructures at the end of the twentieth century presents a daunting, complex task. Vice President Albert Gore has described the U.S. national information infrastructure as consisting of "hundreds of different networks, run by different companies and using different technologies, all connected together in a giant network of networks."[50]

For the purposes of analyzing centers of gravity for strategic information warfare, information infrastructure must be construed to include the myriad privately owned information networks as well as public voice and data networks. Our conceptualization should also include the information resources and people involved in the creation and use of such infrastructures to process, store, and transmit information. Based on Office of Technology Assessment definitions, we will use the term "information networks" here to mean "any set of interconnected electronic information systems (computers, magnetic drives, telecommunications switches, etc.); therefore the network is not restricted to the Internet, corporate networks, the telephone network, and so forth."[51] Our definition for "information infrastructures" will be

> a collective set of computer hardware and software, data storage and generating equipment, abstract information and its applications, trained personnel and interconnections between all these components. According to this approach an international information infrastructure already exists; users in one country can move data that is stored in another country to be used in a computer program in a third country. The infrastructure includes the public-switched telephone network, satellite and wireless networks, private networks and the Internet and other computer and data networks.[52]

This approach to conceptualizing information infrastructure plays an important role in analyzing strategic information warfare. The definition allows us to address the implications of possible digital attacks against all electronically networked information systems relied upon by key sectors of society, not focusing exclusively on the Internet or public telephone networks. Moreover, "a collective set" means that the term "information infrastructure" can be scaled to a wide range of activities from the systems and networks of a small commercial firm or military organization to the aggregated systems and network of an entire nation or even the global community.

We can additionally identify four sets of information infrastructure components of relevance for analyzing strategic information warfare:

• *Physical facilities and hardware equipment* to process, store, and transmit information. This wide and ever expanding set of equipment includes computer processors, keyboards, monitors, printers, video monitors, televisions, telephones, fax machines, network routers, switches, compact disks, video and audio tape, scanners, cameras, twisted-pair wires, co-axial and fiber-optic cable, microwave nets, and satellite systems, among many more.

• *Software and standards* allowing information infrastructure providers and users the capacity to access, manipulate, organize, and apply the information resources available through the infrastructure. Software programs include those used to run communications switches and routers, operating systems for computers, virus checkers, and applications such as databases, network analyzers and word processing, among various other types. Standards and protocols include the open systems interconnection (OSI) model, TCP/IP for networking computers, asynchronous transfer mode (ATM) and synchronous optical network (SONET) standards for fiber-optic transmission of digital information. Although software and standards are not direct targets of disruptive activity, those engaged in strategic information warfare, whether offensive or defensive, must understand standards to operate in the cyberspace environment.

• *Information resources* themselves which may exist in a variety of formats such as video programming, scientific or business databases, sound recordings, archives, and other media.

• *People* who create information resources, develop technologies, applications, and services, construct facilities, and train others to tap the potential of information infrastructures.

Our understanding of strategic information warfare will also involve more than simply potential technologies and targets. We must also address how activity in cyberspace is organized. The creation, operation, and use of information infrastructures for productive ends involves three principal types of activity:

1.   The development and use of underlying technologies, including hardware and software products, and orchestration of standards and protocols used in the information infrastructure.

2.   Provision of networks and services that link underlying technologies to provide information processing, storage, and transmission capabilities for a wide range of users.

3.   Use of the information technologies and networks by individuals and organizations to form an information infrastructure to perform desired tasks.

If an information infrastructure were created from scratch, the optimal process would be to develop the appropriate underlying technological products and standards, then link these pieces together to create networks tailored for the desired uses of specific organizations. Figure 1.1 provides such a simplified picture of flow of activities.

Once information infrastructures are established, however, their evolution occurs through simultaneous activity in all three types of activity. Technology producers develop new products, enhancing the functionality of networks or improving applications desired by users. Network providers develop new ways of linking existing technologies to provide improved services. Users adopt new hardware devices and software applications to accomplish tasks or switch among network providers for various services. As a result, the technological pieces underpinning advanced information infrastructures are pushed out by producers as well as inserted and modified by network providers and infrastructure users. Organizations conducting all three types of activities are responsible for the composition and characteristics of a given information infrastructure. The arrows in figure 1.2 indicate the interactivity between types of activity in the operation of an evolving information infrastructure.

An organization could conduct all three types of activity to optimize a given information infrastructure for its requirements. However, the complexity of the

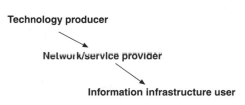

Figure 1.1
Steps in information infrastructure creation

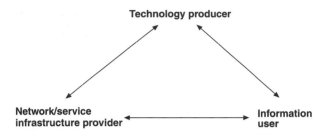

Technology producer

**Network/service
infrastructure provider**

**Information
user**

Figure 1.2
The interactive nature of information infrastructure creation

technologies involved today has resulted in the involvement of a multiplicity of organizations in the creation of most large-scale information infrastructures. Advanced information infrastructures involve products developed, updated, and supported by many producers. Different organizations provide a wide range of choices for computing and network services for a variety of processing, storage, and transmission functions within information infrastructures. The organizational missions and individual tasks users desire to perform with their information infrastructures can evolve at a rapid pace. The multiple types of activities, the roles of different organizations, and the interactivity necessary to sustain the operation of information infrastructures must be kept in mind as one considers the level of understanding necessary to launch disruptive attacks on and conduct defense of information infrastructures as a target. Figure 1.3 provides a sense of the number of different technologies and connections that must be developed, distributed, implemented, and operated by organizations using advanced information infrastructures. The three stages of activity involved in the creation and operation of information infrastructures outlined above are utilized throughout the rest of this work to illustrate the multilevel challenges of conducting strategic information warfare, particularly its defensive aspects.

Significance of U.S. Information Infrastructures

Those individuals and organizations tasked with waging strategic information warfare must understand their own information infrastructures as well as those of their adversaries. As the 1990s progressed, increasingly strong statements were made regarding the significance of information infrastructures in the United States. For example, the Clinton administration's *Agenda for Action* states:

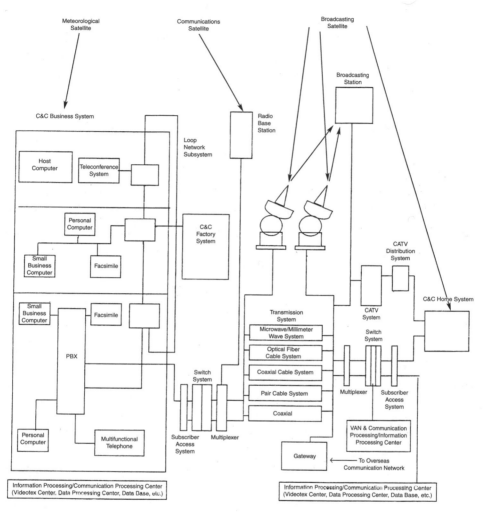

Figure 1.3

Complexity of advanced information infrastructures. Source: Raymond Akwule, Global Telecommunications: The Technology, Administration, and Politics *(Boston: Focal Press, 1992), 5. Reprinted with permission.*

The benefits of the National Information Infrastructure (NII) for the nation are immense. An advanced information infrastructure will enable U.S. firms to compete and win in the global economy, generating good jobs for the American people and economic growth for the nation. As importantly, the NII can transform the lives of the American people—ameliorating the constraints of geography, disability and economic status—giving all Americans a fair opportunity to go as far as their talents and ambitions will take them.[53]

According to Commerce Department figures, capital spending on information systems, such as computers and communications equipment, exceeded capital spending on industrial-age items, such as equipment and machinery for agriculture, mining, construction, manufacturing, and services, for the first time in 1992.[54] According to *Business Week*, the information technology sector contributed 33 percent of the growth in U.S. gross domestic product (GDP) in 1996.[55] More broadly, information systems are a driving force in improving operational efficiency and enabling new organizational forms in activities from car manufacturing, fashion retailing, and managerial consulting, to tax collection, education, and arms control advocacy, as well as warfare.

The volumes of available information regarding the significance of the information technology industry, e-commerce, and the "New Economy" can complicate the task of outlining the significance of information infrastructures. One can easily find examples of how organizations ranging from the Department of Defense (DOD) to Trader Joe's specialty food stores make use of advanced information infrastructures for tasks central to their operations. Yet anyone considering the conduct of strategic information warfare must distill the mass of available information and its complexity into manageable frameworks for analysis. The following list describes the significance of information infrastructures for seven sectors of activity within the United States:

• *National security.* This category includes the DOD, its associated agencies, and the military services as well as the intelligence community, State Department, and other governmental agencies and organizations.

• *Vital human services.* Police, fire, public safety, and emergency response all fall within this category. Although most such services are provided by government organizations at a variety of federal, state, and local levels, some, such as ambulance and 911 emergency notification services, may be privately operated as well. Disruption of these services would have an immediate impact on public safety.

• *Other government services.* This category includes organizations that deliver major government services, such as the Social Security Administration, or those that conduct regulatory activities, such as the Securities and Exchange Commission and others at state and local levels. These organizations conduct activities instrumental to a range of organizations and individuals across U.S. society. Their disruption would, however, generally have a more diffuse, less immediate impact on individuals and organizations than those deemed "vital human services."

• *Public utilities, transportation, and health services.* Government and private-sector organizations that provide electric power, the oil and gas industries, and water and sewage treatment providers as well as the providers of transportation services, such as the airlines and railroads, belong to this category. Disruption of such activities could have immediate impacts, such as widespread physical damage and human casualties.

• *General commercial users.* The broadest of all categories, general commercial users are increasingly reliant on information technology and infrastructures, especially in areas such as the banking/financial sector. The role of information infrastructures may appear less central in other commercial sectors, such as clothing manufacture or the fast food industry. Although the disruptions in this sector may occur quickly and have widespread impact, they generally do not involve threats of physical damage or harm to humans.

• *Commercial information technology producers and providers.* This category includes telecommunications and information technology manufacturers of hardware components, software operating systems, and applications.

• *Commercial network operators and service providers.* Major telecommunications services providers, Internet service providers, and providers of value-added services, such as e-mail or data processing, as well as systems integrators all fall into this category.

Although not intended to be comprehensive, this framework provides an overview of sectors widely identified as potential targets of strategic information attacks. Some of these categories borrow from those established by the President's Commission on Critical Infrastructure Protection (PCCIP) and Presidential Decision Directive (PDD) 63, particularly the characterization of vital human services, other government services, public utilities, and transportation sectors. However, my analysis also addresses the significance of technology providers and general commercial users as sectors of activity related to information infrastructure creation and use outside the scope of the PCCIP and PDD 63 efforts. The wide variance in the degree of sophistication of the information technology usage in, and importance of information resources to, different types of organizations in a given category must be kept in mind. The following sections provide illustrative examples of the significance of information infrastructures for each of the sectors listed above. Those sections do not comprehensively address all organizations or information networks within a given sector, but rather illuminate the breadth and complexity of activities potentially at risk if strategic information attacks were conducted against the United States. Descriptions of the last two sectors, the technology producers and service providers, illuminate the diversity and complexity of activities underpinning information infrastructures in the other sectors. The framework employed here also provides a point of departure for understanding the degree of mutual reliance and different concerns among infrastructure producers, operators, and users.

National Security

The DOD, the intelligence community, and other U.S. agencies with national security responsibilities operate one of the world's largest and most complex information infrastructures. In the late 1990s, the DOD defined the defense information infrastructure (DII) as "a seamless web of communications networks, computers, software, databases, applications, and other capabilities that meet the information processing and transport needs of DOD users in peace and in all crises, conflict, and humanitarian support and wartime roles."[56] The DII supports critical war-fighting functions such as the dissemination of command and control information, collection and transmission of intelligence, and the reprogramming of electronic warfare systems. Information infrastructures are also critical for combat support and peacetime defense planning functions. Information for logistical support and deployment timelines for contingencies all over the world are stored in centralized electronic databases. The organizations responsible for defense budgeting, personnel, and financial affairs are all highly dependent on large, automated computing and communications systems.[57]

By the mid-1990s, the DOD had widely acknowledged that proper functioning of its information infrastructures was fundamental to wartime and peacetime operations. The Joint Chiefs of Staff declared in 1996 that the achievement of information superiority underpins future U.S. efforts to dominate conventional battlefields.[58] The Army has a major program underway to "digitize the battlefield."[59] The Air Force regards achievement of information superiority through the use of air and space forces as one of its core competencies.[60] The Navy and Marine Corps have instituted a program to develop a dedicated intranet that will provide voice, video, and data services to ensure units and personnel around the globe can leverage the national and global infrastructures to reach back to necessary information resources.[61] The DOD's Global Combat Support System (GCSS) initiative will endeavor to integrate computing and communications capabilities for support functions such as logistics, personnel, and medical applications from desktop computers to mainframes and from bases in the United States to deployed units worldwide.[62]

Other national security organizations have also moved toward increased reliance on digital information systems and networks. The intelligence community increasingly relies on computerized information systems to gather, process, and disseminate its products. In 1994, the Director of Central Intelligence and Assistant Secretary of Defense declared that the use of the Internet-based Intelink system would be the strategic direction for the intelligence community's dissemination of its products.[63] The State Department, Coast Guard, Department of Energy, and other federal departments and agencies with national security missions also rely heavily on information networks to perform their missions and coordinate with other organizations.

These defense and intelligence agencies often independently operate portions of their own information infrastructure. Signals and later, communications units, have long been an essential part of the support for combat operations in all the services.[64] These units provide military communications in both peacetime and wartime using a wide array of available transmission means and information systems. During the Cold War, the United States developed nuclear command and control systems as highly reliable, secured systems. Such systems had multiple modes of transmission and very limited connection to commercially operated telecommunications or information systems.[65] Communications at the tactical level on the battlefield were generally accomplished in the past using systems developed and operated by military organizations. The intelligence community also developed and deployed specialized satellite systems designed for specific missions and utilizing highly secured means of information transmission operated by government agencies.[66]

Today, the DII is acknowledged to be heavily connected to commercial information infrastructures as well as reliant on their operation. The DOD has been widely reported to rely on the public networks for transmission of 95 percent of its unclassified communications.[67] The Global Command and Control System (GCCS) will use commercially operated long-distance networks to push operational plans as well as to transmit intelligence, mapping, environmental, and medical data to users requiring such data. The Navy Marines Corps Intranet (NMCI) will be based on services contracted from the commercial sector. The military also relies on internationally operated commercial information networks to provide command, control, and intelligence to forces in theater and logistics support from the United States in conducting operations such as the NATO peacekeeping effort in Bosnia. The Defense Information Systems Agency (DISA) has rented transponders from the INTELSAT and Globestar satellite communications systems to improve telecommunications links to U.S. forces in the Balkans since the mid-1990s.[68] If the U.S. military remains involved in an array of peace operations around the globe, the DOD may rely on commercial imaging systems and information networks for fulfilling the needs of those operations, both to save money and to keep dedicated intelligence and support systems focused on combat operations.

Similarly, the intelligence community has demonstrated an increased willingness to rely on commercial technologies and systems as part of its information networks. The classified Intelink network is based almost entirely on Internet technologies and uses public networks for long-distance transport of communications. The leveraging of commercial technology for such purposes enabled Intelink to go from concept approval to declared operational capability in under two years.[69] Information infrastructures supporting national security activities constitute a primary strategic information warfare concern, especially when crucial activities underlying the operation of the DII and other national security activities are conducted in the commercial sector.

Vital Human Services

The provision of public safety services within the United States today increasingly depends on the proper functioning of information infrastructures. The FBI and law enforcement agencies at all levels are highly dependent on information systems to track and keep records of criminal activity. The FBI operates the National Crime Information Center (NCIC) computer system, which maintains records of arrest warrants, fingerprints, and information on wanted persons and stolen property as well as criminal histories and has more than 80,000 user organizations.[70] A National Law Enforcement Telecommunications System (NLETS) is cooperatively operated and funded by state law enforcement agencies to provide vehicle registration, driver's license, and additional criminal record information, handles more than 400,000 messages daily, and is linked with the NCIC.[71] Firefighters in California use temperature, humidity, and wind speed data fed from remote sensors through satellite links to conduct weather "microforecasting" to assist in their firefighting efforts. The U.S. public relies on 911 telephone systems to report emergencies. As federal and local agencies increasingly focus on how to coordinate their activities to deal with transnational criminal activity as well as domestic and international terrorist threats, the significance of reliable information infrastructures will increase. The National Communications System, managed by DISA, includes provisions to support other government agencies such as the Federal Emergency Management Agency (FEMA) in the event of declared emergencies such as a hurricane or major terrorist attack.[72]

Although federal agencies play key roles in the public services sector, most organizations conducting emergency services activities are highly decentralized, operating at the state, county, municipal, or even precinct level. Less-sophisticated technical resources and management employed at the state and local levels may reduce reliance on digital information networks. Agencies such as police and fire departments as well as ambulance services also tend to operate some of their own information infrastructures, particularly wireless networks to increase flexibility and control over the networks' availability during emergency situations.

Other Government Services

Information systems are crucial to a wide range of other key government operations. Some of these operations are fundamental to other sectors of society, such as the banking and airline industries. The FEDWIRE electronic networks are used by the Federal Reserve to transfer $2 trillion each day.[73] Federal Aviation Administration (FAA) radar systems are highly reliant on both computers and the public-switched telecommunications network. The demonstrated fragility of the air traffic control system in numerous cases in the 1990s has caused major disruptions that threatened catastrophic crashes.[74] The Department of Transportation operates a digital national monitoring network in Orlando, Florida, based on input from railroad operators to oversee the smooth operation and safety of the U.S. railroad traffic.[75]

Increased use of improved information networks figures prominently in reengineering plans to make the government more efficient, effective, and responsive. Provision of many of these services is central to the lives of individual citizens. Vice President Albert Gore's National Performance Review strongly advocates that all government agencies consider using electronic means to transfer funds to government program beneficiaries. The use of information systems and networks will allow the government to improve the planning and efficient use of increasingly scarce public resources. For example, the Department of Housing and Urban Development intends to use commercially available geographic information systems to better understand the distribution of low-income housing in urban areas. State and local governments have implemented a wide range of programs designed to leverage information technology to improve outreach and efficiency. Such programs range from complaint forms on the Internet about traffic lights in New York City to automated searches of public records in Phoenix, Arizona.[76]

Most governmental agencies without national security or emergency response responsibilities do not own and operate their information infrastructures, relying almost completely on commercial-sector telecommunications and information system providers. Analysis of the relevance of this sector to strategic information warfare must address the degree to which these organizations rely on information infrastructures for providing their services. Can Social Security checks be issued and mailed, for example, if electronic benefit transfer systems and networks are unavailable? It should also be noted that the disruption of such services will have a less direct, less timely impact than disruption of most of the other activities described here.

Public Utilities, Transportation, and Health Services

The provision of a wide range of activities included in the categories of public utilities and transportation is highly dependent on information systems. Many public utilities providing electric power, oil, natural gas, water, and sewage treatment dependent heavily on computer-based controls known as supervisory control and data acquisition (SCADA) systems.[77] The scope and duration of the failure of the electric power grid in much of the northwest United States in August 1996 was due in part to limited human involvement in the automated control systems. Although many organizations utilizing SCADA systems today rely on specialized software and private, dedicated communication lines, future upgrades to these systems will likely involve use of standardized Internet-based applications and public data networks.[78] Organizations providing transportation services, such as computerized reservations systems, similarly use information networks to increase efficiency as well as to manage operations and traffic flows within the air and railroad systems.

Another sector with a growing reliance on information infrastructures is health services. Computer-based systems such as computerized axial tomography (CAT) scans and magnetic resonance imagers (MRIs) are central to the diagnosis of patients' illnesses and conditions. Records of individuals and their histories, such as allergies to drugs, are increasingly maintained in digital databases to facilitate their recall and transfer down to the level of neighborhood drugstores. The ability to rapidly transmit such records, as well as information such as X-rays, over electronic networks has enabled physicians in remote locations to call effectively on the services of more comprehensively equipped medical facilities and personnel over long distances.[79]

Information services such as those described above are generally provided by private enterprises using commercially developed information technologies and often rely on commercial public networks. However, the government often plays a major role in this sector through regulation as well as the operation of supporting systems such as the FAA and Department of Transportation (DOT) traffic control systems. In some cases, government organizations actually own and operate services such as metropolitan transportation networks and municipal water supply utilities. The government has a long-standing role in ensuring that public safety is protected in potentially dangerous activities such as the operation of nuclear power plants or gas pipelines or the provision of adequate health care services. Yet deregulation in areas such as provision of electric power may change the degree of emphasis commercial companies place on such concerns. The degree of reliance on information infrastructures remains unclear in most of these sectors. Certain information systems and networks may assist in increasing efficiency but not create fundamental concerns for ensuring safe operation, such as in the provision of oil and gas transport. Therefore, monitoring trends regarding regulation of utilities and health care and the reliability of supporting information infrastructures will prove very important in understanding U.S. strategic information warfare concerns.

General Commercial Users

The reliance of the general commercial sector on information infrastructures has reached staggering levels and grows every day. Measuring the productivity gains achieved and the new types of activities enabled through the use of information technology has proven difficult through traditional means of economic measurement and analysis.[80] Yet service-sector firms have invested heavily in information systems and networks to improve their operations and create competitive advantage. The banking and financial services industries consist largely of organizations whose role is almost purely informational. Their operations depend completely on computers and telecommunications. Banks, mutual fund companies, stock brokerages, and other financial institutions use databases to manage, account for, and transfer most of the world's wealth. According to a 1990 Office of Technology Assessment estimate, an average of $800 billion was transferred among partners in international currency markets every day.[81] As of the mid-1990s, CitiCorp information and communications network connected to more than 100 countries serving seventy million customers.[82] The numbers have undoubtedly increased greatly since then. Large financial institutions increasingly use Internet-based networks both to increase the efficiency of their information management and to reach out directly to customers. Traditional brokerage houses and firms such as Merrill Lynch, Charles Schwab, Amerifrade, and E*Trade are offering their customers the opportunity to place discount trading orders over the Internet. The development of automated-teller and point-of-sale systems along with credit and debit cards have pushed the tools for using electronic networks to access financial resources down to the level of the individual consumer. Large and small firms such as Digital Equipment Corporation and Cybercash are orchestrating arrangements between financial institutions and setting up information networks to allow Internet transactions involving even less than a penny.

Management consulting and legal services also rely heavily on information technology. The U.S. services sector spent more than $750 billion on information technology hardware alone, basically doubling investment in the average worker's information technology (IT) base, during the 1980s.[83] Law firms have come to rely heavily on database systems such as Lexis/Nexis to conduct research central to their core operations. Consulting firms such as McKinsey and Arthur Andersen integrate recommendations about client strategy and operations with information technology expertise to implement required upgrades. Large information systems integrators such as IBM and network providers such as AT&T and MCI have established consulting operations based on their networking expertise. Major accounting firms, including Ernst & Young and Deloitte and Touche, have added information security to the list of services they can provide.

More broadly, manufacturing and distribution of goods and services based on just-in-time inventory and delivery systems have become highly dependent on advanced information networks. General Motors undertook a five-year effort to transform the design and production processes of its automobiles based on integrated computer-aided design, engineering, and manufacturing technologies to beat competitors to market with new products. As the United States auto industry enters the twenty-first century, car makers now increasingly embed connectivity into advanced information infrastructures directly into their products.[84] General Motors offers its satellite-based On-Star driver communication system. General Motors expects the installed base to grow from 100,000 vehicles in 2000 to 3 million in 2003. Ford plans to offer Internet access on some models beginning in 2001. A wide array of Global Positioning Satellite–enabled navigational products have become available as part of the car at purchase or as after-market additions. Levi Strauss can electronically process and produce orders for individually customized jeans at its sales outlets. Most transnational corporations have taken advantage of the increasing capacity of communications networks to carry necessary information to help flatten their organizational structures and orchestrate the activities of far-flung operations. Wal-Mart has been able to reduce its cost of distribution to 3 percent of sales (compared to 4.5 to 5 percent for competitors) through heavy investment and use of advanced information network systems.[85]

The tendency at the dawn of the twenty-first century is to assume that all businesses are rushing headlong into cyberspace and embracing e-commerce. In trying to comprehend the significance of information infrastructures to the commercial sector, we must bear in mind that their use by specific organizations varies widely. We must also remember that all potential uses of information technologies do not become immediately commercially viable. AT&T's efforts dating from the 1930s to promote videoconferencing continually met with less than mediocre results until the 1990s.[86] Chemical Bank's efforts to establish home banking beginning in the 1980s met similar disappointments through the early 1990s.[87] The general trend, however, is clear: The role of information systems and networks has become immensely pervasive and increasingly instrumental in the planning, operations, and coordination of commercial organizations.

The vast majority of the transactions and information flows described above rely on the public-switched networks provided by other commercial enterprises described below. The late 1990s demonstrated a growing use of corporate "intranets" to provide organizations with more direct control over the content and local operation of their information networks. Yet these intranets still rely for long-distance transmission of information on microwave towers, fiber-optic cables, satellites, and other means belonging to major commercial network providers. Such infrastructure components are expensive to construct and operate. Furthermore, the technology and equipment used in intranets is produced by other commercial organizations. Disruption of technology producers and network providers may provide very significant ways of attacking a diverse range of information infrastructure users.

Commercial Information Technology Producers

Understanding the complex web of activities conducted by the organizations that provide the underlying technologies, products, and services for information infrastructures enables us to assess more accurately how these infrastructures operate. The size and projected growth of the producers of information technology products and services highlights the importance of this sector. The Nasdaq, introduced in 1971 as the world's first electronic stock market, has emerged as a major indicator of economic performance because it provides the market for the stock of high-technology firms, including Microsoft, Intel, and Netscape. As early as 1994, the Council of Economic Advisors has reported that the combined telecommunications and information technology sectors of the U.S. economy represented 9 percent of U.S. GDP, and estimated this figure could double in the next ten years.[88] In the summer of 2000, *Wired* magazine reported that information technology–producing industries alone constituted 8.2 percent of the United States GDP in 1999, up from 5.8 percent in 1991. The same article reported that in 1999, the IT industry accounted for 19.2 percent of United States GDP growth.[89] Information technology producers provide the fundamental building blocks for the U.S. move into the information age.

Assessing the significance of specific technology producers requires sophistication regarding the increasingly artificial nature of the categories of hardware and software. Advanced information systems and networks rely on technologies that require integrated physical mediums to transmit, store, and present information (hardware) and digitized processes for processing and formatting information (software). For example, the switching systems for today's networks consist of computer hardware to transmit and store digitized information as well as sophisticated software to route information transmission. Silicon chips that create the necessary computing power for modern information systems are generally considered hardware, however, only 5–10 percent of the production cost comes from materials and energy; the rest accrues from the research, product, and process engineering necessary to create these chips. The technological blocks of modern information infrastructures generally are the product of many organizations involved in multiple stages of a complex process. The activities at all stages are of concern to those who would attack and defend U.S. information infrastructures.

Critical technologies for the creation of information infrastructures currently include Intel Corporation's Pentium microprocessors, Microsoft's Windows operating system, Sun Microsystem's Java programming language, Oracle databases, Dell computers, Cisco Systems' network routers, Corning's fiber-optic cables, Lotus/IBM's Notes groupware, and Hughes Electronics' satellites, as well as countless others. Companies principally based outside the United States, such as Germany's Seimens, Canada's Northern Telecom, Finland's Nokia and Japan's Sony, and their products such as cellular transmission equipment, PBX switches, and flat-panel displays are also central to the technological foundations of information infrastructures in the United States and around the globe. Such organizations and their technology development processes, personnel, and products underpin the performance, reliability, and security of modern information infrastructures. Trade-offs faced by technology producers will be a key theme in understanding the challenges of establishing an effective strategic information warfare defense.

Commercial Information Network and Service Providers

A final sector includes those organizations that provide telecommunications and information networks and services. Such providers link available technologies and products with users to fulfill their information infrastructure requirements. They represent another key sector associated with the creation and evolution of information infrastructures.

The organizations operating public-switched networks (commonly known as PSNs) are at the core of the activities in this sector. For much of the twentieth century, the dominant PSN of concern was the long-distance voice network, and the dominant provider was AT&T. In the past few decades, new technologies for transmission and standards for passing data have emerged that equip new organizations with the capacity to provide long-distance telecommunications. New communications network providers such as Worldcom and Qwest have become major players in just a few years.[90] Many if not most key players in the telecommunications sector of the U.S. economy are in the process of ongoing restructuring through corporate acquisitions and mergers as well as formation of joint ventures and alliances, both internal and external to the United States.

Providers of television and radio networks through wireless terrestrial or satellite broadcast and co-axial cable systems are also major players in the U.S. information economy. To the extent that these networks continue to focus on the transmission of entertainment, news, and education to individual consumers, they do not play a major role in strategic information warfare as considered in this work. As the technological possibilities for using wireless or cable mediums to transmit digital information become more widely recognized, however, these network providers are increasingly relevant to our topic. Very large multimedia companies and joint ventures provide digital information networks to a wide variety of organizations as well as phone services and entertainment to individual consumers, such as the MediaOne venture formed by the acquisition of Continental Cable by the Bell Atlantic phone company. The operations and networks of such organizations may become lucrative targets for actors wishing to disrupt U.S. information infrastructures.

The last decade saw an explosion in organizations providing telecommunications services via privately operated satellite systems. Many of these systems, such as the Hughes Direct TV system, currently focus on broadcast. A growing number of transnational companies, however, use private satellite networks based on Very Small Aperture Terminals (VSAT) to coordinate geographically far-flung operations. Numerous companies and consortiums have established large projects to provide global voice and data transmission services, such as the Motorola-led sixty-six-satellite Iridium project and the forty-eight-satellite Globalstar system led by Loral/Qualcom.[91] Direct-broadcast satellites may be used to provide "channels" of specialized information for U.S. and Allied forces deployed in war-fighting operations. Although highly classified information such as intelligence information and operations plans will likely continue to be carried on systems developed and operated by the Department of Defense, commercial systems may be used to pass crucial weather, logistical, and medical information.[92] Satellites may be used to collect and transmit data to remote locations necessary for the operation of SCADA systems. The organizations that operate satellite services are also increasingly intertwined with providers of others sorts of information networks. The Hughes Electronics effort to create a worldwide mobile voice network involves the use of satellites with twelve ground receiving stations around the globe linked to terrestrial public fixed and mobile networks through partnerships with more than sixty other telecommunications companies in more than forty countries.[93]

Finally, the rapid rise of Internet-based networks for passing information in various digital forms has become a central part of advanced information infrastructures, especially in the United States. The Internet's explosion in terms of numbers of users (see figure 1.4) and activities conducted by users makes its operation and reliability increasingly fundamental to organizations across all sectors of society.

The organizational responsibility for operation of the Internet has evolved significantly since its inception in the 1960s. Originally, the operation of the Internet was independently financed and operated by government agencies such as DARPA and the National Science Foundation. However, the provision of the facilities for the transmission of bits and bytes over the Internet has become increasingly intertwined since the late 1980s with the public-switched networks of the telecommunications providers. Companies like MCI/Worldcom, Sprint, and AT&T provide most of the long-distance or "backbone" carrying capacity of the Internet. A much larger number of smaller commercial providers provide local networks focused on carrying Internet traffic.

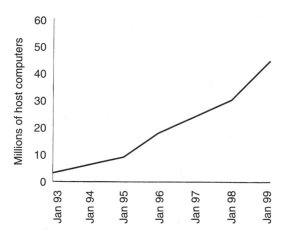

Figure 1.4
Internet growth. Source: Network Wizards Web site (www.networkwizards.com),
January 2000.

Additionally, because individuals and organizations desiring to use the Internet require a connecting point to other networks, a new category of organizations known as Internet service providers (ISPs) has emerged. ISPs in the late 1990s included companies specializing in Internet services, such as America Online, organizations with existing telecommunications expertise and facilities, such as AT&T, and others in the information technology business with relevant expertise seeking to expand their areas of operation, such as Microsoft. As with voice services, a proliferation of small Internet service providers also exists. One estimate of the fragmented ISP market indicated more than 4,000 U.S. companies were providing Internet services in the spring of 1998.[94] Wireless Internet services are also emerging based on both cellular and satellite technology. The operations of Internet service providers are a potential entry point for disruptive activity as well as a locus of vulnerability for the conduct of strategic information warfare.

Other specialized organizations are also involved in the operation of PSNs. Of note, a host of smaller companies has emerged who resell extra capacity from the major telecommunications operators to individuals or organizational customers. Although telecommunications resellers may not be responsible for operating significant hardware or software components of information infrastructures, the services they provide to users may be critical for banking and credit card processing. Also, smaller organizations provide specialized services critical to the operations of the larger telecommunications providers. For example, Illuminet,

Inc., provides signaling services to numerous companies fundamental to the operation of their phone networks. Network Solutions, Inc., assigns domain names, which establish the digital addresses necessary for computers used by individuals and organizations to make use of the Internet. Opportunities to disrupt such organizations provide yet another potential information warfare target as well as a defensive concern.

Sorting out which organizations play what specific role in the provision of the information infrastructures presents a massive task for commercial competitors and strategic information warriors. The wide range of organizations participating in the development, implementation, and use of information infrastructures produces an intricate array of implications for organizing and conducting strategic information warfare. In particular, the complexity creates numerous difficulties in assigning responsibility for problems that arise from the creation and use of these infrastructures, including contractual and antitrust obligations between individuals and organizations. At the broader policy level, efforts to ensure that U.S. citizens and organizations can access and use information infrastructures face an increasingly tough task in simply trying to monitor the organizations providing components and services for these infrastructures, let alone assign responsibility for their assured function.

Salient Features of Information Infrastructures for Strategic Information Warfare

For those concerned with national security, the diversity, fluidity, commercial ownership, and operation of advanced information infrastructures makes protecting or potentially attacking them a significantly different task than conducting past military operations. Building on the preceding overview of the components, operators, and users of U.S. information infrastructures, this section describes five features of advanced information infrastructures central to analyzing strategic information warfare. How these features relate to the vulnerability of information infrastructures to digital attack and challenges for defense will be developed further in chapters 2 and 3. The strengths and weakness of specific efforts to manage the security of U.S. information infrastructures is examined in chapter 5.

Complexity of Interconnection

The myriad interconnections among systems with multiple uses adds to difficulties in articulating clear boundaries between sectors of activity using information infrastructures. For example, the operation of the public phone network is central for the operation of 911 services, which in turn serve as the queuing mechanism for the provision of emergency police, fire, and medical services. Airlines are wholly reliant on the proper functioning of the FAA air traffic control system, which in turn relies on commercially provided telecommunications services. The government's ability to become more efficient through provision of electronic transfer of benefits such as Social Security is predicated on the widespread availability and proper functioning of commercial ATM networks and electronic point-of-sale systems.

A prime example of interconnectivity is the Global Positioning System (GPS), operated by the Department of Defense, which uses over twenty satellites in low earth orbit to provide navigational data. Although originally intended to improve the combat capabilities of U.S. military forces, its uninterrupted function has become central to the positioning and navigational systems of commercial users worldwide. The system has the capability of operating in secure modes accessible only to assigned receivers, degrading the accuracy of navigational information available to others. Yet the U.S. government has entered into an increasing number of agreements not to operate the GPS in this special mode despite potential national emergencies because of the navigational safety concerns of other users reliant on the system. Commercial users have also developed methods to combine GPS signals with other timing mechanisms, which ensures high levels of accuracy even if the reserve mode is activated.[95] Additionally, the timing synchronization systems of most cellular phone networks in the United States rely on the signal provided by the GPS.[96] Disruption of the GPS would affect a wide range of users as well as the provision of other networks and services.

In turn, information systems and networks themselves are reliant in varying degrees on the electric power system, which could also be disrupted through information attacks and sabotage. The National Disaster Recovery Association reported that 90 percent of telecommunications service outages are due to problems with power sources.[97] The timing systems used by telecommunications and computer networks are central to their functioning and could be disrupted through sabotage or attack. The increasing level of interdependence between different networks adds significant complexity to understanding the operation of information infrastructures and the possible effect of their disruption on user organizations.

Civilian-Sector Technological Leadership

Historically, military and national security organizations have been intimately involved with the development of communications and information technology systems. World War I greatly accelerated the pace of technological progress in radio through the added incentives for innovation created by wartime necessity as well as a temporary centralization of R&D efforts. The U.S. Navy assumed the right to order radio equipment using any existing technology from any manufacturer, taking responsibility for all possible patent infringements. This action allowed the development of products that integrated refinements whose patents were held by multiple squabbling inventors and corporations.[98] The development of the transistor and integrated chips was driven in the 1950s and 1960s by military aerospace and NASA space exploration applications.[99] The first imaging, communications, and weather surveillance satellites were all developed for national security applications. The U.S. military research and development community even initiated development of today's Internet.

Yet the U.S. government has always contracted to private organizations the basic research, development, and production of the telecommunications and technologies used by national security organizations. With the notable exception of cryptologic systems, the R&D laboratories of major corporations such as AT&T and IBM pioneered most technological advances in the telecommunications and information technology fields. Bell Labs' status as a national resource during much of the Cold War resulted largely from its role in providing technologies for U.S. defense efforts as well as improving the nation's telephone system. An effort to break up AT&T in the 1950s was defused in large part to allay Department of Defense concerns that such a breakup would impair vital national security–related research being conducted by Bell Labs.[100] The leadership in developing telecommunications and information technologies began to shift decisively in the 1970s as the locus of demand moved firmly into the civilian sector. The cutting edge of technology during the 1990s was driven by commercial applications such as the development of VSATs to enable reception of digital satellite communications or of Java programming approaches to develop new Internet applications.

The U.S. national security community must operate within the context of this reality. In the post–Cold War environment of budget cuts and downsizing of forces, the need to leverage fast-improving civilian information technologies has become a common theme within the Department of Defense. The 1994 Defense Science Board Task Force report *Information Architecture for the Battlefield* recognized that the development and procurement cycles for commercial

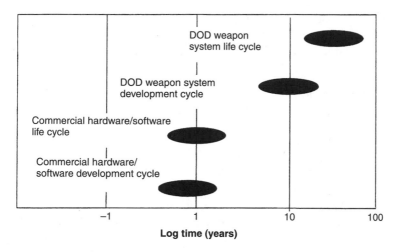

Figure 1.5
Comparison of defense and commercial technology acquisition cycles. Source: Adapted from DSB Task Force, Information Architecture for the Battlefield *(Washington, DC: Department of Defense, October 1994), 41.*

hardware and software products are dramatically shorter than the DOD acquisition cycle geared toward the development and procurement of weapons systems and platforms.[101] Figure 1.5 compares the technology acquisition cycles in the military and commercial sectors. Assistant Secretary of Defense for Command, Control, Communications, and Intelligence, Emmett Paige, concluded in 1996 that "[m]any of the leading-edge technologies critical to success on the battlefield are now driven by commercial markets. Defense must rely more on commercial or dual-use products and the rapid insertion of new commercial leading edge technology into command, control and communications systems."[102] The U.S. national security establishment now stresses adapting commercial technologies to military uses (sometimes called "spin-on") and focusing R&D on military-specific applications rather than efforts to guide and control the general trajectory for information technology development.[103] At the behest of its director, George Tenet, the Central Intelligence Agency has established the widely publicized, In-Q-It, venture capital operation with the intent of forming partnerships with leaders in the information technology industry and academia.[104] The Defense Department and other United States government organizations are pursuing similar approaches.

This shift in technological leadership implies that the military must develop the capacity to monitor information technologies outside its own management and select those that enhance war-fighting capability. More broadly, those concerned with national security must understand how potential technological developments create new challenges and mission areas. In combination with the pace of change and globalization of information technology activity described in the next section, civilian technological leadership will make government control of the application of new developments with national security implications very difficult.

Fast Rate of Change

The emergence of commercial technological leadership in the information technology field has helped cause the development of another significant phenomenon: the rapid pace of change in the performance, operating systems, applications, and modes of use of information infrastructures. The rapid advance in the performance characteristics of computing and communications technologies provides the best evidence of this change. Dramatic advances have occurred in information technologies such as increased computer processing and memory capacity and enhanced transmission capacity of wired, wireless, and satellite communications channels. Figure 1.6 provides an overview of the increases in performance capabilities of computing technology since 1900.

As the price of computing capability continues to drop dramatically relative to performance, users of information technology face choices about how often to replace or upgrade hardware and software technologies to take advantage of new performance capabilities while ensuring continuity of operations and compatibility with existing information systems.[105] For example, switching software for the U.S. West telecommunications network advanced so quickly in the mid-1990s that upgrades were installed every four months.[106] Providers of commercial telecommunication services expect a monthly turnover of 7–8 percent among organizations using their services.[107]

Although the change is less easily measured, software applications have evolved at a similarly dramatic pace. Users of information technologies are confronted with a deluge of new products promising to improve capability to move large quantities of data through networks, allow processing of information in digital formats, increase precision of computer-controlled manufacturing systems, enhance accuracy of inventory systems, or provide greater customization in electronic publishing. These quantitative and qualitative improvements in applications also necessitate improved computing and information transmission capability for their use. Personal and business computer users worldwide faced

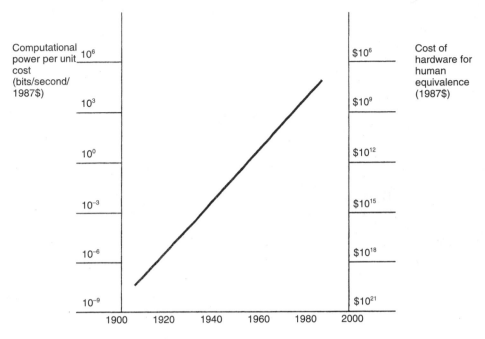

Figure 1.6
Computing trends. Source: Curtis R. Carlson, "The Age of Interactivity," in James P. McCarthy, ed., National Security in the Information Age *(U.S. Air Force Academy, CO: Olin Foundation, 1996), 12.*

this problem throughout the 1990s as it became apparent that to properly use new versions of Microsoft's Windows operating system would require microprocessors with increased capacity, pushing the pace of upgrades. Lt. Gen. Douglas Bucholz, former director of the Joint Staff for Command, Control, Communications, and Computers, has stressed how implementation of new technologies to improve U.S. war-fighting capabilities through the use of digitized maps, images, and even video in real time places ever-growing demands for capacity and flexibility on the defense information infrastructure.[108]

The combination of improved hardware and software capabilities has resulted in continuing shifts in the underlying architectures and modes of use of information networks. Table 1.1 provides an overview of three paradigms for information architectures that have evolved in the past thirty to forty years: mainframe-centric, personal computer (PC)–centric, and network-centric.[109]

In the mainframe age, computers performed very specialized math and engineering functions for highly sophisticated users and organizations.

Table 1.1
Three paradigms of computing

	1960s and 1970s: Mainframe-centric	1980s: PC-centric	1990s: Network-centric
Focus	Engineering (quantitative)	Machine productivity	Individual productivity
Function	Special purpose (math-based)	Broader functions (CAD/CAM/FM)	Cross-functional, enterprise-wide
Operator location	Data center	LANs/WANs	On-line/nomadic
Users	Engineer/scientific orientation	Functional stovepipe (finance, inventory, etc.)	Everyone in the enterprise
Limitations	Speed of bus	Speed of access (cache/RAM)	Speed of network (wireless/ISDN/ATM)

Source: Excerpted from John Woodmansee, Jr., "Applying Information Technology," in James McCarthy, ed., *National Security in the Information Age* (U.S. Air Force Academy, CO: Olin Institute, March 1996), 307.

Operators were located in central data centers, from which data was then transferred in physical formats. The rise of the desktop PC relied on improved, physically smaller processing and memory capabilities and networking software. As a result, PCs could access server databases through dedicated local- or wide-area networks to perform a broader variety of functions, including inventory management, accounting, and finance. Further stimulated by development of common data transmission standards and the rise of the Internet, a network-centric model for information infrastructures has emerged. Using improved hardware and software for connectivity and telecommunications networks with broader bandwidth, remote users rely on networks to access computational resources and data from a much wider range of locations and organizations. These capabilities allow network users to publish whatever information they want and access the information they desire to accomplish many functions with increasing ease.

Rapid evolution continues as new technologies create opportunities for different uses of information in the network-centric era. The advent of CD-ROM technology first created easy access to interactive graphics, voice, and video through the use of powerful PCs. Yet the pictures, sound, and hypertext links of the World Wide Web have also made the Internet a source for interactive multimedia applications for an even wider range of users. The rise in use of Java applets in software applications may increasingly allow users to pull such applications, customized to their particular needs, from networks, reducing reliance on the computing power of the PC. In the telecommunications realm, the advent of fiber optics, modems, and improved switching software has enabled users to access much more data from computers wired to networks. The next wave of innovation in this area may involve improved wireless signal processing to create broadband data connections via low earth-orbiting satellites and cellular communications, allowing users the freedom to access digital information networks without wires.[110]

The trend toward an increasingly mobile, information pull approach to network design and architecture places a premium on open standards and easy access to ensure that new technologies can be accommodated. Information technology producers have very strong incentives to get new products to market as fast as possible and to set de facto standards by establishing patterns of use and reliance. The rapid development of new technologies has forced users of information networks to become increasingly aware of the potential for change and the need for organizational adaptation to take advantage of new information technologies.

The technical skills required to develop and operate information infrastructures are also evolving quickly. Personnel with cutting-edge information technology expertise are an increasingly limited resource. An Information Technology Association of America study published in November 1997 indicated that the United States had 350,000 job vacancies for computer scientists and programmers that were going unfilled.[111] The demand for personnel in three related fields—database administration/computer support specialists, computer engineers, and systems analysts—is expected to grow between 100 to 120 percent from 1996 to 2006.[112] The need for computer programmers became particularly acute in the late 1990s as companies, government agencies, and other organizations struggled with the need to fix their information systems to deal with the Year 2000 problem embedded in a vast range of information systems, With such heavy competition for skilled personnel, salaries for computer professionals are also expected to continue to rise dramatically. The U.S. computer industry successfully campaigned in the late 1990s to get Congress to raise the numerical ceilings on working visas for foreign workers with programming and networking skills.

As the complexity of software applications has increased, their development has become modular. New applications are written to execute new functions or increase performance based on limited modification of and simply adding to existing code. Problems with reliability and security may carry forward over time if technology producers and users do not create procedures to ferret out and constantly remove known problems. The Software Engineering Institute states:

> When vendors release patches or upgrades to solve security problems, organizations' systems often are not upgraded. The job may prove too time-consuming, too complex, or just at too low a priority for the system administration staff to handle. With increased complexity comes the introduction of more vulnerabilities, so solutions do not solve problems for the long-term—system maintenance is never-ending. Because managers do not fully understand risks, they neither give security a high enough priority nor assign adequate resources. Exacerbating the problem is the fact that demand for skilled administrators far exceeds the supply.[113]

Not all components change quickly in large-scale information infrastructures, however. The need to continue to access existing information resources and to sustain current operations requires that existing information systems be "migrated" in planned progressions toward future performance goals and interoperability standards. In cases in which older, "legacy" systems are fundamental to the operation of an organization, they may be replaced very infrequently. For example, the SCADA system used by Manchester Power in New England was deployed in the early 1970s and had not been substantially changed as of 1997.[114] The servicing of such systems involves the expensive prospect of sustaining expertise with software products that vendors no longer support. A lack of personnel capable of programming in languages such as Fortran still present in critical software code in the computer systems of major government agencies and financial institutions exacerbated the human expertise constraints for dealing with Year 2000 problems in those organizations.

The ad hoc evolution of information networks based on the tacking on and patching of new hardware and software components to existing systems also requires development of nonstandard linkages to make the larger network function. Installing new equipment may degrade the preexisting reliability and security features of the original products. The software, hardware, and procedures developed to create interconnections between old and new components often are less well-tested and -documented than standard products developed for commercial markets or government users. New reliability problems and vulnerabilities to outside intrusion may be created through maintenance activities conducted within a large information network.[115]

The changes outlined above and the rate at which they are taking place have fundamental implications for providers and users who manage information infrastructures. The totality of exact sources and dimensions of change in information infrastructures is difficult to track but will prove a central concern of those involved in targeting and defending these infrastructures in the advent of strategic information warfare. However, the pace of change in information technology also contributes to a situation in which large numbers of actors can potentially interfere with the information transmitted through those infrastructures as well as access the tools to conduct disruptive activities through the infrastructures themselves. Additional layers of complexity emerge from the requirement for information networks to reach back to older technologies as they incorporate newer ones. Those grappling with the national security aspects of the growing use and reliance on information infrastructures face trade-offs in managing the benefits of a rapid pace of advance of information technology and ensuring that the new technologies are utilized to create secure networks.

Global Interconnection, Operation, and Production

Information infrastructures have become increasingly global in terms of interconnection between transmission links and networks, development of the underlying technologies, and ownership of the principal operating entities. The increasingly transnational nature of these infrastructures and their operators raises significant issues for strategic information warfare.

Traffic in telecommunications crossing national borders grew at 17 percent per year from 1985 to 1995.[116] Yet historically nations have endeavored to maintain some degree of sovereign control over communications and information that flow across political borders. Long-standing arrangements have protected diplomats and international couriers, whereas spies and agents have illicitly crossed borders to observe and transmit misinformation. Development of the telegraph and telephone in the nineteenth century quickly necessitated the development of International Telecommunication Union (ITU) regulations to deal with transmission of electronic information across borders. Nevertheless, the continued advance of telecommunications and information technologies has made maintaining control of transborder information flows difficult. The advent of radio allowed cross-border transmission of information through the airwaves, which proved much more difficult to monitor and control than telegraph and telephone transmissions.

The launching of communications and broadcast satellites has eroded political control of information transmission even further. The number of privately owned and operated communications and broadcast satellite networks, which were previously operated exclusively by national or international authorities, rose dramatically in the 1990s. A single satellite in geosynchronous orbit has the ability to beam television signals, Internet data, and phone calls over nearly one-third of the earth's surface. If not properly protected, satellite communications, like other wireless means of transmission, can be intercepted, jammed, and distorted by parties outside the control of the communicating parties. Such transmissions cross sovereign borders. At the same time, satellite systems may also require ground stations in multiple countries to provide for control as well as to create connections between parties on opposite sides of the globe. Such facilities may provide a vehicle through which political authorities may exert authority over satellite operators in countries where such ground-based infrastructure is required or desired.

The emergence of packet-switched networks has complicated the situation even further. Modern international telecommunications networks can utilize multiple paths to optimize network carrying capacity by choosing between transoceanic cables, land lines, microwave stations, and a variety of satellites and ground stations to carry transmissions without regard to national borders being crossed. While using these multiple transmission modes, modern information networks also rely on systems and networks operated by multiple organizations to carry a given packet from sender to receiver. These information transmissions leaping around the globe can cross many supposedly sovereign jurisdictions, bouncing into and out of space in the hands of multiple operators for very short periods of time. Such transmissions may prove impossible to put under national or international control, posing severe problems for cooperative defensive approaches to strategic information warfare threats. Use of such transmissions for hostile purposes, such as to create unauthorized access into a computer or disrupt the operation of telecommunications, undermines existing concepts of legal neutrality and responsibility.[117]

Intergovernmental organizations (IGOs) have faced increasing challenges in managing contentious issues involved in growing global interconnectivity. The rapid technological advance and diffusion among worldwide users of new mediums of transmission, especially satellites and digitally switched networks, began to break down the existing structure of international communications governance by the 1980s. Beginning with the United States, many countries have begun to open telecommunications services to competition, although the degree to which international companies have been allowed into domestic markets has varied widely from country to country.[118] The emergence of small digital satellite receivers in combination with high-power transmitters has made it possible for small organizations and individuals to direct video, voice, and data services to areas not served by existing telecommunications and land-based broadcast networks, thereby raising additional concerns regarding trade in telecommunications services. World Trade Organization efforts to resolve these issues have floundered because of differences between major parties, including the United States, Europe, and Japan.[119] Increasingly, the nationalist stances taken by the organization's members have made the process of using IGOs to resolve problems too contentious and too slow to deal with the pace of technological advance.

Despite these difficulties, information technology and telecommunications companies increasingly are deploying cutting-edge technology to take advantage of the possibilities of digital convergence in providing service to customers worldwide. Established national and international governmental institutions are widely perceived as incapable of coping with the dramatic pace of technological and organizational change sweeping through information infrastructures. As a result, providers and users of global networks are attempting to establish standards. Management of the Internet depends on organizations such as the Internet Society, the associated Internet Engineering Task Force, and the World Wide Web Consortium. These organizations rely on an approach in which all interested stakeholders are invited to participate, with a focus on setting open, ad hoc standards to most quickly accommodate the use of technological advances.[120] Such ad hoc mechanisms do not always create adequate levels of coordination, especially when established commercial interests and national competitiveness are involved. For example, different standards have emerged for provision of cellular telephone services in the United States, Europe, and Japan. Lack of widely accepted standards presents a braking force in the rapid pursuit of a tightly intertwined global information infrastructure.[121]

Efforts to control globally networked communications may increasingly focus on recipient networks and addressees of communications within the reach of political authorities, not the originator of the communication or organization(s) carrying the transmission. Throughout the 1990s, China and Singapore attempted to control the access provided through their information infrastructures to the outside world. Concerned about "cultural pollution," Singapore has banned all home satellite dishes and required all ISPs to register with the Singapore Broadcast Authority (SBA). ISPs in Singapore need SBA approval to place political and religious material on the World Wide Web and must block pornographic and objectionable material.[122] In the People's Republic of China, the government permits broadcast only by cable television services whose content it can monitor and bans personal satellite dishes. People with Internet access accounts must register with the police. All Chinese computer networks with Internet services are supervised by government agencies, and international connections must use a channel designated by the Ministry of Posts and Telecommunications and operate under the following requirements: "No organization or individual may engage in activities at the expense of state security. Producing, retrieving, duplicating, or spreading information that may hinder public order are forbidden."[123] Growing global interconnectivity and private-sector involvement obviously does not prohibit individual nations and other actors from undertaking efforts to control the access to global information infrastructures to limit perceived vulnerabilities, despite conventional wisdom to the contrary.

Another aspect of globalization significant for a consideration of strategic information warfare is the increase in the prevalence of mergers, cross-ownership, joint ventures, and strategic partnerships among some of the world's largest corporations. According to a 1997 Harvard Business School study, the privatization of national telecommunication carriers has resulted in "increased equity participation by carriers from one country in the domestic and international markets of another country through global alliances and consortia."[124] In the late 1990s, the AT&T World Partners alliance included KDD (Japan), Singapore Telecom, Telestra (Australia), Unitel (Canada), Korea Telecom, Telecom New Zealand, Hong Kong Telecom, and Unisource—itself a consortium of Telia (Sweden), KPN (Netherlands), Swiss Telecom, and Telefonica (Spain).[125] One must note, however, that these efforts to create global networks focus on regions of the world where projected demand will be the greatest. Certain regions such as Africa and Central Asia have seen much less investment to create connectivity to "global" information infrastructures.[126]

Transnational activities and ownership of the major telecommunications and information network providers varies in degree from provider to provider. Some corporations may have little significant international ownership. The dominant Japanese telecommunications provider, Nippon Telephone and Telegraph (NTT), has engaged in little overseas activity and benefits from well-protected domestic markets.[127] Also, transnational corporations engaged in international strategic alliances have incentives to reach agreements to ensure reliable communications and foster cooperative relationships with host state governments.

Analysts of strategic information warfare must understand the significance of transnational ownership and loyalties of organizations that provide information services and networks. Assigning corporate responsibility and penalties for misuse of networks may be difficult. A hypothetical digital information attack on a U.S.-based organization conducted over the ICO network jointly operated by Hughes and forty other companies could well enter this highly integrated system through the local telecommunications provider in another country. Holding Hughes responsible in United States courts may be legally impossible and possibly counterproductive in terms of co-opting the corporation into national cyber-defense efforts. As the U.S. government endeavors to protect civilian-sector information infrastructures, identifying which commercial entities require and deserve protection, the level of corporate responsibility, and how to achieve cooperation with such organizations will prove a major challenge. Additionally, those responsible for devising strategic information warfare approaches need to consider how cooperative information and technological sharing could result in security leaks and technology transfer because of the transnational nature of participating commercial organizations with transnational ties.

Not only are the means and providers of global information networks increasingly global, but so are the activities of the organizations that provide the underpinning technologies. Companies such as Microsoft, Intel, and Texas Instruments have corporate strategies emphasizing global production and marketing. Very significantly, development and maintenance of software has become a transnational enterprise as digital code is shipped around the globe on information networks in search of cheaper labor and to sustain continuous capabilities to deal with problems. Countries including Ireland, Israel, and India have become increasingly important hubs of activity in the software industry based on the presence of affordable technological expertise. Major U.S. corporations such as Citicorp use Texas Instruments programmers in Bangalore, India, to ensure computer problems receive twenty-four-hour-a-day attention.[128] The Department of Defense has purchased computer security firewalls and network monitoring systems from Israeli firms.[129]

Again, an important caveat regarding the degree of "globalization" in information technology production and expertise must be recognized. The intellectual development of advanced hardware, software, and applications of information technology remains largely directed by organizations in the "triad" of the United States, western Europe, and Japan. Information technology development by commercial firms in other nations, most notably Asian countries such as South Korea, Taiwan, and India, has emphasized technological followership and the development of peripheral hardware and software modification. Past technological competitors such as Russia have slipped further behind in the global information technology competition. Most countries in Africa have little to no capability to develop and produce IT products. Considerable differentiation in expertise across geographic regions and among actors seen as technologically proficient exists, depending on the specific technology involved.

The globalization of corporate activity and ownership associated with information infrastructures has significant implications for strategic information warfare. A wide range of organizations and actors may have access to the technology and human expertise to operate and apply these technologies for either productive or destructive ends. As with the transnational nature of organizations that provide information network services, the globalization of activity conducted by technology providers has implications for strategic information warfare related to assigning corporate responsibility and controlling the flow of technology. Transnational activity in the production of technologies that underpin modern information infrastructures may have significant impact on efforts of national actors to assure their integrity.

How Cyberspace Differs from Operating Environments in Other Forms of Warfare

In addition to supporting a wide range of activities throughout society, information infrastructures also create a distinct new environment. The cyberspace environment of interconnected networks has a specific set of operating locations and principles different from those that govern the operation of other infrastructures. Although other supporting infrastructures, such as the transportation system, at times modify their physical surroundings, such infrastructures generally are used to overcome geophysical constraints to support human activity through improving mobility, providing electric power or heat, and so on. Such infrastructures may shape, but they do not create, the environment for their operation.

Cyberspace is a man-made environment for the creation, transmittal, and use of information in a variety of formats. Changing computer hardware or software systems or operating protocols in an information infrastructure reshapes the environment to a much greater degree than in conventional infrastructures. The electronic networks of the information infrastructure actually provide the physical environment for the provision of information as well as targets of activity intended to disrupt the creation, transmittal, and use of that information.

As a result, the environment for strategic information warfare is much more mutable than that for land, sea, air, and space warfare. For traditional forms of warfare, the environment in which the combat takes place has preexisting physical characteristics that determine the effectiveness of evolving technologies and define organizational competence.[130] Shipbuilders and sailors must understand hydrography, just as designers of airplanes and pilots must understand the aerodynamic characteristics of the earth's atmosphere. Militaries in many states create large organizations and sustained efforts to stay at the leading edge of this required knowledge. Moreover, the presence of armed forces operating in such natural environments is usually clear to opponents. The deep seas and airspace are monitored for the presence of hostile military forces and threatening acts. Efforts to prevent monitoring activity involves quieting submarines or reducing the radar signatures of aircraft as part of technological struggles to increase or decrease transparency. However, such competitions to achieve stealthiness are generally intended to create tactical advantage, not to deny responsibility for military action. When adversaries use these environments to transgress against enemy interests, state governments assume authority over the environment to conduct warfare. Military authorities assume control over all traffic in sea lanes and airspace designated as war zones, dictating where civilian and aircraft vessels may operate. Military control facilitates the use of these same environments to launch and defend against attacks.

The environment for strategic information warfare conducted in cyberspace is substantially different. Warfare in cyberspace would be conducted over a "terrain" that is almost completely man-made. Cyberspace consists of electronically powered hardware, networks, operating systems, and transmission standards. Corrupting, disrupting, or destroying components of digital information networks would actually change the topography of cyberspace, as would changing a system's access procedures or taking it off-line temporarily. Key features of the environment may be under the direct control of the organization and actors engaged in a conflict. The highly complex and interconnected nature of information networks also creates difficulties in determining whether attacks have actually occurred, creating a potential window for actors who wish to avoid responsibility for their actions, as explored in chapter 2.

Technical and operating expertise remain necessary both to conduct and to monitor activity in cyberspace. Although governments could attempt to assume control over cyberspace, such efforts would face the barrier of a lack sufficient technological expertise on the part of the government to operate and monitor the wide range of complex networks and interconnections that create the environment. Infrastructure operators and users confronted with a potential strategic information attack have the ability to change the environment faced by attackers, but coordinating such defensive actions would require unprecedented government-civilian cooperation. The implications of required technological expertise for targeting and attacking information infrastructures, as well as for organizing defensive efforts relevant to strategic information warfare, will be discussed in chapter 3.

The growing concern in the United States and elsewhere regarding the potential for information attacks against critical information infrastructures needs to be addressed in light of both past experience and new conditions. The potential emergence of strategic information warfare can be usefully conceptualized through a comparison to past analyses of physical force as a means to a political end. Attacks on information infrastructures can be and have been launched through a variety of mechanical, radio frequency, and digital means. Digital attacks represent an emerging means for strategic warfare. Although use of digital means for waging strategic warfare creates differences from the past environments for conducting wars, the boundaries for discussion of such warfare still require addressing the actors, their objectives, and issues of legitimacy, as with approaches based on use of nuclear and conventional military forces. Understanding the potential significance of strategic information warfare also requires knowledge of how reliance on information systems, networks, and infrastructures has grown and the significant features of information infrastructures in the early years of the new century. The discussion in this chapter is intended as a point of departure for such awareness, not as a comprehensive survey. The understanding developed here provides the basis for analyzing the possibilities facing the United States for strategic warfare based on attacking and defending information infrastructures.

Suggested Additional Sources

John Arquilla and David Ronfeldt. "Cyberwar Is Coming!" *Comparative Strategy* 12, no. 2 (Spring 1993): 141–165.
One of the earliest articles to identify how an increasingly networked world will allow the development of new forms of warfare. The authors address conflicts based on information infrastructure attacks (Netwars) and the opportunity for increased efforts at perception management (cyberwars).

Alvin Toffler and Heidi Toffler. *War and Anti-War: Survival at the Dawn of the 21st Century.* Boston: Little, Brown and Company, 1993.
Building on the paradigm of three waves of human economic progress developed in Alvin Toffler's earlier works—agricultural, industrial, and informational—this book explores the characteristics of conflict in the "third wave." War and Antiwar was widely read within senior national security circles immediately after its publication and has had significant influence on thinking about how the information age would change the battlefield, the nature of wars, and their resolution.

Winn Schwartau. *Information Warfare.* New York: Thunder Mouth Press, 1994, 1996.
The first major work dedicated to explaining how increasing reliance on information systems and networks creates opportunities for malicious activity across the spectrum of conflict from individuals to nation-states. The first edition was subtitled "Chaos on the Electronic Superhighway" and endeavored to outline the range of new threats. In the second edition, subtitled "Cyber Terrorism: Protecting Your Personal Security in the Electronic Age," Schwartau adds essays by others on a wide variety of information warfare topics.

Martin C. Libicki. *What Is Information Warfare?* Washington, DC: National Defense University Press, 1995.
A concise, articulate effort to categorize the different threads in thinking about information warfare. Libicki illuminates the how some information warfare discussions are natural progressions from those concerning preexisting means of waging conflict and others are wildly speculative.

Rodger C. Molander, Andrew S. Riddle, and Peter A. Wilson. *Strategic Information Warfare: A New Face of War.* Washington, DC: RAND National Defense Research Institute, 1996.
This RAND study is focused on the policy implications of digital attack and disruption. The authors stress how information warfare undermines the United States traditional geographic sanctuary from strategic attack. The book identifies new concerns related to warfare in the cyberspace environment, although it does not delve into how digital warfare translates into political influence for U.S. adversaries.

Zalmay M. Khalilzad and John P. White, eds. *Strategic Appraisal: The Changing Role of Information in Warfare.* Washington, DC: RAND Corporation, 1999.
A comprehensive survey by widely respected authors about information warfare at the end of the 1990s. This work addresses how information warfare will affect national power, notions of deterrence and defense, military organization, opportunities for perception management, and concepts of operation on the battlefield.

Timothy L. Thomas. "Russian Views on Information-Based Warfare." *Airpower Journal* 10 (Special Edition 1996): 25–35; and Wei Jincheng. "Information War: A New Form of People's War." In *Chinese Views of Future Warfare*, ed. Michael Pillsbury, 409–412. Washington DC: NDU Press, 1997.
These two pieces discuss how other nations think about information warfare and shed light on some interesting differences from the U.S. approach.

Lawrence T. Greenberg, Seymour E. Goodman, and Kevin J. Soo Hoo. *Information Warfare and International Law.* Washington, DC: National Defense University Press, 1997.
This work identifies the difficult issues raised by information warfare in relation to international law. The study stresses how past legal constructs may be applied while recognizing that development of the law will lag behind technological advances for the foreseeable future.

David S. Alberts. *Unintended Consequences of the Information Age Technologies.* Washington, DC: National Defense University Press, 1996.
Alberts provides needed tempering to the unabashed enthusiasm in the national security community for jumping wholesale onto the cyberspace bandwagon. In particular, he stresses how new technologies may create vulnerabilities in infrastructures and information overload for decision makers. He recommends a strategy for improved technology insertion and utilization to minimize such potential problems.

William Gibson. *Neuromancer.* New York: Ace Books, 1984.
The science fiction work that coined the term "cyberspace" and conceptualized the Net as a place where human conflicts would be waged in the future. Gibson's works and those of other "cyberpunk" authors generally provide a dark but thought-provoking vision of how information technology combined with biotechnology and nanotechnology will change human existence in the next hundred years.

Tom Standage. *The Victorian Internet.* New York: Berkeley Books, 1999.
Standage examines the evolution of the telegraph in the nineteenth century. The work stresses how the emergence of the Internet constitutes another in a long history of technologically driven information revolutions. He also cautions against "chronocentricity" or the belief that we are the only generation that is blessed or cursed with unique challenges.

Web sites: Internet Society ⟨www.isoc.org⟩ and World Wide Web Consortium (W3C) ⟨www.w3.org⟩.
These two Web sites provide up-to-date information and links on a wide range of technical and policy considerations. The Internet Society is associated with Internet Engineering Task Force that helps manage consensus building about the technological evolution and standards setting for the Internet protocols. The W3C performs a similar function regarding Web technologies.

Notes

1. The rationale for this label is most fully explained in Alan D. Campen, ed., *The First Information War* (Fairfax, VA: AFCEA International Press, 1992).

2. George J. Stein, "Information Warfare," *Airpower Journal* 9, no. 1 (Spring 1995): 32.

3. From John I. Alger, "Introduction to Information Warfare," in Winn Schwartau, *Information Warfare: Chaos on the Electronic Superhighway,* 1st ed. (New York: Thunder Mouth Press, 1994), 12.

4. Dorothy E. Denning, *Information Warfare and Security* (Reading, MA: Addison-Wesley, 1999), 12.

5. Department of the Air Force, *Cornerstones of Information Warfare* (Washington, DC: Headquarters, Department of the Air Force, 1995), 3–4.

6. Joint Pub 3-13, *Joint Doctrine for Information Operations* (Washington, DC: Joint Staff, October 1998), I-1.

7. Statement of George Tenet, Director of Central Intelligence, "Hearing on Current and Projected National Security Threats" to U.S. Senate, Armed Services Committee, 106th Congress, 1st Session, 2 February 1999.

8. See Statement of Jamie S. Gorelick, Deputy Attorney General, to U.S. Senate, Committee on Governmental Affairs, Permanent Subcommittee on Investigations, Hearings on "Security in Cyberspace," 104th Congress, 2nd Session, 16 July 1996.

9. Martin C. Libicki, *What Is Information Warfare?* (Washington, DC: National Defense University Press, 1995), 91.

10. See Richard Szafranski, "An Information Warfare Strategic Information Integrated Operations Plan (SIIOP)" in Schwartau, *Information Warfare*, 2nd ed. (New York: Thunder Mouth Press, 1996), 115–124. Col. Szafranski is a Professor at the Air War College and directed the Air Force 2025 Study which delineated future conflict scenarios, political and economic conditions, and technological developments to guide Air Force planning.

11. Schwartau, *Information Warfare*, 2nd ed., 540. See also Jean Guisel, *Cyberwar: Espionage on the Internet* (New York: Plenum Trade, 1997), esp. chap. 7, "Economics, the New Battlefield," 215–238.

12. President's Commission on Critical Infrastructure Protection (PCCIP), "Interim Report," 13.

13. This topic was addressed by the Commission on the Roles and Missions of the U.S. Intelligence Community, *Preparing for the 21st Century: An Appraisal of U.S. Intelligence* (Washington, DC: Commission on the Roles and Missions of the U.S. Intelligence Community, 1 March 1996), 22–24. On the threat of economic espionage by other means, see John J. Fialka, *War by Other Means: Economic Espionage in America* (New York: W. W. Norton, 1997).

14. Roger C. Molander, Andrew S. Riddle, and Peter A. Wilson, *Strategic Information Warfare: A New Face of War* (Washington, DC: RAND National Defense Research Institute, 1996), xiv.

15. Daniel J. and Julie C. H. Ryan, "Protecting the National Information Infrastructure against InfoWar," in Schwartau, *Information Warfare*, 627.

16. Roger C. Molander, Peter A. Wilson, David A. Mussington, and Richard F. Mesic, *Strategic Information Warfare Rising* (Santa Monica, CA: RAND Corporation, 1998), 6.

17. Frank J. Cilliffo, ed., *Cybercrime . . . Cyberterrorism . . . Cyberrwarfare . . . Averting an Electronic Waterloo* (Washington, DC: Center for Strategic and International Studies, Global Organized Crime Project, 1998).

18. Carl von Clausewitz, *On War*, Michael Howard and Peter Paret, ed. and trans. (Princeton, NJ: Princeton University Press, 1976), 92.

19. Thomas C. Schelling, "The Retarded Science of International Strategy," in *The Strategy of Conflict*, 2d ed. (New Haven: Yale University Press, 1980), 3–20.

20. See Alvin and Heidi Toffler, *War and Anti-War: Survival at the Dawn of the 21st Century* (Boston: Little, Brown, 1993), 242–243, regarding the description of a "soft edged" state.

21. Martin van Creveld, "What War Is Fought For," *The Transformation of War* (New York: Free Press, 1991), 124–156, and John Keegan, "War in Human History," *A History of Warfare* (New York: Vintage Books, 1993), 3–60.

22. Nathan Miller, *Spying for America: Hidden History of U.S. Intelligence* (New York: Dell Publishing, 1989), 46. According to Miller, Franklin forged a document purporting to show the British were buying bales of American scalps from the Indians, including those of women and children.

23. Abraham N. Shulsky, *Silent Warfare: Understanding the World of Intelligence* (Washington DC: Brassey's, 1993), 95–96.

24. Marshall McHulan and Quentin Fiore, *War and Peace in the Global Village* (New York: Bantam Books, 1968), elaborated on the role of the media in the Vietnam conflict. See also Johanna Nueman, *Lights, Camera, War: Is Media Technology Driving International Politics?* (New York: St. Martin's Press, 1996).

25. The possibilities for taking control of TV broadcasts is outlined in Curtis R. Carlson, "The Age of Interactivity With Implications for Public and Private Policy," in *National Security in the Information Age*, ed. James McCarthy (U.S. Air Force Academy, CO: Olin Institute, March 1996), 25–26. See Charles Swett, "The Role of the Internet in International Politics," in Robert L. Pfaltzgraff, Jr., and Richard H. Shultz, Jr., *War in the Information Age: New Challenges for U.S. Security* (London: Brassey's, 1997), 279–306, for an analysis of how the Internet is a becoming a tool for a variety of state and nonstate actors such as the Zapatista rebels in Mexico to use in circumventing traditional political controls in seeking their objectives.

26. The concept of soft power is most strongly associated with Joseph Nye. See Joseph S. Nye, Jr., and William A. Owens, "America's Information Edge," *Foreign Affairs* 75, no. 2 (March/April 1996): 20–36.

27. Phillip Elmer-DeWitt, "Welcome to Cyberspace," as excerpted in Bruno Leone, ed., *The Information Highway* (San Diego: Greenhaven Press, 1996), 19.

28. Richard Power, *Current and Future Danger: A CSI Primer on Computer Crime and Information Warfare* (San Francisco: Report by the Computer Security Institute, 1995), 18.

29. Significant attention in the U.S. national security community has focused on "nonlethal" technologies such as sticky foams and friction-reducing/-enhancing compounds that physically degrade and disable enemy capabilities at the tactical level of conflicts and peace operations. See for example Paul G. O'Connor, "Waging Wars with Non-Lethal Weapons," in Karl P. Mayar, ed., *Challenge and Response: Anticipating U.S. Security Concerns* (Maxwell Air Force Base, AL: Air University Press, 1994), 333–344. Although information attacks possibly could have disabling effects, I treat them as strategic means for waging conflicts distinct from the nonlethal warfare discussions focused on U.S. involvement in peace operations.

30. von Clausewitz, *On War*, 577.

31. Sun Tzu, *The Art of War*. Samuel B. Griffith, trans. (Oxford: Oxford University Press, 1963), 77.

32. Abe Singer and Scott Rowell, *Information Warfare: An Old Operational Concept with New Implications* (Washington, DC: National Defense University, INSS Strategic Forum #99, December 1996), 2.

33. See statement of John M. Deutch, Director of Central Intelligence, "Foreign Information Warfare Programs and Capabilities," to U.S. Senate, Committee on Governmental Affairs, Permanent Subcommittee on Investigations, Hearings on "Security in Cyberspace," 104th Congress, 2nd Session, 25 June 1996.

34. John Warden, "The Enemy as a System," *Airpower Journal* 9, no. 1 (Spring 1995), nn. 1, 43.

35. Molander et al., *Strategic Information Warfare*, 19–20, illuminate the possibility of such alliances between internal and external actors using strategic information warfare as well as the difficulties such a situation would present for the United States.

36. See Anne W. Branscomb, *Who Owns Information? From Privacy to Public Access* (New York, Basic Books: 1994), and Jonathan Roesenor, *Cyberlaw: The Law of the Internet* (New York: Springer, 1997).

37. For a comprehensive review of the law surrounding the technical and legal search issues involved in computer crime cases, see John T. Soma, Elizabeth A. Banker, and Alexander R. Smith, "Computer Crime: Substantive Statues and Technical and Legal Search Considerations," *Air Force Law Review* 39 (1996): 225–259.

38. In the mid-1990s, analysis began to grapple specifically with the relationship between international law and information warfare. Lawrence T. Greenberg, Seymour E. Goodman, and Kevin J. Soo Hoo, *Old Law for a New World: The Applicability of International Law to Information Warfare* (Palo Alto, CA: Stanford University, Center for International Security and Arms Control, February 1997); Sean P. Kanuck, "Information Warfare: New Challenges for Public

International Law," *Harvard International Law Journal* 37, no. 1 (Winter 1996): 272–285; Richard W. Aldrich, *The International Legal Implications of Information Warfare* (U.S. Air Force Academy, CO: Report for Air Force Institute for National Security Studies, October 1995).

39. Greenberg, Goodman, and Soo Hoo, *Old Law for a New World*, 35.

40. Office of the General Counsel, *An Assessment of International Legal Issues in Information Operations* (Washington, DC: Department of Defense, May 1999).

41. Stated in Carter's State of the Union address, 20 January 1980, as quoted in Jeffrey Record, *Revising U.S. Military Strategy: Tailoring Means to Ends* (Washington, DC: Pergammon-Brassey's, 1984), 37.

42. Wei Jincheng, "Information War: A New Form of People's War," in *Chinese Views of Future Warfare*, ed. Michael Pillsbury (Washington, DC: NDU Press, 1997), 412.

43. PCCIP, *Critical Foundations: Protecting America's Infrastructures* (Alexandria, VA: President's Commission on Critical Infrastructure Protection, October 1997), vii.

44. John Arquilla and David Ronfeldt, "Cyberwar Is Coming!" *Comparative Strategy* 12, no. 2 (Spring 1993): 150.

45. Visual signals also underwent a long evolution from smoke signals and mirrors. In 1844, the French semaphore system could pass a message hundreds of miles from Paris to Calais in four minutes. See George P. Oslin, *The Story of Telecommunications* (Macon, GA: Mercer University Press, 1992), 4–5.

46. For the detailed provisions of the 1982 modified final judgment that split up AT&T, see Alan Stone, *Wrong Number: The Break-Up of AT&T* (New York: Basic Books, 1989), 326–335.

47. Anthony G. Oettinger, *The Information Evolution* (Cambridge: Harvard University, Program for Information Resources Policy, P-89-5, 1989), 11.

48. See Martin C. Libicki, *Standards: Rough Road to the Common Byte* (Washington, DC: National Defense University Press, 1995), esp. chap. 4, "To the Gigabit Station," 31–40, regarding the importance and difficulties of the evolution of standards in promoting convergence and widespread use of digitized information.

49. For an overview of the Internet's development and basics about its operation, see Christopher Anderson, "The Accidental Superhighway," *Economist*, 1 July 1995, Survey Section, 1–18. See also Robert E. Kahn, "The Role of Government in the Evolution of the Internet," in National Academy of Engineering, eds., *Revolution in the U.S. Information Infrastructure* (Washington, DC: National Academy Press, 1995), 13–24.

50. Albert Gore, Vice President of the United States, transcript of speech to the International Telecommunication Union Development Conference, Buenos Aires, Argentina, 21 March 1994, 3.

51. Based on Office of Technology Assessment (OTA), *Information Security and Privacy in Network Environments* (Washington, DC: Government Printing Office, 1994), 27.

52. OTA, *Information Security*, 41.

53. Information Infrastructure Task Force (IITF), *The National Information Infrastructure: An Agenda for Action* (Washington, DC: The White House, 15 September 1993), Executive Summary, 2.

54. Curtis R. Carlson, "The Age of Interactivity," 8.

55. "The New Business Cycle," *Business Week*, 31 March 1997, 58–68.

56. Robert L. Ayers (Chief, Information Warfare Division, Defense Information Systems Agency), "Information Warfare and the DII," in *InfoWar Con* (Fairfax, VA: Open Source Solutions, 1995), 13.

57. The central role of information infrastructures and the linkages among the support systems for the DOD have been described in detail by Lt. Gen. Albert Edmonds (Director of the Defense

Systems Agency), "Information Systems Support to the DOD and Beyond," in *Seminar on Intelligence, Command and Control, Spring 1996* (Cambridge: Harvard University, Program on Information Resources Policy, I-97-1, 1997), 181–226. Also see DSB Task Force, *Information Warfare—Defense* (Washington, DC: Department of Defense, November 1996), 2-1–2, on the growing importance of unclassified networks such as the Global Transportation Network (GTN) and its interconnection to crucial war-fighting command and control systems.

58. The central role of "information superiority" is outlined in the Joint Staff, *Joint Vision 2010* (Washington, DC: Joint Staff, 1996), 16.

59. The Army has outlined a vision of future fighting forces that are highly reliant on leveraging information technology, generally referred to as "Force XXI." For a good overview of the Force XXI vision, see Headquarters, U.S. Army, *Army Focus 1994: Force XXI* (Washington, DC: Department of the Army, September 1994).

60. Air Force Doctrine Document 1-1, *Air Force Basic Doctrine* (Maxwell AFB, AL: Headquarters, Air Force Doctrine Center, September 1997), 31.

61. The entire special issue of CHIPS published by the Space and Naval Warfare Center, Charleston, SC, in July 2000 is dedicated to the NMCI initiative.

62. Emmett Paige, Jr., Assistant Secretary of Defense for Command, Control, Communications, and Intelligence (C3I), *Defense Issues* 11, no. 72, 2.

63. Emmett Paige, Jr., *Defense Issues* 11, no. 66, 1.

64. For historical background on the armed services' development of signals and communications units, see Kathy R. Coker and Carol E. Stokes, *A Concise History of the U.S. Army Signal Corps* (Ft. Gordon, GA: U.S. Army Signal Center, 1991); and Linwood S. Howeth, *History of Communications-Electronics in the U.S. Navy* (Washington, DC: U.S. Government Printing Office, 1963).

65. For background on the development of nuclear command and control systems and the relationship to civilian telecommunications systems/information systems, see Ashton B. Carter, "Communications Technologies and Vulnerabilities," in Ashton B. Carter, John D. Steinbrunner, and Charles A. Zraket, eds., *Managing Nuclear Operations* (Washington, DC: Brookings Institution, 1987), 217–281.

66. For descriptions of the development and role of satellite systems in U.S. intelligence efforts, see Jeffrey T. Richelson, *The U.S. Intelligence Community*, 2nd ed. (Cambridge, MA: Ballinger Publishing Company, 1989); and William E. Burrows, *Deep Black* (New York: Berkeley Books, 1988).

67. The 95-percent figure has become a standard in official statements describing the growing interconnection between defense and commercial information infrastructures, including the aforementioned 1994 and 1996 DSB Task Force studies. Interestingly, in trying to resist the breakup of AT&T in 1982, the Department of Defense used an almost identical figure. See "Department of Defense Analysis of the Impact of the Department of Justice—American Telephone and Telegraph Company Settlement to the Department of Defense," 20 April 1982, 3–4, which stated, "The Federal Government today obtains more than 94 percent of its most critical domestic telephone circuits from commercial carriers."

68. This example was provided by Lt. Gen. Albert Edmonds, Director of the Defense Systems Agency, in "Information Systems Support to the DOD and Beyond," 189–197.

69. For details on the development of Intelink, see Paige, *Defense Issues*, 11, no. 66; and presentation by Victor DeMarines, president and CEO of the MITRE Corporation, at the Intelligence and Command and Control Seminar at Harvard University on 16 October 1997. According to DeMarines, the Intelink concept was approved in November 1993 and initial operational capability was declared in December 1994, with expansion of service to 330 servers and 62,000

users by October 1997. MITRE provided the DOD and intelligence community with engineering design and implementation support in the creation of the Intelink network.

70. Author's interview with Susan V. Simens, PCCIP Commissioner from the Federal Bureau of Investigation, 20 June 1997.

71. National Law Enforcement and Training Service, Training Brochure, February 1995.

72. An example of how such capabilities would be used is provide by Chatry Perry, "CATASTROPHIC 1997: An Interagency Disaster Response Seminar," *NS/EP Telecom News*, issue 2 (1997): 3–4.

73. See *Fedpoints*, no. 36, Federal Reserve Bank of New York, available at ⟨www.ny.frb.org⟩.

74. The fragility of this system is discussed extensively in Frederick Cohen, *Protection and Security on the Information Highway* (New York: John Wiley & Sons, 1995), 19. See also PCCIP, *Critical Foundations*, A-17–18.

75. Interview with Lowell Thomas, MITRE Corporation, 24 October 1997. Thomas was a principal analyst in MITRE's efforts to support the PCCIP.

76. "Government and the Web Frontier," *Governance*, January 1998, 42–46.

77. The importance of SCADA systems to support a wide range of infrastructure functions is described by the PCCIP, *Critical Foundations*, 12; and Office of Science and Technology Policy (OSTP), *Cybernation: The American Infrastructure in the Information Age* (Washington, DC: The White House, April 1997), 13–15.

78. This information is from a MITRE Corporation presentation, "Information Operations and Critical Infrastructure Protection," MITRE Corporate Campus, Bedford, MA, 20 November 1997.

79. For overviews of the growing reliance of the medical/health care sector on information infrastructures, see Enrico Coiera, "Medical Informatics," in David S. Alberts and Daniel S. Papp, eds., *The Information Age: An Anthology on Its Impact and Consequences*, vol. 1, part 2, 289–310.

80. For analyses of the difficulty of conventional economics in dealing with the economic impacts of information technology, see Pam Woodall, "Paradox Lost," *Economist*, 28 September 1996, Survey Section, 13–16. For a forward-looking view of how information technology is transforming traditional economics, see Peter Schwartz and Peter Leyden, "The Long Boom: A History of the Future 1980–2020," *Wired*, July 1997, 115–129 and 168–173.

81. OTA, *Information Security*, 1–2.

82. Crook, 274.

83. Quoted in Eduardo Talero and Philip Guadette, "Harnessing Information Technology for Development," *The World Bank*, October 1995, 2.

84. Information on GM's plan to offer information services on its vehicles is outlined in "GM Driving Into Cyberspace," *Washington Post*, 13 January 2000, E1 and E18. Ford Motor Company's Design and Technology plans can be found at ⟨www.ford.com⟩, accessed July 2000. An example of the wide variety of car navigation systems now available through the Automotive GPS Online! Web site ⟨www.teletype.com/gps/autogps/⟩, accessed July 2000.

85. James F. Moore, *The Death of Competition: Leadership and Strategy in the Age of Business Ecosystems* (New York: Harper Books, 1995),

86. A. Michael Noll, "Anatomy of a Failure: Picturephone Revisited," *Telecommunications Policy* (June 1992): 307–316.

87. Peter G. W. Keen, *Shaping the Future: Business Design through Information Technology* (Cambridge: Harvard Business School Press, 1991), 48–50. In general, Keen provides a cautionary note regarding being overly optimistic about assuming that IT would play the central role in gaining competitive advantage at the end of the twentieth century.

88. Cited in presentation by Anne K. Bingaman, Assistant Attorney General, U.S. Department of Justice, to The Networked Economy Conference, September 1994.

89. "Hire Tech: Information Scrutiny and the E-Job Market," *Wired* 8, no. 7 (July 2000): 140.

90. "Spinning Gold from Glass," *Economist*, 14 March 1998, 68–70; and David Diamond, "Building the Techno-Proof Future," *Wired*, May 1998, 124–127 and 178–183.

91. The Iridium project also demonstrates the risky nature of such massive IT projects in a fast-changing environment. The high cost of Iridium services and bulky nature of these phones resulted in few subscribers by summer 2000 and likely bankruptcy for the project.

92. James M. McCarthy, "Managing Battlespace Information: The Challenge of Information Collection, Distribution and Targeting," in Pfaltzgraff and Shultz, *War in the Information Age*, 91.

93. Presentation by Robert B. Rankine, Vice President, Hughes Space and Communications Company, at Harvard University, Cambridge, MA, 9 October 1997.

94. Matthew Rubins, "Telecommunications Venture Investing Opportunities," presentation at the Fletcher School of Law and Diplomacy, Medford, MA, 10 March 1998.

95. Irving Lachow, "The GPS Dilemma: Balancing Military Risks and Economic Benefits," *International Security* 20, no. 1 (Summer 1995): 141–142.

96. MITRE Corporation presentation, "Information Operations and Critical Infrastructure Protection." 20 November 1997.

97. This figure was cited at the 6 June 1997 PCCIP Boston Public Meeting. OSTP, *Cybernation: The American Infrastructure in the Information Age*, 15–16, also stresses the interconnection between the electric power and information and communications infrastructures.

98. Paul F. Capasso, *Telecommunications and Information Assurance: America's Achilles Heel?* (Cambridge: Harvard University, Program on Information Resources Policy, March 1997), 8.

99. Seymour Goodman, *The Information Technologies and Defense: A Demand-Pull Assessment* (Palo Alto, CA: Stanford University, Center for International Security and Arms Control, February 1996), 3.

100. Peter Temin, *The Fall of the Bell System* (Cambridge: Cambridge University Press, 1987), 13–16.

101. The issue is treated in depth in DSB Task Force, *Information Architecture for the Battlefield* (Washington, DC: Department of Defense, October 1994), section on business practices, 37–42.

102. Paige, *Defense Issues* 11, no. 72, 1.

103. See OSTP, *The National Security Science and Technology Strategy* (Washington, DC: The White House, 1996), "Carrying Out the Defense S&T Mission," 18–22, for an authoritative statement of this policy direction.

104. Juliana Gruenwald, "An Unlikely Venture Capitalist: The Central Intelligence Agency," available at the GovExec.com Web site ⟨www.govexec.com/dailyfed/1099/101599b1.htm⟩, accessed 5 January 2000.

105. See particularly James L. McKenney, *Waves of Change: Business Evolution through Information Technology* (Cambridge: Harvard Business School Press, 1995), esp. chap. 7, "Sustaining an Evolving IT Strategy," 205–224, regarding how these challenges are met in the commercial sector. Government difficulties in meshing information systems are detailed in Douglas Stanglin, "Technology Wasteland," *Science and Technology*, June 1996, 67–68.

106. This figure was provided by Mary Olson, Vice President of Service Assurance, U.S. West, in "The Road Ahead: The Role of Business," a presentation at the National Security in the Information Age Conference, U.S. Air Force Academy, CO, 28 February 1996.

107. Rubins, "Telecommunications Venture Investing Opportunities."

108. Douglas D. Bucholz, director of the Defense Information Systems Agency, in a presentation, "The Emerging Joint Strategy for Information Superiority," at the Third International Command and Control Research and Technology Symposium, held at the National Defense University, Washington, DC, 17 June 1997.

109. For discussion of the shifting paradigms in computing, see in particular Nicholas Negroponte, *Being Digital* (New York: Alfred A. Knopf, 1995), 62–85, and Esther Dyson, *Release 2.0: A Design for Living in the Digital Age* (New York: Broadway Books, 1997), 1–10.

110. The changing role of different modes of transmitting information is often referred to as the "Negroponte switch." Negroponte predicts that in the future most information currently transmitted by wire, such as telephone conversations and e-mail, will travel by wireless means and information currently broadcast, such as TV movies or weather reports, will go to the home and office via wire; *Being Digital*, 24–25.

111. An overview of this survey is available on the Internet at the Information Technology Association of America Web site ⟨www.itaa.org⟩, accessed 6 March 1998.

112. Information accessed at Bureau of Labor Statistics Web site ⟨stats.bls.gov/emphome.htm⟩, 28 March 1998.

113. James Ellis, David Fisher, Thomas Congstaff, Linda Pesante, and Richard Pethia, *Report to the President's Commission on Critical Infrastructure Protection* (Pittsburgh, PA: Carnegie Mellon University, Software Engineering Institute, January 1997), 3.

114. The details regarding Manchester Power were provided to the author in the previously cited interview with Lowell Thomas, 24 October 1997.

115. Ellis et al., *Report to the President's Commission*, 3. This challenge was also stressed by Bruce Moulton, Vice President, Information Security Services, Fidelity Investments, in an interview with the author, Boston, MA, 6 January 1998.

116. Vincent Cable and Catherine Distler, *Global Superhighways: The Future of International Telecommunications Policy* (London: Royal Institute of International Affairs, 1995), 1.

117. Greenberg et al., *Old Law for a New World*, 8–9; and Aldrich, "International Legal Implications," 104–108.

118. For analyses of other countries' approaches to telecommunications regulation and deregulation, see Brian Kahin and Ernest Wilson, eds., *National Information Infrastructure Initiatives: Vision and Policy Design* (Cambridge: MIT Press, 1997).

119. See Jeffery F. Rayport, George C. Lodge, and Afroze A. Mohammed, "Global Friction among Information Infrastructures," Harvard Business School Note N9-797-095 (Cambridge: Harvard University, 1997), 18–19, on the negotiating positions and breakdown of negotiations.

120. Lee McKnight and W. Russell Neuman in William J. Drake, ed., *The New Information Infrastructure: Strategies for U.S. Policy* (New York: Twentieth Century Fund Press, 1995), 151–152; Dyson, *Version 2.0*, chap. 5, "Governance," 103–130.

121. Rayport et al., "Global Friction," 14–15; Linda Garcia, "The Globalization of Telecommunications and Information," in Drake, ed., *The New Information Infrastructure*, 80–83.

122. See Poh-Kam Wong, "Implementing the NII Vision: Singapore's Experience and Future Challenges," in Kahin and Wilson, *National Information Infrastructure Initiatives*, 24–60; and Matthew Lewis, "Singapore Moves to Clean Up Information Highway," *The Reuter Asia-Business Report*, 5 March 1996, 2.

123. See Joseph Kahn, Kathy Chen, and Marcus Brauchli, "Beijing Seeks to Build Version of Internet That Can Be Censored," *Wall Street Journal*, 31 January 1996. On China's efforts to control its information infrastructures, see also Milton Mueller and Zixian Tang, *China in the Information Age: Telecommunications and the Dilemmas of Reform* (Westport, CT: Praeger, 1997).

124. Rayport et al., "Global Friction," 4; and see also Douglas Galbi and Chris Keating, *Global Communications Alliances: Forms and Characteristics of Emerging Organizations* (Washington, DC: Report of the International Bureau of the FCC, 1995).

125. AT&T Web site ⟨www.att.com⟩, accessed March 1996.

126. For an index ranking fifty-five countries' relative absorption of information technology, see "The Information Imperative Index," *World Paper*, June 1996, 5.

127. See Joel West, Jason Dedrick, and Kenneth L. Kraemer, "Back to the Future: Japan's NII Plans," in Kahin and Wilson, *National Information Infrastructure Initiatives*, 61–111.

128. John Stremlau, "Dateline Bangalore: Third World Technopolis," *Foreign Policy* 103 (Summer 1996): 152–168.

129. Nina Gilbert, "Israeli High Tech Update: U.S. Military Installs Finjan Security System" *Jerusalem Post*, 16 March 1998.

130. See Carl H. Builder, *The Icarus Syndrome: The Role of U.S. Air Power Theory in the Evolution and Fate of the U.S. Air Force* (New Brunswick, NJ: Transaction Publishers, 1994); and Kenneth C. Allard, *Command, Control and the Common Defense* (New Haven: Yale University Press, 1990), 8–15, on the influence of operating environment on the different theories of warfare that guide each of the U.S. armed services.

One might think of a strategic attack as an entity with well-defined limits. But practice—seeing things in the light of actual events—does not bear this out. In practice the stages of the offensive as often turn into defensive action as defensive plans grow into the offensive.

—Carl von Clausewitz, "The Object of Strategic Attack," in *On War*

Throughout history, people have tried to explain the relationship between warfare and politics. The intertwining of technological and societal changes also influences discussions of the utility of force. Technological developments create new means for waging wars and theories about how to employ these tools. The emergence of an information age that affects society and the technological opportunities for using force may require new approaches to waging conflicts. Strategic information warfare certainly presents a new opportunity and threat facing the United States at the beginning of the twenty-first century.

Those who would consider waging strategic information warfare will confront challenges similar to those military organizations have dealt with in the past. Efforts to attack enemy centers of gravity directly led apostles of airpower to hold out the prospect of avoiding prolonged, bloody conflicts on traditional battlefields. Yet historically, the centers targeted in strategic warfare prove difficult to damage, and adversaries are capable of considerable resistance and adaptation in defending themselves against strategic attack. Despite initial hopes that they would provide political influence on the cheap, nuclear weapons proved so devastating that their use became circumscribed. Estimating the impact of digital attacks against information infrastructures as a center of gravity poses considerable challenges for both offense and defense in waging strategic information warfare as a means for political influence. Actors who wish to adapt successfully to the emergence of this new form of warfare must understand past pitfalls and new complexities.

Dimensions of Strategic Analysis

Two intertwined threads exist throughout writings on strategy: (1) the need to relate means to ends; and (2) the ever-present influence of interacting with an opponent capable of independent action. Although strategic thinkers emphasize these threads to differing degrees, both are central to understanding any possible use of force.

Most strategic analysts address an important distinction between what are referred to as "grand strategy" and "military strategy." According to British strategist B. H. Liddell-Hart, grand strategy "is to coordinate and direct all the resources of a nation, or band of nations, towards the attainment of the political object of the war." It includes the calculation and development of the economic strength and manpower of nations to sustain the fighting services they deploy. Additionally, "fighting power is but one of the instruments of grand strategy which should take account of and apply the power of financial pressure, of diplomatic pressure, and of commercial pressure and, not the least, of ethical pressure." He provides a more narrow definition of military strategy as the "the art of employment of battles as a means to gain the object of a war." At all levels success, for Liddell-Hart, depends, "first and most, on a sound calculation and coordination of the ends and the means."[1]

Strategic choices also involve contemplating the possible courses of action available to one's adversary. The use of force is not simply a linear exercise in orchestrating one's own forces and unleashing them with certain effect against an enemy. Adversaries will attempt to anticipate each other's actions and minimize their detrimental effects. The likely course of an opponent's actions can only be guessed at, however, not determined with any certainty. As eloquently developed by Edward Luttwak, strategy is governed by an interactive logic rather than a linear logic.[2] Approaches that do not appear simple or straightforward may prove the best path of action because they surprise an opponent. Efforts to achieve surprise may also require secrecy and deception, which diffuse limited resources, thereby reducing the impact of one's own action. Additionally, opponents may adapt unexpectedly to mitigate or defeat a particular stratagem. This crucial dimension of interaction is often ignored in theories of strategic warfare.

Strategic analysis also involves actors who have interests in conflict and therefore consider resorting to force. At the extreme, Clausewitz states, "War is an act of force to compel our enemy to do our will."[3] Violent force, however, does not actually have to be used to influence an opponent's behavior in all instances. Schelling describes the strategy of conflict as the study of rational behavior involving independent choices by opposing sides. In situations in which the sides have an interest in limiting their conflict short of a total war of annihilation, strategy is concerned not only with the efficient application of force but also with the exploitation of potential use of force.[4] In conceptualizing strategic information warfare, one must keep in mind that the threat of, as well as the actual use of, such means may have utility in achieving one's objectives.

Waging Strategic Warfare: Past Theories and Practice

The advance of technology has created the possibility of waging warfare intended to affect the will and ability of the enemy to wage war, bypassing an opponent's fielded forces. Such strategic warfare can be accomplished either by holding at risk targets that an opponent values or affecting the ability of an opponent to function at all. By attacking centers of gravity directly, strategic warfare creates new means for influencing an adversary's behavior. The use of strategic warfare, although it involves means designed to avoid the enemy's fielded forces, does not eliminate the battlefield. Instead, waging strategic warfare creates new battlefields and realms of conflict, whether at sea between merchant vessels, U-boats, and U-boat hunters; in the air between bombers, interceptors, anti-aircraft artillery, and surface-to-air missiles; or in space between ballistic missiles and satellite-based interceptors. Conducting operations on such strategic battlefields requires effective intelligence capabilities and command mechanisms to overcome challenges that arise from the inherent difficulties and uncertainty of combat, described by Clausewitz as the "friction" and "fog" of war. The nature of the cyberspace battlefield must be understood as hostile interactions occur in the environment created by information systems.

Thinking about the identification of centers of gravity is most strongly linked to Clausewitz, who made the concept central to his concluding chapter of *On War*, "War Plans." In discussing how an enemy is defeated, Clausewitz states, "One must keep the dominant characteristics of both belligerents in mind. Out of these characteristics, a certain center of gravity develops, the hub of all power and movement, on which everything depends. That is the point against which all our energies should be directed."[5] However, Clausewitz lived in a time when armies were the principal means of European warfare, and he therefore stressed the need to defeat the enemy's army in the field as the primary center of gravity in conflicts between states.

The experiences of World War I led to a broadened conception of how to attack an adversary's centers of gravity. The lack of decisiveness of trench warfare and the devastating casualties that characterized the fighting between well-armed, highly organized, logistically well-supported armies during World War I led to a search for new means by which to achieve military victory. On land, the search for a means of achieving decision focused on the importance of maneuver warfare based on mechanization, epitomized by the German blitzkrieg during World War II. At sea, the Germans attempted to use submarine forces to strategic effect in both world wars. In attempting to strangle the economy of the United Kingdom, the Germans hoped to attack this center of gravity in an effort to coerce it into capitulating so that they could avoid invading the British Isles.[6] Although the submarine proved a potential useful means for strategic attack against enemy centers of gravity, the technological advances of the early twentieth century provided a tool seemingly even more suited to such a use of force. World War I saw the first employment of the airplane in warfare. Airplanes were put to tactical uses such as reconnaissance and artillery spotting almost immediately, but strategic uses also emerged quickly. By 1915, German zeppelin airships were striking cities in England. The zeppelins were later joined by Gotha bombers.[7] The British retaliated against these German efforts with their own strategic bombing efforts against Germany. Visionaries saw the airplane as potentially able to deliver force with the speed, scope, and precision to attack an opponent's centers of gravity without achieving battlefield victory and to win wars without substantial losses. The objective in deploying airpower in such missions was to avoid lengthy, costly wars of attrition by striking directly at the heart of the enemy.

Thinking about strategic warfare using conventional airpower and weapons of mass destruction has continued to evolve since World War I. The next section provides an overview of the thinking and practice of strategic warfare during the twentieth century and stresses the interaction of theoretical development, wartime experience, and technological change in formulating that thinking and practice.

Development of Strategic Air Bombardment Theory

Air power advocates became the early drivers behind the thinking about how to wage strategic warfare against enemy centers of gravity. The development of the theory and doctrine behind strategic warfare has passed through a number of stages as the technological means for such warfare has evolved and historical experience has provided lessons. The first doctrines for strategic bombing were developed in the period after World War I by men who were strong advocates of independent air arms within their nation's military services. The principal early strategic bombing theorist was an Italian, Giulio Douhet.[8] His theory was based on the premise that bomber aircraft could always get through potential defenses and could deliver devastating strikes against a wide range of targets. Douhet believed that the first objective of air forces should be to gain command of the air through all-out first strikes, then attack enemy cities. "A complete breakdown of the social structure cannot help but take place in a country subjected to this kind of merciless pounding from the air," he states. "The time would soon come when, to put an end to horror and suffering, the people themselves would rise up and demand an end to the war." Civilian morale would serve as the primary center of gravity for the next conflict, and strategic airpower was the means for directly attacking this center. In describing the progress of a future Franco-German war, Douhet depicted France suing for peace within thirty-six hours after devastating air attacks against four cities.[9] The independent British Royal Air Forces, led by Air Marshall Hugh Trenchard, firmly adopted Douhet's theory as their vision of future conflict.[10] This theory provided the basis for their night bombing campaign against German cities in World War II.

Chapter 4 addresses in detail the development of U.S. strategic bombing doctrine and its application against Germany in World War II, but a broad outline will help here. Within the United States, the campaign for an air force independent of the Army was led by General William "Billy" Mitchell. However, Mitchell's thinking primarily dealt with proving the effectiveness of bombers at the tactical level of warfare, such as against battleships for coastal defense. Other early leaders in the campaign, such as Mason Patrick and more junior airmen such as Henry "Hap" Arnold, Muir Fairchild, Carl Spaatz, and Haywood Hansell, actually became stronger advocates of the potential and use of strategic air power. During the 1930s, a doctrine for strategic air warfare was elucidated at the Air Corps Tactical School (ACTS), embodying the concept of centers of gravity and the role of air power in striking these centers. Given a more limited set of resources than envisioned by Douhet, ACTS thinkers planned a more focused strategic air campaign designed to achieve economic paralysis by hitting key industrial nodes. Disrupting these nodes would, in turn, undermine the general economy and civilian morale, according to the ACTS approach.

During World War II, the U.S. strategic air campaign planners focused attacks against specific German economic targets. Rather than attack civilian morale, the U.S. campaign was conceived of as a means of reducing the supply of war material to the fielded forces. A group of civilian and military planners in 1943 recognized the difficulty in achieving general industrial collapse and recommended the targeting of critical components of heavy military equipment such as ball bearings and machine tools. Robert Pape describes such an approach as "critical components" theory.[11] This approach has remained a dominant strand in thinking about how to achieve success through waging strategic attacks.

The first phase of strategic warfare thinking received a robust test during World War II. Massive bombing campaigns were launched against differing enemy centers of gravity. These campaigns included the German Luftwaffe against Britain from 1940 to 1942, targeting civilian morale; the British night bombing raids against Germany from 1941 to 1945, targeting morale and industrial production; the U.S. daylight raids against Germany from 1943 to 1945, targeting war materials production and general economic welfare; and the U.S. bombing campaigns against Japan from 1944 to 1945, first a daylight campaign against industrial production and then a night firebombing campaign targeting both industrial production and morale. Debates raged within most military establishments regarding the assignment of available strategic bombing assets to different wartime tasks. For the British and Americans, difficult decisions had to be made in allocating limited numbers of available long-range bombers, which were used in the strategic air campaign against Germany, the antisubmarine war in the Atlantic, and support of Allied ground forces in the European theater as well as U.S. war efforts in the Pacific. Doctrinal differences emerged between the British and U.S. allies regarding how the air campaign against Germany should be waged. The British undertook night area raids to undermine the ability of the general economy to function and to erode German morale. The U.S. conducted daylight precision strategic bombardment to paralyze key sectors of the German war economy. The impact of these attacks on the outcome of the war has received much scrutiny.[12] Yet although debates rage over the effectiveness of these campaigns, most assessments agree that British and U.S. use of strategic warfare did not decisively coerce the enemy to surrender through either crushing civilian morale, or paralyzing the economy until the dropping of the atomic bombs on Japan.[13]

A number of optimistic assumptions made by the early airpower theorists proved incorrect. Bombers confronted robust defenses based on radar, heavily armed interceptors, and anti-aircraft artillery defenses. Command of the air over continental Europe during the day proved difficult to achieve until adequate long-range escort fighters were developed to reduce vulnerability to interceptors. At night, a seesaw electronic war raged as night bombers became reliant on electronic navigation aids to find targets. German defenders used jamming to disrupt these aids and employed radar to locate attacking bombers.[14]

Also, Douhet, Mitchell, and others had grossly overestimated the damage that individual bombing raids would cause. Despite the development of accurate bombsights, difficulties existed for precision delivery targets in the face of tough defenses or bad weather. Delivery of weapons to targets in area bombing proved easier but also had to overcome challenges presented by defenses, weather, and navigation. Further, the industrial infrastructures of targeted states, particularly Germany, proved much more adaptable and robust than expected. Efforts to bomb the wartime industrial base of Japan were hampered by long distances, defenses, and bomb load limitations that forced the Americans to adopt nighttime area bombardment in this theater. Attacks against civilian morale proved ineffective at provoking either a general decline in productivity or political pressure to cause an adversary to sue for peace or a change in the regime. These miscalculations were compounded by the difficulty air campaign planners faced in properly relating strategic bombing target selection to overall wartime objectives. Bernard Brodie criticizes U.S. planners in particular for too much emphasis on panacea targets, such as ball bearings, and for missing the importance of targeting more substantial, underlying infrastructures such as oil and transportation.[15] Others have highlighted the resistance of the Luftwaffe and British Bomber Command to understanding the limitations of area bombing. Assessments widely agree that the bombing campaigns against cities and general economic targets simply did not cause morale to crumble despite the vast resources invested, casualities inflicted, and damage wrought. These evaluations will be covered in detail in chapter 4.

In a more general sense, the early airpower theorists and practitioners created a paradigm for strategic warfare with few political constraints. Conditioned by the totality of World War I, Douhet, Trenchard, and American air planners saw airpower as a military instrument to be unleashed only in pursuit of the goal of completely crushing the opponent. The execution of strategic attacks in World War II was designed to achieve the general political objective of unconditional surrender. Airpower's utility for achieving more limited political objectives was not tested. Neither the risk of reprisal attacks nor the consequences of escalation appear to have influenced German decisions to wage a strategic bombing campaign against the United Kingdom in 1940. Airpower advocates downplayed the role of defenses in the interwar period. Both active and passive defenses were critical, however, in limiting the coercive effectiveness of airpower.

Early airpower theory also neglected the fundamental question of how strategic bombardment translated into political influence. Prewar advocates as well as World War II strategic planners devoted little attention to estimating how or whether destruction of certain target systems would result in changed decision making by opponents. Liddell-Hart initially thought campaigns devoted to such strategic effects would prove effective but later stated that the physical effects of bombing proved too diffuse and their political impacts too slow. Additionally, he assessed that Allied strategic bombing created postwar economic havoc in western Europe that was counterproductive to the grand strategies of Britain and the United States. Luttwak calls the use of airpower a nonstrategy because it was not integrated across the spectrum of concerns from tactical to grand strategic.[16] Overconfidence in the capabilities of evolving technology led to the misleading assumption that bombers would always get through and precisely hit targets. Luttwak argues that such technologically based strategies ignore the difficulties imposed by the fog and friction of war on creating adequate intelligence and orchestrating attacks.

Prior to 6 August 1945, the strategic bombing campaigns of World War II had opened up a new battlefield for conflict based on attrition. These campaigns were neither quick nor decisive. Those assessing the potential for waging strategic information warfare have so far paid little attention to the possibility that its actual use may well confront similar hurdles in terms of requirements for lengthy campaigns and lack of decisiveness.

Nuclear Weapons and Strategic Warfare in the Cold War

The final act of the Second World War laid the foundation for another evolution in thinking about strategic warfare. The dropping of nuclear weapons on the Japanese cities of Hiroshima and Nagasaki created a huge leap in the destructive capacity of military means for achieving political leverage through strategic attacks. The rapid advance in numbers and destructive capabilities of nuclear weapons effectively removed limits on achieving damage to all types of targets: military forces, economic centers, and civilian populations. Theorists dealing with the relationship between the military use of these weapons and their political utility wrote primarily in the context of an evolving nuclear balance between the United States and the Soviet Union. The evolution of nuclear strategy has created a voluminous literature and remains an important focus of defense planners around the world.[17]

This section provides an overview of the evolution of nuclear doctrines and forces in the Cold War relevant to the evolution of U.S. strategic warfare thinking.[18] The United States had a monopoly on atomic weapons until 1949. Although the Soviets possessed nuclear weapons by the early 1950s, only the United States had a significant intercontinental delivery capability in the form of bombers. U.S. nuclear doctrine evolved into an attempt to leverage this advantage in ability to wage strategic warfare through a strategy known as massive retaliation. Based on this strategy, the United States threatened to launch devastating nuclear attacks on the Soviets in an effort to cheaply deter Soviet expansionism. To economize on resources, the U.S. doctrine placed relatively limited emphasis on active or passive strategic defenses. The Soviets, with little ability to strike back against nuclear attacks, initially downplayed the significance of nuclear weapons doctrinally but also undertook large-scale efforts to create air defenses and provide for civil defense.[19] This relative imbalance in emphasis on defense between the two superpowers continued through most of the Cold War.

Yet the ability of the United States to achieve its political objectives via massive retaliation proved extremely limited when such retaliation was provoked by actions that could not justify the use of such devastating means. Nuclear weapons were not used directly in the conflict in Korea, although the influence that nuclear threats may have had in bringing the conflict to a close is debated.[20] The lack of a U.S. military response to the 1956 Soviet invasion of Hungary clearly demonstrated the bankruptcy of the U.S. massive retaliation strategy. Although the United States had the ability to inflict massive damage through strategic attack to protect Hungary from Soviet domination, the inappropriateness of using such means to achieve limited political objectives became increasingly apparent.

The strategic picture between the superpowers had changed by the mid-1950s as the U.S.S.R. developed the means to wage strategic nuclear warfare. The development of Soviet bomber forces to deliver nuclear weapons led in the United States to a short-lived scare about the loss of strategic superiority, known as the "bomber gap." More significant was the rapid progress of the Soviet ballistic missile program, culminating in the launch of Sputnik in 1957, thereby renewing fears of Soviet superiority in the form of a "missile gap." No effective defenses existed in the United States to counter the emerging Soviet ballistic missile threat. National security thinkers again began to address strategic warfare in terms of dominant offensive capabilities, focusing on the use of ballistic missiles to conduct a disarming first strike. The late 1950s and early 1960s became a time of technological arms racing as both sides endeavored to improve their offensive capabilities, placing heavy emphasis on improving the ability to observe the development and capabilities of adversary nuclear forces through satellite reconnaissance and other intelligence means. Systems were also developed on both sides to provide warning of potential surprise attacks by ballistic missiles.[21] Strategic theorists came to concentrate on measures to stabilize this superpower competition to avoid the preemptive first use of nuclear weapons in the event of a crisis.

The rapid development of significant missile and submarine forces combined with early warning systems provided the United States and the U.S.S.R. with the capability to launch a substantial second strike against opponents. Missile and submarine capability on both sides had evolved to the point that the two opponents could threaten unacceptable retaliation against a range of civilian and military targets, if one side chose to use such weapons first. Additionally, the Cuban Missile Crisis in 1962 highlighted to U.S. and Soviet leaders the potential risks of a nuclear war. Command and control systems in the United States were subsequently enhanced to ensure that only the highest political authorities could authorize the use of nuclear weapons. Increasingly during the 1960s and early 1970s, nuclear weapons were not seen as a viable means of waging strategic warfare. Most thinking in the United States and other Western nations about nuclear weapons gradually came to focus solely on their deterrent value. Although the Soviets and a few Western strategists continued to advocate passive defensive measures in case of a failure of deterrence, strategic warfare concepts in the West became dominated by the need to create mutual deterrence based on assured second-strike capabilities.[22] This period also saw the rise of arms control efforts to institutionalize a stable nuclear balance. The Soviets initially appeared to mirror U.S. strategic thinking in their willingness to pursue the Strategic Arms Limitation Treaty (SALT I) accord and particularly the anti-ballistic missile (ABM) treaty. The treaty endeavored to limit the possibility of arms races based on the need for offensive nuclear forces to overcome active missile defenses by severely limiting such systems and reinforcing a situation of mutual vulnerability to devastating attack.

However, the evolving competition between the superpowers in the 1970s raised new issues in managing the doctrine and forces for waging strategic nuclear warfare. Technological advances resulted in the development of multiple independent reentry vehicle (MIRV) systems that allowed ballistic missiles to carry multiple warheads capable of attacking different targets. The advent of MIRVs, as well as cruise missiles, made continued progress in arms control efforts to stabilize the strategic balance between the superpowers more difficult.[23] The Soviets continued their substantial modernization of land- and submarine-based ballistic missile systems, resulting in a growing number of warheads and an increased ability to target U.S. land-based missile systems. Soviet investment in strategic and civil defenses also continued, and a major effort to protect the U.S.S.R.'s political leadership in the event of a nuclear conflict became evident. Fears emerged among some U.S. strategists that the Soviets really believed they could prevail in a politically meaningful sense in a nuclear conflict and that they sought a condition of strategic superiority vis-à-vis the United States.[24] Initially, the United States developed "limited nuclear options" to create the capacity to have a "rational" response to limited Soviet attacks intended to partially disarm the United States. By the end of the 1970s, however, growing concern about Soviet aims had derailed arms control efforts in the form of the SALT II treaty and resulted in the emergence of a "countervailing" nuclear strategy. This strategy was predicated on the development of U.S. retaliatory strategic forces to deter a Soviet attack based on possessing the capability to attack the Soviet leadership, nuclear and conventional military forces, and economic assets.

The early to mid-1980s brought a reemergence of tensions between the nuclear superpowers and a struggle for nuclear superiority. The Reagan administration launched a major strategic offensive modernization program to close the "window of vulnerability" of U.S. intercontinental ballistic missile (ICBM) forces to Soviet attack. The protection of U.S. ICBMs through hardening silos and proposed mobile launcher plans received substantial emphasis as did efforts to upgrade command, control, and communications to operate in the advent of an actual nuclear war. President Reagan reversed past U.S. doctrinal aversion to defense in nuclear weapons strategizing and raised questions about commitment to arms control in announcing the Strategic Defense Initiative (SDI) in 1983. The SDI announcement generated a rancorous debate about the technological feasibility of useful ballistic missile defenses that continues to the present day. Strategic analysts also argued over whether the deployment of such a defense would enhance the U.S. ability to achieve deterrence or create a period of destabilizing uncertainty regarding the balance between offensive and defensive nuclear forces that might increase the chances of a nuclear war.

Yet the political situation continued to shift even as the strategic modernization programs of the Reagan administration began to result in operational deployments. By the late 1980s and early 1990s, the Soviet leader, Mikhail Gorbachev, increasingly recognized the need for internal political and economic reform in the Soviet Union. Gorbachev recognized the economic inability of the Soviet Union to sustain a vigorous strategic competition with the United States. Based on a series of U.S.–Soviet summits and unilateral concessions by both sides, arms control efforts once again came to the fore in maintaining a strategic balance designed to achieve mutually assured deterrence capabilities at ever lower numbers of deployed nuclear weapons. The early Clinton administration substantially scaled back efforts to pursue strategic ballistic missile defense and reaffirmed the U.S. commitment to the principal Soviet successor state, Russia, regarding continued existence of the ABM treaty, albeit with modifications to permit tactical ballistic missile defenses. However, growing concern within Congress and the Executive branch caused yet another shift in U.S. policy on ABM defense and the associated treaty by the late 1990s. The continued pursuit of ballistic missile and nuclear technologies by countries such as North Korea and Iran rejuvenated interest in deploying ballistic missile defenses to protect the continental United States, even at the cost of friction with Russia over arms control agreements including START and ABM treaties. The role of missile defenses and arms control arrangements in managing the U.S.–Russian nuclear relationship will likely to continue a dynamic evolution as we enter the twenty-first century.

During a period lasting more than forty years, then, punctuated by numerous crises and periods of prolonged tension, the world's two superpowers have managed to avoid the use of nuclear weapons and the waging of strategic warfare against one another. Will such a balance also evolve in the new realm of strategic information warfare? Alternatively, does the difference in damage potential posed by digital attacks as compared to a holocaust resulting from nuclear exchange make emergence of a balance of terror with respect to information warfare improbable? To answer such questions, strategists and planners must develop an understanding of the capabilities, vulnerabilities, and objectives of potential adversaries who could engage in a conflict using digital means.

The Reemergence of Nonnuclear Strategic Air Warfare

During the Cold War, armed conflicts were waged in the shadow of a potential superpower nuclear confrontation and the pursuit of arms control. While large-scale conventional wars were held in abeyance by the prospect of nuclear annihilation, limited wars and political movements based on guerrilla warfare were undertaken to pursue objectives using military means. Increasingly, decisive political results were achieved not through strategic attacks or victories on traditional battlefields but through guerrilla action and limited means aimed at long wars of attrition to wear down the will of opponents.

In the limited conflicts of the Cold War, the United States had difficulty in trying to use available non-nuclear airpower to achieve its objectives through strategic warfare.[25] U.S. planners faced major challenges in identifying and attacking the centers of gravity of opponents who did not rely on industrial infrastructures or large logistical support systems for conventional battlefield operations. Strategic air attacks during the Korean conflict proved inadequate to create leverage against an adversary who relied very little on developed infrastructures and was heavily supported by outside powers not subject to attack.[26]

Use of strategic airpower during the Vietnam conflict proved even less fruitful. North Vietnamese and Viet Cong forces were subjected to massive aerial bombardment in numerous air campaigns.[27] Escalating air attacks in the Rolling Thunder campaign during 1965–1968 failed to coerce the North Vietnamese into a peace settlement. As in World War II efforts against the Germans, these strategic attacks efforts to identify and strike significant centers of gravity proved extremely difficult. The North Vietnamese economy was not reliant on its small industrial sector, and efforts to undermine civilian morale or to limit supplies to the guerrilla warfare effort in South Vietnam proved unsuccessful. In fact, the flow of men and material into South Vietnam is estimated to have increased as the conflict progressed. The North Vietnamese had improved their transportation system along the Ho Chi Minh trail so much by 1968 that it could handle three times as much traffic as when Rolling Thunder began in 1965.[28] The massive Linebacker bombing campaigns in 1972 did help end the conflict. Debate continues, however, regarding whether the Linebacker I strikes against the North Vietnamese ground offensive in the spring and summer of that year achieved coercion through denying conventional military victory or the final December Linebacker II bombings actually accomplished coercion through punishing the morale of the adversary.[29]

Developments during the Vietnam War, however, once more laid the foundation for another phase in the theory and practice of strategic warfare by conventional air bombardment. Attacks against bridges in North Vietnam with laser-guided bombs in 1972 allowed precise attacks by limited numbers of aircraft to achieve success in hitting targets that had eluded previous strikes involving hundreds of sorties. These strikes presaged the evolution of technologies throughout the 1970s and 1980s that provided airpower with a new set of capabilities, leading once more to a doctrine based on the ability to conduct decisive non-nuclear strategic warfare. Specific developments included increasingly precise conventional munitions, cruise missiles, stealth strike platforms, and improved intelligence, surveillance, and reconnaissance capabilities.[30] As an integrated system, these capabilities provided airpower advocates with the possibility of launching devastating strikes against centers of gravity by offensive forces with a decisive advantage.

Unlike in previous conflicts, the use of new technological capabilities for waging strategic warfare preceded a fully developed theory about their employment. Confronted by the Iraqi occupation of Kuwait in 1991, the United States developed a plan for conducting the Gulf War that focused on strategic airpower to attack the underpinnings of the Iraqi economy, destroy the Iraqis' ability to use weapons of mass destruction, and decapitate the Iraqi command and control system. Efforts to paralyze the Iraqi war effort would rely on direct strikes against leadership targets as well as efforts to destroy telecommunications networks connecting the leadership with the fielded forces. In the actual conflict, coalition airpower was used with devastating effect against Iraqi fielded forces in Southern Iraq and Kuwait.[31] The Gulf War also evidenced a dramatically faster pace of operations than past strategic air campaigns. Aircraft and pilots often flew multiple missions every day. Providing adequate communications channels to disseminate target assignments, assess damage, and order restrikes to geographically dispersed units proved to be a significant constraint on operations.

As in the period after World War II, debate has raged among military professionals and civilian strategists about the significance of airpower in this conflict.[32] All commentators agree that the coalition air forces did an outstanding job in establishing air superiority to pave the way for both strategic air attacks and those against fielded forces. Attacks against fielded forces severely degraded those forces' ability to fight once the ground war began. After conducting a comprehensive survey of the use of airpower in the Gulf War, Thomas Keaney and Eliot Cohen judged that "[i]f airpower again exerts similar dominance over opposing ground forces, the conclusion will be inescapable that some threshold in the relationship between air and ground forces was first crossed in Desert Storm."[33] Many observers argue that Iraq was coerced into surrendering in large degree because of the ability of airpower to severely degrade the capability of its army to conduct combat operations. Unlike in World War II, the use of independent airpower may have proved decisive in the outcome of the conflict.

Although the Gulf War was too short for attacks on economic centers of gravity, strategic strikes were conducted against leadership, command and control, and the electrical power system to paralyze the Iraqi war effort and cause civilian unrest. According to the Department of Defense's final report on the Gulf War, "[a]ttacks on Iraqi power facilities shut down their effective operation and eventually collapsed the national power grid."[34] Results of attacks on the telecommunications and command and control systems were more ambiguous. The architect of the strategic air campaign, Colonel John Warden, subsequently claimed that "[w]ith fewer than 1 percent of the bombs dropped on Vietnam, the coalition imposed strategic and operational paralysis on Iraq."[35] Keaney and Cohen conclude that "[w]hile the Iraqi regime showed signs of faltering control and its telecommunications were disrupted, a political collapse did not occur, and judging how close the Coalition came [to achieving such a collapse] does not appear possible on the available evidence."[36] The strategic effect of lost power and telecommunications channels on the Iraqi war effort was not clear.[37]

More generally, a cautionary approach must inform efforts to construe the Gulf War experience as heralding an age of dominant non-nuclear strategic airpower. The U.S.-led coalition had near perfect conditions for use of strategic air warfare in the Gulf War (including the desert terrain and weather). The coalition had numerous advantages over the Iraqi forces, including a major technological disparity between the forces, the unilateral advantages held by stealth aircraft on the U.S. side, and the coalition's superior intelligence, surveillance, and reconnaissance efforts. Arguments emerged between national intelligence agencies and intelligence analysts deployed with forces in the Persian Gulf regarding the level of damage inflicted by coalition air strikes on Iraqi forces and civilian targets.[38] Also, postwar assessments indicate that the air plan did not succeed against all important target sets. Targeting efforts faced particular difficulties in locating and destroying dispersed sites for creating weapons of mass destruction capabilities, in finding Iraqi mobile ballistic missiles, and in the dissemination of intelligence to units conducting air strikes.[39]

After the war, Warden evolved a much more theoretical framework of how airpower can be used to conduct strategic warfare against enemy centers of gravity.[40] He asserts that all enemies can be viewed as target systems consisting of five centers of gravity that exist as concentric rings, as depicted in figure 2.1. Extending his analysis beyond states, Warden asserts that other types of actors, such as drug cartels, can also be analyzed using the five-ring model. Emphasizing the utility of strategic concepts and technologies that allow attackers to bypass the adversary's fielded forces, he finds that the essence of war is to create pressure against the leadership of adversaries by threatening their systems with collapse or paralysis through attacking the most vulnerable centers of gravity. Although he recognizes that all states and organizations will have unique centers of gravity and vulnerabilities, he argues that the most critical ring of the five in his model is leadership. Finally, Warden and others argue that technological advances, especially the development of PGMs and stealth airframes, have created a capacity for parallel warfare,[41] which involves "the simultaneous application of force (in time, space, and at each level of war) against key systems to effect paralysis on the subject organization's ability to function as it desires. The object of parallel warfare is the effective control of the opponent's strategic activity."[42] Advocates of parallel warfare believe that airpower no longer needs to wage air warfare based on striking individual targets in succession over months or even years as in World War II and Vietnam. These advocates recognize that

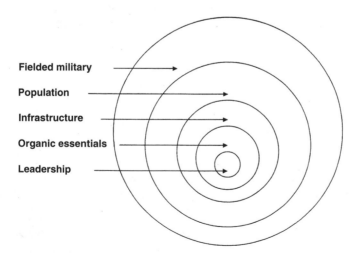

Figure 2.1
Warden's five-ring model

bombardment over an extended period allows defenders to take steps to attenuate the effect of strategic attacks. Using a parallel warfare approach, the new strategic airpower advocates argue that decisive impacts can be achieved in a matter of days, as they believe was demonstrated by the air war in Iraq.[43]

Some debate exists about the ability of U.S. adversaries to develop the capability to wage a parallel war as envisaged by Warden, Barnett, and Allan in the near to mid-term future.[44] Developing intelligence, surveillance, and reconnaissance capabilities to deliver "precision force" guided by advanced command and control systems would require substantial investments by potential U.S. adversaries in both technology and manpower.[45] At the dawn of the twenty-first century, U.S. capability of achieving air superiority and inflicting strategic air attacks against most opponents in the near to mid-term is nearly assured. Again, U.S. strategic airpower advocates have the luxury of considering a situation in which the U.S. homeland and even deployed military forces need not make substantial provisions for retaliation in kind by the enemy for non-nuclear strategic air attacks.

Advocates have emerged within the U.S. national security community for using its dominance in delivering strategic non-nuclear attacks as a means of achieving political influence through deterring and coercing opponents in peacetime. Allan, for example, argues that the United States' improved conventional airpower capabilities can create a type of "dynamic deterrence" that will help bolster U.S. credibility which has atrophied regarding the use of nuclear weapons for deterrent purposes.[46] Ullman and Wade go farther in developing a concept of rapid dominance in which "total mastery achieved at extraordinary speed and across tactical, strategic and political levels will destroy the will to resist. With rapid dominance, the goal is to use our power with such compellence that even the strongest of wills will be awed."[47] Continuing to demonstrate these capabilities and the degree of U.S. superiority will only enhance their political utility, according to such analyses. Allan finds that "both critics and advocates of dynamic deterrence agree that potential aggressors are very likely to assess improperly or totally ignore the value of technological and operational improvements without demonstrations of U.S. capabilities."[48]

The use of airpower to achieve strategic objectives in Kosovo overcame substantial obstacles presented by the weather, the terrain, and the ability of targeted military forces to disperse and hide. The U.S. ability, through the use of air strikes, to force the Bosnian Serbs to the negotiating table in Dayton in 1995 and compel the withdrawal of Serbian forces in Kosovo in 1999 might be considered a validation of the parallel warfare/shock and awe theories. Once more, advocates assert that these cases prove airpower has become the principal means by which the United States can achieve its national goals in conflicts in which vital interests are not threatened but the United States is willing to use force to achieve its objectives. Others argue that air strikes became decisive in Kosovo only after Kosovar rebels forced Serbian ground forces into the open. Additionally, they point out, the continued achievement of U.S. political aims has required the deployment of peacekeeping forces on the ground.

The United States has yet to fully demonstrate its ability to turn dominance in this particular form of strategic warfare into political leverage across the full spectrum of conflict situations presented by the post–Cold War environment. The ability to launch air and cruise missile strikes against Iraq since the war ended in 1991 has proved to have limited influence in stopping Saddam Hussein's efforts to maintain and rebuild biological and chemical weapons arsenals.[49] Even strong advocates of the future use of parallel warfare such as Barnett recognize that certain opponents such as guerrilla movements will be difficult to engage and influence through strategic air attacks.[50] In general, the non-nuclear use of strategic airpower will be constrained in scenarios in which opponents have centers of gravity that are inaccessible because of insufficient intelligence; lack of technological capability; or geographical, political, and legal constraints.

The reemergence of non-nuclear strategic warfare raises important questions for those considering strategic information warfare. Can any actor waging strategic information warfare hope to achieve the level of freedom of action that U.S. air forces seem to have attained in the 1990s? How will situational variables influence the utility of strategic information warfare? How will the damage inflicted in attacks on information infrastructures translate into political influence? As we consider employment of digital means for waging strategic warfare in a new environment, answering these questions will provide useful guidance.

Strategic Warfare and Weapons of Mass Destruction after the Cold War

At the same time that the Cold War superpower nuclear competition was ending and the U.S.-led air forces were demonstrating their capabilities against Iraq, concern was also increasing about the proliferation of weapons of mass destruction (WMD). The spread of nuclear, chemical, and biological weapons as well as of ballistic missiles to new actors, potentially including nonstate actors with the interest and capacity to use them, poses a major security concern for the United States.[51] This section highlights proliferation concerns as we enter the twenty-first century to shed additional light on the dynamics of strategic warfare.

WMD capabilities can provide new actors with the potential to wage strategic warfare against adversaries. Nuclear, chemical, and biological weapons can all cause significant damage against both military and civilian targets in much more limited numbers than conventional weapons. Ballistic missiles can give actors the capability to launch attacks quickly in a way that current defenses have little capacity against. Nontraditional delivery means, such as smuggling weapons into an enemy's territory illegally, may also provide a way to deliver these weapons that requires much less technological sophistication than developing ballistic missiles.

Although concerns about WMD proliferation are not new, the post–Cold War political and technological environment has sharply elevated the level of concern over the spread of such weapons. The ebbing of the superpower rivalry has removed constraints on acquiring WMD from many states who now perceive an increased need to provide for their own security. Meanwhile, the spread of WMD themselves, as well as dual-use technologies associated with these weapons and the basic scientific and engineering knowledge about their creation, has continued largely unabated. The dissolution of the Soviet Union and the subsequent political, economic, and social turmoil has created new sources for all types of WMD materials and technologies, and personnel experienced in their use.[52] Iraqi programs to develop all types of WMD provided a major justification for the U.S. willingness to wage war in the Persian Gulf and facilitated the formation of the Allied coalition. The overt testing of atomic weapons by India and Pakistan and ongoing conflict in the region continue to generate grave fears regarding a nuclear showdown in South Asia. Fear of confronting opponents possessing and willing to use WMD has become a central concern for U.S. strategists and defense planners attempting to pursue interests in various regions around the world.

Other international actors recognize that the difficulty of creating effective defenses to stop the delivery of WMD may represent an Achilles heel for the United States. Most opponents likely believe that they cannot compete on the conventional battlefield with the United States. In terms of waging strategic warfare, they can't hope to develop and compete with U.S. airpower. WMD capabilities may offer such actors a means for achieving political leverage in a conflict with the United States without having to engage on the traditional battlefield.

William Odom finds that "most countries see the futility of investing heavily in air forces if they intend to fly against the United States. No other air force can hope to stand up to it. . . . The rational alternative is to invest in ballistic missiles if one wants to attack the rear areas of U.S. forces."[53] The National Defense Panel report *Transforming Defense* stated in December 1997 that "[d]ue to their availability, relative affordability, and easy use, weapons of mass destruction allow conventionally weak states and non-state actors to counter and possibly thwart our overwhelming conventional superiority."[54]

The threat posed by nuclear, biological, and chemical weapons for use against U.S. forces, allies, or homeland may be sufficient to enable a state such as Iran to deter U.S. military action in a future Gulf War conflict. Terrorist organizations may see the ability to launch strategic attacks with WMD as a means of coercing the United States to achieve political ends. Adversaries may also believe that the United States may be unwilling to retaliate fully in response to a WMD provocation and therefore miscalculate the potential for a devastating U.S. response to such an attack. Various actors will also try to acquire such weapons to manage security concerns not related to the United States.

Both state and nonstate actors may seek to acquire different types of WMD capability. Some may see nuclear weapons and ballistic missile capabilities as offering them the most clearly demonstrable ability to launch devastating effects on an adversary. Yet such weapons and related technologies are generally the most tightly controlled by states currently possessing them and present potential proliferants with the greatest cost and engineering difficulties. Chemical and biological weapons, for instance, have employment limitations, especially in terms of war-fighting applications. Combatants in conflicts ranging from World War I to the Iran-Iraq war during the 1980s have encountered difficulties in using chemical weapons, and their employment has not proved decisive in the outcome of the conflicts. In terms of deterring intervention by outside powers or pursuing coercion through terrorism, however, chemical and biological weapons delivered by nontraditional means may represent a more attractive option compared to conventional weapons for threatening or waging strategic attacks.[55] In most cases, these weapons are likely to be cheaper, technologically simpler, and easier to conceal than nuclear weapons and ballistic missiles.

Vigorous efforts to control the spread of WMD have been undertaken in response to the potential proliferation threat dating back almost to the development of the atomic bomb. Arms control treaties, including the Nuclear Non-Proliferation Treaty and the Biological and Chemical Weapons Conventions, have endeavored to create an international political and legal context within which the possession and use of such weapons is prohibited. Along with treaty provisions, export control supplier regimes have attempted to limit the availability of WMD and related dual-use technologies. Such regimes also provide information regarding what actors may be acquiring and/or developing WMD capabilities. Other contextual factors, such as moral and religious considerations, may constrain the use of weapons with such potentially devastating effects, but these constraints historically have a poor record of success.

As evidence continues to surface that proliferation is occurring despite the efforts to contain it and will prove difficult to stop, the United States has developed programs to deal with the consequences of having to fight adversaries equipped with WMD capabilities. It has been strongly advocated that active tactical and strategic defenses be provided against delivery of WMD by ballistic missiles. In the late 1990s, significant efforts were geared to dealing with ballistic missile threats to U.S. and allied forces in regional contingencies.[56] Also, U.S. concern about WMD attacks delivered against interests at home and abroad by unconventional means has increased, with concerns related to the terrorist use of these weapons receiving growing attention. The National Defense Panel report found that "[t]hese weapons already threaten security at home. The 1995 use of sarin gas in the Tokyo subways stands as a stark and ready reminder of the chemical threat. Biological weapons are even a more serious problem. For example, they could be readily introduced into mass transportation systems and quickly spread to thousands of people with devastating consequences. Small nuclear devices smuggled into population centers could also produce thousands of casualties."[57] Programs to deal with these threats have been instituted by the Department of Defense, the intelligence community, and the FBI. Passive defenses in terms of improving biological and chemical detection and protection capabilities have also received an increasing level of attention and support.[58]

Thankfully, the post–Cold War international environment has seen limited use of WMD capabilities. No nuclear weapons have been used in a conflict since 1945. However, the Aum Shinrikyo attack in Tokyo also demonstrates the growing range of actors with the potential to develop and use WMD. The difficulties in dealing with a diffuse, highly differentiated set of potential adversaries may have significant parallels to those involved in dealing with the potential for strategic information warfare as we enter the new century. The differences in the destructive power of WMD weapons, however, may also mean that the dynamics differ significantly from those of strategic information warfare.

A Brief Critique of Strategic Warfare Theory and Practice

The history of warfare generally and of strategic warfare in the twentieth century in particular demonstrates that successfully waging strategic warfare involves both offensive and defensive dimensions. Past theorists of strategic warfare have emphasized its offensive dimension: the ability to threaten an adversary's assets of value. Strategic warfare's defensive aspects—the ability to protect one's own assets of value from outside attack through active or passive means—historically have been largely ignored, although attention to defensive concerns has grown during the 1990s. In focusing on offense, strategic warfare theorists generally have been influenced by a belief that new technologies will allow attackers to get through and attack key centers of gravity. These theorists assume that adversaries subjected to such attacks have significant vulnerabilities. Strategic warfare theories assume that offensive strikes will prove capable of inflicting sufficient punishment on civilian targets or enough damage on infrastructures supporting military operations to influence adversaries and thereby achieve coercive or deterrent objectives.

Strategic air warfare theorists largely ignore interactions between adversaries in determining the utility of offensive action. Although the issue of relative vulnerability between adversaries is central to strategic nuclear doctrines, it is absent from strategic air warfare theories after Douhet. According to U.S. strategic air warfare theory, offensive strikes will be launched without substantial threat of enemy direct retaliation. Strategic air warfare theory also generally underemphasizes the need to consider the relative level of commitment of adversaries to achieving their objectives in conflicts.[59] As a result, strategic warfare has often been viewed as a panacea for the drawbacks of traditional warfare, able to secure political objectives quickly without lengthy wars or substantial pain and effort.

History has demonstrated, however, that the efficacy of the threat and use of strategic offensive capabilities is intertwined with considerations of strategic defense capabilities, vulnerabilities, and commitment. Achieving air superiority can prove a difficult task if offensive forces enter the fray unprepared for technological and organizational innovations by the opponent's defense. Even more difficult is developing and sustaining the ability to identify, target, and strike enemy centers of gravity with decisive weight in such a way that the attacker's political objectives are quickly and cheaply attained. In the case of nuclear weapons, offensive dominance led to a superpower standoff in which the risks of mutual devastation outweighed pursuit of any useful political objective through the use of these weapons. Neither the ability of intelligence organizations to identify the right targets nor the adequacy of command and control systems for fighting a nuclear war was ever tested. Although faith in achieving such a balance of terror against WMD proliferants has eroded in the 1990s, very limited use of WMD means has yet occurred.

Emerging technological capabilities have primarily driven the development of strategic warfare thinking. Advocates of such technologically driven forms of warfare have tried to advance organizational purposes without sufficient attention to the considerations of grand strategy and political objectives. The experiences of employing strategic airpower in World War II, Korea, Vietnam, and the Gulf War, however, demonstrate the utility of a broader conceptualization of strategic thinking that takes into account additional considerations about the uses of force. The destructive power of nuclear and other weapons of mass destruction has generated much theoretical debate. However, the devastating power of these weapons also has limited their use. Consideration of the emergence of strategic information warfare must be informed by past theory and practice of strategic warfare. The following section outlines a framework of key conditions that enable and enhance for successful use of strategic attack capabilities.

Enabling Conditions for Waging Strategic Warfare

Each of four conditions identified in this section describes a necessary, but not a sufficient, condition for successfully waging strategic warfare. The inability of an actor to achieve one of these conditions would make victory through a strategic warfare campaign unlikely. On the other side of the equation, actors trying to minimize vulnerability to strategic warfare could use the framework as a means of identifying useful strategies for defensive efforts.

1. *Offensive freedom of action.* To be effective, strategic attacks must be able to get through an adversary's defenses and must have the capacity to inflict significant damage on chosen targets. The offense can be favored by the nature of the technological balance in the operating environment or by the ability to bring sufficient mass to bear to overwhelm the defense at critical points of attack. Capacity to achieve surprise, speed, and to sustain the vigor of attacks all work to the advantage of the offense. Of particular concern is whether offensive forces can deliver a disarming or paralyzing first strike, limiting the ability of the adversary to respond.

2. *Significant vulnerability to attack.* The adversary must possess a vulnerable center of gravity that, if attacked, will have political consequences. Centers of

gravity can be exploited through directly attacking and breaking the will of the population, by eroding the political will to fight by destroying the ability of the economy to function, or more specifically by disabling the fielded forces of the adversary through strategic interdiction. Active and passive defenses can reduce vulnerabilities of an adversary's targeted centers of gravity to attack.

3. *Prospects for effective retaliation and escalation are minimized.* Actors initiating strategic warfare need to assess an opponent's likely reactions to a strategic attack and possible courses of action after an attack has been sustained. Such attackers must also assess, prior to initiating attacks, their own vulnerabilities to strategic attack and their adversary's capability to retaliate. The efficacy of an actor's threat or use of attacks will depend on its vulnerability to retaliation both in kind and through other military and nonmilitary means.

4. *Vulnerabilities can be identified, targeted, and damage can be assessed.* Intelligence plays a central role in strategic warfare. Actors considering the use of strategic warfare must be able to discern whether complex targeted systems of the adversary will prove robust and difficult to damage or consist of critical nodes that provide offensive forces with significant leverage in terms of creating damage and pain. Strategists must understand how damaged or destroyed targets within the adversary's perceived centers of gravity will translate into political pressure. If the initial strike does not achieve the desired political influence when a strategic attack is launched, the attacker needs to be able to assess the damage inflicted and the ability of the defender to repair and mitigate that damage. The attackers must then decide whether and how to continue attacks. Accomplishing such intelligence tasks will likely become more difficult once a conflict starts and opponents have greater incentives to hide vulnerabilities and deceive each other.

Those waging strategic war in cyberspace face challenges similar to those encountered in the conduct of strategic warfare in other realms. In particular, policymakers, planners, and operators contemplating the conduct of strategic information warfare will have to address these enabling factors. Thinking about strategic information warfare has emphasized the freedom of offensive forces. Most analysts lament the lack of defensive capabilities. The susceptibility of individual information systems and networks to attack has created assumptions regarding the large-scale, systemwide vulnerability of national information infrastructures. It is widely assumed that digital damage to targeted infrastructures will have significant political consequences in the country attacked. Analysts have not adequately addressed defensive countermeasures and the possibility of retaliation. In addition, political leaders and military commanders waging strategic information warfare must learn how to control new types of weapons and warriors in a new environment.

Waging Strategic Information Warfare

The growing reliance of U.S. society on information infrastructures creates potential new centers of gravity for enemy attack in strategic warfare based on disrupting and defending these infrastructures. This section addresses how actors might wage strategic information warfare. To that end, the section describes the susceptibility of U.S. information infrastructures to disruption and the tools and techniques for attacking and defending advanced information infrastructures.

On the whole, U.S. information infrastructures are quite susceptible to disruption in the early twenty-first century. Many international actors can access technological tools to disrupt them. Yet, strategic information warfare has yet to occur. The conduct of strategic information warfare would require actors to assess, hold at risk, and defend information infrastructures in a complex and dynamic environment. Establishing defenses for information infrastructures requires the ability to understand and protect vulnerabilities, monitor activity within information infrastructures, and react to disruption. Actors contemplating strategic information warfare also face the difficult task of determining the political consequences arising from the disruption of infrastructures across different sectors of society. Those who chose to use such an unproven form of warfare would face significant uncertainties in predicting the effects of their attacks. Depending on the types of attacks pursued, considerable risks of escalation might result. Waging strategic information warfare might prove most useful, then, for actors whose political objectives are limited in scope, who can control vulnerability to retaliation, and who possess a willingness to incur risks.

Susceptibility of U.S. Information Infrastructures to Disruption

Chapter 1 outlined the growing reliance of the United States on information infrastructures. For U.S. adversaries to turn such reliance into a center of gravity for waging strategic information warfare, such infrastructures would have to be susceptible to intentional exploitation and disruption. Disruption of these infrastructures could result from intentional intrusion, use of malicious software code, flawed products, accidents, or simple errors in the configuration and operation of information systems and networks, among other potential causes.

The susceptibility of U.S. information infrastructures to such disruption has become increasingly clear and well documented. In 1991, the National Research Council highlighted its concerns about a society dependent on computer-based information processing systems in a study entitled *Computers at Risk*.[60] Government and private-sector studies conducted throughout the 1990s continued to reinforce these concerns. Much of this work culminated in the formation of the Presidential Commission on Critical Infrastructure Protection (PCCIP), which issued its findings in October 1997. The PCCIP found that U.S. dependence on the information and communications infrastructure "has created new cyber vulnerabilities, which we are only starting to understand. In addition to the disruption of information and communications, we also face the possibility that someone will be able to actually mount an attack against other infrastructures by exploiting their vulnerabilities."[61] This section overviews how U.S. adversaries might attack information infrastructures. While infrastructures across all sectors of U.S. society evidence susceptibility to disruption, systematic evaluations of the significance of large-scale disruptions are sorely lacking.

Digital Intrusion   The same protocols, operating systems, and applications that enable computers systems to interact via networks also make them vulnerable to digital intrusion. Although most information systems have features designed to limit access to authorized users, often these features are improperly configured or can be circumvented. Software systems also can contain flaws that unauthorized users can exploit to gain access to and control over vulnerable computer systems and networks. Even protected information networks have proven susceptible to intrusion, exploitation, and disruption.

The ability of intruders to get into unclassified, yet sensitive, computer systems of the U.S. government has been well documented. A number of the best-known hacker incidents have involved the computer systems of the DOD and other organizations involved in national security. Examples of significant incidents include:

• Intrusion into more than forty sensitive DOD, Department of Energy and NASA computer systems in the late 1980s by a group of German hackers known as the "Hannover hackers." It took more than a year to track down and apprehend this group of German teenagers in the employ of the KGB after their activities were initially detected.[62]

• During the same period as the U.S. involvement in Desert Shield and Desert Storm, hackers from the Netherlands penetrated thirty-four DOD systems, modifying them to obtain full privileges, gain future access and remove indications of their activities. They read e-mail and copied and stored military data on systems at major U.S. universities.[63]

• In early 1994, hackers used a "password sniffer" to gain access to the computer networks at the Rome Air Development Center at Griffis Air Force Base, New York. The two hackers were able to gain access to thirty Rome Laboratories systems that contained research and development files. They also used the Rome systems as a launching point for successful intrusions into other military, government, commercial, and academic systems worldwide, including those of the NASA Goddard Space Flight Center in Maryland, NATO Headquarters in Brussels, and the Korean Nuclear Research Center in Seoul.[64]

• In 1995 and 1996, an Argentinean hacker used access to the Harvard University network to get further access to computer networks at the Naval Research Laboratory and other DOD, NASA, and Los Alamos National Labs computers. The systems accessed contained sensitive research information on aircraft design, radar technology, and satellite command and control systems.[65]

• In February 1998, two teenaged hackers in California, under the guidance of an eighteen-year-old Israeli mentor, gained access to numerous DOD military computer networks. The intruders used a well-known software glitch to tamper with computers required to address and transmit information on these networks (called domain name servers). Before the identity of the hackers was known, DOD and FBI investigators initially explored the possibility that these intrusions may have occurred in response to a U.S. military buildup in the Persian Gulf, referring to the incident as Solar Sunrise. These fears were heightened because the intruders used foreign computer systems, including one in the United Arab Emirates, to launch their attacks. Deputy Secretary of Defense John Hamre called the incident "the most organized and systematic attack" on U.S. defense networks yet discovered by authorities.[66]

As the 1990s progressed, attention increasingly focused on the large-scale susceptibility of the information infrastructures relied upon by the U.S. national security community to digital intrusion. In 1994, DISA began conducting a widely cited series of "red team" tests to evaluate the vulnerability of defense information infrastructures to relatively unsophisticated digital intrusion techniques. DISA tested approximately 12,000 DOD computer networks with well-known digital attack techniques and managed to access 88 percent of these networks. Only 4 percent of these systems' operators recognized they had suffered an intrusion, and less than half of 1 percent of the operators reported the attacks.[67] Evaluations by the Air Force Computer Emergency Response Team (CERT) evidenced similar, although less dramatic, results. The Air Force CERT tested 2,568 computer networks in 1994, of which 41 percent allowed unauthorized access and 24 percent permitted full access. Only 12 percent of the system administrators whose networks were tested reported the efforts at intrusion.[68] The 1996 General Accounting Office (GAO) study *Information Security: Computer Attacks at Department of Defense Pose Increasing Risks* concluded that "the hundreds of thousands of attacks that the Defense has already experienced demonstrate that: 1) significant damage can be inflicted by attackers; and 2) attacks pose serious risks to national security."[69] Yet although these evaluations depict large-scale susceptibility of DOD networks to intrusion, the resultant analyses do not address the value of the systems deemed susceptible to attacks or the overall potential for intruders to disrupt significant activity. The continuing efforts of DOD and the military services to understand and protect their computer networks will be covered in depth in chapter 5.

The information systems of other U.S. governmental agencies besides the DOD are susceptible to disruption as well. The World Wide Web pages of a wide range of governmental organizations including the Departments of Justice and Defense as well as the CIA have been hacked into and changed.[70] In 1998, hackers broke into the U.S. Coast Guard personnel data base.[71] Internet security expert Dan Farmer conducted a survey in December 1996 using a commercially available network analyzer. Farmer found 61.7 percent of federal government Internet hosts susceptible to intrusion, with 38.3 percent of susceptible hosts wide open to well-known attacks requiring less than a minute to gain complete control.[72] The General Accounting Office found in September 1999 through audits it conducted along with inspectors internal to the agencies involved that twenty-two of the largest federal agencies had significant computer security weaknesses.[73]

Private telephone network and Internet service companies have also been the targets of digital intrusion. The National Communications System and the President's National Security Telecommunications Advisory Committee were warned as early as 1989 that the public-switched network is growing more vulnerable to attack and experiencing an increasing number of penetrations.[74] The operations of the telephone network have long been a focus of computer hackers seeking free phone services and serve as a target for honing their understanding of computer networking. In an activity often referred to as "phreaking," individuals have used both physical and digital techniques to gain access to the computer networks of major companies such as AT&T, MCI, and Bell South to make free calls or play tricks on rival hackers.[75] The computer systems of the public telephone companies have been broken into for other malicious purposes. Hackers have intentionally disrupted the operation of 911 emergency notification systems in some localities through misdirecting calls in the phone system.[76] Intercepts of the digital signatures of cellular phones can be used to create "clones" whose recorded usage and its costs are assigned to the unsuspecting victims of the intercept. Such cloned phones are often used to support criminal activity.[77] Digital intruders can also remotely access telecommunication switches, disrupting the activities of a wide range of users. In March 1997, a teenaged hacker penetrated and disabled Bell Atlantic telecommunication switches in the northeastern United States. One of the disabled switches provided phone and data services to the Worchester, Massachusetts, airport control tower, and the incident the shut down the airport for many hours.[78]

Enterprises providing individuals and organizations with Internet services have also suffered numerous incidents of digital intrusion. America Online (AOL), currently the largest ISP, is continually the target of hacker attacks.[79] AOL is not alone. A Florida ISP had to discontinue services for days in 1997 after discovering that hackers had corrupted its operating software. Hackers often also take advantage of weak ISP security to gain privileged access to other computer networks connected to the Internet to cause disruption, as in the well-publicized case of Kevin Mitnick in 1996[80] or that of the California teenagers against the Department of Defense in 1998, discussed above. In December 1994, a group known as the INTERNET Liberation Front was charged with stealing phone data, performing Internet attacks for money, and developing highly sophisticated attack tools. The group attacked numerous information service and Internet providers, including some that support the U.S. government. Its activity included a substantial international component, with members from at least eight countries.[81]

General commercial users of information infrastructures have also proved susceptible to malicious digital intrusion. The banking and financial services industries have received the most attention in this area. Although very reluctant to admit problems with their information systems, such institutions have reportedly suffered increasingly large losses from digital intrusion and fraud. As early as 1978, Security Pacific Bank was victimized by a fraudulent $10.2 million computer wire transfer.[82] By 1999, the CSI/FBI survey found that 62 percent of respondents reported unauthorized use of computer systems within the last twelve months and that an additional 21 percent didn't know if their systems had been misused.[83] Citicorp admitted in a highly publicized incident that a Russian hacker had managed to siphon off $12 million in funds electronically in 1995. Although Citicorp actually managed to recover all but $400,000 of this loss, competitors reportedly used the incident to convince commercial clients to switch banks by instilling a perception of the greater insecurity of Citicorp information systems.[84] The Farmer study found that 68.3 percent of bank Internet hosts tested were susceptible to attack and 35.6 percent of the total were easily exploitable.

The susceptibility of other general users to digital intrusion has received substantially less attention, but reason exists for concern in this area as well. Examples are numerous. According to the White House report *Defending America's Cyberspace*, a hacker in 1991 stole an automaker's future car designs with an estimated value of $500 million.[85] In March 1998, hackers exploited a bug in the Microsoft Windows NT operating system, causing thousands of computers to crash, principally at NASA and major universities. The attack occurred just hours before Microsoft Chairman Bill Gates was to testify in front of the Senate Judiciary Committee regarding his company's exploitation of its dominance in the operating systems market.[86] Surveys have indicated that use of computers to commit crime is on the rise. A 1994 study polling 898 organizations in the public and private sectors indicated 24.2 percent had experienced some verifiable computer crime in the twelve months prior and 20.8 percent had experienced confirmed monetary losses.[87] The situation seems to be getting worse. The 1997 edition of the annual Computer Security Institute/FBI report on computer crime found that of information security managers in Fortune 500 companies surveyed, more than 40 percent reported their companies had suffered disruptive computer intrusions in the previous year.[88]

Overall, as the degree of interconnection and networking between computer and information sectors in U.S. society has risen, so apparently has the amount of susceptibility to intrusion. Data available from the Computer Emergency Response Team/Coordination Center (CERT/CC) at Carnegie Mellon University indicate that the number of reported Internet security incidents rose from 59 in 1989, the first full year of the CERT/CC operations, to 1,280 in 1994, to 4,398 during the first two quarters of 1999.[89] Farmer's study found 64.9 percent of 1,734 Internet hosts surveyed susceptible to attack and 31.1 percent of the overall total easily exploitable. Unfortunately, even less systematic data is available regarding the susceptibility of other important information systems and networks not directly connected to the Internet. However, the susceptibility of telecommunications systems to misuse and those of commercial institutions such as Citibank to intrusion, as well as flaws in operating software such as Windows NT, indicates that significant disruptions can occur.

Other Means of Intentional Disruption   The presence of viruses and other types of malicious software have also caused numerous information infrastructure disruptions.[90] "Malicious software" can be broadly defined as software designed to make computer systems operate differently than intended. The most commonly known subcategory is the "virus," software designed to make copies of itself, spreading from one computer to another. Viruses can be designed to create a wide range of effects on the host computer system once they have spread, ranging from making files difficult to copy to erasing hard drives. Other types of malicious software, such as logic or time bombs, take effect only when certain conditions are met, such as typing in key words, performing certain functions, or reaching a given date. "Worms" are programs that propagate from one computer to another over a network using exploitation means similar to those employed by hackers. In addition to the types of techniques discussed above, digital intrusions may also involve embedding malicious software within systems and networks.

An early event of significance involving malicious software was the 1988 Internet worm unleashed by Robert Morris, which penetrated thousands of computers and shut down Internet services for most of two days. Estimates of the number of computer systems infected by the Morris worm range generally from 2,100 to 6,000. Financial damage estimates range from $100,000 to $100 million.[91] The everyday presence of the large numbers of viruses currently degrades the utility of information infrastructures for many users. The outbreak of the Microsoft Word macro virus in 1995 has plagued millions of users of the world's most popular word processing program with problems of constant infection of working files, transmittal to other users, problems of inaccessible information, and occasional system failures.[92] Virus scares, such as the one created by the overhyped Michelangelo virus in March 1992, can cause computer systems administrators and users problems without even actually "infecting" systems.[93] Within the information technology industry, a significant subsector has emerged whose primary purpose is providing tools to combat the effects of known viruses.

One of the challenges of assessing the potential of viruses to disrupt information infrastructures is the unclear link between the intent of the virus creator and the eventual impact of most viruses. Most viruses encountered so far have been created by individuals intent on exploring the possibilities of software coding and disrupting the cyberspace environment rather than causing targeted disruption against specific organizations. This was the case, for example, with Robert Morris and the Internet worm. Accidental releases of viruses have occurred in numerous widely distributed software products.[94] After the initial unleashing of a virus, its originators lose significant control over the eventual effects on individuals and organizations reliant on infected systems and networks. Viruses can exist for a long time. To defeat antivirus programs, "polymorphic" and "retro" viruses use software code that dynamically changes and adapts to the operating systems of host computers as they propagate.[95] In 1987, there were only 6 known viruses; by 1990 the number had grown to more than 1,000. In 1997, one author found that more than 10,000 computer viruses and strains had been identified.[96] As of mid-1999, one typical commercial virus checker scanned the user's system for 100 different active virus programs.[97]

The virus threat to the information infrastructures of large organizations has varied over time. IBM's worldwide computer network suffered major disruptions for several days as the result of the Christmas Card virus in 1987. However, throughout much of the 1990s, instances of viruses causing a specific organization or institution significant problems were rare. One study in the early 1990s found that viruses accounted for only 2 percent of financial losses due to computer problems.[98] Most known viruses affect the operating systems of personal computers and application programs rather than large, centralized data processing computers or the operating systems of larger information networks.[99] However, throughout 1999 and 2000 a series of virulent outbreaks, including the Melissa, Worm.ExploreZip, and the "I Love You" viruses, disrupted government, commercial, and other private information systems around the globe. A major feature of these viruses has been the traffic overloads created when the viruses propagate vast amounts of e-mail through networked systems. Large organizations reliant on information systems susceptible to disruption by viruses devote significant resources to their control and eradication. The Defense Information Systems Agency has a team devoted to virus detection and developing tools to prevent further outbreaks.[100] Software vendors such as Microsoft and Sun Systems have dedicated efforts to working with customers to detect and eradicate viruses. Viruses and malicious software definitely have the potential to inflict large-scale damage if designed to affect information technology products, systems, and networks that underlie critical information infrastructures.

Individuals within an organization, generally referred to as insiders, can also create intentional disruption. The significant threat posed to information networks and resources by employees and others with sanctioned access is a recurring theme in the information security literature.[101] Reasons for malicious activity on the part of insiders include personal gain, revenge, entertainment, jealousy, and sheer destructiveness. Activity by insiders based on misuse of information systems and networks has proven significantly disruptive in numerous instances. One of the most significant espionage incidents in U.S. history involved a group led by Robert Walker, who provided cryptologic information to the Soviet Union from 1968 to 1985. According to Angelo Codevilla, the material Walker supplied to the KGB provided the Soviet Union with an "advantage comparable to that which the Allies possessed over Nazi Germany through the knowledge of Ultra. [If a war had occurred,] Walker might well have made the difference between a Soviet victory and an American one."[102] The General Accounting Office has reported insider problems in areas of the federal government, including misuse of information in the FBI's National Crime Information Network and by IRS employees.[103] Such problems are also prevalent in the private sector. Illustrative cases include

• A $21.3 million Wells Fargo Bank loss from computer fraud by an officer of the bank.

• Losses of $141,000 by National Bonded Insurance Co. sustained from a Trojan horse installed by a consultant's computer programmer that diverted money orders at the rate of $1,000 a day. The losses necessitated the sale of the business by the family that owned it.

• The loss of 168,000 sales commission records by USPA & IRA, a brokerage and insurance firm, due to a logic bomb that wiped out sections of the main computer's memory.

• The permanent deletion of all of Omega Engineering Corporation's design and production programs, with damage estimated at $10 million, through a logic bomb activated by a network programmer fired in 1996. Omega produced high-technology measurement and control instruments for the Navy and NASA.[104]

All organizations relying on information infrastructures must recognize the potential for disruption caused by insiders whether protecting themselves against individual fraud, the loss of information to competitors, or the potential for malicious flaws that disable systems and networks necessary for the accomplishment of mission-critical functions.

Information infrastuctures can also be disrupted through malicious insertion of flaws in hardware and software products before they are put into use. According to one study, even dedicated efforts to detect and remove software defects have a very difficult time achieving success rates over 95 percent.[105] Such malicious activity could occur at any point throughout the chain of research and development, manufacturing, and distribution. The outbreak of the Pakistani Brain virus in the late 1980s resulted from its purposeful insertion into commercial software reproduced in Pakistan and sold in the United States.[106] Fortunately, the known instances of and overall disruption caused by such malicious corruption so far has proved very limited. Such activity has not yet proved debilitating for a major information infrastructure technology producer, service provider, or user. Inserting preplanned weaknesses into an adversaries' targeted information infrastructures could, however, prove another tool in an orchestrated, large-scale strategic information warfare campaign.

Unintentional Disruption   Information infrastructures are also susceptible to disruption resulting from sources without malicious intent. The complexity of the products, systems, and networks making up advanced information infrastructures has created a situation in which disruptions occur rather frequently across a range of sectors of society. The causes of such unintentional disruption are myriad, including natural disasters; spillover effects from problems in other man-made systems, such as power failures or water main breaks; accidents during maintenance and construction activity; and errors unintentionally inserted in control software programs. The list below provides just a few illustrative examples of the large-scale disruptions of information infrastructure–based activity that have occurred through unintentional disruption:[107]

• In September 1991, an internal power failure due to improper implementation of operating procedures at a Manhattan telephone switching center cut off approximately half of the AT&T long-distance traffic in and out of New York City, The switching center carried some 90 percent of the communications of the New York air traffic control center. Although no airplane accidents resulted, more than 400 flights at three airports over an eight-hour period had to be canceled.

• In September 1993, a crew boring holes for highway road signs in Ohio cut a fiber-optic cable belonging to MCI that carried most of the company's east-to-west traffic. During the seven-hour period in which repairs were made, long-distance phone service was unavailable to millions of residential and business customers.

• In July 1994, a software upgrade to the computers of the NASDAQ stock exchange caused the system to shut down for more than two hours, cutting the day's volume by about one-third and affecting stock exchanges, trading desks, and mutual funds throughout the country. A backup system being upgraded at the same time to maintain compatibility also failed.

• In February 1998, a failure of computer equipment owned by Illuminet, a privately held company that provides signaling services to phone company networks, affected business customers of Teleport Communications Group in sixty-six cities, the mobile phone networks of Bell Atlantic and AT&T, the New York Mercantile Exchange, Columbia Presbyterian Hospital in Manhattan, and WMAR-TV in Baltimore.[108]

• A software glitch in switching equipment caused a major failure in AT&T's frame relay telecommunications service on 13 April 1998, affecting a number of large regional banks and the American Red Cross (ARC) for periods from six to twenty-six hours. In particular, the failure impacted the ARC's automated blood data bank and processing system, delaying the availability of information and blood products to health care providers, including emergency rooms nationwide.[109]

• In May 1998, disruption caused by the failure of a single Pan-American Satellite (PanAmSat) communications satellite crippled most U.S. paging services as well as other data and media communications feeds for hours and, in some cases, a couple of days.[110]

The widespread occurrence of unintentional failures as part of the daily challenges faced by providers and users of information infrastructures raises two important issues in terms of waging strategic information warfare. The first issue is the potential difficulty operators and defenders of information infrastructures face in quickly distinguishing malicious activity from unintended failure. The large-scale failure of the AT&T switching system in 1990 led to a major law enforcement crackdown against suspected hacker groups. The subsequent discovery that the disruption resulted from a software coding error led to a backlash against the law enforcement community that in turn led to the formation of groups such as the Electronic Frontier Foundation to protect privacy and access rights in cyberspace.[111] Alternatively, operators of information infrastructures may delay proper defensive reactions until they can determine the cause of a particular disruption. IBM's uncertainty as to the cause of the disruption wrought in 1987 by its Christmas Card virus delayed response by days, allowing the virus to spread to such a degree that significant damage resulted and significant recovery time was incurred.[112] Questions arise as to where to set thresholds for monitoring activity and authorizing responses. Closely monitoring every system glitch and collecting all possible information about any possible malicious intrusion may impose burdensome costs that must be weighed against the potential costs of an attack's going undetected. Too many aggressive responses to incidents that prove benign could also lead to complacency in the face of a real attack.

The second issue addresses the inherent resilience of organizations to adjust and survive information infrastructure disruptions. Past unintentional disruptions have varied in terms of frequency of occurrence, scope of impact on operations, and costs incurred by information infrastructure providers and users. Very little consolidated data are available on the effects of such disruptions on either information infrastructure providers or users. The PCCIP's overall evaluation in *Critical Foundations* of the U.S. information and communications infrastructure found that "[w]hile rapidly increasing complexity has characterized the I&C [information and communications] infrastructure since the breakup of the Bell System and the advent of the Internet, system reliability has remained extraordinary high. Large scale failures have occurred very infrequently and have been corrected in hours."[113] Does the wide diversity of information processing, storage, and transmission capacity of current U.S. information infrastructures provide both service providers and infrastructure users with substantial capability to adjust to using alternative means? Are the types of activities that are heavily dependent on the proper functioning of information infrastructure of a sort that they can be put on hold until problems are cleared up? Generally, past disruption incidents have resulted from sources that can be identified fairly quickly. Viable plans have been devised at a rapid pace to fix problems. A solution to the problems caused by the Internet worm was implemented within two days. Yet in the case of malicious activity, the perpetrator may try to hide its intent and make recovery from disruption difficult. Dedicated opponents pursuing strategic information warfare may be able to create sustained incidents of disruption for prolonged periods. Thus the ability of information infrastructure providers and users to react to such large-scale malicious activity remains basically untested.

The Situation at the Dawn of the Twenty-First Century

The increasing attention devoted to intrusion incidents since the 1990s has concentrated almost exclusively on characterizing the ability of any potential intruder to gain access to networked information and computing systems. As discussed above, the ability of individual and small groups of hackers to gain access to specific information systems and networks has been well documented. The systematic testing done within DOD and by others and studies of past Internet incidents as well as anecdotal evidence across a wide range of sectors of society make the case that important information infrastructures are susceptible to disruption. Incidents of significant concern have occurred. The hackers that exploited the Air Force computers at Rome Laboratories were able to access computer resources of the South Korean nuclear agency. The effects of the Morris worm, of the AT&T switching software glitch, or of the failure of the PanAmSat satellite, although unintentional, were widespread. The concern is that similar future incidents could potentially be orchestrated intentionally.

Yet so far, large-scale malicious disruptions of key U.S. information infrastructures have not occurred. Efforts to orchestrate significant malicious activity based on digital intrusion for the purposes of piracy of intellectual property and state-sponsored espionage have been identified.[114] Writings by members of the national security communities in other countries have outlined the possibility of future wars waged through strategic disruption by digital means.[115] A significant amount orchestrated activity necessary to gather the intelligence related to waging a strategic information attack could be occurring undetected. However, a large-scale strategic information warfare attack against the United States has yet to occur. The level of U.S. understanding of the strategic information warfare threat is addressed in more depth in chapter 5.

Assertions about the seriousness of the threat posed by the possibility of digital intrusion into the information infrastructures in the new millennium lack force. Why? We lack systematic analysis regarding the significance of systems susceptible to digital intrusion or how potential types of disruption would affect the ability of different infrastructures and the organizations that rely on them to function. Howard's study of Internet incidents finds found that "[n]one of the incidents were tremendously destructive. In terms of financial impact, files lost, time spent by personnel, some incidents were quite disruptive locally. In general, however, most incidents were not destructive, and if they were, the destruction was relatively limited and confined. . . . Most attacks were in the category of a nuisance (although some were a big nuisance), and not something destructive and harmful."[116]

Most analyses of the susceptibility of U.S. information infrastructures to digital attack ignore issues of intent and scale. As detailed in chapter 1, many discussions of information warfare lump any capability to disrupt or exploit information infrastructures together as a national security concern. Current threat assessments by official U.S. government sources differentiate between types of actors responsible for digital attacks, drawing broad distinctions between individual hackers, organized activity by nonstate actors such as terrorist groups, and state-sponsored activity. Those concerned with portraying the digital intrusion threat to the United States have not, however, conducted a structured assessment of the ability of different international actors to conduct attacks systematically to gain political leverage.

Analyses of susceptibility also tend to ignore the range of organizations responsible for creating information infrastructures in the United States. When highlighting the possibility for disruption by digital intrusion, studies recommend increased attention to protecting information infrastructures and provide specific recommendations about steps organizations should implement to provide information security. However, these studies ignore the role of outside organizations that produce underlying technologies, provide network services, or are otherwise digitally connected with a given infrastructure user. The roles and relationships of all organizations involved in producing, operating, and using information infrastructures in undertaking protective measures against attacks needs increased attention. Additional analysis regarding how information infrastructure providers and users should react to attacks and adjust operations once disruption begins is also necessary.

In assessing the potential for strategic information warfare, crucial questions to address include the following: Can attacks on information infrastructures be orchestrated in a way that could cause significant disruption to crucial sectors of society? What can be done to defend key information infrastructures? How will the interplay between offensive and defensive action affect the potential for significant disruption as time progresses? What means are available, both to the United States and to potential adversaries, to retaliate if attacked? Examination of these questions must inform our understanding of the ability of the United States and other actors to conduct strategic information warfare effectively.

Digital Attack

As discussed in chapter 1, attacks on information infrastructures can be launched through a variety of means: mechanical, electromagnetic, and digital. Synergies exist in using mechanical or electromagnetic means in conjunction with digital attacks. The analysis in this section, however, focuses on the potential for remote digital attacks on information infrastructures to forge a new means of waging strategic warfare by U.S. adversaries who cannot achieve the level of physical access necessary to effectively conduct traditional mechanical or radio frequency attacks. The section develops an analysis of the necessary tools for digital attacks, the access that can be created by such attacks, and the disruptive effects that actors can create through use of such attacks. Additionally, the role of insiders in enabling digital attacks and discerning their impact is considered.

Descriptions of the nature of digital attacks on information infrastructures cover a wide range of potential concerns. Lengthy lists of the types of attackers, their motivations, and the tools and techniques used to attack information systems have been developed. Numerous typologies describing the effects of digital attacks on the targeted systems, networks, and infrastructures also exist.[117] Yet efforts to describe attack tools and effects lack a common lexicon. Additionally, taxonomies of hacker tools and techniques rapidly become outdated as these tools and techniques evolve. This section relies on a simplified version of a process-based framework for describing digital attacks developed by John Howard,[118] who outlines a five-step sequence linking the conduct of any digital attack from actor to objective:

Actor > Tools/Techniques > Access > Effects > Objectives

Other types of strategic attacks besides those on information infrastructures require executing a sequence of processes similar to the one Howard describes. The U.S. Army Air Forces in World War II had to establish the necessary tools for its aerial bombing efforts by building aircraft and creating bases in England with the requisite range and bomb loads to attack targets in continental Europe. Bomber formations achieved access by navigating their way to assigned targets and overcoming defenses. The damaging effects inflicted by delivering bombs against targets such as U-boat pens and ball bearing factories were intended to achieve objectives such as degrading the German ability to conduct submarine warfare or produce war materials.

Actors desiring to wage strategic information warfare against the United States to achieve their objectives via digital attacks can use numerous tools and techniques to gain access to targeted information networks and infrastructures to create disruption and damage. Creating access broadly refers to the ability of attackers to identify and take advantage of information infrastructure vulnerabilities. Such vulnerabilities can be exploited to allow digital intrusion into information systems and networks, or insertion of malicious code into logical operating systems. Howard also points out that both unauthorized use by those with authorized access and unauthorized access are means by which attackers gain the ability to achieve desired effects, making insiders another source of potential vulnerability. Insiders could also facilitate insertion of flawed software and hardware into systems and networks. Information infrastructure vulnerabilities can result from the activities of organizations and individuals throughout the technology producer–network provider–information user chain described in chapter 1.

Many authors have described the types of effects likely to be sought through digital attacks. A simple categorization of effects relevant to understanding the use of digital attacks for strategic information warfare includes

· Disclosure of information. The dissemination of information to anyone who is not authorized to access that information.

· Corruption of information. Any unauthorized alteration of files stored on a host computer or data in transit across a network.

· Theft of service. The unauthorized use of computer or network services without degrading the service to other users. Such access can also be used to mislead the security systems of other networks as to the identity of the attacker, allowing access for attacks.

· Denial of service. The intentional degradation or blocking of the use of computer or network resources.

Choices among available tools and techniques allow attackers to achieve different types of effects via digital attacks. Some tools, such as network sniffers, may simply provide information, including passwords and access codes that create the potential for later access. Other tools, known as scanners, can automatically search and identify known types of vulnerabilities in systems and networks. Certain types of attack techniques may focus more on achieving direct effects, such denial-of-service attacks that prevent network operation through e-mail bombardment. Some techniques, such as viruses, may degrade the utility of information networks and systems without disabling them. Digital attacks can enable an attacker to establish continuing access and provide future control to achieve desired effects via what is known as a Trojan horse. A given attack may also involve multiple tools to accomplish multiple tasks more quickly. For example, a program can combine the features of a sniffer and a Trojan horse program to allow an attacker to monitor activity, gain and hide access, and create back doors for future activity. Those concerned with defense against digital intrusions have stressed how attackers on the Internet can use "toolkit" software packages that group together tools for attack in the form of computer command scripts, automated programs, and autonomous agents such as viruses with increasingly user-friendly graphical interfaces.[119]

Attackers can also improve access to information systems and networks for digital attacks through nondigital means. Hacker literature contains reams of information about how to gain direct physical access to systems through breaking into telephone switch facilities. More important for those attackers interested in establishing remote access is the concept of "social engineering." This term refers to the ability to trick those responsible for operating and using information systems into unintentionally providing access information. Attackers can simply call in on the telephone posing as maintenance personnel and request the dial-up modem number for access to the operations of computer routers or telecommunications switches. Attackers and defenders both must therefore concern themselves with physical security and the control of sensitive information.

Insiders and Digital Attacks on Information Infrastructures

Insiders play a potentially crucial role in understanding digital attacks on organizations reliant on information networks and infrastructures. I use the term "insider" to refer to individuals trusted by organizations that create, operate, or use information infrastructures whom an attacker can direct in achieving desired effects against these infrastructures. Such individuals could be employees of the targeted organization corrupted by the attacker or agents of the attacker able to gain the trust of targeted organizations. The knowledge and presence of people actually responsible for the targeted information systems, networks, and infrastructure can enhance the effectiveness of almost any digital attack. Insider access can be critical to providing information on network access, operations, and vulnerabilities, to conducting a physical attack (such as shutting off the power) in conjunction with digital attacks, or to inserting malicious software and/or corrupted hardware. Insiders can also cover up activity conducted by outside attackers as they endeavor to identify vulnerabilities, create access, and achieve effects. To the extent that U.S. adversaries can corrupt insiders or place trusted agents of their own with access to key nodes of targeted information infrastructures, their ability to conduct strategic information attacks may be greatly enhanced.

The Impact of the Cyberspace Environment

In the information infrastructure environment that exists today, attacks based on digital means of intrusion and disruption have certain features that are widely perceived as advantageous to attackers. For one thing, the source of digital attacks can be very difficult to detect. Techniques exist to hide the point of origin of remote attacks conducted over open networks like the Internet thorough means such as IP address spoofing. Sites exist on the Internet that provide users with anonymous addresses. Attackers can also transmit attacks through multiple nodes of transmission, complicating the task of backtracking the activity of digital attackers.[120]

Furthermore, the growing complexity of information networks creates everyday errors and system glitches that allow certain types of digital activity conducted by attackers to remain below the threshold level at which they become noticeable. The German teenagers who had been hacking into a large number of DOD and other computer systems for more than a year were discovered in 1988 only accidentally, as the result of a seventy-five-cent accounting error noticed by a computer programmer at the University at California at Berkeley.[121] If digital attacks can create future access to a variety of important systems and networks without provoking notice, such access greatly enhances the possessor's capacity for unleashing coordinated, surprise attacks. This possibility is often referred to as presenting the United States with the risk of an "electronic Pearl Harbor."

Digital attackers can conduct certain types of attacks very quickly to achieve precise effects. Through the use of automated tools, a digital attacker may be able to scan a network for vulnerabilities, select a tool that creates access, gain control privileges, insert software enabling future access and other effects, and depart the system in a matter of a few minutes. Also, digital attack tools and techniques can create a very high degree of control once certain types of access have been achieved. Many digital attack tools endeavor to provide the user with what is known as "root" access, which allows attackers to assume complete control over the functioning of a given system. Once achieved, root access can be utilized to remove evidence of the initial intrusion and to plant "back doors" that ensure later access for an attacker. In analogy to an attack against an industrial facility, root access would allow an attacker to revisit the plant at the time of the attacker's choosing and completely stop the production of bearings or redirect the shipping address of products. The combined characteristics of stealthiness, speed, precision, and coordination available to digital attackers raise the possibility of waging a digital version of "parallel warfare" as described earlier.

The scope of effects achieved by the use of various types of attack tools and techniques can vary widely depending on the objective pursued. Establishing root access to the server of a local bank system, allowing complete control over account transactions, might prove very lucrative for a criminal. Yet the limited scope of such an attack would have much less utility in creating a level of political concern about national financial systems necessary to achieve strategic information warfare objectives. Conversely, efforts to corrupt the switching software of a major telecommunications provider such as AT&T might provide an attacker with little control over specific effects but could allow the attacker to inflict massive denial-of-service effects on a wide range of users dependent on AT&T networks. The virus that corrupts the save function of the Microsoft Word program has plagued a multitude of individual users but does not disable larger information networks despite the very widespread propagation of the virus. Yet the Morris worm unintentionally severely degraded the functioning of the entire Internet in 1988 by manipulating the routing of transmissions between networked computers. The Melissa and I Love You viruses had similar impacts in 1999 and 2000.

An attacker's ability to control the effects of an attack depends on the techniques and tools the attacker chooses to conduct the attack. Whereas efforts to establish control over specific information networks by establishing root access may allow only very measured effects, e-mail bombardment of an Internet site to deny service may also slow or prevent the transmission of other communications not related to the target. It may be nearly impossible for a potential attacker to determine which information infrastructure users will be affected, and to what degree, when a self-replicating virus is inserted into a widely networked system or piece of software. Attacks designed to achieve precise effects require significant knowledge about how to access and control targeted systems and networks. Tools and techniques for digital attacks that achieve broader effects may require less knowledge about the targeted infrastructure. The effects of such attacks also may well be harder to control, however, as the teenaged hacker who disrupted the Worchester airport phone switch demonstrated.

Digital Attacks at the Level of Strategic Information Warfare

International actors who contemplate conducting digital strategic information attacks face the challenge of creating the capability of using available tools, techniques, and people to orchestrate access and effects against targeted information infrastructures. The challenges in the achieving the level of coordination such an effort requires differ from those faced by other types of potential intruders. Those considering waging strategic information warfare need the technological sophistication to use tools and techniques to explore networks like hackers, to steal information and corrupt individual loyalties like criminals and spies, or simply to break or disrupt systems like an anarchist. However, waging strategic information warfare additionally requires understanding about how the effects of a particular attack will disrupt the operations of a targeted organization. Access to insiders may prove a critical source in creating such an understanding. Actors attempting to establish capabilities of waging digital attacks against the United States may need to engage in a healthy dose of activity associated with espionage and covert action.

Even with insider access, however, those seeking political influence through digital attacks must go a step further in estimating how disrupting the targeted networks, infrastructures, and individuals will translate into political effect. No historical experience or metrics for analysis exist for strategic information warfare. The Achilles' heel of past strategic warfare efforts has been the inability to understand linkages between destruction and disruption of specific target systems and mechanisms for achieving political influence. The challenges of creating the organizational capacity to conduct all the activities necessary to wage offensive strategic information warfare will be addressed in depth in chapter 3.

Defending Information Infrastructures against Digital Attack

As with past forms of strategic warfare, understanding and implementing effective defensive measures can provide protection against digital attacks. Awareness of the need to protect the resources processed, stored, and transmitted via information infrastructures has grown over the past two decades in the United States as reliance on digital technologies has spread and deepened. Led initially by national security organizations concerned with protecting classified information, provision of computer security services and products is a growing sector of the information technology industry. Organizations have been formed both inside and outside of government to help users of information infrastructures respond to malicious activity. The historical background and status of U.S. efforts to protect information infrastructures is analyzed in depth in chapter 5.

The explanation of the conceptual basis for defensive information warfare presented in this section will focus on the ability to control access to, monitor, and respond to and mitigate large-scale digital disruption and destruction of U.S. information infrastructures. Unlike the measures required for defense against conventional air bombardment or weapons of mass destruction, however, many of the same steps necessary to protect information infrastructures against unintentional disruption and malicious activity conducted for purposes other than strategic attack apply to defensive information warfare efforts.

Analyzing the Defense of Information Infrastructures against Digital Attacks

As with past types of strategic warfare, defensive efforts against digital attacks could include both passive and active measures to protect valuable resources. The following process-based framework describes the tasks required for defending information infrastructures against digital attacks:

Establish defender > Control access > Monitor > Respond > Mitigate effects and Prevent future access

According to this framework, the defender is the organization with assigned responsibility for securing the operation of a given information infrastructure. Defenders may range from the system administrator responsible for a small, simple network such as a company's local area network (LAN) to organizations such as the Joint Task Force-Computer Network Defense responsible for the protection of the aggregation of networks comprising the entire Department of Defense information infrastructure. At the level of strategic information warfare, organizations involved in U.S. defensive efforts include all those responsible for the protection of information infrastructures considered potentially significant enough to be considered centers of gravity by an attacker.

Controlling access broadly refers to a defender's capability to ensure that openings for attackers do not exist in the technology product–network provider–infrastructure user chain described in chapter 1. To this end, defenders must be concerned with the security features of underlying hardware and software products, whether produced for general use or developed specifically for use in a given information infrastructure. The connections and operations established by network providers within an information infrastructure must be reliable and free of potential access vulnerabilities. Defenders must ensure that the authorized users of an information infrastructure are not creating access, either intentionally or unintentionally. Defenders must also ensure that insiders are engaging only in authorized activity while they have access to the infrastructure.

As the size and scope of activity for a given information infrastructure increases, multiple organizations will likely field the technology products, provide network services, and use the information infrastructure for many purposes. The typical setup of an Air Force base telephone system provides a simple illustration of the typical network of relationships.[122] An Air Force communications squadron is responsible for providing telephone services to organizations on the base to which it is assigned. The squadron ensures operation of the base telephone system and responds to queries about the availability and quality of the service. The actual equipment, connecting lines, and switches on the base however, are purchased from commercial companies. The main telephone switching hardware is typically on base and owned by the Air Force. Installation, maintenance, and upgrades of the switch hardware and software are typically conducted under contract with a commercial company such as Nortel. Nortel maintenance personnel may well have remote dial-up access to the Air Force switch to conduct normal maintenance and upgrades without having to access the base physically. The contract provisions allowing base telephones to connect from the main base switch to the public-switched network are established with other companies such as AT&T and MCI to provide different services for communication with the world outside the base. All organizations on the base and all their outside customers requiring a functioning telephone system to accomplish their mission thereby rely on a multitude of technology producers and network service providers outside the direct control of the Air Force. The operation and defense of almost all advanced information infrastructures of any size requires managing such complex webs of organizational interrelationships and dependencies.

Defending a specific information infrastructure also requires striking a balance between the availability and functionality of the system and efforts to protect it against attack. Achieving a sound balance in establishing defensive capability depends on the degree of control and coordination between the creators and users of the information infrastructure and the defending organization. At the level of strategic information warfare defenses, the United States has just begun to establish organizations with overarching responsibility for defending those of the nation's information infrastructures that might serve as potential centers of gravity for adversaries, as addressed in chapter 5.

Defenders responsible for operating an information infrastructure require the capability to conduct monitoring efforts. Monitoring refers to the ability to discern whether systems, networks, and people in the infrastructure are functioning properly. This task involves generation of information about activity within an information infrastructure as well as the ability to assess its significance. If operating problems or suspicious activities are detected, monitoring capability allows defenders to discern the cause and potential objectives of such activity and whether it is malicious in intent. One of the key monitoring challenges for defenders of the United States' critical information infrastructures will be determining when evidence of disruption within information infrastructures constitutes part of an offensive strategic information warfare effort and when it falls into other categories of malicious or unintentional activity.

Response to an identified attack on an information infrastructure involves preventing continued unauthorized access, either by intercepting attackers or by identifying and closing access points. Response capability also includes the ability to recover from damage and return the information infrastructure to a desired level of functionality. Finally, response to attacks also involves learning about the access vulnerabilities in the protected infrastructure and developing tools, procedures, and programs to limit these access problems and remove, if possible, the vulnerabilities. As a result, the defending organization must have the capacity to learn from problems encountered and provide feedback to other organizations involved in the information infrastructure's operation to limit future access vulnerabilities. In a situation in which an attacker continues its activities over a period of time, a priority on recovering, learning quickly, and disseminating lessons to limit continuing vulnerability will be fundamental to the overall effectiveness of defensive efforts. The challenges of creating organizational capacity to orchestrate these activities will be discussed in more depth in chapter 3.

Even when attacked, information infrastructures will ideally retain sufficient functionality to prevent or degrade an attacker's ability to achieve its objective. Preferably, of course, defenders stop attacks prior to their achieving any effect on the infrastructure at all. Attacks can be completely disabled either by eliminating access points for attackers or by actively intercepting attacks in progress. However, achieving total control over access or ability to intercept attacks when defending large-scale information infrastructures may prove impossible, for reasons discussed below. Defenders of large-scale infrastructures must therefore weigh the efficacy of available means to limit vulnerability and mitigate damage against the costs of implementing these measures. Similar trade-offs existed in defensive efforts against past strategic attacks, as discussed in the first section of this chapter. In the case of strategic information warfare, the information infrastructures subject to attack by adversaries of the United States must be protected at least to the degree that these infrastructures do not create highly vulnerable

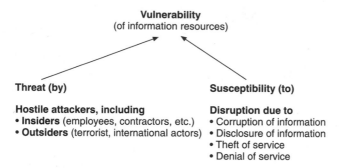

Figure 2.2
Factors affecting vulnerability of information resources

centers of gravity. Assessing the value of different infrastructures, potential threats, and the effectiveness of available remedies will present a major challenge to organizations as they decide how to allocate limited resources to protect their information systems.

Discerning the Level of Effort Necessary to Defend
Information Infrastructures

Daniel Knauf has developed a conceptual framework for assessing the need to protect information resources that highlights the importance of determining both the value of information infrastructures and their vulnerability to disruption.[123] Figure 2.2 depicts the factors involved in assessing information resource vulnerability, and figure 2.3 depicts the larger relationship between

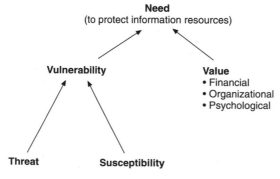

Figure 2.3
Assessing the need to protect information resources

information resource protection needs, the vulnerability of these resources, and their value.

In assessing vulnerability to strategic information warfare attacks, defenders must understand the potential disruption hostile actors might inflict on information infrastructures. These defenders must be able to assess the susceptibility to different types of attacks on the component systems and networks that underpin the operation of information infrastructures of significant organizations in key sectors of society. A distinction must be drawn between susceptibility and vulnerability. Although most modern information infrastructures are susceptible to some disruption, as discussed earlier in the chapter, their susceptibility to sustained, large-scale disruption is indeterminate as of summer 2000. Vulnerability goes beyond susceptibility in additionally requiring the presence of an actual threat. Reliance on information systems and networks alone does not create vulnerability. Assessments of U.S. vulnerability to strategic information warfare should consider which key infrastructures are susceptible to disruption and the capabilities of actors to cause such disruption.

The proper protection of information infrastructures requires that the organizations responsible for such protection undertake significant analysis and effort. However, assessing the value of information resources presents major challenges. Effective metrics to assess the organizational and psychological value of information resources have not yet been developed. Also, the evaluation of an organization's need to protect its information infrastructure has a dynamic dimension, as the components and relative value of infrastructure assets change over time. Performing such evaluations proves increasingly difficult for defenders as the number of information systems and networks with value to an organization increases. Even as early as May 1994, a large commercial company such as Exxon had 261 networks registered on the Internet alone.[124] The Department of Defense information infrastructure in 1996 consisted of more than 2.1 million computers, more than 10,000 local area networks, and more than 100 long-distance networks.[125] The information infrastructures of such large organizations are generally operated and adapted by subordinate organizations whose efforts may be loosely coordinated at best. Establishing programs simply to track and assess the use and value of the disparate components and responsible operating organizations of a large information infrastructure may prove a daunting task. Interviews conducted by the author with individuals responsible for such tasks in the Joint Task Force-Computer Network Defense, Air Force Information Warfare Center, and Fidelity Investments Information Security Services all underscore the difficulty of this task.

Determinations of an information infrastructure's value and the requisite amount of protective effort generally resides with organizational leaders, who allocate scarce resources to create and use the information infrastructures to achieve organizational goals. Such decision makers could include the leadership of government organizations like the Department of Defense or the Internal Revenue Service or chief executive officers (CEOs) of commercial corporations. In some cases, the value placed on information protection may be so high that an organization responsible for defending an information infrastructure may have substantial influence in setting the standards for the level of defensive effort. In the case of U.S. telecommunications systems used to transmit and store classified information, the National Security Agency exerts the dominant influence in decisions about the operational procedures for these systems and the protective measures implemented in the associated information infrastructure. More often, suborganizations responsible for protecting the overall organization's information infrastructure may possess only one voice among many in a debate about the infrastructure's value and vulnerability to attack. Government regulations or corporate policies may be issued to address information security concerns. Users will want to ensure access as well as security. Security programs must compete with other priorities when determining the portion of an organization's limited financial and personnel resources that will be devoted to information infrastructure defense.

An even more complex situation arises when multiple organizations jointly operate critical information infrastructures such as the public-switched networks, including the Internet or long-distance phone systems, which lack a single organization responsible for their control and protection. Coordinating and assigning responsibilities for defense of such infrastructures may require significant levels of interorganizational communication and cooperation. Additionally, the operators and users of information infrastructures rely on the security and reliability features of component technologies making up these infrastructures. Whether technology producers will assume an obligation to ensure that their products contribute to, rather than degrade, the ability of other organizations to defend their information infrastructures is an open question. Efforts to defend information infrastructures may involve co-opting technology producers as well. Organizational challenges central to defensive strategic information warfare are discussed in chapter 3.

Tools and Techniques for Defending Information Infrastructures

A wide variety of technological tools and techniques exist to help information infrastructure defenders in controlling access to, monitoring, and responding to attacks on networks. Passive measures make access more difficult for attackers, and more active measures seek to intercept or prevent attacks.

In controlling access, computer security tools and techniques generally try to create an environment within a protected information infrastructure with the following five characteristics:[126]

- Integrity. Assures users that information has not been modified.
- Authentication. Verification that electronic agreement by party is not fraudulent.
- Nonrepudiation. Undeniable proof of participation in a digital interaction.
- Confidentiality. Only intended agents have access to communication and stored information.
- Availability. Assurance of service on demand.

As attackers can choose among various tools and techniques, so defenders can choose to implement measures to achieve different objectives. Many available tools focus on preventing unauthorized access to and use of a system by outsiders. Computer firewalls endeavor to control access by filtering the types of outside users and digital processes that are allowed on a given information network. Encryption hardware and software can provide users with increased confidence that communications over the system and stored data on the system will remain confidential. Hardware cards can be inserted into computers to provide authentication and ease the use of encryption. Network analyzers allow systems administrators to scan digitally for known access vulnerabilities within information systems and networks. Information systems vendors and computer security organizations also develop solutions to remedy such vulnerabilities, generally known as "patches," which are made available to network providers and users to help in controlling access. Organizations that provide such information in the United States include the CERT Coordinating Center at Carnegie Mellon University. The role of such organizations is discussed at length in chapter 5.

Tools for controlling access by insiders include passwords, challenge and response systems, secure tokens, and biometrics identifiers, which can be used to properly identify users. Risks of insider disruption can also be addressed by placing constraints on access within information systems. Participation of multiple individuals may be mandated for conducting certain types of activities on a system, such as financial transactions or the destruction of cryptographic materials, necessitating collusion for malicious activity to occur. Banks often require employees to take vacations as part of security programs to uncover embezzle-ment with the goal of deterring schemes that require active monitoring and activity by insiders.

Other defensive measures can ensure that authorized users have access to required information resources even if certain assets of an information infra-structure are unavailable or corrupted. Physically and digitally separate backup operating sites can provide insurance against major failure of key infrastructure nodes. Simple programs and procedures can periodically create non-networked copies of valuable information resources on paper or floppy disks. Off-site storage of such backups also complicates the targeting efforts of attackers. Ensur-ing that users have access to redundant processing and transmission capabilities makes an attacker's efforts to deny service more difficult. Although such mea-sures are often implemented to protect against unintentional physical disruptions such as power outages, fires, and floods, tools and techniques that establish redundancy also help mitigate the potential effects of digital attacks. Such mea-sures also involve increased operating costs, however, and possible reduced accessibility to primary operating data, processing, and communications systems. Trade-offs between assured availability and higher costs must be weighed in light of perceived vulnerability to disruption and an organization's information assurance objectives.

Technological tools and techniques also exist to monitor the proper func-tioning of information infrastructures. Virus checkers can determine if certain types of known malicious software exist within an information system. Auto-mated combinations of hardware and software tools can monitor the type of activity being conducted on an information network.[127] These tools can capture data about activity on a network, weigh the degree of threat posed by a given type of network activity using algorithms, filter data about activity for later analy-sis, and cue network operators and defenders when suspicious activity is detected. Like network analyzers and virus checkers, such monitoring tools are generally designed to highlight previously known types of malicious activity. Therefore, access control and monitoring tools need constant updating as new techniques for intrusion and disruption arise and the vulnerabilities of new tech-nologies deployed within information infrastructures change.[128] Monitoring systems currently in use often produce large amounts of data. Users may require specific skills to filter and interpret the output of such systems. The principal network monitoring tool used by the Air Force at the end of the 1990s, the Auto-mated Security Incident Measurement (ASIM) system, provides an example. ASIM provides its users at the Air Force Information Warfare Center with real-time warning of suspicious activity on networks connected to the system, based on detection of known patterns of suspicious activity. The system also captures large amounts of filtered data for downloading on a daily or as-required basis. The Air Force Information Warfare Center as of 1997 employed more than twenty full-time analysts who required a three-month training program to become qualified to analyze ASIM data to investigate important suspicious activity, to recognize new types of possible attacks, and to correlate data across incidents occurring at different locations.[129]

Technological tools can also assist defenders in stopping malicious activity before it has any effect on the underlying system by preventing continued access to information resources, restoring system operations, and assessing the source of attacks. Most antivirus programs allow users to erase discovered viruses before continued operation of the system enables them to have a disruptive impact. Monitoring systems to detect suspected malicious activity can automatically modify network operation to prevent outside access. Such systems also can provide the information necessary to evaluate how an attacker, whether insider or outsider, has gained access to a system to assess how to stop continuing intrusion and disruption as well as to help identify vulnerabilities and devise remedial measures. Other tools help defenders scan systems and networks for evidence of corruption and damage that needs to be fixed. Tools and techniques also exist to backtrack the digital pathways followed by attackers to help identify the point of origin of an electronic attack.

Technological tools for defending information infrastructures have demonstrated very limited ability, however, to proactively prevent digital attacks based on network intrusion.[130] The time required by defenders to determine that a given disruption to information systems and networks has resulted from a malicious attack severely impedes active defense. Most existing defensive tools detect suspicious digital activity based on pattern recognition of previously catalogued digital attacks. The ability of defensive tools and operators to detect new or modified techniques, however, has proven limited. The time required to process monitoring information and confirm whether an observed activity constitutes an intentional attack has made defensive responses reactive rather than anticipatory. By the time an attack is recognized, it may well have been inflicted damage. Defenders could allow automatic monitoring systems to disconnect system users conducting suspicious activity to speed response time and limit damage. As the speed and degree of automation in defensive response increases, however, worries arise about the possibility of falsely identifying activity as an attack and degrading productivity. When attackers are discovered, backtracking against them generally requires access to systems owned and operated by other organizations and individuals, often in other countries, raising legal and political considerations. To precisely identify an attacker's patterns of behavior and point of origin in cyberspace, defenders may have to allow continued intrusions even after the presence of an attack has been detected. Also, in many large organizations, subunits responsible for information security lack direct control or authority over the operation of information systems or networks being protected. Effective responses to attacks require a level of coordination both within and between organizations and across other political and legal jurisdictions that has often proven time consuming to achieve. Yet strong defensive efforts can still deter information infrastructure attackers by making access difficult, enabling faster damage limitation, and improving the efficiency of active responses.

Impact of the Cyberspace Environment

Those responsible for defending information infrastructures against digital attacks in the cyberspace environment are confronted with environmental conditions creating significant challenges. The pace of change and increasing reliance on information infrastructures by organizations across many sectors of society requires defenders to continually reassess the value of specific resources under protection and the overall priority accorded to defense of those resources. Organizations responsible for defense must understand how changing systems, evolving networks, and newly discovered vulnerabilities within an organization's infrastructure create new targets of concern, requiring a shift in the focus of defensive efforts. At a very broad level, the U.S. national security community in the past has focused its information protection efforts on guarding classified information and critical command and control links. Dedicated networks were set up and specialized hardware deployed to make sure that information remained confidential through use of encryption. Availability of information was ensured through redundancy and protection of communications paths. However, increasing reliance on unclassified information and commercial networks for crucial functions such as logistics and transportation planning has resulted in a growing DOD awareness of the need to protect such information resources from attacks. As commercial firms have become increasingly reliant on the use of the Internet to develop closer ties with suppliers and customers, new sources of vulnerability to digital attack have been created that are outside their direct control.

A 1994 survey of access routes for external attacks on corporate networks found that 80 percent of such attacks were conducted over the Internet. A 1995 survey found that 24 percent of companies whose networks were connected to the Internet had suffered from hacker attacks, whereas only 3 percent of those without Internet connection had had such problems.[131] The annual FBI/CSI survey indicated for the first time in 1999 that the number of digital attacks originating from the Internet exceeded those from internal systems.[132] In response, companies have begun to deploy computer firewalls to protect internal networks and encrypting communications to protect against eavesdropping as they use the Internet.

In addition to rapidly changing software and hardware, the degree of organizational reliance on information infrastructures more generally will change the relative value of defending these assets. For example, as described in chapter 1, the financial sector has become increasingly reliant on information systems and networks to conduct almost all aspects of its operations. A recognition of the increasing value of information infrastructures has resulted in a relative shift of security efforts away from protecting physical assets through use of vaults and armed guards to efforts to secure information systems and networks. Such efforts range from improving the ability of automated teller machines to combat fraud, to encryption of data transfers between financial institutions, to establishment of network monitoring operations for critical commercial operations.[133]

Advanced information infrastructures are increasingly reliant on commercial technology producers taking responsibility for enabling network providers or infrastructure users to implement and operate the underlying technologies properly and securely. The corporate producers of underlying technologies such as operating systems like Microsoft's Windows NT are widely perceived as lacking adequate incentives to build security features into their products, as discussed in chapter 5. In particular, the constantly evolving technology and the rapid pace of product development in the information technology industry places a premium on being first to the market with new products to establish operating standards and customer loyalty. The time and cost necessary to create improved security features and test them directly erode perceived competitiveness. Therefore, commercial technology providers have forgone attention to creating products that mitigate intrusion and disruption in the absence of any industry agreements or government stipulations of security standards. As a result, organizations in government and commercial sectors create, use, and even organize their core operations around information networks and infrastructures employing technological building blocks provided by outsiders that almost always lack an adequate foundation for establishing protection.

The proliferation of open networks makes efforts to draw borders around information infrastructures increasingly difficult. Even if an organization can secure its own information systems and networks, if these systems are connected to other systems via an insecure network, such protective efforts may have limited value. Linkages between unclassified systems and classified systems have created a new area of vulnerability for U.S. national security organizations. The connection of Rome Laboratories computers to the Internet not only allowed attackers to gain access to sensitive information but also afforded them the ability to exploit such access to gain further "trusted user" access to other sensitive information networks around the world. A 1996 Defense Science Board study, *Information Warfare—Defense*, highlighted how the classified, protected Global Command and Control System may have significant vulnerabilities because of its interconnections with networks such as the unclassified Global Transportation Network.[134] In the financial industry, the systems for reconciling the daily transactions of banks and trading exchanges require the interconnection of information systems of a large number of banks, trading firms, clearing firms, and other organizations. Such interconnection may compromise the carefully constructed security of one institution's system through breaches in the system of another institution with which it is connected.

On a national scale, increasing complexity of information infrastructures and interconnection with other critical activities, such as the operation of the power system, raise the potential of "cascading" effects of intentional (or other) disruptions. Indeed, the possibility of cascades receives much attention in analyses dealing with U.S. vulnerability to digital attacks.[135] The "cascade" concept refers to the effect of a particular system failure resulting in the promulgation of a much broader set of disruptive effects. A widely cited example is the power outage in the northwest United States in August 1996 resulting from automated shutdown procedures that began when a tree growing into a power line caused a local power system problem. The PCCIP's *Critical Foundations* report stresses the potential threat posed by cascades: "A second threat to infrastructure reliability, less predictable and potentially farther reaching, is system failure arising from increases in the volume and complexity of interconnection and introduction of new technologies. . . . The interaction of complexity and new technologies will almost certainly expand the universe of ways in which system failure can occur, and unlike natural disasters, there is no assurance that such failure will be localized."[136] Information infrastructure disruptions that occur because of loss of electric power may in turn cause financial markets that depend on reliable communications and information to shut down. Both attackers and defenders face a significant challenge in understanding the possibilities for cascades and identifying the potential failure points at which they can be induced.

However, the complexity and openness of interconnections in many systems may also add a degree of "inadvertent robustness."[137] As the number of connections within an information infrastructure grows, necessary information-based functions may be able to flow around a given network node once a disruption in that node is isolated. Diversity among information processing, storage, and transfer systems and networks may also limit the vulnerability of systems to attack. Older systems with overlapping functionality, duplication, and lack of interoperability may provide some measure of protection against intruders exploiting a single point of access and the potential for cascading effects.[138]

In some cases, the impacts of digital attacks may be sufficiently limited in scope, slow enough in propagating effects, and transparent enough to allow information infrastructure users at lower levels to self-correct problems. Other effects of attacks may propagate so quickly and with such complexity that large numbers of infrastructure users across multiple organizations and political boundaries could suffer negative effects, with no capacity to correct the problems on their own. The value of coordinated efforts at assessing vulnerabilities, monitoring, and responding to threats will increase as the size and complexity of the information infrastructure being defended increases.

The time required to implement offensive and defensive efforts also affects the relative difficulty of these tasks. Generally, having time to find and exploit a relatively small number of access points works to the advantage of digital attackers and their efforts. The complex chain of infrastructure creation and evolution that characterizes large, advanced information infrastructures generally creates myriad points for unauthorized access and susceptibility to attack. Defenders of such information infrastructures face the substantial challenge of understanding potential vulnerabilities to digital attacks, analyzing systems and networks to discover potential unauthorized access points, and instituting fixes. A 1997 Software Engineering Institute report from the CERT Coordination Center indicated that in 1995 the CERT/CC "received an average of 35 new [vulnerability] reports each quarter. That average has more than doubled in 1996 and we continue to see the same type of vulnerabilities in newer versions of products that we saw in earlier versions."[139]

Experts generally concur that identifying all potential points of access within large, increasingly open information infrastructures, such as those relied on by the Department of Defense or a large corporation, will prove impossible. Effective defensive efforts should therefore not be geared to eliminating vulnerability with the idea of achieving threat avoidance but instead should focus on managing risk and prioritizing defensive effort. The need to rationalize the allocation of defensive resources to protect critical assets is widely recognized in both the national security community and commercial information security efforts. However, achieving the necessary understanding of the infrastructures under protection as well as institutionalizing operational procedures and defensive programs in various independent suborganizations requires substantial effort.

Defense at the Level of Strategic Information Warfare

Such an effort to understand the infrastructures that need protection and institutionalize procedures to do so would involve conducting national-level assessments of potential centers of gravity based on degree of reliance on these information infrastructures and the adequacy of their existing defensive efforts. Relevant protection efforts would include the activities of large and small organizations with information infrastructure assets deemed significant enough to constitute potential centers of gravity for enemy attack. Organizations at all stages of the technology product–network provider–information user creation chain play significant roles. As described in chapter 1, the entities that provide and operate most key U.S. information infrastructures now reside outside the government. National-level infrastructure defensive efforts must therefore assess mechanisms for coordinating and implementing defensive activities across both governmental and nongovernmental sectors of activity. On the positive side, the efforts of organizations to protect resources against threats from natural disaster, system failures, nonsystematic hacking, insider corruption, financial crime, and economic espionage may provide substantial leverage against the threat posed to those resources by strategic information warfare attacks.

The possibility of strategic information warfare requires defenders of information infrastructures to confront opponents with very different objectives, tools, techniques, and resources than those involved in past threats not of a digital nature. Potential options for improving national-level defensive capabilities would involve different costs and trade-offs for the various organizations involved. A U.S. federal mandate to domestic technology producers requiring that their operating systems incorporate strong information security features would involve very different stakeholders than a U.S. initiative within the International Telecommunications Union (ITU) to establish a set of global telecommunications security standards. The challenges involved in creating the organizational capacity and coordination required to establish strategic information warfare defenses are analyzed more fully in chapter 3.

Ambiguities of Offense and Defense in Waging Strategic Information Warfare

Chapter 1 highlighted some of the unique features of the cyberspace operating environment. The challenges of waging war in cyberspace also include the highly ambiguous nature of the tools and information necessary to conduct strategic information warfare.

The tools and techniques used to conduct digital warfare are often useful to both attackers and defenders. On the one hand, the use of encryption allows defenders to keep communications and stored data confidential while making assets more difficult to corrupt and limiting the ability of attackers to locate access points to attack. On the other hand, the same encryption technologies may allow attackers to protect communications when coordinating their operations in cyberspace. Similarly, tools such as Security Administrator's Tool for Analyzing Networks (SATAN), used to probe networks to identify weaknesses in information systems, are useful to both attackers and defenders. Ambiguity of use and effect of weapons is not new. Indeed, other instruments of war, such as rifles, tanks, and advanced aircraft, can be used for either offensive or defensive purposes on conventional battlefields. In the realm of strategic warfare based on conventional bombardment or weapons of mass destruction, however, the tools and techniques have fairly distinguishable offensive or defensive uses. The difficulty in distinguishing offensive from defensive means of waging strategic information warfare may have significant implications for efforts to control their possession and permissible peacetime and wartime uses.

The complexity and pace of change of information infrastructures also make identifying key resources and vulnerabilities a difficult task for both attackers and defenders. As a result, both sides benefit from information about flaws in operating protocols, system access, network composition, and patterns of use within an information infrastructure. In past instances of strategic warfare, defenders generally had a distinct advantage over attackers in knowing the location of assets to be defended and understanding their weaknesses and significance, and they jealously guarded this knowledge. Attackers had to gather intelligence to gain insight for successful attacks. In a cyberspace environment where organizations responsible for defense lack full knowledge of, and control over, the information infrastructure they are defending, however, gaining such insight while protecting dissemination of information useful to attackers may prove a major challenge.

This dilemma is operative throughout the stages of activity involved in establishing information infrastructures. Companies such as Netscape and organizations such as the CERT/CC publicly disseminate information about the vulnerabilities of software products used in creating information infrastructures. Whereas defenders use such information to understand potential weaknesses in the systems they guard and implement steps to control access, attackers may also use these reports to gain insight into how to achieve unauthorized access to systems and networks. The issue then becomes whether the attackers or the defenders are able to gather and act on such information more quickly and effectively. Additionally, network providers such as AT&T or Worldcom must have information on the composition, physical locations, digital addresses, and access points of infrastructure components such as routers and switches to maintain facilities and use remote access to fix problems and improve performance. As a result, telecommunications providers often openly publish information about the physical locations of facilities and electronic features of their networks. However, improving access and information sources necessary for the efficient, competitive operation of information infrastructures also provides information to evaluate access points, identify key nodes, and attack those same infrastructures. Similarly, databases and maps detailing the users and functionality of a given information infrastructure are useful in understanding the value of assets in terms of allocating defensive effort as well as in deciding where to concentrate attacks. The cyberspace environment for waging information warfare in the new millennium creates a constant struggle to understand weaknesses of information infrastructures of concern. To be effective, attackers must gain an understanding of the available information while limiting the visibility of their intelligence efforts, which might provoke defensive responses. Defenders must control information about vulnerabilities and usage while disseminating such information to enable protective actions.

Accessing the Means to Wage Strategic Information Warfare

The technological tools for attacking and defending information infrastructures outlined above are accessible to a wide range of state and nonstate actors. They are relatively cheap and generally not subject to governmental control, at least in the United States. Even when certain technologies are controlled, as in the case of encryption, their widespread availability and ease of use makes preventing their acquisition by potential adversaries very difficult, as described in chapter 5.

Low Cost and Ease of Availability

Unlike the strategic bombers, interceptors, radar warning systems, ballistic missiles, and satellites for launch detection used in past types of strategic warfare, the tools for strategic information warfare can be created by a wide range of organizations, groups, and individuals at a relatively low cost, as addressed in chapter 1. The United States has spent billions of dollars annually for more than forty years to develop, deploy, and maintain offensive nuclear strike and defensive warning and protective systems for this strategic warfare capability. The increased availability of chemical and biological weapons may provide international actors with the means to wage strategic warfare at relatively low cost with small numbers of weapons. Such weapons, however, are difficult and dangerous to handle and store, and creating large quantities of them can require actors to establish large organizations and expensive programs to manage them, depending on the modes of employment and objectives contemplated.

The technological tools required for waging strategic information warfare, on the other hand, are far more widely available and easier to develop than those needed for other types of strategic warfare. Software tools for digital attacks, such as network analyzers, viruses, password monitors, and rootkit programs, among others, can be easily and anonymously acquired from numerous sources. Publicly available tools such as the SATAN network analyzer and sniffer programs designed to help systems administrators detect attacks can also be acquired by attackers.[140] Programs purposely designed to facilitate intrusion and disruption are legally available on open-access Internet sites maintained by the hacker community. The Joint Task Force-Computer Network Defense estimated that at least 30,000 electronic bulletin boards and Web sites offered such information as of the fall of 1999.[141] The hacker community includes clubs with names like Legion of Doom, Masters of Destruction, and Computer Chaos Club in which members share available hacking techniques and coordinate activities. The community also holds conferences such as DEFCON that serve as a clearinghouse for information on system and network weaknesses and hacking techniques against the latest communications protocols. Virus "clubs" on the Internet facilitate the exchange of information and virus code. Magazines published both in hard copy and digitally such as *Phrack* and *2600* are other widely available sources of information on digital attack tools.[142] CD-ROMs and computer disks with digital attack tools already loaded and ready for use can be ordered from these magazines and other catalogues.

The tools and techniques used for digital attacks require relatively little capacity in terms of commercially available computational power, storage space, and transmission capability. The teenaged British hacker who intruded on the Rome Laboratories computers used a typical home PC. Use of tools such as a rootkit file and network analyzers requires relatively limited processing and transmission bandwidth capabilities. Similarly, creating viruses and inserting intentional flaws into technologies to disrupt targeted infrastructures are not processes that require sophisticated hardware or software capabilities. Some of the most disruptive viruses unleashed in the early 1990s were produced by students using computers with 286 processors at a technical high school in Bulgaria.[143] The information processing, storage, and transmission capabilities necessary to create and use these tools to conduct attacks against most information infrastructures reside on a typical personal computer in the year 2000. A PC with a Pentium processor, a 56.6 kbps modem, and nominal storage capacity provides sufficient capacity for most types of digital attacks for a cost of around $1,000 and is available through thousands of sources worldwide. In describing the threat these relatively simple systems pose to U.S. infrastructures, the PCCIP's *Critical Foundations* report states that in 1996 approximately 32 million devices were capable of accessing the World Wide Web.[144] Slightly more expensive technology would enable attackers to speed the process of understanding access vulnerabilities and designing new tools and techniques for attacks and improve the conduct of attacks. Human expertise and organizational coordination will likely prove the constraining factors in planning and execution of strategic information warfare attacks, not availability of hardware and software tools.

Tools for defense against strategic information warfare attacks may be more technology-intensive, but their cost and availability is generally not prohibitive. Defenders can begin to control access to and monitor information systems and networks with simple tools such as password controls, virus checkers, and encryption capabilities. More complex tools such as firewalls and automated monitoring systems may require defenders to purchase or create separate hardware platforms and software programs, but costs for these tools remain relatively low. Organizations responsible for defense can produce such tools themselves but may choose also to turn to commercial providers. Once software tools to protect information infrastructures are created and property rights for them established, they can be easily replicated and transferred.

A principal concern in creating effective defensive tools will be the degree of effort required to customize available defensive capabilities to features of a particular information infrastructure being defended. These tools and techniques must also be updated to keep up with new technologies installed and the emergence of new techniques for attack. Issues regarding scale of effort also arise in establishing large-scale monitoring and response capabilities. As numbers and types of information infrastructure assets needing to be defended increases, so do the technological requirements for transmitting, storing and processing data, especially if organizations wish to limit the number of personnel involved. Constantly evolving protective technologies and attacker techniques place substantial training demands on defensive organizations. Again, the primary constraint on creating defensive strategic information warfare capabilities is not the dearth of available technological tools but the cost and availability of human expertise to organize, manage, and update these tools. Such expertise will be necessary to evaluate reports generated by access control and monitoring tools, to understand the nature of activity reported, to fix holes, to regenerate systems capabilities damaged by attacks, and to incorporate learning into improved defensive tools, techniques, and procedures.

Difficulty of Controlling Digital Information Warfare Technology

The relative lack of international and domestic controls on the possession and transfer of technological tools for use in strategic information warfare increases their availability. Nation-states have monopolized the ownership of the weapons and delivery means for large-scale WMD and conventional bombardment attacks. International agreements and individual governments endeavor to limit the level of armaments and the transfer of such weapons between international actors. The dedicated technological and organizational infrastructures necessary to conduct large-scale strategic conventional and nuclear operations can be relatively easily observed and monitored. The rising concern about the small-scale possession and use of nuclear, chemical, and biological weapons has provoked efforts to control these weapons as well. International conventions attempt to limit or prohibit the ownership and use of such weapons. States conduct individual and multilateral cooperative efforts to monitor the existence and use not only of such weapons but of technologies related to their production. Because of the differences in national perspectives and the dual-use nature of many of the technologies involved, however, states have encountered obstacles in controlling and monitoring the spread of such weapons and technologies. A major focus of intelligence and treaty monitoring efforts to combat proliferating WMD capabilities is discovering the presence of organizations with the necessary capabilities to deliver and use them effectively.

In contrast, states generally place much less emphasis on the control of tools and underlying technologies potentially used to conduct strategic information warfare. The underlying hardware and software processing, storage, and transmission capabilities required to conduct digital warfare, such as personal computers, modems, and the like, are increasingly part of the everyday life of organizations and individuals across most of the globe. Some countries have banned private ownership of certain generic information technologies such as fax machines and satellite receivers. As described in chapter 1, some countries such as Singapore and China try to control residents' access to global information networks such as the Internet. However, these efforts focus on achieving political control over individual access to communication means, not constraining the acquisition by international actors of the tools for waging strategic information warfare.

Many of the specific tools for strategic information warfare, such as network analyzers and monitors, have important dual-use applications. Used for defensive purposes, such tools are viewed as legitimate by almost all governments, infrastructure operators, and users. The nature of the physical tools for waging digital warfare makes them extremely difficult to observe without highly intrusive measures to monitor and inspect items such as personal computers and individual disks. More importantly, the tools can be transferred electronically through the Internet and other means. Even possession of tools clearly intended for malicious disruption, such as viruses and hacker programs, has not been subject to strict controls.[145] Although domestic laws exist that penalize malicious activity in cyberspace, specific digital attack tools are not outlawed in the United States. The biggest exception to the general lack of control over the tools with potential information warfare uses has been the effort by the United States and other nations to control the use and export of encryption technology. Most analyses have found, however, that controls on such technology have a progressively diminishing impact in limiting diffusion of the technologies while imposing both economic and social costs. The details of U.S. efforts to control encryption technology will be covered in more detail in chapter 5.

The combination of low cost, widespread availability, and lack of controls makes the tools for waging digital warfare highly accessible. Major assessments conducted by the Unites States in the mid to late 1990s concluded that a wide range of potential adversaries had the means and ability to acquire the technological tools to conduct strategic information attacks. Director of Central Intelligence George Tenet testified to Congress in February 1999 that "terrorists and others are recognizing that information warfare offers them low cost, easily hidden tools to support their causes."[146]

Actors desiring to wage offensive information warfare can readily acquire tools capable of disrupting information infrastructures. Similarly, actors and organizations endeavoring to create defensive strategic information warfare efforts also have access to a wide range of technological tools if they can commit adequate financial resources to acquiring and implementing them. The findings of numerous studies examining the security of U.S. information systems, networks, and infrastructures stress that the limited attention paid to technological solutions for providing defense are accompanied by a corresponding lack of societal and managerial concern and effort toward such defense.

Even though the tools and techniques to wage strategic information warfare exist and are readily available, international actors have yet to employ digital force against adversary centers of gravity to win conflicts. The United States and others are engaged in myriad conflicts with numerous enemies. The threat and use of force remain important factors in the international environment. Yet no publicly known conflict waged by strategic information warfare has occurred. I make this assertion despite statements by some such as Deputy Secretary of Defense John Hamre that the 1999 conflict in Kosovo constituted the first cyberwar. Although digital attacks on the DOD's information infrastructure occurred during this conflict, these attacks were quite limited in scope and were not a major factor in Serbian efforts to conclude the conflict on favorable terms.[147] Why did the Serbs not attempt to wage a major strategic information warfare campaign against the United States? Other factors besides the presence of new technological tools must be affecting the perceived utility of strategic information warfare. A full characterization of the strategic information warfare threat to the

United States must identify which actors may perceive waging strategic information as useful for achieving their political objectives.

Using Strategic Information Warfare for Political Ends

The means, availability, and opportunity for waging strategic information warfare leaves open the question of ends served by waging such warfare. State and nonstate actors considering strategic information warfare campaigns would do so in pursuit of differing types of objectives and in different political contexts. As with all types of warfare, considerations related to preparation, timing, and exit strategies would influence how strategic information warfare was waged. The chapter concludes with a framework for assessing the potential utility of strategic information warfare for different types of potential U.S. adversaries.

Phases of a Strategic Information Warfare Campaign

Adversaries who consider strategic information warfare a potential way to threaten U.S. centers of gravity would have to determine how to prepare, wage, and end conflicts in a manner that best matches their available means to their political ends. All the enabling conditions identified earlier in this chapter would determine which actors could successfully wage such a campaign.

Actors contemplating strategic information warfare could conduct both offensive and defensive preparations in peacetime. Attackers would require extensive intelligence on their adversary's reliance on information infrastructures, including access vulnerabilities and the relative significance of different information infrastructures. Intelligence could be collected through digital means as well as through more traditional means such as corrupting insiders and accessing publicly available materials. Assessments would have to be updated regularly as targeted information infrastructures and their significance to the opponents changed. Attackers might develop specific tools and techniques to increase the vulnerabilities of targeted information infrastructures. Preparations might include efforts to insert corrupted software and hardware into targeted information infrastructures to improve access and create desired effects. Also, probes of an opponent's defenses might identify weak points and reaction times. Potential gains from inserting malicious code or probing activity would have to be weighed, however, against the potential risks of their being discovered. Ideally, attackers would be able to develop an understanding of how different degrees of disruption against possible target sets would influence the political decision making of the adversaries' leadership.

Faced with the prospect of a digital attack, defenders of key information infrastructure assets would face the constant challenge of assessing and closing opportunities for unauthorized access as problems became apparent and changed over time. Other tasks would include ensuring the loyalty of insiders as well as coordinating with the defensive efforts of other enterprises. Preparation would also include creating the means to share information about vulnerabilities at all levels of infrastructure creation and warning of possible malicious activities by potential attackers.

Actors considering a strategic information warfare campaign could begin a conflict in a number of ways. An actor might plan and create capabilities to wage digital warfare based on an assumption that the actor could control the initiation of a conflict. Most analyses of the U.S. vulnerability to strategic information warfare are explicitly or implicitly based on this assumption. Digital attacks might occur independently, in conjunction with conventional means of strategic attack, or along with the use of weapons of mass destruction. Actors optimizing their capabilities to conduct a premeditated strategic information attack could concentrate their efforts on refining tools and techniques to achieve maximum access and effect against targets identified as the most critical. An extensive period for preparing an attack could potentially create major advantages for an attacker over the defense in terms of precision, surprise, and synchronization.

However, actors might also need to assess the utility of strategic information warfare capabilities employed in reaction to an unexpected conflict. The dynamic of waging a strategic information campaign with standing forces due to a crisis is a topic noticeably absent from most analyses of information warfare. Offensive forces would have to conduct attacks based on existing levels of access to adversary infrastructures and might have to employ suboptimal reconaissance and attack tools and techniques. Lacking the means to adequately provide precision access to infrastructures of maximum leverage, attackers might be forced to rely on tools and techniques such as unleashing malicious software and launching denial-of-service attacks that create significant collateral disruption of systems that are not intended targets of attack. Efforts to quickly increase the scanning of adversary information infrastructures and probes of defenses as a crisis evolves could heighten awareness among defenders of the existence or imminence of strategic information warfare attack. In the middle of an emerging crisis, preemptive strikes might occur as offensive and defensive forces on both sides attempted to rapidly increase levels of readiness.

The level of activity and length of a strategic information warfare campaign would depend in large measure on an attacker's strategic approach. Three possible campaign approaches are described below. Most past strategic warfare theorists have discussed all-out efforts against the most vulnerable centers of gravity to achieve political objectives as quickly as possible. This approach places a premium on creating maximum disruptive impact. All-out strategic information warfare campaigns would involve high levels of initial activity as offensive and defensive forces engaged in a struggle to establish the upper hand in the cyberspace environment. Cyberspace superiority might be achieved quickly, or the campaign could degenerate into a protracted attrition struggle, as with strategic bombardment in World War II.

In contrast to the all-out approach, an actor confident in a continuing ability to inflict pressure on centers of gravity without risks of retaliation could decide to launch strategic information attacks to demonstrate its intent and capability. The actor could then allow an opponent the opportunity to accede to its demands while holding out the threat of future punishment, as theorized by Schelling and attempted by the United States in the Rolling Thunder campaign.

Finally, an actor might choose to wage a consciously protracted strategic information warfare campaign similar to the protracted warfare strategies discussed earlier in the chapter. The actor would conduct attacks when perceived vulnerabilities offered the maximum opportunity to inflict damage while also minimizing the ability of the targeted actor to retaliate. The goal of such a strategic information warfare campaign would not be to quickly impose unacceptable costs on the adversary but rather to slowly wear down its will to resist.

The choice of strategic approach would depend on the attacker's perceptions of the vulnerability of important centers of gravity. Would the attacker intend to achieve influence through causing economic disruption that the population finds intolerable, resulting in pressure on political leadership? Or could strategic information warfare attacks be targeted against the military communication and logistics information infrastructures of an opponent to paralyze any capacity for military action in a given conflict and thus drive political decisions about employing force? Different targeting choices would have widely varying mechanisms for achieving political influence. The availability of various tools, the strength of an opponent's defenses, and the robustness of the opponent's infrastructure to disruption would shape an attacker's choices about the optimal strategic approach to be employed.

As the conflict progressed, the ability of strategic information warfare forces to attack and defend targeted infrastructures of concern would evolve. In all cases, actors engaged in strategic information warfare would continually assess damage and pain inflicted on the adversary relative to that suffered by their own side. How quickly could the adversary institute defensive adjustments and infrastructure recovery efforts? Could forces tasked with attacking adversaries easily retarget their efforts and sustain the ability to inflict damage? The relationship between the level and timing of pressure achieved against centers of gravity and the resultant political influence would prove crucial in determining the course of the conflict. What level of threatened or actual disruption would be required to achieve political objectives? Would attacks against different information infrastructures serving as centers of gravity achieve political influence quickly or slowly? Could an adversary quickly retaliate and/or escalate the conflict in such a way that the potential gains from information warfare would be outweighed by the costs? The results of the offense/defense interaction and escalatory decisions could dramatically change the tempo and objectives of strategic information warfare campaigns. Strategic approaches previously selected might require adaptation if planned approaches were to prove unworkable. The relevance of strategic information warfare to the outcome of the conflict might be severely reduced if unanticipated escalation to a major conventional struggle or the use of weapons of mass destruction were to occur.

Finally, actors contemplating waging strategic information warfare would have to consider how such conflicts would end. Presumably, if an adversary acquiesced to political demands, an actor would order its forces to cease waging attacks. Attackers using digital warfare tools and techniques would have to evaluate the level of control these means allowed over the disruptive effects inflicted. The effects of some tools such as corrupted software products or viruses might prove difficult, if not impossible, to stop. Also, if insiders and surrogate organizations were involved, adequate means to communicate with, and control, such entities to stop their activities would be necessary. The level of political commitment of actors could change over time, making the achievement of the original political goals of attackers more difficult. Strategic information warfare campaigns resulting in unintended escalation to other means of warfare or causing the involvement of other actors might well increase difficulties involved in halting a conflict. Attacks on information infrastructures that degraded communications with subordinate forces might also impede cessation of a conflict.

Assessing Utility of Strategic Information Warfare for U.S. Adversaries

As a result of the widely accessible means, a variety of state and nonstate actors who may view themselves as potential U.S. adversaries could attempt to conduct strategic information warfare against the United States. Such adversaries might include states viewed as today's international pariahs, such as North Korea, Iraq, Serbia, and Libya, as well as tomorrow's regional powers, such as China or India. Nonstate actors such as terrorist groups, organized crime operations, and ethnic movements might also attempt to develop strategic information warfare capabilities.

Actors in the international system who see themselves in possible competition and conflict with the United States have a wide variety of strategic options for pursuing their objectives. These actors could focus on developing strategic information warfare capabilities as a source of asymmetric leverage against the United States. Actors might also develop these capabilities principally in response to other security concerns but use them in conflict against the United States. For actors deliberating over strategic choices concerning available means for confronting the United States, pursuing a competition based on conventional battlefield capabilities would likely prove very difficult because of U.S. leadership and resource expenditure in that area. The Gulf War demonstrated U.S. strengths in integrating intelligence, surveillance, and reconnaissance systems with advanced precision strike weapons systems to achieve dominance on a conventional battlefield. Although the Persian Gulf environment proved particularly hospitable to such accomplishments, the United States has committed itself to achieving information superiority across the full spectrum of conflicts.[148] According to most observers, the United States will likely continue to dominate conventional battlefields for the foreseeable future. In a 1994 *Foreign Affairs* article, Eliot Cohen states that "only the United States, with its vast accumulation of military capital, better than four times the defense budget of the next leading power, and an unsurpassed ability to integrate large, complicated systems" can fully exploit the revolutionary changes on the conventional battlefield. Cohen believes other countries are aware of such strengths and fearful of U.S. willingness to employ such capabilities.[149] Others observe that U.S. dominance of the conventional battlespace will not last forever and that over time, adversaries may develop an ability to use advanced technologies selectively to acquire niche capabilities that allow them to challenge the United States.[150] But, at the turn of the twenty-first century, U.S. dominance at this level of war is as assured as any military advantage can be.

Actors who feel at a severe disadvantage to the United States on conventional battlefields might elect to pursue the development of weapons of mass destruction as described earlier in this chapter. The chief of staff of India's military has been quoted as saying that "the main lesson of the Gulf war is never fight the U.S. without nuclear weapons."[151] The WMD option may be particularly attractive to nonstate actors incapable of fielding traditional military forces. Even in small numbers, such weapons might create the ability to achieve political objectives vis-à-vis the United States. However, the pursuit of such weapons has both financial costs and political consequences if such programs are discovered. Actors might also believe that the threat or use of such weapons against the United States would precipitate an overwhelming response, limiting the perceived political utility of brandishing WMD capabilities.

Actors who face the prospect of future political conflicts with the United States may therefore view creation of strategic information warfare capabilities as their most viable option. Adversaries could be attracted to such capabilities based on perceptions of a relatively high degree of U.S. reliance on information infrastructures and their susceptibility to attack. The former director of the National Security Agency, Vice Admiral John McConnell, has stated that "[m]assive networking makes the U.S. the world's most vulnerable target for information warfare. . . . The U.S. has orders of magnitude more to lose from information warfare than its competitors."[152]

As noted above, the technological means for strategic warfare are readily accessible, and they are cheap compared to those used to conduct other types of strategic warfare. Opportunities exist to leverage intelligence capabilities through corruption of insiders and inserting spies to improve the effectiveness of these strategic means. The growth and open access of global information networks potentially affords adversaries of the United States an ability to attack key infrastructures remotely. The cyberspace environment makes moving, hiding, even disguising the source of an attack relatively simple compared to other strategic warfare means. Nonstate actors could potentially create strategic information warfare capabilities with a minimal need to be tied to physical locations and resources, thus reducing opportunities for retaliation and escalation. The tools for such warfare might also provide an actor with the ability to tune the level of threatened or inflicted pain more precisely to control retaliatory and escalation risks.

The level of official U.S. concern as to the scope of actors who might engage in strategic information warfare rose considerably in the late 1990s. National Coordinator for Security, Infrastructure and Counterterrorism Richard Clarke stated in October 1999 that numerous foreign adversaries are developing computer attack capabilities and mapping our infrastructure.[153] Analysts are also focusing increased attention on the potential use of digital attacks by nonstate actors, particularly terrorist groups such as the Irish Republican Army (IRA).[154] Renewed hostilities between Israel and the Palestinians in fall 2000 quickly led to digital attacks by hacker groups supporting the two sider. Even those who tend to downplay the strategic information warfare threat recognize the asymmetrical susceptibility of the United States to suffering such attacks. The PCCIP report *Critical Foundations* states that "[past] success in entering networks to alter data, extract financial or proprietary information, or introduce viruses demonstrates that it can be done and gives rise to concerns that, in the future, some party wishing to do serious damage to the United States will do so by the same means."[155]

Yet aligning the necessary contextual factors to make information warfare a useful strategic instrument may not be simple. A useful framework for analyzing the strategic information warfare threat to the United States must include an understanding of the strategic conditions facing potential adversaries. Building on the analysis in this chapter, conditions that would determine the suitability of strategic information warfare as a means for actors to achieve political objectives can be identified as follows:

1.   Does the actor have political objectives achievable through strategic information war?

2.   Which strategic approaches are viable for the actor?

3.   Are the enabling conditions for strategic warfare present?

4.   How will the actor treat risks of failure and retaliation?

First, the nature of political objectives an adversary might pursue using its capability to wage strategic information warfare must be delineated. The level of disruption and damage an adversary would have to be capable of inflicting against specific centers of gravity would directly relate to the objectives an actor might pursue through these means. A state actor might seek to use strategic information warfare capabilities to pursue a wide range of objectives. Such a broad range of functions would requiring a highly developed capability to threaten a range of centers of gravity with varying levels of disruption. A nonstate actor might wage strategic information warfare for much more limited goals, allowing it to more sharply focus the development of its strategic information warfare capabilities.

Actors vary in their proclivity to use different strategic approaches depending on their degree of commitment to a given objective and time constraints. Many state actors place a premium on concluding conflicts quickly to minimize costs of waging war and reduce the potential for retaliation and escalation. Alternatively, certain nonstate actors see the existence of conflict as the norm or even their reason for existence. Desire to conclude conflicts quickly might incline certain actors to view as optimal a strategic approach based on using digital attacks to achieve surprise and with overwhelming force. Other actors might view their environment in such a way that conducting protracted strategic information war would present a much more viable strategic option.

Once the viable objectives and strategic approaches have been determined, the actor would need to examine the enabling factors for strategic information warfare developed in the first section of this chapter. Does the actor perceive that it has an offensive capability against appropriate U.S. information infrastructure centers of gravity? Can it identify and target vulnerabilities within that infrastructure? Can forces be created that threaten key vulnerabilities in a controlled fashion? What ability does the actor have to influence the risks of retaliation and escalation?

Finally, given the high degree of uncertainty in assessing the key enabling factors and constraints on using different strategies, actors' willingness to suffer risks of failure, retaliation, and escalation are also relevant to assessing which may prove most likely to develop and use strategic information warfare capabilities. How important is achievement of the objective to a given actor? Does the actor have alternative means to pursue the objectives that are less uncertain and risky? How painful are the perceived risks of failure, retaliation, and escalation to the actor?

Identifying who might choose to develop and use strategic information warfare capabilities against the United States clearly presents a complex task. Such identifications are fraught with assumptions about difficult questions, such as political intent and risk proclivity. The list of actors who meet the tests outlined here may not necessarily match the list of commonly assumed actors of greatest national security concern to the United States. Differences in the enabling conditions facing state versus nonstate actors or in the various actors' willingness to suffer risks of retaliation may prove much more important in delineating the emerging strategic information warfare threat to the United States than more traditional measures of declared political hostility or economic strength.

Examining Strategic Digital Warfare

Military forces serve international actors to achieve widely varying political objectives. The appropriate use of force depends on both technological considerations and strategic context. The capacity to wage strategic warfare directly against enemy centers of gravity has become a principal means of waging war in the twentieth century. Historical experience with the development and use of strategic conventional bombardment and WMD provides lessons about their political utility and the conditions that enable their successful use.

Government and societal reliance on information infrastructures susceptible to attack has raised concern about the emergence of strategic information warfare as we enter the twenty-first century. Tools for maliciously attacking information infrastructures are widely available, and efforts to defend against such attacks face significant challenges. The potential power of strategic information warfare creates attractive opportunities for its use as a tool of political influence.

Yet the complexities surrounding the use of information technology, the establishment of information infrastructures, and the pace of change in the new century also create significant uncertainties regarding the conduct of warfare in a cyberspace environment. The primary difficulty for potential U.S. adversaries who view strategic information warfare as a means for achieving their political objectives will not be the acquisition of the technological means to conduct such warfare. Rather, the strategic context in which such warfare would be waged will have a large influence on whether the development and use of such means makes sense in light of an adversary's political objectives.

Creating the organizational capacity to use available tools to gather intelligence, to launch successful attacks, and to defend an actor's own assets will prove a difficult hurdle for those considering strategic information warfare as an option. To protect its security in the cyberspace environment, the United States must understand the available means and competing priorities for establishing defenses of its information infrastructures. Additionally, it must consider its ability to threaten adversaries with an unacceptable level of retaliation if attacked. For the United States and its adversaries, the strategic considerations surrounding the political use of force place a premium on creating organizations with technological capabilities that can be properly controlled. The next chapter addresses the challenges involved in developing the necessary organizational capacity to conduct strategic information warfare.

Suggested Additional Sources

Carl von Clausewitz. *On War*. Ed. and trans. Michael Howard and Peter Paret. Princeton: Princeton University Press, 1976. B. H. Liddell-Hart. *Strategy*. New York: Signet Books, 1967. Thomas C. Schelling. *Arms and Influence*. New Haven: Yale University Press, 1966.

The trio are classics on strategic thinking over the past 200 years. Clausewitz wrote after the Napoleonic Wars, and On War *develops the idea of center of gravity fundamental to most subsequent thinking on strategic warfare. Liddell-Hart's work was written after World War II and analyzes how nations can employ a full range of instruments of national power as part of a grand strategy to achieve their objectives. Schelling is a seminal thinker regarding the dynamics of how force might be conceptualized in the nuclear age, particularly regarding deterrence and coercion.*

Lawrence Freedman. *The Evolution of Nuclear Strategy*. New York: St. Martin's Press, 1981. Richard Smoke. *National Security and the Nuclear Dilemma*. 3rd ed. New York: McGraw-Hill, 1993.

These works provide an overview of the development of forces and strategy in the nuclear age. Freedman provides a more detailed historical examination, whereas Smoke focuses more on the implications for U.S. national security policy.

Richard A. Falkenrath, Robert E. Newman, and Bradley Thayer. *America's Achilles Heel: Nuclear, Biological, and Chemical Terrorism and Covert Attack*. Cambridge: MIT Press, 1998.

A very thorough examination of the threats posed by nontraditional delivery of weapons of mass destruction at the end of twentieth century. This work directly addresses the uncertainties involved in estimating the probability and impact of such events and provides useful insights into similar concerns surrounding strategic information warfare.

Robert A. Pape. *Bombing to Win: Airpower and Coercion in War*. Ithaca: Cornell University Press, 1996.

A reconsideration on the strategic use of airpower in light of the Persian Gulf War experience. Meticulously researched and constructed, the book uses both statistics and case studies to address the empirical record of what succeeds in the conduct of strategic bombardment.

Jeffrey R. Barnett. *Future War: An Assessment of Aerospace Campaigns in 2010*. Maxwell Air Force Base, AL: Air University Press, 1996.

Barnett clearly articulates the concept of parallel war as an emerging means by which the United States can quickly conclude conflicts on favorable terms. He also provides useful analyses of how opponents may try to develop asymmetric strategies to undermine U.S. advantages.

Fredrick B. Cohen. *Protection and Security on the Information Highway*. New York: John Wiley & Sons, 1995. Dorothy E. Denning. *Information Warfare and Security*. Reading, MA: Addison Wesley, 1999.

These two works by computer security experts provide an overview of the means and countermeaures involved in digital warfare. Both address the full range of activities from nonmalicious accidents and computer explorations through cybercrime to nation-states waging information warfare. Cohen stresses the organizational dimensions of developing sound computer security. Denning analyzes the computer security problem in a broader context including perception management and nondigital means of disrupting information infrastructures.

Clifford Stoll. *The Cuckoo's Egg.* New York: Simon & Schuster, 1989.
An enjoyable and educational first-person perspective on the challenges of tracking down digital attackers. Stoll was the first individual to recognize the activities of the Hannover hackers against U.S. government and private systems in the late 1980s and assisted the FBI and German law enforcement in tracking them down. Though the book was written over a decade ago, the challenges of responding to digital attackers remain largely the same.

Web sites: ⟨www.infowar.com⟩ and ⟨www.iwar.org⟩.
The first of these two sites is maintained by Winn Schwartau and is very consistently updated with a wide range of material and links on information warfare incidents, conference events, and newly published analyses. The second is the site of William Church's Center for Infrastructural Warfare Studies, which focuses more closely on detailing incidents and the challenges related to waging attacks against infrastructures as discussed in this work.

Notes

1. B. H. Liddell-Hart, *Strategy* (New York: Signet Books, 1967), 321–322. Thucydides similarly stated much earlier in *The Peloponnesian War*, trans. Richard Crowley (New York: Random House, Inc., 1982), 49, "War is not so much a matter of arms as of money, which makes arms of use."

2. Luttwak, in *Strategy: The Logic of War and Peace.* (Cambridge: Harvard University Press, 1987) 61–63, uses the term "paradoxical," rather than "interactive." However, since the interaction between opponents always exists in strategic situations and does not involve a logical paradox, the term "interactive" seems to capture the essence of the concept better for the purposes of this analysis.

3. Carl von Clausewitz, *On War*, Michael Howard and Peter Paret, ed. and trans. (Princeton, NJ: Princeton University Press, 1976), 75.

4. Thomas C. Schelling, *The Strategy of Conflict*, 2d ed. (New Haven: Yale University Press, 1980), 3. His work also addresses the "diplomacy of violence" in considering how actors achieve deterrence and coercion without actually employing force.

5. Clausewitz, *On War*, 595–596.

6. Robert A. Pape, *Bombing to Win: Airpower and Coercion in War* (Ithaca, NY: Cornell University Press, 1996), 41–44.

7. Sources dealing with German strategic bombing efforts in World War I are Raymond Fredette, *The Sky on Fire: The First Battle of Britain 1917–1918 and the Birth of the Royal Air Force* (New York: Holt, Rinehart and Winston, 1966); and Douglas H. Robinson, *The Zeppelin in Combat* (London: G. T. Foulis and Co., 1962).

8. Douhet's central work is *Command of the Air*, trans. Dino Ferrari (New York: Coward-McCann, 1942).

9. Edward Warner, "Douhet, Mitchell and Seversky: Theories of Air Warfare," in *Makers of Modern Strategy*, ed. Edward M. Earle (Princeton, NJ: Princeton University Press, 1971), 492.

10. Phillip S. Melinger, "Trenchard, Slessor and Royal Air Force Doctrine before World War II," in *The Paths of Heaven: The Evolution of Airpower Theory*, ed. Phillip S. Melinger (Maxwell Air Force Base, AL: Air University Press, 1997), 41–78, provides a good synopsis of Trenchard's thinking as well as the Royal Air Force's development of strategic bombing doctrine between the wars.

11. Pape, *Bombing to Win*, 71–72.

12. Useful commentaries include Liddell-Hart, *Strategy*; Bernard Brodie, *Strategy in the Missile Age* (Princeton, NJ: Princeton University Press, 1959); Michael E. Howard, "The Forgotten Dimensions of Strategy," *Foreign Affairs* 57, no. 2 (Summer 1979): 975–986; Pape, *Bombing to Win*; and Luttwak, *Logic of War and Peace*. All these authors rely heavily on the U.S. Strategic Bombing Survey to substantiate their conclusions.

13. Brodie, *Strategy in the Missile Age*, 254–313; and Pape, *Bombing to Win*, 107–144.

14. See R. V. Jones, *The Wizard War: British Scientific Intelligence 1939–1945* (New York: Coward, MaCann & Geoghegan, 1978).

15. Brodie, *Strategy in the Missile Age*, 90–91.

16. Luttwak, *Logic of War and Peace*, 164–166.

17. Seminal works regarding the development of Western nuclear thinking include Bernard Brodie, *The Absolute Weapon: Atomic Power and World Order* (New York: Harcourt and Brace, 1946); Brodie, *Strategy in the Missile Age*; Schelling, *The Strategy of Conflict*; Schelling, *Arms and Influence* (New Haven, CT: Yale University Press, 1966); Herman Kahn, *On Escalation: Metaphors and Scenarios* (New York: Praeger, 1965); and Robert Jervis, *The Illogic of American Nuclear Strategy* (Ithaca, NY: Cornell University Press, 1984). On the evolution of Soviet nuclear strategy, see V. D. Sokolovskiy, *Soviet Military Strategy*, trans. Harriet S. Scott (New York: Crane, Russak & Company, 1968); Jack L. Snyder, *The Soviet Strategic Culture: Implications for Limited Nuclear Operations* (Santa Monica, CA: RAND Corporation, September 1977); Edward L. Warner, *The Defense Policy of the Soviet Union* (Santa Monica, CA: RAND Corporation, 1989); and Thomas E. Symonds, *Of Strategic Designation: The Birth of Soviet Strategic Nuclear Forces* (Washington, DC: Air Force Intelligence Agency, 1989).

18. The historical overview provided in the section is based primarily on Lawrence Freedman, *The Evolution of Nuclear Strategy* (New York: St. Martin's Press, 1981); and Richard Smoke, *National Security and the Nuclear Dilemma*, 3d ed. (New York: McGraw-Hill, Inc., 1993).

19. For the Soviet approach to nuclear weapons through the mid-1950s, see Freedman, *Evolution of Nuclear Strategy*, 110–112. On the role of defenses in the Soviet approach to deterrence, see Sokolovskiy, *Soviet Military Strategy*, esp. chap. 7, "Preparing a Country for the Repulsion of Aggression," 306–333.

20. Smoke, *National Security and the Nuclear Dilemma*, 72; Freedman, *The Evolution of Nuclear Strategy*, 84–85.

21. See William E. Burrows, "Threats, Real and Imagined," in *Deep Black* (New York: Berkeley Books, 1986), 78–107; and Smoke, *National Security and the Nuclear Dilemma*, 96.

22. On Western inattention to the significance of defense in the nuclear age, see Michael E. Howard, "On Fighting a Nuclear War," *International Security* 5, no. 4 (1981): 3–18. For an analysis of how defenses could strengthen nuclear deterrence, see Brodie, *Strategy in the Missile Age*, 173–222.

23. See Forrest Waller, "Strategic Offensive Arms Control", in *Arms Control toward the 21st Century*, ed. Jeffery A. Larsen and Gregory J. Rattray (Boulder, CO: Lynne Rienner, 1996), 104–105, on the difficulties MIRVs posed for the Strategic Arms Reduction Talks (START) II process.

24. See Richard Pipes, "Why the Soviet Union Thinks It Could Fight and Win a Nuclear War," *Commentary* 64, no. 1 (July 1977); and Fritz Ermath, "Contrasts in American and Soviet Strategic Thought," *International Security* 3, no. 2 (Fall 1978): 138–175.

25. Dennis Drew, "Air Theory, Air Force, and Low Intensity Conflict: A Short Journey to Confusions," in Melinger, *Paths of Heaven*, 321–355, provides an analysis of the lack of doctrinal focus of the Air Force on this level of conflict, focusing on the U.S. involvement in the conflict in Vietnam.

26. See Robert F. Futrell, *United States Air Force in Korea: 1950–1953* (New York: Duell, Sloan and Pearce, 1961); and Pape, *Bombing to Win*, 137–173, for discussions of the role and difficulties of employing strategic airpower in Korea.

27. For analysis of the air campaigns during the U.S. involvement in Vietnam from 1965 to 1971, see Mark Clodfelter, *The Limits of Air Power: The Bombing of North Vietnam* (New York: Free Press, 1989); and *The Air War in Southeast Asia* (Maxwell Air Force Base, AL: Air University Press, 1993).

28. Earl H. Tilford, Jr., "The Prolongation of the United States Involvement in Vietnam," in *Prolonged Wars: The Post-Nuclear Challenge*, ed. Karl P. Maygar and Constantine P. Danopolous (Maxwell Air Force Base, AL: Air University Press, 1994), 377.

29. Pape, *Bombing to Win*, 197–210; and Gilster, *Air War in Southeast Asia*, 59–136.

30. See Seymour J. Deitchman, *Military Power and the Advance of Technology: General Purpose Military Forces for the 1990s and Beyond* (Boulder, CO: Westview Press, 1983), for an early view of how sophisticated targeting and precision weapon technologies might greatly increase the effectiveness of conventional forces.

31. See conclusions reached by Thomas A. Keaney and Eliot A. Cohen, *Revolution in Warfare? Air Power in the Persian Gulf War* (Annapolis, MD: Naval Institute Press, 1995), 208–209.

32. Major evaluations of the contribution of airpower to the U.S. victory in the Gulf War include Keaney and Cohen, *Air Power in the Persian Gulf War*; Robert H. Shultz, Jr., and Robert L. Pfaltzgraff, Jr., eds., *The Future of Airpower in the Aftermath of the Gulf War* (Maxwell Air Force Base, AL: Air University Press, 1992); Eliot A. Cohen, "The Mystique of U.S. Airpower," *Foreign Affairs* 74, no. 1 (January/February 1994): 109–124; Christopher Bowie et al., *The New Calculus: Analyzing Airpower's Role in Joint Theater Campaigns* (Santa Monica, CA: RAND Corporation, 1993); Bernard E. Trainor, "Air Power in the Gulf War: Did It Really Succeed?" *Strategic Review* (Winter 1994): 66–68; and Pape, *Bombing to Win*, 211–253.

33. As quoted in David R. Mets, "Bomber Barons, Bureaucrats and Budgets," *Airpower Journal* 10, no. 2 (Summer 1996): 88.

34. Department of Defense, Final Report to Congress, *Conduct of the Persian Gulf War* (Washington, DC: Department of Defense, April 1992), 200.

35. John A. Warden, "Employing Airpower in the 21st Century," in Shultz and Pfaltzgraff, eds., *Future of Airpower*, 78.

36. Keaney and Cohen, *Air Power in the Persian Gulf War*, 61.

37. Pape, *Bombing to Win*, 236–241. See also Daniel T. Kuehl, "Airpower vs. Electricity: Electric Power as a Target for Strategic Air Operations," *Journal of Strategic Studies* 18, no. 1 (March 1995): 237–266.

38. See Department of Defense, *Conduct of the Persian Gulf War*, Appendix C, "Intelligence," section on "Bomb Damage Assessment," C-14–17.

39. See Keaney and Cohen, *Air Power in the Persian Gulf War*, 66–79 and 105–121.

40. See Warden, "Employing Airpower in the 21st Century."

41. See Jeffery R. Barnett, *Future War: An Assessment of Aerospace Campaigns in 2010* (Maxwell AFB, AL: Air University Press, 1996), 13–16, on the concept of parallel war.

42. David A. Deptula, *Firing for Effect: Change in the Nature of Warfare* (Arlington, VA: Aerospace Education Foundation, 1995), 6.

43. See Warden, "Employing Airpower in the 21st Century," 79–81. He coins the term "hyperwar" to describe the speed at which such wars will progress.

44. Barnett, in *Future War*, outlines how niche and near-peer competitors might attempt to choose and employ specific technologies to effectively fight the United States. See also Henry

D. Sokolski, "Non-Apocalyptic Proliferation: A New Strategic Threat," *Washington Quarterly* 17, no. 2 (Spring 1994): 115–127.

45. See James R. FitzSimonds, "The Coming Military Revolution: Opportunities and Risks," *Parameters* 25, no. 2 (Summer 1995): 30–36. The U.S. comparative advantage in this area is highlighted by Joseph S. Nye, Jr., and William A. Owens, "America's Information Edge," *Foreign Affairs*, 75, no. 2 (March/April 1996): 20–36.

46. Charles Allan, "Extended Conventional Deterrence: In from the Cold and Out of the Nuclear Fire?" *Washington Quarterly* 18, no. 3 (Summer 1994): 4–13; and Gary L. Guertner, "Deterrence and Conventional Military Forces," *Washington Quarterly* 16, no. 3 (Winter 1993): 141–151.

47. Harlan Ullman and James Wade, Jr., *Shock and Awe: Achieving Rapid Dominance* (Washington, DC: National Defense University Press, 1996), 14–15.

48. Allan, "Extended Conventional Deterrence," 7. A similar idea called "deliberate capability revelation" has been proposed by Kevin N. Lewis, *Getting More Deterrence Out of Deliberate Capability Revelation* (Santa Monica, CA: RAND Corporation, 1989).

49. For analysis of continuing Iraqi efforts in this area, see David A. Kay, "Denial and Deception Practices of WMD Proliferators: Iraq and Beyond," *Washington Quarterly* 18, no. 1 (Winter 1995): 85–105.

50. Barnett, *Future War*, xiii.

51. Major works on the growing concern with international WMD proliferation include Robert D. Blackwill and Albert Carnesale, eds., *New Nuclear Nations: Consequences for U.S. Policy* (New York: Council on Foreign Relations, 1993); Brad Roberts, ed., *Weapons Proliferation in the 1990s* (Cambridge: MIT Press, 1995); and Keith B. Payne, *Deterrence in the Second Nuclear Age* (Lexington: University Press of Kentucky, 1996).

52. See Graham T. Allison et al., *Avoiding Nuclear Anarchy: Containing the Threat of Loose Russian Nuclear Weapons and Fissile Material* (Cambridge: MIT Press, 1996).

53. William E. Odom, "Transforming the Military," *Foreign Affairs* 76, no. 4 (July/August 1997): 62.

54. National Defense Panel, *Transforming Defense* (Arlington, VA: National Defense Panel, December 1997), 15–16.

55. A good analysis of the factors involved is provided by Brad Roberts, "Between Panic and Complacency: Calibrating the Chemical and Biological Warfare Problem," in *The Niche Threat: Deterring the Use of Chemical and Biological Weapons*, ed. Stuart E. Johnson (Washington, DC: National Defense University Press, 1997), 9–42.

56. See *Exploring U.S. Missile Defense Requirements in 2010* (Cambridge, MA: Institute for Foreign Policy Analysis, 1997).

57. National Defense Panel, *Transforming Defense*, 16. For a detailed analysis of the WMD threat to the U.S. homeland, see Richard A. Falkenrath, Robert E. Newman, and Bradley Thayer, *America's Achilles Heel: Nuclear, Biological, and Chemical Terrorism and Covert Attack* (Cambridge: MIT Press, 1998).

58. In the wake of the Oklahoma City bombing, President Clinton in 1995 issued Presidential Decision Directive 39, "Counterterrorism Policy." The National Defense Panel, *Transforming Defense*, 42, also calls for increased attention to defensive measures organic to our deployed forces and improved detection capabilities as the principal focal points for future U.S. efforts to counter WMD.

59. In an exception, Warden, "The Enemy as a System," *Airpower Journal* 9, no. 1 (Spring 1995), 53, admits that the applicability of his five-ring model for identifying enemy centers of gravity may be somewhat diminished in circumstances where an entire people rise up to conduct a defensive battle against an invader.

60. National Research Council, *Computers at Risk: Safe Computing in the Information Age* (Washington, DC: National Academy Press, 1991).

61. PCCIP, *Critical Foundations: Protecting America's Infrastructures* (Alexandria, VA: President's Commission on Critical Infrastructure Protection, October 1997), 3.

62. Clifford Stoll, *The Cuckoo's Egg* (New York: Simon & Schuster, 1989), contains an extensive description of the activities, discovery, and eventual apprehension of the hackers involved in this incident.

63. Government Accounting Office (GAO), *Computer Security: Hackers Penetrate DOD Computer Systems* (Washington, DC: GAO/T-IMTEC-92-5, 20 November 1991).

64. The Air Force's principal investigator for this case, Jim Christy, provided a detailed description of the events involved in the case to the Senate Committee on Governmental Affairs, Permanent Subcommittee on Investigations, in its Hearings on "Security in Cyberspace," 104th Congress, 2nd Session, 22 May 1996.

65. GAO, *Information Security: Computer Attacks at Department of Defense Pose Increasing Risks* (Washington, DC: GAO/AMID-96-84, May 1996), 25; and "First Computer Wiretap Locates Hacker," *New York Times*, 31 March 1996, National section, 4.

66. For descriptions of the incident, see Bradley Graham, "11 U.S. Military Computer Systems Breached This Month," *Washington Post*, 26 February 1998, A01; James Glave, "DOD-Cracking Team Used Common Bug" and "Pentagon Hacker Speaks Out," both at *Wired Internet* Web site ⟨www.wired.com⟩, accessed 10 May 1998; and Anne Plummer, "DOD Official Says Hackers Are More Sophisticated Since Solar Sunrise," *Defense Information and Electronics Report* 22 (October 1999): 1.

67. Robert L. Ayers, Chief, Information Warfare Division, Defense Information Systems Agency, "Information Warfare and the DII," in *InfoWar Con Report* (Fairfax, VA: Open Source Solutions, 1995), 25.

68. Air Force CERT briefing, "AFCERT Operations," provided to the author at Kelly Air Force Base, TX, July 1997.

69. GAO, *Information Security*, 40.

70. A compilation of incident data from Web site hacks is available on the Internet at Web site ⟨www.hacked.net/exploited.html⟩, accessed 10 January 1998.

71. White House, *Defending America's Cyberspace* (Washington, DC: White House, January 2000), 3.

72. Dan Farmer, "Security Survey of Key Internet Hosts," 18 December 1996, available at Web site ⟨www.trouble.org/survey⟩, p. 2, accessed June 1997.

73. GAO, *Critical Infrastructure Protection: Comprehensive Strategy Can Draw on Year 2000 Experiences* (Washington, DC: GAO/AIMD-00-01, 1999), 6.

74. See National Communications System (NCS), *The Electronic Intrusion Threat to the National Security and Emergency Preparedness (NS/EP) Telecommunications: An Awareness Document* (Arlington, VA: Office of the Manager, National Communications System, September 1993); and National Research Council, *Growing Vulnerabilities to the Public Switched Network: Implications for National Security Emergency Preparedness* (Washington, DC: National Research Council, 1989), for detailed early descriptions of the potential for large-scale disruption posed by digital hacker activity in the public-switched phone networks. The NCS has continued to highlight this concern throughout the 1990s and into the twenty-first century.

75. See Michelle Satalla and Joshua Quittner, *Masters of Deception: The Gang That Ruled Cyberspace* (New York: Harper Collins, 1995), for background on the typical hacking and "phreaking" activities involving the phone network.

76. NCS, *Electronic Intrusion Threat*, 3-3–9.

77. Elaine Shannon, "Reach Out and Waste Someone," *Time Digital*, July/August 1997, 39.

78. Statement of Michael A. Vatis, Director of the National Infrastructure Protection Center, to Senate Judiciary Committee, Subcommittee on Technology and Terrorism, 6 October 1999, available at ⟨www.fbi.gov/pressrm/congress/nipc10-6.htm⟩, accessed December 1999.

79. Jared Sandberg, "Hackers Prey on AOL Users with Array of Dirty Tricks," *Wall Street Journal*, 5 January 1998.

80. The details of the Mitnick case and his apprehension are provided in Tsutomu Shimomura, *Takedown: Pursuit and Capture of America's Most Wanted Computer Outlaw* (New York: Hyperion, 1996).

81. As cited in Defense Science Board (DSB) Task Force, *Information Warfare—Defense* (Washington, DC: Department of Defense, 1996), A-6, from *Trends and Experiences in Computer-Related Crime* (Academy of Criminal Justice Studies, 1996).

82. Richard Power, *Current and Future Danger: A CSI Primer on Computer Crime and Information Warfare* (San Francisco: Computer Security Institute, 1995), 3.

83. FBI/CSI, *Computer Crime and Security Survey—1999* (San Francisco: Computer Security Institute, 1999), 4.

84. Richard Behar, "Who's Reading Your E-Mail?" *Fortune* (3 February 1997): 64.

85. White House, *Defending America's Cyberspace*, 3.

86. "Hacker Attacker Crashes Windows Systems Coast-to-Coast," CNN On-Line at ⟨www.cnn.com/TECH/computing/9803/04/internet.attack.ap/index.htm⟩, accessed 10 March 1998.

87. Ernst and Young LLP/Information Week survey quoted in Power, *Current and Future Danger*, 2.

88. Cited in "Companies Weary of Internal Security Problems," *New York Times*, 1 March 1998.

89. John D. Howard, "An Analysis of Security Incidents on the Internet, 1989–1995" (Ph.D. diss., Carnegie Mellon University, 7 April 1997), 76; and GAO, *Critical Infrastructure Protection*, 4.

90. Analysis of malicious software issues based on Ottmar Kyas, *Internet Security: Risk Analysis, Strategies and Firewalls* (Boston: International Thompson Computer, 1997), chap. 9, "Viruses in Programs and Networks," 105–144; and Dorothy Denning, *Information Warfare and Security* (Reading, MA: Addison-Wesley, 1999), chap. 10, "Cyberplagues," 269–280.

91. See GAO, *Computer Security: Virus Highlights Need for Improved Internet Security Management* (Washington, DC: Government Printing Office, June 1989).

92. Jean Guisnel, *Cyberwars: Espionage on the Internet* (New York: Plenum Press, 1997), 6.

93. Information on virus hoaxes can be found at the Department of Energy's Computer Incident Advisory Capability (CIAC) Web site ⟨www.ciac.org⟩, accessed 7 April 1998.

94. See Anne W. Branscomb, *Rogue Computer Programs* (Cambridge, MA: Harvard University, Program on Information Resources Policy, September 1989), 5–6, on the Aldus peace virus outbreak in 1988 infecting Apple MacIntosh computers with a virus distributed in the Aldus Corporation's Freehand software. Fredrick Cohen, *Protection and Security on the Information Highway* (New York: John Wiley & Sons, 1995), 74, describes an incident in which Novell inadvertently distributed a virus in 1992 to users of one of its products through disks modified to fix a previously discovered software glitch in one of its programs.

95. Kyas, *Internet Security*, 106–107.

96. 1987 and 1990 figures from National Computer Security Association, as quoted in Winn Schwartau, *Information Warfare: Chaos on the Electronic Superhighway*, 1st ed. (New York: Thunder Mouth Press, 1994), 158. 1997 figure from Kyas, *Internet Security*, 106.

97. From the author's own Norton program documentation from software purchased in May 1999.

98. James Lippshultz, "Scare Tactics Exaggerate Actual Threat from Computer Viruses," *Federal Computer Week*, 6 December 1993, 15.

99. According to Kyas, *Internet Security*, 105, "around 70% of viruses affect PCs, with Apple Macintoshes in second place and UNIX systems a long way behind."

100. The DISA team reported 481 virus incidents in 1996. From "Automated Systems Security Incident Support Team (ASSIST)" briefing provided to author at DISA Headquarters, Arlington, VA, briefing materials dated 31 July 1997.

101. The significance of insiders is addressed in Denning, *Information Warfare and Security*, chap. 6, "Inside the Fence," 131–162.

102. Angelo Codevilla, *Informing Statecraft: Intelligence for a New Century* (New York: Free Press, 1992), 176–178.

103. GAO, *National Crime Information Center: Legislation Needed to Deter Misuse of Criminal Justice Information* (Washington, DC: Government Printing Office, July 1993), and *IRS Information Systems: Weaknesses Increase Risks of Fraud and Impair Reliability of Management Information* (Washington, DC: Government Printing Office, September 1993).

104. First two cases from Daniel Knauf, *The Family Jewels: Corporate Policy on the Protection of Information Resources* (Cambridge: Harvard University, Program for Information Resources Policy, P-91-5, June 1991), 113; third from Branscomb, *Rogue Computer Programs*, 8–9, fourth from Schwartau, *Information Warfare*, 163–164; last from "Fired Programmer Zaps Old Firm," available at Web site ⟨biz.yahoo.com/upi/98/02/17/general_state_and_regional_news/nyzap_1.htm⟩, accessed 10 March 1998.

105. For a very good overview of the problems posed by secure software engineering to prevent digital attack, see Paul Strassman, "Poor Software: The Gateways to Cyberterrorism," presentation at National Defense University, July 1999.

106. Branscomb, *Rogue Computer Programs*, 6–8.

107. For more extensive analysis and additional examples of the threats posed to information infrastructures by unintentional disruption, see Cohen, *Protection and Security*, 33–40; Knauf, *Family Jewels*, 101–110; Peter G. Neumann, *Computer-Related Risks* (New York: ACM Press, 1995), chap. 2, "Reliability and Safety Problems," 12–95; and GAO, *Information Superhighway: An Overview of Technology Challenges* (Washington, DC: GAO/AMID-95-23, January 1995), 35–40.

108. Associated Press report, "Phone Outage Hits East Coast," 26 February 1998. The significance of this incident was also highlighted to the author in an interview with Willliam B. Joyce, President's Commission on Critical Infrastructure Protection, Commissioner from the Central Intelligence Agency, Arlington, VA, 25 March 1998,

109. Presentation by Kevin J. Stevens, "Software Bugs, Risks to the Nation's Infrastructure, and Product Liability at the Potomac Institute, Arlington, VA, 16 April 1998.

110. Denning, *Information Warfare and Security*, 71, n. 98.

111. This incident and the subsequent legal and political furor surrounding it are covered in full by Bruce Sterling, *The Hacker Crackdown: Law and Order on the Electronic Frontier* (New York: Bantam Books, 1992).

112. Cohen, *Protection and Security*, 102.

113. PCCIP, *Critical Foundations*, A-3.

114. The most thorough descriptions of such activities are Wayne Madsen, "Intelligence Agency Threats to Computer Security," *Intelligence and Counter-Intelligence* 6 (Winter 1993): 413–488;

John J. Fiakla, *War by Other Means* (New York: W. W. Norton, 1997); and Jean Guisnel, *Cyberwars: Espionage on the Internet* (New York: Plenum Trade, 1997).

115. Numerous theoretical articles on the possibilities of information warfare have been written in the People's Republic of China. Two examples are Wei Jincheng, "Information War: A New Form of People's War," 409–412, and Maj. Gen. Wang Pufeng, "The Challenge of Information Warfare," 317–326, both in *Chinese Views of Future Warfare*, ed. Michael Pillsbury (Washington, DC: National Defense University Press, 1997). Russian views of information warfare have been outlined by Timothy L. Thomas, "Russian Views on Information-Based Warfare" *Airpower Journal* (Special Edition, 1996): 25–35; and Mary C. FitzGerald, "Russian Views on Information Warfare" *Army* (May 1994); 57–59. The former Chief of Staff of the Indian Army, K. Sundarji, has also provided a non-U.S. perspective on information warfare in "Wars of the Near Future," available at the *Asia Week* Web site ⟨www.pathfinder.com:80/Asiaweek/98/1009/feat1.html⟩, accessed January 1998.

116. Howard, "Analysis of Security Incidents," 205–206.

117. Extensive lists of the types of computer and network attacks are provided by Cohen, *Protection and Security*, 40–54; and David Icove, Karl Seger, and William Van Storch, *Computer Crime: A Crimefighters Handbook* (Sebastapol, CA: O'Reilly and Associates, 1995), 31–52.

118. Howard, "Analysis of Security Incidents," 62–69.

119. DSB Task Force, *Information Warfare—Defense*, 2-15–16.

120. See Denning, *Information Warfare and Security*, 241–257.

121. Stoll, *The Cuckoo's Egg*, 1–12.

122. This example is based on an interview with Chuck Flanders, Countermeasures Engineer at the Air Force Information Warfare Center, on 29 July 1997. Lt. Flanders was in charge of the Telecommunications Switching Security Assistance Program, responsible for analyzing and improving the network security of the telephone switching systems installed on Air Force bases.

123. Knauf, *Family Jewels*, 7–25.

124. *Computer Security Journal* (July 1995).

125. DSB Task Force, *Information Warfare—Defense*, 2–7.

126. These five basic characteristics are widely recognized as essential within the information security community. The definitions here are drawn from a National Security Agency pamphlet, *Solutions for a Safer World*, undated, received by author at Ft. Meade, MD, 4 August 1997. The analysis in this section draws on a wide range of background sources on information security cited above as well as interviews at the Software Engineering Institute, Air Force Information Warfare Center, and Defense Information Systems Agency.

127. For an overview of the capabilities of such systems, see Software Engineering Institute, *Detecting Signs of Intrusion* (Pittsburgh, PA: Carnegie Mellon University, 1997).

128. Cohen, *Protection and Security*, 120–129, details the limits of existing defensive technologies in an environment characterized by rapidly evolving vulnerabilities and threats.

129. The description in this paragraph is based on Air Force Information Warfare Center, "Automated Security Incident Measurement Tools" (Kelly Air Force Base, TX: Air Force Information Warfare Center, 12 May 1997); and "AFCERT Operations" and "Information Protect Operations" briefings provided to the author at the Air Force Information Warfare Center, Kelly Air Force Base, TX, July 1997.

130. This assertion is based on the author's interviews at the Air Force Information Warfare Center and with personnel at the Software Engineering Institute at Carnegie Mellon as well as a review of hacker incidents such as the ones outlined earlier in the chapter.

131. The 1994 survey was conducted by the Department of Defense and the 1995 survey by the National Computer Security Association, as quoted in Kyas, *Internet Security*, 3–4.

132. FBI/CSI, *Computer Crime and Security Survey—1999*, 5.

133. For an overview of efforts by the U.S. banking and finance sector to improve security against cyberthreats, see PCCIP, *Critical Foundations*, A-39–41.

134. DSB Task Force, *Information Warfare—Defense*, 2-7–8.

135. See Julie C. H. Ryan, "Information Warfare: A Conceptual Framework," in *Seminar on Intelligence, Command and Control: Guest Presentations 1996* (Cambridge: Harvard University, Program on Information Resources, I-97-1, January 1997), 109–112; and David S. Alberts, *Defensive Information Warfare* (Washington, DC: National Defense University, 1996), 29–30.

136. PCCIP, *Critical Foundations*, A-3.

137. Dr. Martin Libicki of RAND is a principal advocate within the U.S. national security community of the inherent robustness of information infrastructures to large-scale digital disruption. See his *What Is Information Warfare?* (Washington, DC: National Defense University Press, 1995), 52–61, and *Defending Cyberspace and Other Metaphors* (Washington, DC: National Defense University, 1996), 23–29.

138. Office of Science and Technology Policy (OSTP), *Cybernation: The American Infrastructure in the Information Age* (Washington, DC: The White House, April 1997), 19.

139. James Ellis et al., *Report to the President's Commission on Critical Infrastructure Protection* (Pittsburgh, PA: Carnegie Mellon University, Software Engineering Institute, January 1997), 3. In the CERT terminology, a vulnerability is a flaw in a product such as the UNIX operating system that unauthorized users can exploit.

140. Both tools are described in Kyas, *Internet Security*, 181–186.

141. Presentation by Joint Task Force—Computer Network Defense at "Preparing for Cyberwar" Conference, Arlington, VA, 5 October 1999.

142. See Denning, *Information Warfare and Security*, 47–50, for details on such publications.

143. Kyas, *Internet Security*, 109.

144. PCCIP, *Critical Foundations*, 9.

145. See Lynn E. Davis, "Arms Control, Export Regimes and Multilateral Cooperation," in *Strategic Appraisal: The Changing Role of Information in Warfare*, ed. Zalmay M. Khalilzad and John P. White (Washington, DC: RAND Corporation, 1999): 320–334; Kevin Soo Hoo, Lawrence Greenberg, and David Elliot, *Strategic Information Warfare: A New Arena for Arms Control* (Stanford, CA: Center for International Security, 1997); and my "The Emerging Global Information Infrastructure and National Security," *Fletcher Forum of World Affairs* 21, no. 2 (Summer/Fall 1997): 81–99, on the lack of international controls as of the late 1990s.

146. As quoted in GAO, *Protecting Critical Infrastructures*, 10.

147. See Timothy R. Gaffney, "NATO, Serbs Fought in Cyberspace," *Dayton Daily News*, p. 1, for a description on these attacks and their lack of effectiveness.

148. This doctrinal commitment is outlined in the Joint Staff pamphlet *Joint Vision 2010—America's Military Preparing for Tomorrow* (Washington, DC: Joint Staff, 1996).

149. Eliot A. Cohen, "Mystique of U.S. Airpower," 51.

150. See Lloyd J. Matthews, ed., *Challenging the United States Symmetrically and Asymmetrically: Can America Be Defeated?* (Carlisle Barracks, PA: Army War College, 1998); Barnett, *Future Wars*; and Sokolski, "Non-Apocalyptic Proliferation."

151. As quoted in Thomas G. Manhken, "America's Next War," *Washington Quarterly* 16, no. 2 (Summer 1993): 177.

152. John M. McConnell, "The Evolution of Intelligence and the Public Policy Debate on Encryption," in *Guest Presentations—Intelligence and Command and Control Seminar—1996* (Cambridge: Harvard University, Program for Information Resources Policy, January 1997), 168.

153. Clarke made the statement during his presentation at the "Preparing for Cyberwar" Conference, Arlington, VA, 5 October 1999.

154. See Kevin Hoo Soo, Seymour Goodman, and Lawerence Greenberg, "Information Technology and the Terrorist Threat," 135–155, and Andrew Rathmell Richard Overill, Lorenzo Valeri, and John Gearson, "The IW Threat from Sub-State Groups," 164–177, both in *Proceedings of the Third International Symposium on Command and Control Research and Technology* (Washington, DC: National Defense University Press, June 1997).

155. PCCIP, *Critical Foundations*, 3.

THREE
Establishing Organizational Technological Capacity for Strategic Information Warfare

It must be remembered that there is nothing more difficult to plan, more doubtful of success, nor more dangerous to manage than the creation of a new system.

—Niccolo Machiavelli, *The Prince*

The United States, other nations, and a range of nonstate actors in the international system are moving into an information age. The previous chapters detailed how our increasing reliance on information systems, networks, and infrastructures creates new, significant security concerns as well as presenting opportunities for economic and social gains. Digital means have emerged for remotely disrupting the operation of information infrastructures critical to a broad range of activities conducted in technologically advanced societies. A new type of warfare, strategic information warfare, may emerge as a result. The relatively low cost, accessibility of means, and potential effectiveness of this method of warfare could make it attractive to a wide range of actors in the international system. Most analyses addressing the potential for information warfare, however, pay little heed to the challenges faced by actors in developing the technological mastery and organizational capacity necessary to use these new means on a strategic scale to achieve political influence.

The Challenge of Establishing Technological Capability

A wide range of literature addresses the topic of technology, its uses, and the processes of technical change and transfer. Various authors deal with subjects ranging from the use of weapons in war, to competition between transnational corporations operating primarily in technologically advanced states, to decisions by governments in less-advanced nations about appropriate technological choices. The understanding of how people and organizations use technology to achieve their goals provided by this body of knowledge should also inform our analysis of strategic information warfare.

My analysis relies on a broad definition of technology as "any tool or technique, any product or process, any physical equipment or method of doing or making, by which human capability is extended."[1] With respect to waging digital warfare, such technology would include computer systems, software programs that provide access or monitor networks, and techniques such as e-mail bombardment to accomplish a desired objective. Technological knowledge can be conceived of as "information about physical processes which underlie and are given operational expression in technology."[2] The conduct of strategic information warfare would require knowledge of how technological tools and techniques enable attackers to gain access to targeted infrastructures and create the detrimental effects they seek or assist defenders in identifying weaknesses and implementing protective measures. Technological knowledge springs from three primary sources:[3]

• Encapsulated. Technology as artifacts (weapons, consumer and capital goods, etc.).
• Codified. Technology as information (blueprints, operating manuals, tactics guides, textbooks, etc.).
• Experiential. Technology as personal knowledge and skills.

Acquisition of technological knowledge can therefore be defined as acquiring encapsulated, codified, or experiential sources of knowledge with the intent to achieve organizational objectives. Technological knowledge differs from technological assimilation and mastery. Technological assimilation refers to an organization's ability to turn sources of technology into new or increased capacity for accomplishing its objectives within an evolving technology system. A dominant theme regarding technological assimilation suggests that this ability is gained primarily through actual use of the technology. According to Dahlman and Westphal, "experience is the key as achieving [technological] mastery is an iterative effort as the original concept for the technology's use is refined and given practical expression."[4] Technological mastery can be conceived of as operational command over technological knowledge. Mastery provides the possessor with the ability to adapt technology and anticipate changes for future competition. Actors or organizations with a technological mastery of strategic information warfare should be able to acquire, assimilate, and continually adapt technological tools to launch attacks to achieve political aims or protect their information infrastructures against a range of potential threats.

My focus in this chapter is an improved understanding of the acquisition and assimilation of technology for digital warfare at the organizational level. As historians Eliot Cohen and John Gooch explain in trying to come to grips with military failure, "[w]herever people come together to carry out purposeful activity, organizations spring into being. The more complex and demanding the task, the more ordered and integrated the organization."[5] Organizations formed to carry out strategic information warfare activities face the complex and demanding task of developing technological mastery over the tools and knowledge required for waging such warfare successfully.

Military Organizations and Technological Capacity

Weapons have often been a determining influence in battles or even wars. Analyses of technology and military power usually focus, however, on the evolution of increasingly sophisticated weapons and their battlefield use. Discussions of information warfare are particularly prone to stressing software tools and hacker techniques rather than development of organizations and resources necessary for sustained digital warfare. A growing body of work, however, has begun to grapple with how technology drives periods of revolutionary change and how success favors military organizations most capable of doctrinal innovation. Unfortunately, less attention has been paid to the complex processes of technological assimilation that must occur within military establishments to improve organizational capabilities to wage war.

Efforts to analyze technological change and its management for military establishments have occurred only relatively recently in the study of warfare. Classical strategic thinkers such as Sun Tzu and Clausewitz paid little attention to technology. Although occasional innovations such as the longbow had dramatic impact when they appeared, the pace of technological change generally was slow. Military leaders and strategists thought about competing with others as a matter of using available technologies, not of acquiring and assimilate emerging technologies for advantage. Historians and strategic analysts agree that only during the nineteenth century did military organizations seek to institutionalize the management of the development of new, more effective weapons.[6] The confluence of the rise of nationalism, professional military staffs, and the industrial revolution in the nineteenth century made incorporating technological innovations such as the telegraph, railroad, and machine gun crucial to military success. Choices, both good and bad, made by the military establishments of states about how to use available technology to wage war increasingly determined the course of wars and their destructiveness.

The twentieth century saw the pace of technological change and its influence on warfare increase, reaching its apex in the development of nuclear weapons. After World War II, the international political system was dominated by nuclear competition between two superpowers. Every shift in the technological military balance between the United States and the Soviet Union was treated as an event of great significance. Nuclear testing programs, intercontinental bombers, Sputnik, and Polaris submarines became central concerns of political leaders and military strategists alike. Military establishments in both countries made great efforts to set up organizations to develop leading-edge technologies. In the United States, advances including integrated circuits, composite materials, and network computing occurred within the national security research and development community. This community concentrated its efforts on identifying the next wave of breakthrough technology rather than ensuring that user organizations had the capacity to manage and effectively employ the technological tools created. Those concerned with the relationship between technology and military power dealt with issues of quality versus quantity in acquiring weapons systems and discerning which technologies would prove most significant in the next five, ten, or twenty years.[7]

An important understanding emerged in the 1980s regarding the relationship between technological change and doctrinal innovation within military organizations.[8] New work dealt with examinations of technological changes in the period between World War I and World War II. Many of the weapons introduced in World War I, such as the tank and the airplane, matured technologically during this time and became principal instruments of war. The German Werhmacht and Luftwaffe developed the doctrine of blitzkrieg for employing mechanized land forces and tactical air forces to avoid horrendous trench warfare. The British Royal Air Forces (RAF) and the U.S. Army Air Corps developed doctrines of airpower focused on strategic bombing for the same reason. The RAF also developed radar technology and an air defense system that proved capable of defeating an underdeveloped German bomber force. The U.S. Marine Corps developed the doctrine of amphibious assault.

A common theme in all these analyses of technological change stressed the central role of doctrinal innovation in explaining the choices of national military organizations among strategic options as well as their degree of success in employing them. Barry Posen provides the following definition: "Military doctrine includes the preferred mode of a group of services, a single service or a subservice for fighting wars. It reflects the judgment of professional military officers, and of a lesser but important extent, civilian leaders, about what is and is not militarily possible and necessary. Such judgments are based on appraisals of military technology, national geography, adversary capabilities and the skills of one's own military organization."[9] To explain the relationship between capacity for doctrinal innovation and military success, analysts stressed the following considerations:

• The rigidity of military establishments generally makes doctrinal innovation difficult. Posen, in particular, highlights the idea that the uncertainty and risks posed by undergoing significant doctrinal change during periods of transition makes these organizations very resistant to such changes.

• Committed leadership plays a crucial role, especially in achieving revolutionary innovation. Although authors differ on the relative importance of civilian and military roles in fostering doctrinal change, all stress the activities and statements of key leaders.

• Wartime experience and an organizational ability to learn improves prospects for innovation. Most analyses argue that actual battlefield experience with new empolyment concepts has the most direct impact on successful innovation. The experience of surrogates and allies as well as realistic exercises and war gaming can also provide a useful supplement to direct tests of new doctrines in an actual war.

• For an innovative doctrine to succeed, military organizations need to develop a core group of personnel with an understanding of the empolyment concepts and the technologies involved.

Organizations and actors in the twenty-first century wishing to establish the proper doctrine for waging strategic information warfare must formulate new doctrines to use the emerging technologies and employment concepts for waging such wars. The analyses of the interwar period can, however, provide guidance on the challenges facing military organizations in their efforts to accomplish the doctrinal innovation necessary to deal with this new type of warfare.

The Information Age, the Revolution in Military Affairs,
and U.S. Adversaries

The Gulf War brought out another major new thread in thinking about the impact of technology on military operations and organizations. Analysts have increasingly recognized the fundamental advantages gained by the U.S. forces in the Gulf War through use of integrated intelligence, surveillance, and reconnaissance systems and the employment of stealth aircraft and precision weapons. The U.S. military is consciously pursuing an information technology–based capability to wage conventional wars more effectively through achieving "information superiority." The Joint Staff states in the seminal 1996 *Joint Vision 2010*:

> Information technology will improve the ability to see, prioritize, assign, and assess information. The fusion of all-source intelligence with the fluid integration of sensors, platforms, command organizations, and logistic support centers will allow a greater number of operational tasks to be accomplished faster. . . . Forces harnessing the capabilities available from this system of systems will gain "dominant battlespace awareness," an "interactive" picture that will yield much more accurate assessments of friendly and enemy operations in the area of interest.[10]

To capture the magnitude and speed of adaptation required for harnessing new technologies for warfare, the term "revolution in military affairs" (RMA) has been coined.[11] Analyzes of the RMA phenomenon stress that a confluence of factors can create historic periods during which dominant forms of warfare change quickly. The role of technological factors has often proved central to the emergence of such periods, but these analyses also identify the influence exerted by other political, social, and organizational factors. As with the analyses of doctrinal innovation, RMA thinkers also demonstrate sensitivity to the role of organizations in addressing how military establishments employ technology.[12] Most of their findings stress that actors successful during periods of revolutionary change, such as the period between the world wars, orchestrate the use of new technology along with doctrinal innovation and organizational changes. The framework of analyzing doctrinal, organizational, and technological changes within the U.S. national security establishment structures the historical reviews presented in chapters 4 and 5.

Overcoming difficulties involved in adopting and assimilating widely available, relatively cheap but fast-changing information technologies has been acknowledged as a central part of the RMA facing the U.S. military at the end of the twentieth century. Integrating information systems across the services and various agencies of the Department of Defense has proved daunting despite professed desires for "jointness" and "interoperability." A Defense Science Board study concluded in 1994:

> Until policies and processes are put in place to ensure that the joint warfighter interoperability requirements are strongly considered, these well intentioned but unique Service and Agency programs will tend to drift away from migration objectives. In addition to new systems, there are legacy systems that must be either migrated into or interface with common systems. The motivation to diverge from a joint interoperability structure is aggravated by a need to maintain compatibility with service-unique legacy systems.[13]

In explaining the broader unintended consequences of the U.S. military's move into the information age, Dr. David Alberts of the National Defense University notes that "[w]ithout the adoption of a comprehensive and systematic process for introducing and using these [information] technologies, their positive potential will not be realized and the probability of adverse impacts will increase to unacceptable levels."[14]

Even more difficult are the doctrinal and organizational changes required to achieve the desired capacity for leveraging these information technologies. Dr. Andrew Marshall, Director of the Secretary of Defense's Office of Net Assessment, stresses that "being ahead in concepts of operation and in organizational arrangements may be far more enduring than any advantages in technology or weapons systems embodying them."[15] Marshall also acknowledges the difficulty of such transitions given the nature of information technology: "Innovation may be more difficult than it was then [in the 1920s and 1930s]. There may not be any new platforms to rally around. . . . The technologies (informational, computational, communication) that seem central suffuse everything, the same way electric motors did several decades ago, changing everything, but creating no new major systems like the automobile or the airplane."[16]

In 1998, the General Accounting Office reviewed the progress in the Department of Defense efforts to achieve the information superiority objectives stated in Joint Vision 2010. The report's findings stress the technology adoption and assimilation difficulties illuminated by Marshall and others. While finding significant steps had been taken to implement a common C4ISR architecture and through programs such as GCCS and Joint Tactical Radio System (JTRS), the report concludes:

DOD's C4ISR architectural and other information superiority activities are complex undertakings and involve considerable investments in C4ISR systems. In addition, they will require overcoming difficult and long-standing institutional problems and organizational boundaries to be successful.[17]

The military establishments of other states and of nonstate actors will also face complex challenges in attempting to use information technologies to improve their effectiveness. Yet U.S. defense and intelligence analysts appear to assume adversaries can assimilate these technologies with little or no effort. In the mid- and late 1990s, analyses of technology transfer deemed to be threatening to national security spotlighted two technologies, increasingly available to all actors, that could be used to improve precision strike capabilities: commercial satellite imaging and GPS-based navigation systems. As Joseph Nye and William Owens stated in *Foreign Affairs*, "[d]igitization, computer processing, precise global positioning, and systems integration are available to any nation with the money and will to use them systematically."[18] Regarding commercial satellite imaging, many authors argue that the availability of high-resolution imagery will prove militarily useful to actors who could not create such capabilities on their own.[19] Even more strongly stated are assertions that the U.S.-operated GPS system provides adversaries with capabilities they could otherwise not obtain, particularly in the realm of improving the accuracy of cruise missile systems.[20]

None of these analyses raises the question of whether the potential users of these systems will have any difficulty incorporating the technologies into evolving systems and modes of military operations. These discussions lack any analysis whatsoever of the organizational structures and processes as well as human capital necessary to assimilate these technologies effectively into broader military organizations. Satellite imagery requires highly trained technicians to interpret the data and advanced communications architectures for transmitting the information involved. Using GPS navigation on existing cruise missiles will present systems integration challenges to weapons designers, engineers, and technicians in dealing with equipment acquired from numerous different enterprises and countries. A striking common characteristic of these analyses is encapsulated in a statement by Irving Lachow that touches on these concerns without any depth of explanation: "While the information provided by GPS may improve the capabilities of Third World forces, such information is no substitute for training, good morale, or high quality equipment." Lachow neglects, however, to discuss further the difficulty of acquiring the requisite technological knowledge to use the GPS information obtained or establishing the capacity to assimilate new equipment into existing force structures.[21] Most analyses forge on from this point to describe the threat these users of GPS technology pose to the United States and possible technological responses. The very critical concerns of technological assimilation and establishing organizational capacity are dismissed despite acknowledgments that the U.S. military's incorporation of these very same advanced technologies presents substantial challenges.

The vast majority of commentaries describing the diffusion of technologies relevant to strategic information warfare are marked by a strikingly similar set of assumptions. For example, Winn Schwartau states, "When compared to the cost and effectiveness of a well-armed military, almost anyone can play. When we think that drug cartels spend billions of dollars annually to protect themselves, an additional investment in an offensive information warfare strategy would be a relatively minor expense."[22] A summer 1994 Defense Science Board study goes further in finding that "a 'third world' nation could procure a formidable, modern information warfare capability virtually off-the-shelf."[23] The Presidential Commission on Critical Infrastructure Protection concluded in October 1997 that "the basic attack tools [for information warfare]—computer, modem, telephone and software—are essentially the same as those used by hacker and criminals."[24] If the technological tools and skills necessary for strategic information attacks are so easily accessible, actors in the international system have seemingly ignored a fruitful opportunity to develop and use capabilities to conduct strategic information warfare. Significant information infrastructure vulnerabilities and technologies for attacking them are present, yet we have yet to see full-scale strategic information war waged by states, terrorist groups, or other actors. Why?

Using a Broader Base to Assess Organizational
Technological Capacity

A fundamental, implicit assumption of assessments highlighting the U.S. vulnerability to digital attacks is that adversaries can not only acquire the necessary technological capabilities to mount such attacks but also effectively assimilate and employ them. The challenges facing all actors and organizations tasked with the creation of strategic information warfare capabilities needs to be analyzed in a more structured fashion.

Facilitating Factors for Establishing Organizational Technological Capacity

Analyses of the adoption, transfer, assimilation, and diffusion of technologies for a wide range of organizational missions stress that the level of technical mastery required to use acquired encapsulated or even codified technological knowledge does not occur instantaneously or without effort. The challenges of creating organizational technological capacity have received much more comprehensive attention in relation to the use of technology for financial gain and economic development than from defense thinkers. The conditions facilitating development of organizational technical expertise identified below are primarily derived from analyses of the technological capacity building of organizations not involved with national security missions. Significant caution must be taken in building and applying a general framework for understanding organizational technological capacity to the specific case of developing and deploying such capability in the context of information warfare. The approaches of organizations applying technologies for use in productivity improvement and increasing commercial market share may differ substantially from approaches appropriate to developing the capacity to wage war.

This section identifies five facilitating conditions that generally promote organizational success in establishing technological capacity. Analyses of information technology adoption, assimilation, and diffusion indicate that the same general challenges exist as with technology in general. The complexity and rapid pace of change surrounding information technologies in the early years of the twenty-first century makes the presence of these facilitating conditions even more important in enabling organizations to establish technological capacity. Identifying these conditions enhances our ability to understand how military organizations attempt to adopt, assimilate, and improve technology to create strategic information warfare capabilities.

Supportive Institutional Environment   The environment within which an organization operates plays a crucial role in its ability to establish technological capacity. Governmental policies, legal systems, and cultural influences affect the ability of most organizations to achieve technological assimilation and mastery. Certain environments have proven more fertile than others for growing organizations with strong technological capacities for commercial competitiveness and economic growth. Military organizations must additionally deal with the larger contexts of political, legal, and cultural forces that determine organizational mandates, resources, and policies for the establishment of technological capacity.

Governments and legal/regulatory systems vary widely in their ability to adapt to changing technology trajectories.[25] National governments differ in the approach they take in determining when to intervene during technological life cycles to help commercial firms, government enterprises, and other organizations gain advantage through the use of technology. Studies of developing countries' efforts to assimilate technology indicate that too much protectionism or reliance on foreign technological assistance can result in complacency and stagnation due to lack of competition. Peter Drucker points out that removing protectionist barriers to trade to improve a nation's technological assimilation and diffusion capacity requires sacrifices that challenge political and social cohesion.[26]

Technological assimilation also poses challenges of meshing new technologies with existing equipment, infrastructures, and standards. When multiple organizations are involved in the creation, assimilation, and diffusion of technological knowledge, processes to involve and commit multiple stakeholders in both government and private sectors as well as within organizations are needed. The high short-term costs of undergoing change may cause government and commercial organizations to "lock in" certain sets of technology despite the presence of preferable technological options for the longer term. The dominance of particular systems, standards, and infrastructures can make adoption of new technologies involving different systems, standards, or infrastructures difficult. The capability for systems integration and adaptation constitutes a major U.S. asset vis-à-vis both military and commercial competitors in using technology.[27]

Additionally, effective use of technology requires organizations to mesh technology tools and techniques within the cultural and social context in which they are employed. The roles of tradition, fatalism, ethnocentrism, family structures, small group dynamics, and authority structures all affect organizational technological capabilities.[28] Also, communication barriers in the form of both language and conceptual constructs can impede assimilation of technology acquired from outside sources. Although the impact of such factors on technology assimilation and diffusion is difficult to correlate directly, others have detailed the effects of sociocultural forces such as Islamic religious tenets and Muslim traditions on limiting adoption and use of new technologies.[29]

The role of institutional and contextual factors for adoption and diffusion is often denigrated in analyses of how organizations can use technology in the information age. Pundits argue that individuals and organizations can easily use information technology to conduct activities in widely dispersed locations while communicating with ease.[30] Although these assertions are in part true, location and context still matter to a significant degree. Organizations that develop and rely on information technology are thriving in the United States while those in other areas of the developed and developing worlds lag behind. The rise of a significant software industry in Bangalore, India, has much to do with the contextual conditions present in this region.[31] Taiwan and Malaysia have undertaken a major effort to attract foreign investment by planning science parks and cities intended to create a fertile context for information technology–intensive activity. As of the summer 2000, *Wired* magazine identified forty-six high-tech hubs with the right set of contextual factors to make the most significant contributions to the global information technology enterprise.[32] As mentioned previously, China and other states have imposed certain governmental controls on the use of information technologies with yet uncertain impacts on establishing organizational technological capability.

The United States and other nations are undergoing major changes in the legal and organizational structures that regulate public- and private-sector interactions in the telecommunications and information technology sectors of the economy. Analyses during the 1990s highlighted how flexible and pragmatic national policies regarding information technologies and standards succeeded better in fostering innovation and diffusion than those based on government efforts to pick technology winners and national champions.[33] The pace of advance of information technology has increasingly driven the development of products permitting open system architectures, but the dizzying pace of change has made establishing standards for the operation of such architectures a major challenge. Martin Libicki asserts that "[s]tandards become critical for the external systems integration necessary to building tomorrow's networks, which will unite users, instruments, sensors, and software with contributions from governments, corporations and other users."[34] Debate rages within the international telecommunications community regarding the proper role of government institutions both in terms of setting technical standards and in terms of setting policies regarding privacy and content. Goverments face even greater difficulty in establishing policies and standards requiring products to contribute to protecting information security acceptable to the private sector. The current lack of standardization across the wide range of information network and infrastructure implementations makes detecting potential flaws and vulnerabilities in those networks and infrastructures difficult for both those protecting infrastructures and those considering disruption of these systems and networks. Firms, states, and even international organizations that can quickly establish workable policies and standards are likely to achieve advantages in terms of widespread adoption and assimilation of new information technologies for economic development, commercial competitiveness, and national security purposes.

Sociocultural factors also influence the assimilation of information technologies and development of information infrastructures. In examining the dynamics of the semiconductor industry, analysts stress the difference between U.S. and Japanese approaches to fostering innovation and diffusion. Differing approaches have offered advantages to firms based in different places at different points in time. Whereas Japanese firms are thought to tend toward incremental improvements in existing products and technologies, those in the United States are viewed as more likely to attempt revolutionary R&D projects.[35] Additionally, the creation of national and organizational information infrastructures is in large measure culturally driven in terms of the purpose, structure, and effectiveness of those infrastructures.[36]

Demand-Pull Motivation The substantial effort and organizational changes required to achieve effective technological assimilation means that organizations often require substantial motivation, referred to as "demand-pull," to accomplish such assimilation quickly and successfully. This demand-pull can come from a variety of sources: changing customer desires, threats from competitors, or changes in contextual circumstances such as tougher governmental regulation.[37] This theme receives even stronger emphasis in analyses of military doctrinal innovation. Successful assimilation of new technologies during the period between the two world wars was largely driven by defeat in a major conflict or the rise of new threats that created organizational will to enable change.[38]

Outside pressure has proven important in motivating organizations to adopt information technologies, assimilate them, and diffuse them with other technologies. James McKenney's study of three successful commercial efforts to leverage information technology indicates that in all three cases, the organization was initially motivated to accept technological innovation by an impending crisis. For example, the development of the American Airlines computerized reservation system, known as SABRE, was motivated by the company's need to deal with inadequate processing speeds as passenger volumes and demands for last-minute checks on seat availability increased in the 1950s.[39]

Seymour Goodman has highlighted the significance of the demand-pull imperative for the U.S. use of information technology for national security purposes. He notes that "[m]ilitary demands drove the creation of the first operational, large-scale, digital computers. Given the extraordinary complexity of building these machines, it is not clear how or when they might have been built had it not been for the wartime, and immediate postwar, national security driven efforts."[40] Looking into the future, Goodman predicts that the lack of a clear national security mission requiring improved use of information technologies may make assimilation of such technologies more difficult for the U.S. military.

Managerial Initiative Leadership plays a key role in establishing technological capacity and learning. To promote successful implementation of a new technology, the leadership of an organization must articulate a vision surrounding the rationale for acquisition and assimilation of the new technology.[41] Substantial financial resources and commitment are often required to overcome unexpected barriers to successful assimilation. Implementing complex technologies in a new organizational context requires a special form of entrepreneurship that is often in short supply. Managers often must overcome a "not invented here" bias inherent in many organizations regarding the use of new equipment and processes that do not originate within the organizations themselves. Those allocating resources to foster a nation's or organization's ability to adopt and diffuse new technologies must avoid a tendency to overemphasize embodied technology in the form of hardware at the expense of codified and experiential forms of technology. Effective use of technologies may require significant organizational adaptation in terms of new structures, connections with outside organizations, and decentralization of authority that place a premium on committed leadership. Analyses of doctrinal innovation and RMA recognize the importance of new organizational structures for waging new forms of warfare but pay much less attention to the degree of centralization of authority. The proper organizational form varies according to the type of technological activity and the progression of the technology through its life cycle. Choosing the right organizational form presents a major challenge for management in creating the conditions that promote successful assimilation and diffusion.

Increasing reliance on information technology has proven threatening to organizational stakeholders, including workers whose jobs may be altered or eliminated and managers whose roles and missions may change.[42] Successful managers of technologically focused organizations must avoid simply automating access to codified knowledge resources and focus instead on developing knowledge skills in the operating workforce to foster long-term capacity for innovation and diffusion. McKenney indicates that organizations need strong leadership in committing themselves to achieving competitive leadership through the use of information technology. In his analysis, corporate CEOs of organizations adopting major new information technologies were crucial in incubating research, developing internal technological expertise, and evolving strategies for using information technologies as part of normal operations. Strong leadership by these CEOs supported flexible organizational rules, job rotation, and investment in training and career management to achieve the necessary long-term commitment to successfully adopt innovative IT approaches.[43]

Technological Expertise   Creating the right mix of people and skills is consistently identified as central to accomplishing technological assimilation. At the most basic level, an educated, committed workforce with general math and science competency provides a starting point for successful technological assimilation. Technical human capital is necessary in an organization to understand the functional requirements of systems, knowledge of the possibilities, and limitations of technologies involved. As the degree of technological assimilation within an organization increases, the role of specialized skills in that organization becomes increasingly important. The availability and expertise of scientific, engineering, and technical personnel in particular becomes critical. Organizations undergoing significant technological assimilation must also have access to managerial human capital with expertise and commitment to technological change. Bernard and Fawn Brodie come to a similar conclusion regarding the role of human capital in managing the development of military technology: "Men of inventive talent and imagination are scarce in any age, and a full accounting must be made of them."[44]

To assimilate technology successfully, organizations also need a strong base of expertise within the organization to promote understanding of the potential benefits of accessible technologies and properly guide their assimilation. Networks of such expertise can be established through a variety of means including participation in scientific conferences, research consortia, joint ventures, and strategic alliances. Porter advocates creating "early warning systems" to highlight the possibility of technological and regulatory change and as a device for seeking outside ideas and talent for an organization.[45] Locating technologically intensive activities in geographic areas where requisite expertise is concentrated can facilitate access to outside sources for such skills.[46] Personnel with an ability to create networks to outside organizations and individuals with related skills play a particularly important role in building an organization's potential pool of personnel with technological expertise.[47] Although connections to outside sources of expertise can be useful, maintenance of substantial competency within an organization that understands the organization's technology capabilities as well as the mission of the organization is crucial to successful technological assimilation. Such internal expertise can prove particularly critical in situations in which concerns about trade secrets, competitiveness, or national security limit an organization's willingnes to use outside technological expertise.

A limited pool of human resources and experiential knowledge is available to almost all organizations trying to leverage information technology in the early years of the new century. Personnel shortages and changing skill requirements constitute a major barrier to successful information technology assimilation in the United States and elsewhere. The lack of trained information systems engineers and administrators severely constrains the expansion of networking activities and the launching of e-commerce ventures in the United States today. Efforts by Russia to sustain an indigenous capability to produce high-performance computers in the 1990s revolved around maintaining a core of human expertise.[48] Other nations with well-developed scientific and technological educational systems, such as India, have confronted problems created by a "brain drain" of individuals to more attractive opportunities in other countries.[49]

Even more than with most other types of technologies, keeping abreast of information technology developments requires organizations to develop connections with outside sources of information and expertise.[50] Limited availability of people with requisite expertise in information technology means organizations may desire to leverage personnel resources by sharing technological knowledge and participating in networks. Access to outside sources of information technology expertise to benchmark best practices and deepen technological capabilities can assist assimilation and diffusion of information technologies in an organization. Organizations can leverage mechanisms similar to those utilized in pursuing other technologies for establishing such contacts, including cooperative ventures, technology consortiums, and professional societies.

The rapid pace of change of information technologies and challenges created by the managing of open, interconnected information infrastructures also places a premium on creating and maintaining internal technological expertise. Shosanna Zuboff notes that "[a]s the intellective skill base [of an information-intense organization] becomes the organization's most precious resource, managerial roles must function to enhance its quality."[51] The complexity of information technologies requires expertise both in selecting new technologies to augment an organization's existing systems and networks and in determining new possibilities for improving organizational capacity. McKenney identifies two major internal technological players in using information technology: a technological maestro and the technical team. The "maestro" is both an intelligence officer, functioning as a source of information about outside sources of technology, and an organizational champion for the role of information technology within the organization as well. Technological maestros understand both the technology and the organizational mission; according to McKenney, they are in short supply. The technical team provides the critical competence required to change an organization's underlying information architectures constantly to keep the organization at the frontier of technology while supporting several generations of existing systems.[52]

Learning Ability   Most analysts agree that organizational technological capacity is improved through continuous learning by doing and that the process takes time and effort. Numerous authors assert that the ability to learn faster than competitors provides the only reliable source of organizational competitive advantage over another in the late twentieth century.[53] Past analyses have identified the following key features of organizations with a high level of ability to assimilate and diffuse technologies:

- Willingness to upset conventional wisdom and challenge existing ideas.
- Encouragement of experimentation and implementation of mechanisms to integrate results into improved or new organizational capabilities.
- Empowerment of individuals throughout the organization through sharing of information and nonhierarchical decision-making structures.

Organizations possessing the facilitating conditions outlined above should prove more capable of adopting, assimilating, and diffusing technologies to improve their performance than those who lack them.

Within organizations that take maximum advantage of information technology, learning is the heart of productive activity.[54] To succeed, programs to assimilate information technology must have a critical mass of resources at the start and need stability in terms of funding to avoid frequent changes in personnel and programs that impose learning costs. Such programs must also have flexibility to adapt and evolve over time. Increasingly short information technology life cycles will make assimilation of such technology more difficult. As a result, organizations with the highest capacity for learning will have a decided advantage in information technology–based competition.

Information Technology and Organizational Change

Before turning to a focused analysis of the establishment of strategic information warfare capabilities, one more important consideration from past analyses of experience with information technology needs to be examined. Throughout the literature on information technology, the necessity for organizational change in varying degrees in order for organizations to usefully assimilate information technologies provides a central concern. An organization's ability to orchestrate such changes effectively incorporates a number of the facilitating factors identified above, particularly establishing managerial initiative, internal technological expertise, and learning ability within the organization. Yet considering organizational change in an aggregated fashion may provide another useful lens for viewing the challenge of establishing organizational capacity for employing information technology. Simply constructed, three levels of information technology adoption and assimilation can occur:[55]

• Substitution. Simple replacement of existing technology with information technology to accomplish the same tasks.

• Enhancement. Improving processes to make best use of the new technology to improve capability to accomplish existing organizational objectives.

• Transformation. Using technology in new ways to redefine organizational capabilities and objectives.

Studies on information technology also identify barriers confronting those attempting to achieve these differing levels of assimilation. These barriers can be synopsized as follows:

• For substitution, the main barrier may be obtaining sufficient resources to acquire embodied technology.

• For enhancement, the lack of adequate codified knowledge within an organization may require assistance by more experienced practitioners. Acquisition costs of a particular technology may be trivial compared to training costs.

• For transformation, the acquisition of whole new sets of organizational skills may be necessary as well as expensive and painful organizational restructuring.

Actors in the international system who desire to use information technology to improve military capabilities face the same barriers to successful organizational change as any other type of organization. Attempts to leverage information technology to create a wholly new approach to strategic warfare must consider the difficulty of transformational change required to accomplish such a goal. The length of time required to successfully implement such changes may prove substantial. McKenney's analysis of commercial firms who gained competitive advantage through use of information technology found that such firms did not realize significant gains until seven to ten years after they undertook major transformational efforts.[56] As discussed earlier, the literature on doctrinal innovation highlights why military organizations seem particularly resistant to transformative change. Rosen's findings about peacetime doctrinal innovation between the world wars argues that innovation in military doctrine requires that a generation of officers schooled and committed to waging new forms of warfare develop over a period of up to twenty years.[57] So far, no actor has appeared having developed overnight the technological capacity to wage strategic information warfare, despite the hype about such a possibility. Constructive analysis of the emerging strategic information warfare environment facing the United States requires additional assessment of how actors can align the facilitating factors for establishing technological capacity and overcome barriers to organizational change.

Organizational Technological Capacity and Strategic Warfare

Waging digital warfare involves the use of technological tools that minimize requirements for managing large amounts of physical force and energy. Computer viruses spread quickly through the corruption of data stored as magnetic fields on disks and tapes without directly observable manifestations of the change that is taking place. In many cases, the technological knowledge needed to use these tools can be codified in electronic formats and transferred quickly from person to person. Hackers constantly post newly scripted attack tools on Internet sites. In response, commercial firms develop updates for virus checkers and firewalls that clients can quickly download to improve their defenses against electronic attack. As a result, many analyses of strategic information warfare have focused on the low entry costs and decreasing skills requirements for potential actors in such warfare. As discussed above, however, the use of newly acquired technology by any organization requires adaptation and assimilation. The tasks facing organizations engaging in offensive and defensive strategic information warfare require them to establish the capacity for performing new, complex tasks beyond those envisioned by the average hacker group or even a corporate information security team. The knowledge needed to perform these tasks may prove difficult to codify, requiring people with experience geared to functions such as large-scale information infrastructure assessment, intelligence gathering, and economic analysis. Access and exploitation of experiential knowledge may prove central to successfully waging strategic information warfare.

Strategic warfare revolves around the ability of actors to strike directly at enemy centers of gravity to achieve objectives in a conflict without having to engage an opponent's fielded military forces. Given a potential adversary's offensive capabilities to engage in such attacks, actors also endeavor to defend such centers of gravity. Organizations tasked with creating offensive and defensive strategic warfare capabilities face several challenges in using available technological means to accomplish this task. These challenges apply across the range of specific means of waging strategic warfare: submarine warfare, air or nuclear bombardment, or disrupting information infrastructures. The phrase "offensive strategic information warfare capabilities" in this section refers to an actor's ability to disrupt and destroy targeted information infrastructure centers of gravity. Such offensive capabilities can serve multiple political purposes: to coerce, deter, or even defend through preemptive strikes. "Defensive strategic information warfare capabilities" refers to an actor's ability to protect such infrastructures from damage and reconstitute their capabilities, short of measures that achieve defense through preventive, disruptive strikes. Although the distinction made here between offensive and defensive uses of technology can be useful in analyzing the different organizational challenges presented by each, the line between certain offensive and defensive capabilities may be indistinct. Especially in the realm of digital warfare, the technological tools and human expertise involved are often capable of performing either a defensive or an offensive mission.

Achieving the necessary technological mastery for organizations assigned offensive strategic warfare missions requires the development of a number of generic capabilities:

• Ability to analyze an opponent's centers of gravity and potential sources of leverage or points of vulnerability.

• Ability to assess and assimilate available technological means for placing enemy centers of gravity at risk.

• Ability to establish an organizational technological capacity to hold an enemy at risk. This task would include the development and operation of forces capable of inflicting damage, the establishment of target sets, making damage estimates, and developing the command and control system to direct such forces.

• Ability to sustain and adapt organizational technological capability in an environment of changing strategic objectives, adversary reactions, and technological advances.

On the other hand, developing the requisite technical expertise to conduct successful defensive strategic warfare missions presents its own set of required capabilities:

• Ability to survey one's own centers of gravity, assess potential threats, and decide which need protection.

• Ability to assess and assimilate available technological means for defense.

• Ability to establish organizational technological capability to protect key assets. Choices regarding the degree of centralization of defensive activity and expertise will prove crucial when organizations at multiple levels of activity play key roles. Trade-offs involve the degree to which central organizations assume the responsibility and provide means for defense versus the degree to which the means and responsibility for establishing defensive capacity are diffused or decentralized.

• Ability to sustain and adapt the technological capabilities of the organization(s), as with offense.

Differences in Organizational Technological Capacity for Strategic Offense and Defense

The need to assess vulnerabilities and available technological means for attacking centers of gravity creates some similarities in the challenges faced by organizations tasked with offensive and defensive responsibilities for strategic warfare. In some cases, such as in strategic information warfare, the technological tools involved may even be very similar. However, major differences in the scope of responsibility between offensive and defensive strategic tasks may create distinct differences in organizational challenges on opposite sides of the equation.

Organizations tasked with offensive strategic warfare can focus on preparation for waging war. During peacetime, their activity would include gathering necessary intelligence information about potential enemies and honing the skills of individuals and units for the conduct of operations. Historically, nations have established very clear command and control arrangements for employing strategic warfare capabilities. Such capabilities are generally regarded as a military tool authorized for use by only the highest authorities. Military establishments often create new, specialized organizations to ensure the clarity of the chain of command. The advent of nuclear weapons resulted in the formation of new organizations to control these weapons and very elaborate efforts to ensure tight command and control over their use. The specialization of such organizations also allows them to focus on staying at the technological cutting edge for waging such warfare. The development of a doctrine of strategic bombing eventually led to the formation of General Headquarters Air Force units within the Army Air Corps in the 1930s to provide a "strategic" reserve force to be directly controlled by the War Department. The advent of nuclear weapons led to the formation of the Strategic Air Command to organize, train, and operate the nuclear-equipped air forces of the United States and, later, land-based ICBMs. Organizational insularity and focus on technological advantage also led to a perceived need to keep nuclear programs secret not only from adversaries, but also from those at home without a reasonable need to know about them. The technological development of nuclear weapons and delivery systems and the plans for their use, known as the Single Integrated Operations Plan, were accorded the highest degree of secrecy. Establishing organizational technological capacity for offensive strategic warfare must address challenges of assimilation of newly developed technologies and overcoming bureaucratic resistance within the national security establishment to the adoption and assignment of resources to new missions. Issues related to the broad effects of institutional context and the fostering diffusion of technology generally assume less importance.

Organizations tasked with defensive strategic warfare may have responsibility for protecting a wide range of assets and capabilities. For a nation-state, public and private assets not owned and operated by the national security establishment may require defensive protection. Performing such a defensive mission requires a national-level assessment of possible threats and the overall vulnerability of key assets, coordination across a wide range of organizations, and allocation of resources available for defense. Activities requiring protection by nation-states, such as industrial production or the operation of telecommunications networks, will likely evolve during peacetime with little concern about national security threats or missions during a conflict. Germany's military production facilities during World War II were operated with little regard for the possibility of strategic air attack until large-scale Allied bombing operations began to severely threaten production.

Authority for the technological development and operational control of defensive activity may fall outside the purview of national security organizations or even the government. Although changes in authority and responsibility can occur as conflicts emerge, the peacetime activities of defensive strategic warfare organizations will establish the foundation for wartime capability. The need for ongoing efforts to ensure maximum capacity to limit damage and create reconstitution capabilities will be especially important if active defenses are unlikely to be effective. During the 1950s, the United States felt the need to create air defense forces and institute civil defense programs as well as develop offensive nuclear capabilities. Organizations tasked with ensuring damage limitation, providing active defenses, and creating reconstitution capability may develop conflicting opinions regarding the efficacy of different strategic defensive approaches.

Creating the organizational technological capacity necessary to conduct strategic information warfare defense effectively for a nation-state will also require a supportive institutional context and organizational coordination to achieve high levels of capability. Orchestrating defensive efforts demands an understanding of how different organizations view their roles and the role of the government in reacting to various types of threats. Those tasked with ensuring a state's defense against strategic attack must choose the level of governmental control warranted by concerns about potential or actual offensive action. The U.S. government required the participation of the private sector in civil defense efforts in the 1950s in response to the threat of Soviet nuclear attacks. These civil defense efforts atrophied as it became apparent that such efforts could do little to mitigate the devastating damage inflicted in a nuclear attack.[58]

Sharing knowledge of offensive capabilities, technological tools, and techniques across organizations faced with similar threats may improve the cost-effectiveness of overall strategic defensive efforts. The United States has shared defensive responsibilities, technology, and practices for the protection of North American airspace with its Canadian allies through the mechanism of the North American Air Defense Command (NORAD). The challenges of creating the proper institutional context and achieving desired technological diffusion seem much more relevant to strategic defensive efforts of state actors than those involved in creating offensive capability. Nonstate actors may face a much less burdensome set of defense tasks in having to deal only with protecting their own limited infrastructure, rather than endeavoring to protect the assets of an entire society. Such actors may have less concern with issues of institutional context, organizational coordination, and technological diffusion than state actors, as discussed later in the chapter.

Establishing Offensive Strategic Information Warfare Capacities

As described earlier, the embodied and codified technological knowledge of the means for conducting digital attacks is widely available and can be acquired by most actors. Defining the organizational mandate and developing the necessary experiential technological knowledge to conduct such attacks, however, may prove a central challenge for actors endeavoring to establish offensive strategic information warfare capabilities. The analysis here assumes that organizations dedicated to waging offensive strategic information warfare are established within the context of the security establishment of an actor, either state or nonstate.

Moreover, the analysis in this section focuses on strategic information warfare capabilities for achieving objectives substantially independent of the successful use of other military means. Certainly, such capabilities could be used synergistically with other means of strategic attack or in conjunction with battlefield forces. Smaller-scale offensive strategic information warfare efforts could be undertaken with the objective of harassing opponents and providing assistance to other principal means for achieving victory rather than as the primary means of waging war. The analysis here addresses establishing the requisite capacity for strategic digital attacks as a major new mode of warfare, as outlined in chapter 2.

Supportive Institutional Environment

Many of the factors that drive broader adoption and assimilation of technology in the commercial sector of a society, such as the establishment of intellectual property rights, existence of standards, and regulation of competition, will likely have little affect on the development of offensive strategic warfare capabilities. However, legal frameworks for controlling the activities of national security institutions may have a significant impact on offensive strategic information warfare organizations, despite their relative isolation from other institutional constraints.

In the United States, extensive mechanisms exist for congressional involvement in funding, organizing, and even authorizing the most sensitive activities of organizations such as the Central Intelligence Agency and the National Security Agency. Much of this institutional framework evolved from revelations regarding covert activities of the U.S. national security community during the first half of the Cold War. Congress and the public also questioned the legitimacy of U.S. intervention in the internal affairs of other states and the impact on citizens' rights at home during the 1970s and 1980s. The development of offensive strategic information warfare capabilities may require the adoption and use of technologies and techniques that raise similar questions. Legal and institutional frameworks regarding intelligence oversight and covert action may influence the choice of technological means for conducting and permissibility of certain activities during the conduct of strategic information warfare. Such concerns would be particularly operative in the use of digital warfare without a political declaration of hostilities.[59]

Other actors may have much less well-defined institutions and legal frame-works that govern their offensive information warfare activities. For example, most states allow their intelligence organizations much more leeway in the conduct of their activities than does the United States. Nonstate actors such as terrorist groups who conduct activities condemned by the international com-munity are not likely to recognize legal or political constraints on developing, sustaining, or using digital attack.

Demand-Pull Motivation

As discussed in chapter 2, the perceived utility of strategic offensive warfare to actors will be strongly influenced by the availability of other military means to engage in conflict with potential adversaries. Today, nonstate actors or devel-oping states that lack options for competing with advanced industrialized states on the conventional battlefield or by employing weapons of mass destruction may feel a significant pull to develop strategic information warfare capabilities. Given the widely recognized military superiority of the United States, it may experience significantly less of a demand-pull for creating a new capability to wage warfare. Conversely, the demand for a capability to wage "elegant wars" without U.S. causalities and minimal collateral damage to enemies may increase pressure to develop strategic digital attack capabilities. Perceptions about the urgency of the need to develop these capabilities are likely to change as the potential for waging offensive strategic information warfare is demonstrated, especially against the U.S. itself.

The motivation provided by demand-pull to develop capabilities for waging offensive strategic information warfare may be as crucial as in past efforts involv-ing technology adoption and assimilation by military organizations to create the necessary willingness to undergo doctrinal change as well as expend required resources and organizational effort. The level of doctrinal and organizational change required for the United States to develop an organizational technologi-cal capacity sufficient to conduct offensive information warfare is likely to be nothing short of transformational. As described in chapter 2, the development of nuclear weapons in the Cold War caused radical rethinking regarding the significance of strategic warfare and the role of military establishments. Relying substantially on digital warfare tools and techniques to disrupt an adversary's information infrastructures also constitutes an entirely new way of looking at the employment of force. Using information technology to wage strategic war rather than simply to enhance the effectiveness of existing fighting forces may require whole new types of organizations. Past approaches to information in war focused on "force multiplier" effects in inflicting large amounts of physical damage against military forces or an industrial base. Strategic information warfare envisages the use of digital, as well as possibly mechanical and electromagnetic, means to inflict microlevels of physical disruption to create large-scale disruption in an adversary's information infrastructures. The biggest challenge for establishing such organizational capability within a state's national security structure may involve integrating such a new mission and organization(s) into institutional and budgetary frameworks, strategic culture, and established doctrine. Such an effort will require doctrinal innovation on the scale accompanying the development of the blitzkrieg and of amphibious warfare and the pursuit of strategic bombing between the two world wars.

A major choice for state actors such as the United States in developing offensive strategic information warfare capabilities is whether organizations tasked with strategic information warfare missions will be located within or outside of existing military or intelligence organizations. In addition to the institutional context addressed above, determining factors in this choice may include the size of the offensive strategic information warfare organization and its level of openness regarding its existence and mission. The larger the size and the greater the degree of openness, the more likely the choice would be made to locate such an organization in the conventional military establishment, especially if leaders envisage integration of strategic information warfare efforts with more conventional military forces. If secrecy is at a premium and organizational size is small, the choice might be to place an offensive strategic information warfare capability within the intelligence community as part of the nation's capacity for covert action.

Certain state and nonstate actors may possess less rigorously formed organizational and doctrinal constraints challenging the creation of a strategic information warfare organization with a transformational mission than those facing an actor such as the United States. Assessments of the bureaucratic barriers facing such actors would require a well-developed understanding of their security institutions and strategic doctrine. The transparency of actions engaged in by potential adversaries, particularly small, cohesive, secretive nonstate actors, will vary to a considerable degree.

Managerial Initiative

Within a military establishment, creation of new organizations and changing roles and responsibilities generally requires the involvement of senior leadership. Creation of strategic digital attack capabilities within the existing military organizations will require reallocation of personnel and financial resources. In the early stages of evolution, numerous changes to organizational structures and responsibilities may be necessary to most effectively use capabilities. Once established, organizations with the capability to mount strategic digital attacks will require sustained support from senior leaders, who must allocate resources to provide the required tools and personnel.

Establishment of offensive strategic information warfare capabilities will require technologically aware leaders of security institutions who can accept the implications of the information age and foster the necessary organizational adaptation to the new type of warfare. Given the commercial technology leadership in this arena, growing leaders with the necessary skills within state security institutions may be more difficult than in development of strategic bombing and nuclear forces. Building bridges between the military and civilian sector will prove crucial to ensuring that military leaders are cognizant of the trajectories of relevant technologies and organizational approaches being developed in the civilian sector. Technologically astute leaders would play a fundamental role in advancing the vision of how available tools and techniques for conducting digital attacks create a new form of warfare and in developing people with requisite skills.

As discussed by Rosen and McKenney, management commitment is also crucial in creating career paths for those who would specialize in new missions and lead changes to organizational form necessary for useful technological adoption and assimilation. Waging strategic information warfare will require leaders who not only understand the concepts involved in but also have gained a depth of experience in the art of employing digital force in cyberspace. Retaining talented personnel will require the establishment of attractive opportunities for training, advancement, and command responsibility.

Technological Expertise

Establishing the organizational capacity to perform the tasks of understanding available attack tools, assessing infrastructure, and developing and monitoring targets for strategic offensive information warfare requires highly developed human capital. These requirements for technological expertise derive from the nature of modern information infrastructures outlined in chapter 1 as well as the quickly evolving tools and techniques outlined in chapter 2. Factors influencing the types and degree of technological sophistication and required human capital for digital warfare are outlined below. Often overlooked in

descriptions of information warfare, these requirements will be examined in
depth here.

Waging offensive strategic warfare requires people with the ability to use
the available tools and techniques to disrupt adversary information infrastructures. An organization trying to establish such human capital must examine the
level of technological skill required of personnel to accomplish this organizational objective. Conventional wisdom holds that acquiring the technical knowledge to conduct digital warfare has become increasingly easy.[60] Attackers can
employ a significant array of tools and techniques capable of exploiting known
vulnerabilities in deployed information technologies and networks. Codified
attack tools are becoming easier to use as predeveloped scripts of commands
are packaged together in programs that can be executed with graphical interface point-and-click operations. Figure 3.1, taken from the GAO report, *Infor-*
mation Security: Computer Attacks at DOD Pose Increasing Risks, depicts the
evolution of attack technologies and expertise. As discussed in chapter 2,
prepackaged intrusion tools are also widely available through the Internet, mail
order catalogues, personal exchanges, and other means. Using certain of these
tools may require only a limited level of technical sophistication. Other tools and
techniques, such as unleashing certain viruses or denial-of-service attacks
intended to overload Internet servers or telephone switches, also may not require

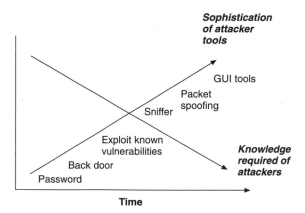

Figure 3.1
Increasing sophistication of digital attack tools and declining human expertise. Source:
Government Accounting Office, Information Security: Computer Attacks at Department
of Defense Pose Increasing Risks *(Washington, DC: GAO/AMID-96-84, May 1996).*

much technological sophistication. However, the utility of such user-friendly attack technologies depends on the nature of the targeted infrastructure and intended effects. Denial-of-service attacks against accessible Internet servers may require low levels of sophistication but may also achieve less controlled effects than attacks based on successful remote access and control of a specific information system or network, which is likely to require a much greater level of technical expertise. Additionally, a defender's ability to assess vulnerabilities and deny access to known digital attack tools and techniques may also increase the level of technological knowledge required for attacking forces. If the key information infrastructures of a target are well protected, achieving surprise and inflicting disruption against significant centers of gravity may require offensive strategic information warfare forces to employ more technological sophistication, time, and effort. The pool of human capital with the ability to develop sophisticated new attack tools or quietly probe strong, attentive defenses is much more limited than the number of individuals capable of running scripted tools or sending multiple e-mail messages to an Internet address. The Centre for Infrastructural Warfare, a think tank focused on information warfare, found in January 1998 that according to recent studies, "most attacks use standard or well-known scripted exploits. Our research reveals less than 1,000 hackers in the world who have the professional programming skills to create their own attack scripts."[61]

The size and complexity of targeted information infrastructures—the number of component technologies, systems and networks—and the wide array of organizations that operate and use these infrastructures will determine the number of potential vulnerabilities and critical nodes that serve as strategic information warfare targets. Increasing complexity of targeted infrastructures may complicate the offensive assessment task but also may create additional vulnerabilities that can be exploited as new technologies and systems are added and patched to existing information infrastructures.

Some information infrastructures are owned, operated, and relied upon by nonmilitary organizations in a nation-state may also be regarded as critical. For some actors, including the United States, disruption of infrastructures with significant impact on the civilian sector may raise policy and legal questions about acceptable levels of collateral damage.[62] Concerns on the part of state or non-state actors with avoiding collateral damage in conducting digital attacks may arise from efforts to adhere to the perceived dictates of the law of armed conflict or simply a desire to avoid escalation of a conflict, complicating the offensive warfare task. Attacking an Internet service provider whose networks transmit logistical data to military forces but also support civilian health care activities may therefore be considered inappropriate by some actors. The transnational reach of many information infrastructures means limiting damage to a particular state actor may be difficult. Disruption of the operations of either satellite broadcast networks or the Global Positioning System could affect the operation of organizations and actors all over the world. If collateral damage is a concern, certain types of infrastructure components, activities, and organizations may be considered off-limits by certain actors. Also, actors may require circumspection in the use of certain digital attack tools and techniques. Attacking targets and infrastructure nodes in a way that causes significant cascading effects, such as disabling power sources or dissemination of viruses, may also be deemed inappropriate. To the extent that specific categories of information infrastructures are considered sacrosanct, an offensive strategic information warfare organization would require the capability to conduct effective operations with a smaller toolkit against more constrained target sets. Such operations would require increased efficiency and precision of assessment and application of digital force as well as the capability for tighter command and control of such force.

Linking the ability to disrupt information infrastructures to gaining a desired level of political influence would require a much greater depth of knowledge about an adversary than that needed to simply create disruption. Developing the requisite ability to orchestrate desired effects using digital attack techniques may prove the most difficult aspect of conducting large-scale digital warfare. In addition to a capability to access and disrupt infrastructures, conducting strategic information warfare necessitates having personnel with the ability to analyze the impact of attacks on targeted sectors that may range from military forces to financial services. In earlier wars, when conventional bombs were dropped or nuclear strikes were planned, estimable physical damage against railroad yards or missile silos was translated through calculations by target experts and systems engineers into estimates of how the centers of gravity of the country under attack would be disrupted. Although initial estimates of probable disruption were frequently overly optimistic, continued analysis and reassessment generally improved such estimates as conflicts progressed. Strategic bombing campaigns during World War II involved large numbers of targeteers, engineers, and systems analysts as well as bomb builders, pilots, and bombardiers. Similarly, nuclear strike planning resulted in the establishment of the Joint Strategic Target Planning Staff and supporting intelligence organizations that understood both the effects of nuclear weapons and the centers of gravity of Soviet military, economic, and political targets.

Contemplating attacks against the information infrastructures of differing centers of gravity such as military organizations, financial institutions, and transportation networks will also require expertise in assessing how disrupting information infrastructures will affect the organizations that use them. Assessing which logistical operations, financial transfers, or transportation nodes have the greatest import within a potential center of gravity requires more than technological knowledge of information systems and networks. Strategic information warfare attacks would require knowledge of the degree to which targets rely on information infrastructures for critical operations and how effectively, quickly, and easily they can switch to backup systems in the event of a primary system disruption. Specific functional area expertise across a range of military and nonmilitary activities would be necessary to discern which target sets offer the most potential leverage in terms of vulnerability to disruption and significance to society. Such knowledge would be necessary to map targeted information infrastructures and address some crucial questions: What are the critical activities and nodes? What are the interconnections between infrastructures? How fast can the adversary improve defensive capabilities and recover the capacity to conduct necessary activity?

The development of target sets and damage estimates will also require administrative and management expertise to catalogue and maintain these information resources. Advanced information technology may ease the processing and maintenance requirements to some degree. However, organizations that rely heavily on information infrastructures for managing target databases and strike plans also create a lucrative strategic information warfare target for an adversary. U.S. and Soviet nuclear plans were among the most closely held secrets during the Cold War. Maintaining desired levels of secrecy required expensive physical infrastructures, detailed handling procedures, and dedicated security personnel. Plans for strategic information warfare campaigns will likely require similar attention.

Even more fundamentally, political and military analysis will be necessary to understand how to translate different targeting and campaign strategies into political influence. In all types of strategic warfare, attackers must answer certain crucial questions: How robust is the will of the adversary's people and leadership? Will the pain inflicted by certain types of attacks simply irritate adversaries or motivate an escalatory response? Past experience with strategic conventional bombardment demonstrates that such estimates are difficult to make. The German bombing of London in the fall of 1940 quickly led the British to retaliate against Berlin. Eventually, the British bombing campaign escalated to raids involving more than 1,000 planes that left German cities such as Hamburg and Dresden devastated. (The specific experiences of the United States in developing the capacity to wage a strategic bombing campaign against Germany are developed more fully in chapter 4.) Individuals and organizations that develop and operate strategic warfare forces have historically produced overly optimistic estimates of the efficacy of such means for achieving political results.[63] Developing expertise to estimate the political impact of strategic information warfare will likely prove even more difficult, given the lack of actual experience with the effects of large-scale attacks on information infrastructures.

The execution of an offensive strategic information warfare campaign will also require personnel and procedures to command and control forces. Communications channels must be established and maintained. Procedures will be necessary to authorize forces to begin operations against specified targets and to coordinate dispersed operating units. Once strategic information attacks are underway, the effective intelligence, targeting, and attack assessment functions may require much more rapid accomplishment. The pace at which such activities need to be conducted would depend on the attacker's expectations regarding the necessary timing to achieve its desired outcome. The challenges for controlling digital warfare operations would be analogous to those faced in the development and dissemination of the Air Tasking Order used by coalition air forces in the Persian Gulf War against Iraq. In that campaign, the unprecedented pace of operations severely stressed available technological means and human expertise for providing targeting information to operating units and assessing damage inflicted by attacks. The potentially accelerated pace of strategic information warfare campaigns, the ability of defending forces to modify the cyberspace operating environment by implementing new operating systems and procedures, and the potential lack of concrete intelligence regarding the effects of attacks, may raise even greater challenges of fog and friction in such campaigns.

Carl von Clausewitz's classic *On War* describes the crucial role of leadership in cutting through the fog and friction of war. Clausewitz refers particularly to the concept of *coup d'oeil*—the ability to make rapid and accurate decisions based on quick recognition of key features of a complex situation—identifying the quality most strongly with Napoleon. Developing commanders able to understand the operating environment and uncertainties involved in strategic information warfare may prove to be a central factor in successfully waging offensive strategic information operations, as it is in all forms of war.

A final type of human expertise useful in conducting offensive strategic warfare operations will be access to insiders. As highlighted in chapter 2, insiders could significantly reduce the effort required by outside attackers to disrupt a particular system or infrastructure by effectively identifying key target and system vulnerabilities and providing improved access for attacks. However, efforts to use insiders will involve inherent risks of compromising intelligence-gathering efforts, telegraphing intended operations, or even suffering from misinformation provided by double agents. My analysis will not address challenges of developing the organizational capacity to run clandestine operations, except to recognize their complexity and risks. The United States needs to explore more fully how the clandestine operations—counterintelligence competition affects strategic information warfare capabilities.

The list below provides a synopsis of human capital requirements for establishing an organizational technological capability for waging large-scale offensive strategic information warfare:

- Operators capable of navigating cyberspace and conducting attacks.
- Computer programmers to design advanced attack techniques and malicious software.
- Information networking engineers to analyze the adversary's infrastructure.
- Targeting experts to estimate probable damage from planned attacks.
- Military, political, economic, and social analysts to assess political influence and reaction.
- Communications operators to operate command and control systems.
- Security, counterintelligence, and administrative personnel to secure, maintain, and update plans.
- Intelligence agents to develop insider information and access to the adversary's infrastructure.
- Commanders with the coup d'oeil for waging digital warfare.

Not all the types of expertise depicted in the list must be present to launch a successful digital attack against every adversary. However, shortfalls in any particular expertise set may constrain targeting options and understanding of the likely effects of a contemplated offensive strategic information warfare campaign.

A number of factors may influence the necessary amount and types of human capital and expertise required to mount an effective offensive strategic information warfare campaign. In general, the requirements for success in this arena will be driven by an actor's potential adversaries and desired objectives. Efforts to target numerous key information infrastructures in a multiplicity of technologically advanced states with the intent of inflicting widespread disruption to accomplish significant coercive objectives, such as preventing U.S. military retaliation, could require a massive effort. Attackers would have to assess the most significant and vulnerable infrastructures to be targeted for attack. Target development would have to progress to a stage at which high levels of disruption and damage could be confidently predicted. Such effort would require the ability to sustain damage and control operations in the face of defensive reactions and retaliation by digital attack and other means. Significant levels of human capital of the types outlined above would be required.

Use of strategic information warfare to achieve more limited objectives however, might require less organizational technological capacity building. The ability of an actor to inflict disruption against limited target sets to achieve lesser objectives than complete discruption of adversery information infrastructures may allow more focused development of digital warfare tools and techniques. Insider assistance could also limit the breadth of technological knowledge necessary to conduct an effective attack. The required level of expertise also would depend on the level of disruption an actor felt was necessary to achieve its objectives. Attack strategies aimed at producing widespread damage intended to undermine the general morale of a population and confidence in its critical information infrastructures could require less in the way of developing sophisticated attack techniques, securing insider access, or developing tight command and control reins. Targeting specific centers of gravity while minimizing collateral disruption and damage, on the other hand, could increase the need for those capabilities. The crucial variable would be the required scope and the degree of disruption an attacker perceived as necessary to attain desired political objectives.

Assessments of required organizational technological capacity are also dependent on choices about campaign strategy and timing of desired effects. Most analyses of strategic warfare focus on conventional bombing or nuclear strikes intended to bring victory as quickly as possible. Similar to air strikes against Japanese cities with the intent of inducing Japan's unconditional surrender, strategic information warfare attacks could be employed with the same objective. Offensive information warfare could also be employed to achieve quick paralysis of an adversary's ability to wage war by execution of overwhelming parallel attacks such as those envisaged by John Warden and arguably executed in the Gulf War. Such information warfare strategies designed to exert overwhelming pressure against a large array of targets in a very short time period would require a great breadth of target development and digital attack skills. Developing the capacity to understand the interactions among targeted nodes within different centers of gravity would also enhance chances for a given attack's success based on achieving cascading effects.

However, an actor could utilize strategic information warfare attacks to wage a protracted war designed to undermine the will of an adversary. Such an approach might permit an actor with a more limited set of expertise and resources to strike targets of maximum vulnerability and pain as opportunity permitted. A strategic information warfare campaign conducted in this manner would be broadly analogous to the strategies of guerrilla warfare addressed in chapter 2. Highly developed hacking skills and expertise about information infrastructures and target sets might prove less important in such a campaign than an actor's ability to shield its attack capacity from retaliation so that it could continue some level of attacks even if their effects are not individually debilitating. Such an approach to strategic information warfare seems most suited to nonstate actors.

Tasking an offensive strategic information warfare organization to consider with multiple adversaries would also increase the human capital and technological expertise to engage in strategic information warfare by increasing the number of specific assessments of key centers of gravity and target sets that would have to be made. One approach might be to focus on developing generic capabilities to disrupt the most common information technologies used as the basis for information infrastructure development across a range of potential adversaries. Such an approach would be similar to fielding conventional strike or nuclear capabilities capable of penetrating most known types of defenses and inflicting damage against any potential adversary. However, the cyberspace operating environment for waging digital attacks will likely be much more specific to particular information infrastructures of the actors involved than the physical environment confronted by forces engaging in other types of strategic attack. Although geography, weather, and other factors vary considerably around the globe, aerospace forces are generally developed to operate in a wide range of environments. The more mutable and dynamic cyberspace environment may make the development of generic digital attack capabilities, independent of the ability to assess and target each adversary's centers of gravity, more difficult.

As part of the conventional wisdom that offensive strategic information warfare organizations will likely be small, many assessments also assume that acquiring the necessary human expertise to wage such warfare will prove relatively easy. This assumption relies on the notion of widespread availability of people with the requisite technological expertise to wage digital warfare. The President's Commission on Critical Infrastructure Protection highlights the significance of "the growth in the number of people having the technical skills necessary to launch such an attack" and that states seventeen million people possessed "cyber attack" skills in 1996.[64] These analyses assume that since the tools and techniques for digital warfare are widely available, finding people to use these tools presents no major barrier. Certain state and nonstate actors, however, would confront challenges in creating an adequate pool of expertise to conduct a strategic information warfare campaign. Many U.S. adversaries who might view strategic information warfare as a useful strategic option might be the same ones who lack easy access to the necessary human resources. Would states such as Cuba, North Korea and Libya be able to establish military and intelligence organizations with the necessary technological expertise to target and attack the complex infrastructures of a large, technologically advanced nation such as the United States? Similarly, could nonstate actors such as the IRA or a Latin American drug cartel recruit, train, and keep the required personnel for such an organization? For certain state actors, indigenously available human capital may be severely limited in numbers and technological sophistication. For nonstate actors willing to use such means, those personnel qualified to conduct such activities for a transnational criminal or terrorist organization might well perceive the risks involved as too grave to justify their participation.

Some analyses have also stressed that despite the lack of local expertise, actors with even moderate financial resources could create strategic information warfare capabilities because of the existence of a globally available pool of "hackers for hire." As Schwartau states, "[t]here are copious and willing populations worldwide from which to recruit assistance."[65] Recruited from the electronic underground, such digital mercenaries would have access to knowledge networks provided by World Wide Web sites, electronic bulletin boards, and hacker conferences. Even without formal recruitment and integration into a strategic information warfare capability, such independent operators could help explore, gather intelligence, and even create access to and conduct attacks against the information infrastructures of potential adversaries.[66]

Yet such conventional wisdom should be regarded with skepticism. One potential barrier to successful recruitment of "hackers for hire" would be that targets of potential strategic vulnerability generally lie outside the realm of the interest of the digital underground. The types of targets an actor may wish to target might be very different from those with which most members of the hacker community would be familiar. Understanding the vulnerabilities and significance of the SCADA systems of utility companies, for example may require the use of technological expertise developed specifically for the purpose of waging strategic information warfare, rather than the types of expertise most hackers would have.

Assuming appropriately qualified personnel could be identified, relying on digital mercenaries for tasks deemed vital to an actor's security poses significant challenges. Strategic theorists dealing with the relationship between political authority and use of military force dating back to Machiavelli and Clausewitz stress the risks involved in employing mercenaries. Numerous questions arise: How would attack planners ensure independent operators utilized secure means to communicate in trying to coordinate activities? If caught, what information would hired hackers divulge? How would an actor ensure that these hackers would not boast of their activities to others or even attempt to get hired by their adversary? Reliance on personnel outside the authority and disciplinary reach of the actor endeavoring to orchestrate an attack could create very significant trade-offs for maintaining desired levels of secrecy regarding strategic information warfare. Actors and organizations with experience in the tradecraft of clandestine operations might be best prepared to evaluate these trade-offs and conduct such sensitive operations.

The actual conduct of strategic information warfare operations would increase concerns involved in using outsiders. How could compliance with targeting and timing schemes be guaranteed? Could secure command and control channels be maintained once a campaign began and the adversary implemented active measures to respond to threats? How would limits on undesirable collateral damage and escalation be implemented? For any number of reasons, many actors might be very leery of taking the risks involved in using digital mercenaries to conduct strategic information warfare. Constraints on the use of hired hackers would vary depending on the strategic situation facing each particular actor. States might perceive very different risks from the potential use of such assets compared to nonstate actors. The type of campaign to be undertaken and objectives envisaged would also determine the usefulness of hired hackers. Campaigns involving tight timelines and highly orchestrated targeting would likely reduce incentives to involve outside actors or capabilities whose activities could only be loosely coordinated.

The challenges involved in establishing the necessary technological expertise in digital warfare might be mitigated for some actors by the similarity in
technological skills required for offensive and defensive strategic information
warfare tasks.[67] Organizations and individuals tasked with defensive missions
must track offensive warfare developments. With lower requirements for secrecy,
defensive strategic information warfare organizations could conduct much more
extensive outreach to stay at the technological cutting edge of digital attack tools
and techniques. Such defensive organizations might provide a conduit of
information and expertise to their own offensive organizations. This knowledge
sharing would be easier for state actors than nonstate actors given state actors'
more developed defensive strategic information warfare efforts. Such liaisons
between offensive and defensive organizations will not occur naturally. Strategic information warfare organizations will have to establish mechanisms to take
advantage of such synergies. It should also be noted that making offensive information warfare activities highly classified will likely constrain information sharing
between offensive and defensive organizations.

Assessments regarding offensive strategic information capabilities generally
ignore the requirement a breadth of skill sets for conducting such operations.
The section of the 1996 RAND study *Strategic Information Warfare* entitled "Low
Entry Costs" states that "[m]any advanced and interconnected networks can be
subjected to attack by a range of entities including skilled individuals; actors that
are not states, such as transnational criminal organizations; and states with a well-
trained cadre of "cyberspace warriors."[68] Most analyses of information warfare
solely address the rapid diffusion of the technological knowledge necessary for
attackers to access and disrupt systems and networks. Few analyze how organizations engaging in such attacks will access and train personnel to collate data
about adversary information infrastructures composition and vulnerabilities,
conduct broad assessments of the significance of these infrastructures and interconnections, and make the strategic judgments required to match estimates of
damage to political objectives.

Requisite skills for identifying digital centers of gravity will not come solely
from training and/or hiring computer scientists, electrical engineers, or members
of the hacker underground. The insights of individuals and organizations responsible for developing technologies, operating networks, and using information
infrastructures will prove useful for broader assessment and targeting tasks. Past
experience with assessing centers of gravity and conducting strategic warfare
operations may afford the best source of expertise for very delicate assessments

that combine military and political judgment. The nontechnical contributions of historians and social scientists may assist in formulating an understanding an how an adversary's political and military leadership and populace might react to different types of infrastructure disruptions and campaign strategies. Again, state actors with experience in orchestrating such large-scale intelligence and strategic warfare operations may have advantages over those who lack such experience if the proper lessons from the past can be drawn. Connections may exist between allied actors conducting similar activities and sharing information, but even these gains may prove highly constrained by the need for secrecy. Analysis of U.S. adversaries' ability to access the necessary human expertise for identifing centers of gravity to be targeted for attack must underlie any sophisticated threat assessments.

Learning Ability

Related to establishing required technological expertise is the need for organizations tasked with offensive information warfare to cope with the rapidly evolving technology involved in such warfare. The pace of change of targeted information infrastructures is also likely to vary widely depending on the adversary and its assessed centers of gravity. Unless critical components of those centers of gravity allow fairly static access and enable significant damage to be easily identified, the complexity of advanced information infrastructures will require offensive strategic information warfare organizations to have a high learning capacity.

The pace of change of targeted infrastructures may significantly influence the amount of technological sophistication and organization effort necessary to identify vulnerabilities and means of access and estimate the disruptive effect necessary to conduct strategic information warfare. Installation of new hardware components or software programs by the entity under attack might well negate any attempts by attackers to exploit vulnerabilities in targeted systems. If a targeted user organization changes network providers or patterns of infrastructure use, attackers must have the capacity to reassess the effectiveness of previously planned attack schemes. Previous efforts to wage war based on conventional bombing of aircraft factories and delivering nuclear weapons against key military and economic targets dealt with much more static target sets and technological tools for attacking them. When the characteristics of target sets changed, such as when German aircraft factories were moved underground in World War II, targeting for offensive strategic warfare became a much more laborious process.

The underlying technologies, the organizations providing network services, and the patterns of use of advanced information infrastructures are changing at a frenzied pace as we move into the new century. Those tasked with assessing the operation and critical features of complex information infrastructures may need significant education about and/or experience with the legacy technologies and networks in those infrastructures as well as the capability to understand the latest technologies implemented by network providers and infrastructure users. The few people who possess the necessary large-scale information networking and management experience to make such assessment are in great demand in the commercial sector. Actors contemplating strategic information warfare will have to provide significant incentives to acquire and sustain such sources of technological knowledge.

An offensive information warfare organization must also constantly adapt its capabilities to assess, target, and disrupt adversaries based on changes in the actor's own objectives and strategic situation. For state actors, the likely placement of offensive strategic information warfare efforts within military or intelligence organizations may impede their development of successful learning organizations, such as a willingness to challenge conventional wisdom, lack of hierarchy, and individual empowerment.

All actors may face social and cultural barriers to assimilation and learning within security institutions regarding the nature of technological tools used for strategic information warfare. For military establishments or terrorist organizations based on fostering a warrior ethic, does digital warfare constitute a viable means of waging "war"? Does the potential lack of direct violent effects undermine confidence in their efficiency? The constraints imposed by such considerations are intertwined with questions about the institutional environment and managerial will to undergo differing degrees of organizational change. Accessing and developing the requisite human capital and technological expertise and making the necessary organizational adjustments to establish offensive strategic information capabilities will likely prove a fundamental constraint for most actors.

Establishing Strategic Information Warfare Defensive Capabilities

As with offensive capabilities, all actors may have fairly easy access to specific embodied and codified technological knowledge relevant to conducting defensive information warfare. However, developing adequate human expertise and overcoming bureaucratic constraints may present significant barriers to establishing the requisite organizational capabilities. Additionally, for state actors such as the United States, defensive strategic information warfare will require establishing protective efforts in numerous organizations engaged in a wide range of activities across different sectors of society. The ability to diffuse available technological tools and knowledge about the nature of the threat, vulnerabilities, and available means of protection will likely prove much more critical for establishing adequate defensive capabilities than for offensive capabilities. A principal feature of efforts to establish adequate defensive efforts will be the actor's ability to orchestrate activities at multiple levels of concern depending on the type of actor involved. For this reason, I analyze state and nonstate actors separately with a decided emphasis on understanding challenges facing large, technologically advanced states such as the United States.

Challenges Faced by Nation-State Actors

Defensive efforts of national actors must consider activity conducted at three levels: individual organizations, sectors of activity, and the actor as a whole. The activities of individual organizations to protect their information resources by ensuring the confidentiality, integrity, and accessibility of their information infrastructures will form the foundation of any strategic defensive information warfare effort undertaken by most technological advanced states in the twenty-first century.

Radars, satellites, and other technological tools allow military establishments to gain substantial visibility with respect to threats from land, sea, air, or space attacks. Warning of attacks allows national authorities to assume responsibility for defense and fight for control over activity in these mediums. Unlike attacks in these arenas, however, the cyberspace environment itself is created and shaped in very large measure by the activities of organizations operating and using the medium. Technological tools to make activities in cyberspace transparent on a large scale are not available as we enter the twenty-first century. Military establishments cannot simply declare that a conflict has begun and exert direct control over cyberspace the way they may be able to do with respect to a war fought on land, on the sea, and in the air. Much of the effectiveness of a national defense against cyberattack may well be determined by efforts conducted at the organizational level to ensure that its ability to access and use cyberspace continues without unacceptable degradation.

Grouping organizations into sectors provides a helpful, but somewhat artificial, level for analyzing the available technological means and knowledge required to orchestrate defensive strategic information warfare. Sectoral groupings consist of organizations conducting similar activities, such as financial markets, air transportation, or fire protection services. The critical infrastructure protection efforts governed by Presidential Decision Directive 63 (discussed in detail in chapter 5) rely heavily on the sectoral approach. Although most sectors lack clearly defined boundaries (the national security sector possibly providing the most coherent example), the conduct of related activities by certain groupings of organizations may present both opportunities for attackers and challenges for defenders. Sectoral frameworks, moreover, are often used to delineate potential centers of gravity, such as provision of electric power, conduct of financial activity, or control of military operations. National efforts toward strategic information warfare defense could establish sectoral entities charged with specific missions and coordinating functions.

For nation-state actors, the aggregate challenge posed by strategic information warfare looms even larger. Nations must manage information infrastructure defenses across key sectors to protect centers of gravity to an acceptable degree. The level of complexity of this task will vary from actor to actor. Technologically advanced nation-states may have multiple sectors of activity whose reliance on information infrastructures and susceptibility to attack creates potential vulnerabilities. National governments may be best suited to address interconnections and dependencies between sectors. For example, discerning the scope and significance of the impact of power failures on the nation's information infrastructures may require a centralized assessment capability.[69] Alternatively, the evolution of information infrastructures and emerging technologies available for redundancy and self-protection may also allow substantial amounts of responsibility to devolve to individual organizations. The national government's fundamental roles include understanding the relative efficacy of different approaches, promulgating best practices, and deciding on the proper level of information infrastructure protection efforts and cost burden at several different levels: the national government, sectors, or organizations.

Certain defensive strategic information warfare concerns can be addressed only at the national level. Even if robust means for passive defenses become available, diverse organizations and sectors may perceive little need to defend against the types of highly sophisticated, large-scale digital attack capabilities possessed by some actors. For example, operators of oil refineries or electric power companies may be the first line of protection and recovery against attack of their facilities by physical sabotage. However, such organizations are not expected to protect themselves against airstrikes from other nations. Similarly, efforts to protect against the digital threat posed by individual hackers or criminal efforts may be undertaken by the organizations that own and operate the information infrastructures at risk for such attack. These same organizations, however, may not develop the capabilities or possess the legal responsibility and legitimacy to take necessary steps to protect against sophisticated, large-scale strategic information warfare attacks. As a result, if left to their own devices, important organizations and sectors of activity may have inadequate capacity to deal with offensive information warfare. Both individual organizations and the state itself may assume that protection against sophisticated attackers with political objectives remains the responsibility of the national government. Protection of nation-states against air and nuclear attacks has necessitated that military establishments develop warning and alerting systems, deploy active and passive defenses ranging from barrage balloons to ballistic missile interceptors, build protective bomb shelters, and orchestrate recovery efforts by emergency services. Protection against strategic digital attacks will likely also require nationally organized efforts to warn of attacks and protect crucial cyberspace-based assets and capabilities.

The complex interrelationships among technology producers, network providers, and infrastructure users involved in creating the cyberspace environment may demand governmental involvement to ensure adequate levels of protection. The activities of one organization may create significant defensive weakness in information systems, networks, and infrastructures relied upon by other organizations. These dependent organizations may have little leverage over those responsible for creating the problems. Technology producers may consistently underemphasize security in the operating systems or routers underpinning key information infrastructures, making the efforts of network providers and infrastructure users to assure adequate levels of security more difficult. Yet providers and users may have an inadequate understanding of security limitations or a limited ability to get producers to improve technology development processes. The inadequate protective efforts of one organization efforts may create vulnerabilities for a wide range of organizations hooked to this weak link of the chain through shared public networks. Such inadequacies in the protective efforts of organizations with which they are linked create "negative externalities" for organizations reliant on advanced information infrastructures to accomplish their objectives. As with pollution control, governments may perceive themselves as having a role in reducing such externalities in establishing defensive strategic information warfare capability. National standards for products or protective efforts by organizations involved in the creation and operation of information infrastructures of public concern may be required to accomplish this goal.

Political authorities may also continue to assert their prerogatives to regulate the possession and use of certain active defensive means, such as monitoring technologies or capabilities to backtrack and eliminate intruders conducting digital attacks. Nations will likely desire to determine the extent which they should authorize and aggregate employment of certain digital defense and response capabilities. The cost and/or availability of requisite technological expertise to develop advanced defensive capabilities may limit their availability. Employing some ostensibly defensive capabilities, such as network analyzers, may require conducting digital activity that can be misconstrued as constituting offensive preparations. Such ambiguity regarding intent may require governments to assert control by taking a role in regulating the possession and employment of certain defensive technological capabilities.

Individual Organizations and Strategic Information Warfare Defense

At the organizational level, establishing the technological capacity and organizational will to self-protect information infrastructure assets and activities adequately provides the principal defensive challenge. Instituting protection programs provides the focal point for most analysis of how organizations should endeavor to achieve good information security. Although programs would necessarily vary by specific organization, table 3.1 outlines commonly accepted features of a good information security program.[70] My discussions with the CERT Coordinating Center at the Software Engineering Institute, the Fidelity Investments Information Security Center, the Air Force Computer Emergency Response Team, and the Defense Information Systems Agency Automated Systems Security Incident Support Team (ASSIST) all indicated that protection efforts for large-scale information infrastructures involving activities across multiple organizations with substantial autonomy rely on a foundation at the level of organizations that operate and use the information systems and networks.

Despite widespread availability of technological tools and managerial expertise to establish effective organizational programs to protect information resources, the level of protective effort undertaken by each specific organization will vary depending on its degree of reliance and perceptions of the level of threat if faces from digital attacks. Individual organizations generally do not in themselves constitute a strategic center of gravity to a state actor, with a few possible exceptions. Examples of such potential exceptions in the United States

Table 3.1
Organizational-level measures for securing information infrastructures

1. Clear and consistent information security policies and practices
2. Valuation of the organization's information resources and activities
3. Vulnerability assessments to identify security weaknesses at separate operating locations
4. Prudent use of physical access controls, electronic firewalls, and other technical solutions
5. Risk assessments and implementation procedures to ensure protection of identified network/system security weaknesses
6. Mandatory and confidential reporting of attacks to help better identify and communicate vulnerabilities and necessary corrective actions
7. Damage assessments to reestablish the integrity of information resources when compromised by an attacker
8. Incident response capability to detect and track intruders and prosecute attackers
9. Awareness training to ensure that computer users understand the security risks associated with networked computers
10. Assurance that network managers and systems administrators have sufficient time and training to perform security functions

include specific organizations that possess information infrastructures so critical to national security or economic activity that their disruption would cause immediate national-level concern, such as Strategic Command's nuclear command and control systems or the New York Stock Exchange.

The U.S. defensive challenge from a strategic information warfare perspective is establishing visibility from the national level to detect the presence and evolution of significant strategic vulnerabilities in information infrastructures as well as widely disseminating information about best practices for information security programs. Influencing individual organizations to undertake protective efforts and establishing mechanisms to acquire and disseminate information regarding threats and proper responses will prove fundamental to the effectiveness of efforts to defend the nation's information infrastructure at a more aggregated level.

Sectors of Activity and Strategic Information Warfare Defense

At the sectoral level, organizations engaged in similar types of activity and use of information infrastructures can be grouped together. The aggregated sectors identified in chapter 1 as important for the United States included national security; vital human services; other government services; public utilities, transport, and health care; general commercial users; commercial technology producers; and commercial network operators. These sectors could be subdivided further in sectoral analysis into categories such as 911 systems, water resource providers, automobile manufacturing, and Internet service providers. The broader the sector, the wider the variation in the activities and role of information infrastructures among specific organizations within the sector. Despite wide variance within some sectors, the grouping of strategic defensive information warfare capabilities at the sectoral level can help to identify some common conditions that affect the vulnerability of a sector's organizations to digital attacks:

1. *General susceptibility to digital intrusion and disruption.* Susceptibility of systems in a given sector to digital attack will be determined by numerous factors. The degree of interconnection to open networks and outside organizations represents a major concern because of potential vulnerabilities such interconnections may create when external organizations fail to take adequate actions to protect their systems. Evaluation of susceptibility must also include how established security programs address the complexity, pace, and management of a sector's changing information infrastructure. The potential for disruption through cascading effects beginning in other infrastructures such as power or emergency services must also be analyzed.[71]

2. *Dependency on information infrastructures for conducting principal roles and missions.* Do redundant systems, networks, and data exist within the sector to perform essential functions if those based on digital processing and communications fail? Examples of redundancy include the presence of gyroscopic inertial navigation systems in aircraft to back up GPS systems, printed maps in the hands of military units in addition to digitized terrain displays, and paper slips documenting trades on the floor of a stock exchange to supplement electronic record keeping. Just as significantly, do the human skills necessary to use these nondigital tools exist? Can aircrews or troops in the field plot positions on a paper map and use sextants or compasses? Can stock market traders conduct business without computer spreadsheets and digitally transmitted news information? Do they periodically practice performing the requisite tasks in their jobs without the aid of the information infrastructures on which they normally rely?

3. *Concentration and standardization of key information infrastructure assets and activities.* The increasing computational power and automation capabilities provided by advanced information infrastructures has allowed a wide range of activities and supporting infrastructures, such as phone network providers and financial services, to consolidate information processing, signaling services, network monitoring, and emergency response in fewer

and fewer locations. Deregulation, corporate downsizing and increased competition also reinforce trends that might place stresses on the reliability of information infrastructures. For example, U.S. West, a major regional telecommunications company, consolidated its network monitoring operations from over fifty separate operating locations in 1984 to two in 1996.[72] Another important consideration involves the degree to which the growing use of common digital control systems and information transmission channels throughout key infrastructures creates common vulnerabilities. A 1997 MITRE Corporation study of the vulnerability of the electric power industry to digital attack indicated that although most providers use proprietary electronic control systems and operator-owned, redundant communications channels, the industry trend toward using common SCADA systems and the Internet for most communications would increase future vulnerability.[73] Consolidation and standardization could potentially simplify tasks for both attackers and defenders by limiting the number of key targets and systems to be assessed, attacked and protected.

4. Capacity for emergency recovery and reconstitution. Generic experience with emergency situations may improve a sector's ability to recover from information infrastructure disruptions. Other relevant efforts would include specific recovery plans to reconstitute necessary information resources and infrastructures, access to specialized response capabilities such as computer emergency and incident response teams, conduct of exercises, and efforts to learn from past experiences with information infrastructure disruption. Certain sectors of activity may place greater emphasis than others on emergency operations and disaster recovery. Lessons provided by efforts to deal with Year 2000 problems are dealt with in the epilogue to this book.

5. Importance of service reliability and assurance of the security of information infrastructures in evaluation of organizational performance. Differences between sectors in which the principal concern is economic competition and those providing emergency services may result in different incentives for assuring reliability of information infrastructures in the two types of sectors. The proclivity to allocate resources to create security and redundancy will vary from sector to sector depending on how organizations in the sector are allocated resources for establishing and protecting information infrastructures. Even within the U.S. national security establishment, the requirement to establish ever greater processing and communications capacity at lower costs drives military organizations to increase their reliance on information systems and networks operated by civilian contractors. A major question for the future success of U.S. defensive efforts is how concerns about digital attacks and the activities of organizations such as the National Infrastructure Protection Center affect how sectors prioritize assurance of security in the creation and use of information infrastructures.

For state actors, analysis of different sectors can provide an understanding of the overall level of vulnerability within the state and assist in managing incentives offered to sectors to improve their capacity to protect significant information infrastructure–dependent activity. Orchestrating such efforts will likely prove difficult since sectors do not constitute discrete entities. However, organizations exist to help diffuse knowledge of technological tools and best practices for information infrastructure protection setup along sectoral lines, including industry and trade associations, research consortia, and standard-setting groups. Examples of such organizations that deal with standard setting in areas of widespread public concern are the National American Electric Reliability Council and the National Fire Protection Agency. Additionally, government agencies often are formed along sectoral lines to help achieve some level of visibility and influence over private organizations conducting activities deemed important to the public interest. For example, the National Security Telecommunications Advisory Committee (NSTAC) was established in 1982 to provide a mechanism for ensuring adequate provision of national security and emergency preparedness communications in the impending breakup of AT&T. The Federal Communications Commission established a Network Reliability Council (NRC) in 1992 in the wake of major telephone provider problems in the previous two years. (The role and activities of the NSTAC and NRC will be addressed in more depth in chapter 5.) Such regulatory agencies and other public institutions provide the United States with an institutional starting point for establishing defensive strategic information warfare efforts at the sector level. However, the existence of agencies at multiple levels of federal, state, and local government with overlapping realms of responsibility can also create confusion, limit coordination, and cause conflict.

Strategic Information Warfare Defense at the Nation-State Level

Although efforts at the organizational and sectoral levels of activity provide important contributions, the national government is responsible for the overall effectiveness of a nation-state's defensive strategic information warfare efforts. During World War II, commercial companies and city governments played crucial roles in providing air raid shelters, fighting fires, manning anti-aircraft artillery, and reestablishing productive activity in the face of air attacks. However, the national government determined how the overall defensive effort affected the ability of the nation to continue the conflict and achieve its political objectives. The same would hold true for national strategic information warfare defense. Successful orchestration of this task implies the capability to understand and monitor organizations and motivate them to play an active role in defending the important information infrastructure–reliant sectors of society against digital attack and to undertake active measures to limit damage, reconstitute capabilities, and identify aggressors when a digital attack has been experienced. The state may also need to create additional capabilities and organizations to fulfill roles and missions present only at the national level.

In attempting to establish strategic information warfare defense capabilities, national governments create a public good by securing from outside disruption information infrastructures relied upon by the entire society. Essentially, the task is the same as any other national security effort to defend against outside attack. Additional government roles in defensive strategic information warfare arise from the requirement to manage how key organizations and sectors that develop information technologies, provide networks, and use information infrastructures conduct their efforts to protect those technologies, networks, and infrastructures. The differences resulting from the role of commercial development of the technologies involved in the cyberspace operating environment may require very different approaches to organizing defensive strategic information warfare compared to other strategic defense efforts to defeat land, air and sea forces. The cyberspace environment requires a national government to face the policymaking challenge of establishing more visibility into the protective practices and activities of non–national security organizations during peacetime and conflicts to accomplish the defensive strategic information warfare mission. Additionally, national security organizations tasked with coordinating efforts of outside sectors to deal with large-scale digital attacks must understand the different technologies used by each of these sectors and establish the required expertise to assess, protect, and recover multiple connected infrastructures.

Facilitating Factors and Nation-State Efforts at Strategic Information Warfare Defense

Establishing effective defensive strategic information warfare efforts will be influenced by the presence of the five facilitating factors for organizational capability developed earlier in the chapter: supportive institutional environment, demand-pull motivation, management initiative, technological expertise, and learning ability. The remainder of this section analyzes the potential degree of influence each of these factors will have on defensive strategic information warfare efforts. My analysis focuses on the United States but endeavors to develop principles in a manner applicable to the broader range of state actors.

Supportive Institutional Environment

Depending on the level of central control a national government asserts, establishing the context for proactive civilian efforts to adopt, assimilate, and diffuse available technology to develop robust, protected information infrastructures may provide the critical first step in establishing strategic information warfare defenses. A spectrum of approaches a central government might employ in accomplishing this task is sketched below, and each approach is discussed in turn:

Own/Operate↔Heavy Regulation↔Coordinate/Assist↔Laissez-Faire

Own/Operate The own/operate approach sits at one end of the spectrum in terms of government involvement in the creation, operation, and protection of information infrastructures. Government-owned telecommunications and information networks systems would operate in close coordination with national security and intelligence agencies. The national government would develop or select appropriate underlying hardware and software technologies for large-scale networks and infrastructures. International connections would be closely managed and could be subject to legally sanctioned widespread monitoring by law enforcement, intelligence agencies, or both. Trade-offs of this approach would include a reduction in information infrastructures' ability to adopt and assimilate the most advanced technologies available. The costs of such non-market-driven information technologies and services would be pushed upward, reducing commercial competitiveness and the pace of economic development. The own/operate approach could also entail severe intrusions into civil liberties such as privacy and free speech. The use of information infrastructures by individuals and organizations could become closely controlled, as it currently is in places like Iran, Singapore, and China. Technologically advanced nations such as France and Japan currently maintain extensive government ownership and control over a wide range of information infrastructure technology implementation and network services. Even in the United States, such a level of government control is not unheard of: The U.S. government nationalized AT&T in World War I to assure control over its operations.

Heavy Regulation Short of direct ownership, national governments could attempt to exert rigorous control over technology development and network service provision through laws and regulatory agencies. Such mechanisms could require strict government control over technologies used in public information infrastructures to ensure adequate security and reliability features as well as the access of governments to monitor activity on information infrastructures. Regulatory agencies would ensure that public needs were met and operators were properly compensated. International connections between telecommunications systems would be the subject of close scrutiny and strict agreement between governments through formal mechanisms such as the International Telegraph Union. The environment in the United States through at least the 1970s could be accurately described as one of heavy regulation, and the government post, telephone, and telegraph monopolies in much of the rest of the world even today could also be so characterized. Until the 1960s, Federal Communication Commission (FCC) regulations allowed AT&T to prohibit the attachment of technologies deemed not to meet AT&T's reliability and security standards to the U.S. public long-distance telephone networks.[74] Significant restrictions on the domestic use and export of encryption technologies were in force in the United States throughout the 1990s. Again, significant trade-offs would occur as a result of a heavy regulation approach, such as reduction in incentives for commercial technology development and implementation, intrusion into civil liberties, and costs passed on to taxpayers and information infrastructure users.

Coordinate/Assist   A coordinate/assist approach would favor commercial implementation and widespread use of information infrastructures with the government maintaining a more limited role in providing assurances of reliability and security. Information infrastructures would be based on architectures that permitted any technology, network, or service provider to hook up to public networks on the basis of open standards. The commercial sector would lead standard-setting activities. Rather than establishing defensive strategic information warfare capabilities based on direct control of the cyberspace environment and operating organizations, the national government would foster attention to such concerns on the part of technology producers, network providers and infrastructure users. Regulatory agencies would focus on ensuring fair commercial competition as well as providing incentive mechanisms to encourage sectors to properly protect privately owned and operated information infrastructures. The government would deemphasize nationally based criteria for ownership and activity. Free trade in information and telecommunications products and services would be encouraged, pursued through international institutions such as the World Trade Organization. The government might endeavor to influence technology trajectories relevant to defensive strategic information warfare by concentrating its R&D efforts in noncommercial areas and encouraging technology sharing and best practices. The coordinate/assist approach is exemplified by the federal government's decision to break up AT&T in the 1980s and the Clinton administration's National/Global Information Infrastructure and Electronic Commerce initiatives as well as congressional efforts to encourage a free-market environment through the Telecommunication Act of 1996. The risks involved in taking such an approach involve greatly reduced control over technological and organizational foundations of information infrastructures. Consequences of the approach may include the consolidation of ownership of key information infrastructure activity and centralization of facilities, technologies, and personnel for control and management of information infrastructures. Increased openness, interconnection, and interoperability within these infrastructures could increase the degree of potential vulnerability posed by an attacker's identification of a few key weaknesses. National-level authorities would have a reduced capacity to assess centers of gravity and vulnerabilities because of the reduced transparency into activities of infrastructure operators. However, the more rapid change and technological diversity possible under such an approach might also create intelligence and targeting challenges for potential adversaries in orchestrating strategic information attacks.

Laissez-Faire   In a laissez-faire approach, market incentives for commercial competitiveness and privacy desires of individuals would drive the development and deployment of technologies and mechanisms to protect information infrastructures without direct government involvement. Such an approach would rely on a proliferation of commercial technologies and providers to create robust information infrastructures based on infrastructure diversity and redundancy. The government might encourage limited legal mechanisms in the realm of liability and insurance to provide incentives for assurance of information system and network performance. The weaknesses of such an approach would include little to no visibility at a central level regarding indications of strategic information warfare threats to key infrastructures and an inability on the part of the national government to discern whether adequate protective steps had been taken to protect crucial information infrastructures. The government would have little ability to assure national security and public stakeholders that it had control over vulnerable centers of gravity and responsible organizations. Historically, national governments place such high importance on the relationship between information infrastructures and the public good that very few have adopted a strict laissez-faire approach.

Nation-State Selection of Defensive Strategic Information Approaches

The spectrum of regulatory approaches outlined above creates broad distinctions between mixtures of various institutional arrangements affecting a nation-state's overall defensive strategic information warfare effort. Generally as one moves to one end of the spectrum, responsibility for decisions and implementation of defensive measures devolve to the organizational level. Movement to the other end implies a greater degree of national government control and access to information about the overall level of vulnerability. The approaches outlined here do not have clear boundaries. The institutions and policies of the United States or other states might involve aspects of more than one approach outlined above.

As with offensive strategic information warfare, certain political institutions and legal edicts may place fairly strong constraints on national government choices in developing organizational capabilities for strategic defense. A governmental system with decentralized political and legal authority for governing key information infrastructure activities could complicate efforts to establish coherent national policies. In the United States, the legal and regulatory powers of state governments mean their activities and decisions may play an important role in orchestrating national strategic information warfare defensive efforts.[75] Moreover, involvement of multiple federal governmental organizations concerned with assessing threats, promoting commercial infrastructure development, and ensuring the public's privacy and service interests could also create coordination challenges for defensive strategic information warfare efforts. Chapter 5 analyzes the specifics of the U.S. case.

Under any of the approaches outlined above, a national government might reserve for itself the role of establishing organizations that employ active defenses against strategic information attacks. However, such national government organizations would have limited effectiveness if nongovernmental information infrastructures were under attack and such defensive organizations had an inadequate understanding of those infrastructures and the threat posed. Alternatively, such active defenses could be set up independent of the traditional military at organizational or sectoral levels to take advantage of more precise knowledge of infrastructures of concern. However, employment of tools and techniques for aggressive response and punishment of actions at the level of strategic information warfare could still require governmental involvement or at least authorization. Command and control of decentralized active strategic information warfare defenses would constitute a key concern.

Furthermore, as a nation moves along the spectrum from peace to crisis to war, the roles of defense institutions and their legal authority to act may require exertion of increased levels of central control. Arrangements similar to those that enable the reserve mobilization of personnel from the National Guard or aircraft from the Civilian Reserve Aircraft Fleet might provide surge or reconstitution capacity for information infrastructures in the case of national emergency.[76] National governments could institute legal requirements to report specific types of information concerning digital attacks to central authorities and to implement directed protective measures as a crisis or conflict evolved. If a government chooses an emphasis on central control and management, the activities and information infrastructures of responsible organizations would present adversaries with a key target for insider corruption and outside disruption.

Governments would also have choices under any of the approaches discussed regarding the establishment of international cooperation and institutions to deal with threats. Legal mechanisms such as treaties and arms control regimes could be pursued to help identify and prosecute sources of digital attacks. International institutions might also play roles in defining whether a given act constituted international aggression or in providing the law enforcement coordination required to track down perpetrators across national boundaries.

Demand-Pull Motivation

Numerous mechanisms might be employed to structuring incentives offered to different organizations and sectors to encourage them to protect their information infrastructures. The use of demand-pull mechanisms to establish defensive strategic information warfare capability would involve addressing all three types of information infrastructure activities: technology producers, network providers, and infrastructure users.

Demand-pull factors relevant to defending information infrastructures can result from laws, regulations, public-private cooperation, and private-sector initiatives. Such mechanisms, though closely related to the influence of the institutional context described above, focus more closely on specific means for influencing sectoral and organizational incentives rather than choices among broad alternatives regarding the role of government. Any specific mechanism might be applied within any of the broad governmental approaches described above. The following list details a range of mechanisms for enhancing the demand-pull on various organizations and sectors for establishing information infrastructure protection in the United States:[77]

• Establish legal liability and insurance. Organizations could be held legally accountable for outside losses sustained because they failed to make responsible efforts to protect information resources and service relied upon by others. Financial or criminal penalties could be imposed. Development of an insurance market covering internal and external losses due to information system and network failures might also help. Such a market could discount the rates of those who implemented proper information security and reliability efforts. The government could assist in the formation of this insurance market by providing financial backing, especially to deal with high-risk pools of key concern.

• Target tax breaks and subsidies for private-sector organizations participating in government programs and/or deemed to meet performance standards to protect designated information infrastructures.

• Support research and development for and assist in diffusing technologies and procedures related to information infrastructure defense. Such activity could include R&D efforts within the government, joint activities with commercial-sector technology producers and network providers, and use by government of commercially developed information security tools and techniques.

• Raise consciousness and educate producers, providers, and users about the types and technological sophistication of potential threats to their activities involving key information infrastructures. Such awareness efforts could occur through legislative and regulatory hearings or by establishing organizations, such as the Software Engineering Institute, to collect and share information. Other activities could involve simulations and exercises involving the technologies, operation, and use of key information infrastructures to identify vulnerabilities, catalogue attack profiles, and test defensive reactions, tools, and techniques.

• Create testing and validation processes for the technology products and network architectures that make up key information infrastructures. Such processes could be provided as a service or mandated as a requirement for certain organizations or sectors of activity. These operations could be run by the government or be established in the private sector like independent audit and accounting firms.

• Create security standards for technology products, network services, and use of information infrastructures. Again, standards could be developed inside or outside the government.

• Ensure provision of redundant capabilities by networks providers and infrastructure users. Redundancy could include backup operating systems and sites, multiple network access or coverage provisions, and data protection. Such capabilities are normally addressed as part of disaster recovery planning. Protective efforts could include designing and implementing technologies with operating characteristics and capabilities reserved for use in a crisis or conflict. Establishing defensive strategic information warfare capabilities would require that orchestrated digital attacks be actively considered in information infrastructure design and implementation plans.

• Establish restoration programs for key infrastructures. If sectors and organizations are attacked, recovery assistance could take the form of direct financial aid or augmentation by personnel and technical assistance through mechanisms such as FEMA or the National Guard.[78] Such agencies could also provide standby telecommunications and other information infrastructure capacity in the case of an emergency, although the utility of such support may be limited by the degree of specific knowledge required. Assistance to individual organizations might be made provisional based on fees or participation in more proactive programs designed to improve strategic information warfare defenses.

Most of the mechanisms outlined above raise crucial questions regarding the degree of governmental intrusiveness and scope of activity. To what degree would participation be mandatory or voluntary by organizations involved in different sectors and types of activities related to information infrastructures? If mandatory, what agencies would be responsible for developing regulations, setting or choosing standards, and ensuring compliance? What penalties would violations invoke? If voluntary, could the government increase levels of participation by enhancing the ease and speed of the processes involved? If activities involve information sharing, how could proprietary information and commercial reputations be protected? How would participants be screened to ensure that information regarding vulnerabilities and defenses is not passed to potential attackers? Whether the programs were mandatory or voluntary, how would such activities be funded? Mechanisms would have to be established to distribute costs of defensive efforts among the government and taxpayers, the resources and shareholders of commercial firms, and consumers of products and ratepayers for services as well. The broader considerations outlined above under institutional context would play a crucial role in such determinations.

Depending on the willingness of organizations with significant information infrastructures to contribute to strategic information warfare defenses, the level of national government involvement may vary by sector. Network providers may invest more in providing service assurance than technology producers more concerned about short product life cycles and establishing market share. Emergency services organizations, such as law enforcement agencies and providers of 911 services, with high levels of public visibility may prove more willing to exchange information about digital vulnerabilities and past attacks than financial institutions worried about their reputation as reliable places for investment. As a result, governments may require flexibility in managing incentive mechanisms and establishing a degree of intrusiveness that matches the differing sectors and activities of concern.

Above the organizational and sectoral levels, the presence of demand-pull incentives will also affect the motivations of different state actors to establish the organizational technological capacity for defensive strategic information warfare. Technologically advanced states like the United States with increasingly open information infrastructures may feel the largest demand-pull because of their high levels of reliance on those infrastructures and their high levels of vulnerability. In the absence of clearly demonstrated offensive information warfare capabilities, on the part of adversaries, however, many actors may find it difficult to justify allocating scarce resources to strategic information warfare defenses. Additionally, concerns regarding diminished economic opportunities and civil liberties may severely constrain the ability of political authorities within the most technologically advanced societies to take strong steps to establish strategic information warfare defenses.

Managerial Initiative

Most analyses highlight the presence of committed leadership as essential in addressing the protection of information systems, networks, and infrastructures. In his comprehensive approach to organizational information protection, Fredrick Cohen notes that "[t]he two most critical functions of protection management are in budgeting and leadership."[79] For defensive strategic information warfare capabilities, such commitment would ideally occur at all levels: organizational, sectoral, and national. At the organizational level, management faces tough trade-offs in determing whether to devote scarce financial and organizational resources to protect information resources not threatened on a daily basis by a strategic information warfare attack. Among technology producers and network providers, the central competitive drive to speed new products and services to market to expand customer and revenue bases may reduce the amount of attention paid to adequate protection of information systems and networks. Such trade-offs require decisions at the highest levels of organizations, not just directives and memorandums from subunits tasked with information security and protection.

Sectoral groupings established for purposes of analysis lack centralized management per se, but government regulators and industry and trade associations may play a central role in establishing protective efforts in the various sectors. In commercial sectors, industry associations or regulating agencies may have to deal with organizations possessing differing perspectives on the importance of secure information infrastructures for the success of their activities or business strategy. In governmental sectors, lack of available personnel or funding may impede defensive efforts. The senior leadership of organizations involved in sectoral management may resist aggressively taking on new issues such as analyzing information infrastructure dependency and vulnerability to digital attack due to perceived cost involved in addressing these complex chellenges. The willingness of regulators and associations to exert pressure on sectors and organizations to provide protection of their information infrastructures may prove crucial in establishing an aggregated strategic information warfare defense.

At the national level, leadership will be necessary to sort out authority relationships between numerous legislative and executive committees, departments, and agencies with potential roles in information infrastructure protection. Instituting policies and developing organizations to implement the incentive mechanisms outlined above will require that political leaders make decisions about requirements for national-level defensive strategic information warfare efforts, assign responsibilities for carrying out those efforts, and establish coordination of the efforts among public and private stakeholders. Governmental initiatives to promote increased reliance on open information infrastructures for commercial gain and social services must be reconciled with calls for increased protection of critical information infrastructures. Establishing a coherent institutional context and orchestrating cost-effective strategic information defenses requires involvement from the highest levels of government.

Many defensive strategic information warfare efforts will not involve the transformational organizational change required by offensive efforts. Defensive efforts at lower levels will seek to enhance an organization's ability to perform an existing mission rather than create new roles. Power companies, airlines, and mutual fund brokers will continue to seek to provide the same basic services while offering customers a greater level of assurance that their underlying information infrastructures are reliable and secure. As such, the task at these levels may principally involve raising awareness and ensuring management attention, proper training, and financial support. Numerous mechanisms are available for developing incentives to motivate leaders in organizations and sectors where protection efforts are deemed crucial. National-level strategic information warfare defenses may establish a strong foundation without instituting wrenching changes to preexisting organizational missions and structures. Creating a U.S. national-level coordinating authority to oversee an effort geared at strategic information warfare defense, however, would constitute a major new national security mission requiring the government to play new roles and possibly affecting the roles and missions of many established organizations.

Technological Expertise

Varying degrees of human capital will be required at the organizational, sectoral, and national levels to establish necessary technological expertise for strategic information warfare defense. To the extent that individual organizations take up protection of their information infrastructures, technological expertise will be necessary at the organizational level to understand the information resources involved as well as to choose and implement protective measures. Some measures may be fairly simple to institute, such as requiring use of passwords or access controls and virus checkers and providing authority to systems administrators to debug hardware and software problems. In large organizations with substantial information technology resources and networks, such as financial institutions or military establishments, defensive efforts may need to employ much more technologically sophisticated means, including real-time network monitoring, red-team exercises involving simulated attacks, and emergency response capabilities as well. All organizations whose important information resources can be accessed and disrupted by insiders will also require expertise to develop and execute personnel security programs.

Industry associations and regulatory agencies operating at the sectoral level may provide a significant locus for establishing the necessary expertise for protecting information infrastructures at that level. Such entities could develop human expertise to analyze and evaluate technological tools for protecting similar information resources, systems, and networks used within a sector of activity. Industry associations might sponsor training programs to enhance the awareness and skills of systems administrators providing the first line of defense at the organizational level.

A major challenge for the United States in establishing national-level defensive efforts will be obtaining sufficient expertise to adequately understand the national information infrastructure. Organizations responsible for national-level defensive efforts will have to understand the significance of infrastructure vulnerabilities across a very wide range of potentially important activities and establish the metrics that will be used to describe and monitor the adequacy of the operation and protection of these infrastructures. Coordinating organizations may require the authority to exert increasingly higher levels of control over various information infrastructures as conflicts emerge and evolve. Personnel in an organization assigned to passive defense missions will require both technological expertise and sufficient knowledge in specific functional areas such as finance, transportation, and power to assess the trade-offs involved in ensuring adequate levels of robustness for the information infrastructure, if attacked. National defensive efforts must involve personnel security expertise and coordination with organizations involved in counterintelligence efforts against insider threats. The legal implications of broadening counterintelligence efforts to include information infrastructure protection in a democratic society such as the United States will also require close attention.[80] Those responsible for providing active defenses will need high levels of specific technological knowledge to understand digital monitoring and intrusion techniques attackers might employ. As with all the other challenges noted, the organization must ensure that its expertise stays up to date as new technologies are installed throughout the information infrastructure and new users emerge to take advantage of the ever changing systems and networks.

Defensive strategic information efforts, like those involved in offensive strategic information warfare, require a pool of human capital with advanced technological skills to assess and protect large-scale infrastructures in the twenty-first century. This pool has a limited number of potential members, as described in chapter 1. Systems administrators, computer programmers, and network engineers are in great demand within all technologically advanced societies as commercial enterprises and governmental agencies try to leverage a deluge of new information technologies for competitive advantage and to improve efficiency. Committing available personnel resources to establish technological expertise to conduct defensive tasks reduces the available personnel resources for accomplishing primary organizational missions. The competition for technologically sophisticated individuals also means that trained personnel may have the ability to quickly find new sources of employment. Organizations with constraints on providing adequate compensation and career opportunities may have difficulty hiring and keeping personnel for long periods.

However, organizations responsible for national strategic information warfare defense will likely have more opportunity to share technological knowledge with outside organizations than those involved with strategic information warfare offense, because of the greater security concerns of the latter. One of the most effective strategies for these defensive organizations may be to form government-industry networks and consortia for sharing information regarding the nature of information warfare threats and technologies for defeating these threats. Such networks would allow multiple organizations to cooperate in assimilating and diffusing the best defensive technological tools and practices. To the extent that such technological knowledge could be codified in software that could be rapidly transferred from organization to organization and infrastructure to infrastructure, defensive technologies may be able to diffuse more quickly. Such cooperative activity could also be orchestrated at an international level. However, limits to such cooperative activities may arise because of commercial competition or the lack of resources and incentives to participate in programs sponsored by regulatory agencies.

Technologically advanced states with substantial security and economic interests in common may wish to cooperate in sharing assessment, protection, and response tools and tactics necessary for the conduct of strategic information warfare defense against other actors of mutual concern. The United States has endeavored to share the burden of efforts to develop active defenses against the increased threat posed by ballistic missiles through shared technology development and other shared efforts with its allies. Cooperative defensive strategic information warfare efforts may be limited, however, by concerns with economic competitiveness and the inherently dual-use nature of technologies involved with digital attacks. Would the United States share vulnerability information and protection expertise with France or Israel, for example, if those nations were also suspected of using digital means to commit economic espionage against U.S. firms? U.S. and European firms such as IBM, Lucent Technologies, and Alcatel have begun to invest in joint ventures to upgrade Russian information infrastructures.[81] Should firms such as IBM be able to employ the latest in information systems protection technology, especially if such technology is also begin used by the U.S. government? Would using such technology better protect investment of predominately U.S.–owned corporations or would such use stand to improve the strategic information warfare capabilities of another major power? By employing Lucent Technologies systems in joint ventures, might the Russian government come to better understand the digital weakness of these systems? As with dual-use nuclear technologies, concerns would emerge about sharing certain technologies with allied or friendly nations if such sharing might result in transfers to third parties considered to be U.S. adversaries.

Questions will arise regarding the desirability of centralizing (within the national-level government) tasks requiring sophisticated technological skills.

Given the limited availability of personnel with such skills, organizations must choose the proper level at which to conduct technologically difficult defensive tasks such as network monitoring and attack assessment. Although systems operators located within individual organizations may be closest to the day-to-day operations of information infrastructures, government leaders must decide whether the technological tools and skills necessary to detect and react to sophisticated digital attacks can be widely diffused and still be effective. If monitoring and response functions are more centralized, on the other hand, can the necessary understanding of specific technologies deployed, localized operating procedures, and value of information resources to operational missions at lower levels be established at a higher level? Does the globalization of information infrastructure technology production and operation require efforts with international participation? Without such efforts, can the products of transnational corporations such as Intel processors and Electronic Data Systems databases be secured? Similarly, will digital attackers simply seek to reside in places with the least ability and willingness to detect and prohibit malicious use of global connections provided by advanced information infrastructures? The establishment of computer emergency response and assistance teams at different levels of activity within the United States and other countries illustrate one approach to dealing with the dilemma of using concentrated technological expertise to deal with protection and response needs throughout information infrastructures with widely distributed vulnerabilities.[82]

Learning Capacity

The need to monitor and assess the evolution of changing information infrastructures over time provides a principal challenge for defensive strategic information warfare efforts. This challenge will occur across the range of levels of activity—organizational, sectoral, and national. Currency of vulnerability and risk assessments, deployment of monitoring and countermeasures technologies, and even strategic choices about the proper level at which to focus defensive efforts will deteriorate over time as the technological base, network architectures, and organizational uses and players evolve. As we enter the twenty-first century, major technological changes, such as the emergence of satellite broadcast and wireless Internet connections, are rapidly shifting the relative importance of the various organizations providing the most significant information technologies and network services. The scramble to provide global services creates a jumble of corporate alliances and joint ventures rapidly formed and just as rapidly disbanded by both governments and corporations. Sectors of activity of fundamental importance to technologically advanced societies, such as health care and biotechnology, may prove sufficiently information infrastructure reliant as to constitute wholly new centers of gravity for adversaries wishing to conduct strategic information warfare. Coordinating procedures for protecting information infrastructures among organizations, within sectors, and between actors will require an ability to adapt quickly to the presence of new technologies and players. Information-sharing arrangements and R&D and technology consortia will have to be flexible enough to allow new entrants and adapt their focus to unexpected technological developments.

Organizations responsible for coordinating national-level defensive strategic information warfare efforts will also need to adapt over time to technological change. The role and activities of the FCC have evolved with new technologies and new conceptions of how to improve societal benefits from telecommunications. The breakup of AT&T resulted in the formation of NSTAC. Will the growth of Internet-based means of providing necessary information infrastructures to the wide range of activities crucial to society require a greater level of government involvement in the deployment of technology and overall management of its operations to ensure security and access? Such an evolution in the roles of national coordinating authorities will require the involvement and education of new organizations and stakeholders. Possibly even more difficult will be reducing or even eliminating the role of fading or ineffective players. Depending on the actors involved, political processes and bureaucratic politics will likely slow the ability of organizations orchestrating strategic information warfare defense at the national level to adapt their form and processes.

In total, the establishment of the organizational technological capacity to mount strategic defensive warfare efforts by state actors faces major challenges that depend on the scope, complexity, and organizational control of the defended infrastructures. Wide variations will obtain across specific nation-states. The particular challenges and efforts involved for the United States in establishing such a capability are addressed in chapter 5.

Nonstate Actors and Defensive Information Warfare

As alluded to earlier, the challenges facing nonstate actors in establishing defensive information warfare efforts may be very different from those faced by state actors. This section briefly addresses the likely paths of divergence.

The principal difference springs from the scope of responsibility for the actor's defensive strategic information warfare program. Unlike state actors involved in strategic information warfare, nonstate actors could limit their defensive efforts to their own organizational information infrastructure with little concern for the diverse range of sectors and activities constituting a state's information infrastructure. Nonstate actors can use access to open, public networks to conduct their activities, eliminating much of the need to engage in defensive activities. To a much greater extent than state actors, nonstate actors can manage the scope of their vulnerability to digital attack and required protection efforts. Nonstate actors such as the Zapatistas or Greenpeace that rely on information infrastructures as a means to coordinate activities, widely disseminate information, and conduct outreach efforts may have to deal with protecting these functions from disruption. For nonstate actors, increasing degrees of reliance on information systems and networks for a wide range of activities creates trade-offs similar to those facing states in weighing security benefits against those of efficiency and achieving coordination. However, nonstate actors may have much more flexibility than state actors to consciously limit their reliance on information infrastructures for nonstrategic information warfare uses and may be able to establish only very small, tightly controlled organizations vulnerable to digital attack. A terrorist organization choosing to develop offensive strategic information warfare capabilities may have little need to conduct additional information infrastructure-reliant activity. The challenges of assessing vulnerability, instituting protection, and evaluating emerging defensive concerns for an organization that makes such a focused use of information infrastructures would be much less than those facing technologically advanced states protecting all sectors of society. The requirements for organizational technological capacity for defensive efforts in such organizations could in fact prove very limited.

Factors that facilitate the establishment of organizational technological capacity for defensive missions may also weigh in very differently for nonstate actors than for state actors. The challenges of establishing managerial initiative and demand-pull motivation within a small organization may prove to be easily met. Cultural and social barriers to effectively establishing organizational technological capacity, however, may prove more significant. Accessing technologically proficient personnel may remain an important challenge depending on the operating locales, membership criteria, and risks posed by involvement with a given actor. The wide variation in the objectives and activities of nonstate actors makes broad generalizations about the specific challenges involved in establishing organizational capacity in such actors for defensive strategic information warfare beyond the scope of the analysis pursued here.

The Fundamental Role of Organizational
Technological Capability

Others have lavished much attention on the impact of technology on warfare. At least in the United States, however, the challenges involved in establishing organizational technological capacity for improving the use of military power have only been partially recognized. Thinking about technology adoption and assimilation for commercial advantage and improving national economic performance has been developed more fully. The time has come for those concerned within the national security establishment to seek outside lessons regarding the establishment of such technological capacity. Increasingly in today's environment, governments and their military organizations have little control over the development or diffusion of information technologies. Nonstate actors have been empowered by the spread of these technologies. The lessons learned by various organizations can be used to understand the conditions that allow the effective adoption, assimilation, and diffusion of information technology. This chapter identified five facilitating factors—supportive institutional environment, demand-pull motivation, managerial initiative, technological expertise, and learning ability—that are central to establishing organizational technological capacity.

Actors attempting to compete in the international security arena using information technology to conduct a new type of strategic warfare will face significant challenges in establishing organizational technological capacity similar to those confronting strategic air and nuclear warfare. Potential difficulties face organizations responsible for both offensive and defensive missions. The chapter outlined how the facilitating factors for establishing organizational technological capacity would affect these missions. As with analysis of the strategic factors driving the emergence of strategic information warfare concerns addressed in chapter 2, the nature of the actor and its objectives have a significant effect on the establishment of requisite organizational technological capability. Coming to grips with these challenges may well prove the most significant factor in determining which actors successfully pursue this new strategic warfare option.

Suggested Additional Sources

Carl J. Dahlman and Larry E. Westphal. "The Meaning of Technological Mastery in Relation to Transfer of Technology." In *Technology Transfer: New Issues, New Analysis.* Ed. Allen W. Heston and Howard Pack. London: Sage Publications, 1981.
This chapter provides a straightforward explanation of the basic idea that technological tools need to be examined in the context of their use. Additionally, the authors provide a lucid explanation of the concept and challenges of achieving mastery over technology.

Barry R. Posen. *The Sources of Military Doctrine: France, Britain and Germany between the World Wars.* Ithaca, NY: Cornell University Press, 1984. Stephen P. Rosen. *Winning the Next War: Innovation and the Modern Military.* Ithaca, NY: Cornell University Press, 1991. Murray Williamson and Allan R. Millet, eds. *Military Innovation in the Interwar Period.* Cambridge: Cambridge University Press, 1996.
These works examine the relationships between technological change, organizations, and military doctrine enabling militaries to effectively evolve their capabilities to fight wars. All three examine facilitating factors and barriers across a range of examples. Posen particularly stresses the degree of threat faced by a nation. Rosen illuminates the need for career paths and generational change to institutionalize innovative change. Williamson and Murray look more closely at innovation across specific technologies. The chapter in Williamson and Murray's book by Alan Beyerchen, "From Radio to Radar: Interwar Military Adaptation to Technological Change in Germany, the United Kingdom and the United States," provides insights tightly linked to the main themes of this chapter.

Stuart E. Johnson and Martin C. Libicki. *Dominant Battlespace Knowledge: The Winning Edge.* Washington, DC: Institute for National Strategic Studies/NDU Press, 1995.
This work provides a good example among many works that call on the U.S. national security community to aggressively pursue the informational aspects of the revolution in military affairs to sustain and further enhance the decisive advantages it enjoyed in the Persian Gulf War.

Seymour Goodman. *The Information Technologies and Defense: A Demand-Pull Assessment.* Palo Alto, CA: Stanford University, Center for International Security and Arms Control, February 1996.
A very insightful analysis of factors driving the U.S. national security community to use information technology since the end of World War II. I relied heavily on Goodman's concept of demand-pull in my analysis in this chapter and will do so again in subsequent chapters. Goodman also challenges the conventional wisdom that the U.S. military will be naturally inclined to invest heavily in information technology as we enter the twenty-first century.

Irving Lachow. "The GPS Dilemma: Balancing Military Risks and Economic Benefits." *International Security* 20, no. 1 (Summer 1995): 126–148. Vipin Grupta. "New Satellite Images for Sale." *International Security* 20, no. 1 (Summer 1995): 94–125.
These two articles provide rare examples of balanced analysis of opportunities and challenges presented by two new technologies: the Global Positioning System and civilian space imaging systems. Both authors address that fact that whereas national security concerns attend civil sector development and reliance on these technologies, economic opportunities largely trump these worries, and that the U.S. has multiple means for mitigating potential threats.

Richard N. Nelson, ed. *National Systems of Innovation: A Comparative Analysis.* New York: Oxford University Press, 1993.
This work provides a framework for understanding national capabilities to effectively develop and facilitate technological advance based on case studies by the premier experts in the field.

James L. McKenney. *Waves of Change: Business Evolution through Information Technology.* Boston: Harvard Business School Press, 1995.
McKenney's book illustrates through case studies the factors involved in the success of and hurdles facing large corporations that undertake major information technology adoption and assimilation programs.

Jennifer Hillmer. "Venture Capitals." *Wired* 8, no. 7 (July 2000): 258–271.
A summer 2000 survey of "high tech hubs." The survey ranks each of 46 regions around the globe on the following: ability of universities and research facilities to train workers and develop

technologies; presence of established corporations to provide expertise and economic stability; drive of local people to start new enterprises; and the presence of venture capital.

Harvard University Information Infrastructure Program Web site (www.ksg.harvard.edu). *The Information Infrastructure Program focuses heavily on research and education regarding the impact of the information age on society and factors influencing its development, particularly government policy. The Web site provides a wealth of material on this topic and links to sites of a wide of organizations with related concerns.*

Notes

1. Frank Bradbury Paul Jervis, Bon Johnston, and Alan Pearson, eds., *Transfer Processes in Technical Change*. (Alphen, aan den Rijn, the Netherlands: Sijthoff & Noordhoff, 1978), 6.

2. Carl J. Dahlman and Larry E. Westphal, "The Meaning of Technological Mastery in Relation to Transfer of Technology," in *Technology Transfer: New Issues, New Analysis*, ed. Allen W. Heston and Howard Pack (London: Sage Publications, 1981), 12. Few works on the use of technology begin with as straightforward an explanation of basic conceptual principles as this one does.

3. This framework builds primarily on the one provided by Rikard Stankiewicz, "Basic Technologies and the Innovation Process," in *Measuring the Dynamics of Technological Change*, ed. Jon Sigurdson (London: Pinter, 1990), 22.

4. Dahlman and Westphal, "Meaning of Technological Mastery," 16.

5. Eliot A. Cohen and John Gooch, *Military Misfortunes: The Anatomy of Failure in War* (New York: Random House, 1991), 21. Cohen and Gooch borrow directly from the literature and examples of failure in business to enhance understanding of why military organizations fail in war. The use here of the broader literature on technology assimilation and diffusion to understand the challenges for military organizations takes a similar approach.

6. Martin van Creveld, *Technology and War* (New York: Free Press, 1989), chap. 15, "The Invention of Invention," 217–234; Trevor N. Dupuy, *The Evolution of Weapons and Warfare* (New York: Bobbs-Merrill, 1980), "The Age of Technological Change," 169–326; and Bernard and Fawn M. Brodie, *From Crossbow to H-Bomb: The Evolution of Weapons and Tactics in Warfare* (Bloomington: Indiana University Press, 1973).

7. On the issue of quality versus quantity, see Seymour J. Dietchman, *Military Power and the Advance of Technology: General Purpose Military Forces for the 1980s and Beyond* (Boulder, CO: Westview Press, 1983); and on the advantages of high-technology and quality forces, see Jeffrey Record, *Beyond Military Reform: America's Defense Dilemmas* (Washington, DC: Pregammon-Brassey's, 1988).

8. The characterization of the literature on doctrinal innovation presented here is principally based on Barry R. Posen, *The Sources of Military Doctrine: France, Britain and Germany between the World Wars* (Ithaca, NY: Cornell University Press, 1984); Stephen Rosen, "New Ways of War: Understanding Military Innovation," *International Security* 13, no. 1 (Spring 1989): 134–168; and Williamson Murray and Allan R. Millet, eds., *Military Innovation in the Interwar Period* (Cambridge: Cambridge University Press, 1996).

9. Posen, *Sources of Military Doctrine*, 14.

10. Joint Staff, *Joint Vision 2010—America's Military Preparing for Tomorrow* (Washington, DC: Joint Staff, 1996), 13. *Joint Vision 2010* has provided the guiding framework for the U.S. military's development of high-technology forces and supporting doctrine and organizational forms in the late 1990s and into the new century.

11. Key works that outline the concept of RMA include Andrew W. Marshall, "Some Thoughts on Military Revolutions" (memorandum, Department of Defense, Office of Net Assessment, Washington, DC, August 1993); Michael Mazarr, *The Military Technical Revolution* (Washington, DC: Center for Strategic and International Studies, 1993); James R. FitzSimonds and Jan M. van Tol, "Revolutions in Military Affairs," *Joint Forces Quarterly* no. 4 (Spring 1994): 24–31; and Andrew F. Krepenvich, Jr., "Cavalry to Computer: The Patterns of Military Revolutions," *National Interest* no. 37 (Fall 1994): 30–42.

12. Strong linkages exist between those authors who address doctrinal innovation and the RMA. Marshall's Office of Net Assessment provided the funding that supported Murray and Millet's *Military Innovation in the Interwar Period.* Rosen has also been active in assessing prospects for an information technology–based RMA. Krepenvich was assigned to the Office of Net Assessment in the early 1990s and was a member of the 1997 National Defense Panel, whose report *Transforming Defense* draws on both threads of thinking regarding the need to revise U.S. strategy at the dawn of the twenty-first century.

13. DSB Task Force, *Information Architecture for the Battlefield* (Washington, DC: Department of Defense, October 1994), ES-6.

14. David S. Alberts, *Unintended Consequences of the Information Age Technologies* (Washington, DC: National Defense University Press, 1996), 13.

15. Marshall, "Some Thoughts on Military Revolutions," 3.

16. Marshall, "Some Thoughts on Military Revolutions," 8.

17. Government Accounting Office, *Defense Information Superiority: Progress Made but Significant Challenges Remain* (Washington, DC: Government Accounting Office, GAO/NSIAD/AIMD-98-257, August 1998).

18. Joseph S. Nye, Jr., and William A. Owens, "America's Information Edge," *Foreign Affairs* 75, no. 2 (March/April 1996): 28.

19. This concern and the trade-offs involved in reaping commercial benefits from satellite imaging are most thoroughly analyzed in Vipin Grupta, "New Satellite Images for Sale," *International Security* 20, no. 1 (Summer 1995): 94–125. Other pieces that analyze the concern over U.S. adversaries' access to satellite imagery are Henry D. Sokolski, "Non-Apocalyptic Proliferation: A New Strategic Threat," *Washington Quarterly* 17, no. 2 (Spring 1994): 123–125; Oliver Morton, "Private Spy," *Wired* (August 1997): 114–199 and 149–152; and John E. Peters, "Technology and Advances in Foreign Military Capabilities," *Fletcher Forum* 19, no. 1 (Winter 1994/95): 125–128.

20. The strongly threatening nature of this development is highlighted in Sokolski, "Non-Apocalyptic Proliferation," 120–123; Peters, "Technology and Advances," 124–128, and Institute for National Strategic Studies, *Strategic Assessment 1995* (Washington, DC: National Defense University Press, 1995), 153–157. A much more balanced approach is presented in Irving Lachow, "The GPS Dilemma: Balancing Military Risks and Economic Benefits," *International Security* 20, no. 1 (Summer 1995): 126–148.

21. Lachow, "GPS Dilemma," 137. Similar examples of this tendency to succinctly write off the challenges of assimilation can be found in Peters, "Technology and Advances," 127; and Institute for National Strategic Studies, *Strategic Assessment 1995*, 161–162.

22. Winn Schwartau, *Information Warfare*, 2nd ed. (New York: Thunder Mouth Press, 1996), 293.

23. DSB Task Force, *Information Architecture*, ES-5.

24. PCCIP, *Critical Foundations: Protecting America's Infrastructures* (Alexandria, VA: President's Commission on Critical Infrastructure Protection, October 1977), 17.

25. Richard N. Nelson, ed., *National Systems of Innovation: A Comparative Analysis* (New York: Oxford University Press, 1993), 509–517; Michael Porter, "The Competitive Advantage of Nations," *Harvard Business Review* 68, no. 2 (March/April 1990): 86–89; Thomas Lee and

Proctor Reid, eds., *National Interests in the Age of Global Technology* (Washington, DC: National Academy of Engineering, 1991), 45–53; and James E. Austin, *Managing in Developing Countries* (New York: Free Press, 1990), 61, all find that these systems are major determinants of the success of enterprises within national technological systems.

26. Peter F. Drucker, *The New Realities* (New York: Harper and Row, 1989), chap. 10, "The Paradoxes of Development," 140–155.

27. See Lee and Reid, *National Interests in the Age of Global Technology*, 59, regarding commercial advantage; and Nye and Owens, "America's Information Edge," 24, regarding military advantage.

28. The crucial impact of the cultural and social context on the adoption, assimilation, and diffusion of technology is a central theme of Everett M. Rodgers, *The Diffusion of Innovations*, 4th ed. (New York: Free Press, 1995). The challenges created by varied cultural and social contexts for the managers of commercial enterprises are discussed in Austin, *Managing in Developing Countries*, 62–68. For more detailed material on this subject, see Steven M. Dunphy, Paul H. Herbig, and Mary E. Howleg, "The Innovation Funnel," *Technological Forecasting and Social Change* 53, no. 3 (November 1996): 282–283.

29. The negative effects of these factors on technology adoption and achieving technological mastery is a major theme of V. S. Naipaul, *Among the Believers: An Islamic Journey* (New York: Vintage Books, 1981). See also Yousef Nassef, "Cultural Impediments to Assimilation of Information Technology in an Arab/Islamic Society: The Case of Egypt" (Ph.D. diss., Fletcher School of Law and Diplomacy, Tufts University, 1996), esp. chap. 3 on the effects of language, 88–122.

30. See Nicholas Negroponte, *Being Digital* (New York: Alfred A. Knopf, 1995); and Robert B. Reich, *The Work of Nations: Preparing Ourselves for 21st Century Capitalism* (New York: Vintage Books, 1992).

31. The factors facilitating the rise of the software industry in Bangalore and future challenges are discussed in John Stremlau, "Dateline Bangalore: Third World Technopolis," *Foreign Policy* 103 (Summer 1996): 152–168.

32. Jennifer Hillmer, "Venture Capitals," *Wired* 8 no. 7 (July 2000), 258–271.

33. See Lee McKnight and W. Russell Neuman, "Technological Policy and the National Information Infrastructure," in *The New Information Infrastructure: Strategies for U.S. Policy*, ed. William J. Drake (New York: Twentieth Century Fund, 1995), 137–154.

34. Martin C. Libicki, *Standards: Rough Road to the Common Byte* (Washington, DC: National Defense University Press, 1995), 48.

35. Marco Insati and Jonathan West, "Technology Integration: Turning Great Research into Great Products," *Harvard Business Review* 97 (May–June 1997): 79.

36. Libicki, *Standards*, 98. The recent lack of productivity gains among Japanese firms from use of information technology has been linked to an unwillingness to diffuse information within organizations due to higher emphasis on authority and hierarchy, as discussed in "Doing It Differently: Wiring Corporate Japan," *Economist*, 19 April 1997, 62–64. See the section in Nassef, "Cultural Impediments to Assimilation," on "General Attitudes towards Modernization," 141–146, regarding Egyptian problems in the same area.

37. Porter stresses these factors throughout "Competitive Advantage of Nations," as do Dunphy et al., "Innovation Funnel," 280–281. See also Curtis Moore and Alan Miller, *Green Gold: Japan, Germany and the United States and the Race for Environmental Technology* (Boston: Beacon Press, 1994), regarding the central role of strict government regulation in stimulating technological advance and diffusion in Germany's environmental sector.

38. Posen, *Sources of Military Doctrine*, 181–186, describes how the German military development of blitzkrieg doctrine was facilitated by restrictions imposed on the German military establishment by the Treaty of Versailles and how RAF development of radars and an effec-

tive fighter command received a crucial push from the British perceptions of the strength of the German Luftwaffe (166–167). Dunphy et al., "Innovation Funnel," 280, provide examples of the impetus World War II provided for U.S. and British development, assimilation, and diffusion of technologies ranging from penicillin to the atomic bomb.

39. James L. McKenney, *Waves of Change: Business Evolution through Information Technology* (Cambridge MA: Harvard Business School Press, 1995), 99–116.

40. Seymour Goodman, *The Information Technologies and Defense: A Demand-Pull Assessment* (Palo Alto, CA: Stanford University, Center for International Security and Arms Control, February 1996), 3.

41. The crucial role of leadership in technological assimilation provides a dominant theme of most authors dealing with such assimilation. See, in particular, Rodgers, *Diffusion of Innovations*, 389–402; and Dunphy et al., "Innovation Funnel," 288–289.

42. Soshanna Zuboff, *In the Age of the Smart Machine: The Future of Work and Power* (New York: Basic Books, 1988), 390.

43. McKenney, *Waves of Change*, 147.

44. Bernard and Fawn Brodie, *From Crossbow to H-Bomb*, 11.

45. Porter, "Competitive Advantage of Nations," 89.

46. See Porter, "Competitive Advantage of Nations," 82–83; and Insati and West, "Technology Integration," 79.

47. Reich, *The Work of Nations*, 108–109, argues that strategic brokers who bring together problem identifiers with problem solvers offer one of three key types of expertise for enterprises that will be able to compete successfully in the global web. See also Thomas J. Allen, James M. Piepmeier, and S. Cooney, "The International Technology Gatekeeper," *Technology Review* (May 1971): 9.

48. Peter Wolcott and Seymour Goodman. "Under the Stress of Reform: High-Performance Computing in the Former Soviet Union," *Communications of the ACM* 36, no. 10 (October 1993): 29.

49. Sanjaya Lall, "Technological Capabilities," in Jean-Jacques Salomon, Francisco R. Sagasti, and Celine Sachs-Jeantet, eds., *The Uncertain Quest: Science, Technology and Development* (New York: United Nations University Press, 1994), 287.

50. Nagy Hanna, Ken Guy, and Erik Arnold, *The Diffusion of Information Technology: Experience of Industrial Countries and Lessons for Developing Countries* (Washington, DC: World Bank, Discussion Paper #281, June 1995), 120.

51. Zuboff, *In the Age of the Smart Machine*, 396.

52. McKenney, *Waves of Change*, 5–6.

53. Ikujiro Nonaka, "The Knowledge-Creating Company," in Ken Starkey, ed., *How Organizations Learn* (London: International Thompson Business Press, 1996), 18; Arie P. DeGeus, "Planning as Learning," in Starkey, *How Organizations Learn*, 94; and Chris Aryglis, "Skilled Incompetence," in Starkey, *How Organizations Learn*, 88–89. For the role of encouraging experimentation in enhancing innovation, see Williamson Murray and Barry Watts, "Military Innovation in Peacetime," in Murray and Millet, eds., *Military Innovation in the Interwar Period*, 410–414. Regarding the role of experimentation in learning in the commercial sector, see Insati and West, "Technology Integration," 75–79.

54. Zuboff, *In the Age of the Smart Machine*, 395.

55. Derived directly from Hanna et al., *Diffusion of Information Technology*, 27–32. Zuboff's study of the effect of information technology on the workplace makes a similar distinction between organizations that simply use information technology to automate existing functions

and those that "informate" an organization, allowing enhancement and transformative effects. See also J. C. Henderson and N. Vankatraman, "Strategic Alignment: Leveraging Information Technology for Transforming Organizations," *IBM Systems Journal* 32, no. 1 (1993): 11–14.

56. Based on major case studies of Bank of America, American Airlines, Frito-Lay, United Services Automobile Association, and American Hospital Supply conducted by McKenney in *Waves of Change*.

57. Rosen, "New Ways of War," 167.

58. For overviews of U.S. civil defense efforts against the nuclear threat, see Samuel Huntington, *The Common Defense: Strategic Programs in National Politics* (New York: Columbia University Press, 1961), esp. chap. 25, "Continental Defense," 326–341; and Thomas J. Kerr, *Civil Defense in the United States: Band-Aid for a Holocaust* (Boulder, CO: Westview Press, 1983).

59. The legitimacy of information warfare actions that fall in the realm of covert action are considered in Lawrence T. Greenberg, Seymour E. Goodman, and Kevin J. Soo Hoo, *Old Law for a New World: The Applicability of International Law to Information Warfare* (Palo Alto, CA: Stanford Univeristy, Center for International Security and Arms Control, February 1997), "Peacetime Use of Information Warfare and Problems of Definition," 13–20.

60. This assertion is made in a number of authoritative studies, including the DSB study *Information Warfare—Defense* (Washington, DC: Department of Defense, 1996), 2–16; PCCIP, *Critical Foundations*, 19; and in my interviews with representatives of the Software Engineering Institute's Network Survivability and Security Program and CERT Coordinating Center and the Air Force Information Warfare Center.

61. *CIWARS Intelligence Report*, 2, no. 1 (4 January 1998), published by the Centre for Infrastructural Warfare.

62. See Greenberg Goodman, and Hoo, section on, "International Humanitarian Law," 9–12; and Richard W. Aldrich, *The International Legal Implications of Information Warfare* (U.S. Air Force Academy, CO: Report for Air Force Institute for National Security Studies, October 1995), 9–14. This issue was a particular concern addressed in the Office of the General Counsel, An Assessment of International Legal Issues in Information Operations (Washington, DC: Department of Defense, May 1999).

63. This point is made strongly by Robert A. Pape, *Bombing to Win: Airpower and Coercion in War* (Ithaca, NY: Cornell University Press, 1996), "Why Strategic Bombing Persists," 326–329; and Luttwak, *Strategy*, "Claims of Autonomy: Strategy by Bombardment," 164–168.

64. PCCIP, *Critical Foundations*, 9. Other assessments that stress the ease of acquiring human expertise are GAO, *Information Security: Computer Attacks at Department of Defense Pose Increasing Risks* (Washington, DC: GAO/AMID-96-84, May 1996), 4; and Roger C. Molander, Andrew S. Riddle, and Peter A. Wilson, *Strategic Information Warfare: A New Face of War* (Washington, DC: RAND National Defense Research Institute, 1996), 20.

65. Schwartau, *Information Warfare*, 543.

66. John Arquilla and David Ronfeldt, *The Advent of Netwar* Santa Monica, CA: RAND Corporation, 1996), and Schwartau, *Information Warfare* (1st ed., 1994, as well as 2nd ed. previously cited), develop the possibilities of this idea most fully.

67. The potential experiential synergies in having organizations with offensive and defensive roles was recognized as early as National Research Council, *Computers at Risk: Safe Computing in the Information Age* (Washington, DC: National Academy Press, 1991), 14; as well as in the DSB study *Information Warfare—Defense*, 6-5.

68. Molander et al., *Strategic Information Warfare*, 17. Other significant examples of focusing principally on "hacker" expertise include the GAO, *Information Security*, 12–15; and PCCIP, *Critical Foundations*, 9–10.

69. This conclusion is stressed in PCCIP, *Critical Foundations*, 22; and Office of Science and Technology Policy (OSTP), *Cybernation: The American Infrastructure in the Information Age* (Washington, DC: The White House, April 1997), 29.

70. For guidelines on how such programs should be instituted, see Fredrick Cohen, *Protection and Security on the Information Highway* (New York: John Wiley & Sons, 1995), "An Organizational Perspective," 132–146; and Dorothy E. Denning, *Information Warfare and Security* (Reading, MA: Addison-Wesley, 1999), 371–396.

71. OSTP, *Cybernation*, 15–17, provides historical examples of cascading effects across infrastructures and a good conceptual description of the significance of these interconnections.

72. Mary Olson, Vice President for Service Assurance, U.S. West, "The Road Ahead: The Role of Business" in *National Security in the Information Age*, ed. James McCarthy (U.S. Air Force Academy CO: Olin Institute, March 1996), 259.

73. MITRE Corporation presentation, "Information Operations and Critical Infrastructure Protection," Bedford, MA, 20 November 1997, based on a study that MITRE performed for the PCCIP.

74. Carol L. Wienhaus and Anthony G. Oettinger, *Behind the Telephone Debates* (Norwood, NJ: Ablex, 1988), 16–17.

75. See Paul F. Capasso, *Telecommunications and Information Assurance: America's Achilles Heel* (Cambridge MA: Harvard University, Program on Information Resources Policy, March 1997), 49–50, on the important role state public utility commissions could serve in U.S. defensive strategic information warfare efforts.

76. The National Communications System already has arrangements with the major telecommunications providers to provide extra capabilities in the case of emergencies. Lt Gen. Albert Edmonds (ret.), who as director of DISA also directed the NCS, addresses this subject in "Information Systems Support to the DOD and Beyond," in *Seminar on Intelligence, Command and Control, Spring 1996* (Cambridge: Harvard University, Program on Information Resources Policy, I-97-1, 1997), 208–209. The National Defense Panel, (NDP), *Transforming Defense*, (Arlington, VA: National Defense Panel, December 1997), 55, has recommended considering a specific role for the National Guard in information infrastructure protection.

77. The list of mechanisms presented here is principally derived from the following studies: NRC, *Computers at Risk*; Office of Technology Assessment (OTA), *Information Security and Privacy in Network Environments* (Washington, DC: Government Printing Office, 1994); PCCIP, *Critical Foundations*; OSTP, *Cybernation*; and Stephen J. Luksiak, *Public and Private Roles in the Protection of Critical Information-Dependent Infrastructures* (Palo Alto, CA: Stanford University, Center for International Security and Arms Control, March 1997).

78. PCCIP, *Critical Foundations*, 62; NDP, *Transforming Defense*, 55.

79. Cohen, *Protection and Security*, 133. The fundamental role of management is also addressed in NRC, *Computers at Risk*, in the section on "Developing Policies and Appropriate Controls," 59–61.

80. PCCIP, *Critical Foundations*, 87–88.

81. Details of such joint ventures are provided in a special edition of the U.S.–Russian Investment Symposium (U.S.–RIS) newsletter entitled Russian Information Technology News available on the Web at <www.ksg.edu/USRIS/newpage6.htm>, accessed August 2000.

82. See Joint Staff, *Information Warfare: Legal Regulatory, Policy and Organizational Considerations*, 2nd ed. (Washington, DC: Joint Staff, July 1996), A-317–319, for more information on the range of different CERT-type organizations and their activities.

FOUR
Development of U.S.
Strategic Airpower,
1919–1945: Challenges,
Execution, and Lessons

*The road ahead promised to be a
stormy one. Feasibility of effective and
sustained air attack as the key to
victory could not be demonstrated by
past experience. Victory through air
power alone was pure theory.*

—Haywood Hansell, on the creation
of the first U.S. strategic bombing
plan, AWPD-1 in 1941

As World War I ended, airpower advocates announced the advent of a new
technology as a decisive means for avoiding the protracted attrition of trench
warfare. In the United States and elsewhere, civilians and military officers discussed the ramifications of this technological advance. Airpower leaders clam-
ored for the formation of new organizations and the resources to bring visions
to fruition. By the mid-1930s, the United States had developed a doctrinal construct for conducting strategic bombing through precision, high-altitude attack
against industrial centers; an organization committed to independent air operations, the General Headquarters Air Force; and a technological tool to wage this
new form of warfare, the B-17. However, when the United States entered World
War II, the strategic bombardment campaign against Germany took more than
two hard-fought years to achieve significant effects. Even at the conclusion of
the conflict, the U.S. Strategic Bombing Survey offered the following assessment:
"Airpower in the last war [World War I] was in its infancy. Behind its dogfights
and hit-and-run tactics there were some glimmerings of the concept of using airpower to attack the sustaining resources of the enemy, but these bore only a

hint of future developments. In this war, airpower may be said to have reached a stage of full adolescence. Its growth and development still continue."[1] The impact of strategic airpower, adolescent after twenty years of peacetime development and a global conflict involving all the world's major powers, fell short of the expectations of its proponents.

As with any effort to use historical analysis to guide understanding of a contemporary challenge, inevitable differences exist between the past and present cases. Development of strategic warfare capabilities based on airplanes required massive material mobilization to produce the large forces necessary to achieve desired levels of mechanical destruction. Acquiring the physical means for conducting digital attacks is likely to prove easier than producing bombers and other supporting equipment. Microforce applied against the digital vulnerabilities of information infrastructures may well require much less material mobilization and energy expenditure for waging conflict. In strategic air warfare, much of the required technology was embodied in the airplanes and bombs. In strategic information warfare, the experiential requirements in the form of highly trained personnel may prove the principal mobilization concern. Relative geographic isolation during the 1919–1945 period meant U.S. strategic air defenses were never tested. The ability of digital attacks to attenuate such geographic barriers is a major reason behind the concern within the United States regarding strategic information warfare in the twenty-first century.

However, this case of air-based strategic warfare also presents significant similarities to the challenges facing the development of strategic information warfare capabilities in the twenty-first century. In both cases, the rapid advance of technology created a potential new means of waging strategic warfare. Analysis of the interwar period and that of the period around the dawn of the new millennium evidences untested visions guiding choices in doctrine, organization, and technology to conduct these new forms of warfare. The increasing pace of technological change involving commercial industry in both periods influenced the development of strategic warfare capabilities. Although other countries besides the United States also wrestled with the development of strategic capabilities in the interwar period, the use of the U.S. experience additionally allows for the comparison of U.S. institutional and cultural influences across periods.

The wartime experience of World War II permits evaluation of choices made in the establishment of strategic air warfare capabilities and their use in a conflict. The bombing campaign against Germany was chosen for analysis here because it was the focus of U.S. initial war planning, lasted the longest time, was waged against a robust opponent, and has received the most thorough historical evaluation. Therefore, this campaign provides an excellent case for examining the different enabling factors and the interplay between offensive and defensive actions in waging strategic warfare.

Development of U.S. Strategic Airpower Doctrine, Organization, and Technology

World War I provided only a limited wartime experience for the United States regarding the use and potential of airpower, as the United States entered relatively late in the conflict. Its air forces were woefully behind those of the other principal combatants in terms of size and technological sophistication. The Air Service was part of the Signal Corps and depended heavily on its British and French allies for advice, doctrine, and training to create a combat-ready force. Although an ambitious mobilization and production program was established, because of manufacturing delays the United States relied almost exclusively on combat aircraft from allies.[2] The U.S. forces deployed in France in World War I (known as the American Expeditionary Forces (AEF)) were led by General John Pershing. The AEF air component was under the command of Brigadier General William "Billy" Mitchell. The two leaders received little guidance from either the War Department or Air Service headquarters in Washington, D.C., about how to employ airpower in the war effort. Whereas Pershing viewed air forces as a means for direct support of ground operations, Mitchell quickly became a strong advocate of consolidating air forces to establish superiority in the skies.[3] Mitchell and the AEF airmen had also created plans for grandiose strategic bombing operations in 1919 in conjunction with the RAF.[4] The close of World War I left U.S. airmen with a strong taste of the possibilities for waging war from the air. The U.S. return to an isolationist foreign policy, however, created a strategic context that lacked any necessity to exploit such a capability. This section gives an overview of the period between the world wars to examine how the evolution of U.S. strategic airpower doctrine, organization, and technology resulted in successes and failures in realizing the potential of strategic airpower. The appendix at the end of this chapter provides dates of and organizational charts depicting major changes within the Army air arm from 1919 to 1941.

Doctrine: Emergence of a Precision Strategy

The development of U.S. strategic bombing doctrine between the two world wars has been a topic of much historical scrutiny. As explained in chapter 3, doctrine is the preferred mode for fighting wars among a group of services, a single service, or a subservice. The analysis here highlights how emerging doctrine played a central role in shaping the capabilities of the United States for conducting strategic air operations during World War II.

During the 1920s, the possibilities for strategic air warfare were given voice in the United States and Europe. Bomber aircraft would range freely throughout the skies, operating unhampered by geography and independent of armies and navies to strike directly at the enemy's warmaking capacity and will. In analyzing the development of U.S. air doctrine, historian Thomas Greer refers to the period from 1919 to 1926 as the "heroic age of doctrinal development." Captivated by technological possibilities and a desire to create independent organizations and resources to pursue these visions, airmen who flew in World War I argued that the airplane would completely change the character of future wars.

The initial visions for this change emanated from Europe. The book *Command of the Air*, published in 1921 by Italian general Giulio Douhet, provides the most comprehensive early articulation of strategic air warfare theory.[5] Driven by the experience of World War I, Douhet viewed airpower in the context of struggles between entire peoples. Believing that the vastness of the sky made defense against air attacks impossible, Douhet argued that airpower was inherently offensive and could dominate land and sea operations. Command of the air would be secured by an intense campaign against the opponent's air bases. Once established, air supremacy would be used to strike at the will of the opponent by destroying or neutralizing a country's "vital centers." Douhet identified five basic target systems: industry, transportation, communications, government buildings, and the will of the people. He asserted that civilian morale was the most important and fragile target for air attack.[6]

Airmen in Britain also played an important role in developing early concepts of strategic bombardment. By the end of World War I, the Royal Air Force had already become an independent service. The RAF's first chief, Hugh Trenchard, became another staunch advocate of strategic airpower directed against the will of the populace. As early as 1919, Trenchard argued that in bombing cities, "the ratio of morale to material effect was 20:1."[7] Early U.S. airpower advocates during the 1920s clearly were cognizant of European views on the future role of airpower. Mason Patrick, the first chief of the Army Air Corps, liberally quoted British and French thinkers on the future of airpower in published articles and addresses to the Army War College.[8]

The most vocal and prominent early advocate of airpower in the United States was William Mitchell, who returned from World War I to become assistant chief of the Air Service. A strong advocate of an independent air service from 1919 onward, Mitchell carried on an ongoing crusade to raise awareness of the revolutionary nature of airpower. His vision encompassed the importance of airpower in providing close air support on the battlefield to extending U.S. coastal defenses.[9] Mitchell incited significant public attention with successful demonstrations of airpower's capability against naval forces, sinking the captured German battleship Ostfriesland and other warships in 1921. As with his European contemporaries, Mitchell saw airpower principally as an offensive weapon that would make wars sharp and short, inexpensive for the victor but terrible for the vanquished. He wrote in 1919 that the main value of bombardment would come from "hitting an enemy's great nerve centers at the very beginning of the war so as to paralyze them to the greatest extent possible."[10] He also recognized that advancing technology would eventually put the United States within striking range of the European and Asiatic powers. Therefore, Mitchell advocated that "national safety requires the maintenance of an efficient air force adapted for acting against the possible enemy's interior."[11] By 1930, Mitchell clearly advocated that airpower constituted a dominant new form of war: "[The] advent of air power which can go straight to the vital centers and entirely neutralize them has put a completely new complexion on the old system of war. It is now realized that the hostile main army in the field is a false objective and the real objectives are the vital centers."[12] Unlike his European counterparts, however, Mitchell initially felt pursuit aviation still had a key role to play in achieving the air superiority necessary for successful offensive operations. In 1921, Mitchell advocated a balanced air force consisting of 60 percent pursuit, 20 percent bombardment, and 20 percent attack forces.[13] Although Mitchell and others would eventually come to see advocacy of bombardment superiority as the sole way to justify establishing an independent air force, the United States continued to maintain a substantial commitment to pursuit aviation throughout the 1920s.

Mitchell was not alone within the Air Service in trumpeting airpower as a dominant new mode of warfare. Though not as controversial as Mitchell, other leaders during the period also advocated a strategic role for airpower. In particular, Maj. Gen. Mason Patrick, chief of the Air Service, argued that the "airplane alone could jump over enemy armies and strike directly at the seat of the opposition will and policy."[14] Like Mitchell, Patrick felt that airpower ought to be organized centrally under airmen for its potential to be properly exploited. Patrick made the following recommendation to the War Department: "[F]ormation of a force of bombardment and pursuit aviation and airships should be directly under General Headquarters for assignment to special or strategical missions, the accomplishment of which may be either in conjunction with the ground forces or entirely independent of them. This force should be organized into large units insuring great mobility and independence of action."[15]

The 1920s also saw the emergence of the Air Corps Tactical School as the driver for airpower doctrine within the United States. The school was founded at Langley Field as the Air Service Field Officer's School to train students on air tactics and techniques necessary for direction of air units in cooperation with other branches. It was renamed ACTS with the formation of the Air Corps in 1926 and moved to Maxwell Field, Alabama, in July 1931. The last ACTS course ended in June 1940, when the school was disbanded during the mobilization effort for World War II. By the mid-1920s, ACTS was becoming an important breeding ground for the new theories regarding strategic bombardment. As early as 1926, an ACTS lecture on the "Employment of Combined Air Forces" stated that air attacks constitute "a means of imposing will with the least possible loss by striking vital points rather than by gradually wearing down an enemy to exhaustion."[16] The same lecture stressed the characteristics of airpower mobility and the need to concentrate forces to successfully conduct strategic strikes.

While a visionary doctrine was emerging in the Air Corps, official U.S. military doctrine regarding the role of the Army air arm changed little. The Army-Navy Joint Board Report on the Ostfriesland bombing tests states that "[t]he Battleship is still the backbone of the fleet and the bulwark of the Nation's sea defense and will remain so long as safe navigation of the sea for the purposes of trade or transportation is vital to success in war."[17] Army Training Regulation TR 440-15, "Fundamental Principles of the Air Service," stated in 1926 that the mission of the air service was to aid ground forces in achieving decisive success by destroying enemy aviation, attacking surface forces, and protecting friendly ground units from hostile air reconnaissance or attack. The regulation stated that air units would usually operate as organic elements of ground commands, allowing that some units might indirectly support the battle area at a remote distance.[18] Throughout most of the interwar period, the Army and Navy conducted a constant bureaucratic rearguard action to limit the doctrinal development of an independent air force. The organizational competition in this period is addressed later in this chapter.

The role of strategic bombardment as the principal means for employing airpower achieved complete ascendancy during the 1930s within the Air Corps. Past analyses of the development of doctrine during the period consistently highlight the central role of the ACTS. According to Greer, "[t]he function of the school was not only to develop new ideas but, more importantly, to attempt to coordinate individual notions into a unified and consistent body of doctrine."[19] Although the activities of operational units and decisions made in Washington, D.C., also played crucial roles in the development of the Army air arm during the period, thinking about the nature of future war and the airpower's role was dominated by ACTS. The official history of the Army Air Forces (AAF) in World War II provides the following summary of "air war" theory expounded at the ACTS:[20]

1.   The national objective in war is to break the enemy's will to resist and force him to submit to our will.

2.   The accomplishment of this objective may entail the actual destruction of his power to resist, or merely the threat thereof, but in either case requires an offensive form of warfare.

3.   The immediate mission of the armed forces may be: defeat of the enemy's army, navy or air force; the occupation of his homeland; pressure against his national economy; or operations against vital centers within his country.

4.   These military missions are best carried through by the co-operation of the three arms: air, ground and naval. Each has its peculiar functions and limitations. Of the three arms, only aviation can contribute significantly to all the designated missions.

5.   The special mission of the air arm then should be to attack the whole of the enemy national structure. Under conditions of modern warfare, the military, political, economic and social aspects of a nation's life are closely and absolutely interdependent, so that dislocations in any one will bring disturbances of varying degrees of intensity in all other aspects.

6.   Modern war with its extravagant material factors places a special importance on a nation's economic structure and particularly on its "industrial web." A nation may be defeated simply by the interruption of the delicate balance of this complex organization, which is vulnerable to the air arm and directly to neither of the other arms.

7.   Future wars will begin with air action. This fact makes it necessary to maintain an adequate air force, since it would be impossible to build one if the enemy

ever gained air control over our territory. Conversely, we should strike at his industry as early in the war as possible.

8.   An attack against his industrial fabric requires more than random strikes at targets of opportunity, and so it is a function of peacetime strategy to weigh the war potential of possible enemies and uncover those relatively defenseless areas which can be profitably exploited by our attack.

The doctrine outlined above emerged gradually during the period but with an admirable coherence. The curriculum at ACTS was constructed around an annual schedule of instruction. The same basic courses were taught each year with occasional additions and substitutions. The lecture materials available from the period indicate that instructors annually reviewed and added to material presented the previous year. Also, key instructors stayed at the school for a prolonged period to lead the development of doctrinal concepts.[21] The Air Corps trained a cadre of future World War II leaders based on a very strongly articulated but untested doctrine.

This emphasis on offense detrimentally affected defensive considerations and the need to develop pursuit aircraft. As doctrine increasingly focused on future wars, the lessons learned by the air forces of the AEF about the utility of specialized airplanes for ensuring air superiority were gradually forgotten at the ACTS.[22] Although thinkers within the Air Corps continued to believe in the need for air superiority, operational concepts in the United States came to mirror the earlier thoughts of Douhet and Trenchard concerning the inability of pursuit aviation to intercept and destroy bomber aircraft. As the performance characteristics of bombers began to improve rapidly in the early 1930s, doctrine came to assert that the achievement of air superiority would occur through the development of fast, high-flying, self-protected aircraft. (The effect of technological progress in the 1930s between offense and defense will be addressed more fully below.) Then Major Henry "Hap" Arnold, future Chief of the Army Air Forces in World War II, in 1933 stated that "[t]he bomber was the basic type of aircraft and other branches should be built around it."[23] Some advocates of the role of pursuit aviation in intercepting attacking forces and escorting friendly bombers fought the prevailing wisdom at ACTS through the early 1930s. By 1935, however, the doctrinal primacy of the bomber as the main weapon of the Army Air Corps was clearly established, as the 1936–1937 ACTS lecture entitled "Offense and Defense" shows: "We can apparently conclude that analysis of the relative merits of the air force defense and the air force offense based upon what we can hope to accomplish in war shows that the defense is inherently a false illusion and that by itself can accomplish nothing of conclusive value, nothing of ultimately decisive importance in war."[24] Later reflections by bomber advocates at ACTS and planners of the U.S. strategic bombing campaigns lamented the lapse in attention to pursuit aviation, but the doctrine that would dominate the thinking of most AAF leaders in World War II had formed well prior to the conflict.

The emphasis throughout the 1930s within the Air Corps on strategic bombardment remained distinctly different from the perceived role of Army air units as understood in the War Department and outlined in official manuals. One area of doctrinal mismatch regarded the relative priority of independent air operations vis-à-vis those for direct support of ground operations. The General Staff continued to stress ground support as the principal role for Army aviation throughout the period. The 1935 version of TR 440-15 stated that "[A]ir forces further the mission of the territorial or tactical command to which they are assigned."[25] Even when the Air Corps issued its own Field Manual 1–5 in 1939, entitled "Employment of the Aviation of the Army," the manual emphasized the protection of the continental United States in support of the Army and Navy, with only a vague reference to "other operations in which the Army engaged."[26]

The role of the Army air arm in coastal defense was also important in determining the types of planes the Army should develop. Throughout the 1920s, both Mitchell and Patrick had been strong advocates of airpower's role in protecting U.S. sea approaches. Following the Ostfriesland demonstrations, Patrick pressed the War Department to revise the Joint Army and Navy Board directives in 1923–1924 regarding the offshore role of the Air Service, arguing that "the Army Air Service should be definitely charged with all [air] operations conducted from shore."[27] As resources tightened in the late 1920s, the Air Corps increasingly looked to long-range coastal defense as an official justification for continued development of bombardment capabilities. The General Staff War Plans Division and Office of the Chief Air Corps issued a finding in 1933 entitled "The Employment of Army Aviation in Coast Defense" that decreed that during the first phase of a conflict the Air Corps would attempt to "locate, observe and destroy enemy vessels."[28] At the same time, the Navy attempted to reserve all over-water air operations for itself, whether land- or sea-based. A 1935 Joint Board decision permitted the Air Corps to have a role in long-range over-water operations in "direct defense" of the coast and in "support of naval forces." These provisions were generally interpreted within the Air Corps as justifying a requirement for long-range bombers to attack surface vessels when the main fleet was engaged elsewhere.[29]

The Air Corps focus on strategic bombardment continued in the latter half of the 1930s as the United States began to recognize the threat posed by events in Europe and the Pacific and mobilize for war. By the late 1930s, the industrial web theory born at ACTS had been fully developed. Based on growing bombing accuracy in peacetime tests, the doctrine stressed identifying especially sensitive points of failure within complex, specialized industries of an enemy. Because very little information was available on potential adversaries such as Germany and Japan, detailed analyses were conducted using the U.S. economy. ACTS used the U.S. economy as an example target for strategic air attack beginning with the 1933–1934 course. During its last year of operation, ACTS developed sufficient information about Japan to conduct a lecture in the 1939–1940 air force course on targeting the Japanese industrial system. No indication exists, however, that the material on the Japanese economy was used in later war planning efforts.[30]

Emphasis was placed on targeting key nodes in systems such as electric power, the steel industry, and rail transportation. The 1938 ACTS text *Air Force— Air Warfare* offered the following principles regarding the employment of strategic air forces:[31]

1. The economic structure of modern nations is highly integrated.
2. The destruction of one Vital Element will bring a succession of collapses in allied spheres of industry or finance until the entire nation is prostrated or a disheartened population forces its government to sue for peace.
3. The ultimate objective of air forces is the destruction of such vital elements. Air forces so employed accomplish the aim of air strategy by assuming the strategic offensive, and exploit to the maximum their outstanding capability which is to reach and destroy distant surface objectives of whatever character.

Haywood Hansell provides the following commentary on the ACTS thinking about target selection:

The classic example of the type of specialization and hence, vulnerability, literally fell into our laps. . . . The delivery of controllable pitch propellers had fallen down. Inquiries showed that the propeller manufacturer was not behind schedule. Actually it was a highly specialized spring that was lacking, and we found that all the springs for all the controllable pitch propellers of that variety in the United States came from one plant and that plant in Pittsburgh had suffered from a flood. There was a perfect and classic example. To all intents and purposes a very large portion of the entire aircraft industry in the

United States had been nullified just as effectively as if a great many airplanes had been shot up, or a considerable number of factories had been hit. That practical example set the pattern for ideal selection of precision targets in the United States doctrine for bombardment. That was the kind of thing sought in every economy.[32]

ACTS thinkers did not analyze how critical nodes in the industrial systems in the United States might differ from those of potential adversaries. Consideration of the possibility that adversaries might adapt their systems once placed under attack was also not in evidence. The implications of strategic bombing doctrine based on the identification and destruction of critical nodes became a major focus in U.S. planning for World War II and is covered later in this chapter.

Organizing to Employ Airpower: Evolution of an Independent
Operating Force

As the doctrine of strategic airpower emerged and was refined, bureaucratic battles were also fought that helped determine the capabilities of the U.S. air forces upon their entry into World War II. Inextricably connected to concepts of doctrine and rapidly changing technological possibilities, the evolution of the Army air arm between the world wars provides important lessons about how organizations evolve to deal with these intersecting concerns.

After World War I, the initial concerns regarding the organization of the Air Corps revolved around the question of whether a separate air force should be established, modeled on the British Royal Air Force. In 1919, Representative Charles Curry introduced a bill in Congress calling for an independent Department of Aeronautics. The Curry Bill envisioned a combat air force capable of independent or joint operations and received the support of Mitchell and other air advocates. In response, the War Department initially established a board headed by Assistant Secretary of War Benedict Crowell to examine what the World War I experience might indicate about how to organize military aviation in the United States. After traveling to England, France, and Italy to interview wartime participants, the board Crowell convened to conduct the examination also recommended formation of a separate Department of Aeronautics. Under this scheme, the Department of Aeronautics would train and equip all air forces during peacetime. Air combat units would transfer to Army and Navy control in wartime. Dissatisfied with this recommendation, Secretary of War Newton Baker set up yet another board consisting of the nonflying director of the Air Service and four artillery officers. Not surprisingly, the Baker Board found that the air arm could not be employed decisively against ground forces and must come under the control of the Army. Now satisfied, Secretary Baker approved this report and forwarded it to the Senate, where any concurrent legislative action to match the Curry Bill was blocked.[33]

After the initial defeat of the independent service initiative, the period of the 1920s was characterized by a crusade led by Mitchell, Benjamin Foulios, and others within the Air Service to get Congress to establish a unified Department of Defense with coequal air, army, and navy branches. Mitchell's voice became increasingly shrill in criticizing his superiors in the War and Navy Departments for a lack of vision. Yet Mitchell inspired a number of disciples who were staunch defenders during his court-martial in 1926, including Hap Arnold, Carl Spaatz, and Ira Eaker. These men would later become principal players in the development of U.S. strategic air power and jointly led the strategic bombing campaign against Germany.

Other air leaders, particularly Mason Patrick, who became chief of the Air Service in 1921, took a more moderate approach. Patrick focused on establishing an independent air strike force within the Army and postponed arguments about independence. In 1923, Patrick advocated an increase in air service size and the establishment of a General Headquarters reserve force to ensure availability of adequate means to create air supremacy in the event of a war. These recommendations were approved by a board led by Maj. Gen. William Lassiter that same year. Although the Lassiter Board report did not result in legislation, its findings came to represent War Department policy regarding Air Service organization.

The prospects for an independent air force again became ripe in the mid-1920s.[34] Congress established the Lampert Committee in 1924 to examine the role of airpower in the nation's defense. Calling on more than 150 witnesses over an eleven-month period, the committee recommended on 14 December 1925 the establishment of a unified air force independent of the Army and Navy. Cognizant of the activity in Congress, the War and Navy Departments convinced President Calvin Coolidge to form yet another board, this one under the direction of Dwight Morrow, to conduct a similarly broad reaching review. Mitchell and other advocates of an independent air service including Foulios, Arnold, and Spaatz testified to both boards. The Morrow Board stole the initiative from the Lampert Committee by issuing its recommendations on 30 November 1925. It found that a separate air force would increase complexity and breach the principle of unity of command and instead recommended that the Air Service be renamed the Air Corps, that it receive special representation on the General Staff, and that an Assistant Secretary of War for Air Affairs be established. The Army acted quickly on the Morrow Board's advice to create air sections within each of the five divisions of the General Staff. In July 1926, Congress approved the Air Corps Act implementing the major recommendations of the Morrow Board.[35]

After the recommendations of the Morrow Board carried the day, the issue of establishing a separate air force generally remained fallow until after World War II. Yet the continued desires of Air Corps leaders for greater autonomy and the doctrinal imperatives of strategic bombardment led to a continued push for an independent air strike force not subordinate to the Army corps commanders. During the early 1930s, the Air Corps used its assigned coastal defense mission to push for establishment of a General Headquarters (GHQ) aviation unit intended to operate as a strategic reserve in the defense of the United States. War Department boards headed by Hugh Drum and Newton Baker convened in 1933 and 1934 to consider the issue of organizing military aviation. Supported by the Navy, the Drum and Baker Boards found insufficient reason to make large-scale organizational changes. However, the Baker Board report issued in July 1934 recommended the "formal establishment of a GHQ air force made up of all combat units, trained as a homogenous force and capable of either close support or independent action."[36]

Acting on these recommendations, the War Department established the GHQ Air Force effective 1 March 1935. The new organizational structure consolidated the air combat units of several corps areas under a newly appointed commander, Maj. Gen. Frank Andrews, who reported directly to the Army Chief of Staff.[37] The GHQ Air Force was separated from the Air Corps, which continued to provide units for support for ground operations as well as to have overall responsibility for recruitment and training of personnel. Yet no provision was made for a separate air arm budget, and the War Department remained in control of resource allocation for research, development, and procurement. The organizational separation between the Air Corps and the GHQ Air Force presented few problems until the imperatives of mobilization and expansion came to the fore in 1939. The initiation of a series of increasingly ambitious plans for expanding the Army's air forces, particularly bomber forces, began to demonstrate weaknesses in the bifurcated organizational structure. Differences between GHQ Air Force and Air Corps priorities created difficulties in establishing a coherent leadership voice for the air forces in the quickening mobilization and war planning.

These difficulties were smoothed fairly quickly through a fortuitous blend of foresight, accelerated action, and the personalities involved. After an abortive attempt to place the GHQ Air Force under the Air Corps, the situation was resolved in late 1940 through a less formal approach. The Chief of the Air Corps, Hap Arnold, was also made Acting Deputy Chief of Staff of the Army, with responsibility for coordinating the activities of both elements of the Army air arm. Robert Lovett was appointed to the long-unfilled position of Assistant Secretary of War for Air in March 1941, where he would prove invaluable in improving procurement procedures and ties with private industry.[38] Soon afterwards, Arnold and Lovett orchestrated a reorganization of the Army air arm in June 1941 at the direction of Secretary of War Henry Stimson and the Army Chief of Staff George Marshall. Arnold assumed sole command as chief of the Army Air Forces. Under this structure, the Air Corps retained responsibility for training and equipping air forces, while an Air Force Combat Command (AFCC) was established to assume the former role of the GHQ Air Force in controlling combat units. In February 1942, Arnold was made an official member of the Joint Chiefs of Staff.

The development of combat organizations within the Army air arm also underwent a number of restructurings as the war approached. In 1940, defensive forces were established within AFCC as a part of an Air Defense Command organized along geographic lines.[39] Four continental air districts were established with the dual mission of providing forces for air defense as well as training incoming personnel (see the appendix, Chart 3). An Office of Civil Defense was also formed. The units with defensive roles in the AFCC quickly became overwhelmed with responsibilities to form cadres for combat units rather than maintaining proficiency for defensive operations. The AAF units at home quickly became a training force for the development of offensive air forces destined for deployment overseas. Yet despite the heavy doctrinal emphasis on strategic bombardment, no dedicated bomber force was formed prior to the war.

After World War II began, all AFCC and Air Corps units based in the United States were incorporated into a Zone of the Interior organization that reported directly to Headquarters, Army Air Force.[40] Numbered air forces were established in the European and Pacific theaters that reported directly to the theater commanders. Arnold also ensured that these air forces were closely tied to AAF Headquarters.

Technology: Developing the Tools for Air Warfare

The ability of airpower to deliver on doctrinal visions and organizational missions during the interwar period was heavily influenced by rapidly changing technology. As commander of GHQ Air Force, Frank Andrews described the relationship as follows: "The tactical and strategical employment of Air Forces and the status of development of aeronautical science exercise a profound influence, each upon the other. The needs of employment spur designers and manufacturers to produce equipment that can meet those needs, and likewise, the equipment on hand, or definitely foreseen, limits and extends the sphere of influence of Air Power."[41] The rates of advancement in performance of air warfare technologies varied over time. The doctrine of strategic bombardment would play a central role in determining which technologies were pursued and ignored as the United States geared up for World War II.

As the Air Service entered the 1920s, the technological possibilities of airpower were largely unknown. The rapid advances in aircraft performance during World War I greatly excited airpower advocates in both military and civilian sectors. However, resources for developing new aircraft and supporting technologies were severely limited. The Air Service consolidated its research, development, and procurement activities during the period at Wright Field in the area surrounding Dayton, Ohio, but also pushed the development of a commercial aviation industry in the United States. Billy Mitchell recognized the need for a synergistic relationship between civil and military activities related to the use of airpower. In *Winged Defense*, he states that "[t]he substantial and continual development of airpower should be based on a sound commercial aviation."[42] In a lecture to the Army War College in November 1923, Mason Patrick also called attention to "the intimate relation between the commercial and military air fleets, the readiness with which commercial aircraft can be transformed into military aircraft" and stressed that "therefore, in measuring the air strength of a country due weight must be given to both of these components."[43]

During the immediate post–World War I period, the Air Service placed substantial emphasis on improving the performance of all types of aircraft. Increasing speed and range were primary concerns. According to an active participant in the interwar technological development of the Army air arm, James Doolittle, the involvement of the Air Service in air races and competitions "was for two purposes: one was research and development and the other was to bring aviation to the American public."[44] In announcing the U.S. military participation in air races in 1922, a public release by the Secretaries of War and Navy stated that "[t]he encouragement of an aeronautical industry and of aeronautical activity outside the military forces is considered by every nation developing aeronautics the most economical method for developing air power."[45] The flight of Army MB-2 bombers around the world in 1924 and Lindbergh's Atlantic crossing in

1927, as well as experiments with refueling, explored the possibilities for improving the range of aircraft.

Throughout the period, the Air Service, then the Air Corps, experimented with aircraft of all types—pursuit, bombardment, attack, and observation. In the area of pursuit aviation, the emphasis was on improving speed through use of larger engines while continuing to use the biplane as the standard design. The Air Service conducted considerable experimentation with both single-seat and two-seat pursuit aircraft. The principal pursuit model in the mid-1920s was the Curtiss PW-8A Hawk with a top speed of 178 miles per hour and a cruising range of 335 miles.[46]

Air Service attention to bombardment aviation in the 1920s generally evidenced a steady decline. Despite radical visions being articulated about the possibilities for strategic bombardment, the official Army doctrine of supporting surface operations and the general isolationist mood of the country resulted in very limited resource allocation in this area. Development efforts concentrated on two-engine biplanes with minimal performance improvements. The principal bomber of the mid-1920s, the Curtiss NSB-4, had a top speed of only 100 miles per hour. One reason for the slow progress in bomber development was the lack of adequate equipment for necessary tests and studies at Wright Field. The Air Corps decide to forgo development of four-engine aircraft given limited resources, a perceived high production cost, difficulty of operation, maintenance problems, and higher fuel consumption.[47] In March 1928, the Air Corps Procurement Planning Board decided to emphasize the purchase of light LB-6 bombers rather than heavier XB-2 bombers with superior range, payload, and maneuverability. The reasons for the decision included the lower production and operating costs of the LB-6 as well as the fact that the XB-2 bombers could not fit in existing hangar facilities.[48] At the close of the first interwar decade, the technological tools available for strategic bombardment clearly lagged behind doctrinal expectations.

The early 1930s saw the rapid introduction of a number of important technological developments that permitted rapid advances in all types of aircraft, such as all-metal airframes; improved structural strength, which allowed single-wing designs; turbo-charged engines; variable-pitch propellers; and reliable navigation gear. These advances enabled improvements in aircraft speed, payload, and range. The quickening pace of technological advance also meant that existing aircraft obsolesced more quickly.

The increasing range and speed of bomber aircraft in the early 1930s had the apparent result of confirming the concepts laid out by Douhet and the Air

Corps Tactical School regarding the superiority of offense in the air. A debate emerged in the late 1920s between the Air Corps and the War Department on the proper path for development of future bombers. The Air Corps argued the need for two distinct types of bombers: (1) a plane of high speed, short range, heavy defensive power, and small bomb load for use in day operations, and (2) a bomber of minimum defensive strength to carry heavy bomb loads over longer distances in night operations. The War Department, however, mandated the development of a single, all-purpose bomber for reasons of economy.[49] The joint Air Corps Bombardment Board and ACTS response called for development of a fast, long-range, day bomber in 1929. As a result of this effort, in 1932, the Air Corps took delivery of two new all-metal, single-wing, two-engine bombers with vastly improved capabilities: the Boeing B-9 and the Martin B-10. The B-10 was capable of a speed of 207 miles per hour and had a ceiling of 21,000 feet, making it the fastest, most powerful bomber in the world.[50] The development of these bombers indicated that aerodynamic efficiency could be increased with size and paved the way for even larger bombers.

The Air Corps issued a design proposal in 1933 for an advanced multi-engine bomber. Within two years, Boeing delivered a new four-engine bomber to the Air Corps. Weighing in at 35,000 pounds, the XB-17 had a top speed of 250 miles per hour, a ceiling of 30,000 feet, and a range of 2,260 miles with 2,500 pounds of bombs.[51] The Air Corps was so impressed that it immediately ordered sixty-five B-17s for delivery in 1936. Hap Arnold remarked in his memoirs, "This was the first real American airpower. . . . For the first time in history, airpower that you could put your hand on."[52] In the same year, the Air Corps also received delivery of Norden and Sperry bombsights that allowed precise, daylight bombing at altitudes that at the time were beyond the reach of anti-aircraft artillery and made interception by pursuit aircraft difficult.[53] With this delivery occurring at about the same time as the establishment of GHQ Air Force, the mid-1930s became a period in which doctrine, organization, and technology apparently all came together to realize the visions of strategic bombardment advocates.

As a result of their confirmed faith in the technological dominance of the offense, both the Office of the Chief of the Air Corps and GHQ Air Force began a sustained campaign to procure heavy bombers and pursue research for ever larger, longer-ranged aircraft. Advising the Secretary of War on procurement matters, the chief of the Air Corps wrote in 1937, "the primary need of the Army for airplanes is in the category of long-range bombers—aircraft which would insure the Army's responsibility in defending the United States."[54] Yet until 1939, the procurement and development of heavy bombers was constrained by the Army's General Staff. After the crash of the only XB-17 in late 1935, the Army cut back the initial order for B-17s from sixty-five to thirteen. During the late 1930s, the General Staff canceled research on airplanes with a longer range than the B-17 and resisted Air Corps efforts to buy more B-17s. The Army Staff notified the Air Corps in the summer of 1938 that developmental expenditures for fiscal years 1939 and 1940 would be "restricted to that class of aviation designed for the close support of ground troops and protection of that type of aircraft."[55] The Air Corps requested 206 B-17s and 11 extra-long-range B-15s between October 1935 and June 1939. Because of War Department reductions and cancellations, however, the Air Corps had only fourteen B-17s when war broke out in Europe in September 1939. Although crucial technological progress had been made in developing the tools for strategic bombing, actual capabilities to wage such a form of warfare were severely limited by the number of weapons available.

Pursuit aviation did not evidence the same pace of technological advance as bomber development in the United States during the early 1930s. The speed and ceiling of the B-10 and the XB-17 gave the appearance that bombers might simply be able to outrun pursuit aircraft. The top-of-the-line Boeing P-26 produced in 1933 was capable of only a top speed of 235 miles per hour and a range of 360 miles. Exercises held at Wright Field and on the Pacific Coast made the Air Corps fundamentally question the role of pursuit aviation. Brigadier General Oscar Westover, then assistant chief of the Air Corps, remarked in 1933 that

> [d]uring these exercises, observation aircraft appeared woefully obsolete in performance as did pursuit aviation in speed characteristics. Since new bombardment aircraft possess speed above two hundred miles an hour, any intercepting or supporting aircraft must possess greater speed characteristics if they are to perform their missions. In the case of pursuit aviation, this increase in speed must be so great as to make it doubtful whether pursuit aircraft can be efficiently or safely operated either individually or in mass.[56]

Development of pursuit aircraft fell into a period of marked decline because of this perceived ineffectiveness. The advocacy of Major Claire Chennault at ACTS for improved interceptors and escort aircraft increasingly fell on deaf ears.[57] Chennault departed the Air Corps in frustration in 1935, remarking in his memoirs that "[t]he Office of the Chief of the Air Corps adopted the slogan 'Fighters are obsolete,' and funds for their development and procurement were greatly reduced."[58] Air Corps debates in the late 1930s over the required types of pursuit aircraft slowed progress even further. Although attention was given to single-seat fighters in the form of the P-38, P-39, and P-40, considerable effort was also expended on developing a multiseat fighter. This type of large fighter was believed to have the size to keep up with the range and speed of bombers such as the B-17. The resultant Bell XFM-1 never went beyond the design stage due to its slow rate of climb, low speed, and poor maneuverability. Despite the XFM-1's flaws, the Chief of the Air Corps, the ACTS, and the Air Force Board continued to support the idea of a multiseat escort fighter through at least the summer of 1940.[59]

The problems of improving pursuit performance were compounded by the lack of attention by commercial firms to improving airframe designs and engines for small aircraft. As the civilian air transport industry began to grow during the 1930s, firms such as Boeing and Douglas had much larger incentives to pursue technologies used for bomber aircraft for the Air Corps and transports for the airlines. The lack of research expenditures within the Air Corps caused the P-39 and XFM-1 to suffer from poor engines and performance. Even the P-38 and P-40 fighters produced in 1940–1941 were much less capable than the Me-109s, Spitfires, and Zeros produced respectively by Germany, Britain, and Japan.

The Air Corps also ignored air defense technologies that would enable development of capable air defense systems. The capabilities of radar for improving warning and interception networks were ignored in the United States and most other countries except Great Britain. The development of anti-aircraft artillery (AAA), barrage balloons, and passive defenses as responses to the threat posed by strategic bombardment received very little attention in the United States.

When events in Europe resulted in U.S. decisions to pursue mobilization with a heavy emphasis on airpower, the Air Corps and civilian industry had difficulties creating the massive forces called for by President Franklin D. Roosevelt. The Army air arm went through a rapid succession of plans involving ever larger projections of combat groups, planes, and manpower as follows:[60]

· Spring 1939—Expand to 24 combat ready groups by June 1941

· May 1940—Revise 24 group program upward to 41 groups

· July 1940—Expand to 54 groups with 4000 combat aircraft and over 200,000 personnel

· Autumn 1941—Victory Program with 84 groups and 40,000 personnel by June 1942

Production of strategic bombardment forces received the greatest emphasis. The lack of emphasis on long-range bomber production during the late 1930s, however, resulted in the engineering and production capabilities of the United States aircraft industry being severely overtaxed. As of October 1941, the Army Air Force could field only eighty-three B-17s. Significant resources were allocated for R&D beginning in 1939, but the lack of trained technical personnel and test facilities limited the initial progress of such efforts.[61] The success of the RAF during 1940 in defending Britain against the Luftwaffe caused Arnold and others to pay renewed attention to the development of pursuit aircraft. However, the available P-38, P-39, and P-40 designs lacked sufficient performance and range for escort missions. The ill-conceived commitment to multiseat escort fighters left the United States without any prospects for a capable long-range fighter.

During the course of World War II, these initial difficulties in mobilization of air forces were overcome. The scale and effectiveness of U.S. wartime efforts to create the planes, manpower, and supporting infrastructure for waging all types of air warfare far exceeded that of any other nation. From 1941 to 1945, the United States produced more than 200,000 aircraft and the Army Air Forces reached a maximum size of 2,372,000 personnel.[62] Despite this impressive showing in mobilization of men and material, the initial U.S. strategic bombardment operations were plagued by problems of insufficient force levels and execution of flawed doctrine. Before turning to the conduct of U.S. strategic bombing against Germany, we will look at lessons provided by the U.S. interwar experience regarding the establishment of organizational technological capacity.

Establishing Organizational Technological Capability for Strategic Air Warfare

This section explores the U.S. interwar experience of establishing strategic airpower in light of the facilitating factors addressed in chapter 3. Not unexpectedly, the history of the U.S. army air arm from 1919 to 1941 provides both positive and negative lessons about how strategic warfare capabilities can be nurtured during peacetime. In this case, although substantial progress occurred between the two world wars in articulating a doctrine for the conduct of strategic bombardment, the actual capacity created by the start of World War II was very limited. Also, the doctrinal focus established by the mid-1930s tended to blind U.S. airmen to technological developments and practical lessons that proved very important to the conduct of such operations during the war.

Institutional Context: Managing the Emergence of a New Military Capability

The interplay of the president, Congress, and the military services played a central role in shaping the organizational structure of the Army air arm during the interwar period. The view of different institutions regarding the strategic context of the United States also influenced the environment in which doctrine was shaped and determined the resources available to turn doctrinal visions into war-fighting capabilities.

Civilian political authorities in the United States after World War I "wanted aircraft to be able to fulfill the maximum that air theory promised."[63] Congressional initiatives to create an independent air service in 1919 and 1925 resulted in evaluations of how the emerging capabilities of airpower might require changes to organizational structure. Congress's role in investigating the problems the Air Corps had in delivering air mail in 1934 also provided an important impetus to Army decisions to drop this peripheral mission and establish the GHQ Air Force as a designated strategic air combat unit. Although the War Department successfully avoided the establishment of an independent air force until much later, Congress fostered the slow emergence of the Air Corps with a separate combat mission. The formation of the Morrow Board by President Coolidge in 1925 was a major factor in defusing the drive by Congress and Billy Mitchell for an independent service.

In the 1930s, President Roosevelt's sense of impending conflict played a fundamental role in the belated scramble to establish significant U.S. strategic airpower capabilities. Roosevelt sent Congress a special request in January 1939 for additional defense funds to meet the rising threat from overseas. Referring particularly to the Air Corps, he declared that current estimates for production needed to be revised upward.[64] Public and Congressional support for wartime mobilization followed the initiative of the president. For the United States, civilian legislative and executive institutions will always play a critical role in shaping strategic warfare capabilities.

Within the defense establishment, the isolationist position of the United States meant that the theories of strategic bombardment developed at ACTS lacked official validation until 1941. The result was a doctrinal disconnect of the Air Corps from the larger military establishment and a struggle with the War Department and Army lasting two decades. Whereas official manuals outlined the primary role of the Air Corps as one of direct support for ground and sea operations, a cadre of future leaders were trained to believe that the purpose of airpower was to launch precision strikes against the enemy's vital centers. The

Navy was also particularly leery of the establishment of significant long-range bomber forces within the Army as a potential challenger to its role in coastal defense and managing over-water air operations. The joint Navy and War Department resistance to the doctrine of strategic bombardment resulted in a crucial slowdown in Air Corps procurement of heavy bombers. The failure to obtain heavy bombers severely handicapped training, the development of tactical doctrine, and the building of a strong, ready-to-go offensive force. As a result, available bomber capabilities did not match the role envisioned for airpower in initial war plans for the defeat Germany.

Finally, the interwar period was one in which numerous boards and commissions evaluated emerging military capabilities based on a new technology. These boards were generally composed of individuals from within the military departments and civilian aviation industry. They became forums for mobilizing arguments and presenting controversial positions to either change or protect the status quo. The reviews by Congress and the War Department discussed above proved the most influential means for addressing challenges presented by questions of air service independence, procurement priorities, and combat roles. The Joint Army/Navy Board was the vehicle used to establish compromise between the War and Navy Departments regarding the role of the Air Corps in coastal defense as well as to retard procurement of B-17s in the late 1930s. Within the Air Corps, internal boards were also formed to deal with emerging concerns ranging from improving bombing accuracy, to procurement priorities, to the strategic role of airpower.[65] The deliberations and recommendations of the Air Corps boards during the late 1930s were especially pivotal in dealing with new challenges presented by mobilization and in defining the strategic role played by the Army air arm as the threat of war became increasingly clear. Although the activities and recommendations of such committees are often denigrated, during this period they generally provided a positive mechanism for conducting debate, establishing consensus, and achieving evolutionary organizational change.

Demand-Pull: Impact of Perceived Missions and the Role of the Air Force

The strategic context of the United States during the interwar period had a major impact in determining the types of capabilities pursued to perform perceived U.S. airpower missions. Until the late 1930s, U.S. bombardment aircraft development revolved around coastal defense. Mitchell's demonstration against the former German battleship Ostfriesland in 1921 proved the ability of aircraft to successfully attack major surface units and clearly established a role for airpower in defending approaches to the U.S. coast. Throughout the 1920s and 1930s while the doctrine of strategic industrial attack was being refined, the United States lacked a clearly identified enemy. The Air Corps and the GHQ Air Force necessarily relied on the coastal defense mission to justify the expenditure of scarce resources on bombers. The designated purpose of these bombers resulted in a technological focus on their capability to achieve precision bomb delivery against relatively small, moving ships on the ocean while flying at a high altitude to avoid anti-aircraft fire. Range was at a premium, as it allowed bombers to intercept enemy naval forces at as great a distance as possible from the coast. Aircraft carriers also emerged during this period, and although they were capable of launching defending interceptors, the increasing speed of bombers led U.S. airmen to denigrate the possibilities of intercept. The Air Corps consistently downplayed the need to sacrifice weight, payload, and speed to provide bombers with robust self-defense armament. The great range requirements for such operations reinforced the belief that escorts would not be able to accompany the bombers.

The rapid emergence of real concern about conflict with Germany and Japan caused a shift in the perceived role for U.S. strategic airpower. Offensively, the rationale for strategic bombing, so long advocated at ACTS, finally emerged. Initially, the strategic bombing mission was portrayed in terms of hemispheric defense. The influence of airpower in the German diplomatic success at the Munich conference in 1938, the initial blitzkriegs in Poland and France, and the beginning of the air campaign against Great Britain caused a sudden rise in the level of concern about the possibilities of air attacks launched on the United States.[66] The principal concerns were that the Germans would be able to influence Latin American nations to allow bombers to be based in their territory or, if Great Britain fell, bases would be seized in the northeastern portion of Canada. The Air Corps Board completed a study entitled "Air Corps Mission under the Monroe Doctrine" in October 1938. This study stated that the primary role for airpower was defense against hostile efforts to operate from air bases established in the Americas. According to the official AAF history, this concept subordinated both antishipping strikes and offensive strategic bombardment to counter–air strikes and exerted "a tremendous influence over air planning and designing aircraft during the emergency years of 1939–1941."[67] By June 1940, the Air Corps described its role as consisting of the following six missions (in order of priority):[68]

1. Deny the establishment of hostile air bases in the Americas
2. Defeat hostile air forces lodged in the hemisphere by attacking their bases

3.   Defeat hostile air forces by aerial combat

4.   Prevent the landing of expeditionary forces by attacking transport and supply ships

5.   Co-operate with the mobile army in ground operations

6.   Operate in support of or in lieu of U.S. Navy forces against hostile fleets

Throughout this period, the strategic emphasis was placed on achieving defensive objectives through preemptive operations. Therefore, resources were devoted to the development and procurement of long-range bombers. The utility of passive defenses such as dispersal or hardening to protect key assets within the United States received little attention.

The establishment of air defense of the United States lagged during this period because of political, service, and public indifference. Although concern rose in the late 1930s, an Air Defense Command was not established until February 1940. Little attention was given to defensive systems such as radar, observer networks, and radio communications systems. The attack on Pearl Harbor led to a short-lived surge in effort to develop air defense capabilities. Volunteer ground observers, information and filter centers, anti-aircraft and radar sites, and interceptor squadrons were all established. During the war, the defensive capabilities of these forces were never tested. The demands for limited material and manpower resources and the lack of a clear threat meant such efforts never received significant priority. The Joint Chiefs of Staff took the calculated risk of further reducing the effort expended on defense of the continental United States in 1943.[69]

The most significant development influencing the eventual role of U.S. strategic airpower in World War II was the fall of continental Europe while the United Kingdom maintained its independence. During 1941, the civilian and military leadership of the Western allies increasingly focused on strategic air bombardment as the only available means for striking directly at Hitler's war-making capability, as examined later in this chapter.

Management Initiative: Advocacy, Approach, and Emphasis

The establishment of both the organizations and technology required for waging strategic air warfare was a principal concern of Army air arm leaders. Uniformly, these men were believers in the growing significance of airpower as a means for waging war and the need for airmen to lead centrally controlled offensive striking forces. However, interwar U.S. air leaders took different approaches to advocacy. These differences centered on the degree to which conflict with superiors and the War Department was useful in achieving desired aims. As exemplified by the actions of Mitchell in the 1920s and Frank Andrews in the mid- to late 1930s, many airmen openly criticized superiors as lacking vision and aggressively courted Congress and the U.S. public to create the desired momentum for an independent air arm. Others, particularly Mason Patrick in the 1920s and Arnold in the late 1930s, used a more moderate approach within existing institutional structures. Their efforts created the de facto autonomy and freedom for the Army air arm to develop organizations such as the GHQ Air Force and technological tools such as the B-17 to fulfill doctrinal visions related to strategic warfare. The record of the 1919–1941 period seems to validate the value of an approach of incremental organizational change and improving functional capabilities. Although more widely publicized than the actions of others more moderate, the critiques of Mitchell and Andrews actually had the counterproductive effect of provoking pronounced negative reactions in the War Department. Patrick and Arnold managed to achieve progress on the organizational front (leading to the establishment of the Air Corps and Army Air Forces respectively) while also mobilizing resources for the expansion of the size and role of the air arm.

Arnold's role within the War Department in the immediate pre–World War II period was particularly significant. Until late 1938, the leadership within the War Department and Army inevitably took positions that slowed the growth of the Army air arm and its role. This was particularly true in the late 1930s and severely constrained funds for the B-17 and other long-range bombers. As Chief of the Air Corps after 1939, Arnold demonstrated an invaluable ability to work with President Roosevelt, Secretary of War Stimson, and Army Chief of Staff Marshall to put airpower at the forefront of the U.S. mobilization efforts and war plans.

The air leaders who did have an influence on the development of the Army air arm were all strong advocates of the primacy of the bomber. Dating back to the early advice of Mitchell about the inherently offensive nature of airpower, the most influential Air Service/Air Corps leaders of the period, including Patrick, Westover, Andrews, and Arnold, all saw the future of airpower in the doctrinal visions regarding the role of strategic bombardment. Emphasizing the ability of airpower to revolutionize warfare was a strong motivation within the Air Corps and in co-opting congressional and civilian allies. Those in the Air Corps who resisted such a one-sided view of airpower, such as Claire Chennault and Alexander de Seversky, were shunted aside.[70] The development of pursuit aviation lacked advocates within the Air Corps. The resulting inattention severely handicapped the early phases of U.S. strategic bombing campaigns in World War II.

Technological Expertise: Pilots, Bombers, and Missing Support Systems

    The development of technological expertise within the Army air arm during the period clearly followed the impetus created by doctrine and the organizational leadership. The emphasis throughout the 1920s and 1930s was on the development of fast, long-range aircraft that could demonstrate the potential of airpower to political leaders and the public. During the 1920s, the Air Corps was heavily involved in air races and setting speed records with aircraft funded through experimental programs. Long-range flights and refueling experiments were conducted to demonstrate the range and endurance potential of aircraft. Technologies supporting doctrinal emphasis on strategic bombing and the recognized mission of coastal defense were also stressed. The speed, range, and operating ceilings of bomber aircraft steadily improved from the B-2 to the B-10 to the B-17. By 1933, the Air Corps had tested the Norden and Sperry bombsights that provided the basis for war plan assumptions of precision daylight strikes against industrial facilities. Peacetime exercises with improving bombsights created a belief that sufficient accuracy to "hit a pickle barrel at high-altitude" could be achieved.[71]

    The development of technological tools within the Army air arm was also enhanced by the presence of relatively junior officers who progressed during the 1930s and early 1940s to assume major roles in leading the Army Air Forces in World War II, particularly the strategic bombing campaign against Germany. The nature of the U.S. Army air arm was that pilots dominated the officer corps and were intimately involved with the evolving technology. The Air Corps Act of 1926 mandated that no more than 10 percent of the officers in the Air Corps be nonpilots, which contributed to difficulties in building supporting engineering and technical expertise.[72] Pilots such as Arnold, Spaatz, Eaker, and Doolittle were all active in the experimental efforts to push aircraft technology forward during the 1920s. These men played the role of technological maestros within the Air Corps of the 1930s, linking a first-hand knowledge of the technology with an understanding of organizational missions and emerging doctrine. Again, the focus of these future air leaders on the possibilities for bombardment led them to push technological developments within the Air Corps in this direction, resulting in the steady progress evidenced in the B-10, B-17, and B-29. However, little room existed for men like Chennault and de Seversky to play a similar role for pursuit and defensive technology developments. Chennault's memoirs recount how, as a member of the pursuit development board within the Air Corps during the 1930s, he fought a losing battle against the development of a multiseat fighter advocated by bomber pilots.

The Air Service and Air Corps also maintained sound connections with the commercial aircraft industry during the interwar period that would work to its later advantage. Of particular importance was the recognition that the fledging civilian aircraft industry would not be able to survive on its own without government support. The Air Corps allowed the principal responsibility for research and development on experimental aircraft to remain with commercial firms to facilitate the maintenance of a diverse technology base instead of creating a major R&D program within the military. The Air Corps of the late 1920s and early 1930s kept the detail of solicitations for designs and prototypes for future aircraft to a minimum. The 1933 circular for industry proposals that resulted in the B-17 simply identified the need for "an advanced multi-engine bomber."[73] While most firms created two-engine designs, Boeing was able to propose and convince the Air Corps to pursue a four-engine aircraft. The Air Corps and commercial firms also cooperatively shared responsibility for identifying the specifications for developmental aircraft such as the B-17. Men like Doolittle and de Seversky maintained ties with the Air Corps during the 1930s while pursuing roles in commercial aviation that facilitated cooperative relationships.[74]

As mobilization became the primary challenge, the benefits of such a close relationship became apparent. The Air Corps "adopted various methods of acquainting manufacturers with new types of aeronautical equipment, of spreading the production among more firms, and of increasing the capacity of the industry. 'Educational orders' were placed with manufacturers, existing facilities were enlarged by the aid of government financing and new plants were built by the government for operation by private firms."[75] Such ties were enhanced by the appointment of Robert Lovett, formerly a vice president at General Motors, as Assistant Secretary of War for Air, creating firm links with commercial industry. Historians give the Army air arm high marks for their ability to sustain ties with the civilian sector. Richard Overy notes that

> the British and American experience was united, on the importance
> of involving officers and civilians with technical and engineering

experience in the air forces. The engineering officers were of equal status with those in combat and administrative positions. In most cases, career air officers already possessed a considerable amount of technical training. Where gaps existed during the war, civilians were brought in to organize technical and engineering functions, and in the AAF in particular considerable emphasis was laid on the engineering staffs, on whose contribution the combat staffs were largely dependent.[76]

As a result, the United States entered World War II with an Army Air Force and industry capable of managing the type of mobilization that would create material dominance over its adversaries. However, underdevelopment of defensive technologies and supporting activities to enable strategic bombardment and measure its effectiveness would undermine wartime efforts.

A crucial problem area was a lack of attention to the supporting technologies that would prove necessary to enable strategic bombers to conduct daylight operations without prohibitive losses. Such problems began with inadequate defensive armament on the bomber aircraft developed in the 1930s.[77] Experience during World War I had indicated the need for large-caliber, all-aspect self-defense armament for bomber aircraft. For two decades, the Army air arm ignored the lesson for a variety of reasons. An adequate .50 caliber machine gun had been developed for aircraft self-defense in the early 1920s. However, this weapon was rarely installed because of the need to save on the procurement costs and operating expenses that the heavier weapon required. The lack of adequate gunnery ranges meant defensive armament received little testing, and the shortcomings of smaller .30 caliber guns were not discovered. No incentive existed for commercial enterprises to develop systems such as powered gun turrets without funding from the Air Corps. The pilots who dominated the Air Corps during the 1930s concerned themselves principally with matters of flying performance.[78] The focus on improving speed, range, and ceiling received even more emphasis as the belief grew that bombers could defend themselves by outrunning pursuit aircraft. This belief directly contributed to a downgrading of attention to defensive armament within the Air Corps development efforts in the mid- to late 1930s. The addition of guns and external blisters, which expanded the field of fire for such weapons, came at the cost of weight and "prohibitive drag," which the Aircraft Laboratory at Wright Field deemed a poor trade-off.[79] The first three service models of the B-17 (A, B, and C) were armed with only five .30 caliber machine guns and lacked a tail gun. The Air Corps rejected Boeing proposals for improved armament on the B and C models as "aerodynamically unacceptable." British crews flying the B-17C model during 1941 suffered dearly in combat as a result.[80]

By 1940, the wartime experience of the RAF had managed to convince Arnold and the Air Corps Board to stress to Wright Field engineers the need to provide improved defensive armament on the B-17 and other bombers. The Armament Division at Wright Field initially proved incapable of absorbing the rush of funding provided as part of the U.S. mobilization effort. Initial efforts at designing powered turrets and tail guns were flawed, wasting valuable time in fielding defensive armament as war approached. Not until the B-17E model, armed with ten .50 caliber machine guns, six placed in powered turrets, began to roll off the production line in 1942 did the U.S. possess the type of bomber that could fulfill the doctrinal visions of U.S. airmen. Large numbers of these aircraft did not become available, however, until 1943. When deep strikes began against Germany in the summer of that year, the bombers would inflict significant losses on attacking German fighters. However, without fighter escort, even robust defensive armament would prove inadequate to enable cost-effective strategic bombing.

The story of the evolution of U.S. long-range escorts for the strategic bombardment campaign is largely one of wartime reaction and improvisation. In relation to this analysis of interwar development of technological means and expertise for waging strategic bombardment, suffice it to say the Army air arm refused in the interwar period to establish engineering expertise and undertake efforts to design and build adequate escort fighters. During the mid-1930s, the Air Corps believed the development of airplanes with the range and speed to escort long-range bombers would likely prove technologically impossible. The one effort during the pre–World War II period to design such an aircraft took a fatally flawed approach. When confronted by crisis, the AAF was fortunate to be able to upgrade the powerplant of the P-51 Mustang, an aircraft originally not designed for use by the AAF, with British Rolls-Royce engines.[81] Another crucial development, fuel tanks that could be jettisoned for combat, was pioneered in the early war years by the Navy and by Army Air Force units for use in tactical operations in New Guinea.[82] The unplanned availability of these technologies allowed U.S. strategic bombing efforts against Germany to recover the initiative in 1944, as detailed later in this chapter.

Beyond inattention to supporting technologies, the initial U.S. strategic bombardment efforts were also hampered by the underdevelopment of human expertise. A principal reason for this underdevelopment was the challenge of training large numbers of personnel to perform a whole range of necessary functions. Even prior to the expansion of the late 1930s, Army air arm leaders had consistently lamented the lack of enough experienced personnel.[83] When the expansion program began in 1939, simply recruiting and teaching enough pilots to fly the tens of thousands of planes envisioned in the mobilization plans required the revamping of training procedures and curriculums. The Army Air Forces came to rely heavily on civilian schools for this purpose and had difficulty sustaining the level of instructor expertise desired.[84] The situation regarding the establishment of training programs for bombardiers, navigators, radio operators, gunners, and ground crews was even more difficult.[85] The specifically military tasks in which these personnel engaged lacked any basis in the civilian sector and far fewer qualified personnel to conduct the necessary training existed within the prewar Air Corps. Throughout the mobilization period and war, the United States suffered from a lack of qualified instructors for bombardiers and navigators, relying on RAF schools and observers to provide lessons based on combat experience. Maintaining the skill base of instructors for teaching aircraft repair and maintenance also proved difficult because these personnel were pulled toward better paying jobs in depots and factories.

Even when personnel began to move out of initial training programs, establishing combat units proved a daunting challenge. Regular units based in the United States often were unable to sustain any inherent combat capability due to the continuing transfer of experienced personnel overseas. A postwar report on "Combat Crew and Unit Training in the AAF" indicates that, "[b]ecause of the pace of expansion in the late 1930s, the shortage of airplanes and equipment, the low level of experience of most pilots, the relative experience of maintenance personnel, and the rapid change in air tactics, even the older groups had difficulty in approaching the level of proficiency required."[86] Generally, establishing strategic bombardment capability was initially limited by the challenges of assimilating and diffusing a wide range of experiential skills necessary to operate the B-17s and B-24s that rolled off production lines in ever greater numbers. As with aircraft production, the wartime development of the U.S. system for training aircrews and most other supporting skills eventually developed into a fundamental strength. However, the official AAF history states, "It would take a nation at arms several years to produce the aircraft and crews, bases, and technicians called for."[87] The doctrine of the 1930s called for quickly establishing air superiority and incapacitating the opponent's industrial web through large-scale strategic bombardment. The U.S. Army Air Forces in World War II required a lengthy period to turn available technological tools and small, standing forces into a significant capability to wage strategic warfare under such a doctrine.

The U.S. also lacked the capability to conduct adequate target analysis and intelligence for employing strategic airpower due to inattention during the interwar period. As early as Douhet and Mitchell, advocates of strategic bombing recognized the need for proper target identification to maximize its effect.[88] ACTS lectures detailing precision attacks against critical nodes of an enemy's industrial system also stressed the significance of this task.[89] Neither the Army nor the Air Corps itself made a significant effort to establish either organizations or personnel with such skills. For most of the Army leadership, World War I had created a perspective that defined air intelligence as the use of aircraft to collect information to support ground operations. Intelligence support for the air arm was the responsibility of the General Staff G-2 branch in Washington, D.C.[90] Yet, according to General Omar Bradley, Army intelligence during this period was "a dumping ground for officers ill suited to line command."[91] The General Staff G-2 focused on gathering intelligence for surface operations and pointedly resisted efforts to create inroads to its sole responsibility for military intelligence in war planning.[92]

Attachés responsible for providing information on overseas developments and potential targets were often from privileged social backgrounds and provided little useful information. Consider a proposal in the mid-1920s that air attachés be required to attend the Air Service Engineering School. The Air Service decided against this initiative in 1925 due to fears of dispersing the already limited pool of available aviation engineering expertise.[93]

Despite the dictates of ACTS doctrine, little effort was made within the Air Corps to develop adequate intelligence capabilities for waging strategic warfare during the interwar period. During the 1930s, the Office of the Chief of the Air Corps included a small Information Section whose responsibilities included public affairs, keeping information on air fields, flight routes, and counterintelligence, as well as providing intelligence about adversaries. The intelligence staff concentrated on collecting reports by attachés and observers regarding the size and technical capabilities of other nations' air forces and the conduct of air operations in places like Ethiopia, Spain and China.[94] The GHQ Air Force lacked dedicated intelligence support for its role as an independent air strike force and often was at odds with the Office of Chief of the Air Corps Intelligence Division.[95]

The ACTS instructors developing the industrial web concept had no economists or industrial engineers within the Air Corps to analyze the likely effects of strategic bombing. Efforts to garner support from the G-2 Military Intelligence

Division in Washington proved fruitless. The War Department even went so far as to forbid independent ACTS examination of the economies of foreign countries, arguing that such was the responsibility of the MID.[96] This reinforced the tendency of the school to use the U.S. economy as a basis for its critical node thinking. ACTS instructors eventually turned to the Army Industrial College in the late 1930s for analyses such as the effect of targeting electric power facilities.[97]

Growing concern over the approaching war and the recognition of the potential role for airpower lead to a struggle within the G-2 for creation of an independent intelligence capability for the Army's air forces. A separate section was set up within G-2 for aviation intelligence activities, and the Information Division within the Air Corps staff was renamed the Intelligence Division in November 1940.[98] As early as 1939, a tiny economic analysis branch had been set up and even began work on target folders.[99] However, in June 1941, the General Staff G-2 complained to the Army Chief of Staff, General Marshall, that practically all phases of military intelligence were being duplicated by the Air Corps staff and demanded a delineation of responsibilities. A War Department directive that would remain in effect throughout the war resolved the situation in September 1941. The directive gave the G-2 responsibility for collection, evaluation, and dissemination of all military information, including information relevant to the Army Air Forces. Air Staff intelligence agencies would limit their activities to technical and tactical intelligence.[100] The Army Air Forces began its first formal training course for intelligence personnel focused solely on imagery intelligence on 8 December 1941, the day after Pearl Harbor.[101] According to Hap Arnold, the arrangement would prove "one of the most wasteful weaknesses in our whole setup . . . our lack of a proper Air Intelligence Organization."[102]

The Army air arm entered the war without a dedicated intelligence capability to support the targeting and damage assessment tasks necessary for waging strategic air warfare and therefore lacked the capacity to effectively manage the initial bombing campaigns. This challenge would remain central to the results of strategic bombardment throughout the war.

Learning Ability: Impact of Doctrinal Fixation

The ascendancy of the belief in high-altitude, precision strategic bombardment by the 1930s skewed learning within the Army air arm regarding the lessons of peacetime exercises in the United States and the wartime conduct of air operations by others. The importance of exercises held on the West Coast in 1933–1934 establishing the rationale for the primacy of the bomber was addressed earlier. As commander of the principal bomber group involved in those exercises, Hap Arnold reported that "[p]ursuit or fighter aircraft . . . will rarely intercept a modern bomber except accidentally."[103] Other key air leaders during the 1930s, including Westover and Andrews, echoed these lessons in the immediate aftermath of the experience. By the mid-1930s, the lessons taught by this set of experiences, combined with doctrinal precepts, contributed to the dismissal of potential lessons from later exercises. Exercises held at Ft. Bragg, North Carolina, in 1938 demonstrated the feasibility of establishing a warning net enabling pursuit aircraft to intercept bombers.[104] Yet these exercises received no attention from the bomber advocates. The demonstrated potential for effective air defenses had little impact on World War II air planners considering either hemispheric defense or German opposition to U.S. long-range bombing plans. Arnold and the other U.S. air leaders took the view into World War II that "the whole concept in the Air Force is offense: to seek out the enemy, to locate him as early and as far distant from our vital areas as we can."[105]

Peacetime impediments also inhibited learning about the requirements for the conduct of offensive strategic bombardment operations. The use of the United States as a model for understanding the industrial web concept proved problematic. Lacking clearly identified adversaries and adequate intelligence, the ACTS theorists analyzed U.S. infrastructures and cities. Beginning in 1935, detailed analysis of the supporting electric, transportation, and communications systems for New York City became the principal model for refining their ideas. Major Muir S. Fairchild presented a lecture in the 1935–1936 course at ACTS that used New York City as an example of how attacks could be launched on major cities. Fairchild's lecture analyzed key nodes in rail transportation, water, and electric power systems. Utilizing this analysis, lectures at the ACTS argued that bombs from just eighteen aircraft could cause an electrical power outage that would bring the whole city to a halt.[106] Interestingly, the President's Commission on Critical Infrastructure Protection in 1997 also used an analysis of New York City electric power as an infrastructure vulnerable to strategic digital attack.

Peacetime understanding of the size of bomber forces and weight of weapons necessary to destroy targets was based on expected high accuracy and mathematical calculations of the required numbers of planes. U.S. airpower advocates generally ignored past practical experience with the fog and friction of war. The quest for mathematical precision in the conduct of bombardment operations dates back as far as Douhet, who asserted that when ten planes carrying a total of twenty tons of bombs strike a target with a diameter of 500 meters in diameter, "we have mathematical certainty that the target will be destroyed."[107] Within the United States, the infatuation with bombing accuracy was reinforced by Billy Mitchell's successes in destroying the Ostfriesland and other naval vessels in the early 1920s. By the late 1930s, the Air Corps Board had issued a study entitled "Delivery of Fire from Aircraft" that asserted that the size of a bomber force necessary to destroy a given target could be quantified "with a reasonable assurance of success" while avoiding overkill.[108] U.S. airmen developed a faith in the ease of calculating the required forces and achieving desired damage against any targets. This highly precise, mathematical approach dominated air war planning for the strategic bombing against Germany.

The well-established belief in the ability of unescorted bombers to conduct long-range bombardment also limited the degree to which the Army air forces were able to learn from the experience of others. Numerous reports flowed into the United States from attachés and interested observers regarding the use of air forces by the Italians in Ethiopia, the Russians and Germans in the Spanish Civil War, and the Japanese in China. U.S. airmen extracted from these reports lessons to fit the ACTS precepts regarding the use of airpower. In addressing the Army War College in 1936, the GCHQ commander, Frank Andrews, argued that Italian airpower had virtually transformed the Mediterranean into an Italian lake and possibly "prevented England from openly assisting Ethiopia in its war with Italy."[109] In reviewing the Sino-Japanese war in 1937, Hap Arnold concluded, "The employment of the Japanese Air Force is directly in line with the most up-to-date teaching of our own Air Corps Tactical School and with the doctrines of our own GHQ Air Force."[110] The impact of perceived Luftwaffe bomber strength in influencing the outcome at Munich was also widely recognized within the Air Corps.

Yet although they recognized the value of offensive striking power, senior U.S. airmen largely ignored the growing evidence that technological develop-ments overseas were beginning to give the defense the advantage. A 1938 Air Corps analysis of air operations in the Sino-Japanese war found that "the senti-ment that bombardment has not sufficient power to penetrate unprotected against pursuit opposition is nearly universal."[111] Yet the report apparently received little notice. Even when war began to rage in Europe and Britain became directly involved, the technological advances in interceptor aircraft and the British air defense network received inadequate attention in the United States. Observers outside the Army air arm such as de Seversky pointed out that American fighter planes had become inferior to those of the other world powers. De Seversky wrote in 1942 that "[n]o one in his senses would pretend the P-40 is a match for the Messerschmidt or Spitfire."[112] More significantly, little attention was paid to British advances in radar that played a critical role in defeating the Luftwaffe in the Battle of Britain. Incredibly, Haywood Hansell would later portray ignorance of British advances in radar as beneficial to the United States, stating, "If our air theorists had a knowledge of radar in 1935, the American doctrine of strategic bombing in deep daylight penetrations would surely not have evolved. Our ignorance of radar was surely an asset at this phase."[113] Hansell here neglects the possibility that airpower doctrine could have been modified to acknowledge the need for escort aircraft to overcome air defenses while remaining focused on bombardment for destroying the enemy's warmaking potential.

Numerous influential U.S. airmen including Hansell, Spaatz, and Eaker visited Great Britain to observe the conduct of the air war in Europe and met with RAF leaders as early as 1940. Exchanges of information occurred in almost every conceivable area of doctrine, organization, and technology. Direct exposure to the implications of combat prodded the United States to accelerate development of certain technologies such as defensive gunnery.[114] More generally, however, the U.S. observers tended to downplay the difficulties the Germans and British faced in waging successful strategic bombing campaigns. Hansell indicated that "both German and British bombers proved vulnerable to fighters but then they were medium bombers, poorly armed, and flying at relatively low altitude. . . . American bombers were much better armed and they would be flying at high altitude."[115] Reviewing German difficulties, Spaatz would argue that the Germans had misunderstood how to conduct strategic bombing. Despite demonstrated British resilience and ability to adapt, he argued the Germans could have reduced the British to a shambles in 1940.[116] A similar resistance to learning is demonstrated in the evaluation of British bombing efforts during this period. U.S. assessments of British bombing efforts stressed the damage done by daylight raids while assessing that area night bombing attacks were inefficient. An U.S. Army Air Forces assessment of the first "1,000 plane" night raid found that, although massive damage had been inflicted, "population displacement, unaccompanied by direct damage to industrial establishments, transportation and power sources appears to be an ineffective and uneconomic means of achieving strategic bombing results." The AAF authors concluded that "[t]he most economic as well as the most certain method of accomplishing an effective concentration of bombardment effort is precision bombing."[117]

The result of allowing doctrinal precepts to constrain learning was that U.S. airmen during World War II would use assumptions about the nature of strategic bombardment operations that proved hard to modify and costly in terms of both men and machines. Yet expectations regarding the ability of organizations to learn about the proper fashion of waging strategic warfare during peacetime should rightfully be tempered. Regarding the difficulty of successful learning, Richard Overy concludes in *Air War 1939–1945* that "[b]y the 1930s, the lessons of the earlier conflict had been turned from hasty empiricism into a refined doctrine. However, by 1939 even the refined doctrine was becoming obsolescent, overtaken by scientific and strategic events."[118] Williamson Murray's study of interwar innovation in strategic bombing notes that "[i]f the strategic air war looked quite different from prewar concepts in reality, that was largely due to its complexity and the relative paucity of prewar experience."[119] Looking ahead to the ability of planners and operators to understand the nature of strategic information warfare at the start of the twenty-first century, such inherent limits to understanding should also be kept in mind.

U.S. Strategic Bombing Campaign against Germany: 1942–1945

This section provides an overview of the U.S. planning and execution of a strategic bombing campaign against Germany during World War II. This campaign has received much attention from historians and commentators on strategic affairs. The analysis here does not attempt a comprehensive review of events. Rather, the section describes the evolution of strategic bombardment plans, reviews the challenges encountered in executing these plans, and assesses how the campaign contributed to the Allied war effort. The history of this effort highlights the difficulties involved in successfully waging strategic warfare and provides possible lessons for the conduct of strategic information warfare.

Planning for Aerial Victory: The Development of AWPD-1 and Its Successors

The development of U.S. war plans against Germany was heavily influenced by the close relationship between President Roosevelt and British Prime Minister Winston Churchill. Roosevelt's decision to provide the British with aid through the lend-lease program in 1940 led to growing contact and coordination between the military establishments of the two countries. Exchanges of intelligence information began while U.S. and British planners started to discuss how war might be jointly waged in Europe. The first set of common strategic principles was arrived at by delegations of the British and U.S. chiefs of staff in February and March 1941. The plan produced in these sessions is usually referred to as ABC-1. Recognizing the possibility of simultaneous war with Japan, the planners recommended defeating Germany first as the predominant member of the Axis powers. Offensive actions to be taken against Germany included "a sustained air offensive against German Military Power, supplemented by air offensives against other regions under enemy control which contribute to that power" in preparation for a ground campaign. The Allied air forces would seek to achieve "superiority of air strength over that of the enemy, particularly in long-range striking forces." According to ABC-1, "U.S. Army air bombardment [would] operate offensively in collaboration with the Royal Air Force, primarily against German Military Power at its source."[120]

The War Plans Division of the Army General Staff was simultaneously developing a U.S.-only plan for a war involving both Germany and Japan known as RAINBOW-5. In the plan approved by the Joint Board in May 1941, the role of strategic airpower was much less clearly defined in RAINBOW-5 than in ABC-1. In RAINBOW-5, Army Air Forces bombardment forces were committed to hemispheric defense and support of naval operations, rather than strategic offensive operations against the adversary.

The potential divergence between these plans became apparent in August 1941 during a high-level conference involving President Roosevelt and Prime Minister Churchill. The official document produced at this summit was the political declaration known as the Atlantic Charter. Military exchanges during this conference included a concerted effort by the British to assert the necessity of a major strategic air campaign against Germany. The Western allies agreed that they would be unable to launch a ground offensive in Europe prior to 1943. The British argued that a concentrated bombardment campaign against morale, transportation, and industrial centers could severely weaken the German war effort and even possibly induce Germany to sue for peace. The U.S. senior military leadership was very reserved about supporting such a strategy. The formal Joint Chiefs of Staff response to the British in September 1941 stated that such an emphasis on strategic bombardment would significantly diverge from the principles originally outlined in ABC-1.

At the same time, U.S. planning efforts in Washington also began to involve grandiose visions for the strategic air campaign. On 9 July 1941, President Roosevelt requested the Secretaries of War and the Navy prepare an estimate of overall production requirements required to defeat U.S. potential enemies. Though Roosevelt envisioned this estimate simply as a determination of material and logistical requirements for U.S. mobilization, the Army Air Forces produced a document outlining a vision for conducting a strategic air war against

Germany. The responsibility to answer the President's directive was nominally the task of the War Plans Division of the General Staff. However, the growing autonomy of the AAF had led Hap Arnold to form a separate Air War Plans Division within the Air Staff. This organization quickly assumed responsibility for determining the Army's aviation requirements.[121] The resultant document, known as AWPD-1, was produced by a committee of four men, led by Col. Harold George and including Lt. Col. Kenneth Walker, Maj. Laurence Kuter, and Maj. Haywood Hansell. All had been associated with the ACTS during the 1930s. Walker, in particular, had helped articulate and advocate the doctrine of strategic bombardment. The efforts of this committee produced a plan within a frenzied week from 4 to 11 August. Given the time pressure to comply with the president's directive, AWPD-1 was quickly reviewed and approved by the War Plans Division, Gen. Arnold, Gen. Marshall, Lovett, and Stimson and included as part of the Joint Board's report to the president on 11 September.

The result of this hurried effort provided a more complete vision of how U.S. airpower would contribute to the war effort than the simple statements of strategic principles and aggregated numbers of personnel and material provided by the Army and Navy. According to AWPD-1, the air mission in Europe would be offensive from the start. Support of ground operations would occur only if it became necessary to invade the continent. According to Hansell, the plan's objective statement leaned heavily toward victory through airpower but allowed for air support of an invasion if the air offensive should not prove conclusive. Although AWPD-1 also assessed the aircraft requirements for defending both coasts and for conducting operations in the Pacific theater, it focused primarily on outlining operational assumptions and aircraft requirements for waging a strategic bombardment offensive against Germany. Based on the industrial web doctrine and the assumption that the German offensive against Russia begun in June 1941 had placed great strain on the German economy, AWPD-1 stated that "[d]estruction of that economic structure will virtually break down the capacity of the German nation to wage war. The basic conception on which this plan is based lies in the application of airpower for the breakdown of the industrial and economic structure of Germany."[122] The plan called for precision attacks on industrial targets at first. It also stated that as morale in Germany began to crack, area bombing might become effective.

AWPD-1 provided the first systemic identification of key targets for the strategic air campaign against Germany. The planners settled on four basic systems comprised of 154 total targets as detailed below:

1. Electric power (fifty generating plants and switching stations).
2. Transportation (forty-seven marshaling yards, bridges, and locks).
3. Synthetic petroleum production (twenty-seven plants).
4. The Luftwaffe, especially fighters (eighteen aircraft assembly, twelve aluminum and magnesium plants).

The importance of achieving air superiority was recognized in identifying the German Air Force as an intermediate objective of overriding significance. The Luftwaffe's defeat would be necessary to achieve success against the other "primary" objectives.

However, despite the implied precision of the numbers produced, little is known about how the planners decided on target systems and numbers of targets. The plan called for targeting facilities associated with objectives vital to the continued German war effort and to the means of livelihood of the German people. The AAF would tenaciously concentrate all bombing toward those facilities. Hansell's account of the planning process and other histories lack any description of how such "vital objectives" were identified. Formal intelligence support was seemingly nonexistent. These histories make no mention of efforts to use the target folders being developed within the Air Intelligence branch of the Office of the Army Air Corps. The best source of information available to the AWPD-1 planners was intelligence provided to Hansell by the British earlier in 1941, which was particularly focused on the German transportation and aviation industries. Additionally, U.S. banks provided information about the German electric industry based on documents received when construction loans had been made in the 1920s.[123] In a very rushed effort to target the German industrial web, the seminal U.S. strategic war plan apparently focused on targeting systems for which information was most readily accessible rather than relying on well-developed databases or systematic analysis of key nodes. Also, the AWPD-1 planners paid little heed to German capacity to harden, disperse, or reconstitute different target systems or how inflicting damage on these systems would specifically affect Germany's warmaking capability or morale.

Based on their identification of targets, the AWPD-1 planners proceeded to determine the number of aircraft required. The plan states, "War time errors [are] assumed to be 2.25 times those of peace time. The force required in war [to achieve 90 percent probability of damage requirements] is thus 2.25 squared or 5 times that for peacetime bombing." After a brief description of British problems dealing with German AAA and fighter defenses, the AWPD-1 indicates that, "[b]y employing large numbers of aircraft with high speed, good defensive fire-power and high altitude, it is feasible to make deep penetrations into Germany during daylight."[124] Based on such assumptions, the resultant plan called for the establishment of ninety-eight total bomber groups. The scheduled bombing campaign would begin in 1943 with the principal effort to start in 1944. For the protection of air bases, a total of sixteen pursuit groups would be located around bases in Britain and the Near East. Although the potential requirement for escort fighters was identified, the plan simply proposed experiments with the flawed multiseat design, and no production figures for escorts were provided.[125] In total, AWPD-1 was largely based on factors the planners felt confident in estimating: aircraft production, bombing accuracy, and attrition rates. Consideration or even identification of the uncertainties such as weather or defenses facing those who would execute this plan due to the fog and friction of war was not in evidence.[126]

After the unexpected Japanese attack on Pearl Harbor in December 1941, continuing efforts to achieve coordination with British allies and competing demands on resources resulted in inevitable modification of the plans for the U.S. strategic bombing campaign. Ira Eaker, who would assume command of the U.S. Eighth Air Force bomber forces, and several staff officers were sent to Britain early in 1942 to consult with the RAF regarding the planned joint bombardment campaign.[127] Having begun their efforts at the Atlantic conference the previous summer, the British continued to try to convince the Americans that their planned bombing campaign would prove unworkable. They recommended that U.S. bomber forces join British forces engaged in nighttime area attacks. The early British daylight bomber efforts had suffered heavy losses during unescorted strikes in 1939–1940. Conducting daylight operations with the protection of available escorts had severely limited the target set and convinced the British that long-range fighters could not hold their own against defending short-range fighters. RAF efforts to use B-17Cs and B-24s received from the United States in the summer of 1941 also resulted in unacceptable losses. By 1942, the RAF, under the command of Air Marshall Arthor Harris, were firmly committed to a strategy of nighttime area bombardment designed to undermine the German war effort by crushing civilian morale.[128]

British pleas to newly appointed American air leaders fell on deaf ears. Dedicated to a doctrine of daylight, high-altitude precision bombardment, the U.S. leaders continued to plan for deep strikes against Germany without fighter escort. A report issued in January 1942, based on unopposed exercises conducted in the cloudless southwest U.S. desert, confirmed the confidence of U.S. air leaders in the ability of U.S. bombers to conduct precision strikes.[129] Clear evidence that both the Luftwaffe and RAF had found achieving accuracy diffi-cult under wartime conditions was ignored. Eaker led a review of RAF bombing doctrine and efforts, issuing his report in March 1942. Although it acknowledged that British bomber losses had been reduced by conducting nighttime opera-tions, the report found that attacks against morale would take a prolonged period to achieve desired effect. Eaker recommended that U.S. air forces be employed in "operations of the type for which [their] equipment and training had been designed." He did stress the value of a coordinated day and night campaign in conjunction with the RAF. Eaker's report placed little emphasis on the require-ment to develop fighter aircraft.[130] Lacking a capable fighter for this mission, efforts to convert B-17 and B-24 airframes into heavily armed escorts would prove a dismal tactical failure.

Although early ABC documents had called for escalating the magnitude of the strategic bombing campaign as early as possible, other events and wartime priorities soon cut into efforts to execute this strategy. Through the spring of 1943, a critical conflict raged in the Atlantic as German submarines took a ter-rible toll on Allied shipping. To take some burden from the Russians, the Western allies decided to conduct an invasion of western North Africa. Japanese suc-cesses and domestic pressure in the United States also made minimizing war efforts in the Pacific difficult. Despite efforts by Arnold and the AAF staff to resist, these considerations resulted in the diversion of heavy bombers initially desig-nated for the AAF bomber forces in England. These wartime exigencies resulted in the promulgation of a revised U.S. planning document known as AWPD-42, issued in August 1942. AWPD-42 differed from its AWPD-1 predecessor in detail-ing requirements in material and manpower for strategic bombing campaigns against both Germany and Japan. This plan called for the U.S. strategic bombing forces against Germany to strike 177 targets with the following priorities: (1) the German air force, (2) submarine yards, (3) transportation, (4) electric power, (5) oil, and (6) rubber.[131] Significantly, AWPD-42 now called for the destruction of two military target sets before the strategic centers of the economy suffered the weight of attack. Additionally, targeting rubber was identified as a useful means of hampering the efforts of ground forces rather than dislocating the German industrial web. AWPD-42 planning was based more directly on available intelli-gence, particularly that provided by the British Ministry of Economic Warfare. However, the planners wrongfully assumed that the German war economy was "already strained to a breaking point and incapable of further expansion."[132]

Another significant modification to U.S. strategic bombing plans occurred the following spring in the wake of the North African campaign. A major U.S.–

British war planning conference was held off Casablanca in January 1943. At the Casablanca conference, the Combined Chiefs of Staff called for the conduct of "a joint U.S.-British air offensive to accomplish the progressive destruction and dislocation of the German military, industrial and economic system, and undermining the morale of the German people to a point where their capacity for armed resistance is fatally weakened."[133] By April 1943, this directive had been turned into a plan known as the Combined Bomber Offensive (CBO). The U.S. plan for conducting the CBO identified the following six systems comprising seventy-six precision targets. The priority among target systems was as follows:

1. Intermediate objectives
    - German fighter strength
2. Primary objectives
    - Submarine construction yards and bases
    - German nonfighter aircraft industry
    - Ball bearings
    - Oil
3. Secondary objectives (in order of priority)
    - Synthetic rubber and tires
    - Military motor transport vehicles

Walking a tightrope between the contending views of Allied air leaders, the plan validated the approaches of both the AAF and the RAF regarding strategic bombardment. Increasingly stressing the strategic interdiction of war materials, the CBO plan demonstrates a very conscious effort to identify key nodes within the German industrial web. The plan reduced the number of targets to be struck and endeavored to identify systems with more immediate impact on German war efforts rather than targeting systems generally supporting the economy. The projected effect of bombing the ball bearing industry is described as follows: "The concentration of that industry makes it outstandingly vulnerable to attack. 76 percent of the ball-bearing production can be eliminated by destruction of the targets selected. This will have immediate and critical repercussions on the production of tanks, airplanes, artillery, diesel engines—in fact, upon nearly all the special weapons of modern war."[134] In summary, the planners said, "In view of the ability of adequate and properly utilized air power to impair the industrial source of the enemy's strength, only the most vital considerations should be permitted to delay or divert the application of an adequate air striking force to this task."[135]

Despite the shifting target sets outlined in these plans, U.S. airmen, including Arnold, Spaatz, and Eaker, maintained a faith that strategic bombing could prove decisive, possibly eliminating the need for a major ground effort. However, the air campaign was always conducted within the context of a greater war effort. Although these airmen fought the diverting of strategic bombardment resources, other "vital considerations" arose numerous times as the land and naval wars raged simultaneously. The prewar doctrine of directing maximum airpower efforts against industrial centers of gravity suffered from a continuing recognition that fighting a global war with important allies required flexibility in determining how limited heavy bomber assets were employed. Also, although theoretically committed to a coordinated effort, differences between the RAF and U.S. air leaders often resulted in basically independent strategic bombing efforts. The impact of the U.S. strategic bombing campaign fell short of the war-winning possibilities envisioned in its war plans.

Executing the Strategic Air War Plans: A Slow Start and Forced Adaptation

The story of the U.S. Eighth Air Force strategic bombing campaign against Germany, with its initial crescendo in October 1943, seems full of missteps and miscalculations. Under the command of Spaatz and Eaker, the Eighth Air Force underwent a slow buildup and a piecemeal commitment to action during 1942 and the first half of 1943. The first air strike, involving eighteen Eighth Air Force aircraft B-17s and aircrews escorted by RAF fighters, was conducted against a railroad yard in Rouen, France, on 17 August 1942. Small strikes were conducted against other targets in France and along the north German coast throughout the fall of that year. The establishment of large bomber forces in England was slowed severely, however, by the diversion of aircraft to North African invasion forces, to the Pacific theater, and to the U.S. Navy and British Coastal Command to conduct long-range antisubmarine patrols in the Atlantic. Efforts to quickly step up the pace of Eighth Air Force bombing operations were also delayed by the need to provide significant in-theater training to crews. Pilots needed to learn combat formations. Prior to their arrival in England, inexperienced gunners had never fired weapons or operated turret systems while flying.[136] The decision was made to accumulate combat experience and test the defensive capabilities of the B-17 slowly in well-protected missions in which the RAF fighters provided cover. Winter weather basically put a stop to significant combat operations. The lull allowed an incremental buildup in Eighth AF bomber assets. However, the antisubmarine campaign had reached a critical phase during the spring of 1943. U.S. bombing efforts remained concentrated on submarine bases and construction yards until June 1943. Finally having turned the corner in the Battle of the Atlantic and built up substantial forces, the Eighth Air Force began to conduct strategic bombing missions deep inside Germany by midsummer. The first of these raids did not occur until more than eighteen months after the United States entered the war.

Spaatz and Eaker lacked intelligence support as the Eighth Air Force began its planning of the strategic bombing offensive against Germany. Eighth Air Force operations initially relied on the British for target photoreconnaissance.[137] An A-2 organization was established within the staff with responsibility for intelligence about enemy order of battle, capabilities, and potential targets. Eventually, in December 1942, the decision was made to consolidate targeting efforts within the A-5 (Plans) portion of the staff. The A-5 targeting organizations relied heavily on the British Ministry of Economic Warfare, the U.S. Board of Economic Warfare, and the Research and Analysis Branch of the U.S. Office of Strategic Services throughout the war. This organization proved innovative in establishing methods to develop detailed studies of optimal routes, defenses, and industrial components of specific targets, known as "aiming point" reports, drawing on available intelligence, mapping information, and aircrew debriefings. However, as the strategic bombing campaign began in earnest, the efforts of the Eighth Air Force and its supporting organizations to analyze economic systems and assess target damage assessment proved fraught with difficulty and uncertainty.

The U.S. strategic bombing efforts in August–October 1943 consisted primarily of efforts against German fighter aircraft and ball bearing production. Despite growing defensive opposition and losses in missions against coastal targets in north Germany, Eaker and other Eighth Air Force leaders believed an unescorted force of more than 300 bombers could attack any target within range at an acceptable attrition rate of 4 percent or less.[138] This assumption proved disastrously flawed. A raid in August against the aircraft factories at Regensburg and the ball bearing plants at Schweinfurt resulted in the loss of 60 of 276 bombers, comprising 10 percent of the Eighth Air Force bomber inventory and 17.5 percent of the crews. The Eighth Air Force returned for raids deep over Germany in the second week of October. During three days of raids on 8–10 October, a total of 88 bombers were lost, at an average lost rate of over 8 percent for these missions. The culminating point arrived with the 14 October mission against Schweinfurt, when 65 of 291 bombers dispatched were shot down and more than 600 airmen were lost.[139] Although the attacks had inflicted severe damage on the

Schweinfurt ball bearing plants and other plants involved in fighter production, the losses proved so unacceptable that the United States decided to halt deep raids into Germany for the rest of 1943.

Numerous factors contributed to the failure of the first major U.S. strategic bombardment effort against Germany. Ignoring the experience of the RAF and their own early raids, U.S. air leaders' faith in self-protecting bomber formations resulted in efforts to use forces incapable of performing the assigned mission without prohibitive losses. The Germans understood the range limits of escorting fighters and waited to attack until the bombers were on their own. As Haywood Hansell would later acknowledge, "[i]t was a near-tragic deficiency of the Air Corps Tactical School that proponents of long-range escort fighters did not come forward to demand the development of such a fighter with the same insistence, enthusiasm and determination which led the bomber people to get the [B-17] Flying Fortress."[140] The piecemeal employment of the Eighth Air Force for over a year had allowed the Germans to probe weaknesses in the defensive armament and tactics of U.S. bomber formations. The Germans developed tactics to exploit these weakness, including the use of rockets and massed fighter attacks against the underprotected nose of the B-17 and B-24 bombers and concentrating on one group at a time. Rampant inflation by AAF aircrews of German fighter losses inflicted by U.S. heavy bombers also played a role in the Eighth Air Force's inability to understand the cost and benefits of the attrition air war that was occurring.[141] From the beginning of their liaison with the RAF until late 1943, the AAF leaders demonstrated a doctrinal fixation and painfully slow learning curve that cost its airmen dearly.

In addition to sustaining unacceptable losses in the air, U.S. strategic bombardment efforts could not achieve the desired impact on the ground. The targeted aircraft and ball bearing industries proved very capable of adapting to the damage produced by the raids in the fall and summer of 1943. One reason for this unexpected adaptability was that wartime bombing accuracy was much lower than the air campaign planners expected based on the Air Corps' experience with peacetime exercises. According to the U.S. Strategic Bombing Survey.

> Before the war, the U.S. Army Air Forces had advanced bombing techniques to their highest level of development and had trained a limited number of crews to a high degree of precision under target range conditions, thus leading to the expressions "pin point" and "pickle barrel" bombing. However, it was not possible to approach such standards of accuracy under the battle conditions imposed over Europe.

Many limiting factors intervened; target obscuration by clouds, fog, smoke screens and industrial haze; enemy fighter opposition which necessitated defensive bombing formations, thus restricting freedom of maneuver; antiaircraft artillery defenses, demanding minimum time exposure of the attacking force to keep losses down; and finally, time limitations imposed on combat crew training after the war began. . . . While accuracy improved during the war, Survey studies show that, in the overall, only 20 percent of the bombs aimed at precision targets fell within the designated target area.[142]

In addition to contributing to inaccuracy, the weather over Europe also made the conduct of simple daylight precision bombing operations impossible for prolonged periods, especially during the winter months. Haywood Hansell later proclaimed that "bombing accuracy was heavily degraded by even partial cloud cover of the target. The weather was actually a greater hazard and obstacle than the German Air Force."[143] As a result of the limitations imposed by weather, combined with the need to recover from heavy losses, the initial U.S. strategic bombing campaign never put constant pressure on the systems under attack.

Even when bombers delivered their weapons on target, the U.S. doctrinal and planning assumptions that the German war economy constituted a taut, inflexible web proved fundamentally flawed. According to the summary findings of the U.S. Strategic Bombing Survey:

Because the German economy throughout most of the war was substantially undermobilized, it was resilient to air attack. Civilian consumption was high during the early war years and inventories in trade channels and consumers' possession were also high. These helped cushion the people of the German cities from the effects of bombing. Plant and machinery were plentiful and incompletely used. Thus it was comparatively easy to substitute unused or partially used machinery for that which was destroyed . . . labor was sufficient to permit the diversion of large numbers to repair of bomb damage or the clearance of debris with relatively small sacrifice of essential production.[144]

The German ability to take advantage of existing slack and to regenerate production was not evident in the thinking of those planning the U.S. strategic bombing campaign in 1943. U.S. war plan estimates regarding Schweinfurt indicated that more than 50 percent of German ball bearing production was located at this one target and that the destruction of these facilities would reduce overall German war production by 30 percent. After the Schweinfurt raid, Hap Arnold publicly stated, "Our attack was the most perfect example in history of accurate distribution of bombs over a target. It was an attack which will not have to be repeated again for a very long time if at all."[145] Yet despite heavy damage inflicted in the August and October 1943 raids, the Germans were able to relocate their ball bearing production facilities, and war production suffered little. The Strategic Bombing Survey found that despite the fact that the 1943 raids reduced production at Schweinfurt to 35 percent of preraid levels, the suspension of attacks for more than four months meant the Germans were able to recover through concerted efforts to disperse industry, relocate machines and tools (which suffered much less than structures), draw on substantial stocks, and redesign equipment to substitute other types of bearings. Production by autumn 1944 exceeded prewar levels.[146] The success of such German efforts at adaptation and regeneration were basically opaque to those U.S. operators and intelligence agencies evaluating the impact of industrial bombing during the war, for reasons discussed later in this section.

The failure of 1943 prompted a substantial adaptation by the United States to restore the viability of its strategic bombardment campaign and achieve significant impact against German war efforts. The winter weather, bomber losses, and demoralized aircrews required a lull from November 1943 to February 1944 that allowed the U.S. air forces in Europe to institute of a number of operational changes to the campaign. The Fifteenth Air Force was organized around substantial bomber assets in Italy, providing another axis of attack against Germany. As detailed earlier, fortuitous events also made possible the large-scale deployment of the P-51 long-range fighters and the use of drop tanks to provide adequate escort for bombing operations deep into Germany. U.S. fighter forces also developed sweep tactics to aggressively engage the Luftwaffe in an accelerated attrition contest, both in the air and through attacks against aircraft on the ground.

The combined Eighth Air and Fifteenth Force, now renamed U.S. Strategic Air Forces in Europe (USSTAF), successfully renewed the effort called for by the CBO plan to establish air superiority through the bombing of aircraft production facilities and direct engagement of the Luftwaffe in February 1944. Even though heavy damage against aircraft factories was inflicted, evaluations of this phase of the campaign strongly indicate it was won in the air, not through limiting German fighter production, as envisioned by the CBO. General Galland, commander of the German fighter forces, reported in mid-1944 that "[b]etween January and April 1944 our daytime fighters lost over 1,000 pilots. They included our best squadron, Gruppe and Geshwader commanders. Each incursion of the enemy is costing us some fifty aircrew. The time has come when our weapon is in sight of collapse."[147] Losses of German pilots meant that available airframes stood idle while the intensity of Allied bombardment efforts increased throughout the rest of the war. German fighter aircraft production did not peak until September 1944.[148] Yet crucial mistakes by Hitler, particularly in delaying the production of jet fighters, contributed to the establishment of Allied air superiority over France and Germany by summer of 1944.

Having finally established command of the air, the U.S. strategic bombardment campaign again confronted constraints on its ability to employ available forces. Most importantly, the Allied air forces were controlled directly by Gen. Dwight D. Eisenhower from April to July 1944 to prepare for and assist Operation Overlord, the invasion of France on 6 June. Another distraction emerged in the form of the German V-1 and V-2 missile campaigns. The Operation Crossbow bombing attacks against missile launch and production facilities provided Allied leaders with a means of response to assuage the British populace. These attacks may also have actually delayed large-scale deployment of the V-1.[149]

The record of U.S. strategic bombing from the fall of 1944 through the spring of 1945 demonstrated the potential of a strategic air campaign to inflict significant damage when waged with the proper operating conditions and when the right targets were attacked in a sustained fashion. Major campaigns were conducted against the German oil and transportation industries. After limited attacks beginning in May, the sustained bombing of German oil facilities began in earnest in July 1944. Combined with the Russian occupation of Romanian oil fields in August, the oil attacks quickly began to have a significant impact. Production dropped from 316,000 tons a month when the attacks started to 17,000 tons a month in September.[150] In response, the Germans implemented adaptation measures similar to those utilized in response to attacks on the ball bearing and aircraft industries. In this case, however, the success of such German efforts was severely limited by the fact that production was already near capacity and the size and complexity of synthetic oil plants prevented their easy dispersal. Albert Speer, the German Armaments Minister, wrote in his memoirs: "I shall never forget the date May 12, 1944. On that day, the technological war was decided. Until then we had managed to produce approximately as many weapons as the armed forces needed, in spite of considerable losses. But with the attack of 935 daylight bombers of the American Eighth Air Force upon several fuel plants in central and eastern Germany, a new era in the air war began. It meant the end of German armaments production."[151] Additionally, repeated U.S.

attacks prevented the recovery of oil production. The Strategic Bombing Survey highlights the case of the largest German synthetic oil plant at Leuna, which was hit twenty-one times by the Eighth Air Force between May 1944 and March 1945, with the result that production during the period averaged 9 percent of capacity. According to the Strategic Bomber Survey, "To win the battle with Leuna a total of 6,552 bomber sorties were flown against the plant, 18,328 tons of bombs were dropped and an entire year was required."[152] The campaign against oil production also created cascading effects against a range of critical German war-making activities. The lack of aviation gas limited Luftwaffe air defense and pilot training activity. Nitrogen and methanol, by-products of oil production, were essential for the manufacture of explosives, which helped create a general ammunition shortage on all fronts by the end of the war.[153]

The heavy bomber attacks in preparation for Operation Overlord focused on disrupting rail traffic and attacking marshaling yards in northern France to inhibit the German ability to reinforce forces defending against the invasion. In September, a systematic campaign was launched against the central German transportation system, including rail yards, bridges, lines, individual trains, and the canal system. As with the sustained effort against oil, attacks on this economic system proved less susceptible to German efforts to adapt. Inability to ship coal had a dramatic impact on production in all industries by December 1944 as well as on the ability of the rail system itself to function. Movement of military units and equipment became increasingly uncertain.[154]

By 15 March 1945, Albert Speer would report to Hitler that the German economy was "heading for inevitable collapse within 4–8 weeks."[155] Yet by this time, Allied land forces had already occupied much of Germany. Questions were raised by both the U.S. and the British about the cost-effectiveness of the strategic air war in securing the defeat of Germany. The significance of strategic bombardment in World War II would become a hotly debated topic for historians and airpower theorists. Rancor continues to this day.

The Impact of Intelligence on Strategic Bombing Operations

Throughout the strategic bombing campaign, discerning the actual impact of attacks against the German war effort proved difficult for both the AAF and the RAF. Although this analysis deals only with the difficulty faced in measuring the impact of precision bombing on industrial production, the RAF faced similar problems in its campaign to crush German morale. U.S. difficulties arose in part from the fact that the Army Air Forces never developed an indigenous intelligence capability to wage strategic warfare. The Air Staff Intelligence Division continued its prewar focus on order of battle and technical intelligence. Although the Intelligence Division was eventually assigned responsibility for continuing assessment of the strategic air operations, little evidence exists that such activity was ever conducted.[156] The Eighth Air Force developed a more robust target intelligence capability in terms of creating folders and documenting the weight of bombing effort applied to specific targets. However, the intelligence staffs of the Eighth Air Force and later the USSTAF did not endeavor to measure production levels or impacts on the German war effort. Arnold and the other strategic planners within the AAF eventually came to rely on the analysis of other organizations when deciding on targets to hit and for discerning the impact of the bombing campaign.

The responsibility for understanding German industrial systems and potential targets within the Air Staff was assigned to an organization known as the Committee of Operations Analysts (COA), in part owing to the lack of such capability within the Air Staff intelligence organization.[157] In late 1942, the Joint Intelligence Committee (JIC) of the Joint Chiefs of Staff began to question some of the assumptions the Air Staff planners had used in developing AWPD-42, which motivated Arnold to form a new organization. The COA consisted primary of civilians with experience in economics and industry as well as military experts in and out of uniform.[158] The initial COA report to Gen. Arnold in March 1943 provided the baseline for the targets identified in the Combined Bomber Offensive.[159] The report recognized the possible fallibility of its analysis and recommended "that there should be continuing evaluation of the effectiveness of air attack on enemy industrial and economic objectives in all theaters."[160] Once the bombing campaign began in earnest in the summer of 1943, however, systematic analysis of the effects was lacking.

Arnold and the other U.S. Joint Chiefs received reports from a variety of organizations, including their own JIC Board of Economic Warfare and the U.S. Office of Strategic Services, as well as the British Joint Chiefs Intelligence Committee, regarding the progress of the strategic bombardment effort against Germany. Yet U.S. reports consisted almost completely of enumerating the number of bomber sorties flown, tons of bombs dropped, photo intelligence estimates of the percentage of each target facility destroyed, and resultant predictions of reduced production. Some reports also utilized German press clippings and reports from field agents to draw conclusions about the state of German morale. Little transparency into the state of the German war effort was ever achieved by the COA or other intelligence efforts. The COA analysis incorporated into the CBO plan simply confirmed the tenets of the industrial web doctrine and made little allowance for the possibility of dispersal and substitution. Assuming that German industry was stretched to its limits, U.S. estimates of the impact on German production during the war proved well wide of the mark. According to the AAF official history: "The average monthly production of German single seat fighters during the last half of 1943 was 851, as against Allied estimates of 645. For the first half of 1944, on the other hand, actual production reached a monthly average 1,581, whereas Allied intelligence estimated only 655. Allied estimates were even further off in dealing with the antifriction-bearing industry."[161] The difficulties of accurately estimating the effects on overall production increased as the Germans began to disperse their production facilities and move them underground. The Strategic Bombing Survey report "The German Anti-Friction Bearing Industry" states that

> [t]he first lesson of the German experience is the indispensability of adequate and firm economic intelligence on the location and output of plants. The Allies knew exactly the anatomy of the industry in 1943 and early 1944 and their attacks on these facilities were responsible for a 50 percent drop in production. By October 1944, the factories we considered worth attacking represented only 20 percent of the industry's output and bombing had little effect. In July we had known of only one dispersal plant, and we had falsely identified the product of that one. In early 1945 we knew the names of a dozen dispersal sites, but confused store-rooms with productive units, major factories with minor ones, assembly points with machine shops; and we were deceived by the false names used by the enemy for his new plants.[162]

The result was severe miscalculation of the success of the campaigns against ball bearings and fighter production that became apparent only in retrospect. Even the access to the signals intelligence provided by exploiting the compromised German Enigma cryptography system provided little transparency into the actual effects of the bombing campaign on most of the German war effort.[163] Ultra was most useful in providing information on the state of the Luftwaffe. However, information regarding industrial capacity and conditions rarely passed through military channels, limiting the utility of intelligence provided through Ultra channels to planning the strategic bombardment campaign against other target sets.[164]

By the fall of 1944, Arnold and some other senior air leaders had come to have doubts about the prospects for decisive strategic bombardment.[165] In January 1945, Arnold made the following assertion to his senior staff:

Great damage by bombing has already been inflicted on German military installations and industry. Nevertheless, the German Army and the German Air Force continue under these circumstances to fight with an effectiveness that would have been considered impossible a few years ago. . . . It would appear to me that new yardsticks for measuring the ultimate effect of our bombing on the German military effort must be used. Certainly we are destroying German industry and facilities from one end of the country to another. Also, certainly this destruction is not having the effect upon the German war effort we had expected and hoped—not the effect we had all assumed would result.[166]

Maj. Gen. L. S. Kuter, an AWPD-1 planner and now the Director of Plans on the Air Staff, responded to Arnold as follows: "Your own staff may be criticized for pressing the combat units for higher and higher numbers of sorties and large bomb tonnages resulting in quantity rather than quality operations. Furthermore, your staff has unquestionably failed to properly advise you on the military results to be expected from scheduled operations."[167] As a result of initiatives emanating from both Washington and Europe, a major effort to evaluate the effectiveness of the Army Air Force strategic bombing campaigns was launched. The previously cited U.S. Strategic Bombing Survey (USSBS) was created in late 1944. The USSBS would continue its work through 1947 and issued reports through that year. The USSBS was conducted under civilian leadership but received intense scrutiny from the leaders of Army Air Force, Army, and Navy. The reports of the survey have served as the basic point of departure for continued reassessments of the conduct and significance of the U.S. strategic bombardment campaigns during World War II.

Postwar Debates and the U.S. Bombing Effort against Germany

Efforts to sort out the contribution of U.S. strategic bombardment in defeating Germany are complicated by the timing and circumstances surrounding the German collapse. The weight of the U.S. bombing campaign really began to take effect only by the middle of 1944, well after the tide had turned in Russia and the Western allies has already successfully landed in Normandy. By late 1944, land forces on both fronts had occupied territory that also substantially reduced the capacity of the German war economy. Also, the U.S. strategic bombing campaign was conducted simultaneously with a major RAF effort aimed generally at cities that also stressed the German war effort. The war did not end until virtually all of Germany had been occupied. The ambiguities in the relative contributions of different nations and services to winning the war has proved fertile ground for historical debate. The conduct of the U.S. strategic bombing campaign has raised at least two important issues that have remained a source of contention: the contribution of bombing to reducing the German ability to wage war, and whether more efficient targeting could have increased the impact of the bombing campaign.

Many argue the U.S. bombing campaign was not worth the resources and lives invested in it. Their analyses stress the ability of the Germans to sustain and often increase production of war materials through most of the war. Not until late 1944 did production of crucial goods by Germany decrease significantly, by which point the war was already basically won on the ground.[168] Others have answered that although not debilitating, the U.S. strategic bombing effort required the Germans to divert crucial resources to air defense, and that industrial dispersal and reconstitution programs significantly reduced the productivity that German mobilization efforts could have achieved in its absence.[169]

In any event, despite its contributions, strategic bombing did not play the decisive, revolutionary role envisioned in prewar doctrine. Elimination of the need to invade Europe discussed in the AWPD-1 plan and planning for the Combined Bomber Offensive did not occur. Conventional strategic air bombardment alone proved incapable of bringing the enemy to its knees. The German war economy did not crumble quickly when attacked, and major campaigns had to be waged on land and sea, as well as in the air, to secure victory.

Other assessments of the U.S. strategic bombing efforts against Germany highlight how opportunities were missed to make the campaign more effective through better target selection. Apologists, led by AWPD-1 contributor Haywood Hansell, argue that other taskings interfered with the buildup and execution of the U.S. strategic bombing effort. Plans were modified in such ways that valuable time and resources were expended against targets that were not vital centers of gravity. In particular, the decision to forgo attacks against the German electric power system initially identified in AWPD-1 has been criticized.[170] The Strategic Bombing Survey stressed how U.S. efforts initially failed to comprehend the need to sustain attacks against key target systems to achieve a lasting impact. Although they acknowledge and lament mistakes, the critiques of Hansell and others provide little understanding of the cause of such miscalculations. Postwar accounts of those involved do not address the continuing difficulty of establishing capabilities to discern critical target sets and of assessing whether attacks are achieving the intended impact. The final section of the chapter analyzes the U.S. strategic bombardment campaign against Germany in light of the enabling factors elaborated in chapter 2. Lessons are drawn regarding the establishment of strategic information warfare capabilities.

Experiential Lessons about the Enabling Conditions for
Strategic Warfare

The advocates of strategic bombing during World War II entered the fray with a highly specific, but untested, doctrine. The plans developed for strategic bombardment lacked an appreciation of the full complexity of waging such campaigns. Chapter 2 elaborated four enabling conditions for success derived from the theory and practice of strategic warfare: (1) offensive advantage, (2) significant vulnerability of centers of gravity to attack, (3) minimal prospects for retaliation and escalation, and (4) identifiability and targetability of enemy vulnerabilities and assessibility of damage inflicted. Only one of these enabling conditions presented relatively little difficulty for the U.S. strategic air campaign planners and operators in attacking Germany. The challenges presented by the other three proved very difficult for the AAF to surmount. This section analyzes which factors created difficulty in waging the daylight precision bombing campaign against the German war economy and how these experiences may relate to waging strategic information warfare.

Minimal Prospect for Retaliation and Escalation

The U.S. effort was only marginally affected by the German prospects for retaliation and escalation. By the time the Eighth Air Force began major efforts against the German war industry in mid-1943, the United States faced very little prospect of German retaliation against the bomber bases in the United Kingdom. U.S. home territory was out of range of any efforts to escalate the conflict. Whereas the British night bombing campaign grew out of an escalatory response to the German blitz in 1940–1941, the U.S. air effort in Europe was generally not geared toward managing interactions with German strategic warfare capabilities. The exception was the need to divert some U.S. strategic bombardment effort in 1944 and 1945 to attack V-1 and V-2 missile facilities. These missiles did not pose a direct threat to U.S. operations or homeland. However, the coalition war aspect of World War II meant the employment of U.S. strategic forces was also affected by the vulnerabilities of its British ally to retaliation and escalation.

The prospect for strategic information warfare in the late 1990s presents the United States with a very different context. Given the ability of adversaries to use digital information warfare with global points of access to attack information infrastructures throughout its homeland, the United States will likely be subject to retaliatory and escalatory attacks in any digital war in which it is involved. The U.S. geographic sanctuary from strategic attack may be severely undermined by these attacks. The ability to defend its centers of gravity will necessarily be part of U.S. calculations about the utility of and methods for conducting strategic information warfare.

Difficulty in Establishing Offensive Advantage

The U.S. airmen conducting the strategic air campaign against Germany faced difficult problems. In larger measure, these challenges had not been adequately confronted in establishing the doctrine, organizations, and technology to conduct such warfare. The fundamental condition of offensive freedom of action was not initially present. In contrast to expectations created by the theories of Douhet and the teachings of the Air Corps Tactical School, the B-17 and B-24 bombers of the Eighth Air Force sustained prohibitive losses during unescorted strikes in 1943. U.S. air planners and commanders underestimated the impact of numerous defensive innovations such as radar that improved warning, better radios for coordinating defensive responses, and the ability of high performance, heavily armed interceptors to intercept and destroy larger aircraft. Point defenses in the form of AAA also added to losses and reduced the ability of bombers to hit targets. The Germans estimated that flak decreased the effectiveness of U.S. bomber raids by 25 to 33 percent.[171] Commitment to existing concepts of operations from the late 1930s through 1943 blinded the Army Air Force to significant evidence that bombers would not be able to operate effectively during unescorted daylight operations over Germany. Learning this lesson proved very costly for the aircrews of the Eighth Air Force over targets like Schweinfurt and delayed the ability of the U.S. strategic bombardment effort to inflict significant damage. The inability of the U.S. air forces to establish control of the daylight skies over Germany required a lull in offensive action during the winter and spring of 1944 to regenerate bomber forces and bring escort fighter capabilities to bear in a massive attrition campaign against the Luftwaffe. The most effective strategic campaigns against German oil and transportation did not really disrupt the German economy until the fall of 1944, by which time the outcome of the conflict was already being decided on the ground.

Unlike in World War II, offensive freedom of operation may prove an easier condition for the United States to establish in waging twenty-first century strategic information warfare. The complexity of modern information infrastructures creates many avenues for attack unless a target implements very concerted protective efforts to assess and minimize vulnerabilities. The digital tools available for conducting attacks make effective active defenses difficult to implement. Yet the possibility for the emergence of technologies and techniques for improving defensive visibility and the effectiveness of active defenses remains present in the realm of strategic information warfare. The painful lessons of an unfounded faith in offensive dominance that plagued the Army Air Forces should provide sufficient reason for continued attention to both sides of the offense-defense equation.

Limited Vulnerability of Centers of Gravity to Strategic Air Bombardment

The U.S. bombers over Germany confronted difficulties in hitting targets even when freedom of action was established. Beginning with the first planned raid in 1942, weather created friction for the conduct of sustained operations necessary to achieve severe disruption of the German economy.[172] The weather in the winter of 1943–1944 contributed to the Germans' ability to disperse ball bearing and aircraft production facilities. Poor weather in March 1944 meant that strategic bombing halted for weeks after air superiority had been achieved over Germany. By the time the weather cleared, the U.S. strategic bombers were committed to supporting Operation Overlord until July. Even when strikes could be conducted, weather played a key role in limiting bombing accuracy and damage. The passive defense measures implemented by the Germans on the ground also limited vulnerability to strategic bombing. Smoke generators, hardening walls, and moving production facilities underground all reduced the effect of bombs dropped against targets. Dispersal efforts limited the impact of strikes against individual facilities. Dedicated recovery efforts brought production back on line more quickly than U.S. planners expected. Most significantly, the slack that existed in the overall German war economy made certain sectors (such as ball bearing and aircraft production) much less vulnerable to precision air attack against a few key nodes. After the conflict, the Strategic Bombing Survey stressed the importance of sustained attacks against targets that were difficult to disperse. In general, a variety of factors reduced the vulnerability of the German economy to strategic bombing. These factors had been ignored or downplayed by airpower thinkers and U.S. campaign planners.

This experience provides very important lessons for those contemplating similar efforts regarding strategic information warfare. The conduct of large-scale attacks against information infrastructures may create conditions of noise and confusion in the cyberspace environment that are analogous to poor weather in bombing campaigns and that degrade the ability of attackers to navigate and access targets via digital means. Even if offensive forces can operate in a relatively unconstrained fashion, defenders can also undertake passive defensive measures to limit vulnerability. By making access as difficult as possible, dispersing processing and communications activities in important information infrastructures, installing backup systems, creating redundancy, and investing in reconstitution capabilities, targets can severely attenuate the impact of attacks against certain information infrastructures. Offensive forces should understand the significance of selecting target systems with the least flexibility in terms of response and recovery. Evaluating the ability of attackers to sustain damage against targeted infrastructures in the face of defensive responses must not be ignored.

Inability to Identify and Target Centers of Gravity and Assess Damage

The unanticipated ability of the Germans to limit vulnerability was closely related to the problems the U.S. strategic planners had in identifying and attacking the most significant target systems. The authors of AWPD-1 and later plans including the CBO had little understanding of the degree of slack and flexibility in the German economy. Hansell and the other American planners had expected to "find a taut industrial fabric, striving to sustain a large Nazi war effort."[173] Yet the fact that the Germans had not conducted a full wartime mobilization until 1942 was not evident to either the British or United States. Similarly, the ability of the Germans to redesign systems to minimize use of items like ball bearings and disperse production in the aircraft industry did not figure into targeting schemes. The Strategic Bombing Survey would later conclude that "[t]he recuperative powers of Germany were immense; the speed and ingenuity with which they rebuilt and maintained essential war industries in operation clearly surpassed Allied expectations"[174] In particular, the U.S. effort to identify critical nodes for production of finished war materials to minimize the number of required targets proved flawed. Attacking underlying systems proved to have a higher payoff. As stated by the Survey, "[t]he importance of careful selection of targets for air attacks is emphasized by the German experience. The Germans were far more concerned over attacks on one or more of their basic industries and services—their oil, chemical, or steel industries or their power or transportation networks—than they were over attacks on their armaments industry or the city areas. The most serious attacks were those which destroyed the industry or service which most indispensably served other industries."[175]

Very similar challenges will face those who wage strategic information warfare. The complexity of modern information infrastructures will make the effects of large-scale attacks difficult to estimate. The ability of the adversary to recuperate must be analyzed. Strategic information warfare planners must evaluate which sectors or systems within an infrastructure constitute centers of gravity with the greatest leverage.

The ability of the U.S. strategic bombing campaign to attack the German vulnerabilities identified in war plans was also constrained by the continuing tug of war regarding available heavy bomber assets. The result during the first phase of the campaign was a piecemeal commitment of assets to strategic attacks that had very limited effect and may well have allowed the Germans to achieve substantial learning in responding to the threat of heavily armed but unescorted bomber attacks. The continual shift between target systems—from submarines to aircraft and ball bearings to supporting the Normandy invasion to the eventual concentration on oil and transportation—allowed the Germans considerable latitude for reconstitution and recovery until the final phase of the campaign. In the context of information warfare, available assets capable of conducting information attacks may well also be able both to support battlefield operation and to conduct strategic attacks. If the United States engages in a conflict with a significant conventional warfare aspect, plans for waging strategic information campaigns should similarly expect a competition for resources and possible diversions of effort.

Once the U.S. strategic bombing campaign was under way, its effectiveness also suffered from an inability to assess the damage it was inflicting. The Army Air Force lacked an intelligence capacity to conduct its own assessments. The assessments conducted by others, such as the Committee of Operations Analysts and the Joint Intelligence Committee, looked to identify future targets without adequately assessing the available information about the effects of attacks already conducted. Estimates measured bombing campaign progress in terms of the numbers and weight of the attacking force, not the effects on the targeted system. As a result, the combined U.S. and British intelligence estimates on the effects of the strategic bombing campaign proved susceptible to wide miscalculation and deception. Even if intelligence-gathering efforts had been improved, the task of understanding the effects of bombing and the German efforts at recovery and substitution were immense. The U.S. Air Force history study on intelligence and Army Air Force Operations in World War II stresses the tendency to overestimate damage based on photoreconnaissance and the difficulties posed by the

German program to disperse industrial production.[176] Daniel Pape concludes that "[i]nformation was inadequate to produce reliable macroeconomic analysis, let alone comprehensive microeconomic analysis required for strategic interdiction by precision bombing."[177] Even when a thorough analysis such as the Strategic Bombing Survey for Germany was conducted, the assessments of such a report were deemed inconclusive in terms of guiding the conduct of the strategic air campaign against Japan. Those responsible for waging strategic information warfare campaigns should pay heed to the difficulty of constructing capacity for damage assessment adequate to conduct a new type of warfare. Intelligence organizations with the proper skills and analytic tools must exist if planners desire to adapt and improve their strategic information warfare targeting plans as a campaign progresses.

In total, those contemplating waging a strategic information warfare campaign probably confront at least as many challenges in establishing the enabling conditions for success as faced the planners and leaders of the U.S. strategic bombing effort against Germany in World War II. Although achieving offensive advantage may prove easier in the cyberspace environment, meeting the other three conditions will present difficulties requiring attention if such campaigns are to prove effective. The lessons of the past should be kept prominently at the forefront of thinking about how to establish information warfare forces and wage this type of strategic warfare.

The Importance of Peacetime Preparations and Wartime Learning

The conduct of U.S. strategic bombing operations during World War II reflected significantly different wartime conditions than those outlined in the doctrine developed within the Army air arm prior to the conflict. The emergence of sophisticated defenses, the adaptability of the German economy, and the difficulty of assessing the impact of strategic bombing were largely unaccounted for in the industrial web doctrine developed at ACTS and the preparations of the operational forces in the Air Corps and GHQ Air Force. The U.S. Army Air Forces entered the war with a very underdeveloped organizational technological capacity for waging strategic warfare, both in terms of numbers of weapons and personnel and in terms of the breadth of technologies, skills, and organizations required as well. The quest of airmen to define a unique mission for air forces and achieve autonomy of operations led to the development of a narrowly conceived offensive doctrinal concept. These airmen were also inattentive to defensive developments that changed how strategic bombardment forces could be effectively operated. The absence of a clearly identified enemy and pace of technological change contributed to the significant challenges faced by the U.S. Air Corps in trying to develop doctrine and weapons for waging a new type of warfare in a peacetime environment.

Even after the U.S. strategic bombardment campaign began, the learning process was slow and very painful. The conduct of strategic bombing campaigns and efforts to protect against their effects involved massive efforts by all combatants.[178] The U.S. Army Air Forces in Europe dropped almost 1,500,000 tons of bombs, flew more than 750,000 bomber sorties, and reached a peak strength of about 620,000 personnel. Losses of nearly 10,000 bombers and almost 80,000 personnel were incurred. In conjunction with the British area bombing campaign, massive physical damage and enormous casualties were inflicted on the Germans. Yet the effect of the strategic bombing campaign was only contributory. Airpower alone did not have the decisive impact on the war's outcome that had been predicted by prewar doctrine and the leaders of the air campaign. The conditions for conducting the type of campaign airpower advocates had envisioned were inhibited by technological shortcomings, operational difficulties, and the demands of competing strategies. When the conditions for a successful air campaign existed during the last year of the European war, the U.S. bombing efforts eventually did take a major toll on the German warmaking effort. The speed at which the United States learned how to adjust prewar expectations to the realities of the combat environment proved a principal determinant of the payoff achieved by the investment in the strategic bombing effort against Germany.

The first report of the Strategic Bombing Survey made the following recommendation in September 1945:

> In maintaining our peace and our security, the signposts of the war in Europe indicate the directions in which greater assurances may be found. Among these are intelligent long-range planning by the armed forces in close and active cooperation with other government agencies, and the continuous active participation of independent civilian experts in peace as well as war; continuous and active scientific research on a national scale in time of peace as well as in war; a more adequate and integrated system for the collection and evaluation of intelligence information, that form of organization which clarifies functional responsibilities and favors a higher degree of coordination and integration in their development, their planning, their intelligence, and their operations; and finally, in time of peace

as well as in war, the highest possible quality and stature of the personnel who are to man the posts within any such organization, whatever its precise form may be—and in this, quality, not numbers, is the important criterion.[179]

We should heed these sound recommendations from over half a century ago as we analyze the challenges presented by a new form of strategic warfare. U.S. efforts to establish strategic information warfare capabilities face a similar context of strategic uncertainty, rapid technological change, and constrained defense resources to that which challenged U.S. airmen during the interwar period. The hard-won lessons from World War II could admirably serve our current efforts.

Appendix: Organizational Development of the Arm Air Arm
1907–1942

Redesignations of the Army Air Arm, 1907–1942[180]

Aeronautical Division, Signal Corps
Created 1 August 1907 by Office Memo No. 6, Office of the Chief Signal Officer, 1 August 1907.

Aviation Section, Signal Corps
Created 18 July 1914 by act of Congress.
(Air Service, American Expeditionary Forces was created on 3 September 1917 by HQ AEF GO 31 and remained in being until demobilized in 1919. Air Service, AEF, however, was distinct and apart from the evolution of the air arm within the War Department.)

Director of Air Service
Appointed on 28 August 1918 by Secretary of War, and given supervision and direction over the Division of Military Aeronautics and Bureau of Aircraft Production. Director of Air Service given complete control of DMA and BAP in March 1919 by Executive Order of 19 March 1919.

Army Air Service
Given statutory recognition and established as a combatant arm of the Army by the Army Reorganization Act of 2 June 1920.

Army Air Corps
Created by Air Corps Act of 2 July 1926.

GHQ Air Force
Established as a coordinate component with the Air Corps on 1 March 1935 by TAG letter of 31 December 1934.

Army Air Forces
Created on 20 June 1941 by Army Regulation 95–5.
(The AAF was to coordinate the activities of the Office of Chief of Air Corps (OCAC), the Air Force Combat Command (AFCC), (Formerly GHQ Air Force), and other air units.)

Army Air Forces
Reorganized as one of the three major army commands, and OCAC and AFCC abolished, by War Department Circular 59, 9 March 1942.

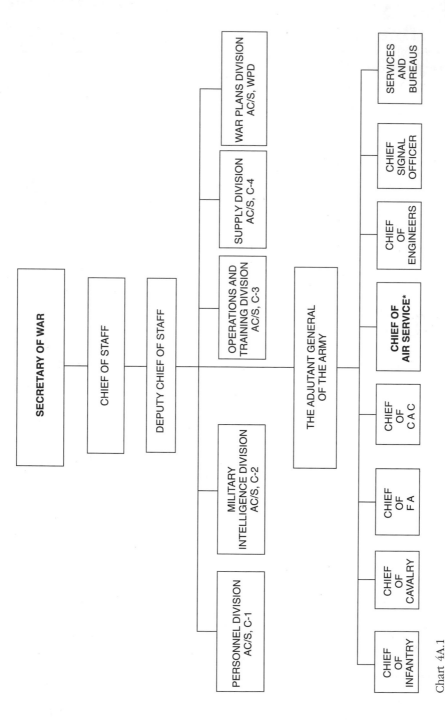

Chart 4A.1

Aviation in Army organization (1920–1934). Source: Greer, Development of Air Doctrine, 144. Reprinted with permission.
*Chief of Air Corps after 1926.

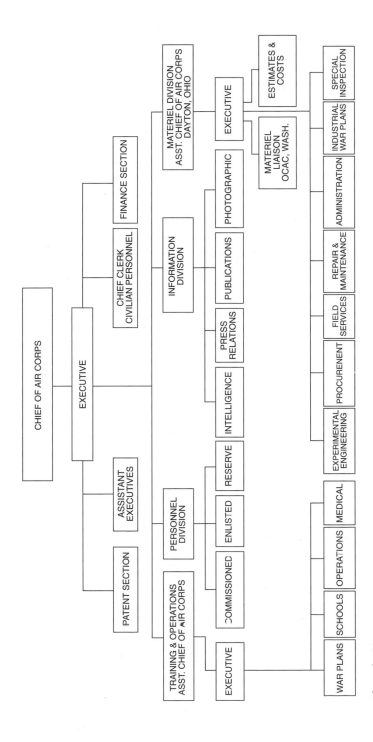

Chart 4A.2*

The Army Air Arm. Source: Greer, Development of Air Doctrine, 145. Reprinted with permission. *Organization of the Air Corps as of 26 November 1926. The organization of the Air Arm fluctuated during the period 1920–1934, but this chart is representative of the organization for the period.

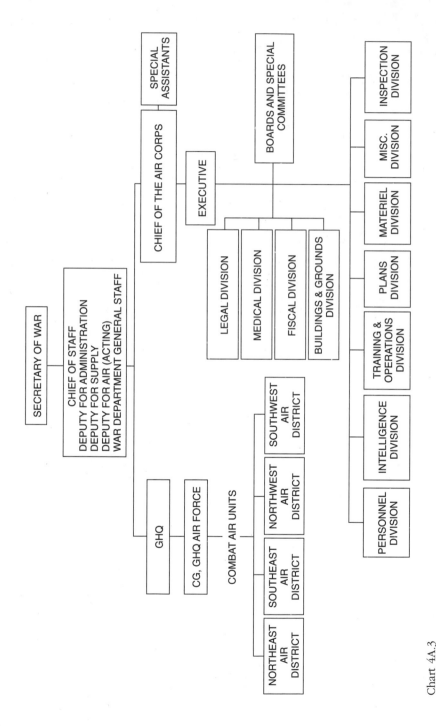

Chart 4A.3
The Army Air Arm (late 1940). Source: Greer, Development of Air Doctrine, 147. Reprinted with permission.

Suggested Additional Sources

U.S. Strategic Bombing Survey. Ed. David MacIssac. New York: Garland Publishing, 1976.
A massive effort that began before the conclusion of the war, the Survey was intended to evaluate the impact made by U.S. strategic bombing campaigns. Specific volumes provide overall summaries of the bombing campaigns against Germany and Japan. Completed in 1947, the USSBS provides an exhaustive source of detailed statistics on the level of effort and impact of U.S. bombing against various types of targets.

Wesley F. Craven and James L. Cate, eds. *The Army Air Forces in World War II.* Washington, D.C.: Government Printing Office, 1948.
The six-volume official history of the AAF in World War II. The work provides extensive background on the prewar period as well as combat operations. The history provides an even-handed appraisal of the U.S. effort, especially in discussing the lack of Army Air Corps readiness for World War II and the difficulties of mobilization.

Thomas H. Greer. *The Development of Air Doctrine in the Army Air Arm, 1917–1941.* Washington, D.C.: Office of Air Force History, 1985.
Greer compiles a convincing case regarding the fixation of the Air Corps on unescorted, daylight strategic bombing prior to World War II and the resultant negative impact on the development of pursuit aviation and other capabilities.

Richard J. Overy. *The Air War 1939–1945.* New York: Stein and Day, 1980.
This work delves beyond a simple accounting of the day-to-day air war to examine the systemic factors that determined the outcomes. He highlights how the strength of the U.S. economic base and skill in its management allowed the Allied air forces to overwhelm their adversaries by attrition.

Phillip S. Meilinger, ed. *The Paths of Heaven: The Evolution of Airpower Theory.* Maxwell Air Force Base, AL: Air University Press, 1997.
This volume compiles well-researched and written essays that examine the central tenets of airpower thinkers, including Douhet, Mitchell, and Trenchard.

Haywood S. Hansell. *The Air Plan that Defeated Hitler.* Atlanta: Higgins-McArthur, 1972.
Written by an architect of the first plan for the strategic bombing of Germany, this work shows the faith U.S. airmen retained in the doctrine developed prior to World War II. It provides a first-hand account of the formulation of this plan and how it was implemented.

Barry D. Watts. *The Foundations of U.S. Air Doctrine.* Maxwell Air Force Base, AL: Air University Press, 1984.
A well-argued critique of the continuing Air Force belief in the efficacy of strategic bombing based principally on the failure to acknowledge the inherent fog and friction of war.

Robert F. Futrell. "U.S. Army Air Forces Intelligence in the Second World War." In *The Conduct of the Air War in the Second World War: An International Comparison.* Ed. Horst Boog. 527–552. New York: St. Martin's Press, 1992.
A detailed examination of the failure of Army Air Force intelligence to properly prepare to support the projected strategic bombing called for in its doctrine. This work also reviews the difficulties inherent in providing intelligence to assess whether strategic bombing campaigns are achieving their intended effects.

Air Force Historical Research Archives, Maxwell Air Force Base, Alabama.
For those with an interest in primary source materials on the Air Force, this archive provides a wealth of material. The staff is very helpful. The files dealing with Air Corps Tactical School and interwar activities of the Army Air Corps are particularly strong.

Notes

1. U.S. Strategic Bombing Survey (USSBS), Vol. 2, "Overall Report—European War" (New York: Garland Publishing, 1976), 1. Subsequent citations to USSBS in the 1976 Garland compilation are referred to by USSBS, the volume title, and the page number within the volume. (First citations to a specific volume will also include the volume number.)

2. Lawerence R. Benson, *Acquisition Management in the USAF and Its Predecessors* (Wright-Patterson Air Force Base, OH: Air Force History and Museums Programs, 1997), 4–5.

3. See Thomas H. Greer, *The Development of Air Doctrine in the Army Air Arm, 1917–1941* (Washington, DC: Office of Air Force History, 1985), 5. According to Greer, Billy Mitchell and Hap Arnold both resisted initiatives prior to World War I to create an independent air service despite friction with the Signal Corps.

4. For details of the RAF strategic bombing efforts in World War I, see W. Raleigh and H. A. Jones, *War in the Air*, vol. 6 (Oxford: Clarendon Press, 1937), 118–174; and Alan Morris, *First of Many: The Story of the Independent Force, RAF* (London: Jarrolds, 1968).

5. See Giuilo Douhet, *Command of the Air*, trans. Dino Ferrari (New York: Coward-McCann, 1942).

6. Douhet, *Command of the Air*, 47–48. A principal reason for Douhet's belief in the devastating effects of air attacks against cities is that he believed such attacks would make use of incendiary weapons and poison gas. After World War I, Mitchell also believed that these types of weapons would be used. See Brig. Gen. William Mitchell, Asst. Chief of the Air Service, "Notes on the Multi-Motored Bombardment Group Day and Night," 1919, 83, in Air Force Historical Research Agency (AFHRA) file no. 248.222-57.

7. Maj. Gen. Sir H. M. Trenchard, "Report on the Independent Air Force," Tenth Supplement to the *London Gazette*, 1 January 1919, 134–135.

8. See Greer, *Development of Air Doctrine*, 48–51; David MacIssac, "Introduction to USSBS" (New York: Garland Publishing, 1976), ix. Patrick quoted from Frenchmen Marshall Foch and General Duvall in a 1927 speech to the American Legion and from British General P. R. C. Groves in a lecture to the Army War College in 1923. Transcripts are available in National Archives Record Group (NARG), 18, file no. 229.

9. Mitchell's writings include *Our Air Force: The Key to National Defense* (New York: Dutton, 1921); *Winged Defense* (New York: G. P. Putnam's Sons, 1925); *Skyways* (Philadelphia: J. B. Lippincott, 1930); and *Memoirs of World War I* (New York: Random House, 1960).

10. Mitchell, "Tactical Application of Airpower," 5 January 1919, AFHRA file no. 167.4-1.

11. Mark A. Clodfelter, "Molding Airpower Convictions: Development and Legacy of William Mitchell's Strategic Thought," in *The Paths of Heaven: The Evolution of Airpower Theory* ed. Phillip S. Meilinger (Maxwell Air Force Base, AL: Air University Press, 1997), 99.

12. Mitchell, *Skyways*, 253.

13. Mitchell, *Our Air Force*, 15. The Army air arm in the interwar period included four general categories of planes: pursuit planes to shoot down other aircraft, bombers to deliver bombs over a long distance, attack aircraft using guns and smaller bomb loads to provide tactical support for ground forces, and observation planes to conduct reconnaissance. My analysis focuses on the development of pursuit and bomber aircraft.

14. Speech to Army War College, March 1922, in NARG 18, file no. 229.

15. See memorandum from Patrick, "Air Service vs. Air Force Distinction," to War Department, 10 April 1923, in NARG 18, file no. 228.

16. As quoted in Greer, *Development of Air Doctrine*, 41, from Air Service Tactical School manual *Employment of the Combined Air Force*, 6 April 1926.

17. Office of the Chief of Naval Operations, *Report of the Joint Board on Results of Aviation and Ordnance Tests* (Washington, DC: Government Printing Office, 1921), 7.

18. Greer, *Development of Air Doctrine*, 40.

19. Greer, *Development of Air Doctrine*, 47–52.

20. Wesley F. Craven and James L. Cate, "The Army Air Arm," in *The Army Air Forces in World War II*, vol. 1, ed. Wesley L. Craven and James L. Cate (Washington, DC: Government Printing Office, 1948), 51–52. These authors derived this set of principles from a review of ACTS lecture materials from the period available at AFHRA. My review of the same materials leads me to believe this presents an accurate synopsis of the major tenets of ACTS thinking.

21. Important figures included then Maj. Donald Wilson and 1st Lt. Kenneth Walker in charge of the ACTS bombardment course. Walker went on to become a principal player in development of the immediate pre–World War II air war plans and was first commander of the air forces supporting General Douglas MacArthur in the southwest Pacific. Maj. Muir Fairchild was responsible for the extensive development of the industrial web theory in the Air Force course during the late 1930s.

22. See Williamson Murray, "Strategic Bombing: The British, American and German Experiences," in *Military Innovation in the Interwar Period*, ed. Williamson Murray and Allan R. Millet (Cambridge: Cambridge University Press, 1996), 96–143, regarding the inattention to the lessons of World War I at ACTS in the 1930s.

23. From "Report of the GHQ Air Force (Provisional)," 1933, as quoted in Greer, *Development of Air Doctrine*, 56.

24. Lecture in AFHRA file no. 248-2018A-8.

25. Training Regulation no. 440-15, "Employment of the Air Forces of the Army" (War Department, Washington, DC, October 15, 1935), 4, in AFHRA file no. 248.2018A-4.

26. Greer, *Development of Air Doctrine*, 114–115.

27. As quoted in Greer, *Development of Air Doctrine*, 36.

28. Craven and Cate, "The Army Air Arm," 63.

29. Joint Board 350 (ser. 514), "Joint Action of the Army and Navy" (1935), 1718, as quoted in Greer, *Development of Air Doctrine*, 70. On the role of General Headquarters air forces, see lecture by Maj. Gen. Frank Andrews, Commander GHQ Air Force, to Army War College, 9 October 1937, 15–22, in AFHRA file no. 415.201. Andrews asserts that joint exercises held with the Navy demonstrated the effectiveness of B-10 and B-17 bombers in coastal defense.

30. See AFHRA file no. 248.50090.

31. ACTS text in AFHRA file no. 248.501-3.

32. Haywood Hansell, "The Development of U.S. Concept of Bombardment Operations," lecture, Air War College, 19 September 1951, 10–12, quoted in Greer, *Development of Air Doctrine*, 81. Hansell was an ACTS instructor from 1934 to 1938. He was also a principal author of the first U.S. strategic air war plan and commanded 21st Air Force in the strategic bombing campaign against Japan.

33. Review of the developments involving the Curry and Baker boards based on Greer, *Development of Air Doctrine*, 20–22.

34. The description of the events leading up to the Air Corps Act of 1926 is based primarily on Irving B. Holley, *Buying Aircraft: Material Procurement for the Army Air Arm* (Washington, DC: U.S. Army Center of Military History, 1989), 46–49; and Craven and Cate, "The Army Air Arm," 28–30.

35. Air Corps Board Study no. 28, "The Air Force Expansion Program," 1937, 3–4, in AFHRA file no. 248.2019-1A.

36. R. Earl McClendon, "The Question of Autonomy for the U.S. Air Arm, 1907–1945," Air University Documentary Research Study, Maxwell Air Force Base, Alabama, 157–163.

37. Air Corps Board Study no. 28, 8.

38. In *Global Mission* (New York: Harper and Brothers, 1949), 172, Hap Arnold credits Lovett as "one of the most helpful people in doing [my] job."

39. For a detailed examination of the air defense organization and activities of the United States, see William A. Gross, "Air Defense of the Western Hemisphere," in Craven and Cate, *Army Air Forces in World War II*, 271–309.

40. Gross, "Air Defense of the Western Hemisphere," 295.

41. Memorandum to the Assistant Secretary of War, "Procurement Program for the Air Corps 1940–1945," 24 November 1937, as quoted in Craven and Cate, "The Army Air Arm," 60.

42. Mitchell, *Winged Defense*, 95–96.

43. Untitled lecture, 27 November 1923, in NARG 18, file no. 229.

44. Jacob Neufeld, *Research and Development in the U.S. Air Force* (Washington, DC: Center for Air Force History, 1993), 20.

45. Memorandum for public release by the Secretary of War and Secretary of Navy on Pulitzer Trophy race, 9 October 1922, in NARG 18, file no. 229.

46. Greer, *Development of Air Doctrine*, 37–38.

47. Army Historical Study no. 6, "Development of the Heavy Bomber, 1918–1944," 63–66, as quoted in Greer, *Development of Air Doctrine*, 39; and Holley, *Buying Aircraft*, 49–51.

48. "Proceedings of Air Corps Procurement Training Board," 5 March 1928, in NARG 18, file no. 222.

49. Craven and Cate, "The Army Air Arm," 58.

50. Greer, *Development of Air Doctrine*, 46.

51. Specifications cited here from Greer, *Development of Air Doctrine*, 46–47.

52. Arnold, *Global Mission*, 153.

53. David MacIssac, "The United States Strategic Bombing Survey 1944–1947" (Ph.D. diss., Duke University, 1970), 16.

54. Maj. Gen. Westover, memorandum to the Secretary of War 12 November 1937, in AFHRA file no. 145.93-23. Maj. Gen. Frank Andrews, Commander GHQ Air Force, made a similar plea in a lecture to the Army War College in October 1937, 7, in AFHRA file no. 415.201.

55. Robert F. Futrell, *Ideas, Concepts, Doctrine: A History of Basic Thinking in the United States Air Force, 1907–1964* (Maxwell AFB, AL: Air University Press, 1974).

56. "Report of the GHQ Air Force (Provisional)," 1933, quoted in Craven and Cate, "The Army Air Arm," 65.

57. Claire L. Chennault, *Way of a Fighter* (New York: G. P. Putnam's Sons, 1949), 23–27.

58. Chennault, *Way of a Fighter*, 26. After he left the Air Corps, Chennault would command the Flying Tigers under Chiang Kai-Shiek in China against the Japanese and rejoined the AAF in 1942 to command U.S. air forces in China.

59. Greer, *Development of Air Doctrine*, 87, 121.

60. James L. Cate and E. Kathleen Williams, "The Air Corps Prepares for War, 1939–1941," chap. 4 in Craven and Cate, *Army Air Forces in World War II*, 104–107.

61. Greer, *Development of Air Doctrine*, 118–120.

62. Richard J. Overy, *The Air War 1939–1945* (New York: Stein and Day, 1980), 139 and 150. In Overy's authoritative treatment of the economic, scientific and organizational basis for mobilizing air power, he finds the U.S. and British superiority across these dimensions

was the key to their eventual success in the air wars in both the European and Pacific theaters.

63. Overy, *Air War 1939–1945*, 17.

64. Greer, *Development of Air Doctrine*, 100.

65. The authority for the Air Corps boards was established by the Air Corps Act of 1926. This assessment of the significance of the Air Corps boards in influencing doctrine and policy decisions derives from my review of numerous Air Corps board studies at the Air Force Historical Research Agency and the weight placed on this organization by the official Air Force histories of the period.

66. See, for example, Lt. Col. Donald Wilson, memorandum to Office of Chief of the Air Corps, "Long-Range Airplane Development," 1938, in AFHRA file no. 167.4.

67. From Craven and Cate, "The Army Air Arm," 50, citing Air Corps Board Study no. 44, 17 October 1938.

68. "Requirements of Army Aviation for Hemisphere Defense," 3 June 1940, in Army Archives Group 381, "War Plans," as quoted by Cate and Williams, "Air Corps Prepares for War," 119, n. 54.

69. William A. Gross and P. Alan Bliss, "Air Defense of the United States," chap. 3 in Craven and Cate, *Army Air Forces in World War II*, 78–118.

70. De Seversky would single out Hap Arnold for blame in not emphasizing the development of escorts as the United States entered World War II. See Meilinger, ed., *The Paths of Heaven*, 251, n.41.

71. The perceived improvement in bombing accuracy during the 1930s is highlighted in a memo to Gen. Hap Arnold, "Subject: Bombing," 1938, in AFHRA file no. 248.222-31.

72. Holley, *Buying Aircraft*, 113.

73. Neufeld, *Research and Development in the U.S. Air Force*, 23–24.

74. During the late 1930s, Doolittle managed Shell Oil's aviation department and de Seversky owned his own aircraft manufacturing company.

75. Cate and Williams, "Air Corps Prepares for War," 106.

76. Overy, *Air War 1939–1945*, 136.

77. This paragraph on the Army air arm development of defensive armament is based on Irving B. Holley, "The Development of Defensive Armament for U.S. Army Bombers 1918–1941: A Study in Doctrinal Failure and Production Success," in *The Conduct of the Air War in the Second World War: An International Comparison*, ed. Horst Boog (New York: St. Martin's Press, 1992), 131–147.

78. James Doolittle comments on the lack of coordination between Army pilots desiring improved speed and range and the engineering efforts at Wright Field in Neufeld, *Research and Development in the U.S. Air Force*, 19–20.

79. Holley, "Development of Defensive Armament," 137, quotes a memorandum from the Chief, Aircraft Laboratory, to the Chief, Armaments Laboratory, on "Machine Gun Mounts," 29 October 1940.

80. Edward Jablonski, *Flying Fortress* (Garden City, NY: Doubleday, 1965), 28–31.

81. Barry D. Watts, *The Foundations of U.S. Air Doctrine* (Maxwell Air Force Base, AL: Air University Press, 1984), 76.

82. Williamson Murray, "The Influences of Pre-War Anglo-American Doctrine," in Boog, *Conduct of the Air War in the Second World War*, 240.

83. For evidence of such concerns, see lecture by Maj. Gen. Frank Andrews, Commander, GHQ Air Force, to Army War College, "The General Headquarters Air Force," 9 October 1937,

3, in AFHRA file no. 415.201; and his lecture to ACTS, "Problems Met by the GHQ Air Force and Solutions to Some of Them," April 1938, 5, in AFHRA file no. 248.2019A-19.

84. See "Conclusions," 112, of Army Air Force Historical Studies, no. 61, "Combat Crew and Unit Training in the AAF 1939–1945," in AFHRA file no. 101-61.

85. "Tentative Principles Governing Specialized Training," GHQ Air Force, Office of the Commanding General, Langley Field, VA, 16 December 1938, in NARG 18, file no. 247; and "Individual Training in Aircraft Armament by the AAF 1939–1945," AAF Historical Offices, Army Air Forces Headquarters, in AFHRA file no. 101-60.

86. "Combat Crew and Unit Training," 5.

87. Cate and Williams, "Air Corps Prepares for War," 150.

88. Douhet, *Command of the Air*, 50; and Mitchell, *Winged Defense*, 16–17.

89. See 1935–1936 ACTS lecture on "National Economic Structure," 3, in AFHRA file no. 248-2017A-11.

90. See ACTS study, "Military Intelligence for Initial Operations of Air Units," 1938, in AFHRA file no. 248.501-25; and memorandum to Col. Ira Eaker, 30 October 1939, "Subject: Air Intelligence," in AFHRA file no. 142.025-2.

91. As quoted in Robert F. Futrell, "U.S. Army Air Forces Intelligence in the Second World War," in Boog, *Conduct of the Air War in the Second World War*, 529. On the same page, Futrell quotes Eisenhower as stating that attachés of the period were "socially accepted gentlemen" who "knew few essentials of Intelligence work."

92. Futrell, "U.S. Army Air Forces Intelligence," 530.

93. John F. Kreis, *Piercing the Fog: Intelligence and Army Air Force Operations in World War II* (Washington, DC: Air Force History and Museums Program), 19–20.

94. This conclusion is based on my review of available intelligence reports in the Air Force Historical Research Archives in September 1997. For examples of the analyses of these operations, see "Foreign Air Forces," AFHRA file no. 248.2020A-20.

95. Kreis, *Piercing the Fog*, 25–26.

96. Haywood Hansell, *The Strategic Air War vs. Germany and Japan: A Memoir* (Washington, DC: Office of Air Force History, 1986), 12.

97. Greer, *Development of Air Doctrine*, 81.

98. Concern about the inadequacy of the War Department G-2 capability to provide intelligence reports was addressed in a memorandum by Brig. Gen. George V. Strong to the Chief of the Air Corps, "Subject: Air Corps Intelligence," 5 October 1939, in AFHRA file no. 142.0201-1. See also Futrell, "U.S. Army Air Forces Intelligence," 531.

99. MacIssac, "The United States Strategic Bombing Survey 1944–1947," 36. As of 9 December 1941, only eleven people were assigned to the enemy objectives unit of this branch. My research and Hansell's account provide no indication that the target folders developed by the Intelligence Section were used by the AWPD-1 planners.

100. Futrell, "U.S. Army Air Forces Intelligence," 531.

101. See Kreis, *Piercing the Fog*, 127–131, on the history of Army Air Forces intelligence training during the war.

102. Arnold, *Global Mission*, 168–169.

103. Memorandum from Lt. Col. H. H. Arnold to Chief of Air Corps, 26 November 1934, quoted by Holley, "Development of Defensive Armament," 134.

104. Greer, *Development of Air Doctrine*, 85.

105. Overy, *Air War 1939–1945*, 16.

106. Lecture in AFHRA file no. 248.2017A-12.

107. Douhet, *Command of the Air*, 3. This theme is also stressed in Watts, *Foundations of U.S. Air Doctrine*, 6–7 and 18–22.

108. Air Corps Board study, "Delivery of Fire from Aircraft," 10 June 1939, in AFHRA file no. 167.86-4.

109. Address by Andrews to Army War College, 15 October 1936, in AFHRA file no. 145.93-107.

110. Address by Arnold to Army War College, 8 October 1937, in AFHRA file no. 4743-64A.

111. Intelligence Section, HQ Air Corps, report by Capt. Patrick W. Timberlake, "An Analysis of the Air Operations in the Sino-Japanese War," 1938, 17 and 24, in AFHRA file no. 248.501-65A. See also Martin Byrd *Kenneth N. Walker: Airpower's Untempered Crusader* (Maxwell Air Force Base, AL: Air University Press, 1997), 72, regarding similar conclusions from Spanish Civil War that were also ignored.

112. See de Seversky's response in the *New York Herald Tribune*, 25 August 1942, to earlier statements made by Arnold regarding the essential equivalence of the P-40 to the Spitfire, quoted in Meilinger's chapter on de Seversky in *The Paths of Heaven*, 252.

113. In a lecture to Air War College in 1950 by Hansell, cited in Greer, *Development of Air Doctrine*, 60.

114. See memorandum to Chief of the Air Corps, "Initial Meeting with the British Technical Commission," 28 August 1940, in AFHRA file no. 142.025-3. Holley, "Development of Defensive Armament," 136, stresses the importance of contact with the British in providing the impetus to improve U.S. defensive armament on bombers.

115. Hansell, *The Air Plan That Defeated Hitler* (Atlanta: Higgins-McArthur, 1972), 53–54.

116. Greer, *Development of Air Doctrine*, 110.

117. HQ Army Air Forces, Director of Intelligence Service "Special Studies of Bombing Results no. 2—RAF Attacks on Cologne," 19 October 1942 in, AFHRA file no. 142.035.6 6–7.

118. Overy, *Air War 1939–1945*, 5.

119. Murray and Millet, *Military Innovation*, 98.

120. Cate and Williams, "Air Corps Prepares for War," 138.

121. See Hansell, *Air Plan That Defeated Hitler*, 61–99, for a first-hand account of the formation of the Air War Plans Division and the activities surrounding the creation of AWPD-1. The APWD-1 plan itself is available as Air War Plans Division, Air Staff, "Graphic Presentation and a Briefing: AWPD/1, Munitions Requirements of the Army Air Forces to Defeat Our Potential Enemies," August 1941, in AFHRA file no. 145.82. For a good summary of the planning process and contents of AWPD-1, see Watts, *Foundations of U.S. Air Doctrine*, chap. 3, "The First U.S. Strategic War Plan," 17–23.

122. "Graphic Presentation and a Briefing: AWPD/1."

123. Futrell, "U.S. Army Air Forces Intelligence," 532–533, on Hansell's information from the British. See Overy, *Air War 1939–1945*, 111, on the involvement of the U.S. banks with the German electric industry.

124. "Graphic Presentation and a Briefing: AWPD/1." Hansell would later admit that he and his associates were never fully appraised on available technical intelligence on German Air Force capabilities (Kreis, *Piercing the Fog*, 49).

125. Summary of required production figures based on Cate and Williams, "Air Corps Prepares for War," 148–149.

126. Watts, *Foundations of U.S. Air Doctrine*, 21–22, critiques the overly scientific approach of AWPD-1. See also Thomas A. Fabyanic, "A Critique of United States Air War Planning, 1941–1944" (Ph.D. diss., St. Louis University, 1973).

127. Alan J. Levine, *The Strategic Bombing of Germany 1940–1945* (Westport, CT: Praeger, 1992), 74–75.

128. Murray, "Influence of Pre-War Anglo-American Doctrine," 239–240. The British became doctrinally locked into area night bombing, never experimenting with drop tanks and sticking with area bombardment despite the development of improved navigational aids.

129. James C. Cate, "Plans, Policies and Organization," in Craven and Cate, *Army Air Forces in World War II*, 605.

130. Conclusions of Eaker report from Cate, "Plans, Policies and Organization," 605–607; and U.S. Air Force Oral History Interview with General Carl A. Spaatz, 21 February 1962, in AFHRA file no. K239.0512-754.

131. Haywood Hansell, *The Strategic Air War vs. Germany and Japan: A Memoir* (Washington, DC: Office of Air Force History, 1986), 58–60.

132. Kreis, *Piercing the Fog*, 151.

133. The complete briefing given by Lt. Gen. Eaker to the Joint Chiefs of Staff on 29 April 1943 on the Combined Bomber Offensive plan is transcribed in Watts, *Foundations of U.S. Air Doctrine*, 133–150.

134. Eaker briefing in Watts, *Foundations of U.S. Air Doctrine*, 137.

135. Eaker briefing in Watts, *Foundations of U.S. Air Doctrine*, 146.

136. Rodger A. Freeman, *The Mighty Eighth* (Oscola, WI: Motorbooks International, 1991), 4, 11.

137. Kreis in the section entitled "The Air War in Europe: Organizing Eighth Air Force's Intelligence," chap. 3 of *Piercing the Fog*, 132–140, provides a detailed history of the efforts summarized in this paragraph.

138. As quoted in Williamson Murray, *Strategy for Defeat: The Luftwaffe 1933–1945* (Baltimore, MD: Nautical and Aviation Publishing, 1985), 170.

139. See Dana J. Johnson, *Roles and Missions for Conventionally Armed Heavy Bombers—A Historical Perspective* (Santa Monica, CA: RAND Corporation, 1994), 20, for details on the U.S. losses in the raids discussed in this paragraph.

140. This quote is from MacIssac, "Introduction to the USSBS," xxviii, n. 5. Hansell's admission is contained in a letter MacIssac received from Hansell in 1975.

141. For detailed analysis of U.S. Army Air Forces' miscalculation of German losses, see Watts, *Foundations of U.S. Air Doctrine*, 62–71.

142. USSBS, "Summary Report—European War," 4–5.

143. Hansell, *Air Plan That Defeated Hitler*, 121.

144. USSBS, "Summary Report—European War," 2.

145. As quoted in Charles Webster and Noble Frankland, *The Strategic Air Offensive Against Germany 1939–1945* (London: HMSO, 1961), 66.

146. USSBS, "Summary Report—European War," 4–5.

147. Cajus Bekker, *The Luftwaffe War Diaries*, trans. Frank Ziegler (Garden City, NY: Doubleday, 1968), 522.

148. USSBS, "Overall Report—European War," 19.

149. USSBS, "Summary Report—European War," 12.

150. USSBS, Vol. 3, "Effects of Strategic Bombing on the German War Economy," 78–81.

151. Albert Speer, *Inside the Third Reich* (New York: Macmillian, 1970), 346.

152. USSBS, "Summary Report—European War," 9.

153. USSBS, "Effects of Strategic Bombing on the German War Economy," 81–83.

154. For very detailed analyses of the effect of the bombing campaign against the German rail system, see USSBS, Vol. 200, "The Effects of Strategic Bombing on German Transportation"; and Alfred C. Mierzejewski, *The Collapse of the German War Economy 1944–1945: Allied Air Power and the German National Railway* (Chapel Hill: University of North Carolina Press, 1988).

155. As quoted in the USSBS, "Summary Report—European War," 13.

156. Based on this author's review of available Air Staff intelligence documents at the Air Force Historical Research Archives and conclusions drawn in Futrell, "U.S. Army Air Forces Intelligence"; and MacIssac, "United States Strategic Bombing Survey 1944–1947," 41–42.

157. Kries, *Piercing the Fog*, 7.

158. MacIssac, "United States Strategic Bombing Survey 1944–1947," 39–41.

159. See Eaker's briefing on the CBO in Watts, *Foundations of U.S. Air Doctrine*, 134.

160. MacIsaac, "United States Strategic Bombing Survey 1944–1947," 42.

161. Arthur B. Ferguson, "Big Week," in Craven and Cate, *Army Air Forces in World War II*, vol. 3, 45. See also Office of Strategic Services, Research and Analysis Branch, Report no. 1044.1, "Bomb Damage Report," 18 September 1943, 17, in AFHRA file no. 142.035-3, which found that "the concentrated assaults on the German air position during July and August appear to have reversed the long-term growth trend in German fighter strength."

162. USSBS, Vol. 53, "The German Anti-Friction Bearings Industry," 20.

163. General conclusion reached by Watts, *Foundations of U.S. Air Doctrine*, 75. Overy, 198–199, *Air War 1939–1945*, notes that Ultra provided useful information on the effects of attacks on synthetic oil production but little visibility into other sectors of the German war economy. Murray, *Strategy for Defeat*, 244, also found that Ultra provided key intelligence on pressure exerted on the German fighter forces by AAF sweep tactics but no information on aircraft production.

164. Kreis, *Piercing the Fog*, 74–80.

165. In a memorandum, "Subject: Priority of Targets, Europe," 19 October 1944, in AFHRA file no. 145.81-161, Gen. Arnold states, "I am concerned over our present target priorities in the European Theater." In this memorandum, Arnold requests from the Air Staff Director of Plans, Maj. Gen. L. S. Kuter, an "estimate of what our target priority list should be in order to bring the war with Germany to an end by 1 January 1945."

166. Memorandum from H. H. Arnold, "Subject: Bombing Targets," 8 January 1945, in AFHRA file no. 145.81-162.

167. Memorandum to Gen. Arnold from Maj. Gen. Kuter, "Subject: Air Operations against Germany," 11 January 1945, in AFHRA file no. 145.81-162.

168. Robert A. Pape makes this argument most strongly in *Bombing to Win: Airpower and Coercion in War* (Ithaca, NY: Cornell University Press, 1996), esp. 281–282. As detailed by MacIssac, "Introduction to USSBS," xviii–xxv, this criticism of strategic bombing was also a theme in the immediate postwar histories in Britain, which made extensive use of the USSBS material.

169. Defenders of the efficacy of U.S. strategic bombing efforts include MacIssac, "Introduction to USSBS," xviii; Overy, *Air War 1939 1945*, 118 123, and Hansell, *Air Plan That Defeated Hitler* and *Strategic Air War vs. Germany and Japan*.

170. The USSBS, in "Effects of Strategic Bombing on the German War Economy," 126, states that "the results of bombing the enemy's power system might well have been far greater than the results of bombing alternative industrial or city targets." See Hansell, *Air Plan That Defeated Hitler*, 262. Another supporter of this idea is Greer, *Development of Air Doctrine*, 125.

171. Johnson, *Roles and Missions for Conventionally Armed Heavy Bombers*, 25.

172. Arthur B. Ferguson, "Rouen-Sottereville," in Craven and Cate, *Army Air Forces in World War II*, 661. The first bombing raid by the Eighth Air Force planned for 9 August 1942 had to be canceled due to weather. See Watts, *Foundations of U.S. Air Doctrine*, 61–62, on general significance of weather as a source of friction for U.S. efforts.

173. Hansell, *Air Plan That Defeated Hitler*, 197.

174. USSBS, "Summary Report—European War," 16.

175. USSBS, "Summary Report—European War," 16.

176. Kreis, *Piercing the Fog*, 202–203.

177. Pape, *Bombing to Win*, 275.

178. Figures provided in this paragraph are from USSBS, "Overall Report—European War," table 1, p. x.

179. USSBS, "Summary Report—European War," 15–16.

180. From Greer, *Development of Air Doctrine*, 149.

FIVE
The United States
and Strategic
Information Warfare,
1991–1999: Confronting the
Emergence of Another
Form of Warfare

We are at risk. Increasingly, America depends on computers. They control power delivery, communications, aviation, and financial services. They are used to store vital information, from medical records to business plans to criminal records. Although we trust them, they are vulnerable—to the effects of poor design and insufficient quality, to accident, and perhaps most alarmingly, to deliberate attack. The modern thief can steal more with a computer than with a gun. Tomorrow's terrorist may be able to do more damage with a keyboard than with a bomb.

—National Research Council,
Computers at Risk, Opening
Statement, 1991

    The United States in the 1990s again entered a period full of new opportunities and challenges. Like the 1920s, technological and economic optimism were again ascendant. The explosive growth of networked computing and revolutionary new means of telecommunication transformed commercial activity and influenced the daily lives of many people. Gas stations installed satellite dishes to provide data to corporate headquarters. Pagers and cellular phones provided constant contact with professional associates and families. Both the government and the private sector championed the information superhighway as the new engine of economic growth and a vehicle for social improvement. Economists argued about the applicability of old models based on measuring physical production of goods and mass-market activity. Futurists predicted that the United States and other technologically advanced nations had slipped the bonds that constrained growth during the previous two decades and emerged into a new era of prosperity based on an emerging information age.

The 1990s also saw the development of wholly new possibilities for warfare waged through use of information technology. As the airplane created a new realm for combat, cyberspace increasingly began to serve as a place for military operations. Visions abounded of digital Pearl Harbors, cyberstrikes against air traffic control systems, and the manipulation of stock markets. Possibilities were perceived for military and economic institutions to grind to a halt as political leaders pondered an attacker's demands. The potential for intrusion, manipulation, and disruption via digital means across globally intertwined information infrastructures also created a transformative opportunity for strategic strikes. The more an actor relied on its information infrastructures, the greater the potential these infrastructures provided as a center of gravity worth attacking and defending.

This chapter builds on the analysis and frameworks developed earlier to evaluate the development of strategic information warfare capabilities in the United Stated from 1991 through the end of 1999. The year 1991 marks a confluence of events central to the emergence of U.S. concerns about strategic information warfare. The Gulf War, labeled by some as the "first information war,"[1] provided a substantial push for the U.S. national security establishment to understand the relationship between the information age and the use of force. The commercial and scientific sectors also recognized at about the same time that the convergence of computing and communications could create national-level concerns regarding disruption of information infrastructures. The Internet worm incident in 1988 resulted in the production of a National Research Council study entitled *Computers at Risk: Safe Computing in the Information Age* in 1991. Large-scale outages in AT&T networks in both 1990 and 1991 resulted in public expressions of concern by telecommunications companies and law enforcement agencies about the threat posed by hackers. The resultant backlash against hacker groups (who turned out not to be responsible for the outages) also provided a major impetus to the formation at this time of advocacy groups within the United States for freedom of use and privacy in the world of cyberspace.[2] Organizations such as the Electronic Frontier Foundation and the Center for Democracy and Technology have since become major voices in national debates over telecommunications deregulation and encryption controls.

Publicly available information about U.S. development of strategic offensive information warfare capabilities remains very limited as this book is being written. U.S. military doctrine states the requirement to develop offensive information warfare capabilities, but details regarding specific organizational arrangements and technologies employed are generally classified. Discussions of possible offensive use of U.S. digital information warfare capabilities in the Kosovo conflict in 1999 have emerged, but details are few and no official confirmation has occurred so far.[3] I will discuss U.S. doctrine development as it addresses all aspects of strategic information warfare but will primarily focus on the organizational and technological challenges involved in establishing defensive strategic information warfare capabilities, a topic for which a wealth of sources is available. This chapter balances the analysis conducted in chapter 4, which explored challenges in creating offensive strategic airpower capabilities in the period between the two world wars.

Historical Background

U.S. national security concerns about the development and use of telecommunications and information technologies did not arise overnight at the end of the twentieth century. As addressed in chapter 1, the historical development of information infrastructures has been closely related to their exploitation for military purposes.

The development of electronic means for information transmission such as the telegraph, telephone, and radio since the mid-nineteenth century forced the U.S. government to recognize the relationship between the national security and telecommunications. World War I resulted in the assumption of direct federal government control over AT&T. The 1934 Communications Act established the Federal Communications Commission to streamline the government's regulation of the communications industry. The Act also gave the president authority to take control of telecommunications assets to satisfy defense needs in case of a national emergency and remains the principal basis for federal governmental involvement in this area. During World War II, President Roosevelt managed U.S. telecommunications through the Board of War Communications.[4] Through mid-century, the U.S. government focused on ensuring that AT&T provided sufficient telecommunications capacity to meet military requirements, not on protecting these assets against outside attack.

The development of the computer during World War II began to broaden the relationship between ensuring national security and the use of information technology. The Department of Defense became increasingly reliant on information technologies as part of the Cold War competition with the Soviet Union.[5] Computer-based processing assumed a central role in the intelligence game as a means of encrypting and decrypting classified communications and in launching, orbiting, and operating surveillance satellites. The rush to improve the designs of nuclear warheads and delivery systems, along with the space race, pushed the development of advanced information technologies in both computing and communications during the 1950s and 1960s. Technologies such as the first solid-state transistors and digital telecommunications switches were created in commercial research laboratories by AT&T and IBM for use by the Department of Defense. Eventually, the advance of information technology also became crucial to sustaining a U.S. high-technology edge for its numerically inferior conventional forces. Advanced-strike and air superiority aircraft required the use of cutting-edge microelectronics and computer processing. The Navy's ability to operate aircraft carriers and maintain the upper hand in antisubmarine warfare depended on leadership in electronic countermeasures and signal-processing technologies. Even the design of tank armor and fire control relied on the use of advanced computer processing and simulation. In the telecommunications arena, the technological basis for today's Internet resulted from Defense Advanced Research Projects Agency efforts initiated in 1968. Computer networking was promoted as a means of improving information flows between government agencies, research labs, and universities performing defense-related research and development.

The strategic importance of the United States' growing reliance on information infrastructures as a source of national security vulnerability also became apparent in the Cold War. Most attention focused on the need to ensure secure nuclear command and control and continuity of government in the event of a nuclear showdown with the Soviet Union. Throughout the 1950s and 1960s, the close relationship between AT&T and the federal government meant such concerns were addressed primarily through informal accords.[6] Additionally, a series of initiatives began in the Kennedy Administration to create a national-level system for assuring capacity to respond to a military or civil emergency.

These initiatives resulted in the establishment of a National Communications System (NCS) to ensure survivable communications for supporting continuity of government in emergencies ranging from nuclear war to natural disasters.[7] The divestiture of AT&T during the early 1980s necessitated the creation of a more formal mechanism of government coordination and control over private-sector telecommunications operations. In advance of the impending breakup, President Ronald Reagan issued Executive Order 12382 establishing the National Security Telecommunications Advisory Committee as the focal point for interaction between the government and private sector regarding national security and emergency preparedness (NS/EP) communications. Comprised of approximately thirty members, the NSTAC "provides information and advice to the President on issues and problems relating to implementing national security emergency preparedness policy."[8] During the remainder of the 1980s, NSTAC primarily focused on ensuring command and control and continuity of government in the event of a nuclear conflict with the Soviet Union.

The vulnerability of U.S. telecommunications also became a source of increasing concern during the Cold War. Exploitation and protection of communications provided the basis for creating of the National Security Agency (NSA) in 1952.[9] The NSA assumed responsibility for oversight of the Communications Security Board, which dealt with all classified national security communications. Adversarial (particularly Soviet) interception of long-distance telephone traffic in the United States was recognized as a possibility in the 1970s. U.S. officials worried about the loss of "strategic economic information in the form of privately held, unclassified data about technological developments, industrial processes and investment plans" to its Soviet adversaries.[10] As a result, President Carter issued Presidential Directive 24 establishing efforts to improve protection of both classified national security and government commercial nonclassified information.

During the Reagan administration, tensions grew as NSA's role in information security was strengthened. Other federal departments and the private sector expressed concerns about NSA's authority, prompting direct congressional involvement through the 1987 Computer Security Act,[11] which redefined the role of federal government agencies in providing information security. NSA reverted to establishing guidelines and procedures specifically for classified national security information and systems. The National Institute of Standards and Technology (NIST) within the Commerce Department was given responsibility for developing policies and overseeing programs related to the protection of unclassified, but sensitive, federal government information. The Act specifically allowed, but did not require, NIST to provide assistance to organizations outside the federal government. Combined with the divestiture of AT&T, the Computer Security Act largely eliminated any direct government mechanisms for assuring security and reliability of an increasingly diverse U.S. information infrastructure by the end of the 1980s.

U.S. Concepts, Doctrine, and National Strategy for
Waging Strategic Information Warfare

Establishing capabilities to engage in a new form of warfare requires developing concepts, doctrine, and strategies regarding its nature and relevance. The conduct of strategic information warfare involves other government and civilian organizations to an unprecedented degree, especially in orchestrating defensive efforts. For this reason, understanding military doctrine and DOD policies as well as the activities of other U.S. government and private-sector entities sheds light on strategic information warfare.

Emergence of Information Warfare Concepts, Policy,
and Doctrine within DOD

Information warfare emerged within the U.S. military establishment as a concept closely associated with the revolution in military affairs. Two levels of significant change confronted the U.S. military establishment. In the near term, the integration of advanced intelligence, surveillance, and reconnaissance systems with stealthy, long-range, precision weapons systems would establish dominance in future traditional battlefield engagements. For the longer term, RMA thinkers stressed the importance of a loosely articulated concept known as "information warfare," emphasizing the ability to degrade or even paralyze an opponent's command, control, communications and intelligence (C3I) systems.[12]

During the 1990s, the U.S. military pursued both major thrusts of the RMA with varying degrees of vigor. Doctrinal constructs, organizational changes and acquisition programs were strongly emphasized to leverage improvements in information technology to enhance traditional military operations. Multiple initiatives sought to improve the ability to link sensors to shooters to improve the speed and precision of employing strike forces. In the late 1990s, advocates of the RMA called for a shift from "platform-centric" to "network-centric" warfare to achieve information superiority. These advocates continued to focus on "use of high-capacity, multimedia networks of sensors, shooters and commanders to achieve the power of a truly integrated force."[13] Yet in isolation, efforts geared toward using information technology to enhance the capability to employ conventional "precision force" did not require doctrinal development regarding information warfare as a new area of strategic thought and military operations.

The DOD grappled mightily in the 1990s with definitions and the scope of what constitutes information warfare. The classified DOD directive TS3600.1, entitled "Information Warfare," published in December 1992, provided the earliest official framework.[14] Initial efforts to establish information warfare doctrine involved revising existing command, control, and communications countermeasures doctrine. Chairman of the Joint Chiefs of Staff Memorandum of Policy (MOP) 30, "Command and Control Warfare (C2W)," published in March 1993, provided seminal guidance.[15] MOP 30 defined C2W as "the military strategy that implements information warfare on the battlefield and integrates physical destruction. Its objective is to decapitate the enemy's command structure from its body of combat forces." The memorandum stressed both offensive action to seize the initiative and also protecting friendly command and control (C2). The means for achieving these goals included "operations security, psychological operations, military deception, electronic warfare and destruction (hard kill and weapons effects)." Actions affecting adversary computer-based networks were not specifically covered because of classification considerations at the time.[16] Soon after MOP 30's publication, the Joint Electronic Warfare Center at Kelly Air Force Base in Texas was renamed the Joint Command and Control Warfare Center (JC2WC) to support the development of C2W strategy and capabilities.[17] MOP 30 also tasked the individual services with developing C2W programs and combatant commanders with incorporating C2W into operational war plans.

MOP 30 did not articulate a concept of strategic information warfare. The scope of C2W included only attacks against C2 targets, ignoring the full range of military operations and civilian-sector activities supported by information infrastructures. Efforts to paralyze an adversary's military C2 potentially could constitute offensive strategic information warfare. However, MOP 30 primarily expanded upon previous concepts of electronic warfare and how information warfare considerations would affect war-fighting commanders-in-chief, not how such warfare could independently provide political influence in a conflict. Also, the document did not discuss the requirement to protect U.S. national information infrastructures.

Realizing the Potential for Strategic Information Warfare

Offensive information warfare began to be viewed after the Gulf War as a potential means of minimizing exposure and collateral damage in situations otherwise requiring the use of conventional forces. Discussions about using digital information warfare techniques to strike targets beyond the traditional battlefield began occurring outside the government. Works such as Alvin and Heidi Toffler's *War and Anti-War: Survival at the Dawn of the 21st Century* received increasing attention within national security circles.[18] The Tofflers addressed a wide range of military challenges presented by the information age, including digital attacks to disrupt information infrastructures and perception management as means available to state and nonstate adversaries. U.S. defense officials also began to stress the potential benefits of a broader information warfare concept beyond battlefield operations. The Assistant Secretary of Defense for Command, Control, Communications and Intelligence (ASD/C3I) at the time, Duane Andrews, was quoted by the Tofflers as outlining the possibility for strategic "knowledge warfare" in which "each side will try to shape enemy actions by manipulating the flow of intelligence and information."[19] General John Sheehan, then commander in chief of the Atlantic Command, advanced the possibility of detering conflict through "changing [an adversary's] perception so clearly that before he decides to start a conflict he knows deep down he is going to lose" at the opening of the JC2WC in October 1994.[20] Yet these initial articulations dealt much more with use of perception management than with digital attacks on information infrastructures.

In the context of the intensifying U.S. debate over the efficacy of economic sanctions, especially as applied to Iraq, national security analysts also began to address directly how information warfare might be used to sharpen the pain inflicted on adversaries. Timothy Sample of the Hudson Institute said in 1994 of this use of information warfare, "The goal of this avenue of coercion would be to engage the voice of the targeted country's business to confront its government. For example, the ability to access a company's computer network and manipulate design, production and marketing data, or go into accounting records and "zero-out" entries would have a devastating effect on operations."[21] Gen. (ret.) James McCarthy outlined at the U.S. Air Force Academy late in the same year how the United States and potential coalition partners "might deny electronic access to foreign accounts or alter internal financial records of the [adversary's] elite to cause confusion or frustration."[22] The Department of Defense did not acknowledge offensive strategic information warfare concepts in official documents, however, until 1996.

During the same period, the U.S. national security establishment was increasingly forced to recognize the significant challenges presented by the defensive aspects of strategic information warfare, primarily because of concerns about the vulnerability and protection of the defense information infrastructure. Although the DOD computer systems had long been the target of hackers, international incidents involving digital intrusions in the early 1990s significantly raised the level of anxiety. Between April 1990 and May 1991, hackers from the Netherlands penetrated thirty-four Department of Defense sites, resulting in a congressional investigation and hearings in late 1991.[23] Although these events do not appear to have directly influenced early information warfare policy or doctrinal development, DISA did establish a Vulnerability Analysis and Assessment Program in 1992 to identify weaknesses in defense information systems.[24] Using publicly available digital attack tools, DISA began testing large numbers of DOD systems for such weaknesses. The early results of these tests indicated not only that systems were often vulnerable to attack, but also that successful attacks were rarely detected, and detected attacks rarely reported. In 1994, the Air Force Information Warfare Center Computer Emergency Response Team (AFCERT) began an on-line survey program focused on Air Force systems that yielded similar initial results. Both organizations also tracked an increasing number of outside computer intrusion incidents as part of their vulnerability assessment efforts.

The growing level of understanding and concern about protection against digital intrusion was reinforced by a series of more than 150 Internet intrusions during April and May 1994 against the Air Force command and control research facility at Rome Laboratory at Griffiss Air Force Base, New York.[25] In this incident, two hackers were able to seize control of Rome's computer support systems for several days and compromised an air tasking order research project at the labs. Masquerading as Rome Labs–based trusted computer users, these individuals successfully accessed systems at other government facilities, including NASA's Goddard Flight Space Center and Jet Propulsion Lab, Wright-Patterson Air Force Base, and Army missile R&D facilities, as well as those of two defense contractors. Even more significantly, the attackers were able to access computer systems of the Korean Nuclear Research Agency in Seoul. The FBI and British law enforcement agencies managed to track down the intruders in the United Kingdom. The incident brought home the real possibilities posed by outside digital intrusion and disruption for the Air Force and Department of Defense leadership.[26]

The report of a 1994 Defense Science Board (DSB) Summer Study Task Force, *Information Architecture for the Battlefield*, provided a major impetus to official efforts and concerns surrounding a strategic level of information warfare. Going well beyond its mandate, the report delineated two levels of concern regarding information warfare. At the level labeled "information in war," the DSB report stressed the need to support U.S. commanders and forces conducting conventional military operations with flexible, high-bandwidth, commercially leveraged information systems. The report outlined the need for war-fighting forces to reach back to information systems in the United States through the use of both military and civil information infrastructures and identified a second level of concern, which it labeled "information warfare" based on digital attacks, as a direct threat to the United States. The report states that "Information Warfare then is a national strategic concern. Our economy, national life and military capabilities are very dependent on information—information often vulnerable to exploitation or disruption."[27]

A major policy push began inside DOD to address information warfare concerns within a larger, national construct, particularly regarding defensive concerns. An Information Warfare Directorate was established within the ASD/C3I.[28] Statements by senior DOD leaders began to reflect an understanding of a broader relationship between information warfare and national infrastructure assurance. The Information Security office within the ASD/C3I staff was renamed the Information Assurance office "to promote awareness, build consensus and provide direction for defense of our DOD systems from exploitation."[29] DOD statements about information warfare during 1995–1996 began to include diagrams depicting the interrelationship between the DII, the national information infrastructure (NII), and the global information infrastructure (GII) similar to the one depicted in figure 5.1.[30]

Yet these initial responses did not alleviate the continuing concerns about the DII and NII as sources of vulnerability in the assured conduct of U.S. military operations. DISA and Air Force efforts, although they increased awareness, made slow progress in reducing the vulnerability of defense information systems and networks. Another major DSB effort was initiated in October 1995. The Task Force on "Information Warfare—Defense" focused "on protection of information interests of national importance through the establishment and maintenance of a credible information warfare defensive capability."[31] The task force's report,

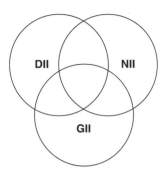

Figure 5.1
Overlaps between the DII, NII, and GII

issued in November of 1996, found that the DII clearly constituted a strategic center of gravity subject to paralyzing attacks that could impede the ability of the nation to employ its military forces. The task force criticized U.S. defensive efforts up to that point, stressing that "[t]he reality is that the vulnerability of the Department of Defense—and of the nation—to offensive information warfare attack is largely a self-created problem. Program by program and economic sector by economic sector, we have based critical functions on inadequately protected telecomputing services. In aggregate, we have created a target-rich environment and U.S. industry has sold globally much of the generic technology that can be used to strike these targets."[32] The task force found that defensive information warfare efforts were characterized by confusion. Management mechanisms and programs formed to deal with information warfare concerns were assessed as inadequate. The report highlighted the need to establish organizational capabilities to perform necessary intelligence, infrastructure planning, and protection functions and noted that "because of our [the United States'] perceived lead in offensive information warfare capabilities, not everyone understands the need for defensive information warfare preparations."[33]

The Department of Defense also actively participated in efforts during the late 1990s to understand the larger challenges presented by the need to protect the U.S. national infrastructures against cyberattacks. The department provided most of the funding and much of the analytical expertise for the President's Commission on Critical Infrastructure Protection.[34] Subsequent to the issuance of Presidential Decision Directive 63 on critical infrastructure protection, DOD formed a dedicated effort led by the ASD/C3I to ensure that its efforts to protect the defense infrastructure sector against cyber- and physical attacks were integrated into larger national efforts. These efforts are discussed in depth later in the chapter.

Computer intrusion incidents also have continued to focus the attention of senior DOD leadership on the need to protect the DII from digital attack. The incident known as Solar Sunrise, involving teenaged hackers who intruded upon key networks elements in the spring of 1998, which was described in chapter 2, provided a major impetus for the formation of Joint Task Force-Computer Network Defense discussed later in the chapter. This incident was followed by another orchestrated effort in 1998–1999, known as Moonlight Maze, to access DOD scientific and technical information that highlighted continued defensive information warfare weaknesses. Michael Vatis, the director of the National Infrastructure Protection Center, told the Senate Judiciary Subcommittee on Technology and Terrorism in October 1999 that these intrusions resulted in the compromise of "unclassified but still sensitive information about essentially defense/technical research matters. . . . About the furthest I can go is to say the intrusions appear to originate in Russia."[35] Assistant Secretary of Defense for Command, Control, Communications and Intelligence Art Money stated in the same month at the National Information Systems Security Conference that "[o]ver a year, the severity has increased dramatically . . . the kids [responsible for Solar Sunrise] essentially found a well-known vulnerability and came in that way. Moonlight Maze brings a whole different, much more sophisticated approach. But it also brings another dimension—we are no longer dealing with hackers, but with the problem of state sponsored attack."[36]

At the end of the 1990s, the Department of Defense clearly recognized the emergence of strategic information warfare as a national security concern. Most of the discernible effort addressed the degree of DOD information infrastructure vulnerability and developing mechanisms to coordinate defensive responses to defend the DII. Additionally, the department acknowledged that it needed to link its efforts into a broader national strategy and improve organizational capacity for defensive strategic information warfare. At the same time, the services and the Joint Staff have integrated information warfare into doctrine specific to military operations.

Formal Military Doctrine Related to Strategic Information Warfare

Within the U.S. military establishment during the 1990s, both the Joint Staff and the individual services (Air Force, Army, Navy, and Marines) formulated doctrine to guide military operations involving information warfare. According to the definition used earlier, in chapter 3, military doctrine is the preferred mode for fighting wars of a group of services, a single service, or a subservice. The formation of doctrine for information warfare has engaged all these institutions. The approach of the different services and the Joint Staff to strategic information warfare varies considerably.

Among the services, the Air Force was the first to grapple with formulating information warfare doctrine. The Air Force identified information warfare as a priority in April 1993 after the issuance of the initial DOD directive on information warfare. The service renamed its Air Force Electronic Warfare Center the Air Force Information Warfare Center (AFIWC) in September 1993, designating for the new organization a focus on "battlefield information dominance."[37] During 1994–1995, attention to the topic flourished within the Air Force, which held a summit of its four-star generals in August 1994 to discuss the issue. The generals agreed that offensive operations would provide a multiplier for future forces but that serious defensive concerns had already emerged.[38] Most of the initial Air Force discussion centered on the importance of information warfare in enhancing the ability of U.S. forces to exploit decision-making advantages on the battlefield though provision of better information support to friendly forces while disrupting enemy systems.[39]

The Air Force's first effort to formalize a doctrinal foundation for information warfare culminated in the publication of a white paper, *Cornerstones of Information Warfare*, in August 1995. The culmination of a long development process, the document endeavored to explain how the Air Force needed to deal with military implications of the information revolution.[40] *Cornerstones* describes information warfare in a manner that "views information itself as a separate realm, potent weapon and lucrative target." According to the paper, information attacks involve "directly corrupting information without visibly changing the physical entity within which it resides. . . . Direct information warfare affects information through altering its components without relying on adversary's perceptions or interpretations." Although it acknowledges defensive concerns as constituting the "the other edge of sword," the document generally stresses exploiting potential offensive opportunities. *Cornerstones* recommends that information warfare be incorporated into Air Force doctrine without trying to define a separate mission area, approaching information warfare as another means for accomplishing the Air Force missions of aerospace control, force application, force enhancement, and force support. Although it continues to focus on affecting adversary military operations and decision making, the paper addresses the possibility of strategic information attack analogous to strategic air attack. *Cornerstones* highlights the significant possibilities of remote, digital attacks but does not directly address them as a new means for waging war.

The Air Force continued to refine its doctrinal construct in another white paper entitled, simply, *Information Warfare* in 1996.[41] The paper outlines information attack as a distinctly new means of applying force. It focuses on support for conventional operations, not strategic information warfare. In building organizations and personnel for information warfare, the expressed goal is support for theater commander-in-chief campaign objectives. Significantly, although it identifies protection as one of three goals for mastering information warfare, *Information Warfare* does not call for defensive measures to mitigate adversary digital attacks or address Air Force dependence on private-sector information infrastructures.

The progress of Air Force efforts to integrate information warfare into its mainstream doctrine was reflected in the revised *Air Force Basic Doctrine*, published in September 1997. This document stresses air and space power but acknowledges that "information is now considered another medium in which some aspects of warfare can be conducted."[42] The document identifies achievement of information superiority as an Air Force core competency, continuing to stress the achievement of decision-making superiority over adversaries through more effective command and control of military forces. *Basic Doctrine* describes information warfare as "involving such diverse activities such as psychological warfare, military deception, electronic combat and both physical and cyber attack." Yet the definition of strategic attack in this document makes no reference to the possible use of digital means.

The Air Force codified its vision regarding information warfare with the publication of Air Force Doctrine Document (AFDD) 2-5, *Information Operations*, in August 1998.[43] AFDD 2-5 stresses that information warfare has both offensive and defensive dimensions with an increased emphasis on the defense as the "Air Force's #1 IW [information warfare] priority." Although it recognizes the existence of a strategic level of information warfare, AFDD 2-5 states that "Air Force efforts will focus on implementing IW capabilities through warfighting component commands in support of joint warfighting commands." It acknowledges the reliance of the Air Force on non-DOD information infrastructures, but the section on information assurance emphasizes securing military computer and communications systems against digital attack. *Information Operations* does not mention offensive digital warfare. The final chapter describes the need to focus Air Force information warfare efforts on creating forces to meet the needs of theater commanders and the use of the Joint Forces Air Component Commander to manage such forces.

As of the end of 1999, the Air Force had integrated digital information warfare into its doctrine but shied away from creating a vision of future conflict involving the conduct of strategic information attacks. Since the publication of *Cornerstones* in 1995, the Air Force doctrinal orientation toward information warfare has become increasingly focused on supporting traditional battlefield operations.

The other services have shown even less inclination to address a strategic level of digital information warfare than the Air Force. The Army has grappled with war in the information age through two major initiatives. The Chief of Staff of the Army declared in the spring of 1994 that "the Army's institutional response to the demands of the information age is Force XXI, a structured effort to redesign the Army—units, processes and organizations—from those of the industrial age to those of the information age."[44] Within the Force XXI vision, the Army stresses the need to leverage information technologies in support of operations on a digitized battlefield.[45] The Force XXI thrust emphasizes the need to win the battlefield information war through "increasingly integrated systems to collect, disseminate and rapidly act on information."[46] The Army has instituted an "Army After Next" program as a follow-on to Force XXI with the same general focus on attaining superiority on the digitized battlefield.[47]

The Army also established "information operations" doctrine in the 1990s. Beginning with the publication of an Army Training and Doctrine Command pamphlet in August 1995, the Army identified information operations (IO) as "the integrated approach to gaining and maintaining the information the warfighter requires to fight and win, while denying that same information to the enemy."[48] The information operations concept was formalized a year later in FM 100-6, *Information Operations*. Adopting a very broad approach, FM 100-6 defines IO as "continuous military operations within the military information environment that enable, enhance, and protect the friendly force's ability to collect, process and act on information to achieve an advantage across the full range of military operations. IO include interacting with the global information environment and exploiting or denying an adversary's information and decision capabilities." The Army explicitly adopts the term "information operations" "to recognize that information issues permeate the full range of military operations (beyond just the traditional context of warfare) from peace to global war."

Significantly, the Army approach recognizes that the Army's capability to conduct information operations resides within a global information environment largely outside its control. The original FM 100-6 explicitly highlights the news media as the principal non-DOD organization of concern within this environment. In outlining threats to information infrastructures, FM 100-6 addresses the ability of both state and nonstate groups to launch remote hacker attacks against civil as well as military targets but evidences even greater concern with an adversary's capability to manipulate the news media. The document does not address an Army role in conducting strategic digital warfare.

Generally, Army doctrine related to information operations/information warfare in the 1990s also predominantly focused on the need to achieve battlefield advantage and information dominance, with little concern about the possibility of war waged totally or primarily through digital strikes against centers of gravity.[49] However, the broader approach to information operations influenced the formation of joint service doctrine. The Army doctrine calls for protecting military and national information infrastructures as a prerequisite for effective operations but does not provide an approach for accomplishing such broader defensive missions.

The Navy and Marine approaches to information warfare remained exclusively focused in the 1990s on improving battlefield operations. Although the Navy generally avoided explicit articulation of doctrine, a number of sources provide insight its vision for war in the information age. In 1990, the Navy outlined its "Copernicus" concept, focused on improving the effectiveness and responsiveness of command, control, communications, computers, and intelligence (C4I) support to naval warfighting forces.[50] As the Copernicus vision evolved in the 1990s, the Navy addressed command and control warfare (C2W) and information warfare through a focus on providing sensor-to-shooter links and integrated information networks in a joint environment for deployed Navy and Marines forces. This emphasis on combat operations was reinforced with the 1994 publication of *Sonata*, which outlines a strategy for space and electronic warfare as part of the Copernicus vision that avoids any acknowledgment of digital warfare. However, the document does detail how growing reliance of U.S. space and electronic warfare forces on global, commercially operated information infrastructures could constitute a tactical center of gravity for potential U.S. adversaries.[51] In April of the same year, the Navy issued an Operating Instruction outlining Information Warfare/C2W responsibilities based very heavily on the MOP 30 approach of considering C2W as the military application of information warfare.[52]

The most detailed articulation of the Navy's concept of information warfare is provided by its 1998 *Information Warfare Strategic Plan.*[53] The plan places the Navy's information warfare efforts firmly "in the context of traditional military activities" to enhance "the ability of naval forces to successfully execute joint military operations." It recognizes the need to defend the NII, but finds that policy and legal constraints prohibit the DOD from taking an "overly proactive role." Although the Navy's plan calls for establishing information warfare as a formal warfare area and creating official doctrine, this had yet to occur at the end of 1999.

The Navy approach to information warfare involves conducting offensive and defensive information warfare as well as protecting infrastructure assets against adversary action.[54] Interestingly, the Navy has addressed strategic information attacks affecting both military and civilian information infrastructures in its Global Wargames held at Naval War College dating back to the early 1990s. The service's policy statements and plans, however, do not address any active Navy role in conducting strategic digital force application or defense. The Marine Corps was nearly silent on the subject of information warfare in the 1990s, preferring to limit its approach to C2W as "better defined and orientated to the tactical and operational levels of war and, therefore, more coincident with Marine Corps missions."[55]

By the end of the 1990s, the military services still had not openly wrestled with the doctrinal implications of strategic information warfare. Service information operations and warfare doctrine remained predominately concerned with supporting traditional war-fighting operations. None of the services advocated launching independent attacks against adversary centers of gravity. Although service doctrines generally recognized the possibility of remote digital attacks and their potential to disrupt nonmilitary information infrastructures, the primary goal of these doctrinal statements was achieving information superiority against enemy military forces and commanders. The services addressed to varying degrees the interrelationship of military and civil infrastructures.

The Joint Staff holds responsibility for developing overarching U.S. military doctrine. Joint doctrine guides the military employment of U.S. forces of all services and operations with allies.[56] During 1993–1999, U.S. joint information warfare and later, information operations doctrine publications evidenced a substantial broadening in conceptual approach. The Joint Staff more clearly articulated strategic information warfare concerns for involving the U.S. military. However, even in Joint doctrine, the military's role in defending the nation's information infrastructure remained limited.

After the publication of MOP 30 describing C2W in 1993, the Joint Staff played a minor role in the following two years in developing doctrine about information warfare as services wrestled with creating their own conceptualizations. Formal Joint Staff doctrine remained focused on enhancing traditional battlefield operations, as outlined by the Joint Staff pamphlet *C4I for the Warrior*, published in 1994. In May 1995, the Joint Staff released Joint Publication 6-0, *Doctrine for C4 Systems Support to Joint Operations*. This document highlighted the importance of a global infrastructure in providing adequate support to U.S. overseas military operations but addressed DOD-operated systems without acknowledging defensive concerns or their interrelationship with civil information infrastructures.[57]

The growing ferment about information warfare did, however, lead to the formation of organizations within the Joint Staff to deal with the broader range of concerns. Within the Operations (J-3) Directorate, an Information Warfare-Special Technical Operations Branch (J-39) was formed and in the Command, Control, Communications, and Computer Systems Directorate (J-6), an Information Assurance Branch (J6K) was established.[58]

The Joint Staff began to play a guiding role in the formation of information warfare doctrine beginning in 1996. The first major step was the release in February of that year of Joint Publication 3-13.1, *Joint Doctrine for Command and Control Warfare*.[59] This document endeavored to clarify the relationship of C2W to information warfare while stressing that "the full dimensions of IW policy and its implementation are still emerging." As in MOP 30, the conceptualization of C2W remains in Joint Publication 3-13.1 as "an application of IW in military operations and is a subset of IW." More significantly, the document begins with an articulation of "the merging of civilian and military information networks and technologies" and the recognition that "the DII, NII and GII are inextricably intertwined." Joint Publication 3-13.1 highlights the fact that "although these technologies and techniques offer a significant increase in the efficient application of military power, they also increase the risk to military forces or even entire societies if not protected." The publication states that information warfare "supports the national military strategy but requires support, coordination and participation of other United States Government (USG) departments and agencies as well as commercial industry. Although DOD information flows depend on civil information infrastructures, the protection of these infrastructures falls outside the DOD. A USG interagency effort is necessary to coordinate the protection of civil information infrastructures critical to DOD interests. Offensive IW actions also require interagency deconfliction and cooperation." This for the first time provided a doctrinal statement relating information warfare to the strategic implications of national information infrastructures. Moreover, it highlighted the limits of DOD's role in U.S. infrastructure protection and the need for a broader national approach.

The role of the Joint Staff in doctrinal formation was enhanced by its publication of *Information Warfare—A Strategy for Peace—The Decisive Edge for War* in the summer of 1996. Based on the definition used in Joint Publication 3-13.1, this document stresses that information warfare "applies across all phases, the range of military operations and at every level of warfare."[60] Reiterating the significance of the intertwined DII and NII, *Information Warfare* calls for a team approach to developing a comprehensive strategic defensive IW strategy, emphasizing that "[w]e must assist in demonstrating to [commercial] service providers the compelling need for a collaborative, teamed approach in crafting solutions— not just to support the Department of Defense and to protect our national security but to protect their proprietary interests as well."[61] The document clearly identifies tasks for strategic defense of DOD information infrastructures, including threat assessment, providing indications and warnings, and responding to attacks. In describing the threat and necessary defensive responses, this Joint Staff document emphasizes remote, digital means of attacks, not kinetic or electromagnetic means, and stresses the crucial role of intelligence support.

Information Warfare describes the possibility of offensive information warfare that "applies traditional perception management disciplines such as psychological operations and information system attack to produce a synergistic effect against the remaining elements of an adversary's information systems, information transfer links and information nodes."[62] The document describes the potential strategic role of information warfare for deterring crises and avoiding escalation and outlines the use of information warfare against nonstate actors, such as through attacks on a drug cartel's communications. The examples of information warfare targets outlined in the document, as depicted in figure 5.2, clearly indicate the desire to wage strategic information warfare. The document establishes the Joint Staff as the lead agent for developing joint information warfare doctrine. Moreover, *Information Warfare* hammers home the importance of establishing broader efforts across the U.S. government and U.S. industry to ensure adequate protection of information infrastructures. In total, the document provides the clearest doctrinal statement to date about the significance of both strategic offensive and defensive information warfare for the DOD and the nation as a whole.

Examples of IW targets

Leadership
• Key personnel
• ADP support
• Strategic communications
• Power base

Military infrastructure
• Commanders
• C2 communication (links/nodes)
• Troops
• Intelligence collectors

Civil infrastructure
• Communications (links/nodes)
• Industry
• Financial
• Populace

Weapons systems
• Planes/ships
• Artillery
• Precision Guided Munitions
• Air defense

Figure 5.2
Information warfare targets

Since the publication of *Information Warfare*, the Joint Staff has continued to broaden the scope of the information warfare rubric and its integration with more traditional military operations. The Joint Staff reinforced guidance related to defensive information warfare tasks by issuing, in May 1996, Chairman of the Joint Chiefs of Staff Instruction 6505.1A, "Defensive IW Implementation," which expanded the scope of previous implementing instructions narrowly focused on communications security to a broader focus on infrastructure protection.[63] The Joint Staff publication *Joint Vision 2010—America's Military: Preparing for Tomorrow*, released in summer 1996, also directly linked the use of both offensive and defensive information warfare to the achievement of "information superiority."[64] *Joint Vision 2010* has become a touchstone document regarding the U.S. military's vision of future wars.[65] It mentions the use of digital offensive and defensive warfare and calls for increased strategic level programs in those areas. However, *Joint Vision 2010* retains the legacy of the C2W approach in strategic attacks on "enemy military decision-makers" and does not address defense of the DII or NII as military missions.[66]

In late 1996, the DOD/Joint Staff adopted the term "information operations" in place of "information warfare." The principal rationale for the switch of terminology appears to be that whereas information warfare definitions and discussions tended to be very inclusive of peacetime operations and defensive preparations, the term "warfare" was more generally perceived as a more specific term dealing with actions in a crisis or conflict.[67] The term "information operations," previously in used only by the Army, was officially adopted by the Department of Defense in the December 1996 DOD directive S3600.1 "Information Operations (IO)," which replaced the previous TS3600.1 "Information

Warfare."[68] The adoption of the information operations framework established a broader rubric to support DOD efforts to achieve interagency and civil-sector coordination in achieving protection of intertwined information infrastructures. According to the directive, information operations must "secure peacetime national security objectives, deter conflict, protect DOD information and information systems and shape the information environment."[69]

After a lengthy drafting and review process, the Joint Staff followed the DOD directive with Joint Publication 3-13, *Joint Doctrine for Information Operations*, in October 1998.[70] This document delineates information operations and information warfare as follows: "IO involves actions taken to affect adversary's information and information systems while defending one's own information and information systems. IO applies across all phases of an operation and the range of military operations, and at every level of warfare. IW is IO conducted during time of crisis or conflict to achieve or promote specific objectives over a specific adversary or adversaries." Describing information operations as an "integrating strategy," the document stresses many of the same issues identified in the earlier *Information Warfare* pamphlet regarding the need to achieve close U.S. government coordination and a partnership with industry in the conduct of strategic information operations and information warfare, particularly for assurance of information security. Computer network attack, according to the document, can be used as a tool for offensive information operations as are psychological operations, deception, electronic warfare, and physical destruction.[71] Offensive information operations "at the strategic level of war will be directed by the National Command Authorities and planned in coordination with other organizations outside the DOD . . . these operations may be conducted to influence or affect all elements (political, military, economic, or informational) of adversary national power."[72] Defensive information operations represent a "process that integrates and coordinates policies and procedures, operations, intelligence, law and technology to protect information and defend information systems."[73] The very broad focus of Joint Publication 3-13 includes within information operations actions to enhance friendly C4I capabilities and conduct perception management. Although it identifies the importance of the DII-NII interface, the chapter dealing with defensive information operations focuses primarily on concerns of military joint force commanders, not on broader issues of DII and NII protection and the role of DOD organizations. Digital warfare means are not stressed as either offensive or defensive concerns. Taken as whole, Joint Publication 3-13 continues the general trend toward an expansive treatment of the activities considered under the information warfare/information operations label. Despite acknowledgement of strategic offensive and defensive considerations, the overall thrust remains improvement of traditional U.S. military operations.

At the end of 1999, U.S. military doctrine encompassed the potential significance of a strategic level of information warfare in both offensive and defensive dimensions. However, the doctrine remained burdened by an expansive conceptualization of what constitutes information warfare and operations. This breadth was necessary to enable the DOD and services to grapple with the many concerns raised by the information age for military operations. Yet with a few exceptions like the two DSB Task Force reports and the 1996 Joint Staff *Information Warfare* pamphlet, the focus of doctrinal development in the 1990s was on enhancing traditional military operations. The possibilities for waging strategic information warfare, although apparent, did not become a major thrust of U.S. doctrine for fighting future wars. Additionally, the U.S. military establishment recognized policy and legal constraints on a DOD–led approach to conducting national-level defensive strategic information warfare efforts.

Increasing National Attention to Infrastructure Vulnerability and Protection

The increasing reliance of U.S. society on networked computers and other information technologies has resulted in an evolution in the relationship between national security and use of information infrastructures. Instead of restricting its interest to protecting classified and sensitive information from espionage and ensuring minimal essential telecommunications in the event of a nuclear conflict, the U.S. government has shifted to a broader set of national security concerns surrounding information infrastructure protection and assurance. Through a learning process involving external prodding and growing internal awareness, the U.S. government outside the military establishment in the 1990s developed an appreciation of the potential threat of digital warfare and began to orchestrate a response.

The 1991 National Research Council (NRC) report *Computers at Risk* provided an early notice of new challenges that had arisen in protecting U.S. information infrastructures. The committee responsible for the report was comprised primarily of individuals involved with information technology development and the academic community.[74] A response to the 1988 Internet worm incident, *Computers at Risk* looks beyond protective efforts of individuals and separate organizations to address the broader problems of securing the nation's information infrastructures. The report discusses how the evolution of distributed networks means that the overall security of information resources is largely determined by weak links in the chain of networked computers capable of digital communication and interaction. The market-driven weakness of the security features in most information technology products of the early 1990s and the lack of useful means to assess protective features are stressed throughout the NRC findings.[75]

Significantly, the report also distinguishes between the different threats posed by unorganized hackers and by an organized, sophisticated adversary intent on disruption. Describing past threats in terms of espionage, the report notes that "[t]he rapidly decreasing cost of computer resources, rapid spread of computer technology and increased value of information-based assets make it likely that high-grade threats will be encountered from other sources and with other aims than traditional espionage."[76] The NRC's report also explains why developing and instituting protective measures against such sophisticated threats involves substantial time and expense. *Computers at Risk* clearly addresses the emerging security concerns related to advanced information infrastructures as well as difficult policy and economic trade-offs that must be made in grappling with them.

During the early 1990s, organizations responsible for U.S. national security telecommunications also developed an awareness of civil information infrastructure vulnerability and endeavored to raise broader awareness within the federal government. A series of early efforts conducted under the auspices of the NCS made clear that the U.S. government's NS/EP communications were increasingly at risk. The NCS Office of the Manager issued a report in 1993 stating that "[t]he threat that contemporary computer intruders pose to the public switched network (PSN) is significant and rapidly changing."[77] NS/EP communications rely on the public-switched network. The report noted the growing skills of intruders but did not describe the threat in terms of strategic information warfare. NCS activities focused principally on the provision of telecommunications services, not the larger set of activities involved in information infrastructure assurance. Throughout the mid- and late 1990s, NCS and NSTAC studies stressed the linkage between national security and commercial telecommunications networks.[78]

The community concerned with protecting national security information also began in the 1990s to reevaluate the effects of the changing international environment and nature of information resources on security concerns. One official responsible for DOD information assurance programs, Ralph McMillian, describes the early 1990s as a "boutique" period for discussions of information warfare. According to McMillian, the period involved an emerging understanding of threats posed by digital attacks against unclassified information and networked information systems.[79] The new challenges in the securing of information resources were squarely addressed in 1994 in a report by the Joint Security Commission (JSC), which was established by the Secretary of Defense and the Director of Central Intelligence to deal with changing concerns about the protection of national security information in the post–Cold War environment. The JSC report, *Redefining Security*, made the following observation:

> The policies and standards upon which the Defense and Intelligence Communities base information systems security standards were developed when computers were physically isolated. As a result, policies and standards:
>
> • Were developed based on a philosophy of complete risk avoidance and so do not deal effectively with information systems and security as part of a balanced mix of countermeasures.
>
> • Do not provide the flexibility needed to address the wide variations among systems in use today and planned for tomorrow.
>
> • Do not differentiate between the security countermeasures needed within and among protected network enclaves and those needed when information must travel to and from less protected or unprotected parts of the infrastructure.
>
> • Are beginning to combine computer science and public key cryptography.
>
> • Are not capable of responding to dynamically evolving technology.[80]

Even more broadly, the JSC found, "if instead of attacking our military systems and databases an enemy attacked our unprotected civilian infrastructure, the economic and other results would be disastrous."[81] The report demonstrates a clear awareness of a new national security threat and of the difficulties posed by the changing character of the nation's information infrastructure. The JSC recommendations resulted in the September 1994 Presidential Decision Directive (PDD) 29, "Security Policy Coordination," establishing the Security Policy Board (SPB).[82] Chaired by the Assistant to the President for National Security Affairs, SPB membership included the Deputy Secretaries from Defense, State, Justice, Energy, and Commerce, the Director of Central Intelligence, and the Vice Chairman of the Joint Chiefs. The Board became a principal mechanism for educating a broader range of federal government actors about this emerging national security concern.[83]

Awareness of the national security dimension of information infrastructure protection was also publicly highlighted in speculative analyses performed outside the U.S. government. The Tofflers' *War and Anti-War* raised interest in high-level DOD audiences about the broad impacts of the information age on warfare and the possibilities of digital warfare. Winn Schwartau's *Information Warfare*, first published in 1994, heightened awareness of the threat and of the need to provide protection for the U.S. information infrastructures.[84] As detailed in chapter 1, Schwartau utilizes a sensationalist tone to outline the increasing reliance of individuals, businesses, and the nation on information infrastructures, as well as the wide range of means and potentially highly disruptive effects that digital attackers could inflict. He provides an in-depth discussion of the possibility of digital attacks waged as strategic warfare by both state and nonstate actors. Schwartau does not, however, analyze the many challenges faced by attackers or the difficulties involved in national defensive efforts. Others, including Tom Clancy, in *Debt of Honor* and his series of *Net Force* novels, and well-regarded journals, such as *The Economist*, added fuel to the fire with additional speculation regarding the possibility of future adversaries waging large-scale digital attacks on U.S. financial markets and transportation systems.[85] Such works set the stage for a period of ferment about the degree of national vulnerability and the adequacy of U.S. responses. These authors, as well as their apostles and critics, subsequently held discussions in a range of forums involving futurists, military and civilian national security officials, academics, and concerned individuals from the commercial sector.

In 1995, a series of events and activities catalyzed a larger push within the U.S. government beyond the traditional national security establishment to address the protection and assurance of the nation's information infrastructure. Within the DOD community, the 1994 DSB Task Force provided impetus to develop policies and approaches based on protecting nonclassified resources and managing the risk posed by heavy reliance on information infrastructures, rather than trying to completely eliminate the presence of vulnerabilities. Information and computer security efforts became part of a larger approach, known as "information assurance," which dealt with both classified and unclassified information resources related to national security.[86]

The need to clarify the foreign information warfare threat to the nation led the newly formed DOD Information Warfare Executive Board to request a national intelligence estimate from the intelligence community in early 1995.[87] The ASD/C3I Information Warfare directorate also pushed the development of a broader, coordinated approach by drafting a Presidential Decision Directive regarding national information warfare concerns and responsibilities. Although this effort stalled, the momentum grew for addressing infrastructure protection across the range of stakeholder agencies in the federal government.[88]

Another major initiative of the Information Warfare Executive Board and the ASD/C3I staff was sponsorship of a continuing study by RAND Corporation that specifically addressed the subject of strategic information warfare.[89] The series of exercises begun in early 1995 known as "The Day After in Cyberspace . . ." endeavored to illuminate the defensive challenges faced by national security policymakers. The "Day After" scenario confronted participants with a series of potentially malicious disruptions of different U.S. information infrastructure–dependent activities including military mobilization and provision of transportation and electric power, as well as adversaries' use of the Internet and World Wide Web to conduct perception management efforts. The RAND effort explicitly focused on strategic information warfare as an emerging realm of conflict "wherein nations utilize cyberspace to affect strategic military operations and inflict damage on national information infrastructures."[90] According to the 1996 RAND report based on these exercises, entitled *Strategic Information Warfare: A New Face of War*, "participants represented various levels of industry, academia, the analytic and research communities, the intelligence community, national security policymakers and the military services."[91] Exercises involving individuals at the Deputy Secretary level within the government and industry CEO level had been held by the late spring of 1995.

The RAND report acknowledged the lack of comprehensive risk assessment regarding the vulnerability of U.S. national information infrastructures. In grappling with the question of who should provide a focal point for such an assessment, *Strategic Information Warfare* offered possibilities, including the intelligence community, the National Communications System or a federal government interagency effort. It identified challenges of inadequate resources and sensitivity to mixing law enforcement and intelligence community activities in conducting such an assessment. The report recommended an effort to define and protect a "minimum essential information infrastructure" or MEII, required for support of key military, governmental, and civilian functions that would form the baseline for initial efforts at establishing a U.S. strategic information warfare defensive capability.[92] The report also found that existing national military strategy did not address how to cope with and respond to the threat posed by strategic information warfare. An important aspect missing in the RAND exercises, however, was a clear articulation of the military and political objectives sought by attackers through the use of strategic information warfare. By avoiding the specific objectives of attackers, the RAND findings overplayed the degree of ambiguity involved and the dilemmas facing U.S. policymakers in responding to such attacks.

Another push came from an unexpected source as bombings at the World Trade Center and in Oklahoma City resulted in major initiatives to deal with terrorist threats within the United States. President Bill Clinton issued PDD 39, "U.S. Policy on Counterterrorism," in June 1995, which stated, "The Attorney General, as the chief law enforcement officer, shall chair a Cabinet Committee to review the vulnerability to terrorism of governmental facilities in the U.S. and critical national infrastructure[s] and make recommendations."[93] In response, an interagency effort known as the Critical Infrastructure Working Group (CIWG) was formed in the fall of 1995 under the direction of the Deputy Attorney General, Jamie Gorelick. Its membership also included the Deputy Secretary of Defense, the Deputy Assistant to the President for National Security Affairs, the Director of the FBI, and the Director of Central Intelligence. This group was tasked with identifying critical infrastructures, the scope of threats to these infrastructures, existing government mechanisms to deal with such threats, and long-term and interim options for addressing the threats. The group identified eight critical infrastructures, one of which was telecommunications. These critical infrastructures were deemed "so vital that their incapacity or destruction would have a debilitating impact on a regional or national level."[94] Very significantly, the group also divided the threats into two general types, physical attacks and "cyber" attacks. The CIWG characterized the "cyber" threat as "electronic, radio frequency, or computer-based attacks on the information or communications components that control critical infrastructure. Logic bombs, viruses and other computer-based attacks may disrupt, manipulate or destroy the information upon which our defense, security, economic and societal fabric depends."[95] The activities of the CIWG subsequently molded U.S. efforts to deal with strategic information warfare defense. The group's efforts to establish the baseline categories of critical infrastructures and two main threat categories were used in Executive Order 13010 in July 1996 to establish the PCCIP. Concern about strategic attacks waged by digital warfare were clearly addressed. The CIWG identified numerous threats, including "malicious hackers, disgruntled insiders, organized criminals, foreign terrorists and nation-states."[96] However, the CIWG focus on critical infrastructures also constrained the federal government's role in information infrastructure defense to the activities conducted by telecommunications networks and network service providers. The role of technology producers and concerns about general commercial users, on the other hand, subsequently received inadequate emphasis in developing policies or organizational mechanisms for national information infrastructure defense.

The Executive Branch as a whole began to recognize the necessity of protecting U.S. information infrastructures at the national level in the mid-1990s. In December 1995, the Security Policy Board issued a white paper on "security-related challenges presented by the emergence of the NII."[97] The board highlighted the perceived vulnerability of defense and other government and commercial information infrastructures as well as the inadequacy of efforts to respond. Stressing the results of the RAND "Day After" exercises, the paper notes, "There is no single entity with sufficient breadth of vision, responsibility and resources to effectively manage the Executive Branch's goal of information assurance." The SPB felt the U.S. government lacked a "fair court" to balance legitimate, but competing, national security, law enforcement, commerce, and private interests. Furthermore, it found that separate NII security-related activities in the DOD/NSA, Commerce/NIST, and the Information Infrastructure Task Force were not coordinated, and noted that limited resources in the Executive Branch "appear to be inefficiently, ineffectively and illogically scattered."[98] To create mechanisms for coordination of NII security and assurance, the SPB paper recommended the formation of a focal point within the SPB, the NSTAC, or the National Security Council. A growing chorus of voices called for national-level leadership to deal with protection of U.S. information infrastructures.

The Department of Justice also initiated a concerted effort in the mid-1990s to cope with the emerging threat to the nation's information infrastructure by simultaneously upgrading efforts focused on computer crime and improving infrastructure protection. Concern with cybercrime and its international dimensions had grown within the FBI through the mid-1990s, especially during the FBI's extensive cooperation with the Air Force during the Rome Labs incident. Cyberthreats became the responsibility of the FBI's Computer Investigations and Threat Assessment Center in 1995.[99] Throughout 1995–1996, Deputy Attorney General Gorelick went on a major campaign to stress cyberthreat awareness and motivate efforts to respond. Her public speeches and congressional testimony outlined the "high potential for crippling strikes aimed at vital U.S. computer and/or energy systems by terrorists" and the need for "hardening vital infrastructures against computer and physical attacks."[100] The Department of Justice also emphasized its new mission to deal with the threat to information infrastructures in the spring of 1996 by announcing its successful pursuit of an Argentinean hacker who had spent months using Harvard's computer systems to gain access to DOD and NASA networks. An Infrastructure Protection Task Force (IPTF) was formed by Executive Order 13010 in July 1996, in conjunction with the PCCIP. The Justice Department assumed leadership of IPTF with the operational mission of coordinating the provision of expert guidance from inside and outside the government to deal with detecting threats to and protecting critical infrastructures. The Department of Justice/FBI role remained central in U.S. efforts to establish a coordinated, national strategic information warfare defense throughout the 1990s.

During the same period, the popular press in the United States picked up on the growing concern in the government and in society more generally with national-level digital attacks. Media reports drew on government sources such as congressional testimony by intelligence officials, the DISA vulnerability testing, and the 1994 DSB Task Force and NCS reports, highlighting the growing concern about threats to the United States and the lack of clear protection strategy. Most significant was a July 1995 article published by Neil Munro in the *Washington Post*, entitled "The Pentagon's New Nightmare: An Electronic Pearl Harbor." Munro alleged that "if the civilian computers stopped working, America's armed forces couldn't eat, talk, move or shoot . . . [and] military officials acknowledge they have no ability to protect themselves from cyberattacks and no legal or political authority to protect commercial phone lines, the electric power grid and vast databases against hackers, saboteurs and terrorists."[101] *Time* soon followed with quotes from the director of the NSA, Vice Admiral John McConnell, stating, "We're more vulnerable than any nation on earth."[102] The popular press continued to stress the vulnerability created by strategic digital attacks throughout the remainder of the decade.

Prompted by DOD concerns and rising attention in the national media, Congress contributed the national debate over the significance of strategic cyberattacks. Following up on previous investigations conducted after the Gulf War, the General Accounting Office launched another probe into DOD computer security. The 1996 GAO report resulting from this probe noted that "attacks on Defense computer systems are a serious and growing threat."[103] Based largely on DISA data and analysis of the Rome Laboratory incident, the report stated that "[t]he potential for catastrophic damage is great. Organized foreign nationals or terrorists could use 'information warfare' techniques to disrupt military operations by harming command and control systems, the public switched network, or other systems and networks the Department of Defense relies on." This GAO report and a series of subsequent efforts provided another voice of awareness regarding the weakness of defense and other U.S. government infrastructures to digital attacks.[104]

Congress also began to take more direct legislative action to prompt protection of the larger NII in the mid-1990s. The Senate Select Committee for Intelligence report on the Intelligence Authorization Bill for FY 1996 (S.922) called on the DCI and Secretary of Defense to issue a comprehensive report on threats to government and private computer and communications systems and develop a plan with legislative and programmatic recommendations to deal with these threats. The same year, Senators Kyl and Leahy co-sponsored S.982, "The NII Protection Act." Although the Senate did not pass this bill, it provided the foundation for a key provision of the 1996 Defense Authorization Bill known as the Kyl amendment, which required that "[n]ot later than 120 days after the date of enactment of this act [March 1996], the President shall submit to Congress a report setting forth the results of a review of the national policy on protecting the national [information] infrastructure against strategic attacks."[105]

Additionally, Congress sponsored a National Defense Panel (NDP) to address a broad range of post–Cold War national security concerns. Its December 1997 report, *Transforming Defense*, recommended major changes in emphasis for U.S. force structure planning. The NDP report stressed the importance of responding to asymmetric threats to the U.S. homeland rather than preparing for another Gulf War–type scenario. The panel argued that DOD needed to proactively prepare to play a role in homeland defense against such threats. The asymmetric threat of most concern in *Transforming Defense* was weapons of mass destruction, but digital threats and information warfare also received significant attention. The report stated that "[t]he potential for an enemy to use attacks on information infrastructures as a means of undermining our economy and deterring or disrupting our [military] operations abroad is of increasing concern. As threats to commercial and defense networks increase, the defense of our information infrastructure becomes crucial."[106] The NDP explicitly separated consideration of information operations for enhancing traditional military forces from efforts geared to protect U.S. information infrastructures. Although it described the active role DOD should play in defending information infrastructures, the NDP sidestepped the issue of how the department should deal with this mission by recommending support for implementation of the PCCIP's recommendations. Significantly, the NDP also recognized that a transformative change to focus the U.S. military on homeland defense would require radical shifts in organizational responsibilities and even a new legislative basis for some DOD missions. In particular, *Transforming Defense* called for the formation of a Homeland Defense Command "for such missions as augmenting border security operations, defending North America from information warfare attacks and air and missile attacks, and augmenting consequence management of natural disasters and terrorist attacks."[107] The panel's recommendations for reducing expenditures on the DOD industrial base and infrastructure did not take into consideration the need to establish secure technological foundations for information infrastructures, nor did the panel recommend the allocation of funds for such an undertaking. The NDP findings were a major force behind changes to the U.S. military's Unified Command Plan in 1999, discussed later in the chapter.

By 1996, strategic information warfare had become an issue requiring attention at the highest levels of national security policy. That year's *National Security Strategy* states for the first time that "the threat [of strategic information warfare] to our military and commercial information systems poses a significant risk to national security."[108] More importantly, under pressure from departments and agencies within the Executive Branch and with legislative calls for action issued by Congress, the President issued Executive Order 13010 on 15 July 1996 establishing the PCCIP.[109]

The formation, activities, and recommendations of the PCCIP became the central focus of national efforts to understand and respond to strategic information warfare threats from the fall of 1996 through the end of the following year. The PCCIP activities overlapped and largely subsumed efforts by other entities dealing with the problem within DOD, NSTAC, and the Justice Department. Chaired by retired Air Force Gen. Robert T. Marsh, the commission included twenty representatives from inside and outside the federal government. The process of appointing commissioners proved difficult, especially finding representatives from outside government. In fact, few people from actual commercial organizations were involved, which limited private-sector receptiveness to the PCCIP's eventual recommendations.[110]

Embarking on an unprecedented task, the commission spent considerable effort on trying to adequately understand the nature of activities and threat concerns in each of the infrastructure sectors. It brought to bear on the problem a wide range of sources, including general literature and briefings by industry experts and organizations as well as sponsoring studies and exercises related to specific threats to and vulnerabilities of different infrastructures. The commission also conducted an extensive series of public meetings and made extensive use of electronic means to solicit input from all interested parties.[111] The slow start and extensive learning process required led the PCCIP to request and receive a ninety-day extension to the original twelve-month deadline for issuing its findings. The final PCCIP report, entitled *Critical Foundations*, was released on 13 October 1997.

Despite the physical acts of terrorism that had prompted the national concerns with infrastructure protection, the *Critical Foundations* report focused its attention predominantly on the cyberthreat to the nation's infrastructure and how the United States should respond. Its foreword states that "[o]ur infrastructures are exposed to new vulnerabilities—cyber vulnerabilities—and new threats—cyber threats. And perhaps most difficult of all, the defenses which served us so well in the past offer little protection from the cyber threat. Our infrastructures can now be struck directly by a variety of cyber tools."[112] The report stresses the lack of available information about the nature and significance of cyberthreats and how this information deficit may result in private organizations making ill-informed decisions about risk management. Additionally, the report details the growing interconnections between infrastructures and the possibility that minor and routine disruptions might cascade throughout infrastructures in an unexpected fashion, creating significant problems. The report strongly urges building partnerships between government and the private sector to increase understanding of and establish national priorities and investment in infrastructure protection from cyberthreats.

Acknowledging the rising significance of the cyberthreat, *Critical Foundations* does not directly address strategic information warfare. Instead, the report makes little distinction between the threat posed by different categories and digital attackers with different objectives. Despite finding no immediate threat sufficient to warrant declaring the situation a national crisis, it also asserts, "A personal computer and a telephone connection to the Internet Service Provider anywhere in the world are enough to cause harm."[113] The report downplays the challenges facing those who would conduct digital attacks while stressing how ambiguous attacks by substate actors present new challenges for the intelligence community. Further, *Critical Foundations* makes no effort to identify how disruption achieved through cyberattacks relates to the political objectives that might be pursued by specific U.S. adversaries.

The PCCIP report quickly resulted in the formation of a National Security Council interagency group tasked with making recommendations to the president concerning concrete actions to institute a national infrastructure protection program, which resulted in PDD 63, "Critical Infrastructure Protection," in May 1998. The PCCIP itself was disbanded, in late 1997 but many of its personnel formed a transition group to support the NSC deliberations and assist with the formation of federal infrastructure protection efforts.[114]

The direction provided by PDD 63 closely followed the recommendations provided by the PCCIP.[115] Critical infrastructures designated as essential to the minimum operations of the economy and government included telecommunications, energy, banking and finance, transportation, water systems, and emergency services in both the government and private sector. The president declared the United States would take all necessary measures to eliminate swiftly any significant vulnerability to both physical and cyberattacks on our critical infrastructures, including especially our cybersystems. The directive called for a cooperative effort between federal, state, and local governments and the private sector to create and conduct critical infrastructure protection efforts. The president mandated establishment of an initial operating capability for a national cyberdefense by 2000. The directive stated that by 2004 the United States would have the ability to protect critical infrastructures from intentional acts that would significantly diminish the ability to provide for national security, ensure public health and safety and the orderly functioning of the economy, and deliver telecommunications, energy, financial, and transportation services. PDD 63 provides the core direction for strategic information warfare defense efforts as the United States enters the twenty-first century. The specifics of PDD 63, organizational roles, and implementation efforts are discussed below.

The president and Congress established in the mid- and late 1990s that digital attacks pose a distinct threat to the United States. PDD 63 recognized that the changed nature of the cyberspace environment and the actors that can operate in this environment require a new type of protective effort involving a wide range of government actors and a necessary partnership with the private sector. However, the continuing inability of governmental organizations to articulate the plausible goals of an adversary's cyberattacks has left the planned U.S. response short of a clearly focused effort aimed at defensive strategic information warfare. *Transforming Defense* acknowledged homeland defense, including protection against digital attacks, as a new DOD mission but lacked clear guidance about how military resources should be committed to this new mission.

Law enforcement concerns continue to outweigh emphasis on protecting centers of gravity from strategic digital attack by adversaries in establishing U.S. information infrastructure protection efforts. Additionally, the critical infrastructure focus of the CIWG, the PCCIP, and PDD 63 meant the significant role of technology producers in establishing the cyberspace environment was not addressed. National security concerns posed by digital information warfare have yet to be matched by a focused effort to avert the threat at the strategic level. In large measure, this situation arises from choices made in the U.S. government and the private sector to emphasize other priorities.

Working at Cross-Purposes: U.S. Government Efforts to
Leverage Advantages from the Information Age

The United States clearly established its leadership during the 1990s among global efforts to move into the information age. Commercial firms such as Microsoft, Intel, Cisco, and Sun Microsystems dominated much of the world's computer and networking markets. U.S.-based telecommunications companies including AT&T, Worldcom, and BellSouth aggressively competed for customers at home and abroad. U.S. individuals and corporations were the most prolific users of the Internet and other advanced technology applications at the close of the decade. The federal government attempted to foster international leadership in this realm through policy initiatives, legislative action, and negotiations. Motivated principally by desires for economic advantage and opportunities for social gain, these activities also influenced the environment for national security efforts to deal with strategic information warfare.

The National Information Infrastructure initiative undertaken by the Clinton Administration provided clear evidence of the U.S. government's simultaneous pursuit of differing priorities. The initiative stressed five principles: promoting private-sector investment, extending universal service, assuring information resources are available at the lowest prices, promoting technological innovation and new applications, and promoting a seamless, interactive, user-driven operation of the NII.[116] Launched in September 1993, the NII initiative was managed by the interagency Information Infrastructure Task Force (IITF), led by the Secretary of Commerce with significant involvement as well by the Vice President, Albert Gore. Despite concerns about security and reliability, the IITF consistently stressed efforts to make U.S. information infrastructures open to competition among more telecommunications providers, foster implementation of new technologies, and provide more access to individuals. These efforts did not envision mechanisms and procedures to assure that new telecommunications and network service providers entering the market have implemented adequate security procedures or that new technologies installed on the nation's information infrastructures are reliable and difficult to corrupt. The potential risks of allowing more access to networks received little initial emphasis.

The IITF effort most closely linked to national security was the Reliability and Vulnerability Working Group (RVWG). Responsible for NS/EP concerns, the RVWG established linkages with the NSTAC and issued a report entitled *NII Risk Assessment: A Nation's Information at Risk.* Echoing previous efforts by the National Research Council and the NCS, the RVWG report stressed the lack of available information about possible threats and vulnerabilities, requiring the establishment of information exchanges among all NII users. Yet challenges posed by strategic information warfare were not evident in this report or any IITF effort. The RVWG was disbanded in 1996 when the PCCIP was formed.[117]

The Clinton administration, again under the leadership of Vice President Gore, also internationalized U.S. efforts to promote openness and competition with the 1994 Global Information Infrastructure initiative. Also directed by the IITF, the GII initiative laid out a similar set of guiding principles without attention to achieving network assurance and protection against malicious disruption. In International Telecommunications Union and World Trade Organization forums, the Commerce Department and the FCC emphasized U.S. efforts to open telecommunications and information technology markets in other countries for competition involving U.S. companies. The administration has shown an inclination to address law enforcement and cybercrime concerns in international forums such as the Organization for Economic Cooperation and Development (OECD) and through cooperation with initiatives under development by the Council of Europe.[118] However, the United States still has failed to address strategic information warfare as part of its international cooperative efforts, despite calls for such action by the Department of Defense and the PCCIP. The "Framework for Global Electronic Commerce" released in the summer of 1997 opens with the principle that the private sector should lead information infrastructure development. The framework asserts "[t]he need to preserve the Internet as a non-regulatory medium, one in which competition and consumer choice will shape the marketplace."[119] The framework does not address national security concerns.

Other Clinton administration activities also downplayed defensive concerns as part of the larger NII agenda. In October 1996, the administration launched an initiative known as Next Generation Internet (NGI). The White House identified three NGI initiative goals: establishing high-speed network connections for universities and national labs, promoting experimentation with networking technologies, and demonstrating new applications to meet important national goals and missions. Interestingly, national security missions were couched in terms of achieving "dominant battlefield awareness which will give the U.S. military a decided advantage in any conflict. . . . This will require orders of magnitude more bandwidth than currently is commercially available."[120] The initiative made no mention of digital disruption threats or national defensive concerns related to the use of the Internet.[121]

The U.S. government also had the task in the 1990s of preparing the nation for potential problems posed by the Year 2000 rollover in date-reliant computing and information systems. In addition to efforts by federal departments and agencies, the White House worked to raise the awareness of state and local governments as well as the private sector about potential Year 2000 problems. Remediation efforts geared at ensuring software code and embedded devices would function properly resulted in creation of a National Y2K Coordinator and the expenditure of billions of dollars across the federal government.

Although the timing and scope of this work prohibits a detailed analysis of the many concerns surrounding the Y2K event, it highlights two key considerations. As discussed elsewhere, remediation efforts may have offered opportunities for potential U.S. adversaries to insert malicious code and back doors into software systems and information infrastructures. Although the U.S. government recognized this as a concern, the scope and cost of the remediation efforts prevented comprehensively checking all code for such devices. Additionally, as 1999 came to a close, the federal, state, and local governments had also developed consequence management efforts to deal with problems that might arise during Y2K rollover periods. Increasingly, newly created critical infrastructure protection organizations such as the National Infrastructure Protection Center (NIPC) and in the Department of Defense established linkages with organizations responsible for dealing with Y2K concerns. In October 1999, the Government Accounting Office published a report entitled *Critical Infrastructure Protection: Comprehensive Strategy Can Draw on Year 2000 Experiences.*[122] The report usefully described how government Y2K preparations set priorities, developed understanding of cross-sectoral linkages, and improved incident identification and coordination capabilities. The ability of the United States to address Y2K-related events and to learn lessons from the experience may provide a very useful window into our capacity to address defensive strategic information warfare concerns. The epilogue to this book makes an initial effort to draw such insights.

As of the end of 1999, the wider government policy initiatives of the Executive Branch still emphasized making U.S. information infrastructures easily accessible and adaptable. Beyond the recognized needs for authentication and reliability to promote electronic commerce and Y2K preparation, efforts within the NII/GII/NGI rubric to ensure the safety of the nation's information infrastructures from strategic information attack have received very low priority.

Regulatory and legislative trends in the 1980s and 1990s reinforced conditions that increase the difficulty of instituting national-level defenses of the U.S. information infrastructures. The actions of the FCC to foster an open network architecture (ONA) for the nation's information infrastructure were particularly significant in this respect. In the wake of the AT&T divestiture in the 1980s, the ONA initiative began in 1986 to require operators of public-switched telecommunications networks (PSTNs) to allow independent service providers to have access to the PSTN operators' basic communication services on an equal basis and cost. To accord with the ONA provisions, outside providers had to be given real-time access to network control software. As early as 1989, the National Research Council stressed the potential security concerns arising from implementation of an ONA approach:

> First, ONA increases greatly the number of users who have access to network software. In any given universe of users, some will be hostile. By giving more users access to network software, ONA will open the network to additional hostile users. Second, as more levels of network software are made visible to users for purposes of affording parity of network access, users will learn more about the inner workings of the network software, and those with hostile intent will learn more about how to misuse the network.[123]

Yet the general tide of actions to foster openness and access to maximize gains from competition and technological innovation continued in the 1990s. With the support of the Clinton administration, Congress added its weight to efforts to enhance competition in telecommunications service and equipment as well as broadcast markets within the United States with passage of the 1996 Telecommunications Act.[124] The act deals only with issues of commercial competition and public decency in the development and use of information infrastructures. It completely ignores national security concerns. Pushing toward even greater interconnection and access, the act requires public network providers to facilitate interconnection to U.S. communications networks at any point that is technically feasible. This provision of the act has generated concerns about network security and reliability arising from the interconnection of new providers with preexisting carriers, particularly among the regional Bell companies. The PCCIP found that

> [t]he unbundling of local networks mandated by the Telecommunications Act of 1996 has the potential to create millions of new interconnections without any significant increase in the size or redundancy of network plants. Unbundling will be implemented at a time of rapid and large scale change in network technologies. The interaction of complexity and new technologies will almost certainly expand the universe of ways in which system failure can occur and, unlike with natural disasters, there is almost no assurance that such failures will be localized.[125]

Outside the telecommunications arena, other regulatory agencies may inadvertently hurt defensive efforts by creating openness and forcing information infrastructure users to use less-secure public networks and technologies. For example, the recent ruling by Federal Energy Regulatory Commission (FERC) to provide for equal transmission access to public electric grid for power generation enables a growing number of power providers, transmission providers, and consumers to use the Internet-based Open Access Same-Time Information System (OASIS) to advertise and purchase power and transmission capability.[126] The PCCIP also critiqued the FAA's Federal Radionavigation Plan calling for national airspace controls completely dependent on the GPS system as creating a significant vulnerability through reliance on a single system.[127]

In total, U.S. government actions outside the defense, intelligence, and law enforcement communities in the 1990s demonstrated a lack of attention to national security issues arising from the increasing reliance upon and potential vulnerability of U.S. information infrastructures to outside attack. A broad range of actors such as the IITF, FCC, FERC, FAA, and Congress actively pursued certain conditions that made instituting effective strategic information warfare defenses more difficult at the end of the 1990s than it had been at the beginning. The race to leverage the efficiency provided by emerging information technology and networking opportunities and promote commercial competition and innovation may have unintended negative consequences.

At Arm's Length: The Private Sector and Protecting U.S.
Information Infrastructures

Characterizing the private sector's efforts and willingness to engage with the government enables us to develop a better understanding of the overall progression of U.S. national efforts to create strategic information warfare defenses. The first three chapters described the roles played by infrastructure users, network service providers and operators, and technology producers in the creation and protection of information infrastructures, and this section relies on the same framework. So far, most private-sector technology producers, infrastructure operators and users seem generally to have ignored concerns with information infrastructure protection at the level of strategic information warfare.

Similar to the emergence of concern about cybervulnerabilities within the DOD during the 1990s, commercial-sector users evidence a growing recognition about the dangers posed by increasing reliance on openly networked computers. Numerous surveys indicate that the amount of computer crime and the costs of disruptive activity in the U.S. commercial sector increased significantly during the 1990s.[128] The American Society for Industrial Security found that the monthly rate for proprietary business information theft rose 260 percent between 1985 and 1993.[129] Surveys in the mid-1990s regarding the incidence of computer crime and disruption over the prior twelve months indicated significant numbers of organizations were suffering disruptions. A 1995 Ernst and Young/Information Week survey reported that 50 percent of organizations surveyed had suffered losses due to lack of availability of systems or telecommunications.[130] The 1999 Computer Security Institute (CSI)/FBI *Computer Crime and Security Survey* indicated that 62 percent of respondents had definitely suffered unauthorized use of their computer systems in the prior twelve months and an additional 21 percent did not know if they had.[131] Available survey results highlight the important role played by insiders as a source of disruption but also indicate that outside threats to organizations were equally important. Results of the 1999 CSI/FBI survey revealed that 19 percent of organizations surveyed reported sabotage of data or networks and 14 percent reported financial fraud. Survey results and analysis also indicated that the amount of foreign involvement in these incidents has become a major source of concern, especially in terms of corporate- or government-sponsored espionage. A report by Kessler and Associates, an investigative consulting company, indicates propriety information theft increased over 100 percent between 1997 and 1999.[132] Statements by the FBI in the late 1990s

continued to stress the significance of the use of computer intrusions and information resources as part of the foreign commercial espionage threat.[133]

The increasing number of incidents and instances of losses have spurred
a growing awareness in the private sector of the significance of risks posed by
reliance on advanced information technology and digital intrusion and disruption. According to the Ernst and Young/Information Week survey, more than 72
percent of corporations surveyed perceived that risks to data had increased over
the prior five years, with less than 10 percent of respondents stating that such
risks had declined. The 1999 CSI/FBI survey found that 93 percent of public and
private organizations responding had access control programs, and 98 percent
indicated they use antivirus software. Mainstream business publications, such
as *Fortune* and *Business Week*, provide anecdotal evidence of the risks and
challenges posed by computer hackers.[134] Advertising for information technology products such as Nokia cellular phones or IBM networking services began
in the late 1990s to stress security as a selling point.

A March 2000 opinion survey by computer publication firm Ziff-Davis indicated that concern over the threat of Internet attacks has grown within the public
at large.[135] Ninety-three percent of respondents voiced some concern about computer break-ins by foreign governments or anti-American groups were a cause
for concern with 30 percent characterizing such threats as "an extremely real
threat." Eighty-eight percent of respondents thought that computer systems of
the U.S. government, the financial establishment, and power utilities were at least
"somewhat vulnerable" to attack.

Despite the increase in general awareness regarding commercial computer
crime and digital disruption, most assessments remain skeptical of the amount
of effort actually devoted to information and computer security and the effectiveness of programs to address information security issues. The 1996 survey
based on the use of commercially available tools to test the security of public
and private Web sites conducted by computer security expert Dan Farmer discussed in chapter 2 found disappointing results in terms of the vulnerabilities
of Web sites and reactions of systems operators to those vulnerabilities. Broad
assessments conducted by U.S. government agencies, although often com-
mending an increased awareness, generally characterize information protection
efforts within most private sectors as inadequate. During the 1996 congressional
hearings on "Security in Cyberspace," the Senate minority staff drew the following general conclusions based on interviews with security experts from the
private sector: "Computer security personnel in the private sector do not have a

strong voice in corporate and management decisions. In the private sector the computer security experts are usually at odds with the business leaders of their companies. Generally, the computer security function is buried in the administrative support area of the business. The pressure to automate and connect systems almost always takes precedence over the need to protect."[136] The PCCIP arrived at a nearly identical finding. The 1999 CSI/FBI survey found that "[o]rganizations need comprehensive information protection programs."[137] Additionally, the survey found that only 32 percent of organizations experiencing computer intrusions reported them to law enforcement. The relative lack of effort given the potential risk has been stressed in the general press as well.[138]

We must keep in mind that general survey data, overarching assessments, and other anecdotal evidence provide only a very sketchy picture regarding the degree of vulnerability and adequacy of private-sector efforts to protect their information systems. The resistance of the private sector to allow transparency into its computer security efforts has been stressed by all studies endeavoring to characterize the problem, beginning with the 1991 NRC *Computers at Risk* study. The PCCIP noted that "[i]ndustry representatives expressed reluctance to share information about vulnerabilities because of fear it might be made public, resulting in damage to their reputations, exposing them to liability, or weakening their competitive position."[139] The 1999 CSI/FBI survey effort involved sending out 3,670 questionnaires, from which only 521 responses were received, a participation rate of only 14 percent. Even of those who responded to this survey, 48 percent indicated that they did not publicly report incidents because of fear of negative publicity and actions of competitors.

The private-sector investment in protecting information resources and infrastructures varies dramatically by organization, yet available analyses are highly aggregated. Although some sectoral analysis has been conducted, available information does not permit an understanding of the relationship between the overall significance to society of various privately owned and operated information infrastructures, their degree of vulnerability, and the appropriate level of effort required to protect them. Also, the available information addresses concerns related to casual hackers, espionage, computer crime, and discontented employees. Therefore, we have a very limited understanding of how the private sector perceives its vulnerability and conducts protective efforts related to orchestrated attacks intent on inflicting large-scale disruption.

The major telecommunications service providers are acutely aware of the vulnerability of their systems to malicious digital attacks and demonstrate greater willingness to undertake protective efforts. These companies have been actively involved with the evolution of national security concerns related to the information infrastructure through the NSTAC and the NCS. The series of studies conducted by these organizations during the 1990s detailed earlier in the chapter highlighted the vulnerability of public-switched networks to digital intrusion and disruption. These studies involved active participation by major telecommunications industry players that are aware of their own vulnerabilities. Government regulators and commercial network operators have also demonstrated awareness of the need to address information infrastructure assurance. The FCC has established the Network Interoperability and Reliability Council (NIRC), a federal advisory committee to exchange information and consider PSTN reliability issues.[140] The council conducts studies about PSTN reliability focusing primarily on accidental threats to operations. Significant levels of cooperation through mechanisms such as the NSTAC and NIRC enables the federal government to identify vulnerability concerns and assurance priorities to senior industry representatives.[141]

However, ISPs and small telecommunications companies do not yet have a significant role in either the NSTAC or NIRC, whose activities focus on public telecommunications networks. The susceptibility of ISPs such as America Online to digital intrusion and disruption have been well publicized. Yet very little systematic information is available about the vulnerabilities to digital attack of such organizations or their efforts to protect themselves from such attacks. If smaller network operators and Internet service providers increasingly prove central to the operation of key U.S. information infrastructures, however, they will also necessarily need to be involved in national planning. Understanding the evolution of the organizations of most significance within the network provider sector should be emphasized more strongly in the future within efforts aimed at establishing strategic information warfare defenses.

In a very significant oversight, technology producers have yet to receive substantial attention in efforts to protect and assure U.S. national information infrastructures. The hardware and software products as well as standard-setting activities of companies such as Microsoft, Cisco Systems, Nortel, Bay Networks, and innumerable other organizations underpin the operation of advanced information infrastructures, as addressed in chapter 1. Yet this sector has been criticized in a wide range of assessments for creating products and establishing standards with weak security and with vulnerabilities that are easy to discover and exploit. The reasons cited for this apparent inattention to security issue among technology producers focus on market-driven incentives of producers and lack of user awareness and concern. The Software Engineering Institute provided the following illustrative assessment in 1997:

> There is little evidence of improvement in the security features of most products; developers are not devoting sufficient effort to apply lessons learned about sources of vulnerabilities. The CERT Coordination Center routinely receives reports of new vulnerabilities. In 1995, we received an average of 35 new reports each quarter. That average has more than doubled in 1996, and we continue to see the same types of vulnerabilities in newer versions of products we saw in earlier versions. Technology evolves so rapidly that vendors concentrate on time to market, often minimizing that time by placing a low priority on security features. Until their customers demand products that are more secure, the situation is unlikely to change.[142]

Similar findings lament the lack of security features of the technologies implemented in almost all advanced information infrastructures, including those of the Department of Defense.[143]

Yet these technology producers are conspicuously absent in the evolving dialogue about the proper level of national security concern regarding information infrastructure protection and assurance, and this sector of commercial activity has remained largely outside of government regulation. The major exception has been the Department of Justice antitrust action in the fall of 1997 against Microsoft Corporation regarding its use of a monopolistic position regarding its Windows operating system to create leverage with computer suppliers to provide its Internet Explorer Web browser. Pursuing antitrust concerns may indirectly help increase diversity in the technology product sector, but as of this writing, neither the Department of Justice action nor the ruling issued by Judge Thomas Penfield Jackson in June 2000 has directly addressed information infrastructure protection. Such antitrust efforts may actually work against other U.S. federal government actions designed to engender cooperation in improving the defenses of the NII. Although the features of information technology products are central to the security of telecommunications and computer networks, most key technology producers are not included in organizations such as the NIRC or NSTAC. Outside of the mandate of "critical infrastructure protection," the PCCIP and PDD 63 also demonstrated a notable lack of attention to this sector.

The distance of technology producers from the government results in part from the wariness in the information technology community about national security and law enforcement–related activity. The cyberelite made up of individuals such as Bill Gates, Mitch Kapor, and Esther Dyson emerged from a computer culture in the 1970s and 1980s that denigrated the government's role in the information age as that of an Orwellian big brother. Throughout the 1990s, this culture continued to stress the value of individual freedom, innovation, and resistance to government intervention or leadership. Esther Dyson believes that, "[t]he greatest structural impact of the Net is decentralization, things and people no longer depend on a center to be connected."[144] A dominant concern of the cyberelite regarding government involvement is the protection of privacy rights. Numerous advocacy organizations such as the Electronic Frontier Foundation (EFF), the Center for Democracy and Technology (CDT), and the Electronic Privacy Information Center (EPIC) receive strong support from technology producers in efforts to resist the establishment of government controls over activity in cyberspace. Technology producer leadership and organizations have remained leery of stepping into the fundamental role they must play in efforts aimed at establishing strategic information warfare defenses.

The rancorous debate over the U.S. government role in the development, implementation, and control of encryption technology has contributed greatly to the resistance of technology producers to engage with the government in efforts at national information infrastructure protection. The use of encryption technologies to secure information transmission and storage represents a possible area of convergence for those concerned with producing technologies and those concerned with national security. To the extent customers wish to have the features provided by encryption in their information technologies, producers will want to provide products with enhanced security. To the extent the implementation of such technology would improve protection of key information infrastructures from digital attacks, those concerned with national security from strategic information warfare attacks would also have in interest in widespread use of encryption. However, the government's simultaneous desire to monitor communications and ensure access to information for law enforcement and foreign intelligence activities has resulted in U.S. policies designed to allow access to domestic and foreign communications through controls over the export of encryption technologies. Such policies have been the subject of much criticism by privacy advocates, commercial software firms trying to compete in global markets, and those who believe that widespread use of strong encryption would help secure information infrastructures.

Early contention centered on what is popularly referred to as the "Clipper Chip."[145] In 1993, the Clinton administration initiated a voluntary program to improve the security and privacy of private communications while meeting the needs of law enforcement. The U.S. government offered to provide for commerical use a hardware-based strong encryption system for providing secure voice, data, and fax services. The hardware chip and its encryption algorithm were developed by NSA, which refused to declassify the algorithm. The master keys for each encryption device using the NSA-developed technology were to be deposited with NIST for release, if necessary, to law enforcement. Despite loudly voiced concerns that the government would be able to immediately decipher encrypted communications using the proposed system and lack of industry interest in using the technology, the Commerce Department and NIST approved the chip and algorithm as a voluntary national standard known as the Encryption Escrow Standard (EES). Development of strong encryption technologies in the commercial sector was permitted, but technologies not based on the EES would not receive federal government approval for export.

The U.S. government efforts to prohibit the export of strong encryption technologies became a rallying point for private-sector criticism of the federal government's attempt to control cyberspace. The commercial sector decried the government's willingness to sacrifice commercial competitiveness for gains in law enforcement and intelligence capability. The events surrounding the development of the Pretty Good Privacy (PGP) encryption algorithm by Phil Zimmerman brought this controversy into sharp focus. Zimmerman independently developed the PGP algorithm in 1992 for use in the private sector and without federal government involvement. The PGP algorithm was sufficiently sophisticated to be considered "strong encryption" and therefore was prohibited from export. However, Zimmerman posted software on the Internet that allowed free access to PGP and published a book describing the algorithm that made PGP available internationally. Despite widespread international availability of the PGP algorithm and availability of "strong" encryption technologies from non-U.S. sources, the FBI charged Zimmerman with violation of U.S. export control laws.

A prolonged court battle mobilized both privacy advocates and the software industry in support of Zimmerman.[146] Privacy advocates, represented by organizations such as the EFF and EPIC, stressed the right of all citizens to encrypt their private communications without the threat of government eavesdropping. More importantly for efforts to protect the national information infrastructure, U.S. software manufacturers, such as the Business Software Alliance and Software Publishers Association, argued that increasingly important business operations and commerce were conducted over electronic networks requiring the protection encryption provided from commercial and industrial espionage. They asserted that customers in the global market, especially large, transnational corporations, increasingly demanded strong encryption as a necessary feature of advanced software products. The U.S. software industry became increasingly vocal about how international competitors were able to produce strong encryption and would capture important market share from U.S. firms. Business users complained about the increased risk and complexity of conducting transnational operations with "U.S.-only" versions with strong encryption and "export" versions with weaker, incompatible software.[147] The law enforcement and intelligence communities provided little public information regarding the benefits of maintaining export controls as the controlled technology becomes widely available from overseas sources.[148] In the face of intense public scrutiny, the Justice Department dropped the Zimmerman case in 1995.

Faced with the lack of private-sector willingness to use EES-based products and its defeat in the Zimmerman case, the Clinton administration revised its approach to ensuring that the government could maintain its access to encrypted communications for law enforcement purposes. In 1995, federal agencies proposed establishing "key escrow," which would ensure that keys to encrypted communications and stored data would be maintained by a "trusted third-party" (TTP).[149] Although such TTP organizations could conceivably be created in the private sector, any TTP would be required to grant the government access to the keys for legitimate law enforcement purposes. Key escrow proposals generally require TTPs to provide immediate, around-the-clock government access without notice to key users, again raising crucial privacy concerns. The private sector has again balked at developing and implementing technologies to facilitate such a scheme. Additionally, the scientific and academic communities have strongly criticized proposals for key escrow schemes as technologically difficult, very expensive to implement, and creating new security vulnerabilities. In 1996, the Organization for Economic Cooperation and Development rejected the idea of mandated key escrow, stating that "[t]he deployment of global key recovery-based encryption infrastructure to meet law enforcement's stated specifications will result in substantial sacrifices in security and greatly increased cost to the end-user."[150]

Numerous U.S. government and outside studies have reinforced the position of the software industry that U.S. encryption control policies and key escrow initiatives continue to hurt commercial development of encryption technology and commercial competitiveness. Vice President Gore proposed an initiative in October 1996 to allow the export control limit on general commercial encryption products to increase from 40-bit to 56-bit strength if the producer formally committed to the establishment of a TTP key escrow system within two years. This initiative transferred power over export control decisions from the State Department to the Commerce Department, but also gave the Justice Department a veto in the export licensing process.[151] Few U.S. information technology producers took Gore up on the offer.

The government has painfully recognized that the U.S. policy debate on encryption also affects the broad defensibility of its information infrastructure. Such awareness was clearly stated in the 1996 Senate hearings on "Security in Cyberspace." Computer security expert Peter Neumann testified at those hearings that "U.S. cryptographic policy has not been sufficiently orientated toward improving the infrastructure, in that it has been more concerned with limiting the use of good cryptography. U.S. cryptography policy has acted as a deterrent to better security."[152] The 1996 DSB Task Force *Information Warfare—Defense* report directly addressed the detrimental effects of the encryption control controversy, observing that "[t]he nation has focused a lot of attention and energy on the encryption policy debate. . . . The Task Force believes the policy debate has been a distraction from efforts to enhance the resiliency of the critical national information services."[153] An expert group of cryptographers and computer scientists reported in May 1997 that implementing a key-management infrastructure to support law enforcement would probably pose important risks in terms of broader information infrastructure protection goals.[154] The Internet Architecture Board of the Internet Society and the Internet Engineering Task Force issued a joint statement in 1998 that key escrow policies "are against the interest of consumers and the business community and are largely irrelevant to issues of military security."[155] The PCCIP found that strong encryption mechanisms were an essential element for establishing information infrastructure security, yet it recommended the pursuit of a key escrow scheme to support law enforcement. As a result, the reaction of privacy groups and commercial technology producers to the PCCIP report focused press criticism on the commission's position in the highly charged encryption debate.[156]

In September 1999, the Clinton administration once more revised its policy.[157] The new policy allows U.S. telecommunications and Internet service providers to use any encryption product to provide services and eased restrictions on export of strong encryption products to commercial users (except in seven countries associated with support of terrorism) upon review by the Commerce Department. Strong encryption exports to foreign governments could be approved under a specific license. Yet the privacy lobby continued to criticize the administration's policy, particularly regarding the requirement for a governmental review of commercial encryption products prior to export. The Electronic Frontier Foundation planned to continue its First Amendment challenge to unconstitutional restrictions on encryption publishers. The defense and intelligence communities continued to argue that reducing the barriers to export of U.S. commercial encryption products would impact intelligence collection and possibly increase cost of defending U.S. national security systems.[158]

At the end of 1999, the federal government continued to struggle with these competing priorities. Despite the strongly voiced objections of important private-sector stakeholders and recognition of national security trade-offs, most observers found that U.S. encryption policy consistently prioritized the interests of law enforcement and national security.[159] This rancorous debate burned, rather than built, bridges between the government and the private sector.

Overall, the private sector's role in creating and using information infrastructures remains weakly linked to the establishment of U.S. defensive strategic information warfare capabilities. Although concerned about cybercrime and protection of their information resources, most private-sector activities and organizations have yet to engage actively in efforts designed to improve the protection of broader information infrastructures. Through the activities of the PCCIP and other organizations such as the NSTAC and NIRC, the federal government has initiated the process of raising threat awareness and establishing a cooperative dialogue with some private-sector owners and operators of critical infrastructures. The gap has yet to be bridged, however, between general commercial users and national infrastructure protection organizations. Detrimental to U.S. long-term efforts in this area is the confrontational relationship between commercial information technology producers and government agencies with leading roles in establishing a strategic information warfare defense.

Strategic Information Warfare and U.S. National Security:
Dawning Awareness

By the end of the twentieth century, the traditional U.S. national security community had recognized the potential emergence of strategic information warfare in both its offensive and its defensive dimensions. The possibility of conducting remote, digital attacks to disrupt a broad range of information infrastructure–based activity has been acknowledged in general analyses of post–Cold War national security concerns and through official DOD statements. The military has encountered a good deal of difficulty in sorting out the dimensions of a "strategic" level of warfare from broader concerns addressed under the labels of "information warfare" and "information operations." U.S. doctrine during the 1990s recognized a strategic level of information warfare/operations. Most doctrinal statements, however, stressed information warfare as a means for improving traditional battlefield effectiveness. Moreover, the Department of Defense and intelligence community remained leery of articulating any role in protecting the nation's information infrastructures outside their direct control.

At the national level, certain federal agencies and private-sector organizations have become aware of increasing threats to their activities based on the potential disruption of information infrastructures. Many studies identify a high potential for disruption to a range of centers of gravity via digital attacks. However, analyses almost uniformly avoid grappling with what U.S. adversaries would seek through waging such attacks, and descriptions of the strategic information warfare threat generally remain vague and devoid of specifics.

The governmental efforts to grapple with defensive strategic information warfare concerns from the mid-1990s to end of the decade increasingly focused on critical infrastructure protection. However, these programs paid inadequate attention to the activities of technology producers fundamental to the creation and evolution of the infrastructures. U.S. government initiatives to leverage the economic opportunities of the information age have also fostered conditions that make information infrastructure protection more difficult. The debate over encryption policy has contributed to distance between the government and key stakeholders whose participation is necessary for establishing national strategic information warfare defenses. Recent efforts, as embodied in the PCCIP and PDD 63, have begun to establish policy and coordination mechanisms for infrastructure protection. The lack of clarity about strategic information warfare challenges and trade-offs involved, however, is reflected in the underdevelopment of organizational structures to grapple with this emerging form of warfare.

Organizing for Defensive Strategic Information Warfare: Initial Pieces and Putting Together a Larger Puzzle

Waging strategic information warfare necessarily involves establishing organizations capable of performing offensive and defensive missions. The United States continues to wrestle with establishing clear conceptual and doctrinal frameworks for fitting strategic information warfare into its national security policy. In the case of airpower, doctrinal clarity preceded organizational development and refinement. The establishment of organizations to deal with transformative military missions has historically proven very difficult. U.S. efforts to manage organizational challenges regarding strategic information warfare evidence a similarly slow trajectory of progress. Because most information on the subject is highly classified, little public information is available regarding specific organizational arrangements for U.S. offensive information warfare efforts. Therefore, this section focuses on the development of organizations related to U.S. defensive strategic information warfare efforts.

As discussed in chapter 3, the establishment of national defensive strategic information warfare capabilities involves efforts at multiple levels: national, sectoral, and organizational. The analysis here will deal with development of organizations with national-level responsibilities for protecting the broad range of key U.S. information infrastructures. A comprehensive analysis of the myriad activities at lower levels related to the protection of U.S. information infrastructures is beyond the scope of this analysis. The section concludes, however, with examples of organizational-level defensive programs to illustrate how efforts at lower levels contribute to U.S. strategic information warfare defenses.

Organizing for National Policy Development and Coordination

The historical background of different organizations involved in national policy development and management of U.S. information infrastructure protection has already been touched upon. This section outlines the key organizational players in policy development and coordination related to defensive strategic information warfare, with a focus on reviewing organizational responsibilities and proposals for change. Although the U.S. recognizes the potential threat posed by strategic information warfare, it has made slow progress in establishing broadly inclusive mechanisms for policy development and coordination.

One set of U.S. government organizations with missions in this area develops and implements policies related to information and computer security. Another set assures adequate communications capabilities, especially in time of crisis. The broad impact of convergence between telecommunications and computing technologies and activities over the past few decades has greatly blurred distinctions between these two categories of activity. However, legislation and executive orders defining the authority and missions for organizations engaged in these areas developed separately. As a result, the United States has created a complex and overlapping set of policy formulation processes and organizational roles. Recent recognition of problems and gaps created by increasingly artificial distinctions between information and computer security has resulted in recommendations for establishing national level-policy coordination.

The most overarching governmental authority for information and computer security resides with the Office of Management and Budget (OMB), designated by legislation in 1995 and 1996 as having the broad authority to publish and enforce information resource management policies for the federal government. Yet OMB has yet to play an active role in policy formulation related to national-level information security concerns. Below the level of OMB, the basic organizational responsibilities for information and computer security were outlined by the 1987 Computer Security Act and remain in place. Figure 5.3 depicts the relationships between organizations in this area.

The organizational structure for formulating information and computer security policy carried forward from the 1987 act left critical holes in responsibilities for addressing private-sector information infrastructures. Even within the

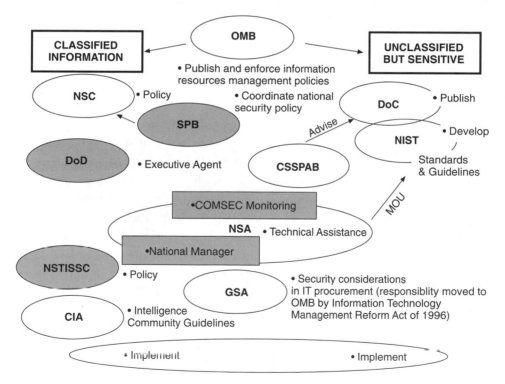

Figure 5.3
Policy responsibilities for information systems security. Note: Shading indicates organizations with nonstatutory responsibilities. Source: Joint Staff, Information Warfare—Considerations *(Washington, DC: Joint Staff, 1996), 2–41.*

government, policy coordination in this area is hampered by the lack of an organization perceived as an impartial judge to weigh the various interests involved.
Security Policy Board efforts in the mid-1990s to establish an Information
Security Committee were stymied by perceptions within other federal departments and agencies that the board was an arm of the national security community.[160] The SPB's December 1995 White Paper describes two groups of
organizations holding opposing views:

• The civil agencies, OMB, the information industry, and those primarily
focused on the personal freedom/libertarian dimensions of the information age,
believe it is neither wise, desirable nor legal (citing the Computer Security Act
of 1987) to combine policy making across the "classified" and "unclassified" communities. With respect to protecting the NII, a sizable portion of this group would
hold that the Federal Government has little or no direct role to play, but should
lower/reduce certain export controls and "get out of the way."

• The defense, intelligence, national security and emergency preparedness/
public safety communities, believe that with the explosion of digital networking
across both communities and all parts of the NII, it is anachronistic, unwise and
unworkable to continue to address the NII security/assurance issues and policy
making in a fractured manner. This group also tends to focus more on national
level threats to the NII, and sees a significant role for the Federal Government
to play in assuring its health and security.[161]

The board found that breaking this impasse would require "action at a
higher level," calling for presidential and congressional leadership.

Yet at the broader level of trying to establish national information and computer security policies that include private-sector activity, no organization has
been created with mandate or means to coordinate efforts related to the defense
of national information infrastructures. The 1987 act still provides NIST with sole
authority to conduct outreach activities to the private sector. Yet, NIST's publication of *Generally Accepted Systems Security Practices* (GSSP) in 1996 had little
impact, either within government or the private sector. The efforts of NIST to
build bridges into the private sector lack adequate resources to make much of
an impact.[162] Also, NIST's activities in the realm of information and computer
security are not geared to concerns related to large-scale, malicious digital
attacks. The August 1999 report by the Joint Security Commission also indicates
progress on establishing policy responsibilities has proven slow. The report
states:

> The Board had not succeeded in addressing information systems secu-
> rity (INFOSEC), having been unable to create the intended INFOSEC

committee, nor has it established a mechanism for oversight as PDD-29 provides.[163]

Organizational arrangements governing the formation of national policies for infrastructure reliability and assurance are at least as complex. Instead of delineations based on classified and unclassified systems and information, the roles of different federal agencies spring from the existence of national emergencies, particularly those with a national security aspect. Figure 5.4 diagrams organizational responsibilities in this area.

The Communications Act of 1934 provides the basic authority for federal involvement in information infrastructure assurance for national security purposes. The act states that the war powers of the president include authority to direct telecommunication providers to give priority to national defense communications and authorize the employment of the armed forces to prevent obstruction of interstate or foreign communications. Significantly, the 1996 Telecommunications Act completely sidestepped issues related to NS/EP policy formulation and program development, leaving in place an increasingly antiquated legislative foundation for U.S. efforts to protect its information infrastructure.

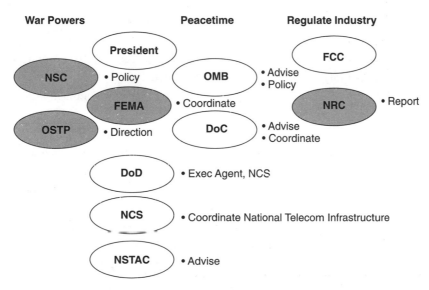

Figure 5.4
Policy responsibilities for information infrastructure assessment and assurance. Note: Shading indicates nonstatutory responsibilities. Source: Joint Staff, Information Warfare—Considerations *(Washington, DC: Joint Staff, 1996), 2–41.*

The basic policy formulation mechanisms for national security and emergency preparedness to implement the 1934 act were laid out during the Reagan administration and remained operative as of the end of 1999. Executive Order 12742 gave the National Security Council responsibility for policy direction and the Office of Science and Technology Policy authority to direct the exercise of presidential power in implementation of the NS/EP program.[164] This order also outlined the specific mission of the National Communications System to coordinate the activities of federal departments and agencies responsible for the operation of telecommunications facilities of significance to national security and emergency preparedness. The Secretary of Defense was made the executive agent of the NCS and given authority to appoint the manager of the NCS, a responsibility currently assigned to the director of DISA. The NSTAC was also established in the early 1980s by a separate directive, Executive Order 12382, to provide the president with information and advice with respect to the implementation of national security telecommunications policy. The involvement of senior DOD officials, particularly the ASD/C3I and the director of DISA, in both the NCS and the NSTAC facilitates a close linkage between the activities of these organizations.

Additionally, other organizations have been assigned roles related to national information infrastructure protection. FEMA has potentially significant responsibilities related to information infrastructure assurance because it develops plans to ensure the continuity of the federal government during national emergencies and to respond to major terrorist incidents. Yet FEMA's emphasis on responding to natural disasters means it has played little or no role in the development of policy or planning related to defending the nation's information infrastructure against digital attack.[165]

The 1934 Communications Act also established peacetime roles of the federal government in the management of the nation's telecommunications system. It appointed the Secretary of Commerce as the principal advisor to the president on telecommunications policy as well as advancement and regulation of the telecommunications industry. Additionally, the act created the FCC as the federal government regulatory agency responsible for managing the public interest related to the telecommunications industry. In general, the FCC has shown little interest concerning telecommunications/information infrastructure assurance.

Through the mid-1990s, the number of organizations involved and their diffuse responsibility rendered ineffective the U.S. government's organizational structure for coordinating and developing policy for defending key national information infrastructures. The NSC had overarching responsibility but lacked adequate staff and interested key players and so did not provide significant leadership on this issue.[166] Yet organizations including the SPB and NSTAC clearly highlighted the need for a central focal point for policy coordination. Bridges to the private sector remained underdeveloped throughout the 1990s. NIST's inadequate resources and ties to the private sector prevented it from creating a national approach to information and computer security. The NSTAC provided firmer linkages with the big telecommunications industry players regarding information infrastructure assurance, but its activities did not involve the technology producers or new types of information network providers and operators. Policy formulation efforts in the infrastructure assurance area throughout the early and mid-1990s were disjointed and definitely not focused on strategic information warfare concerns.

Rising awareness of the threat to information infrastructures, however, eventually led to action. In late 1995, PDD 39 established the interagency CIWG under the leadership of the Department of Justice, significantly raising the level of leadership involvement regarding national policy development for the protection of critical infrastructures. In March 1996, the CIWG recommended formation of a presidential task force to study infrastructure assurance issues and recommend national policy. The CIWG recommendations, along with prodding from Congress and other sources, resulted in the establishment of the PCCIP in July 1996. Although the PCCIP's mandate was somewhat different than the defense against strategic information warfare, as previously discussed, its activities did focus on cyberthreats and did consider how to develop policy relevant to dealing with digital attacks against a wide range of information infrastructures. As discussed earlier, the commission's *Critical Foundations* report provided the conceptual foundation for the issuance of PDD 63, "Critical Infrastructure Protection," in March 1998.

PDD 63 represented the first effort to establish an integrated national policy development structure relevant to strategic information warfare defense across the federal government that explicitly pursued private-sector and state and local government involvement. The directive recognized that "the elimination of our potential vulnerability requires a closely coordinated effort of both the government and the private sector. To succeed, this partnership must be genuine, mutual and cooperative." To guide the federal government effort and establish linkages to the private sector, PDD 63 created the organizational structure

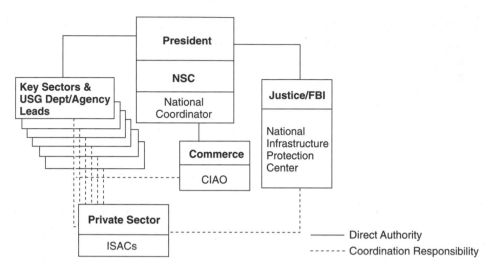

Figure 5.5
PDD 63 structure for U.S. critical infrastructure protection

detailed in figure 5.5. The key offices for policy development and coordination in this organizational scheme include the National Coordinator for Security, Infrastructure Protection and Counterterrorism on the National Security Council; the Critical Infrastructure Coordination Group; and the National Infrastructure Assurance Council (NIAC). Other organizations in the figure with roles and responsibilities primarily related to threat assessment, infrastructure assessment and assurance, indications and warnings, and recovery and response are described in later portions of the chapter. The principal roles and responsibilities of policy development and coordination organizations under PDD 63 can be summarized as follows:

• The national coordinator has overall responsibility for U.S. government policy formulation, oversight of government activities in infrastructure assurance and security issues, and coordination of support to existing and planned decision-making processes in the law enforcement, national security, counterterrorism, and intelligence areas. The national coordinator also is the NSC lead for the development of counterterrorism policy, as outlined in PDD 62, "Protection against Unconventional Threats to the Homeland and Americans Overseas," issued on the same day as PDD 63. Richard Clarke was appointed the first national coordinator in 1998.

• The Critical Infrastructure Coordination Group (CICG), chaired by the national coordinator, is responsible for ensuring interagency coordination of critical infrastructure protection efforts. The CICG includes representatives of the

Lead Agencies for Sector Liaison and Special Functions (addressed later) as well as other federal departments and the National Economic Council. The CICG receives assistance from the Security Policy Board and the National Security Telecommunications and Information Systems Security Committee (NSTISSC).

• PDD 63 calls for development of a national plan coordination office, which was established as the Critical Infrastructure Assurance Office (CIAO) within the Department of Commerce. The CIAO provides support to the national co-ordinator in creating a national plan and assisting in the coordination of U.S. government analyses of its own dependencies on information systems plus networks. Additionally, the CIAO would help support the ONIA in managing the Information Sharing and Analysis Center and in dealing with the sector co-ordinators, whose roles are addressed below. Jeffery Hunker was appointed as the first director of the CIAO. Initial CIAO personnel included commissioners and staff from the PCCIP.

• The NIAC would consist of presidentially appointed CEOs from throughout the critical infrastructures, senior federal officials, and representatives of state and local government. The chairman would be appointed by the president and the national coordinator would serve as Executive Director. The NIAC would meet to provide a forum for high-level discussion of proposed policies for infra-structure assurance, encourage public-private partnership, and make recommendations to the president. As of the end of 1999, no efforts had been made to establish the NIAC.

The structure depicted in figure 5.5 and outlined above clearly establishes a single focal point for critical infrastructure protection at the highest level of government, the NSC. It also recognizes the central role of forging firm partnerships with the private sector. The establishment of the CIAO in the Commerce Department was a positive step in recognizing the private sector's role. However, as noted above, the NIAC has yet to be established. Also, the critical infrastructure mandate constrains the range of private-sector partners that can be recommended for inclusion in the nascent policy formulation partnership. The future membership of the NIAC and the activities of the national coordinator must become more inclusive of technology producers as essential to infra-structure assurance and must endeavor to co-opt the participation of leading software and networking companies. The implementation efforts associated with PDD 63, especially the development of a national plan for critical infrastructure protection against cyberthreats, have yet to adequately recognize the funda-mental import of this additional task.

Of critical concern is the emphasis that defensive strategic information warfare efforts will receive in the future among the broad range of activities associated with critical infrastructure protection. The mandate of the national coordinator and Critical Infrastructure Coordination Group includes physical and cyberprotection from accidents and malicious disruption and support for law enforcement and counterintelligence purposes, as well as missions related to strategic information warfare defense. Additionally, the national coordinator has very substantial responsibilities for overseeing counterterrorism activities throughout the U.S. government. Limited time, resources, and political capital will require trade-offs in policy development geared to pursue different objectives. Emphasis on preventing computer-based computer crime or counterterrorism may limit attention devoted to other concerns more important to defending against digital attacks for strategic purposes. The CIAO must establish effective interfaces with the national security and law enforcement communities in addition to reaching out to the private sector. No public proposal has yet been made to create an organization solely concerned with developing policy for and coordinating efforts geared to the establishment of U.S. strategic information warfare defenses.

Organizations Conducting Defensive Strategic Information Warfare Operations
National policy development and coordination will serve a useful purpose only if operational capabilities are established as a result. The United States has only begun to develop the organizations and resources required for conducting a national strategic information warfare defense. The analysis in this section focuses on the development of national-level organizations to perform threat assessment, infrastructure assessment and assurance, indications and warning, and recovery and response missions. Certain subnational organizations, however, particularly in the national security community, have developed capabilities to conduct operations related to defensive strategic information warfare. The activities of these organizations are discussed in brief.

Threat Assessment The intelligence community has been tasked with the responsibility of collecting information on and characterizing the strategic information warfare threat to the United States. Limited unclassified information exists about the exact nature and capabilities of specific organizations involved in strategic information warfare intelligence collection and assessment. The analysis here, however, outlines broad organizational responsibilities identified in the public record and provides some indication of the difficulties the intelligence community has had in coming to grips with this new task.

The intelligence community got a relatively late start in grappling with foreign information warfare programs. An initial community-wide assessment of the foreign information warfare threat was made in 1995 to provide a point of departure for a more comprehensive national intelligence estimate (NIE). The director of Central Intelligence at the time, John Deutch, stated to Congress in 1996 that the intelligence community had initiated new collection activities to uncover evidence of foreign intent to attack U.S. systems but "unfortunately, obtaining information on foreign information warfare plans and programs will take some time."[167] Outside evaluations also indicate that the national intelligence community efforts to form organizational capabilities to perform its role in this area have emerged fairly slowly. In March 1996, the Commission on the Roles and Missions of the U.S. Intelligence Community stated that "[c]ollecting information about 'information warfare' threats posed by other countries or groups to U.S. systems is . . . a legitimate mission of the Intelligence Community. Indeed it is a mission that has grown and will become increasingly important. It is also a mission which the Commission believes requires better definition. While a great deal of activity is apparent, it does not appear well coordinated or responsive to an overall strategy."[168]

Multiple reasons exist for the slow development of intelligence community efforts in this area. Most significantly, U.S. intelligence organizations lack the proper sources and methods to observe adversary capabilities related to conducting digital warfare and characterize strategic information warfare organizations. The 1996 DSB Task Force described the challenge in this way:

> Information Warfare is a whole new game from the Intelligence dimension. We have precious few real data from which to derive "patterns of activity." This is made all the more difficult because so many "indicators" we have used in the past have involved some physical phenomena. In IW, at least in the computer and networked components of it, evidence is fleeting at best and usually not observable. The Intelligence Community is working hard to address some of these issues; but progress is hampered by organizations, processes and systems optimized for situations found in the past, not the future.[169]

Senior officials and outside studies have strongly recommended that the intelligence community improve linkages with outside sources of information, including law enforcement agencies, computer emergency response teams, and the commercial sector.[170] By 1998, the Director of the CIA, George Tenet, had stated that understanding foreign information warfare threats was a "top intelligence priority."[171] Yet such efforts to coordinate domestic activities among agencies are hampered by the legal limits of U.S. operations in the foreign intelligence community, the legacy of animosity between intelligence and law enforcement agencies, and a reluctance on the part of commercial-sector organizations to share information with the government. Within the defense intelligence community, the need to assess adversary digital attack threats and capabilities against information infrastructures is recognized but competes with requirements to support U.S. military information operations geared toward conventional operations.[172] The Defense Intelligence Agency (DIA) appointed a Defense Intelligence Officer for Information Operations in 1998 to ensure that activities related to supporting information operations were integrated into the DOD intelligence plan, but only limited steps toward accomplishing this goal had occurred by the end of 1999.[173]

The FBI established a National Infrastructure Protection Center (NIPC) in February 1998.[174] PDD 63 reinforced the role of the NIPC as a the organization for coordinating "timely warnings of intentional threats, comprehensive analyses and law enforcement investigation and response." The NIPC staff includes members of the Department of Defense, the intelligence community, and other government agencies such as the Secret Service in addition to FBI personnel. The NIPC must also establish relationships with the private sector to accomplish its missions. As envisioned by its creators, the NIPC will bridge the gap between the defense, intelligence, and law enforcement communities, serving as a national focal point for gathering information on threats to the infrastructures. So far, the NIPC principal efforts have centered on leading responses to high-profile intrusion incidents and endeavoring to raise awareness regarding the general cyberthreat.[175] As of the end of 1999, the center had not yet provided publicly available assessments of U.S. adversaries with the capacity to conduct digital attacks at the level of strategic information warfare.

As a result of the slow formation of organizations with assessment capabilities, U.S. policymakers have lacked a coherent description of the digital threat to the United States, especially at the level of strategic information warfare. U.S. government estimates generally portray the information warfare threat as large and growing. Available estimates describe a spectrum of information warfare threats ranging from individual hackers to the types of structured, politically motivated attacks described in this analysis as strategic information warfare. Figure 5.6 provides an illustrative example of the information warfare threat spectrum from the PCCIP *Critical Foundations* report.

National Security Threats	Information Warrior	**I**	Reduce US Decision Space, Strategic Advantage, Chaos, Target Damage
	National Intelligence	**N**	Information for Political, Military, Economic Advantage
		S	
Shared Threats	Terrorist	**I**	Visibility, Publicity, Chaos, Political Change
	Industrial Espionage	**D**	Competitive Advantage
	Organized Crime	**E**	Revenge, Retribution, Financial Gain, Institutional Change
		R	
Local Threats	Institutional Hacker	**S**	Monetary Gain, Thrill, Challenge, Prestige
	Recreational Hacker		Thrill, Challenge

Figure 5.6
Information warfare threat spectrum. Source: President's Commission on Critical Infrastructures Protection. Critical Foundations: Protecting America's Infrastructures *(Washington, DC: President's Commission on Critical Infrastructures Protection, October 1997), 20.*

A July 1998 pamphlet published by the Defense Intelligence Agency describes threats posed by hackers, organized crime, espionage, terrorists, and foreign countries, without evaluating their relative significance.[176] Lacking a well-developed analytical capability, available public estimates usually portray worst-case pictures based on large numbers of potential adversaries and on the ease of digitally intruding into U.S. information infrastructures. Substantive estimates of the scale of damage adversaries may be capable of inflicting are notably absent.

The only publicly available estimate directly addressing the timelines for emergence of a strategic information warfare threat is the 1996 DSB Task Force report. The task force stated that development of even a limited strategic information warfare threat by probable U.S. adversaries would be unlikely before the year 2005. The task force's estimate was based on the difficulty an adversary would face in developing an adequate knowledge of the complex and heterogeneous U.S. information infrastructure to ensure a high level of confidence that cyberattacks would cause large-scale disruption.[177] Yet even this analysis does not detail the types and significance of the political influence and objectives that U.S. adversaries might seek to pursue through digital warfare. Diffused efforts to deal with the very broad range of cyberthreats usually identified may limit the effectiveness of the U.S. intelligence community in understanding adversary efforts to wage digital attacks for strategic purposes.

Infrastructure Assessment and Assurance In addition to understanding the threat posed by adversaries, the United States must develop organizations with the ability to assess information infrastructure reliance and vulnerability across key sectors of society to establish effective strategic information warfare defenses. Moreover, such organizations must have the ability to implement protective policies for and programs to address weaknesses in the security provisions of information infrastructures. Dedicated organizations and programs contributing to this mission have already formed to assure telecommunications for national security purposes. Other preexisting organizations, such as regulatory agencies and industry associations, may play a role in helping to assess and protect information infrastructures in key areas. To achieve national-level understanding and improved information sharing for infrastructure assurance, however, the United States requires broader coordinating organizations and mechanisms.

The NSTAC and the NCS are the most well developed organizations in this area.[178] In addition to roles in policy coordination and development, the NSTAC involves both government and private-sector actors in assessing the vulnerability of the nation's telecommunications infrastructure to digital attack. The responsibility of the NCS to provide NS/EP telecommunications means this organization has also been actively involved in conducting such assessments since the early 1990s. The numerous studies conducted by these organizations and their findings have been detailed earlier in this chapter. The assessments of the NSTAC and NCS regarding U.S. reliance on the PSTN for national security purposes and its growing vulnerability to digital attack have proved important in increasing awareness of such vulnerability in the U.S. government. The establishment of a Network Security Information Exchange (NSIE) by both organizations has created "a process that enables telecommunications and information industry members to share sensitive, competitive information regarding threats, vulnerabilities and intrusions without violating antitrust restrictions. This process, based on extensive non-disclosure agreements and a hierarchy of information sensitivity, also allows government and industry to share similar information."[179]

Yet in the past, NSTAC and NCS organizations and activities have made only limited progress in furthering U.S. national assessment and assurance tasks related to protecting all of the nation's key information infrastructures. First, the NSTAC/NCS and the activities of the NSIE have focused principally on the operation and vulnerabilities of telecommunications networks as support for NS/EP programs without a broader consideration of the increasing role the Internet plays in enabling other government and private-sector activities. A principal limitation of the NSTAC involves the composition of its membership. As of late 1999 the committee included all the large telecommunications communications providers as well as a few significant technology producers and information systems integrators such as IBM, Motorola, and Electronic Data Systems (EDS). This limited membership has resulted in the recognition that the NSTAC does not provide a voice for emerging players in the information technology sector. Companies focused on providing Internet services are not generally represented. Also notably absent are major software producers such as Microsoft and Oracle. Small companies are not on the NSTAC, nor are representatives of the many major user organizations. The NSTAC membership therefore brings to the table only a limited portion of the stakeholders involved in national-level information assurance and assessment efforts.[180]

Additionally, as an advisory committee to the president, the NSTAC lacks a mandate or the resources to actually implement or enforce recommended policies and programs to improve information assurance within the private sector. Although the NSTAC serves as an increasingly strong organizational mechanism for information exchange and conducting assessments, as constructed at the end of 1999, it has little capacity to perform broad-based assurance efforts. Although the NCS has succeeded in encouraging telecommunications providers to ensure the provision of national security/emergency communications, the organization has no authority outside this narrow scope.

As in other areas, the general inadequacy of national-level efforts became increasingly clear in 1995–1996. Reports issued by the Security Policy Board, the Joint Staff, the Defense Science Board, Congressional hearings, and the NSTAC itself highlighted the following sets of concerns regarding the status of national capabilities for information infrastructure assessment and assurance against digital attack:

• Past efforts had lacked common frames of reference and terms to accurately compare data on information infrastructure reliance, vulnerability, or assurance efforts.

• Outside the telecommunications sector, no organizational structures or processes existed to facilitate sharing of sensitive information for infrastructure assurance. In particular, civilian organizations were leery of becoming involved in U.S. government efforts related to assessing specific incidents and the state of vulnerability because of their concerns about loss of proprietary information and damaging disclosures about their information security posture.

• Limited resources had been dedicated to these efforts given the growing scope and significance of security concerns. Because of their relatively small size and influence, information assurance/security organization staffs inside and outside of the government were stressed.

• Establishing coordination among efforts within government and linkages to outside efforts was difficult because of wide difference in organizational perspective on the significance of the problem and the effectiveness of various approaches to achieving information assurance.

• Given the lack of economic and technical feasibility of closing all vulnerabilities in large information infrastructures, assurance efforts needed to focus more attention on establishing resilience and reparability.

Most of these studies presented a relatively dire perspective on the state of U.S. national efforts to assess and assure its key information infrastructures. The moderating voice in the clamor was the 1996 DSB Task Force, which found that although infrastructure assessment efforts had yet to progress very far, the complexity of such assessments also offered some measure of protection and assurance against structured digital attacks.[181]

The formation of the CIWG provided the basis for the first national efforts designed to enhance the critical infrastructure protection area. Most importantly, the CIWG provided a baseline for the formation of the PCCIP, which particularly stressed assessment and assurance activities. A significant portion of the PCCIP efforts involved assessments of the significance of the level of reliance on information infrastructures and vulnerability to cyberthreats of the critical infrastructures: information and communications, physical distribution/transportation, energy, banking and finance, and vital human services. Yet after fifteen months of activity and a presidential mandate, the commission increasingly recognized that its assessments constituted only a "prologue to new era of infrastructure assurance."[182]

Building on the PCCIP recommendations, the PDD 63 construct focused heavily on promoting a partnership between government and infrastructure operators to share information on infrastructure threats, vulnerabilities, and interdependencies. The PDD 63 established a framework of organizations to promote the necessary information sharing to achieve effective national infrastructure assessment and assurance efforts. The major organizations and their roles are listed below:

• *Information sharing and analysis centers (ISACs).* These centers are established by private-sector owners and operators in each identified critical infrastructure sector. Their key role is to gather, analyze, and disseminate properly sanitized information on threats and vulnerabilities to industry, the NIPC, and federal lead agencies for the sectors. The first ISAC was established in October 1999 by the banking and finance sector. According to the national coordinator, Richard Clarke, the Information and Communications sector had agreed to set up an ISAC and the federal government was in discussions with other sectors as of the fall of 1999.[183]

• *Federal lead agencies.* PDD 63 designated specific federal agencies to take the initiative in developing approaches to protect specific critical infrastructure sectors in coordination with the national coordinator. The agencies establish cooperative relationships with private-sector actors in each of the critical infrastructure sectors and work together with private-sector counterparts in the development and implementation of a vulnerability awareness and education program. They also are responsible for developing critical infrastructure assurance plans for each of the sectors as components of the National Infrastructure Assurance Plan. Lead agencies identified by PDD 63 and the sectors for which they are responsible are as follows:

   • Commerce: Information and communications
   • Treasury: Banking and finance
   • Environmental Protection Agency: Water supply
   • Transportation: Aviation, highways, mass transit, pipelines, rail, and waterborne commerce
   • Justice/FBI: Emergency law enforcement services
   • FEMA: Emergency fire services, continuity of government services
   • Health and Human Services: Public health services
   • Energy: Electric power, oil and gas production and storage

Additionally, PDD 63 designates lead agencies for special functions that must be performed chiefly by the federal government. Like the other lead agencies, these agencies are responsible for interagency coordination and producing sector assurance plans. These agencies and their responsibilities are as follows:

   • Justice/FBI: Law enforcement and internal security
   • CIA: Foreign intelligence

- State: Foreign affairs
- Defense: National defense

Initial sector and special function critical infrastructure assurance plans were submitted by lead agencies in late 1998 and early 1999. At the end of 1999, the national coordinator was endeavoring with the assistance of the CIAO to pull these together into the first comprehensive national plan, as called for by PDD 63.

PDD 63 also addressed a number of additional tasks necessary to improve national critical infrastructure protection efforts. In particular, it directed the national coordinator to commission studies on numerous initiatives to improve implementation of the PDD 63 structure, particularly in regard to information-sharing arrangements between the government and private sector. The directive calls for public outreach activities by the White House, the national coordinator, and the National Academies of Science and Engineering. The national coordinator and NAIC are directed to encourage private-sector risk assessments. The Departments of Commerce and Defense are required to work with the private sector to offer expertise in developing security-related best practice standards. Specific federal departments and agencies are tasked with improving existing programs to increase the overall effectiveness of the government's critical infrastructure assurance efforts.

An in-depth evaluation of PDD 63 implementation regarding infrastructure assessment and assurance at the end of 1999 would have been premature. In the eighteen months between the issuing of the directive and the end of the decade, the federal lead agencies focused on producing initial critical infrastructure assurance plans for the sectors, establishing their own organizational structures to accomplish required tasks and programming for the necessary resources. So far, the establishment of ISACs has proven to be a slow process. Effective relationships between the federal government and private sector (beyond those already established though the NSTAC and other preexisting mechanisms), although often emphasized, have not yet matured to a significant level that they improve the U.S. government's capability to provide strategic information warfare defense.

Properly implemented, PDD 63 should provide a sound construct for improving infrastructure assessment and assurance efforts that would greatly improve U.S. capabilities to establish defensive strategic information warfare capabilities. In addition to fostering necessary interaction between the government and private sector, the ISACs' role in consolidating and analyzing information from across interconnected infrastructures would provide a capability to identify possible information infrastructure vulnerabilities to cascading effects from the disruption of electric power or in other areas. Lead agencies would also provide the organizational structure to implement policies and programs to improve the overall defensive stance of the United States against strategic information warfare attacks. The directive rightfully acknowledges private-sector confidentiality concerns in the information-sharing mechanisms and the need for legislative changes. Yet its focus on critical infrastructures still does not address the need to conduct assessment and assurance tasks for other potential centers of gravity for digital attack, especially commercial activity outside the banking and finance sector. Even more significantly, the role of technology producers in providing the foundations of advanced information infrastructures is not directly addressed within the PDD 63 construct or the associated implementation efforts. This fault remains the fundamental weakness in U.S. efforts to create a strong capability to wage effective defense at the level of strategic information warfare.

Indications and Warning Given the widely scattered policy development within the Executive Branch and legal constraints on national security and low enforcement activities, no federal agency had a mandate to address such a task at the national level prior to 1995. Awareness of the growing threat from digital attacks resulted in recognition that the United States government lacked the capacity to assess disruptions in information infrastructures, to provide warning to appropriate U.S. government and private-sector leaders when an attack is detected or suspected, and to assess the responsible actors, scope, and likely intent of such an attack. The 1994 DSB Task Force report noted that, "[a]lthough there are limited efforts underway to detect and counter the unstructured threat, there is no nationally coordinated capability to counter or even detect a structured threat."[184] The issuance of PDD 39 in late 1995 and the establishment of the Critical Infrastructure Working Group in early 1996 created organizations with a broader role in this area. The CIWG was given the mandate to handle the interim infrastructure assurance mission for both physical and cyberthreats and to facilitate rapid access to existing physical and cybersecurity efforts and expertise inside and outside the government.[185]

The Department of Justice, FBI, and Department of Defense have made efforts to establish organizations responsible for national indications and warning and attack assessment missions. In 1997, the FBI established a Watch and Threat Analysis Unit within its Computer Investigations and Threat Assessment Center (CITAC). This multiagency unit was responsible for issuing warning notices on threats to the nation's critical infrastructures.[186] Attorney General Janet Reno upgraded the status of the FBI coordination function related to cyberwarning in February 1998 through the establishment of the NIPC and requested $64 million in funding for the center in fiscal year 1999.[187]

Under the PDD 63 construct, the NIPC plays the central role in providing indications and warning against cyberattacks. The directive calls on the NIPC to issue attack warnings and alerts for threats to both government and private-sector infrastructures, and the center has established an Analysis and Warning Section.[188] The NIPC-led indications and warning construct stresses the synergy between the FBI's conduct of investigation and prosecution of cybercrime and its activities for counterintelligence and protection of the United States against terrorism. The NIPC has worked to establish linkages with other organizations in the federal government responsible for warning of cyberattacks. In particular, the NIPC has developed strong relationships with the Defense Department's Joint Task Force-Computer Network Defense and U.S. Space Command. Other agencies represented at the NIPC include the Central Intelligence Agency, the Departments of State and Energy, and the Secret Service to help provide warning information. According to the director of the NIPC, Michael Vatis, the center issued twenty-two warnings, alerts, or advisories between January and September 1999.

Additionally, in conjunction with the National Security Council, the NIPC has launched an initiative to create an indications and warning system for other federal government departments and agencies known as FIDNET (Federal Intrusion Detection Network). FIDNET would mirror the intrusion detection approach pursued by DOD through linking intrusion detection sensors to warn of cyberattacks on critical networks throughout the civilian federal information infrastructure. FIDNET would rely on sensors at key nodes feeding a General Services Administration (GSA)-managed federal Intrusion Detection Analysis Center (FIDAC), which would then feed law enforcement and warning information to the NIPC. However, the announcement of the FIDNET concept in the summer of 1999 raised significant concerns among privacy advocates and members of Congress that such a system could create an unlawful intrusion into the privacy rights of U.S. citizens.[189] As of the end of 1999, the NIPC planned to continue to pursue the FIDNET program and hoped to convince Congress and other groups that the system can be operated in a fashion that protects computer systems but does not monitor personal communications. Whatever the outcome, FIDNET raises issues that go to core challenges faced by the NIPC in establishing the technological capabilities as well as the broad-based trust necessary to effectively fulfill an indications and warning role.

As of the end of 1999, the FBI/NIPC linkages to the private sector centered on pilot programs such as the InfraGard and Key Asset Initiative programs.[190] The InfraGard program establishes a "chapter" run by each of the fifty-six FBI field offices, linking local government and private-sector members to an alert network via encrypted e-mail, a secure Web site, and local meetings. The Key Asset Initiative facilitates response to threats and incidents by building liaison and communication links with owners and operators of individual companies in critical infrastructure sectors and assisting in contingency planning. Additionally, the NIPC has established a publicly accessible Web site to provide warning reports of possible cyberthreats.[191] The future effectiveness of the NIPC in this role will depend heavily on the success of the emerging private-sector ISACs in providing the principal bridge both for pulling key private-sector information into an overall national indications and warning picture and for pushing out relevant warning of significant cyberattack activity.

Tracking the indications and responding to a cyberattack in coordination with other government agencies constitutes a major mission for the NIPC. Additionally, the center must combat computer crime and build connections with the private sector. The relatively recent assignment of its cyberindications and warning mission, the broad scope of computer crime activities, and limits on building human expertise all limit the center's ability to quickly establish the required internal capabilities and external networks.[192] Congressional scrutiny in early 1996 led to the assessment that the FBI generally lacked technical expertise related to computer-based activity and raised concerns about whether the FBI would be perceived as an honest broker by other government agencies and private-sector actors involved in national information infrastructure protection.[193] The legal constraints on aggressively pursuing the indications and warning mission have also been highlighted. Most importantly, current laws limit the ability of law enforcement agencies to backtrack hackers through cyberspace given privacy concerns and ownership issues related to computing resources in cyberspace.[194] Moreover, the FBI remains focused on cyberthreats in the form of computer crime, espionage, and terrorism. Although it has a mandate to grapple with indications and warning of strategic information warfare, such concerns were not central in efforts to develop organizations within the CITAC.[195] As of the end of 1999, the most well-developed expertise in the NIPC resided in the Computer Investigations and Operations Section as well as National

Infrastructure Protection and Computer Intrusion squads at each of the FBI field offices. Public warnings issued so far by the NIPC have focused on specific computer vulnerabilities to digital intrusion or the emergence of threatening viruses such as Melissa, without any characterization of specific adversaries or objectives. Whether the NIPC has the ability to establish an effective framework for identifying and characterizing strategic digital attacks against the United States remains an open question.

The Department of Defense has also developed organizations with important roles in national-level indications and warning. DIA has been given national-level responsibility within the intelligence community for developing indications and warning capabilities related to foreign information warfare attacks against the United States.[196] DISA maintains a capability to warn of disruptions to the wide range of governmental and nongovernment activities supporting the DII, the NCS, and the FBI as part of its Global Network Operations and Security Center (GOSC).[197] The NSA supports the DISA GOSC for purposes of warning against cyberattacks through its National Security Incident Response Center (NSIRC). The NSIRC is tasked with fusing incident data with intelligence, other source information, and technical analysis to assist in determining the nature of a specific attack as well as with producing and issuing warning of impending threats to U.S. networks.[198]

As a result of numerous self-assessments, exercises such as Eligible Receiver in 1997 (discussed later in the chapter), and the Solar Sunrise event in spring 1998, the Secretary of Defense established the previously mentioned Joint Task Force-Computer Network Defense (JTF-CND) as the focal point for coordinating and directing the defense of the defense information infrastructure.[199] The JTF-CND created an initial operating capability in December 1998 and reached full capability in June 1999. The initial focus has been on "providing indications and warning of adversary attack preparations or the attacks themselves, determining when system(s) are under strategic attack, assessing impact to military operations capabilities, and notifying National Command Authorities (NCA) and the user community."[200] The JTF-CND provides coordination with the NIPC and the National Communications System to perform its mission. In October 1999, the Department of Defense 1999 Unified Command Plan gave responsibility for the computer network defense mission to U.S. Space Command (USSPACE-COM).[201] The initial U.S. Space Command implementation plan envisages that the JTF-CND will remain the operational entity responsible for providing indications and warning and directing response while the Command's staff develops the capability to conduct longer-term planning, develop requirements, and advocate for resources.

The mandate of USSPACECOM and the JTF-CND directly addresses the need to focus on strategic attacks. Both organizations recognize that they may need to play a supporting role in national cyberdefense efforts. However, DOD indications and warning efforts remain focused on protection of defense information infrastructures. The DOD focus results from both the roles and responsibilities outlined in PDD 63 and recognition of the department's limited resources, which restrict it to simply creating a capability to address security requirements of the DII.[202]

As with infrastructure assessment and assurance, the PDD 63 construct establishes an organizational structure designed to bring the private sector into national attack warning and assessment efforts. However, the increasingly central role of the FBI in managing national cyberthreat indications and warning may have drawbacks as part of a larger effort to establish strategic information warfare defenses. FBI efforts in the area of critical infrastructure protection have been spurred principally by concerns with terrorism and espionage, not the potential for strategic information warfare. The bureau's natural tendency to focus on criminal prosecution may shape the way a warning center under its direction develops efforts to gather and handle information regarding cyberthreats. Management of the large-scale analytic and technological development efforts necessary to improve techniques and tools related to providing the U.S. with warning against sophisticated, large-scale digital attacks falls well outside the scope of past bureau expertise and its inherent focus on law enforcement concerns. If strategic information warfare becomes a higher priority for the United States, the Department of Defense and intelligence communities may be required to assume a more explicit national-level role. Moreover, given private-sector hesitation regarding FBI leadership because of the encryption policy debates and information-sharing concerns, the bureau's ability to build crucial bridges may prove limited. Finding a widely accepted "honest broker" to lead the U.S. national indications and warning effort will prove a difficult but fundamental challenge to establishing an effective capability in this area.

Response and Recovery from Digital Attack Establishing organizational structures for national-level recovery and response efforts to deal with a strategic information attack generally lagged behind efforts to provide for indications and warning in the 1990s. As in other mission areas, the most well developed organizations prior to the issuance of PDD 63 involved national security organizations, particularly the NCS. In the words of its former director, Lt. Gen. Albert Edmonds, the NCS provides capabilities to "meet the critical telecommunications requirements of the federal government for NS/EP under all circumstances."[203] The NCS involves a confederation of twenty-three federal departments and agencies based on use of more than ninety networks as well as emergency management authority over commercial telecommunications providers contracted for services. Specific NCS organizational activity related to recovery and response roles for the United States includes the following:[204]

• The National Telecommunications Management Structure (NTMS), which provides a comprehensive, survivable, and enduring management capability for coordinating, restoring, and reconstituting U.S. telecommunications resources. In the event of wartime exercise of the NTMS's functions, the director of OSTP is responsible. The focal point of the NTMS is the National Coordinating Center (NCC), which can be activated to coordinate the activities of commercial telecommunications providers in the event of a required NS/EP response. The NCC is staffed by government and telecommunications industry representatives.

• The Government Emergency Telephone System (GETS), established in 1995 to facilitate NS/EP communications during disasters by using surviving public-network resources.

As discussed earlier, the NS/EP system established in the 1980s focused on the U.S. capability to ensure nuclear command and control and continuity of government and critical military operations during a major war. During the 1990s, the NCS-managed NCC also played a growing role in disaster responses such as in the Oklahoma City bombing, the Northridge, California, earthquake, and numerous hurricanes. In general, the NCS recovery and response organizations remain dedicated to facilitating communications in the event of a physical attack or natural disaster. Although the NCS has recognized its critical infrastructure protection and information assurance missions, it has principally focused on supporting NSTAC and NSIE activities rather than creating dedicated efforts to provide response and recovery capabilities in response to digital attacks on telecommunications systems themselves.[205] Also, the NCS coordinating mechanisms such as the NTMS and NCC involve the major telecommunications companies such as AT&T, MCI, and Motorola. The NCS organization does not create linkages with Internet service providers such as AOL, nor does it provide support to infrastructure users who may be the targets of digital attacks.

FEMA could also play a role in conducting recovery and response operations related to a strategic digital attack. Yet FEMA has committed very limited resources to such activities.[206] FEMA funds emergency programs, offers technical assistance and deploys federal resources in time of disasters. It also has responsibility for developing the Federal Response Plan, which details the roles of various federal agencies in ensuring government continuity in a national security emergency and federal responses to terrorist events. However, FEMA's role in the PDD 63 construct is limited to serving as sector lead for emergency fire services and continuity of government, rather than a broad response and recovery mandate as advocated by the PCCIP.

Another set of organizations, usually labeled computer emergency response teams (CERTs) or computer incident response teams (CIRTs), provide specific capabilities to conduct response and recovery activities related to digital attacks on information infrastructures. At the national level, the Software Engineering Institute at Carnegie Mellon University hosts the CERT Coordinating Center.[207] As detailed earlier, the CERT/CC was formed by the Defense Advanced Research Projects Agency in 1988 as a response to the disruption caused by the Internet worm incident. The CERT/CC organization mission includes operating a twenty-four-hour-a-day point of contact to respond to security emergencies on the Internet. Additionally, the CERT/CC serves as a model for facilitating the development of other computer security incident response teams. Below the national level, a wide variety of organizations have formed CERT-type organizations to provide computer incident response, and their capabilities are briefly discussed later in this chapter. According to its manager, Richard Pethia, the CERT/CC responded to more than 7,600 security incidents between 1989 and 1996 affecting tens of thousands of Internet-related sites.[208] The role of the CERT/CC in incident response involves[209]

· Assisting sites, on a confidential basis, in identifying and correcting problems in their systems and policies.

· Coordinating with other sites affected by the same incident and notifying the Internet community of widespread attacks through the CERT/CC's advisory service.

· Assisting law enforcement agencies in addressing computer crime concerns.

· Notifying interested parties about systems vulnerabilities discovered and working with technology producers to develop patches.

Although very active on a day-to-day basis, the CERT/CC does not constitute an organizational vehicle for national-level U.S. response and recovery efforts related to strategic information warfare attack. It remains a private, non-profit organization without strong links to the organizations responsible for U.S. national security threat assessment or indications and warning. More importantly, its focus is mitigating damage and recovering from limited, specific incidents, not managing responses to large, malicious attacks on a nationwide scale. The CERT/CC has no authority over government agencies, private-sector service providers, or infrastructure users to dictate their actions during an attack. Also, the CERT/CC employs only about twenty people.

The legislatively mandated role of the director of OSTP in directing NTMS activities in the advent of a large-scale digital attack on the United States generally receives little attention. Although a system was created in the mid-1990s to exercise the crisis response capability of OSTP in assuming direction of the NTMS, OSTP's role in response and recovery is missing from the PDD 63 construct.

PDD 63 addresses the need for response and recovery capabilities after large-scale attacks on information infrastructures in two ways. First, the NIPC exists primarily to coordinate the federal government's response to such an incident. It views its key role as investigating intrusions to identify the responsible actor and providing warnings about potential attacks against information infrastructures.[210] Recovery has not been a major focus of NIPC efforts except for the Key Assets Initiative mentioned earlier. If an attack is determined to have foreign origins and presents a severe threat, the president may place the NIPC in a support role to the Department of Defense or the intelligence community. However, PDD 63 does not directly address authorities in the event of digital attacks constituting a national security emergency or war. Response and recovery missions are directly tasked only as part of lead agencies' critical assurance plans for the various sectors. Although the directive places substantial emphasis on outlining responsibilities for warning and information sharing, it does not provide an adequate construct for establishing national-level control over response and recovery activities. The deeper challenges of resourcing and building actual organizational capacity to adequately perform these missions is completely sidestepped.

In addition to PDD 63, other initiatives have significant potential for improving organizational capacity for U.S. national recovery and response to large-scale information warfare. As previously highlighted, the NDP's *Transforming Defense* report strongly urged DOD to focus more on its role in homeland defense, including responses to digital attacks on critical infrastructures. Specifically, the report recommended that the Army National Guard provide forces whose roles would include defense of information infrastructures.[211] The Army Reserve has formed a unit in Vermont dedicated to defensive information warfare.[212] The Washington State Air National Guard has created a unit focused on information security based on the high levels of technological expertise within its organization.[213] As part of a Secretary of Defense study on the use of reserves, the Joint Staff and services are also exploring the establishment of a "virtual" joint service unit responsible for conducting information assurance and computer network defense missions.[214] These Guard and reserve initiatives have focused principally on assisting ongoing DOD vulnerability assessment and intrusion monitoring efforts. If actual conflicts based on strategic information warfare occurred, however, well-developed digital warfare capabilities in the reserve and Guard components of the Armed Forces might provide very effective organizations capable of national-level tasking for recovery and response missions.

The U.S. government must further articulate the role of nondigital military responses to a strategic warfare attack. National command authorities have the responsibility for making decisions to employ military forces in response to a digital attack on the United States. However, RAND war games, military exercises, and operational experiences continue to indicate that the organizational mechanisms that exist within the national security community are underdeveloped and insufficient to link an understanding of the nature and scope of a disruptive attack against the U.S. information infrastructure with determinations of the appropriate responses to mitigate the effects of the attack. The United States has yet to establish a declaratory deterrence policy related to how it will respond to digital attacks against its information infrastructures. PDD 63 declined to address the recommendation of the PCCIP that the NSC develop such a deterrence policy by defining U.S. retaliatory responses.

As of the end of 1999, the U.S. lacked a coherent organizational structure capable of managing response and recovery activities in the advent of a strategic information warfare attack. PDD 63 focuses on how NIPC leads response to cybercrime or terrorism. Although the directive envisaged Department of Defense and intelligence community roles in the case of attack by foreign actors, it ignores the development of capabilities to recover from strategic information warfare attacks. If the National Guard and reserves, building on the initiatives already begun, should develop significant capabilities in terms of response and recovery to digital attacks, organizational mechanisms to prioritize the assignment of these resources to the sectors of greatest need would require development Certain sectors, such as the national security community, telecommunications providers, and commercial organizations, especially financial institutions, have developed response and recovery capabilities to respond to digital attacks against their own information infrastructures. Other critical sectors, such as transportation or emergency services, lack such capabilities. The focus on law enforcement-led incident response has crowded out efforts to respond and recover in a digital war.

Efforts to Protect Information Infrastructures below the National Level

Organizations below the national level also play an important role in defending U.S. information infrastructures. As with the larger national effort, at the end of 1999, the sectoral and organizational programs that existed to protect information infrastructures were designed primarily to deal with threats from accidents, individual hackers, computer crime, and espionage rather than large-scale attacks by U.S. political adversaries. Yet these efforts to assess vulnerabilities, institute security measures, and protect sectors' and organizations' information resources provide the baseline capabilities upon which larger national efforts must be built. A comprehensive survey of myriad programs and capabilities developed by the very diverse government and private-sector organizations conducting decentralized assessment, assurance, and recovery activities is beyond the scope of this analysis. The discussion in this section simply provides a brief overview of organizations and programs that have developed in the Department of Defense and the military services to defend one key strategic information warfare center of gravity, the DII, and the generic types of organizations in the private sector that have sprung up to deal with information security and infrastructure protection.

Within the Department of Defense, many organizations have roles in infrastructure protection in addition to the previously discussed U.S. Space Command and the JTF-CND. Efforts within the DOD initially focused on the use of centralized centers of excellence to establish defensive capabilities, with a more recent push to establish programs at lower levels involving a broader set of network operators and infrastructure users. DOD Directive TS3600.1 in 1992 called upon the director of DISA to "ensure the DII contains adequate protection against attack."[215] According to the Joint Staff Operating Instruction on "Defensive Information Warfare," DISA also has the responsibility for implementing DII security architecture and information systems standards.[216] In May 1993, DISA created a Center for Information Systems Security (CISS) to implement its defensive information warfare program. The CISS, later renamed the Automated Systems Security Incident Support Team (ASSIST), and now the DOD CERT as part of the DISA Global Operations and Security Center, provides operational protection, detection, reaction and vulnerability analysis for the DII and supports the JTF-CND.[217] GOSC performs high-level correlation of computer and information systems incidents DOD-wide, provides technical investigative support, and is the DISA liaison to other DOD, government, and civilian CERTs, intelligence agencies, and law enforcement agencies. Additionally, DISA instituted a program in fiscal year 1996 to integrate intrusion detection systems throughout the DOD. Efforts to standardize these programs across the DII's heterogeneous networks and systems have progressed slowly.[218] The current JTF-CND/DISA concept focuses on developing a capability to fuse information from multiple different sensors deployed by the military services and DOD agencies to provide an integrated intrusion detection picture. Finally, in early 1997 DISA sponsored the formation of the Information Assurance Technology Analysis Center (IATAC), which provides a central data repository for information on assurance techniques, intrusion detection tools, security alerts, and conducting training and conferences.[219]

At the Joint Staff level, the Information Assurance Division, C4 Directorate (J6K) manages important DII protection efforts. J6K has developed numerous information assurance initiatives as part of implementing the mandate in *Joint Vision 2010* to achieve "information superiority."[220] The Joint Staff actively sought out the participation of the DOD Unified Commands beginning in 1996 as part of a larger joint vulnerability assessment process. J6K programs provide for training and licensing of systems administrators and users, conducting advanced technology demonstrations for information assurance systems, and sponsorship of Joint Staff and CINC exercises involving red team efforts to test and demonstrate DOD system vulnerabilities. Of particular significance was the Joint Staff–sponsored exercise known as ELIGIBLE RECEIVER conducted in early summer 1997.[221] In this exercise, with three months of preparation, a red team proved capable of significant intrusions against DOD systems. In combination with simulated digital attacks against supporting electric power and telecommunications providers, the attackers in ELIGIBLE RECEIVER were assessed to have disrupted operations at military bases to an extent that U.S. ability to deploy and sustain its forces was degraded. The PCCIP and numerous other studies have highlighted this exercise as a prime example of the significance of cyberthreats.

The J6 went a step further in early 2000, issuing a detailed "Defense-in-Depth" vision.[222] Analogizing the protection of the DII to defense of a medieval castle, a pamphlet describes the need to protect local computing environment or "enclaves," enclave boundaries, networks linking enclaves, and the supporting infrastructures. The J6 vision recognizes roles for people, operations, and technology, focusing on the availability of technologies to shore up DII defenses. The document portrays a range of threats recognizing the "special danger of stealthy, widespread, sustained, penetrating, high loss Computer Network

Attack," but also stresses the disruptions that result from the natural environment and man-made physical hazards.[223]

The Unified Commands have also begun to establish their own organizations for information assurance efforts. Strategic Command established the first command-level computer emergency response team in 1997. Within the Unified Command structure, Regional Security and Operations Centers (ROSCs) have been established at European Command, Pacific Command, and Transportation Command. The Joint Publication 3–13 construct for conducting information operations calls for the development of information operations cells in support of joint military operations.[224] The mission of these cells includes conducting information assurance and other defensive information warfare activities. Information operations capabilities were employed by European Command to support U.S. operations in the former Yugoslavia, and their activities included the enhancement of the security and protection of information infrastructures supporting U.S. and allied forces in that operation.[225] In the future, under the DOD's 1999 Unified Command Plan, the U.S. Space Command will coordinate DOD-wide computer network defense (CND) operations in support of the other Unified Commands and respond to specific command requests for CND support.[226]

In addition to the Unified Commands, the military services also have developed organizations for information infrastructure defense based upon the same approach of establishing a center of excellence and following up with efforts at decentralizing capabilities and responsibilities. Of the four services, the Air Force has most aggressively developed organizations and programs for information protection. The Air Force CERT was established in 1992, and its activities have expanded to encompass a wide range of programs as part of the larger Air Force Information Warfare Center established in 1993. In January 1999, the AFCERT became the lead Air Force liaison to the JTF-CND. The AFCERT conducts remote-survey and on-site vulnerability assessment of Air Force installations to evaluate the state of Air Force defenses against digital attack. It also conducts incident response and operates the Air Force's Automated Security Incident Measurement program, employing intrusion detection technology to capture and analyze data on possible digital attacks on Air Force networks at all major Air Force installations. The AFCERT has strong ties to law enforcement organizations through the Air Force's own Office of Special Investigations.[227] The AFIWC's capabilities also include an organization known as the Countermeasures Engineering Team (CMET). The CMET develops technologies to improve Air Force capabilities for vulnerability identification and intrusion detection and assists in the development of new Air Force weapons programs and information systems with improved built-in security.[228]

The Air Force has also endeavored to establish organizations at more decentralized levels to conduct infrastructure protection operations. The 609th Information Warfare Squadron (IWS) was formed on 1 October 1995 at Shaw Air Force Base in South Carolina as part of the Ninth Air Force, whose mission is to support to Central Command.[229] Information protection was a major focus of the IWS's activities. The IWS construct proved the value of information warfare units directly integrated into other war-fighting organizations. In the summer of 1998, the Air Force decided on a revised construct, known as information warfare flights (IWFs), for integrating information warfare capabilities into its war-fighting commands. The IWFs leverage resources available in the AFIWC and Air Intelligence Agency to provide capabilities integrated with those of all Air Force war-fighting operations. The IWFs are manned with approximately thirty personnel in peacetime, augmented to seventy in the case of a major contingency. Two IWFs were established in fiscal year 1999 and four more were slated for development in fiscal 2000. When the 609th IWS was closed in June 1999, its mission was assumed by a new IWF. Additionally, the Air Force is trying to devolve certain responsibilities for information infrastructure defense to individual installations through the creation of Network Operations and Security Centers (NOSCs) at major command headquarters and Base Network Control Centers (BNCCs) at all major Air Force installations. These NOSCs and BNCCs are intended to provide focal points at the major commands and at bases for ensuring the provision of networked communications and implementation of additional layers of security technology and monitoring.[230]

The Army and Navy have established similar organizations and programs for information infrastructure defenses. The Army has created its own CERT within its Land Information Warfare Activity that provides incident response capabilities, liaison with other DOD CERT/JTF-CND, and red team capabilities to test Army field units.[231] The Army Director of the Information Systems for C4 established a Command and Control Protect Working Group in January 1995. The director also developed a C2 Protect Program Management Plan in 1996 as part of the overall Headquarters, Department of the Army Information Operations campaign plan. The Army has leveraged DISA expertise in acquiring defensive technologies for vulnerability assessment, network monitoring, and infrastructure protection. It has also established regional CERTs, with the first having been formed in Europe in February 1996 to support Operation Joint Endeavor, and these CERTs provide automated monitoring of theater-based computer networks. The Army provides support to its deployed forces and exercises through Information Operations Field Support Teams (FSTs), which have been actively engaged in supporting U.S. operations in the former Yugoslavia.

The Navy has split its expertise related to information warfare into two centers. The Fleet Information Warfare Center (FIWC) provides the Navy Computer Incident Response Team (NAVCIRT) for both deployed fleet operations and shore-based commands, serves as liaison with DISA and other services, and conducts vulnerability analysis and infrastructure assessment programs. The FIWC has initiated development of an automated security incident detection system for classified systems in naval battle groups. The Naval Information Warfare Activity provides the Navy with technical threat analysis and capabilities to evaluate new technologies and advanced concepts for defensive information warfare systems.[232] The Marines have also recently developed a CERT capability in support of the JTF-CND.[233]

This overview of organizations with responsibilities for protecting information infrastructures in the military services illustrates a number of important features of each branch's approach to providing such protection. Most notably, the diffusion of responsibility for the operation and control of advanced information infrastructures creates imperatives for both centralization and decentralization of defensive efforts. Organizations endeavoring to provide improved protection for information infrastructures for which they are responsible range from the most central levels of the Joint Staff and U.S. Space Command down to the BNCCs at the Air Force base level. Centers of excellence within responsible organizations provide a focal point for coordination and a repository for technical expertise related to defending information infrastructures. However, many of these organizations, with the exception of DISA's CISS/ASSIST/DOD CERT and AFIWC's AFCERT, have come into existence since 1995. Establishing command and control relationships under the JTF-CND has proven a positive development.[234] Figure 5.7 captures the DOD incident reporting and response structure as of February 2000.[235] However, assessments of the process of establishing adequate manning and organizational linkages indicate development of capabilities had progressed slowly at the end of the 1990s. The development of an effective "Defense-in-Depth" requires substantial human expertise and technology deployment throughout the DII. Also, efforts to diffuse expertise and responsibility to lower organizational levels bear scrutiny regarding lessons on how to best develop localized capabilities to improve the effectiveness of the overall defense of the DII. Interviews with individuals in these organizations in 1997–1999 indicated that

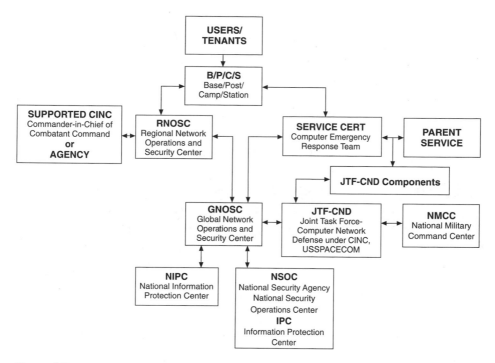

Figure 5.7
DOD Incident Reporting and Response Structures

although substantial progress had been made in initiating decentralized activity for DII protection, actual improvements in overall capabilities were both difficult to measure and probably fairly limited.[236]

Organizations involved in providing protection of information infrastructures in other U.S. government and private sectors present a much more diverse, less hierarchically defined realm of activity than those protecting the DII. The overview presented here simply identifies generic types of organizations in these sectors that undertake significant information infrastructure protection activity, including a few examples of well-known organizations.[237]

As previously discussed, numerous computer emergency and incident response teams exist in the private sector in addition to the national CERT/CC located at the Carnegie Mellon University Software Engineering Institute. These organizations provide vulnerability reports and advisories regarding flaws discovered in certain technologies, identify and assess virus outbreaks, develop and disseminate information on technological responses to identified problems, and provide incident response capabilities. Examples of organizations that have developed CERT-type organizations to help protect their information infra-structures include the Department of Energy, Purdue University, the Boeing Corporation, MCI Communications, and Goldman Sachs Company.

Closely related to the CERTs are the commercial organizations within technology producers assigned the task of conducting research and assistance related to improving the security and reliability of information technology products. CERT-type organizations in both the government and civilian sector often work with such organizations once vulnerabilities are discovered to engineer solutions that can be transferred to users, either from the technology producers themselves or from CERTs. Examples of technology producers with such organizations include Microsoft, Sun Microsystems, and Hewlett-Packard. Other organizations have been set up specifically to establish capabilities to understand viruses and develop software that detects and eradicates them. Companies such as McAfee and Symantec have developed substantial commercial operations in this area. Other government and private-sector organizations have subunits within larger information security/CERT operations dedicated to dealing with viruses. The providers of antivirus software often work very closely with the CERT community in both government and the private sector in responding to virus outbreaks, such as Melissa in the spring of 1999.

Numerous associations dealing with computer and information system security have emerged in response to growing perceptions of the need to protect such systems. These associations provide mechanisms for member organizations to share information about infrastructure protection and also provide training and publish reports and studies. Examples of important associations in this area are the International Institute for Information Integrity (IFOR) operated by Stanford Research Institute, the Computer Security Institute, and the National Computer Security Association.

Increasingly, organizations specializing in providing information and network security capabilities have also begun to spring up in response to the growing demand for such services. Independent commercial organizations such as iDefense and Internet Security Services, as well as units within larger information systems integrators such as IBM and Unisys, technology providers such as Cisco, and major consulting firms such as Booz-Allen & Hamilton, Science Applications International Corporation, Ernst & Young, and Deloitte & Touche will all provide information security advice and technologies for a fee. These firms develop technologies such as intrusion detection and network monitoring systems, conduct red team exercises, and provide security posture assessments.

These companies can also be contracted to provide ongoing information security services for organizations that wish to avoid developing their own internal capabilities.

Large organizations, especially in the banking and financial services sector, usually have significant internal information security organizations to ensure protection of key information resources. For example, Fidelity Investments, the world's largest mutual fund company, has a corporate Information Security Services Group (ISSG) that serves as the center of excellence for the company in protecting its information infrastructure.[238] The ISSG provides other Fidelity business units with expert advice and training about risk assessment, security standards, configuration management, and appropriate technologies such as access controls and firewalls, as well as assistance in incident response. Not directly responsible for providing, implementing, or operating Fidelity's information systems and networks, the ISSG instead endeavors to raise awareness and establish sound policies and procedures throughout the business units regarding information systems security concerns. Each business unit and technology group provides its own resources to create the requisite organizational and administrative capacity for information security. Fidelity's approach is, therefore, decentralized. Other companies use a more centralized model for administration, and both models are common.

Overall, within the private sector, a very diverse range of organizations has evolved to provide network operators and infrastructure users across all sectors with a rich spectrum of information, services, and technological products for use in their specific protection efforts. Yet the private-sector investment in information infrastructure protection in terms of developing organizations and allocating resources clearly remains driven by risk assessments involving threats to day-to-day operations rather than part of a national defensive effort.

Assessing Organizational Development: Hesitant Moves in
Dealing with New Concerns

At the end of the 1990s, the U.S. had yet to develop a coherent organizational structure for grappling with the tasks relevant to defense against strategic digital attack. National government organizations responsible for infrastructure assurance focused on risks to major telecommunications providers. Information security organizations concentrated on the protection of classified national security information. Organizations capable of establishing widely acceptable policies, standards, and technologies for protecting information infrastructures had not emerged. These problems have been recognized, but implementing major changes in organizational roles and responsibilities has occurred slowly at the national level. Below the national level, organizations within the DOD and elsewhere have created decentralized capabilities for information infrastructure protection but these efforts require coordination if the U.S. is to establish a national defensive strategic information warfare capability.

The U.S. government has initiated the development of national-level organizations to improve the protection of information infrastructures outside the national security sector. The PDD 63 construct stresses the role of owner-operators in protecting their own information infrastructures and how the federal government can provide assistance to these organizations. Yet the directive avoids crucial measures necessary to improve defensive efforts by the private sector. It stops far short of establishing organizations with intrusive mandates and regulatory authority to ensure protection measures are implemented. The directive's stress on the leadership role for the FBI, rather than the DOD, reflected the perception in the late 1990s that threats were related more to computer crime and espionage rather than actions requiring robust defenses against a strategic information warfare attack.

The United States has emphasized incremental changes to existing organizations and missions rather than efforts to establish a radically new mission assigned to independent strategic information warfare organizations. The late-1990s focus on critical infrastructure protection enabled the federal government to orchestrate a required policy consensus across a wider range of stakeholders to make initial organizational changes to begin to create a national defensive capability. The formation of the Air Corps and the General Headquarters Air Force also involved similar interim steps in the development of strategic bombardment capabilities in the period between the two world wars. Yet the absence of mechanisms to involve technology producers in these efforts may well limit their effectiveness. The evolution of technological trends related to establishing organizational capabilities for protecting U.S. information infrastructures provides our next topic.

Technology and U.S. Strategic Information Warfare
Capabilities: Underlying Forces and Their Influence on
Offensive and Defensive Trends

The development of U.S. capabilities to conduct offensive and defensive strategic information warfare operations requires doctrine and organizations that are properly aligned with the technological considerations involved. The Air Corps' ability to develop and conduct strategic air operations in the interwar period depended on advancing capabilities of bomber aircraft as well as supporting technologies such as bombsights, defensive armament, and intelligence collection systems. The evolution of offensive and defensive technologies clearly interacted with doctrinal developments and organizational arrangements in the interwar period and influenced the effectiveness of operations in World War II. Future employment of digital microforce will also involve wielding available offense and defensive weapons to fulfill objectives established for strategic information warfare organizations. However, unlike those employed in strategic air warfare, offensive and defensive technologies for waging and protecting against digital attacks are widely available to actors outside of national military establishments. Additionally, the man-made fabric of the cyberspace environment presents an additional challenge for those contemplating warfare in this realm. The basic nature of the air and space environments is relatively static, whereas the cyberspace "ground" on which strategic information warfare will be waged is constantly changing. Planning for strategic information warfare involves understanding the technological trends affecting information infrastructures as decisions are made about effective doctrinal constructs, organizational formats, and digital tools and techniques to conduct operations.

This section builds on the understanding of the cyberspace environment developed in chapter 1 and the nature of technological tools for strategic warfare discussed in chapter 2. The analysis here focuses on the trends over the past decade affecting the vulnerability of U.S. information infrastructures, the offensive technologies openly available to U.S. adversaries, and the development of defensive technologies both within and outside the U.S. national security establishment. The section analyzes how certain underlying forces, particularly weak security features in fast-changing technological foundations, compound the difficulty of establishing effective strategic information warfare defenses in the late 1990s.

Forces Affecting the Evolution of U.S. Information Infrastructures

Two major trends have contributed greatly to the growing U.S. reliance on information systems and networks: implementation of openly networked information architectures and increasing automation of control systems within information infrastructures. In the past, organizations tended to develop information infrastructures customized to their own needs and with little interconnection to those of other organizations. By the early 1990s, however, technologies began to diffuse that permitted organizations to link their information systems and networks more easily, improving the exchange and processing of information. Network providers and infrastructure users have increased openness in the information infrastructure by implementing technologies such as common protocols and compatible hardware and software. These technologies facilitate the ease of interaction between connected information systems and networks. Particularly important has been the move toward systems and networks linked by the use of Internet protocols and transmission facilities as a basis for conducting critical activities, as described in detail in chapter 1. The U.S. military plans to use Internet-based systems for everything from supporting major force deployments to improving the ability of the Marines to conduct urban combat operations. The PCCIP noted in 1997 that a wide range of U.S. critical infrastructures, such as the air traffic control system and electric power distribution, are increasingly shifting from closed, proprietary information systems and telecommunications networks to information infrastructures based on the Internet. Commercial organizations increasingly use open networks to conduct outreach to customers, coordinate with suppliers, and manage internal operations. Also crucial is the growing openness of public-switched telecommunications networks to control by a very wide range of organizations providing network and information services. Exact measurement of the speed and degree to which key information infrastructures can be characterized as "open" remains elusive because of the pace of change, the diversity of activity of concern, and the proprietary nature of the information involved. However, increasing openness in constructing advanced information infrastructures is a basic tenet of U.S. government policy as expressed in the NII/GII initiatives and the 1996 Telecommunications Act.

Increased openness in the use of information technology has arisen from the need of organizations to facilitate the exchange of information between infrastructure users. This increasing openness additionally means a wide range of organizations interact with each other through these infrastructures, sometimes without their knowledge. Such openness in information infrastructures allows malicious activity to occur if users do not take protective steps to manage the degree of interaction allowed with other systems connected to shared networks. According to the National Research Council in 1991:

> Interconnection gives almost an ecological flavor to security; it creates dependencies that can harm as well as benefit the community of those who are interconnected. . . . Just as average citizens have only a limited technical understanding of their vulnerability to pollution, so also individuals and organizations today only have a limited under-

standing of the extent to which their computer systems are put at risk by those systems to which they are connected, or vice versa. The public interest in the safety of networks may require some assurances about the quality of security as a prerequisite for some kinds of network protection.[239]

The effectiveness of technological approaches and the level of organizational implementation in establishing a national information infrastructure defense will be greatly influenced by the degree of openness in the infrastructure. In establishing air and space defenses, the necessary technological tools for defense could be developed and wielded by a central national security organization. However, the increasingly open, interconnected U.S. information infrastructures create an operating environment in which implementing defensive technologies, techniques, and procedures must necessarily involve the many organizations involved in creating, operating, and using the systems and networks.

Coincident with the increasing openness of information infrastructures is the growing degree of automation involved in the use of information infrastructures. According to the Office of Science and Technology Policy (OSTP) in its 1997 *Cybernation* report: "Today's infrastructure has a fundamental, indeed momentous, distinguishing characteristic: *it is automated.* From routing of telephone calls to the distribution of electrical power; from the separation of aircraft to the electronic transfer of funds, the domestic infrastructure operates through automatic information networks. . . . This trend towards cybernation has been building for decades, but it has accelerated dramatically in recent years."[240] The information infrastructures necessary to support U.S. "information superiority" in the military realm involve high levels of automation in the collection, fusion, transmission, and display of information to establish sensor-to-shooter links and improved battlespace displays. In the commercial sector, store computers automatically restock shelves based on inventory control systems using point-of-sale data. The increasing level of automation occurs as a means of making control systems for different activities more accessible and responsive. At the level of strategic information warfare, however, the growth of automation based on digital information infrastructures can clearly provide opportunities for adversaries who would attack organizations reliant on such automation. Automated controls rely on inputs from a number of subsystems. According to the OSTP study, "[c]omputer controlled subsystems often have little tolerance for variations—in sequence, content or timing—in the interactions they undertake with other subsystems. Small margins, like highway tailgaters, are vulnerable to dangerous chain reactions. Subsystems which have small margins—often called tightly coupled systems—are a reality within complex computer networks."[241] A U.S. adversary who could understand critical computer interactions could dramatically increase the possibility of disruptive effects through launching digital attacks designed to achieve cascading effects by exploiting the small margins of these tightly coupled systems. A crucial factor in managing the potential negative consequence of growing automation is the tightness of coupling within automated systems. Strategic information warfare defenses would be enhanced by infrastructure operators and users who implemented technology approaches that loosened the coupling between important automated systems, just as increasing the spacing between cars on the highway decreases chances of chain-reaction accidents. Technological heterogeneity and establishing redundancy based on access to distinctly different capabilities would reduce the likelihood of tight coupling and the possibility of cascades.

The increase in use of open information systems and automation is intertwined with other forces driven by organizations that seek to improve operational efficiency by reducing the cost of using information infrastructures. In both government and the private sector, these forces have led to increased use of commercial off-the-shelf (COTS) technologies. Implementing COTS technologies in adaptable, open networks allows infrastructure users to keep up with the fast-moving, leading edge of available information technology without having to go through the expensive and time-consuming process of designing and implementing customized systems and networks. Using COTS technologies also means, however, that technologies fundamental to operating information infrastructures are widely available to those who would disrupt their operation.

The use of Internet-based technologies is particularly attractive for those implementing open systems and automation today. As a means of linking systems and networks, the Internet provides users with cheap transmission means for digitized information. Organizations reliant on use of Internet technologies have established nongovernmental forums, such as the Internet Engineering Task Force and the World Wide Web Consortium discussed earlier, to ensure standardization and reduce costs of implementing new technologies. These forces tend to create convergence by service provider and infrastructure users on products such as the UNIX or Windows NT operating systems and standards such as the IP/TCP protocol suite to allow maximum connectivity. Although competition still exists in many areas, a very significant portion of providers and users rely on a very limited number of technologies. More than 90 percent of personal computer workstations throughout homes, in corporations, and in the government rely on the Microsoft Windows operating system and Intel Corporation microprocessors.[242] The more common a given networking technology becomes, the more widely known and exploitable are its vulnerabilities.

Deregulation, particularly in telecommunications and energy sectors, has allowed new entrants to legitimately gain access to control networks that were previously proprietary or carefully protected. As part of deregulation, the automated control systems for the public-switched networks and electrical grid have been moved toward greater standardization to facilitate interconnection for any potential provider of such services.[243] The FERC ruling on the Open Access Same-Time Information System driving electric power providers to common Internet-based control systems and the FCC's Open Network Access requirement for telecommunications providers offer examples of the standardization forces created by deregulation.

All in all, the dominant technological trends driving the establishment and use of the U.S. information infrastructures increasingly add to the burden the wide range of service providers and infrastructure users face in conducting their own security and assurance efforts. Taking advantage of advanced information infrastructures means using an open, automated cyberspace environment in which control and security are increasingly distributed to other unknown providers and users. The management of technological implementation has been pushed to lower and lower organizational levels. In terms of enhancing the protection of the United States against strategic information attacks, the overall robustness of these infrastructures would be increased if network providers and users implemented technologies with security features that minimized the difficulty of managing vulnerability arising from ever-increasing automation and interconnection. Yet during the 1990s, the dominant networking technologies often had weak security features.

The construction of the advanced information infrastructures of increasing significance, particularly the Internet, generally does not prioritize efforts to make implementing security measures easier for service providers or infrastructure users. Chapter 3 detailed the forces that have historically caused information technology producers to pay minimal attention to security. The following list highlights the security weaknesses attending the development of a few key technologies:

• The deployment of analog cellular phone technology in the 1980s prioritized improving network capacity, lowering end-user cost and increasing robustness of operation, despite known risks of easy interception if identification codes were transmitted along with voice communications in the clear without encryption. Cellular phone users and providers have subsequently been plagued with massive problems related to stolen identification codes and fraudulent use. The movement to digital cellular technology will involve better quality and a broader range of services, especially data communication and Internet access. The implementation of a new wave of technology has provided producers of such technology with an opportunity for renewed attention to security features. Yet although most technology producers and network providers plan the use of encryption to provide security, studies find users cannot easily configure security features. Also, certain standards for digital cellular transmission can be easily compromised.

• The UNIX computer operating system that dominated network computing in the early 1990s was developed in an ad hoc fashion through cooperative efforts across government, academe, and industry. The development emphasized simplicity and improving ease of computer interconnection with little to no concern with security. The UNIX code was made openly available to systems developers and hackers alike to evaluate and test improved techniques. Many of the widely used digital attack tools and techniques exploit UNIX-based flaws, although vendors and computer security organizations have over time developed a significant capacity to identify vulnerability and develop fixes. The principal successor to the UNIX operating system, known as LINUX, also relies on openly available source code. New concerns have arisen because of the rapid diffusion of Microsoft's Windows-based operating systems throughout the networked computing base. Expert evaluations indicate Microsoft's security features are not robust, and the vulnerabilities of this operating system have quickly emerged. Security expertise to deal with Windows-based vulnerabilities has taken time to develop.[244] As Microsoft's Windows 2000 operating system is widely implemented throughout information infrastructures, hackers and security personnel will renew their learning competition to understand the system's flaws.

• The explosion of the World Wide Web as a means of accessing and displaying information available through the Internet requires the use of software programs known as Web browsers, such as Netscape Navigator or Internet Explorer. Yet the intense competition in this very important market has meant a very fast rate of release for new products and technology that emphasize linkage to other recent Internet developments such as image framing and Java-based programming. Security again seems to have taken a back seat. Browsers have been plagued with a series of demonstrated vulnerabilities. Also, the international World Wide Web Consortium's (W3C's) development of common protocols for use of the Web stresses efforts "to enhance interoperability." Although the W3C approach includes privacy and authentication functions for electronic commerce and intellectual property protection within new protocols, its efforts do not appear to take into consideration threats posed by digital attacks for the purposes of infrastructure disruption and denial.[245]

• The principal standard for use of Internet-based computer networks, known as TCP/IP, also emerged through an open, cooperative process with the same priorities as described for UNIX.[246] Flaws in these protocols create some of the most widely known vulnerabilities for Internet-connected infrastructures, such as through "IP spoofing" and "syn" attacks, described below. Awareness of protocol-based security problems has grown. The next version of the basic Internet protocols, Iv6, will implement features to reduce susceptibility to known sorts of attacks. Yet proactive efforts to implement security features in the basic Internet technologies to avoid the emergence of future digital threats do not seem to be a priority of the Internet Engineering Task Force or even of the U.S. government's own Next Generation Internet initiative.[247] As other advanced telecommunication protocols such as ATM and SONET have begun to be implemented, indications are that hackers have already begun to identify their vulnerabilities.

• The cutting edge of information network technology, such as Java and Active X software code, allows users of advanced information infrastructures to pull necessary applications software and data from other systems as necessary. Security problems in network-based applications have begun to crop up because of problems in the way such applications are accessed by Microsoft and Netscape Web browsers and other software applications.

The above review does not intend to advocate that the U.S. should adopt a policy to restrain the development and implementation of new technologies in its advanced information infrastructures. Rather, the analysis points out that processes that underlay the very aggressive and successful U.S. development and implementation of information infrastructures in the 1990s helped determine the security foundations of these infrastructures. At best, efforts to implement security features in evolving information technologies confront very difficult challenges because of the decentralized private-sector development of these technologies and the rapid emergence of standards and dominant products. At worst, technology developers may consciously minimize attention to security in products because of lack of consumer demand for security features or of any other incentives to devote attention to security. As a result, the current technology development process makes efforts to defend advanced information infrastructures more difficult.

A related problem in securing and assuring advanced information infrastructures is the difficulty of configuring COTS products in complex systems and networks. The Software Engineering Institute notes:

> Systems are very "trusting" in their out-of-the-box configuration to make installation convenient and easy for the end user, but the default settings expose the user to break-ins. The system can be broken into before the owner takes the time needed to reconfigure the system more securely.... There is a continuing movement to distributed, client-server, and heterogeneous configurations. As the technology is distributed, the management of the technology is often distributed as well. In these cases, systems administration and management also fall upon people who do not have the training, skills, resources or interest to operate their systems securely.[248]

In short, the producers of information technologies that are easily assimilated and diffused among infrastructure providers and users do not create adequate security foundations for advanced information infrastructures.

Additionally, most end-users of advanced information technologies and products lack a cost-effective means of evaluating the security features of either individual products or the complex systems that are constructed from these pieces. Existing U.S. government information security standards and technology evaluation mechanisms within the NSA and NIST are perceived as too slow and inattentive to commercial concerns for use by the private sector. Even within the government, growing use of COTS has made such mechanisms inadequate to assess security and assurance features of large-scale information infrastructures involving connections to open, unclassified networks. The implementation of COTS software means that users often lack access to the underlying code of the system developer, which even further limits efforts to assess vulnerability problems and conduct effective system and network security accreditation.[249]

The labor-intensive nature and costs of software development in the late 1990s also means that the development of many software products has included significant involvement by organizations and individuals outside the United States. Recent reports indicate that use of Russian, Indian, Israeli, and Irish programmers has increased dramatically. The lack of available U.S. programmers led to the growing use of Russian, Israeli, and Indian programmers to help U.S.-based companies and organizations fix Year 2000 problems in their computer software programs.[250] The National Coordinator for Counterterrorism, Infrastructure Protection and Security, Richard Clarke, has noted the lack of background checks on foreign individuals doing this work and the possibility that these programmers could insert "back door" accesses into revised code.[251] The ability of the U.S. government to create incentives for sound software development practices and implementation of strong security features may well be reduced by the transnational development of products.

The need to mitigate these problems was recognized in the early 1990s. Numerous organizations such as the National Research Council, the Software Engineering Institute, DARPA, and the NSA developed programs designed to address technological challenges posed by the emergence of insecure foundations for U.S. information infrastructures. At least four basic technological approaches were being advocated by the end of the 1990s:

1. Improve the capabilities of engineers and commercial firms to design adequate security and reliability features into the systems, networks, and standards underpinning information technologies. The Software Engineering Institute has established programs to provide materials to train programmers in techniques that will enhance the reliability and security of products. PDD 63 mandates a national-level review of the status of education in the information security field and identification of necessary responses to meet increased demand for such skills.

2. Improve capabilities to evaluate the security and reliability of products and even network configuration through establishing effective certification and accreditation organizations. Although past efforts in this area have fallen short in terms of effectiveness and widespread acceptance, especially in the commercial sector, calls for creating such organizations continue to be issued by the PCCIP and others. PDD 63 does not address such an initiative. Moreover, the willingness of technology producers or users outside the critical infrastructure sectors to voluntarily participate in such programs proved limited during the 1990s.

3. Use the power of the federal government to create incentives for information technology producers to develop technologies with stronger security features. One such incentive would involve leading by example by requiring strong security and reliability in the products the U.S. government purchases. Advocates of such efforts posit that if the government provides technology producers with sufficient incentives to create a set of products with security and reliability features, commercial users would then also gravitate to these products and foster a market demand-pull for security and reliability features to which producers would respond. According to Lt. Gen. Kenneth Minihan, then Director of the National Security Agency, use of government procurement to establish a viable commercial technology market to ensure the future security of the U.S. information infrastructures would be analogous to U.S. efforts to lay the keels for U.S. Navy vessels during the 1930s that would prove instrumental for victory in World War II.[252] However, establishing such a process would buck the prevailing technology development trends that prevailed in the 1990s.

4. Establish programs to educate users about the significance of the security problem and the need to properly implement technologies with appropriate security and reliability features. The Software Engineering Institute asserts that "in the long term, consumer education is the best means to cause market forces to address this situation."[253] Such programs are stressed in PDD 63, which recommends a broad range of awareness programs, including White House–led conferences. The National Coordinator for Security, Infrastructure Protection and Counterterrorism and the directors of the CIAO and NIPC have all made substantial efforts to conduct public outreach and education in this area.

However, technology producers pay little attention to improving design processes. Efforts by organizations such as the Software Engineering Institute suffer from difficulty in developing adequate personnel and technical resources to understand and disseminate information security of emerging technologies.[254] Government attempts to establish customer demand for security have also been constrained by similar pressures on government information technology acquisitions that stress reduced costs and the need to improve interconnection over paying for strong security features. Educational efforts should therefore focus on improving awareness on the part of commercial network providers and infrastructure users of the importance of establishing secure technological foundations. Yet even within the relatively robust information assurance programs in the DOD, those responsible for awareness programs believe the educational process has only begun to affect overall vulnerability.[255] Most evaluations of advanced information infrastructures indicate that past efforts to increase attention to security and reliability in implementation of underlying technologies did not match the increasing sophistication of attackers and the importance of these infrastructures in the late 1990s.

The resultant vulnerability and robustness of different key U.S. information infrastructures to strategic information warfare remain unknown. Such assessments require additional knowledge of the deployment of varying technologies across different infrastructures, their degree of susceptibility to attack, and costs of implementing protective measures. These assessments can provide an improved focus for future U.S. defensive efforts. Those who create the technological foundations for U.S. information infrastructure-based centers of gravity, however, are not attentive to security and assurance concerns. Halting efforts have been made to influence the information technology development process, but the slow rate of progress during the 1990s indicates the existence of significant barriers to change. Given that the technologies implemented in U.S. information infrastructures will remain susceptible to attack for at least the near future, we now turn to an analysis of specific offense and defense technology trends for waging digital strategic information warfare.

Technological Trends for Waging Strategic Information Warfare

Efforts to identify information warfare trends can cut a very wide swath across the whole range of advanced information technology developments. A 1995 Institute of Defense Analysis study of baseline information warfare technologies identified more than fifty broad categories ranging from protein-based computers to integrated optical-digital correlation. The study's conception of information warfare activity ranged from improved logistics to identification of battlefield targets to detecting malicious software code.[256] My analysis here, in contrast, describes the evolution only of basic technology categories for digital strategic information warfare described in chapter 2 and assesses their capabilities related to changes in the underlying technology base described above. The analysis in chapter 2 provided a background on the conduct of digital warfare and technological means for offensive and defensive operations. The analysis below builds on the descriptions of tools in chapter 2 to develop an understanding of how their development over the past two decades affects the overall defensibility of U.S. information infrastructures.

My description of development of technologies to wage strategic information warfare relies solely on assessments of publicly acknowledged and available technologies. It does not address technology development within the national security establishment of the United States or any other specific actor. Rather, it relies on the same approach used in the unclassified studies conducted by the U.S. government and outside analysts, which assumes that adversaries will access and build on the wide array of publicly available digital intrusion and attack techniques. The analysis here does not involve a detailed description of the characteristics and effects of specific digital tools, but rather focuses on the relationship between the underlying infrastructure and broad categories of offensive and defensive means. Examples of different technologies are used to illuminate the major trends in offensive technological capabilities.

Offense: The Emergence of Sophistication and Availability   Concern about digital intrusion and attacks during the 1980s revolved around tools and techniques developed by relatively small, sophisticated groups of hackers.[257] Digital intruders initially focused on developing means to gain access to the public-switched telephone network, as well as the national security and academic computer networks, such as DARPAnet and NSFnet. Many of the technological tools in use at the time focused on gaining access through password exploitation. Software programs known as war dialers were developed to identify network access points such as dial-up ports for test and maintenance activities. Other programs, known as password crackers, could automatically test accessed systems with a long list of likely passwords. The hacker literature of this period also detailed many nondigital techniques such as "dumpster diving," "social engineering," and physically breaking into telephone switching facilities. Dumpster diving refers to searching through trash bins and collecting other unprotected waste outside the targeted organization in hopes of finding useful information such as passwords or network configuration diagrams. Social engineering refers to efforts to gain system or network access by fraudulently acquiring protected information by techniques such as by posing as a telecommunications company repairperson. Activity focused mainly on gaining digital access as a means for exploration and minor telephone toll fraud. More malicious criminal and espionage activities also evolved during this period through use of these technologies to achieve access to telephone, bank, and government networks. However, little activity occurred during the 1980s that employed digital attack tools to create denial-of-service effects that intentionally disabled targeted information systems and networks. Execution of digital attacks at the time required a degree of technological sophistication. Therefore, the numbers of individuals with sufficient experiential knowledge to engage in such attacks remained fairly small. However, hackers during this period began to congregate in groups, often through illegitimate access to electronic networks, to exchange knowledge of tools and techniques, as detailed in chapter 2. These groups also began to codify the knowledge and techniques they had acquired and to publish it electronically and in print, accelerating the pace of development of attack technologies as well as the skill base of digital intruders.

The next major technological development came with the surge of virus outbreaks in the late 1980s and early 1990s. The problems caused by the release of the Morris worm and the advent of IBM Christmas Card and Pakistani Brain viruses were discussed in chapter 2. Viruses became increasingly common during the early 1990s, on occasion inflicting dire effects such as system crashes and destroying the data of limited groups of users. The period also demonstrated that skills for developing viruses were widely distributed as places like Bulgaria and Malaysia were uncovered as the sources of many of the most disruptive viruses.[258] Recent outbreaks and scares still plague information technology users and require preventive and reactive efforts to eradicate problems. During much of the 1990s, viruses faded somewhat as a major concern in large-scale information infrastructure protection efforts as means were developed to contain their effects. However, as described in chapter 2, the Melissa virus and ExploreZip worm unleashed in the spring of 1999 and continuing with the I Love You virus in 2000, has quickly brought this type of malicious software back onto the list of critical defensive information warfare concerns. Although these outbreaks were not assessed to be part of an orchestrated attack, the potential effects of technologically sophisticated U.S. adversaries unleashing an orchestrated set of virus-based attacks are even more worrisome.

The explosion in the use of Internet and other networking technologies in the early 1990s quickly came to dominate the attention of hacker groups. At the same time, the technologies for conducting digital attacks began to take on an increasing degree of sophistication while also becoming more accessible and easy to use. The development of digital intrusion and attack tools began to rely on analysis of flaws in the computer source code of technologies that underpin advanced information infrastructures. This activity began with hacker groups stealing and examining software code gleaned primarily from telecommunications providers such as AT&T and BellSouth. However, the scope of development of intrusion techniques also quickly extended to the packet-switched networks, especially the Internet, because the software development tools for the operating systems and communications protocols of the networks were readily available. Attack tools were developed based on customized software programs that could target access to and effects against specific computers or network elements, as discussed in chapter 2. These programs began to include techniques such as "Trojan horses" and "sniffers" that could be inserted into information systems of target organizations or placed at Internet junctions to monitor passwords and other activities. As the 1990s progressed, the sophistication of digital attack technologies increased rapidly. Techniques emerged such as "sendmail" attacks based on inserting code in electronic mail, allowing attackers to gain total control within targeted systems, or "IP spoofing," based on programs that allow attackers to appear as if their activities come from an Internet address trusted by the targeted computer system. Attackers have developed techniques based on inserting code within graphics or encrypted text to make detection more difficult.

Additionally, attackers have increasingly used technologies and techniques geared simply to disrupting targeted computer systems and making them unavailable, generally referred to as denial-of-service (DOS) attacks. Sophisticated approaches include a technique known as a "syn attack," whereby a program takes advantage of the message-synchronize function built into Internet protocols to establish multiple network connections and deny users access to a particular computer or system. A technologically simpler attack involves simply orchestrating a group of attackers with Internet access to flood a targeted computer system with e-mail messages at a predetermined time to overload the system.

Efforts to package tools together in programs have facilitated the diffusion of offensive technology and increased the speed with which digital attacks can occur. The 1996 DSB Task Force report provides the following two descriptions of such tools:

> Rootkit: a medium technology software command language package which, when run on a UNIX computer, will allow complete access and control of the computer's data and network interfaces. If this computer has privileges on a network, the network can be controlled by the Rootkit user.

> Watcher T: a high technology Artificial Intelligence engine, which is rumored to have been created by an international intelligence agency. It is designed to look for several thousand vulnerabilities in all computers and networks including PCs, UNIX (client/server) and mainframes.[259]

Such tools can now be used through graphical user interfaces, reducing the required technological sophistication of users. The precision of such tools in achieving system control conceivably allows timed, overwhelming attacks, as discussed in depth in chapter 2. Attacks can also be conducted very quickly. According to the Software Engineering Institute, "in as little as 45 seconds, intruders can break into a system, hide evidence of the break-in, install their programs, leaving a back door so they can easily return to the now-compromised system and begin launching attacks on other sites."[260] The Netbus and Back Orifice tools provide attackers with the ability to conduct "remote administration" of computers compromised by "trojan horse" programs.[261] The Back Orifice 2000 tool was released in summer 1999, before Microsoft had even released the Windows 2000 operating system in the marketplace. In late 1999, new techniques for distributed denial-of-service attacks were also emerging. These techniques create large networks of hosts controlled by a limited number of master servers to launch coordinated packet-flooding denial-of-service attacks for specified periods of time.[262]

Assessments indicate technological expertise in using attack tools is available internationally. As early as 1993, a NCS study had identified more than twenty countries, mostly European, as having an active computer underground involved in developing and using such technologies.[263] The best-known attacks on U.S. national security and banking computer systems during the 1990s involved international participation. As detailed throughout this work, many analyses stress the increasing numbers of actors hostile to the United States and their increasing capability to use these technologies for criminal, espionage, and strategic information warfare purposes.

Much more uncertainty revolves around the breadth of information infrastructure vulnerability to such packaged digital attack technologies. Making a determination about the breadth of such vulnerability would involve comparing the access created and effects caused by a given tool set within systems utilized for key functions in a targeted infrastructure. Also, as technologies including hardware, software, and communication protocols within a targeted information infrastructure change, the access and effects a given set of attacks tools can achieve will likely atrophy. Little analysis exists of the rate of declining effectiveness for digital attack tools. Increasing understanding in these areas is required to discern the actual threat posed by such tools when conducting infrastructure risk assessments and evaluating the level of appropriate defensive effort.

Defense: The Challenges of Protecting an Open, Fast-Changing Environment
Defensive technologies that protect and assure the availability of information infrastructures have evolved in response to growing reliance on open network technologies and the evolution of perceived threats. Although the national security community has historically led technological development in this area, the technologies discussed in this section are now being developed and implemented by other government and private-sector organizations in the United States and elsewhere. Defensive technologies fall into broad two categories: those limiting an attacker's access to protected information resources and those for detecting, monitoring, and responding to attacks. The nature of passive and active approaches to defending information infrastructures was discussed in depth in chapter 2. This section highlights how defensive tools and techniques emerged and their relative state of development.

Technologies and techniques to passively protect protection information infrastructures have progressed the farthest of all the defensive technologies available. Commercial companies and government agencies have developed password control and user authentication systems that helped defeat the early generation of digital attacks. Such technologies include systems requiring one-time password use, computer-generated "challenge and response" systems, requirement for users to have secure tokens as a means of authentication, and even biometric devices based on fingerprint or retinal identification. Other techniques limit the number of password entry attempts allowable by remote users. In general, although password attacks continued to succeed in the late 1990s as a means of access, their continued viability results more from inadequate implementation of password control procedures than inadequacy of technological tools to combat the problem.

Technological means to control viruses have advanced over time to provide significant capabilities. A significant commercial industry has emerged that catalogues virus outbreaks and develops programs to detect and eradicate software code that matches the profile of known viruses. Virus checkers can automatically scan computer systems or networks on a periodic basis or may be directly triggered by users. The information security programs of many organizations also internally monitor virus outbreaks and respond with technological expertise to help users minimize any resulting disruption. New viruses continue to emerge at a fairly rapid pace, requiring that virus checkers be updated regularly to remain effective. The social engineering aspects of viruses such as Melissa also pose new challenges for defensive efforts. Virus creators have begun to use deceptive subject lines and content to trick recipients of e-mail messages into opening attachments that enable viruses to spread. As with access controls, good organizational procedures and user awareness must supplement simple availability of technological tools for combating particular problems.

Even more substantial challenges for defensive technologies have emerged with the requirement to protect information infrastructures based on openly networked systems. A variety of technological responses to these challenges have been mounted within the national security community and elsewhere. One approach heavily emphasized by the government in the early and mid-1990s was the implementation of multilevel secure (MLS) systems.[264] The intent of MLS systems is to use trustworthy hardware and software technologies to process information with different levels of classification, allowing simultaneous access to multiple users of a given system but denying access to specific information based on the user's predetermined level of authorization. DOD implementation of MLS technologies has proven a prolonged process, especially regarding certification of such systems to carry the most sensitive information. The approach has not been viewed as widely applicable outside national security organizations.[265]

Encrypting information as a technological means to achieve information security has a long history, especially in the national security context. In the context of protecting information resources in open networks, encryption technologies make it difficult for adversaries to use attack techniques that rely on reading network traffic to discover passwords and access points as long as the encryption cannot be compromised by eavesdroppers. According to an analysis conducted at the CERT Coordinating Center, approximately half of the security incidents to which the center responded in 1989–1997 could have been avoided through the use of encryption.[266] Encryption can also protect stored information from compromise by attackers and can be used to help authenticate transactions with others, ensure data integrity, and establish confidentiality. Encryption algorithms are available within the national security community as well as through commercial vendors in the United States and abroad, as discussed earlier. In the 1999 CSI/FBI Computer Crime and Security survey, 46 percent of respondents stated their organizations required users to utilize encrypted login procedures and 61 percent protected files through encryption.[267] Both studies and expert opinion almost unanimously find that efforts to protect information infrastructures would be enhanced by having all users implement encryption technologies to protect communications and stored data.

Yet implementation of encryption technologies will not provide a panacea for the threat of digital attacks.[268] Encryption technology efforts led by the national security establishment have underemphasized user authentication and data integrity functions crucial to information infrastructure security in the private sector. Although commercially developed technologies are beginning to address these concerns, implementation of robust encryption outside the national security community remains constrained by limited standardization and the costs imposed by significant public key infrastructure requirements.[269] Also, encryption does not provide protection against denial of service attacks. Finally, the uncertainty produced by continuing struggles over encryption escrow policies has slowed the widespread adoption of encryption techniques and their integration into underlying communications, data processing, and storage technologies in many key U.S. information infrastructures.

Computer firewall systems provide another technology designed to limit risks from using open information infrastructures. These devices filter incoming network traffic and endeavor to stop potentially harmful traffic from affecting protected systems.[270] The filters employed in these devices are generally based on rules that reject network traffic coming from undesirable digital addresses or that prohibit certain types of digital transactions on the network by users either outside or inside the firewall that are known to pose risks of malicious disruption. Firewall implementation has increased dramatically since the mid-1990s, and the use of firewalls is a major part of DOD efforts to secure its DII.[271] Commercial firms establishing intranets and extranets also depend heavily on firewalls to limit their exposure to outside digital disruption. The 1999 CSI/FBI survey found that 91 percent of respondents had instituted firewalls.[272]

Firewalls have crucial limitations, however. Generally, firewall technologies lack versatility in adjusting to implementation of additional services such as new communication protocols, often requiring expensive system replacement to maintain desired levels of security when changes occur. Additionally, firewall systems necessitate continual updates to their filtering rules and address lists to adjust to threats posed by the connection of protected systems to the fast-changing web of outside networks. New addresses and types of attacks must constantly be added to firewall algorithms. Firewalls can create bottlenecks for network traffic and a potential single point of failure for both security and inter-connectivity if compromised. Use of firewalls can also limit services available to users. Firewall settings must sometimes be changed to allow users to improve productivity based on technological advances. Organizations often acquire or develop software systems to perform their missions that require specific pro-tocols or operating system services. To allow such systems to function, system administrators must create "tunnels" through firewalls to permit necessary inter-actions across the boundary, creating opportunities for intruders. Trade-offs quickly arise between security and functionality in the design and use of infor-mation infrastructures protected by firewalls. Effective long-term implementation of firewall systems requires strong decentralized management.

Network analyzers provide another tool for mitigating the significant risks of advanced information systems. These analyzers are designed to detect flaws in technological systems and configurations implemented within an information infrastructure. Among the most publicized is the SATAN tool described in chapter 2. Organizations such as DOD CERT and the AFIWC also have developed similar network analyzers to conduct remote security surveys and vulnerability assess-ments. Generally, these analyzers rely on a scripted compilation of known flaws and hacker attacks to allow defenders to test vulnerabilities of networked systems. However, some tools, like SATAN, also allow users to take control of compromised systems to implement fixes. To effectively identify vulnerabilities, such testing tools must also be updated to account for the emergence of new attack techniques as well as changing technologies in the information infra-structure under assessment. Also, the public availability of such tools has created a significant debate within the information security community about whether attackers may not receive greater benefit from employing network analyzers than the defenders for whom such tools are ostensibly developed.[273]

Recognition of the limitations and risks inherent in technologies such as firewalls and network analyzers has led to the development of network monitoring and intrusion detection systems. Such systems highlight suspicious digital behavior related to a protected network and allow defenders to reduce access or to endeavor to digitally trace the source of suspicious activity. Efforts to detect, monitor, and backtrack digital attackers have been well publicized, at least as far back as Clifford Stoll's campaign to catch the Hannover hackers in 1989.[274] Such efforts have stressed automating the detection function by allowing defensive technologies attached to protected networks to profile known digital attacks, such as auditing commands that disable systems or multiple password attempts. Additionally, monitoring can occur based on detecting patterns of traffic within a network that deviate from previously established norms. Once a system highlights suspicious behavior, its defenders can choose to change the operating parameters of the information infrastructure under protection to reduce or cut off access of potential attackers. Alternatively, defenders can allow suspicious activity to continue with the intention of backtracking and identifying and stopping attackers by apprehending or eliminating them. Employing techniques known as "honey pot" and "fishbowling," defenders try to divert attackers into a decoy system where no real threat is posed by intrusion and the attackers' activity can be monitored.[275]

In contrast to the development of encryption technologies, the government has worked closely with the private sector to develop improved network monitoring and intrusion detection systems. The Air Force's Automated Security Incident Monitoring system is based on technology originally developed at University of California at Berkeley in a partnership with Trident Data Systems. The Net Ranger security software made available for commercial use by the Wheelgroup Corporation built on technology developed by corporate personnel while they were members of the Air Force Information Warfare center. This center, DISA's Information Assurance Technology Assessment Center, and many others help evaluate COTS intrusion detection systems for DOD use and to help sustain their technical expertise. Creating synergies between related efforts in this area leverages limited fiscal and human resources to improve defensive technologies for information infrastructure protection.

The relatively recent emergence of monitoring and intrusion detection systems, however, means these tools have limitations in providing robust protection to different networks within large, rapidly changing information infrastructures. As with firewalls, the level of protection provided by a particular detection system depends on the types of operating systems the system can handle. As the number of different computer operating systems and communications protocols a given monitoring and intrusion detection system can address increases, so do the processing demands of the system, thereby increasing costs and possibly affecting overall network efficiency.[276] The Department of Defense has initiated efforts to develop systems, such as the Automated Intrusion Detection Environment, that can fuse and portray intrusion data from multiple sensors across a diverse information infrastructure to allow a more diverse set of sensors to cover a broader range of systems.[277] By the end of the 1990s, such systems still did not have the ability to detect previously unknown types of attacks not preprogrammed into detection algorithms. As with all technologies related to the defense of open, advanced information infrastructures, effective implementation of monitoring and intrusion detection systems requires that they be updated and modified constantly. Also, as described in chapter 2, the data provided by current monitoring systems are voluminous. Effective use of these systems requires the development of advanced filtering techniques or highly developed human expertise. Operators of such systems describe the difficulty of discerning between trivial, unintentional suspicious activity and sophisticated efforts to probe information infrastructures while sophisticated attackers remain undetected using nonstandard techniques. One analyst at the DISA CERT noted that intrusion detection systems may detect the presence of Cessnas intruding upon the DII but miss the incoming B-2.[278]

The development of technological solutions for responding to digital attacks confronts institutional tradeoffs to enabling speedy, effective mitigation and elimination of potential threats. One potential technological approach to improving defenses would be to link intrusion detection systems with other network control systems. If intrusion detection systems identified suspicious behavior profiled to be sufficiently threatening, defenders could allow automated commands to change the access allowed by firewalls and other systems controls. Yet issuance of false alarms and overreacting to low-grade threats degrades efficiency. Determinations regarding how much automation to employ in intrusion detection systems boils down to concerns over organizational authority and risk-use trade-offs given assumptions about the likely threat. Interviews with individuals involved in DII protection efforts indicate that as of late 1999, operators of intrusion detection systems still relied on contacting network operators and system users to confirm that intrusions had occurred and to implement defensive responses.

Technological tools could also allow defenders to identify the source of digital attackers by tracing and electronically backtracking the electronic trail left by attackers along the path they used to make the attack. However, such a response may mean intruding into systems, quite likely outside U.S. borders, utilized by attackers without the knowledge of their owners and operators. Again, interviews and official studies stress the legal constraints of using such techniques.[279] As addressed in chapter 2, such constraints on the use of aggressive backtracking techniques might well be relaxed if the severity of attacks were deemed to constitute strategic information warfare against the United States.

Another major challenge facing U.S. efforts to protect key information infrastructures is the development of technological responses to DOS attacks intended simply to make systems unusable. Although not prevalent in digital intrusion activity for purposes of exploration, crime, or espionage, DOS attacks on computer systems of government agencies, nonprofit organizations, and corporations have emerged as a means of political protest in the United States and elsewhere, typified by the distributed denial of service (DDOS) attacks described in the epilogue.

DOS attacks are widely touted as a potentially effective strategic information warfare attack technique.[280] Such attacks do not require creating digital access inside targeted systems and networks. Rather, techniques such as syn attacks and e-mail bombardment seek to overload the access points and connections of the targeted system or network to other systems or networks that require interconnection to perform their function. Firewalls and monitoring and intrusion detection systems are often not designed or configured to deal with DOS attacks. Such attacks generally leverage weaknesses in network communications protocols and the underpinning technologies implemented in information infrastructures. Therefore, the most effective counters to DOS attacks involve efforts to improve the features of underlying standards and operating systems. Responses focused on mitigating the effects of DOS attacks must address difficulties in increasing the attention of technology producers to security and assurance concerns and getting network operators and infrastructure users to implement the most robust security technologies available.

Research and development for advanced tools and techniques to provide security and protection of information infrastructures received emphasis in both the 1996 DSB Task Force and the 1997 PCCIP recommendations. PDD 63 designated the White House Office of Science and Technology Policy as the federal lead for research and development related to critical infrastructure protection.

The Defense Advanced Research Projects Agency has led a major program to explore approaches to information assurance and survivability since 1995.[281] This program assumes advanced information infrastructures will continue to have porous technological foundations from the security point of view based on increasing levels of openness and distributed control. The DARPA program is addressing a broad range of concerns, including cybercommand and control, strategic intrusion assessment, intrusion-tolerant systems, and autonomic information assurance. The program has also examined responses built on biological and social models for identifying and responding to disruptive activity when it occurs while enabling systems and networks to continue to function effectively. Technological areas of emphasis within the DARPA program include[282]

• Software code "wrappers" that would be used during transactions between computing bases to ensure that disruptions do not occur as a result of activities of unknown and less-trusted operators and users of advanced information infrastructures. Wrappers would be generated by highly trusted systems and would allow easy detection of tampering with the contents of information they are designed to protect.

• Techniques to proactively identify anomalous software code before such code could create disruptions, similar to the human body immune system. Unlike virus checkers, firewalls, and monitoring systems available as of the late 1990s, such technologies would allow identification of and protection against previously undetected attack tools and techniques.

• Use of abundant computing power and information storage capacity to create diversity of software systems and redundancy among them. Efforts along these lines stress techniques and models that allow networks to dynamically move critical functionality away from disrupted subsystems to other available resources on the network. Increasing diversity would limit vulnerability from a single type of attack. Such diversity could be implemented through changing logical processes rather than requiring implementation of a variety of different hardware and software products.

Reaping the technological fruits of such R&D efforts will require attention to the concerns of the network providers and infrastructure users who must implement new tools and techniques. The DARPA program specifically focuses on improving protection of defense information systems. If such technologies are also to be used to protect other key infrastructures, the private sector must have a means and an opportunity to voice its requirements. Advanced defensive technologies that both improve daily life and provide protection against strategic information warfare threats, such as digital authentication for electronic commerce, stand the best chance of widespread assimilation and diffusion. Technologies providing redundancy and diversity will engender very little voluntary implementation if they are expensive and/or degrade interoperability and flexibility. As with all research and development efforts, linking conceptual efforts with user concerns must remain a principal focus of improving available defensive technologies for strategic information warfare.

Most assessments, at the end of 1990s, described the balance of offensive and defensive technologies involved in strategic information warfare in terms of asymmetries that favored the attacker. Offensive tools and techniques have increased the speed, stealthiness, ease, and precision of digital attacks. The technological foundations of advanced information infrastructures provide a wide range of potential vulnerabilities for attackers to exploit. As of the end of the 1990s, defensive tools that quickly eliminate such vulnerabilities were not readily available. The Software Engineering Institute describes the situation in the following manner:

> As we face the rapidly changing and complex world of the Internet, comprehensive solutions [to achieve security] are lacking. Among security-conscious organizations, there is increased reliance on "silver bullet" solutions, such as firewalls and encryption. The organizations that have applied a "silver bullet" are lulled into a false sense of security and become less vigilant, but single solutions applied once are neither foolproof or adequate. Solutions must be combined and the security solution must be constantly monitored as technology changes and new exploitation techniques are discovered.[283]

Those responsible for developing and conducting strategic information warfare defenses lack simple technological means to guarantee absolute protection and must use available tools to manage risks posed by potential attackers. Technological approaches to improving defenses could include efforts to shore up foundations by (1) producing and implementing underlying technologies that are more secure and robust, (2) increasing diversity and redundancy to improve survivability if disruption occurs, and (3) increasing the ability to detect and stop attacks. The adoption of each of these approaches imposes burdens differently among the various organizations involved in creating, operating, using, and protecting U.S. information infrastructures. Efforts to improve technological foundations place responsibility on technology producers and the establishment of organizations to assess and validate technologies. Approaches that emphasize diversity and redundancy focus on the actions taken by owners, operators, and users to ensure that such characteristics are present in technologies implemented in their infrastructures. Creating defenses that can react to and mitigate specific attacks may allow more centralization of responsibility for technological development and implementation but may also require infrastructure operators and users to relinquish some control.

As a nation, U.S. efforts to employ technologies for defending infrastructures have focused principally on employing specific tools by designated information security organizations, with limited attention given to securing the technological foundations of the infrastructures to be protected or stressing diversity and redundancy. This approach has emerged from the failure by policymakers to take a more comprehensive approach that involves technology producers, network providers, and general users in defending the U.S. information infrastructure. Technological challenges, such as implementing strong encryption technologies or ensuring stronger security features in the next version of Windows or Internet protocols, will require non–technologically driven trade-offs. Sound policy to guide development of defensive technologies requires assessing the appropriate levels of government involvement, understanding the significance of individual, and commercial privacy rights, and reaching agreements over who should pay different costs for implementing improved capabilities. Development of the technology to establish effective U.S. strategic information warfare defenses is not simply an engineering exercise in developing the best technologies. Such an effort also requires effective policy management to ensure widespread diffusion of appropriate technologies.

Facilitating Factors and the Establishment of U.S.
Organizational Technological Capability for
Defensive Strategic Information Warfare

The United States had made limited progress in developing doctrine, organizational structures, and technology for defensive strategic information warfare by the close of the 1990s. The nation's highest leaders have expressed concern about the need to protect the nation's information infrastructures. Yet, the U.S. government has vaguely articulated the threat posed by digital warfare at the strategic level. The Department of Defense and other national security institutions have only begun to secure their own information infrastructures and have demonstrated limited interest in providing nationwide defensive capability. The PDD 63 construct provides a basis for action but does not address key sectors of activity. The growth in networking and the accelerated process of developing products and standards mean that the technological foundations of advanced information infrastructures have developed features that make protecting them more difficult. The progress of offensive digital warfare technologies seems to provide attackers with a significant advantage over defensive efforts in terms of exploiting weaknesses. This section analyzes the reasons for the current state of affairs in development of the U.S. capacity for defensive strategic information warfare, using the facilitating factors for establishing organizational technological capacity developed in chapter 3. The framework addresses five factors: supportive institutional environment, demand-pull motivation, management initiative, technological expertise, and learning ability. The limited presence of these factors provides insight into why U.S. efforts to establish defensive strategic information warfare capabilities have progressed fairly slowly.

Institutional Environment: Priorities in Information Infrastructure Use and Protection

The establishment of effective organizational capabilities to defend U.S. advanced information infrastructures has been critically influenced by the nature of the institutional environment. Defensive strategic information warfare requires the orchestration of activities at multiple levels: national-level policy; understanding the degree of reliance of different sectors on infrastructures; shaping incentives for individual organizations to produce technology products and operate networks; and utilizing infrastructures in a manner that improves, rather than degrades, overall security. In the United States, the federal government has only recently addressed the relationship of national-level policy and institutions to coherent efforts to defend centers of gravity from digital strategic attack. These nascent efforts to provide a supportive institutional context still involve substantial areas where important institutions have yet to even acknowledge that significant trade-offs constrain the ability of the United States to prioritize the establishment of strong defensive strategic information warfare capabilities.

The U.S. national security sector has clearly recognized the significance of strategic digital attacks as an offensive means and a defensive concern. Yet the development of information warfare/operations concepts and doctrine within the Department of Defense and U.S. military has focused primarily on improving traditional battlefield operations, not developing doctrine based on waging strategic war in the uncharted reaches of cyberspace. In the cyberspace arena, no military service has pushed to aggressively develop new concepts of warfare or demonstrated a willingness to undergo major institutional changes similar to those undertaken by the interwar Army air arm in the 1920s and 1930s. While firmly establishing programs to improve defense of the DII and raise awareness about national concerns, the U.S. military establishment has consciously shied away from asserting an active role in protecting the U.S. national information infrastructure. According to numerous policy and doctrinal statements, the U.S. military establishment believes that such efforts must be conducted by a broader range of federal organizations in conjunction with the private sector. The Department of Defense has recognized the tremendous challenges involved in improving the security and reliability of the DII alone and has increasingly focused its effort on this more limited concern. It has gratefully left responsibility for leading the development of national-level institutions to emerging efforts surrounding critical infrastructure protection, particularly the NIPC. The leadership of the U.S. national security establishment, expressed though findings of the Security Policy Board and the Defense Science Board, has explicitly recognized that institutions such as the National Security Agency will not be seen as honest brokers of policy debates surrounding national defensive efforts.

Within the rest of the federal government, few institutions have demonstrated a desire to engage actively in efforts to improve U.S. capabilities for defensive strategic information warfare. Organizations such as FEMA, the FCC, and NIST do have established roles related to information infrastructure protection. Yet such organizations view large-scale threats posed to the United States by international actors for political purposes as both outside their mission, given limited resources, and traditionally the responsibility of the national security establishment. Organizations such as the FCC and the Commerce Department may well view efforts to improve information infrastructure protection as detrimental to implementing policies such as telecommunications deregulation and improving U.S. international economic competitiveness. The exception to this hands-off approach has been the leadership of the Department of Justice and FBI in the critical infrastructure protection area. The involvement of these two organizations is based on their counterterrorism role and a desire to combat computer crime and espionage more effectively.

In the private sector, explicit recognition and attention to defense of U.S. information infrastructures has also proven very limited. Awareness of the threat posed by strategic information warfare has begun to develop only through growing attention in the public press and through outreach efforts conducted by the Departments of Defense and Justice. In a few sectors, particularly telecommunications, institutional mechanisms such as the NSTAC and the NCS have provided a basis for establishing policy development and implementation mechanisms to address national-level defensive concerns. PDD 63 envisions development of organizational mechanisms to orchestrate defensive efforts against cyberthreats to a broader range of critical infrastructures. However, the key roles of technology producers, Internet service providers, and general commercial users remained largely ignored at the end of 1990s. Federal policies on encryption have even alienated many of these players and made them reluctant to become involved in the development of U.S. government efforts to protect information infrastructures.

Chapter 3 laid out a spectrum of institutional approaches to establishing strategic information warfare defenses. The United States falls in the portion of the spectrum between coordination and laissez-faire. The continuing push toward deregulation in telecommunications and other industries with critical information infrastructures since the early 1980s has hampered the ability of the federal government to assess infrastructure protection and assurance efforts. Efforts to promote competition have increased the openness of information infrastructures and the development of common standards that create challenges for establishing effective defenses. The lack of government intervention also has encouraged a fast-moving technological environment. The Clinton administration's NII, GII, and electronic commerce initiatives have emphasized a hands-off approach by government to infrastructure development and management. The principal exception has been in the area of encryption policy, where efforts in the 1990s to encourage commercial adoption of government controls on these technologies through export regulations resulted in little private-sector cooperation, acrimonious debate, and slowed implementation and use of these technologies.

Yet efforts to create a federal government role in coordinating the protection of the nation's information infrastructures gathered some momentum as the 1990s drew to a close. The numerous studies conducted by organizations such as the NRC, the NSTAC, and the Department of Defense have established an incremental process of building awareness and dialogue among a growing number of institutions. The PCCIP engaged in the broadest effort to understand concerns across various sectors of U.S. society involved in protecting the nation against strategic digital attacks. Organizational change in this area has similarities to the evolution of the Army air arm in the 1920s and 1930s. Changes to organizational structures in the Army air arm in the interwar period emerged slowly through a series of different boards and studies trying to figure out the proper role of an organization focused on a new mission within the national security establishment. The organizational structure envisioned for national cyberdefense under PDD 63 deals primarily with law enforcement and counterterrorism concerns. The strategic air warfare mission envisioned by those as

Mitchell and Arnold for Army air arm in the 1920s and 1930s only became a reality as a result of World War II. Similarly, strategic information warfare defense roles and responsibilities remain in the background of the start of the twenty-first century. Important stakeholders have yet to be given or to assume a positive role in the process.

The U.S. institutional context facilitates private-sector leadership in developing and implementing advanced information infrastructures. U.S. policies support the development of advanced information technologies and provide the basis for sustained advantages in economic competitiveness. The responsibility for protecting information infrastructures in the United States has generally devolved to the organizational level, where the level of efforts toward such protection has varied widely. The generally hands-off approach of the federal government may mean that U.S. information infrastructures having significant robustness because of the resulting technology diversity and redundancy, but such features have proven resistant to measurement.

The commercial incentives and lack of government involvement in the development of the technology underpinning most key information infrastructures renders the laissez-faire approach risky in ensuring adequate cyber defenses. Government agencies encounter great difficulty in discerning and managing vulnerabilities to digital intrusion and attack. Trends toward deregulation and minimizing government intrusiveness mean private-sector organizations lack strong incentives to provide information regarding infrastructure reliability, threats, and protection or to undertake defensive measures beyond protecting against everyday risks. The institutional context at the end of the 20th century did not offer the U.S. government a window on the degree of its vulnerability to strategic information warfare and could provide no assurance about the effectiveness of defensive efforts if the nation were to suffer such attacks. Such a situation of heightened awareness but limited institutional development for protecting information infrastructures could be ripe for a damaging overreaction that constrains economic competitiveness and privacy without facilitating well-planned improvements to defensive capability if the United States were to suffer a major digital attack in the near future.

Demand-Pull: Lack of an Immediate, Demonstrable Threat

The slow emergence of national-level capabilities for strategic information warfare defense has been influenced in large measure by how stakeholders in both government and the private sector perceive their responsibilities and incentives. Evidence of the possibilities for digital attacks on information infrastructures and growing awareness of the degree of reliance on and vulnerability of these infrastructures has provided motivation for Department of Defense and Justice efforts, congressional involvement, and the issuance of PDD 63. Other sectors of U.S. society continue to perceive strategic information warfare as a limited threat and the need to undertake defensive efforts as correspondingly small. As a result, government agencies outside the national security and law enforcement sectors have not engaged in substantial efforts to promote protective measures throughout the private sector. Nor have the president and Congress felt sufficient motivation to direct the formation of a comprehensive U.S. defensive strategic information warfare program.

What demand-pull incentive does exist to create stronger organizational technological capacity for strategic information warfare has arisen largely because of a series of key incidents that have been discussed throughout this work. The 1988 Internet worm incident resulted in the formation of the U.S. national CERT Coordinating Center at the Software Engineering Institute and the 1991 *Computers at Risk* study. The intrusions by Dutch hackers in 1992 and the 1994 Rome Lab incident provided the Department of Defense with impetus to vigorously assess its vulnerabilities and helped awaken congressional concern about the security of critical information infrastructures. The 1995 electronic theft involving Citibank allowed those concerned with raising awareness about security issues to highlight the digital threat to the commercial sector. The terrorist attacks on the World Trade Center and in Oklahoma City, though not directly involving information infrastructures, provided a major impetus for increased concern about U.S. vulnerability to terrorism at home and generated the initial efforts geared to critical infrastructure protection that blossomed into PDD 63. Accidental outages, from the 1991 AT&T switching failure to the 1996 power outage in the northwestern U.S., became vehicles for promoting understanding of the growing degree of automation and interconnection in critical infrastructures and the potential for large-scale cascading effects in the face of malicious attacks on such infrastructures. The observable, disruptive consequences caused by these events have provided most of the analytical fodder and organizational impetus behind efforts relevant to the establishment of strategic information warfare defenses.

These events and intrusion incidents precipitated follow-up activities, particularly within DOD, the Department of Justice, and Congress, that provided a demand-pull for national-level defensive efforts. As the Department of Defense came to recognize the centrality of the DII in accomplishing its traditional war-fighting missions, it discovered vulnerabilities in the DII and the difficulty involved in defending it through efforts such as the DISA Vulnerability Analysis and Assessment Program and the Air Force CERT on-line surveys. The national security establishment also became worried about the susceptibility of U.S. defense information infrastructures to intrusion as well as the inability of the system operators to detect attacks. Concerned parties used these findings to stress the need for increased attention in the crucial 1995–1996 timeframe. The PCCIP promoted the Eligible Receiver exercise in 1997 as "a glimpse at future forms of terrorism and war," similar to the way Billy Mitchell used the sinking of the battleship Ostfriesland in 1921 to demonstrate the potential of airpower in warfare.[284] The FBI has also begun to engage in active efforts to raise awareness of the threat posed by digital attacks, focusing on computer crime and espionage through studies involving the Computer Security Institute, in congressional testimony, and through public statements by its director.

Congress also has played a key role in creating a demand-pull on the President to directly address concerns related to national-level information infrastructure protection.[285] The Kyl Amendment forced the president to address the question of the adequacy of U.S. defenses in the face of digital strategic information attack. Senator Sam Nunn and others followed up by holding the June–July 1996 Senate hearings on "Security in Cyberspace." These congressional demands provided the principal impetus for the establishment of the PCCIP. That commission's recommendations, in turn, now provide the basis for a national-level effort to extend strategic information warfare defensive efforts into the private sector.

Yet demand-pull motivation framed primarily in terms of national security and, more recently, antiterrorism and law enforcement concerns has excluded potentially important players who have felt their direct involvement was unnecessary to address these problems. In particular, the U.S. government has taken very limited concrete steps to motivate significant private-sector involvement in a national defensive effort geared to establishing more defensible information infrastructures. The implementation of PDD 63 may change this situation but only in certain areas. Chapter 3 identified mechanisms that a national government could employ to increase the involvement of private-sector organizations. The following list delineates some potential incentives for private-sector involvement in U.S. information infrastructure protection and evaluates the degree to which such mechanisms have been implemented and/or proposed as part of efforts to develop such protection:

- *Legal liability and insurance.* No major government effort undertaken or envisioned.

- *Tax breaks and subsidies.* No major government effort undertaken or envisioned.

- *Research and development.* U.S. government efforts have been established to improve risk assessment techniques and develop defensive technologies, principally within the Department of Defense. Funding for programs directly accessible to the private sector, particularly at NIST, remains at low levels.[286] Diffusion to the private sector of technology and of lessons from government efforts at improving information infrastructure protection seems limited.

- *Raising awareness through education and information-sharing efforts.* Significant efforts have been established for private-sector activities with ties to the national security community, such as through the NSTAC/NCS mechanisms. The Department of Justice and FBI have broadened efforts to improve understanding potential vulnerabilities and security concerns within private-sector organizations that deal with what have been defined as critical infrastructures. The PDD 63 construct provides a very strong framework for improving awareness of the need to improve cyber defenses in the critical infrastructure area if aggressively implemented. Efforts to engage other stakeholders, such as technology producers and general commercial users, have received little attention and remain outside the thrust of the government's critical infrastructure protection activities.

- *Creating testing and validation processes and standards for information systems and networks.* Available processes and standards provided by NIST and NSA have not broadly engaged the private sector and therefore contribute only to a limited degree to improving the security and reliability of information infrastructures outside government. PDD 63 did not address PCCIP recommendations for a decentralized standards development process to engage owner-operators of these infrastructures. No mandated involvement by technology producers and general commercial users is envisioned.

- *Ensuring redundancy and diversity.* No significant government programs currently exist in this area. The recent push for deregulation and increasing competition in telecommunications and other areas may actually diminish the degree of technological redundancy and diversity implemented by organizations involved in operating information infrastructures, although detailed assessments need to be conducted. Antitrust actions initiated against Microsoft and Intel Corporation may inadvertently provide more diversity in certain market sectors. The PDD 63 construct of utilizing ISACs to conduct risk assessments and to encourage implementation of best practices across sectors with critical infrastructures may involve recommendations to improve redundancy and diversity in those infrastructures. The onus for expending resources and for implementation remains, however, on owner-operators, who have proved very reluctant.

• *Establishing restoration programs.* The NCS provides funding and issues regulations to ensure that the major telecommunications companies are engaged in efforts to assure national security and emergency preparedness communications. These efforts, however, do not extend to restoration capabilities for private-sector activities in the event of a major digital attack against public-switched networks. The government has also provided assistance for restoration efforts to deal with digital intrusion and disruption related to the Internet by creating and supporting the CERT/Coordinating Center and through its sponsorship of the Forum of Incident Response Teams (FIRST) by NIST and DARPA. The CERT/CC and FIRST activities have motivated limited development of similar organizations in the private sector and provide a liaison to technology producers regarding the identification and patching of vulnerabilities in information systems. Implementation of recent initiatives to develop information infrastructure response and restoration capacity within the reserve and National Guard components of the military services could potentially make a substantial government contribution to supplementing efforts developed in the private sector.

• *Requiring involvement in U.S. government defensive efforts.* The principal federal efforts in this area again revolve around the major telecommunications providers' involvement with the NCS. Beyond the telecommunications sector, some regulated organizations such as electric power providers and financial markets have reporting requirements regarding information infrastructure disruptions, but these mechanisms are not intended to help identify and organize responses to orchestrated digital attacks. The PDD 63 structure for involving sector coordinators in a national indication and warning system would considerably improve private-sector integration into defensive efforts but suffers from the previously discussed limitations in terms of scope of activity covered.

Generally, the U.S. government has employed only limited mechanisms to encourage private-sector participation in improving information infrastructure defenses and shied away from heavy-handed efforts at regulation or mandated involvement. Its efforts have focused primarily on the telecommunications sector, with few incentives for other private-sector organizations to become involved. PDD 63 envisions significant government leadership to engender positive participation across the private-sector organizations involved in the ownership and operation of critical infrastructures. The directive explicitly avoids new regulatory schemes, as technology producers and other private-sector organizations remain consciously leery of burdens that involvement in efforts to establish national strategic information warfare defenses would entail and thus remain distanced from them. Federal government creation of negative incentives to involve these sectors could well bring weighty political and economic costs.

Finally, no crisis has yet faced the U.S. information infrastructure that has threatened national security or placed a significant burden on U.S. society. Computer security expert Peter Neumann described the effects of the absence of such a crisis as follows: "Another factor which has slowed progress in security is that despite very considerable vulnerabilities and risks in today's telecommunications infrastructures, digital commerce and national security systems, serious disasters have not yet struck critical systems. Major security-related events have not occurred that in their effects on public awareness might be considered to correspond in scope to a Chernobyl, Bhopal or Exxon Valdez."[287] A hypothesized "digital Pearl Harbor" remained only a theoretical possibility at the end of the twentieth century. The actual resiliency of key U.S. information infrastructures in the face of orchestrated, malicious attacks remains unknown. The U.S. faced no major threat to drive the development of strategic airpower in the interwar period. Similarly, advocacy for establishing national strategic information warfare defensive capabilities faces the same critical obstacle of a lack of a real crisis to motivate action. Efforts to develop such capabilities require proactive investment to prepare for waging the next war, rather than simply mitigating currently pressing problems. The clear costs of implementing a comprehensive effort in this area have so far apparently outweighed the demand for establishing a national strategic information warfare defense. The willingness of federal departments and agencies as well as the private sector to take steps to implement aggressively the proactive measures outlined in PDD 63 will provide a measure of the perceived concern operating at the highest levels of U.S. government.

Management Initiative: Requirement for Presidential and Congressional Leadership to Coordinate Difficult Trade-Offs

The willingness of leaders in the U.S. government and private sector to engage the difficult challenges of providing information infrastructure protection has varied across different sectors. In the private sector, rising awareness of the potential for digital disruption has led in some areas to organizational initiatives to reduce risks. Within the government, the most visible management initiatives to deal with the problem have been undertaken within the Departments of Defense and Justice. Yet even within these efforts, strong policy declarations about the need for improved infrastructure protection remain less than fully supported in terms of allocated resources or organizational development. At the highest levels of the federal government, the leadership necessary to create a national-level coordinating authority for strategic information infrastructure defense has yet to emerge because of competition with other priorities.

A detailed analysis regarding management initiatives within the private sector to improve information infrastructure protection is beyond the scope of this work. Generally, initiatives have emerged most prominently among commercial organizations that perceive the greatest threats of digital intrusion and disruption, particularly in the financial sector and among providers of information and telecommunications network services. In-depth analysis of differing perceptions and the role played by corporate management in creating these initiatives could provide important lessons regarding how to establish a broader private-sector response to information infrastructure protection challenges.

Management initiative clearly played an important role in establishing efforts within the national security community in the 1990s to deal with defensive strategic information warfare concerns. The general potential for information technology to change the nature of future conflicts was recognized early during the Clinton administration by the senior DOD leadership, including Secretary of Defense William Perry.[288] Other senior DOD officials, including Vice Chairman of the Joint Chiefs of Staff William Owens and the director of the Office of Net Assessment, Andy Marshall, aggressively advocated concepts such as the "systems of systems" and "the revolution in military affairs" designed to leverage information technologies for U.S military advantage. These conceptual developments culminated in the issuance in 1996 of *Joint Vision 2010* and the drive for "information superiority."

This generally forward-looking approach by DOD management helped to identify the vulnerability of the DII to digital disruption and promoted DOD engagement in efforts to improve defenses in the last decade. Senior officials in the ASD/C3I, the Joint Staff J-6, DISA, NSA, and the Air Force directed efforts to implement vulnerability assessments of DOD's assets. Efforts sponsored by the ASD/C3I and the Office of Net Assessment such as RAND's "The Day After in Cyberspace . . ." began to address the broader aspects of strategic information warfare. The DOD leadership also directed the Defense Science Board to conduct the very important 1994 and 1996 task force studies that provided baselines for organizational initiatives such as formation of the Information Warfare Executive Board and red team exercises such as Eligible Receiver. Within the ASD/C3I, the DOD has endeavored to conduct outreach efforts to the private sector since 1996 through the formation of the Highlands Group, which brings together senior officials from the U.S. government and individuals from the information technology industry and academe and other leading intellectuals to identify and discuss emerging security concerns resulting from the rapid advance of the information age.[289] The efforts of the Joint Staff, especially the J-6, led to the clear identification of the requirement for a cooperative effort between the government and the private sector to create strategic information warfare defenses in official U.S. military doctrine.

The changes in DOD leadership in early 1997 and the focus on the PCCIP caused a brief lull in management initiative to enhance the department's emphasis on defensive strategic information warfare. The Defense Reform Initiative released in the fall of 1997 recommended the breakup of the ASD/C3I organization into other elements of the Secretary of Defense staff.[290] However, this breakup never occurred. The attention of the Deputy Secretary of Defense, John Hamre, and the ASD/C3I, Art Money, have clearly returned ability to defend the DII to the top of the defense agenda. The formation of the JTF-CND and changes to the Unified Command Plan endeavor to address strategic defense concerns. Within the ASD/C3I organization, the Defense Information Assurance Program was created in 1998 to manage DOD information assurance efforts and support PDD 63 implementation.[291]

Within the rest of the federal government, the Department of Justice and FBI have also provided a significant push since 1995 to address the U.S. need to establish information infrastructure defenses as part of its role in identifying and leading national critical infrastructure protection efforts. Attorney General Janet Reno and FBI Director William Freeh have campaigned to raise awareness of threats posed by cybercrime and cyberterrorism. Deputy Attorney General Jamie Gorelick was appointed as the head of the interagency Critical Infrastructure Working Group and led its efforts, which led to the establishment of the PCCIP.[292] The formation of the National Infrastructure Protection Center in March 1998 provided evidence of the continuing Department of Justice and FBI willingness to commit resources to these efforts as the 1990s drew to a close. The NIPC plays a central role in the PDD 63 construct but its focus on computer crime may leave larger critical infrastructure protection concerns unattended.

At the highest levels of U.S. government, the president and Congress have undertaken initiatives to address the protection of the United States against strategic information attacks while simultaneously making this task more complex through initiatives to serve other purposes. Congressional initiatives in the 1990s, especially in the Senate, highlighted national-level concerns about inadequate efforts to protect information infrastructures and motivated presidential action. Yet the much more notable passage of the 1996 Telecommunications Act ignored national security dimensions in its restructuring of activity in the U.S. telecommunications sector. The act's provisions increased access to U.S. information infrastructures while reducing the government's visibility regarding the activities of operators of these infrastructures.

Within the White House, a similar disconnect has occurred in the pursuit of initiatives that affect the use and protection of U.S. information infrastructures. The NII, GII, and electronic commerce initiatives to promote open, privately owned and controlled, rapidly advancing information infrastructures for economic gain and social improvement have avoided addressing national security concerns in a fashion very similar to the 1996 Telecommunications Act. The federal government's response to Y2K initially was independent of strategic information warfare and critical infrastructure protection efforts. In the fall of 1999, however, the GAO and others began to stress how Y2K remediation and consequence management efforts might provide insight to those trying to create defensive capabilities to respond to cyberattacks.[293] The lessons of Y2K for strategic information warfare are addressed in the epilogue. Initial calls by the Department of Defense, the Security Policy Board, and the NSTAC for the nation to grapple with growing awareness of national information infrastructure vulnerabilities were not met with aggressive action by the administration. Yet the formation of the CIWG and the expansion of its efforts to deal with cyberthreats indicated an emerging willingness to engage these vulnerabilities. The formation of the PCCIP followed by the issuance of PDD 63, under pressure both from Congress and within the Executive Branch, constitutes the single major initiative launched by the administration to address protection of U.S. information infrastructures. However, both the PCCIP and PDD 63 shied away from acknowledging difficult trade-offs in establishing strong strategic-level defenses. By focusing concern only on critical infrastructures, the directive avoided grappling with the issue of how to improve the security and reliability of the underlying technologies that constitute U.S. information infrastructures. Moreover, PDD 63 relied on improved awareness to establish voluntary participation and resource allocation by private-sector owner-operators, despite a poor historical record for such an approach.

The debate over encryption policy shines the brightest light on the apparent schizophrenia within the U.S. political leadership in the 1990s concerning information infrastructure protection issues. Despite a dominant emphasis on U.S. commercial competitiveness in other industries and the widespread belief that unrestricted use of encryption would improve information infrastructure security, the Clinton administration continued to support policies that industry saw as retarding widespread commercial development and implementation of encryption technology.

Establishing strategic information warfare defenses demands that U.S. national leadership directly address the difficult trade-offs involved in information infrastructure development. Steps toward accomplishing this could include increasing government research and development into key technologies that prioritize both improved use and protection of information systems and networks. Motivating protective action by infrastructure operators and users in government and the private sector, however, could require steps perceived to constrain efficiency and economic gains as well as infringe on privacy rights. So far, this conflict has largely been avoided by allowing issue advocates to march along separate paths. When their paths cross, however, as over encryption policy, voices become strident and compromise difficult. Aggressive implementation of PDD 63 in the near term would provide evidence of national leadership commitment to improved protection of U.S. information infrastructures. Over the longer term, establishing effective information warfare defenses will require the political leadership to engage a broader range of stakeholders concerned with the evolution of information infrastructures in a manner that allows reasonable trade-offs between divergent goals.

Technological Expertise: Difficulties in Developing, Sustaining, and Allocating a Limited Resource

As with waging strategic air warfare, developing organizations with the proper sets of technological expertise provided a fundamental challenge in establishing strategic information warfare capabilities in the 1990s. Although the availability of digital information technologies and the knowledge necessary to use them has expanded dramatically over the past couple of decades, the availability of human expertise remains a constraint throughout government and in the private sector. Given the development of advanced information infrastructures without strong security and reliability features, network providers and infrastructures users face the task of establishing expertise in identifying vulnerabilities and implementing protective measures. As operation of advanced information infrastructures becomes increasingly decentralized, conducting defensive efforts at lower levels of organizations could improve evaluation of fundamental use versus protection trade-offs. Yet if organizations faced with protecting information infrastructures have very limited access to the expertise necessary to implement defensive technologies, centralization of defensive resources may be required. Struggling with this dilemma has played a major role in efforts, including national-level plans, to protect a wide range of U.S. information infrastructures.

The best available information on this challenge comes from the national security sector. Efforts by DISA and the military services to understand vulnerabilities and protect information infrastructures have evolved through the use of a "center of excellence" approach. Limited available technological expertise has been pooled in centralized organizations such as the DOD CERT and the service information warfare centers to provide computer emergency response teams, vulnerability assessment cadres, red team capabilities, and countermeasures engineering sections. These centers have brought together personnel with expertise in networking and computer programming to address specific defensive tasks for parent organizations. Many of these efforts have made significant progress in establishing baseline vulnerability data, creating monitoring systems, and reducing impacts of digital intrusion and disruption.

However, employing centralized pools of technological expertise to protect the large, diverse information infrastructures of the Department of Defense and the military services presents major challenges. In the case of Air Force Information Warfare Center, for example, the organization has responsibility for a very broad range of activities, including tasks such as electronic warfare countermeasures development and countering tactical deception, in addition to digital warfare. Also, the number of personnel assigned to deal with digital warfare remains relatively limited given the breadth of the information infrastructures they are assigned to protect. As of December 1999, the AFIWC Countermeasures Engineering Team responsible for managing the development of new defensive technologies for the protection of Air Force information infrastructures had a staff of fewer than twenty people. Additionally, the DOD CERT community has generally focused its efforts on monitoring day-to-day activity and responding to specific, limited incidents. Interviews with personnel in these organizations indicate that efforts to employ available expertise to provide indications and warning, attack assessment, and management of recovery and response operations in the face of a strategic information warfare attack have yet to develop fully. The JTF-CND, collocated with the DISA CERT, was established in late 1998 to help accomplish this mission. However, the JTF employs less than twenty-five full-time personnel and is focused on protection of the DII, not the broader U.S. NII.

These information warfare organizations also do not have direct responsibility for the protection and operation of defense information infrastructures overall. As a result, the DOD and services have endeavored to make operators and users of their information infrastructures more capable of self-protection against digital attack. The services have developed awareness and education programs to explain the threat posed by digital intruders. Significant initiatives have aimed at improving the technological skills of systems and network administrators to conduct protective efforts. DOD has come to recognize that establishing strong capabilities for large-scale information defenses requires a balance between centralization and decentralization of technological expertise. Centers such as those at DISA and in the individual military services are needed to perform large-scale vulnerability assessment, develop technological fixes, manage efforts to improve technological foundations for defense, and provide assistance when incidents occur. Diffusing expertise among infrastructure operators and users is necessary to implement vulnerability reduction efforts, improve indications and warning of attacks, mitigate damage during incidents, and conduct recovery operations.

Yet despite efforts to establish and diffuse relevant technological expertise within the DOD, overall evaluations of the state of defensive expertise for protecting the DII have remained highly pessimistic.[294] These assessments address concerns both at the level of assuring local information infrastructure protection and in producing a core of highly developed technological expertise to implement overall defensive efforts as well.

Numerous studies and expert analyses continue to lament the generally poor state of training and expertise within DOD systems and of network administrators. Illustrative are the following examples cited by the General Accounting Office in 1996:

- In interviews with individuals responsible for operating and securing DOD computer networks, sixteen of the twenty-four interviewees told the GAO they lacked the time, experience, or training to do their job properly.

- An Air Force survey of systems administrators found that 325 of 709 respondents were unaware of procedures for reporting vulnerabilities and incidents, 249 of 515 had not received any network security training, and 377 of 706 reported that their security responsibilities were ancillary duties.

- The Army noted in its August 1995 Command and Control Protect Program Management Plan that it had approximately 4,000 systems administrators, but few of these had received formal training in security issues.[295]

This underdevelopment of expertise at the systems administrator level results from the lack of resources for training and the low priority assigned to information systems security concerns at all levels of DOD management.

Although efforts to address these concerns were underway within DOD by the late 1990s, the inability to attract and retain skilled personnel remained a critical limitation.[296]

The inadequate opportunities for personnel to develop substantial technological expertise related to defensive information warfare and inadequate rewards for doing so constitutes a significant problem. Junior Air Force officers interviewed by the author at the AFIWC and DISA indicated that the lack of a specific career field dealing with digital information warfare was a major problem. As communications officers, these officers felt career advancement would require them to move out of activities related to digital warfare and infrastructure protection into other areas. Managers in organizations in the DOD responsible for digital defenses have highlighted the difficulty of retaining personnel within the defense establishment once they have been provided with training in information networking and information security that allowed them to earn substantially greater salaries in the private sector. Congressional staff reported during the "Security in Cyberspace" hearings that "[i]t has become commonplace for government agencies involved in information security to lose their best and brightest personnel to private firms engaged in the same type of mission. While there is nothing wrong with a natural migration of civil servants to the private sector, numerous persons within government and in the private sector have acknowledged that the "brain drain" of government experts to private industry seriously hampers our government's ability to respond to computer attacks."[297] An example of this phenomenon is the Wheel Group Corporation in San Antonio, Texas, comprised primarily of former Air Force officers and defense contractors who previously worked for the AFCERT. Wheel Group provides network security services, conducts vulnerability assessments, and develops network monitoring tools for commercial organizations.[298] Cisco Systems bought out Wheel Group in 1998 to improve its ability to provide router technologies with improved security. In terms of developing a larger organizational technological capacity for defending the broader range of U.S. information infrastructures, diffusion of such technological expertise out of national security into the private sector needs to receive greater attention. A mechanism for developing human expertise within the federal government, particularly the DOD, may even prove useful to the nation as a whole, especially if the government is unwilling to directly support or mandate protective efforts in the private sector. Also, the government has begun to turn to the private sector as a source for information and network security tools and technologies such as network monitoring systems. Developing public-private webs of expertise and contacts may prove increasingly important in achieving cross-sectoral technology assimilation and diffusion.

The ability of other federal departments and agencies to protect their own information infrastructures, as well as assist the private sector, is generally less well developed than that in the Department of Defense. When asked to provide information about its internal information security and assurance effort in 1996, FEMA responded that a single individual supervised this activity for the entire agency.[299] A State Department Inspector General audit of the department's unclassified mainframe system found that the department had no security plan and that many computer systems administration functions relied on foreign nationals because of salary constraints. Other federal computer security programs have been found to be understaffed, and federal computer security personnel generally have very little experience or training.[300] Career progression and brain drain problems also exist outside DOD. As previously discussed, NIST's capability to perform its assigned role to lead efforts to provide security to unclassified federal government information, systems, and networks has been hampered by the limited number of personnel and resources assigned to it. NIST created a federal CERT capability in 1996 to improve responses to computer intrusion incidents within the federal government. NIST relies on the national CERT at Carnegie Mellon for day-to-day operations, however, further taxing the limited resources of this organization.[301] These constraints have led NIST to require reimbursement for CERT services from the organizations that use them, which creates a disincentive to requesting organizations to seek assistance.

Although limited availability of information about commercial-sector efforts in this area make a comprehensive review impossible, a similar situation generally seems to exist in the commercial sector with regard to establishing technological expertise. Pooled centers of information security expertise have developed both within organizations and as independent operating entities. Further efforts to understand the development of technical expertise for defending private-sector information infrastructures need to examine the extent of development and effectiveness of these nongovernmental webs of information and expertise.

Overall assessments of efforts to develop technological expertise for information infrastructure defense within the private sector also find the same limitations as those faced by agencies in the federal government in meeting the challenges posed by increasingly sophisticated attackers and the growing reliance on more open networks.[302] The security awareness and skills of most systems administrators remain underdeveloped, thereby creating significant vulnerabilities in most private-sector systems and networks. Managers in organizations that are network providers or infrastructure users face an allocation trade-off in using an increasingly limited, expensive pool of people to enhance their profit-making operations or utilizing the expertise to provide information protection and assurance. According to a 1997 Computer Security Institute study, most commercial organizations spend only 1–3 percent of their investment in information technology on protection.[303]

Individuals and organizations concerned about inadequacy of private-sector efforts consistently highlight the need to develop an information security profession. The lack of educational programs and widely accepted credentials for individuals involved in information security has hampered efforts to employ personnel effectively. The Software Engineering Institute stressed the problem to the PCCIP in 1997:

> Building, operating and maintaining secure networks are difficult tasks; and there are few educational and training programs that prepare people to perform them. Training will also enhance the ability of administrators and managers to use available technology for configuration management, network management, auditing, intrusion detection, firewalls, guards, wrappers and cryptography. . . . In the long-term, there should be undergraduate-level and master's-level specialties in network and information security.[304]

Programs of the Software Engineering Institute have stressed the need to develop engineering expertise that provides more solid technological foundations for information infrastructures. The limited programs instituted by the institute to provide training and materials to engineers to improve software development processes are resource-constrained and must contend with the rapid pace of technological advance in trying to develop materials for such purposes. Additionally, these programs are focused on improving engineering programs at universities, not at the engineers in commercial information technology firms such as Microsoft.[305] Despite continuing calls for establishing a professional cadre and credentials in information security and engineering development, limited progress was made on this front during the 1990s. On a positive note, evidence of growing capability in this realm exists. James Madison University has established a master's degree program in information security in conjunction with the National Security Agency's Information Systems Security Organization. Ideally, additional educational initiatives and programs related to information security called for under PDD 63 will be implemented over the next decade.

Employing expertise to establish strategic information warfare defenses competes with a high demand in the private sector for people with information technology skills. A limited pool of expertise creates prioritization challenges at many levels: information security efforts within organizations; allocation of human resources for coordinating and assisting in national defensive assessment, warning, and response; and the creation of new educational programs. The costs of developing and retaining personnel to defend information infrastructures may make achieving desirable decentralization of defensive efforts difficult. Mechanisms to effectively disseminate and diffuse knowledge accumulated in centers of excellence would improve the organizational capabilities for large-scale information infrastructure protection. In addition, establishing organizations in the Guard and reserve components of the armed forces to quickly mobilize and deploy technological expertise for defensive tasks may provide a means to augment day-to-day use of limited expertise and protective efforts in response to a strategic information warfare attack.

Learning Ability: Threats, Maps, and Developing a Deeper Level of Understanding

The U.S. military establishment increasingly has recognized that adjusting to the post–Cold War world and conducting military operations in the information age will require increased organizational learning ability. Those who have identified the emergence of a revolution in military affairs have recognized the need to adapt doctrine and organizations to leverage the advantages of the information age. These themes have become enshrined in official declarations such as *Joint Vision 2010* calling for "organizations and processes agile enough to exploit emerging technologies and respond to diverse threats."[306] The National Defense Panel went even further to stress the necessity of organizational adaptation and learning to achieve transformational changes in U.S. military forces. These visions encourage experimentation, the utility of conducting exercises and war games, and allowing leaders to risk failure in developing new systems and approaches. The growing emphasis on attaining information superiority and conducting information warfare/information operations provides an indication that the U.S. military establishment will endeavor to adapt and learn in providing national security in a rapidly changing international environment.

Important progress has been made in the U.S. military in establishing capabilities for strategic information warfare defenses through the use of vulnerability testing and simulated exercises. Data from the vulnerability testing programs conducted by DISA and the Air Force indicate that previously tested sites have become more difficult to penetrate. These testing programs also indicate that fixes are implemented to reduce vulnerabilities identified through such testing,[307] which provides organizations with a learning mechanism about information infrastructure vulnerabilities and implementation of improved protective measures. Yet the Air Force has noted a disturbing trend in these otherwise generally positive data. In the mid-1990s, Air Force on-line survey data indicated that the already limited reporting by sites of the type of intrusion activity detected during testing had actually declined.[308] If this trend indicates that improved awareness of digital intrusion threats creates a perception among local systems and network administrators of increased culpability if problems are discovered, such an assessment process could raise learning barriers to efforts to comprehensively identify vulnerabilities and the scope of malicious activity. Additionally, Air Force survey results from the late 1990s indicated stagnation in learning at the base level concerning how to defend properly against digital attacks.

Conducting exercises based on digital attacks has played a very significant role in heightening awareness and motivating senior DOD managers and the political leadership to address the protection of defense information infrastructures. Specific demonstrations such the Joint Staff's Eligible Receiver exercise have provided more concrete object lessons of exactly how adversaries could disrupt U.S. military operations through use of digital strategic information warfare. The RAND "The Day After . . ." scenarios provided illustrations of the policy challenges created by broader strategic information warfare attacks involving civilian information infrastructures as well as lessons for incorporation into the efforts of the Department of Defense, the NIPC, and the National Coordinator for Security, Information Protection and Counterterrorism.

Vulnerability assessments and red team testing have also emerged as learning tools in commercial sector. Only limited aggregated data regarding the extent of such efforts has become publicly available, however, because of the continuing reluctance of private-sector organizations to divulge information that could create legal liability or prove harmful to their reputation. Commercial-sector leaders have become involved in the larger efforts at assessing information infrastructure vulnerabilities and protection needs through activities such as those sponsored by the NSTAC, NCS, RAND Corporation, and the PCCIP. PDD 63 stresses the important role played by private-sector participation.

The learning ability of those responsible for defending the United States from strategic digital attack has also been constrained by limited efforts so far to conduct detailed assessments of the actual degree of reliance of key sectors and organizations on their information infrastructures. Although accidents, hacker incidents, results of vulnerability surveys, and weaknesses identified by exercises point out specific types of problems within governmental and private-sector infrastructures, fundamental questions remain unanswered about the significance of such vulnerabilities. Malicious attackers, organizations conducting vulnerability assessments, and even managers of monitoring efforts may all have limited knowledge of the functions of the systems targeted by digital attacks. As discussed in chapter 2, the conduct of effective risk management of an information infrastructure requires an evaluation of the infrastructure's value as well as its potential vulnerabilities and potential threats to it. Within the DOD, efforts to "map" the information networks and their import have began in the 1990s, but only subsequent to the hue and cry about massive vulnerability within the DII. The Joint Chiefs of Staff established requirements for the commanders of the U.S. Unified Commands to conduct assessments of their infrastructure dependencies in 1996. The Air Force has also implemented a program requiring that Base Network Control Centers map the use of information infrastructures at individual Air Force installations. Interviews with managers involved with both programs indicate that these mapping efforts still had a long way to go, as the decade drew to a close, to comprehensively identify the resources and their relative significance within defense information infrastructures.[309] Although managed by organizations responsible for protecting the DII within the DOD, these mapping efforts require the network providers and infrastructure users who operate these information infrastructures to expend time and resources to identify specific dependencies and evaluate their significance. Therefore, mapping efforts involve trade-offs between the use and protection of information resources. Less data is available regarding the conduct of information infrastructure mapping in other government and private-sector organizations. Mapping efforts also confront the challenges of rapid information infrastructure evolution identified in chapter 1. The validity and value of a given information resource and reliance map as a tool for defensive resource prioritization will atrophy quickly over time, and dynamic means are necessary for updating and disseminating information between increasingly distributed sets of operators, users, and defenders. As of the end of 1999, nascent efforts to establish strategic information warfare defense were limited by constraints on melding information about technological vulnerabilities with underdeveloped knowledge about which systems, networks, and activities are most important. Mapping information infrastructure use and evolution will provide very important learning tools for defensive efforts.

Last, establishing effective information infrastructure mapping and defenses will require defenders of specific systems and networks to understand relationships of those specific systems and networks to larger information infrastructures as well as their dependencies upon other types of infrastructure. The DOD has recognized its fundamental reliance on the DII as part of larger national and global information infrastructures but has yet to develop sufficient learning ability to track the technological trajectories affecting these infrastructures and the organizations responsible for their evolution and operation. Efforts such as those of the ASD/C3I Highlands Group to bring together individuals and organizations from across many sectors to develop understanding of likely future technological and social trends provides a model of the mechanisms required to promote the requisite understanding of information infrastructure interrelationships and interdependencies. Yet the great complexity of this task more often has resulted in DOD recommendations to focus protective efforts on establishing a "minimal essential information infrastructure" or simply to focus on protecting the DII. Such recommendations leave to higher authorities the more difficult learning tasks required to effectively institute national information infrastructure management and defenses.[310] The OSTP and PCCIP have more aggressively advocated the need to understand linkages across infrastructure sectors, especially between information and electric power infrastructures, and have made recommendations to improve learning capacity in these areas. Establishing learning ability about the technological trajectories of advanced information infrastructures will prove fundamental to the ability to effectively guide research and development efforts geared to establishing improved U.S. defensive strategic information warfare capabilities. An understanding of the evolution of organizational responsibilities and cross-sectoral dependencies will be required to properly assess overall national levels of risk and properly allocate the burden of defense among the changing array of stakeholders.

Organizations with the ability to provide learning synergies and central coordination across different infrastructure sectors have developed slowly. Since the early 1990s, a growing number of government studies, congressional investigations, and outside critiques have identified the need for improved cooperation between the public and private sectors to enable implementation of effective defensive responses to digital threats to U.S. information infrastructures. At the end of 1999, the problem no longer remained one of recognizing the need to improve the learning ability within organizations that protect information infrastructures. Rather, competing priorities and the absence of a concrete manifestation of a sufficiently compelling threat resulted in the absence of the resource investment and managerial support necessary for developing requisite expertise to assess information infrastructure vulnerability or establish organizations to achieve information sharing and coordination. Effective implementation of the PDD 63 construct would provide positive evidence about the nation's learning ability regarding requirements to protect its information infrastructures.

The U.S. Capability for Strategic Information Warfare in the Late 1990s: Evaluating Progress and Trade-Offs

In the early 1990s, the leaders of the U.S. national security community faced rapidly changing strategic circumstances. The nation had emerged victorious from the Cold War and assumed a position of leadership in the global advance into the information age. The U.S. military, and society as a whole, began to invest ever more heavily in information technology and its underlying infrastructures as means of improving efficiency and gaining competitive advantage. As the decade progressed, the potential challenges confronting a superpower reliant on information infrastructures when conducting its economic and military affairs also became increasingly evident.

The emergence of highly interconnected, computer-driven infrastructures to process, transmit, and store information in the last two decades has created the possibility of a new form of warfare based on digital attack and defense. Willingness on the part of the U.S. military establishment to formally recognize the possibility of strategic information warfare has emerged slowly. Regarding offensive operations, U.S. military doctrine has stressed employing a wide range of information warfare techniques to improve support for conventional military operations. The doctrinal development regarding information warfare/operations includes the use of means such as psychological operations and deception geared to achieving perception management along with direct physical, electromagnetic, and digital attack to disrupt information infrastructures. This breadth of concern continues to blur analyses of what constitutes the significantly different aspects of strategic information warfare/operations. The national security establishment has recognized the potential to use digital attacks to gain leverage over centers of gravity distinct from traditional battlefield operations but lacks doctrinal or organizational advocacy for conducting independent strategic information warfare operations as a vital means of securing the nation's interest.

The lack of public information about U.S. organizations and technologies for offensive strategic information warfare make it difficult to empirically evaluate progress in creating such capabilities. Yet the analysis outlined in chapters 2 and 3 indicates substantial challenges confront such an effort, similar to those facing the creation of strategic bombardment capabilities in the period between the two world wars.

On the defensive side of information warfare, the U.S. security community has recognized the significant threat posed by digital attacks to both traditional military operations and the nation's well-being. Yet national security doctrine has avoided addressing the fundamental role played by the private sector in the creation of vulnerabilities in the nation's information infrastructures. Statements regarding the threat posed to the nation's information infrastructures by digital warfare lump together a very wide range of threats without adequately distinguishing the relative likelihood and risks posed by different categories. Most assessments concentrate on what U.S. adversaries could potentially disrupt, with very little attention devoted to understanding underlying political objectives of possible adversaries, the degree to which disruption would cause serious damage, or the management of response and recovery efforts after an initial attack. The U.S. government has instituted laws, regulations, and public initiatives that work at cross-purposes to expressed concerns about protecting the nation's infrastructures against cyberattacks. The private sector remains largely unmotivated to address its role in strategic information warfare defensive efforts.

Capabilities for strategic information warfare defense have developed slowly. "We are vulnerable" has been a constant refrain for those advocating improved defensive efforts since the early 1990s. Yet for most of that decade the U.S. lacked an aggressive approach to establishing mechanisms to orchestrate coordination and capabilities across the wide range of government and private-sector actors who would have to conduct strategic information warfare defense. The construct outlined by PDD 63 in the spring of 1998 provided a good start on which to base future development of national-level protection against digital attacks. However, effective implementation of the directive will continue to buck difficult forces. Little support has developed for transformative organizational change or the heavy resource allocation necessary to establish more robust defensive strategic information warfare capabilities.

Within the government, and certainly in the private sector, the government's hands-off approach to information infrastructure development has clear benefits that no one wants to constrain. Consensus building about trade-offs and cost burdens to improve protective efforts has proven a difficult and lengthy process, especially the inclusion of reluctant new constituencies, such as software producers. The approach used in the 1990s may establish a level of redundancy and adaptability on its own, but inadequate technological tools and organizational coordination impede measurement of these properties. Also, most analyses of the challenges posed by digital attacks have dealt with improving defenses against lower-level threats such as espionage and anonymous terrorism, which makes determinations of legal boundaries, governmental role in infrastructure defense, and employing offensive military capabilities in a measured response to provocations more difficult. The strategic digital warfare envisioned in the analysis in this book may well involve adversaries whose involvement in attacks is distinguishable. Limited U.S. organizational capabilities to defend against such attacks have developed. However, the actual large-scale vulnerability and robustness of the range of U.S. information infrastructure centers of gravity to such attacks remains unclear. The possibility of employing other military means to deter and respond to strategic information warfare waged against the United States may also affect the appropriate level of defensive efforts.

A comparison to the evolution of strategic airpower capabilities in the period between World War I and World War II may help put into perspective progress in the 1990s regarding strategic information warfare capabilities. Strong advocates for organizational independence pushed development of U.S. airpower between the two world wars. During a fifteen-year period, the Army air arm created an offensive strategic air doctrine in advance of the technological means and organizational structures to wage the war envisioned by the doctrine. Technological and organizational developments for offensive strategic air warfare capabilities were constrained by a national security establishment that lacked incentives to devote limited resources to developing such capabilities or to undergo transformational changes. Development of defensive capabilities languished because of the lack of a clear threat and leadership commitment to the doctrinal and technological superiority of the offense. After more than two decades of endeavoring to improve the Army air arm, the United States would enter World War II with an underdeveloped capability for strategic air warfare.

In the second half of the 1990s, the subject of strategic information warfare provoked a great deal of discussion within the U.S. national security establishment, but capabilities did not emerge to make it a dominant new means of waging war. Offensively, strategic information warfare capabilities evolved without a clear target, given the limited vulnerability of U.S. adversaries to digital attacks. Also, no corps of specialists, such as the airmen who led the development of U.S. strategic bombing doctrine, has taken up the sword of digitally based warfare. On the defensive side, the significance of the information warfare mission has become increasingly clear but efforts to establish organizational technological capabilities still lack adequate support. The new environment for waging defensive digital warfare requires development of a supportive institutional context involving not only the traditional national security establishment but also the private sector. Simply sorting out the appropriate roles and coordinating mechanisms necessary to bring the diverse range of stakeholders together has absorbed much of the effort devoted to establishing strategic information warfare defenses. Insufficient demand-pull motivation has meant that many stakeholders have avoided substantial investment or even involvement in the process of orchestrating U.S. national information infrastructure protection. Efforts to understand the significance of digital warfare threats and educate those at risk have constituted most of the effort to establish increased management initiative. An adequate cadre of technological experts to create and operate secure, robust advanced information infrastructures has yet to emerge in either the national security establishment or the private sector. The learning ability of organizations tasked with strategic information warfare missions has suffered from underdeveloped bridges between sets of human expertise, experiential lessons, and technological developments present in different sectors of activity.

The United States has taken an extended period to align the facilitating factors necessary to develop strategic warfare capabilities, offensive or defensive. After World War I, the requisite confluence of doctrine, organizations, and technology to achieve the visions of strategic bombardment advocates was not achieved until the mid-1930s. Even these capabilities were severely hampered by unanticipated flaws when later tested in World War II. At the end of the 1990s, efforts to develop strategic information warfare capabilities had existed for an even shorter time. The U.S. has undergone only very limited development of doctrine, organizations, and technologies necessary to provide capabilities for strategic information warfare defense. Yet if one measures progress only from the early 1990s, past experience indicates that the record of progress should not be evaluated too harshly. Ongoing efforts provide hope that improved capabilities will emerge as the United States moves further into the twenty-first century.

Suggested Additional Sources

National Research Council. *Computers at Risk: Safe Computing in the Information Age.* Washington, DC: National Academy Press, 1991.
Conducted in the wake of the 1988 Internet worm incident, this study outlines with great clarity how the growing reliance on, and interconnection of, information systems would pose risks for our society. The study also does a much better job than almost any of the many that followed

in detailing how the technological foundations of advanced information infrastructures deter-mine their vulnerability and outlining the difficulties in motivating commercial technology pro-ducers to place greater emphasis on security.

Defense Science Board Task Force. *Information Architecture for the Battlefield.* Washington, DC: Department of Defense, October 1994. Defense Science Board Task Force. *Information Warfare—Defense.* Washington, DC: Department of Defense, November 1996.
Together these two DSB reports provided much of the direction for DOD information warfare efforts in the mid-1990s. The 1994 report covered a greater scope of concerns than the title indi-cates, including making the distinction between "information in war," focused on improving traditional war-fighting operations, and "information warfare," emerging as a new form of warfare conducted over digital networks. The 1996 report focused more closely on the chal-lenges of defending the defense information infrastructure.

Joint Staff. *Joint Vision 2010—America's Military: Preparing for Tomorrow.* Washington, DC: Joint Staff, 1996.
The culmination of a major effort to rethink how to shape the U.S. military to fight future wars, Joint Vision 2010 remained a touchstone for planning throughout the rest of the 1990s. The document stresses the importance of achieving information superiority as a enabling condition for U.S. military success in future wars.

General Accounting Office. *Computer Security: Virus Highlights Need for Improved Internet Security Management.* Washington, DC: Government Printing Office, June 1989. *Computer Security: Hackers Penetrate DOD Computer Systems.* Washington, DC: GAO/TIMTEC-92-5, 20 November 1991. *Information Security: Computer Attacks at Department of Defense Pose Increasing Risks.* Washington, DC: GAO/AIMD-96-84, May 1996; *Information Security: Serious Weaknesses Place Critical Federal Operations and Assets at Risk.* Washington, DC: GAO/AIMD-98-92, 23 September 1998. *Critical Infra-structure Protection: Comprehensive Strategy Can Draw on Year 2000 Experiences.* Wash-ington, DC: GAO/AMID-00-01, 20 September 1999.
This series of GAO reports has proved crucial to motivating congressional and Executive Branch action to acknowledge and respond to risks posed by computer system vulnerabilities and dis-ruptions. These reports provide background on key computer intrusion incidents and the efforts of federal departments and agencies to deal with them, facilitating an improved debate on the proper policy and resource investment strategies to deal with these concerns.

President's Commission on Critical Infrastructure Protection. *Critical Foundations: Protecting America's Infrastructures.* Washington, DC: President's Commission on Critical Infra-structure Protection, October 1997.
The final report based on the findings of the eighteen-month-long inquiry conducted by the PCCIP. The commission's report brought together a description of the cyberthreat to U.S. infra-structures, detailed examination of U.S. reliance on, and vulnerabilities of, identified critical infrastructures and a comprehensive array of policy proposals to address the problems. Its recommendations stressed the crucial need to establish a government-private partnership to succeed in national cyberdefense. The report also provided the baseline for the deliberations that resulted in PDD 63.

National Defense Panel. *Transforming Defense* Arlington, VA: National Defense Panel, December 1997.
The NDP report addressed homeland defense and information warfare in the context of whole-sale efforts to reform U.S. defense efforts to adapt to a post–Cold War world. The report's rec-ommendations were a major force behind the changes in the 1999 Unified Command Plan that realigned command responsibilities and included giving the U.S. Space Command responsibil-ity for defending the department's computer networks.

Oliver Morton. "The Softwar Revolution." *Economist*, 10 June 1995, Survey Section, 1–20.
Very illustrative of the popular press descriptions of information warfare. The article provides useful insight into key areas, such as the military's growing reliance on commercial information technology developments and the possibility of war waged by digital attacks on infrastructures. Morton's speculation about information warfare possibilities, unbounded by historical analysis or empirical data, also illuminates how hype surrounding the subject can make informed debate more difficult.

Esther Dyson. *Release 2.0: A Design for Living in the Digital Age.* New York: Broadway Books, 1997.
Dyson provides a broad overview of societal impacts of the digital age on individuals, business, and governments. Much broader in scope than books authored by leaders of information technology corporations, Dyson's book addresses how transition into an information age will affect work, communities, education, government, privacy, security, and treatment of intellectual property.

Hal Abelson et al. *The Risks of Key Recovery, Key Escrow and Trusted Third Party Encryption: A Report by an Ad-Hoc Group of Cryptographers and Computer Scientists.* Washington, DC: Center for Democracy and Technology, May 1997.
This report by a senior group of technologists involved with the U.S. encryption policy debates lays out the core policy issues in a manner that the layperson can understand. The report also clearly illustrates the implementation problems and risks involved with government-controlled, centralized encryption and key management schemes.

Office of Science and Technology Policy. *Cybernation: The American Infrastructure in the Information Age.* Washington, DC: The White House, April 1997.
This short report provides a sound approach to examining the impact of automation on and the complexity of interconnection in U.S. information infrastructures. The report discusses how this complexity may cause hidden vulnerabilities and enable cascading disruptive effects but also illuminates features of inherent robustness and adaptability possessed by such infrastructures.

Computer Security Institute/Federal Bureau of Investigation. *Computer Crime and Security Survey.* San Francisco: Computer Security Institute. (Survey results have been released annually 1996–1999.)
The most comprehensive survey effort so far to track computer security problems and responses in the private sector. As time progresses, the survey will also provide a much-needed perspective on how threats and responses evolve over time.

Web Sites

Center for Democracy and Technology ⟨www.cdt.org⟩, Electronic Frontier Foundation ⟨www.eff.org⟩, and Electronic Privacy Information Center ⟨www.epic.org⟩.
These sites provide extensive information on policy concerns related to privacy, especially material related to the encryption policy debate.

U.S. National Computer Emergency Response Team (CERT/CC) ⟨www.sei.org⟩ and Forum of Incident Response Teams ⟨www.first.org⟩.
The CERT site provides advisories regarding computer vulnerabilities, models for software engineering practices to improve reliability and security, information on courses offered by the Software Engineering Institute, research papers on concepts for survivable infrastructures, and evaluations of information security technologies. The FIRST site provides information on the forum's mission, sponsored information security events, and how to contact member organizations.

Joint Doctrine ⟨www.dtic.mil/doctrine⟩.
Provides official Joint Doctrine documents as well as links to doctrine sites of the military services.

National Infrastructure Protection Center ⟨www.fbi.nipc⟩.
Provides background on NIPC activities and advisories about cyberthreats to critical United States infrastructures.

Notes

1. The label comes primarily from Alan Campen, ed., *The First Information War* (Fairfax, VA: AFCEA International Press, 1992).

2. The story is best told in Bruce Sterling, *The Hacker Crackdown: Law and Order on the Electronic Frontier* (New York: Bantam Books, 1992).

3. See Gregory L. Vistica, "Cyberwar and Sabotage," *Newsweek*, 31 May 1999, 38; Robert Berwin, "Kosovo Ushered in Cyberwar," *Federal Computer Week*, 27 September 1999, 1; and Robert Wall, "USAF Expands Infowar Arsenal," *Aviation Week & Space Technology*, 15 November 1999, 102.

4. Paul F. Capasso, *Telecommunications and Information Assurance: America's Achilles' Heel?* (Cambridge, MA: Harvard University, Program as Information Resources Policy, March 1997), 11–13.

5. A good overview of this particular subject is provided in Seymour Goodman's *The Information Technologies and Defense: A Demand-Pull Assessment* (Palo, Alto, CA: Stanford University, Center for International Security and Arms Control, February 1996), section 2, "A Brief History of the Information Technologies in the Cold War," 3–6.

6. George H. Bolling, *AT&T and the Aftermath of Anti-Trust: Preserving Positive Command and Control* (Washington, DC: National Defense University Press, 1983).

7. President Jimmy Carter reinvigorated the NCS in the late 1970s with PD-39. Capasso, *Telecommunications and Information Assurance*, 20–23.

8. James B. Bean, Co-Chair, Wireless Services Task Force of the NSTAC, "The Role of the National Security Telecommunications Advisory Committee," in *National Security in the Information Age*, ed. James McCarthy (U.S. Air Force Academy, CO: Olin Institute, March 1996), 188.

9. See James Bamford, *The Puzzle Palace* (New York: Penguin Books, 1982); and George A. Brownell, *Origins and Development of the NSA* (Laguna Hills, CA: Aegean Park Press, 1981), for history of the NSA.

10. Greg Lipscomb, *Private and Public Defenses against Soviet Interception of U.S. Telecommunications: Problems and Policy Points* (Cambridge: Harvard University, Program on Information Resources Policy, P-79-3, 1979), 2.

11. Lipscomb, *Private and Public Defenses*, 13–18, details the activities of Congress during the 1970s related to NSA accountability and privacy. See Susan Landau and Whitfield Diffie, *Privacy on the Line: The Politics of Wire Tapping and Encryption* (Cambridge: MIT Press, 1998), 68–69, regarding concerns that led to the 1987 legislation.

12. This two-level characterization is based on Andrew W. Marshall, "Some Thoughts on Military Revolutions" (memorandum, Department of Defense, Office of Net Assessment, Washington, DC, August 1993), 3–4; and Thomas G. Manaken, "War in the Information Age," *Joint Forces Quarterly* no. 11 (Winter 1995–96): 34–39.

13. Joint Staff, *C4I for the Warrior: A Vision for C4I Interoperability* (Washington, DC: Joint Staff, January 1998), 20–21. See also Vice Admiral Arthur K. Cebrowski, Director, N6, Space,

Information Warfare, Command and Control Directorate, Headquarters, Department of the Navy, "Sea Change," *Surface Warfare*, November/December 1997, 5.

14. Brian E. Fredricks, Chief, Information Operations Division, Headquarters, Department of the Army, "Information Warfare at the Crossroads," *Joint Forces Quarterly* no. 17 (Summer 1997): 97. Fredricks comments on the prolonged lack of public details regarding information warfare policy guidance. Directive TS3600.1 was updated as S3600.1, "Information Operations," in December 1996.

15. Chairman of the Joint Chiefs of Staff, Memorandum of Policy 30, "Command and Control Warfare," Washington, DC, 8 March 1993. This MOP replaced "Command, Control and Communications Countermeasures," 17 July 1990.

16. John I. Alger, Dean of the National Defense University School of Information Warfare and Strategy, "Declaring Information War," *Jane's International Defense Review*, July 1996, 54.

17. The JC2WC was renamed the Joint Information Operations Center (JIOC) in October 1999 and resubordinated under the direction of the U.S. Space Command.

18. I used the Tofflers' book to co-teach a course with Gen. (ret) James McCarthy, "Strategy and Arms Control," in spring 1994 at the U.S. Air Force Academy. The following summer, Gen. McCarthy became the co-chair of the very influential Defense Science Board Task Force on Information Architecture for the Battlefield. Senior military and civilian leaders within the Department of Defense, such as the Army Chief of Staff, Gordon R. Sullivan, relied heavily on the Tofflers' model. See Gordon R. Sullivan and James M. Dubick, "War in the Information Age," *Military Review*, April 1994, 46–62.

19. Alvin and Heidi Toffler, *War and Anti-War: Survival at the Dawn of the 21st Century* (Boston: Little, Brown, 1993), 141.

20. Fredricks, "Information Warfare at the Crossroads," 98.

21. Timothy R. Sample, "New Techniques of Political and Economic Coercion," in *U.S. Intervention Policy for the Post–Cold War World*, ed. Arnold Kanter and Linton F. Brooks (New York: W. W. Norton, 1994), 168. Also see H. D. Arnold, J. Hukill, and J. Kennedy, "Targeting Financial Systems as Centers of Gravity—Low Intensity Conflict to No Intensity Conflict," *Defense Analysis*, September 1994, 181–208.

22. Gen. (ret.) James P. McCarthy, "Alternatives to the Use of Military Force: New Tools for a New World Order" in *John M. Olin Lecture Series in National Security and Defense Studies*, ed. Gen. (ret.) James P. McCarthy (U.S. Air Force Academy: Olin Foundation, 1994), 14.

23. General Accounting Office (GAO), *Computer Security: Hackers Penetrate DOD Computer Systems* (Washington, DC: GAO/T-IMTEC-92-5, November 1991).

24. Defense Information Systems Agency briefing, "Automated Systems Security Incident Support Team (ASSIST)," provided to author at DISA Headquarters, Arlington, VA, 4 August 1997.

25. A good summary is provided in GAO, *Information Security: Computer Attacks at the Department of Defense Pose Increasing Risks* (Washington, DC: GAO/AMID-96-84, May 1996), 22–25.

26. The significance of this incident was stressed in the author's interview with Lt. Gen. Kenneth Minihan, Director of the National Security Agency, Cambridge, MA, 14 November 1997. At the time of the incident, Minihan was the director of the Air Intelligence Agency, responsible for the Air Force Information Warfare Center that led the response to the incident. The incident was highlighted in numerous DOD and GAO studies conducted in 1994–1996.

27. DSB Task Force, *Information Architecture for the Battlefield* (Washington, DC: Department of Defense, October 1994), 24.

28. Author's interview with Capt. (USN) Richard O'Neill of ASD/C3I Information Operations office, Pentagon, Arlington, VA, 24 March 1998.

29. Roger M. Callahan, Director for Information Assurance, ASD/C3I, "Information Assurance: A Community Wide Challenge," *Information Technology Assurance Newsletter* 1, no. 1 (March 1997): 1.

30. From presentation by Robert L. Ayers, Chief, Information Warfare Division, Defense Information Warfare Agency, "Information Warfare Briefing," at Conflict in the Information Age Conference, held by the Air Force Institute for National Security Studies, Washington, D.C., 26 July 1995.

31. DSB Task Force, *Information Warfare—Defense* (Washington, DC: Department of Defense, November 1996).

32. DSB Task Force, *Information Warfare—Defense*, 2-2.

33. DSB Task Force, *Information Warfare—Defense*, 6-16.

34. Based on my interviews with the PCCIP Chairman and other PCCIP personnel in the summer of 1997.

35. As quoted in Jim Wolf, "FBI Traces Cyber Raids to Russia," *Reuters News Report*, 6 October 1999.

36. As quoted in Anne Plummer, "DOD Official Says Hackers Are More Sophisticated since Solar Sunrise," *Defense Information and Electronics Report* (22 October 1999): 1.

37. *Air Force Issues Book* (Washington, DC: Headquarters, Department of the Air Force, Office of Legislative Liaison, 1994), 30.

38. "AF Information Protection" briefing slides provided to the author at the Air Force Information Warfare Center, Kelly Air Force Base, TX, 31 July 1997.

39. Many analyses dealt with achieving superiority over adversaries in a time-based competition to conduct observe-orient-decide-act functions (outlined by John Boyd and known as the "OODA" loop). For example, see Edward Mann, "Desert Storm: The First Information War?" *Airpower Journal* 8, no. 4 (Winter 1994): 3–14; and Owen E. Jensen, "Information Warfare: Principles of Third Wave War," *Airpower Journal* 8, no. 4 (Winter 1994): 35–43.

40. Department of the Air Force, *Cornerstones of Information Warfare* (Washington, DC: Headquarters, Department of the Air Force, 1995). Although the document was not released until mid-1995, I was aware of the drafting process as early as November 1994.

41. Department of the Air Force, *Information Warfare* (Washington, DC: Headquarters, Department of the Air Force, 1996).

42. Department of the Air Force, *Air Force Basic Doctrine* (Maxwell Air Force Base, AL: Headquarters, Air Force Doctrine Center, September 1997).

43. Air Force Doctrine Document 2-5, *Information Operations* (Maxwell Air Force Base, AL: Headquarters, Air Force Doctrine Center, August 1998).

44. Sullivan and Dubick, "War in the Information Age," 61. See also Gordon R. Sullivan and Anthony M. Coroalles, *The Army in the Information Age* (Carlisle, PA: Army War College, Strategic Studies Institute, March 1995).

45. For detail on the Army's Force XXI plans, see Department of the Army, *Force XXI: America's Army of the 21st Century* (Fort Monroe, VA: Office of the Chief of Staff of the Army, Louisiana Maneuvers Task Force, 15 January 1995); and Mark Hanna, *Task Force XXI: The Army's Digital Experiment* (Washington, DC: National Defense University, INSS Strategic Forum no. 119, July 1997).

46. Department of the Army, *Decisive Victory: America's Power Projection Army* (Washington, DC: Headquarters, Department of the Army, October 1994), 20.

47. See *Strategy, Force Structure and Defense Planning for the Twenty-First Century* (Cambridge, MA: Institute for Foreign Policy Analysis, May 1997), 23–24.

48. Department of the Army, Field Manual 100-6, *Information Operations* (Washington, DC: Headquarters, Department of the Army, 27 August 1996). This field manual was updated in June 1999.

49. This conclusion was reinforced through the author's discussions with representatives of the Army staff and the Army's Land Information Warfare Activity in 1998–1999.

50. Department of the Navy, *Copernicus . . . Forward C4I for the 21st Century* (Washington, DC: Headquarters, Department of the Navy, 1990), 1–2.

51. Department of the Navy, *Sonata* (Washington, DC: Headquarters, Department of the Navy, 1994), 6.

52. Chief of Naval Operations, Operating Naval Instruction 3430.25, "Implementing Instruction for Information Warfare/Command and Control Warfare (IW/C2W)," Office of the Chief of Naval Operations, Washington, DC, 1 April 1994.

53. Department of the Navy, *Information Warfare Strategic Plan* (Washington, DC: Department of the Navy, 1998).

54. Bruce Wald and Alan Berman, *Information Operations and Information Warfare: N3/N5 Responsibilities and Opportunities* (Alexandria, VA: Center for Naval Analysis, June 1997), 10–11.

55. Quote from Marine Corps input to Joint Staff, *Information Warfare—Considerations*, A-49.

56. Joint Publication 1-01 can be found, along with all other approved Joint Doctrine publications, at the Joint Doctrine Web site ⟨www.dtic.mil/doctrine⟩.

57. Joint Publication 6-0, *Doctrine for C4 Systems Support to Joint Operations* (Washington, DC: Joint Staff, 30 May 1995).

58. Joint Staff, *Information Assurance: Legal, Regulatory, Policy and Organizational Considerations*, 4th ed. (Washington, DC: Joint Staff, August 1999).

59. Joint Publication 3-13.1, *Joint Doctrine for Command and Control Warfare* (Washington, DC: Joint Staff, January 1996).

60. Joint Staff, *Information Warfare—A Strategy for Peace—The Decisive Edge for War* (Washington, DC: Joint Staff, 1996).

61. Joint Staff, *Information Warfare—A Strategy for Peace*, 4.

62. Joint Staff, *Information Warfare—A Strategy for Peace*, 12.

63. Chairman of the Joint Chiefs of Staff Instruction (CJCSI) 6505.1A, "Defensive Information Warfare Implementation," Joint Staff, Washington, DC, 31 May 1996. This instruction has been updated, most recently in August 1998, as CJCSI 6510.01B, which changed the title to "Defensive Information Operations Implementation" but retains the same basic thrust.

64. Joint Staff, *Joint Vision 2010—America's Military: Preparing for Tomorrow* (Washington, DC: Joint Staff, 1996), 16.

65. See the entire issue of *Joint Forces Quarterly* no. 14 (Winter 1996/1997), which is devoted to analysis of, and service perspectives on, Joint Vision 2010. Both major planning efforts conducted in 1997 in the DOD's Quadrennial Defense Review and the congressionally sponsored National Defense Panel use Joint Vision 2010 as a principal reference point.

66. The tactical focus of Joint Vision 2010 is critiqued by Carl Builder, "Keeping the Strategic Flame," *Joint Forces Quarterly* no. 14 (Winter 1996/1997): 76–84.

67. Based on the author's interviews with Lt. Gen. Kenneth Minihan, Director, National Security Agency, Cambridge, MA, 14 November 1997; Capt Richard P. O'Neill, 24 March 1998; and Maj. Joseph Means, Joint Staff J6K, Information Assurance Division, 26 November 1997.

68. Fredricks, "Information Warfare at the Crossroads," 97.

69. Fredricks, "Information Warfare at the Crossroads," 100.

70. Joint Publication 3-13, *Information Operations* (Washington, DC: Joint Staff, October 1998).

71. Joint Publication 3-13, *Information Operations*, I-1, II-13.

72. Joint Publication 3-13, *Information Operations*, II-18-19.

73. Joint Publication 3-13, *Information Operations*, I-19.

74. NRC, *Computers at Risk: Safe Computing in the Information Age* (Washington, DC: National Academy Press, 1991). The membership of the study committee listed on p. iii shows no direct DOD involvement, although individuals from RAND, the Stanford Research Institute, and Rockwell Corporation were members. The committee also included industry leaders from commercial corporations such as Digital Corporation and BBN Incorporated.

75. NRC, *Computers at Risk*, in particular chap. 6, "Why the Security Market Has Not Worked Well," 143–178.

76. NRC, *Computers at Risk*, 283.

77. National Communications System (NCS), *The Electronic Intrusion Threat to the National Security and Emergency Preparedness (NS/EP) Telecommunications: An Awareness Document* (Arlington, VA: National Communications System, Office of the Manager, September 1993), ES-1.

78. Besides the NCS's *The Electronic Intrusion Threat* report, see National Security Telecommunications Advisory Committee, *An Assessment of the Risk to the Security and of the Public Network* (Washington, DC: NSTAC Network Security Information Exchange, December 1995).

79. Author's interview with Ralph A. MacMillian, Deputy Director, Information Assurance, ASD/C3I staff, Office of the Secretary of Defense, Pentagon, Arlington, VA, 4 August 1997.

80. Joint Security Commission, *Redefining Security: A Report from the Secretary of Defense and the Director of Central Intelligence* (Washington, DC: Joint Security Commission, 28 February 1994), 104–105.

81. JCS, *Redefining Security*, 103.

82. Presidential Decision Directive 29, "Security Policy Coordination," The White House, Washington, DC, 16 September 1994.

83. Interview with John Deutch, former Director of Central Intelligence (1995–1996) and Deputy Secretary of Defense (1994–1995), Cambridge, MA, 30 March 1998. See also Joint Security Commission, "Report by the Joint Security Commission II" (Washington, DC: Joint Security Commission, 24 August 1999).

84. Winn Schwartau, *Information Warfare: Chaos on the Electronic Superhighway*, 1st ed. (New York: Thunder Mouth Press, 1994).

85. Oliver Morton, "The Softwar Revolution," *Economist* (10 June 1995), Survey Section, 1–20. Tom Clancy's works, which deal with information warfare concerns, include *Debt of Honor* (New York: Putnam Publishing Group, 1994) and *Net Force* (New York: Berkley Books, 1999).

86. The term "information assurance" was formalized in the 1996 DOD Directive S.3600.1 as information operations "that protect and defend information and information systems by ensuring their availability, integrity, authentication, confidentiality and non-repudiation. This includes restoration of information systems by incorporating protection, detection and reaction capabilities." As quoted in Fredricks, "Information Warfare at the Crossroads," 100.

87. Joint Staff, *Information Warfare—Considerations*, A-11.

88. Interview with Capt. Richard P. O'Neill, 24 March 1998.

89. Roger C. Molander, Andrew S. Riddle, and Peter A. Wilson, *Strategic Information Warfare: A New Face of War* (Washington, DC: RAND National Defense Research Institute, 1996).

90. Molander et al., *Strategic Information Warfare*, 1.

91. Molander et al., *Strategic Information Warfare*, 9.

92. Molander et al., *Strategic Information Warfare*, 37–40. Although the MEII idea was also picked up by 1996 DSB Task Force on Information Warfare—Defense, the emphasis on such a concept seems to have atrophied during the late 1990s. A critique of the MEII idea is offered in John Arquilla, "The Great Cyberwar of 2002," *Wired*, February 1998, 122–127 and 159–170.

93. Department of Justice/Federal Bureau of Investigations briefing, "Computer Investigations and Infrastructure Threat Assessment Center," Cambridge, MA, May 1996.

94. Gorelick statement at "Security in Cyberspace" Hearings, 4.

95. Statement of Jamie S. Gorelick, Deputy Attorney General, to U.S. Senate, Committee on Governmental Affairs, Permanent Subcommittee on Investigations, Hearings on "Security in Cyberspace," 104th Congress, 2nd Session, 16 July 1996, 6.

96. Department of Justice/Federal Bureau of Investigations briefing, "Critical Infrastructure Protection: CITAC and the Interim Mission," 7. Briefing materials provided to author at the School of Information Warfare and Strategy, National Defense University, Washington, DC, May 1997.

97. SPB, "White Paper on Information Infrastructure Assurance," dated December 1995, available at Web site ⟨www.fas.org⟩, accessed 24 July 1996. My assessment of the role of the SPB and the White Paper findings was confirmed in an interview with Daniel Knauf, who was a member of the SPB staff and drafted the White Paper, at Ft. Meade, MD, 26 March 1998.

98. SPB, "White Paper on Information Infrastructure Assurance," 2–3.

99. Interview with Michael J. Woods, Assistant General Counsel, Department of Justice, at Department of Justice Headquarters, Washington, DC, 25 March 1996.

100. Gorelick statement at "Security in Cyberspace" hearings. Numerous individuals interviewed by the author also confirmed her key role in creating momentum for critical infrastructure protection.

101. Neil Munro, "The Pentagon's New Nightmare: An Electronic Pearl Harbor," *Washington Post*, 16 July 1995, C3.

102. Mark Thompson and Douglas Waller, "Onward Cyber Soldiers," *Time*, 28 August 1995, 44.

103. GAO, *Information Security*, 2.

104. GAO, *Information Security*, 35; *Information Security: Serious Weaknesses Place Critical Federal Operations and Assets at Risk* (Washington, DC: GAO/AIMD-98-92, 1998); and *Critical Infrastructure Protection: Comprehensive Strategy Can Draw on Year 2000 Experiences* (Washington, DC: GAO/AIMD-00-01, 1999).

105. The text of the Kyl Amendment is provided in full in Joint Staff, *Information Warfare—Considerations*, 2-59.

106. National Defense Panel (NDP), *Transforming Defense* (Arlington, VA: National Defense Panel, December 1997) 27.

107. NDP, *Transforming Defense*, 72.

108. White House, *National Security Strategy of Engagement and Enlargement* (Washington, DC: Government Printing Office, February 1996), 13.

109. Executive Order 13010, "Critical Infrastructure Protection," White House, Washington, DC, July 1996.

110. Based on author's telephone interview with Gen. (ret.) Robert T. Marsh, PCCIP Chairman, 1 April 1998. The commissioners are listed in President's Commission on Critical Infrastructure Protection (PCCIP), *Critical Foundations: Protecting America's Infrastructures* (Alexandria, VA: President's Commission on Critical Infrastructure Protection, October 1997), iii.

111. The diversity of sources and efforts at public outreach was stressed to the author in an interview with Gen (ret.) Robert T. Marsh, 20 June 1997, and in interviews with other PCCIP commissioners and staff on the same date.

112. PCCIP, *Critical Foundations*, vii.

113. PCCIP, *Critical Foundations*, x.

114. Interview with William B. Joyce, PCCIP Commissioner from Central Intelligence Agency, Arlington, VA, 24 November 1997.

115. My descriptions of the provisions of PDD 63 are based on the White House press release "Protecting America's Critical Information Infrastructures: PDD-63," 22 May 1998; and the White Paper, "The Clinton Administration's Policy on Critical Infrastructure Protection: Presidential Decision Directive 63," 22 May 1998.

116. This document is available, along with a wealth of information on the IITF, its activities, and published reports, at the IITF Web site ⟨www.iitf.nist.gov⟩.

117. Information Infrastructure Task Force, Reliability and Vulnerability Working Group, *NII Risk Assessment: A Nation's Information at Risk* (Washington, DC: Information Infrastructure Task Force, 29 February 1996).

118. A detailed analysis of the OECD and Council of Europe efforts is provided by Richard W. Aldrich, "International Information Terror: Does It Call for an International Treaty?" Research Paper for the Air Force Institute for National Security Studies, U.S. Air Force Academy, CO, May 1999, 14–43. See also Clifford Krauss, "Eight Countries Join to Combat Computer Crime," *New York Times*, 11 December 1997.

119. From "A Framework for Electronic Commerce," Executive Summary, 1, available at Web site ⟨www.iitf.nist.gov/eleccomm.htm⟩, accessed 28 January 1998.

120. "Next Generation Internet Initiative" Concept Paper, available at the NGI Web site ⟨www.ngi.gov/pubs⟩, accessed January 1998.

121. Interview with Thomas A. Fuhrman, a member of the White House, Office of Science and Technology Policy, National Security Division staff from 1994 to 1997, McLean, VA, 25 March 1998. Fuhrman stated that OSTP's National Security Division was unaware of the NGI initiative until its public announcement.

122. GAO, *Critical Infrastructure Protection*.

123. NRC, "Growing Vulnerability of the Public Switched Networks," as cited in Joint Staff, *Information Warfare—Considerations*, 2-65.

124. "Telecommunications Act of 1996" (P.L. 104-104, 8 February 1996).

125. PCCIP, *Critical Foundations*, A-3.

126. The OASIS example was provided in the author's telephone discussion with Lt. Col. Steven Rinaldi, White House, Office of Science and Technology Policy, National Security Division staff, 3 April 1998.

127. PCCIP, *Critical Foundations*, A-19.

128. Surveys used in this analysis are those conducted by the Computer Security Institute, the FBI, the American Society for Industrial Security, and Ernst and Young/Information Week, cited in Richard Power, *Current and Future Danger: A CSI Primer on Computer Crime and Information Warfare* (San Francisco: Computer Security Institute, 1995).

129. As cited in Power, *Current and Future Danger*, 1.

130. As cited in Power, *Current and Future Danger*, 2.

131. CSI/FBI, *Computer Crime and Security Survey—1999* (San Francisco: Computer Security Institute, 1999), 4.

132. Sylvia Dennis, "Information Theft Soars," *Computer Currents Online*, 4 January 2000, available at Web site <www.currents.net/newstoday/00/01/04/ndws13.html>, accessed January 2000.

133. For examples, see "Economic Spies Took $300 Billion Toll in '97," Associated Press, 12 January 1998; and Johnathan T. Cain, "Congress Eyes Federal Criminal Code Changes," *Washington Technology*, 22 January 1998.

134. Richard Behar, "Who's Reading Your E-Mail?" *Fortune* (3 February 1997): 57–70.

135. Survey results were reported in Matthew Rothenburg, "Poll: How Worried Are You?" ZDNet, 29 March 2000, available at Web site <www.zdnet.com/special/stories/defense/0,10459,2487277,00.html>, accessed April 2000.

136. Statement of Senate Minority Staff to U.S. Senate, Committee on Governmental Affairs, Permanent Subcommittee on Investigations, Hearings on "Security in Cyberspace," 104th Congress, 2nd Session, 5 June 1996, 21.

137. CSI/FBI, Computer Crime and Security Survey—1999, 3.

138. Frank Barbetta, "Concern for Security High: Action Remains Low," *Business Communication Review* (January 1998): 59.

139. PCCIP, *Critical Foundations*, 28.

140. Office of Science and Technology Policy (OSTP), *Cybernation: The American Infrastructure in the Information Age* (Washington, DC: The White House, April 1997), 11.

141. The activities of the NSTAC and NRC are addressed extensively by Steve Rinaldi, Senior National Security official at the White House Office of Science and Technology Policy, in "Sharing the Knowledge: Government–Private Sector Partnerships in Information Age Warfare," a research paper for the Air Force Institute of National Security Studies, U.S. Air Force Academy, CO, October 1999.

142. James Ellis et al., *Report to the President's Commission on Critical Infrastructure Protection* (Pittsburgh, PA: Software Engineering Institute, 1997), 3.

143. See, in particular, Testimony of Duane Andrews to U.S. House of Representatives, National Security Committee, Subcommittees on Military Procurement and Military Research and Development, Hearing on "Information Warfare," 105th Congress, 1st Session, 20 March 1997.

144. Esther Dyson, *Release 2.0: A Design for Living in the Digital Age* (New York: Broadway Books, 1997), 8. See also Bill Gates, *The Road Ahead* (New York: Viking, 1995), 271–274, on how the information age will diffuse political power.

145. My review of the early stages of the Clinton EES initiative is primarily based on Office of Technology Assessment (OTA), *Information Security and Privacy in Network Environments* (Washington, DC: Government Printing Office, 1997), chap. 4, "Government Policies and Cryptographic Safeguards," 111–183; GAO, *Information Superhighway: An Overview of Technology Challenges* (Washington, DC: GAO/AMID-95-23, January 1995); and Dorothy E. Denning, "The Case for 'Clipper': Resolving the Encryption Dilemma," *Technology Review*, May 1995, 46–56.

146. An overview of the Zimmerman case in provided in Landau and Diffie, *Privacy on the Line*, 205–206. Also see materials available on the Web sites for the Electronic Frontier Foundation ⟨www.eff.org⟩ and the Center for Democracy and Technology ⟨www.cdt.org⟩.

147. Bill Gates, *Road Ahead*, 269–271, provides a good overview of the software industry's general concerns and stance regarding U.S. government encryption policy.

148. See evaluation in OTA, *Information Security*, 159. The most extensive official treatment of law enforcement concerns is provided by the Federal Bureau of Investigation, *Encryption: Impact on Law Enforcement* (Quantico, VA: FBI Engineering Research Facility, June 1999). However, this document was produced long after the debate began and negative relationships developed with privacy advocates and the information technology industry.

149. The characterization of key escrow initiatives here is based on NRC, *Cryptography's Role in Securing the Information Society* (Washington, DC: National Academy Press, 1996); and Hal Abelson et al., *The Risks of Key Recovery, Key Escrow and Trusted Third Party Encryption: A Report by an Ad-Hoc Group of Cryptographers and Computer Scientists* (Washington, DC: Center for Democracy and Technology, May 1997).

150. The excerpt of the OECD report is available on the Electronic Privacy Information Center Web site, section entitled "Encryption Policy Resource Pages," at ⟨EPIC.org/crypto⟩, accessed 20 January 1998.

151. See Department of Commerce, "Interim Rule on Encryption Items," *Federal Register*, 61 (30 December 1996): 68572.

152. Statement of Dr. Peter Neumann, Moderator of the Internet Risks Forum, to U.S. Senate, Committee on Governmental Affairs, Permanent Subcommittee on Investigations, Hearings on "Security in Cyberspace," 104th Congress, 2nd Session, 25 June 1996, 6–7.

153. DSB Task Force, *Information Warfare—Defense*, 3-6.

154. Abelson et al., *Risks of Key Recovery*, 18.

155. Statement quoted on Electronic Privacy Information Center Web site, accessed February 1998.

156. See Jeri Clausing, "Head of Cyber-Terrorism Panel Says Encryption Rules May Be Needed," *New York Times*, 6 November 1997, A5; and Chris Oakes, "A New Crypto Furor," *Wired News*, at ⟨www.wired.com⟩, accessed November 1998.

157. The review in this paragraph is based on material available at Electronic Frontier Foundation and Electronic Privacy Information Center Web sites.

158. Colin Clark, "Opponents Rap Eased Export Rules on U.S. Encryption Technologies," *Defense News*, 15 January 2000.

159. See Todd Lapin, "Cyber Rights: Too Close for Comfort," *Wired*, December 1997, 51; and Declan McCullagh, "Jacking in from the 'Recurring Nightmare' Port: Shadow Cryptocrats," at ⟨www.well.com/~declan/pol.tech⟩, accessed February 1998.

160. Interview with Daniel Knauf, Ft. Meade, MD, 26 March 1998.

161. SPB, "White Paper on Information Assurance," 5.

162. GAO, *Critical Infrastructure Protection: Fundamental Improvements Needed to Ensure Security of Federal Operations* (Washington, DC: GAO/T-AIMD-00-7, October 1999), 6.

163. Joint Security Commission, "Report by the Joint Security Commission II," 3.

164. Information on the OSTP program to exercise presidential authority over telecommunications in case of a war or other national emergency is from the author's interview with Thomas Fuhrman, then assigned to the National Security Branch, OSTP, Washington, DC, 25 March 1998.

165. W. Oscar Round and Earle L. Rudolph, Jr., *Civil Defense in the Information Age* (Washington, DC: National Defense University Press, Strategic Forum no. 46, September 1996), 3.

166. Interview with James Hearn, former Deputy Director for Information Security, National Security Agency, 1988–1994, at Ft. Meade, MD, 26 March 1998.

167. Statement of John Deutch, Director of Central Intelligence, to U.S. Senate, Committee on Governmental Affairs, Permanent Subcommittee on Investigations, Hearings on "Security in Cyberspace," 104th Congress, 2nd Session, 25 June 1996, 6.

168. Commission on the Roles and Missions of the U.S. Intelligence Community, *Preparing for the 21st Century: An Appraisal of U.S. Intelligence* (Washington, DC: Commission on the Roles and Missions of the U.S. Intelligence Community, 1 March 1996), 27.

169. DSB Task Force, *Information Warfare—Defense*, 6-5.

170. See, in particular, Deutch statement at "Security in Cyberspace" hearings, 7; Department of Justice/Federal Bureau of Investigations briefing, "Computer Investigations and Infrastructure Threat Assessment Center."

171. Lou Anne DeMattei, "Developing a Strategic Warning Capability for Information Defense," *Defense Intelligence Journal* 7, no. 2 (Fall 1998): 94.

172. Defense Intelligence Agency, *Information Operations: Intelligence Support for the Security of the United States and U.S. Military Forces* (Washington, DC: Defense Intelligence Agency, July 1998).

173. Joint Staff, *Information Assurance*, 5-5.

174. National Infrastructure Protection Center Fact Sheet, 1998.

175. Statement of Michael A. Vatis, Director of the National Infrastructure Protection Center, to Senate Judiciary Committee, Subcommittee on Technology and Terrorism, 6 October 1999, available at ⟨www.fbi.gov/pressrm/congress/nipc10-6.htm⟩, accessed December 1999.

176. DIA, *Information Operations*, 4.

177. DSB Task Force, *Information Warfare—Defense*, 2-12.

178. The NSTAC, NCS, and NSIE are explained in detail in Rinaldi, "Sharing the Knowledge," 62–67.

179. Joint Staff, *Information Warfare—Considerations*, 2-23–24.

180. Interviews with Robert T. Marsh, Arlington, VA, 1 April 1988; and James Hearn, Ft. Meade, MD, 26 March 1998. Both agreed that composition of the NSTAC has yet to catch up with the fast-changing array of important players creating and operating the U.S. information infrastructure.

181. DSB Task Force, *Information Warfare—Defense*, 2-4.

182. PCCIP, *Critical Foundations*, 101.

183. Presentation by Richard Clarke at "Preparing for the Cyberwar" Conference cosponsored by the National Infrastructure Protection Center and Joint Task Force—Computer Network Defense, Arlington, VA, 5 October 1999.

184. DSB Task Force, *Information Architecture*, 25.

185. Interviews with Michael Woods, Washington, DC, 25 March 1998; and Daniel Knauf, Ft. Meade, MD, 26 March 1998.

186. Department of Justice/Federal Bureau of Investigations briefing, "Computer Investigations and Infrastructure Threat Assessment Center."

187. Heather Harreld and Torsten Busse, "Cybercenter Will Trace Net Intrusions," *Federal Computer Weekly*, 2 March 1998, 1 and 48.

188. Detailed information on NIPC activities is available in the Vatis statement to the Senate Judiciary Committee, 6 October 1999.

189. John Schwartz, "GOP Joining Opposition to U.S. Plan to Fight Hackers via Computer Monitoring," *Washington Post*, 4 August 1999, A12.

190. These programs are outlined in the Vatis statement to the Senate Judiciary Committee, 6 October 1999.

191. The NIPC Web site is located at ⟨www.fbi.gov/nipc⟩.

192. Interview with Michael Woods, Washington, DC, 25 March 1998.

193. Senate Minority Staff statement at "Security in Cyberspace" Hearings, 44–45.

194. Gorelick statement at "Security in Cyberspace" Hearings, 15; DSB Task Force, *Information Warfare—Defense*, 6-28; PCCIP, *Critical Foundations*, 85.

195. The focus on crime as opposed to digital attacks is addressed in M. J. Zukerman, "FBI Takes on Security Fight in Cyberspace," *USA Today*, 21 November 1996, 4B.

196. DIA, *Information Operations*, 2.

197. Joint Staff, *Information Assurance*, D-67.

198. DOD Chief Information Officer, "Annual Information Assurance Report," Office of the Assistant Secretary of Defense Command, Control, Communications and Intelligence, Washington, DC, May 1998, 6.

199. Information about roles and responsibilities of the JTF-CND and USSPACECOM are provided in the Department of Defense, "JTF-CND Charter," Office of the Secretary of Defense, Washington, DC, October 1999; and Joint Staff, *Information Assurance*, 5-2–3.

200. "JTF-CND Charter," 1.

201. U.S. Space Command Press Release 19-99, "USSPACECOM Takes Charge of DOD Computer Network Defenses," Peterson Air Force Base, CO, 1 October 1999.

202. This assertion is based on the author's review of Department of Defense, "JTF-CND Charter"; and "Computer Network Defense Implementation Plan," U.S. Space Command, Peterson Air Force Base, CO, September 1999).

203. Albert J. Edmonds, Director, Defense Information Systems Agency, "Information Systems to Support DOD and Beyond," in *Seminar on Intelligence, Command and Control, Spring 1996* (Cambridge: Harvard University, Program on Information Resources Policy, I-97-1, 1997), 208.

204. For additional information on the role of the NCS in U.S. national telecommunications recovery and response activities, see National Communication System, *National Communications System: 35th Anniversary* (Arlington, VA: National Communications System, 1998); Office of the Manager, *FY 1998 National Communications System* (Arlington, VA: National Communication System, 1998).

205. See section on information assurance in Office of the Manager, *FY 1998 National Communications System*, 3–21.

206. Analysis in this paragraph based Round and Rudolph, *Civil Defense in the Information Age*, 3–4.

207. The overview of CERT/CC presented here is based on a CERT/CC briefing, "Computer Security Incident and Vulnerability Trends," Pittsburgh, PA, July 1997, and interviews with CERT/CC personnel, Pittsburgh, PA, July 1997.

208. Statement of Richard Pethia, Manager of the CERT/CC, to U.S. Senate, Committee on Governmental Affairs, Permanent Subcommittee on Investigations, Hearings on "Security in Cyberspace," 104th Congress, 2nd Session, 5 June 1996; and the author's interviews with CERT/CC personnel in July 1997 and December 1999.

209. Based on Pethia statement at "Security in Cyberspace" Hearings and interviews with William Fithen, 8 July 1997, and Mark T. Zajicek, 7 December 1999, both at Software Engineering Institute, Carnegie Mellon University, Pittsburgh, PA.

210. Vatis statement to Senate Judiciary Committee, 6 October 1999.

211. NDP, *Transforming Defense*, 55.

212. Brig. Gen. Bruce M. Lawlor (Army National Guard), "DOD Needs to Tap the Civilian Expertise Resident in Its Reserve," *Armed Forces Journal International* (January 1998).

213. "Washington Air National Guard Information Security Team," concept paper, Washington National Guard, October 1999.

214. Joint Staff, "Concept of Operations for the RCE-05 Joint Virtual IO/IA Proof of Concept," Washington, DC, 21 October 1999.

215. Robert L. Ayers, Chief of Information Warfare Division, DISA, "Developing the Information Warfare Defense: A DISA Perspective," presentation, 4 December 1995.

216. CJCSI, "Defensive Information Warfare Implementation," C-8.

217. The summary of DOD CERT activities presented here is based on the author's discussions with ASSIST/CERT personnel, 5 August 1997; DISA briefing, "Automated Systems Security Incident Support Team (ASSIST)"; and Joint Staff, *Information Assurance*, A-70–72. Rod Laszlo and Bruce Gardner, "Monitoring and Protecting the Global Network," *IAnewsletter* 3, no. 2 (Fall 1999): 20–21.

218. Ayers, "Developing the Information Warfare Defense."

219. "IATAC Basic Services," *Information Assurance Technology Newsletter* (March 1997): 5.

220. Maj. Joseph Means, Joint Staff, Information Assurance Directorate, J6K, "Information Operations: A Guided Discussion," presentation made to author at Pentagon, Arlington, VA, 26 November 1997. Information on Joint Staff and Unified Command activities also provided in DOD Chief Information Officer, "Annual Information Assurance Report," Office of the Assistant Secretary of Defense Command, Control, Communications and Intelligence, Washington, DC, May 1999.

221. PCCIP, *Critical Foundations*, 8.

222. Director of Command, Control, Communications and Communications Systems, *Information Assurance Through Defense in Depth* (Washington, DC: The Joint Staff, February 2000).

223. Director of Command, Control, Communications and Communications Systems, *Information Assurance Through Defense in Depth*, 6.

224. Joint Publication 3-13, *Information Operations*, chap. 4.

225. See Berwin, "Kosovo Ushered in Cyberwar."

226. U.S. Space Command, "Computer Network Defense Implementation Plan."

227. Air Force Information Warfare Center briefing, "AFCERT Operations," provided to author in October 1999 at Air Force Information Warfare Center, Kelly Air Force Base, TX.

228. Air Force Information Warfare Center briefing, "Countermeasure Engineering Team," provided to author in October 1999 at Air Force Information Warfare Center, Kelly Air Force Base, TX.

229. 609th Information Warfare Squadron, "609 IWS: A Brief History, October 1995–August 1997" (Shaw Air Force Base, SC: 609th Information Warfare Squadron, September 1997).

230. The discussion of the IWF, NOSC, and BNCC constructs is based on U.S. Air Force, *Information Warfare Concept of Operations* (Washington, DC: Headquarters Air Force, December 1999).

231. Discussion of Army activities is based on Land Information Warfare Activity brochure, U.S. Army, 1998.

232. Details regarding these organizations are provided in the Navy's *Information Warfare Strategic Plan*.

233. Joint Staff, *Information Assurance*, A-48 and; E. H. Ted Steinhavser, "Marine Forces Computer Network Defense: MARFOR-CND," *IAnewsletter* 3, no. 2 (Fall 1999): 16–17.

234. The status of the JTF-CND and each of the service component is surveyed in the fall 1999 edition of *IAnewsletter* 3, no. 2.

235. Director of Command, Control, Communications and Communications Systems, *Information Assurance Through Defense in Depth*, 16.

236. Based on GAO, *Information Security*; Senate Minority Staff Statement at "Security in Cyberspace" Hearings; DSB Task Force, *Information Warfare—Defense*; DOD Chief Information Officer, "Annual Information Assurance Report"; and author's interviews with personnel at the JTF-CND, DISA DOD CERT, AFCERT, and the Joint Staff Information Assurance Division.

237. Sources for this overview include numerous discussions with Bruce Moulton, Vice President, Information Security Services, Fidelity Investments; interviews with personnel at the Software Engineering Institute's CERT/CC; and a review of general literature on information security

in the commercial sector, especially Frederick Cohen, *Protection and Security on the Information Highway* (New York: John Wiley & Sons, 1995); Peter G. Neumann, *Computer-Related Risks* (New York: ACM Press, 1995); and Dorothy E. Denning, *Information Warfare and Security* (Reading, MA: Addison-Wesley, 1999).

238. This characterization was developed in conjunction with Bruce Moulton.

239. NRC, *Computers at Risk*, 17.

240. OSTP, *Cybernation*, 6. Italics in original.

241. OSTP, *Cybernation*, 13.

242. "Squeeze Gently," *Economist*, 30 November 1996, 65–66.

243. Stressed in MITRE Corporation, "Information Operations and Critical Infrastructure Protection," presentation at MITRE Corporate Campus, Bedford, MA, 20 November 1997.

244. Based on interviews with CERT Coordination Center personnel. See also Deborah Radcliff, "Target NT," *Computer World*, available at ⟨www2.computerworld.com/home⟩.

245. Based on a review of materials on World Wide Web Consortium Web site ⟨www.w3.org⟩.

246. See Internet Society's "History of the Internet" at ⟨www.isoc.org⟩; and Martin C. Libicki, *Standards: Rough Road to the Common Byte* (Washington, DC: National Defense University Press, 1995), 21–22.

247. Based on review of activities on the Internet Society and Information Infrastructure Task Force Web sites, previously cited.

248. Ellis et al., *Report to the President's Commission*, 3.

249. DSB Task Force, *Information Warfare—Defense*, 6-9–12.

250. "Companies Wary of Internal Security Problems," *New York Times*, 1 March 1998; and Neil Winton, "Y2K Seen as Possible Cover for Cyberwars," *Reuter News Report*, 8 October 1999.

251. Clarke presentation at NIPC/JTF-CND "Preparing for Cyberwar" Conference, Cambridge, MA.

252. Interview with Lt. Gen. Kenneth Minihan, 14 November 1997.

253. Ellis et al., *Report to the President's Commission*, 22.

254. Based on interviews with Software Engineering Institute personnel and the Software Engineering Institute presentation at the Information Vulnerabilities Conference, Pittsburgh, PA, January 1998.

255. Based on interviews with personnel in Joint Staff, Information Assurance Directorate (J6K); JTF-CND; DOD CERT; and Air Force Information Warfare Center.

256. Joint Staff, *Information Warfare—Considerations*, 2-96–98.

257. NCS, *The Electronic Intrusion Threat*, 3-11–12; NRC, *Computers at Risk*, section on "Risks and Vulnerabilities," 61–62.

258. Cohen, *Protection and Security*, 70.

259. DSB Task Force, *Information Warfare—Defense*, 2-16.

260. Ellis et al., *Report to the President's Commission*, 8.

261. CERT/CC Summary CS-99-01, 23 February 1999, available at ⟨www.cert.org⟩.

262. CERT/CC Incident Note IN-99-07, "Distributed Denial of Service Tools," 8 December 1999, available at ⟨www.cert.org⟩.

263. PCCIP, *Critical Foundations*, 3–4.

264. A good overview of the DOD's Multi-Level Information Systems Security Initiative (MISSI) is provided by Jan M. Lodal, Deputy Undersecretary of Defense for Policy, "Implications for National Defense," in McCarthy, *National Security in the Information Age*, 98–99.

265. Landau and Diffie, *Privacy on the Line*, 217–218.

266. Figure cited by Jean Camp, Assistant Professor of Public Policy, "Cryptography Policy," presentation at Harvard University, Cambridge, MA, 6 April 1997.

267. CSI/FBI, *Computer Crime and Computer Survey—1999*, 3.

268. See NRC, *Cryptography's Role*, and U.S. Congress, Senate, Committee on Governmental Affairs, Testimony of LoPht Heavy Industries on Computer Security, 106th Congress, 2nd Session, 19 May 1998.

269. Abelson et al., *Risks of Key Recovery*, 17–18.

270. Ottmar Kyas, *Internet Security: Risk Analysis, Strategies and Firewalls* (Boston: International Thompson Computer, 1997), 184–187.

271. Albert Edmonds, DISA Director, "Protection and Defense of Intrusion," in McCarthy, *National Security in the Information Age*, 172–175.

272. CSI/FBI, *Computer Crime and Security Survey—1999*, 3.

273. See Radcliff, "Target NT," available at ⟨www2.computerworld.com/home⟩, accessed January 1998.

274. Clifford Stoll, *The Cuckoo's Egg* (New York: Simon & Schuster, 1989).

275. These techniques were described by Howard Shrobe, former Director of the Defense Advanced Projects Agency Project on Information Survivability, "How Can the U.S. Survive Information Warfare?" presentation at Massachusetts Institute of Technology, Cambridge, MA, 9 February 1998.

276. Efforts to improve the capabilities of the Air Force–developed host-based intrusion monitoring system have been constrained by the system's increased processing requirements as its capabilities are extended. Based on interview with Lt. Chuck Flanders, Countermeasures Engineer, Air Force Information Warfare Center, Kelly Air Force Base, TX, 29 and 30 July 1997.

277. Brian T. Spink and Brad Jobe, "Automated Intrusion Detection Environment," *IAnewsletter* (Summer 1999): 14–15.

278. Lt. Brian Dunphy (USAF), interview, DISA Headquarters, Arlington, VA, 4 August 1997.

279. See, in particular, PCCIP, *Critical Foundations*, 68–87; and DSB Task Force, *Information Warfare—Defense*, 6-27–28. Author's interviews with AF CERT, DISA DOD CERT, and National Infrastructure Protection Center personnel also stressed the significance of these constraints.

280. Ellis et al., *Report to the President's Commission*, 4–5; Schwartau, *Information Warfare*, 265–269; Cohen, *Protection and Security*, 76–78.

281. Based on Sami Saydjari, DARPA Information Assurance Project Manager, "DARPA Information Assurance and Survivability Programs," presentation to author on 25 October 1999, Arlington, VA.

282. Based on Shrobe, "How Can the U.S. Survive Information Warfare?"

283. Ellis et al., *Report to the President's Commission*, 3–4.

284. Example provided by Capt. Jay Healy of the DOD Joint Task Force—Computer Network Defense.

285. The direct relationship of congressional pressure in causing the president to act on the issue of national information infrastructure protection is addressed by John M. McConnell, "The Evolution of Intelligence and Public Policy Debate on Encryption," in Guest Presentation—Intelligence, Command and Control Seminar, 178.

286. Martin C. Libicki, "Protecting the U.S. in Cyberspace," in Allan D. Campen, Douglas H. Dearth, and R. Thomas Gooden, eds., *Cyberwar: Security, Strategy and Conflict in the Information Age* (Fairfax, VA: AFCEA International Press, 1996), 101.

287. Neumann statement at "Security in Cyberspace" Hearings, 10.

288. Secretary Perry's leadership role stressed was in an interview with Capt. Richard P. O'Neill, Pentagon, Washington, DC, 24 March 1998.

289. See Dyson, *Release 2.0*, 262; the activities of the Highlands Group were also detailed for the author in numerous conversations with Capt. (USN) Richard P. O'Neill, who was responsible for running the Highlands Group for the ASD/C3I and now runs the group as a private organization.

290. William S. Cohen, Secretary of Defense, *Defense Reform Initiative Report* (Washington, DC: Office of the Secretary of Defense, November 1997), 23. The ASD/C3I position vacated in the summer of 1997 was left unfilled through fall and most of the winter 1997–1998.

291. DOD Chief Information Office, "Annual Information Assurance Report," May 1999, 2.

292. See Gorelick, "Protecting Critical Infrastructures." The Senate Minority Staff statement at the "Security in Cyberspace" Hearings, 45, praised Reno and Gorelick, as well as the Justice Department more generally, for playing a leadership role in fostering national-level concern on this issue. When Gorelick left the Justice Department in the spring of 1997, she served on the Steering Committee for the PCCIP in the summer and fall of 1997.

293. GAO, *Critical Infrastructure Protection.*

294. See, in particular, Statement of Duane Andrews, Chairman of the 1996 DSB Task Force on Information Warfare—Defense, to U.S. Congress, House National Security Committee, Subcommittees on Military Procurement and Military Research and Development, 105th Congress, 1st Session, Hearing on "Information Warfare," 20 March 1997.

295. GAO, *Information Security*, 34–35.

296. The systemic hurdles facing the government in resolving these problems are driven home in Elizabeth Shogren, "U.S. Tries to Plug Computer Worker Drain," *Los Angeles Times*, 23 November 1999, 1.

297. Senate Minority Staff statement at "Security in Cyberspace" Hearings, 49.

298. Behar, "Who's Reading Your E-Mail?" 58.

299. Joint Staff, *Information Warfare—Considerations*, A-222.

300. Senate Minority Staff statement at "Security in Cyberspace" Hearings, Pittsburgh, PA, 22.

301. Interview with Mark T. Zajicek, Software Engineering Institute, 7 December 1999.

302. This assessment is based on my interviews with Bruce Moulton, Vice President, Information Security Services, Fidelity Investments, Boston, MA, 10 August 1997 and 6 January 1998; Cohen, *Protection and Security*; and R. T. Gooden, "Business Strategy in the Information Age," in Campen, Dearth, and Gooden, *Cyberwar*, 133–146.

303. This figure was provided in the MITRE corporation presentation "Information Operations and Critical Infrastructure Protection"; and the same 1–3 percent figure was cited in FBI/CSI, *Computer Crime and Security Survey—1997* (San Francisco: Computer Security Institute, 1997).

304. Ellis et al., *Report to the President's Commission*, 20.

305. Interview with Mark T. Zajicek , Software Engineering Institute, 7 December 1999.

306. Joint Staff, *Joint Vision 2010*, 31.

307. Based on DISA "Automated Systems Security Incident Support Team (ASSIST)"; and Air Force Information Warfare Center, "AFCERT Operations."

308. Air Force Information Warfare Center, "AFCERT Operations."

309. Interviews with Maj. Stephen J. Walsh, Information Assurance Directorate, J6K, Joint Staff Pentagon, Washington DC, 26 November 1997; and Robert Adams, CERT Operations at Air Force Information Warfare Center, Kelly Air Force Base, TX, 30 July 1998.

310. Molander et al., *Strategic Information Warfare*, 38–39; and DSB Task Force, *Information Warfare—Defense*, 6-22–24.

Conclusion

General Lessons about Technology, Organizations, and Warfare

History demonstrates that technology continually changes the nature of warfare. Developments from the discovery of bronze to the advent of networked computing have presented opportunities to gain decisive military advantages. Those who adapt best have won wars and extended their influence. According to Italian Air Marshall Giulio Douhet, "Victory has gone to those who succeeded in changing from the traditional ways of war, and not to those who clung desperately to them."[1] Yet nation-states and other groups who consider establishing new military capabilities to leverage technological advances confront a situation of considerable complexity and uncertainty. As one observer has found, "Unfortunately, history also makes it clear that, for every technological visionary who gets the future right, there are at least ten who get it wrong."[2]

The question is how to beat these odds. Successful efforts to gain advantage through adaptation to emerging technological forces should consider the lessons of the past as well as visions of the future. To begin with, any international actor must link such efforts to a continuing understanding of military force as a means to achieve its ends. How will new weapons and military organizations interact with those of adversaries in a conflict? Technological change may enable an actor to establish strategic warfare capabilities to strike at an adversary's center of gravity in new ways, creating previously unavailable political leverage. Yet by the same token an actor's own centers of gravity can also become vulnerable to attack and require protective efforts matched to the emerging threat. Knowledge of past efforts to wage strategic warfare can provide guidance in weighing the opportunities and risks as new technologies appear to loom large on the horizon.

Bringing together ideas about the future conduct of wars and the organizational change necessary to apply new technologies presents difficult challenges. Waging conflicts in a new environment, whether on the seas, in the air, or through cyberspace, requires that organizations learn fundamental lessons about the new technological tools and operational constraints on their employment. How do weather conditions affect air operations? How will implementation of new communications protocols impact digital warriors? Do offensive or defensive forces appear to have fundamental advantages? Effective adaptation to technological change also requires weighing the strident arguments of advocates of new doctrines, organization, and technologies against those made by entrenched institutions with a vested interest in the status quo. Decisions about adaptation are made all the more difficult when leaders must deal with emerging technologies without actual wartime experience to illuminate the inherent complexities involved in employing military forces. Military institutions that emerge victorious from major conflicts involving the first use of new technologies have capacity to learn during wartime as well as to prepare properly during periods of peace.

Understanding the Development of
Strategic Information Warfare Capabilities

The United States must deal with the challenges that technological change throughout the 1990s has brought. The international environment is in flux. Conventional and nuclear military strength limits the traditional security threats to the nation's vital interests. As the sole remaining superpower, the United States has reluctantly assumed obligations in establishing conditions of increased democratization and political stability around the globe. The drivers of economic growth are undergoing a fundamental shift as technological advances contribute to the emergence of global markets and systems of production. Transnational corporations and international consortiums that influence technological trajectories provide a cross-cutting web of interests when superimposed on the world's political map as drawn up by nation-states.

The emergence of an information age assumed center stage in the pursuit of U.S. interests in the late 1990s. In the realm of global economic affairs, the U.S. showed a great capacity for adaptation, adjustment, and leadership throughout the decade. U.S.-based corporations such as Microsoft, Intel, and Cisco Systems clearly established themselves as leaders in the creation and implementation of the technologies of the information age. Other U.S. companies as diverse as Wal-Mart and AT&T downsized, informated organizations, and aggressively sought competitive advantage through technological leverage. The information revolution also overtook the U.S. military establishment in the 1990s. Emerging from the spectacular battlefield success of the Gulf War, the U.S. military establishment recognized the emergence of a revolution in military affairs that requires the use of advanced information technology and organizational agility to dominate the conventional battlefields of the twenty-first century.

At the intersection of these varied activities lies information warfare. Military adversaries on the battlefield or economic competitors in the marketplace can exploit information to improve employment of resources and endeavor to limit the utility of information to others. U.S. efforts to achieve commercial and conventional battlefield advantages at the beginning of the twenty-first century require advanced information infrastructures. At the same time, these infrastructures could well constitute centers of gravity subject to attack. Theories and scenarios regarding the nature and significance of information warfare are receiving increasing attention. Everything from jamming Serbian air defense radars to manipulating Rwandan radio broadcasts to stealing computer-generated plans for Boeing's next airliner has been thrown into the mix.

This work has delineated *strategic* information warfare through an analysis of the objectives, means, and actors who might wage conflicts based on disrupting information infrastructures as a center of gravity as an extension of past uses of force. The establishment of advanced information infrastructures allows the use of digital attacks based on micro applications of force to potentially have strategic influence. Powerful offensive tools for employing micro force can be wielded by much smaller organizations and even individuals. Yet the disruption caused by digital attacks may prove much more difficult to estimate. The rapid pace of technological change within advanced information infrastructures makes efforts to understand centers of gravity more difficult than for past forms of strategic warfare.

Many options exist for conducting strategic information warfare campaigns. Such campaigns could involve efforts to overwhelm an adversary, as attempted during World War II or envisaged as the goal of nuclear exchanges between the superpowers. However, actors might also use new digital warfare means to conduct prolonged conflicts to wear down an adversary's capabilities and will, similar to strategies adopted by guerrillas and terrorists. The likely success of different campaign strategies and utility of strategic information warfare will remain as contextually dependent as for other types of force. Bomber aircraft and nuclear weapons have not proven useful for all military purposes of all actors. Likewise, actors considering the development of strategic information warfare capabilities must consider their political objectives, their strategic situation, and their ability to establish sufficient means to achieve their goals.

The widespread availability of the means for disrupting information infrastructures has led to a common belief that almost any actor can obtain and employ the tools required for waging strategic information warfare. Yet establishing effective offensive and defensive military capabilities has rarely proved so easy. An understanding of the opportunities and challenges posed by the development and control of the requisite technological knowledge for waging digital warfare can build on known theoretical approaches and past experience. Therefore, this work has established a framework of conditions that facilitate the development of organizational technological capability.

This framework of facilitating conditions is designed to identify foreseeable challenges involved in the development of strategic information warfare capabilities. Widely available tools and lack of protective efforts may create numerous potential vulnerabilities to digital attack. However, developing the offensive means to assess and target centers of gravity may prove very difficult because of the fast-changing information infrastructure of an adversary. Understanding the significance of different vulnerabilities and their potential influence on the disruption inflicted by digital attacks will require the same type of difficult evaluations that plagued many past efforts to employ strategic attacks. Defensively, the commercial technological leadership and control of the evolving cyberspace environment requires national governments to establish coordination between organizations across multiple sectors of society whose reliance on information infrastructures creates centers of gravity for attack by opponents. Making choices about the degree of government involvement may necessitate negotiating extremely difficult trade-offs with other national priorities, including economic competitiveness and individual rights. State and nonstate actors with little reliance on information infrastructures may find the defensive challenges much simpler. Minimal vulnerability to digital attack may also present a situation of asymmetric advantage for certain actors considering the development of strategic information warfare capabilities. For both offensive and defensive missions, the availability of the required human expertise and the ability to learn quickly will likely prove vital to establishing effective organizational capabilities.

Evaluating U.S. Efforts to Establish Strategic Warfare Capabilities

Historical comparison of the U.S. development of its strategic air arm during the early twentieth century to efforts during the 1990s to grapple with the emergence of the potential for strategic information warfare demonstrates the challenges of establishing organizational technological capabilities. Difficulty in aligning the factors necessary to establish doctrinal constructs, develop organizational structures, and manage technological advances slowed progress in both efforts.

Doctrinal conceptualization of digital strategic information warfare remains underdeveloped as the United States begins the twenty-first century. Though recognizing its potential, the national security community has yet to explain fully how such warfare might constitute either a fundamentally new means for employing offensive military force or a major defensive challenge for the United States, or both. Yet the lack of doctrinal clarity regarding strategic information warfare should not be seen as unexpected. The full articulation of strategic airpower doctrine in the United States required almost two decades after the idea surfaced in World War I. The dominant U.S. nuclear doctrine of mutually assured destruction and well-articulated concepts of deterrence similarly did not emerge until the late 1950s and early 1960s despite the fact that atomic weapons were first used in 1945.

Open consideration of the concept of strategic information warfare within the United States dates back only to the early 1990s. Even today, such warfare remains only a theoretical possibility. Information warriors do not have lessons from an empirical record of large-scale, digital information infrastructure attacks on which to base their theories and doctrine. Discussions of information warfare within the Pentagon still focus on traditional battlefield advantage through use of a wide range of means. Military doctrine and broader federal policy approaches regarding strategic information warfare defenses continue to lump together consideration of all threats to U.S. information infrastructures, with wholly inadequate distinctions made between categories of intent and capability. Not yet ready to protect these infrastructures, the U.S. government has proved reluctant to address the requirement for a coherent, national information infrastructure defense against strategic digital attack. Arguably, the challenges of conducting such an attack may provide some breathing room in terms of when such a threat will emerge for the United States. However, the lack of U.S. progress in developing a doctrine for defensive strategic information warfare does not appear to be based on a well-developed capacity to assess the capabilities or likelihood that adversaries might conduct such an attack in the near future.

Establishing organizations and allocating the necessary resources to create new capabilities to conduct strategic warfare has also proven difficult. Between the world wars and during the 1990s, the lack of a clear strategic warfare mission impeded the willingness of existing institutions to invest in developing new capabilities. In the interwar period, the geographic and political isolation of the United States hampered arguments by William Mitchell and the Air Corps Tactical School about the need to invest limited military resources in untested, revolutionary new airpower capabilities for fighting future wars against far distant adversaries. Amidst the shrinking defense and federal government budgets of the 1990s, investment in information warfare focused on improving prospects for "dominant battlefield awareness" and "information superiority" on battlefields that loom large in places like the Persian Gulf and the Balkans. Efforts to create the organizational mechanisms and make the resource commitments necessary to assess information infrastructure vulnerabilities and establish defenses for the homeland have fought an uphill battle.

Organizational capabilities progressed incrementally in both periods through similar processes. Events such as Mitchell's bombing of the Ostfriesland or hacker intrusions against U.S. Air Force's Rome Laboratories created ammunition for advocates to use in heralding the significance of new strategic warfare missions. Studies and reviews, such as those of the 1926 Baker Board on the future of the Air Corps and the 1997 President's Commission on Critical Infrastructure Protection, provided the impetus for change. The proposals of zealous advocates for wholesale transformations of organizations and reassignment of national security missions were not embraced. However, more even-handed proposals produced progress in adjusting existing organizational structures to better address new missions.

The development of strategic air and information warfare capabilities also confronted similar challenges in assimilating and understanding complex, fast-changing technologies. Establishing the appropriate pools of technological expertise provided a major challenge in both areas. During the interwar timeframe, bomber pilots came to dominate the development of doctrine, organizations, and technologies that provided the Army air arm with strategic air warfare capabilities. Technological tools such as the B-17 were built, albeit in small numbers, prior to the start of World War II. The dominance of pilots within the Air Corps also meant, however, that critical pools of supporting expertise in terms of bombardiers, navigators, and intelligence personnel were lacking as the United States contemplated its strategic air campaign against Germany. Developing expertise for defensive strategic information warfare in the 1990s confronted similar limitations. Both the national security community and the commercial sector established centers of excellence to react to digital attacks. Optimally, it was believed, defensive technological expertise diffused to the lowest-level operation would improve overall protection of information infrastructures. Yet constraints on developing such a broad skill base limited the success of such efforts. Even more sorely lacking were organizations and personnel with the capacity to organize and conduct broad assessments of information infrastructure reliance and vulnerability.

Additionally, the trajectory of technological development in both cases required linkages to the commercial sector and capacity for organizational learning. U.S. airmen in the interwar period benefited from close ties to the commercial aviation industry in terms of understanding the technological potential of tools related to strategic air warfare. However, the very limited willingness of the "bomber mafia" to learn after the early 1930s resulted in a technological fixation with fast, long-range bomber aircraft that blinded them to key defensive technological developments they would confront over the skies of Europe in World War II. Government efforts in the 1990s to establish bridges to the commercial sector also encountered great difficulty. Military officers and national security officials responsible for protecting defense and other information infrastructures had no natural ties to the commercial technology producers and network operators so crucial in creating the technological environment for this type of warfare. Implementation of the PDD 63 construct promised to improve the development of required public-private bridges and promote cooperative learning regarding the nature of information infrastructure vulnerabilities and improving defensive measures. Yet the U.S. government did little to proactively manage the processes of technology development and implementation that provide major hurdles for establishing effective strategic information warfare defenses.

The following list compares U.S. preparations for strategic warfare involving digital information in the 1990s to those involving airpower in the interwar period.

SIMILARITIES

• Doctrinal advocacy for new technology's military potential was a factor in both periods.

- The technology in both instances has significant dual-use applications.
- Both underwent a period of rapidly advancing technological performance and short technology life cycles.
- Organizational adaptation was slow in both periods, given the lack of a demonstrable outside threat.

DIFFERENCES

- Digital warfare tools diffuse much more readily to lesser states and nonstate actors.
- Digital warfare offers greater opportunities for asymmetric strategies.
- The cyberspace environment is not controlled by governments of sovereign states.
- Information warriors must understand technology and activity outside their direct control.
- Offensively, identifying centers of gravity and limiting damage are more difficult in information warfare.
- Defensively, the government must cooperate with the private sector, and organizational coordination and adaptability are crucial, in information warfare.

Implications and Recommendations for Strengthening U.S.
Strategic Information Warfare Defenses

The lessons of the past and U.S. experience in developing strategic information warfare capabilities during the 1990s sound a very strong cautionary note about understanding the outcomes of unleashing such a new form of warfare. The first campaigns involving strategic information warfare may well be confused, messy affairs with limited effect, as were the initial uses of strategic airpower in World War II. Efforts to develop a peacetime understanding of the effectiveness of technological tools and level of forces necessary to wage strategic warfare and the nature of the centers of gravity involved have historically proven less than successful. The establishment of effective organizational capabilities to wage new forms of warfare has often also had to rely on painful wartime lessons.

Yet, the emergence of strategic information warfare as a new means of military force has been attended by much optimism about its potential to achieve decisive impacts. The type of warfare described herein has beguiling characteristics. Disruptive digital attacks are certainly feasible. The cost of acquiring the necessary means is low, especially in relation to conventional forces and most

WMD alternatives. A much wider range of actors can consider employing such a form of warfare. The United States currently possesses dominant capabilities across the range of other types of military force. U.S. adversaries may view the possibility of remote, digital attacks directly against U.S. centers of gravity as their best way of achieving some type of political influence if a conflict seems destined to come to blows.

The United States has publicly announced concern about its degree of vulnerability to digital attacks. Newspapers put hacker intrusions against the Pentagon and Citicorp on the front page. Presidential commissions, congressional hearings, and national security studies bemoan the inadequacy of protective efforts. However, no one possesses an adequate understanding of the overall risks involved. Very few analyses stress the complexities of successfully orchestrating such attacks. The uproar within the United States may reinforce its adversaries' belief that a significant strategic opportunity has arisen.

Various actors will likely attempt to wage strategic information warfare in the future, and such conflicts may well involve the United States. For many actors, strategic information warfare capabilities seem to hold out real potential for political utility. Yet establishing firm estimates of when adversaries might effectively develop and employ such capabilities have proven and will continue to prove difficult. Technological means for waging digital attacks exist today, along with significant challenges to turning these means into viable capabilities to conduct strategic warfare, but these difficulties are not insurmountable. For some actors, pursuit of objectives through strategic information warfare may seem viable. An actor may miscalculate the influence its offensive capabilities will actually provide or its own vulnerability to retaliation. Alternatively, an actor may recognize its strategic information warfare capabilities are limited but may judge that these means offer it the only potential leverage it has in a confrontation. For U.S. national security planners, these considerations remain basically unknowable at the dawn of the twenty-first century. Future strategic information warfare attacks against U.S. information infrastructures pose a real concern. Prudence would indicate the necessity for improvements to U.S. strategic information warfare defenses. The question remains how to tackle this knotty problem most effectively.

U.S. efforts to address protection of its information infrastructures have yet to be cast specifically in terms of defense against strategic warfare attack. Past approaches and recommendations are geared to a wide spectrum of concerns, including natural disasters, teenagers exploring computer networks, and malicious disruption. Yet strategic information warfare presents certain unique challenges in terms of defense. What steps should be taken, then, to improve future U.S. defensive strategic information warfare capabilities? One approach would be to return to an analysis of the enabling conditions for successfully waging strategic warfare established in chapter 2. If the United States can implement adequate, robust barriers to an adversary's ability to achieve these conditions, its strategic information warfare defenses will prove more effective.

Reducing Offensive Advantage

Successful strategic attacks rely on the ability of offensive forces to gain access to targeted centers of gravity. This work has stressed the fundamental defensive challenge posed by the continuing development and installation of technology products that create weak security foundations for U.S. information infrastructures. Widely used products contain vulnerabilities to digital disruption that are easily identified, and the characteristics of these vulnerabilities as well as the tools and techniques to exploit them are quickly disseminated among potential attackers. Those responsible for protecting information infrastructures across sectors of U.S. society have had a difficult time keeping up with the identification of problems and implementation of fixes to limit the access of attackers to information systems.

U.S. national policy to improve strategic information warfare defense must stress the timely, voluntary disclosure of vulnerabilities once discovered by the broad range of technology producers, network operators, and infrastructure users. PDD 63 identifies approaches to deal with vulnerabilities in designated critical infrastructures. However, efforts to reduce the weakness of technological foundations of information infrastructures across U.S. society must more broadly involve technology producers and general commercial users. Lessons learned from the active efforts in the U.S. national security community to protect its own information infrastructures could also be usefully fed into the process. To motivate responses across all sectors of society, the president and the national security community can also clearly articulate the threats posed by strategic information warfare beyond those posed by everyday computer security risks.

The U.S. government must strengthen institutions that collect information on infrastructure vulnerabilities and develop measures to remedy those vulnerabilities. Individuals and organizations across all sectors who are willing to report problems need guarantees that such reports will remain confidential to minimize their concerns over reputation, legal liability, privacy, national security, and potential punitive action. Again, implementing the PDD 63 recommendations would improve progress in protecting certain sectors of activity. Within the national security sector, the efforts of JTF-CND, DISA, and the military services in forming defensive information warfare centers of excellence deserve continuing emphasis. However, institutions such as the CERT Coordinating Center at Carnegie Mellon have a broader focus across all types of information infrastructure operators and users. These institutions should continue to receive attention and resources as critical information infrastructure protection efforts develop. Increasing the support for these organizations would enable better cross-flow among the growing number of CERT-type organizations developing across different sectors of activity. National CERT-type organizations responsible for collating information on vulnerabilities must rely on their reputations as trusted agents, avoiding perceptions that they are instruments of groups narrowly focused on law enforcement or intelligence gathering. These institutions can also provide mechanisms for assisting technology producers in developing fixes to identified problems that can be quickly and broadly disseminated, especially if other linkages to these producers remain underdeveloped.

Improving efforts by operators and users to implement fixes to problems and vulnerabilities that have been identified would also reduce the systemic sources of vulnerability to strategic attack within U.S. information infrastructures. U.S. policies designed to create legal requirements for "due diligence" in establishing security by operators and users should receive more attention. Fundamental to such efforts would be generally accepted information and computer security and reliability standards and practices. Policies designed to foster acceptance and implementation of such standards should consider combining both positive and negative incentives. One possible stick would be implementation of legislation and regulations that establish liability for negligence in compliance. In the area of positive incentives, the federal government should continue fostering educational programs to improve the skills of security specialists and systems administrators responsible for assessing and fixing security problems throughout the U.S. information infrastructure. Government agencies should also initiate efforts to learn how the civilian sector applies its limited computer and information security expertise to the problem of infrastructure protection.

Reducing Vulnerability across Key Sectors

Strategic warfare attacks succeed only if adversaries actually possess vulnerable centers of gravity dependent on information infrastructures. Reliance on information technology, systems, and networks has increased across U.S. society, and the susceptibility of such technology, systems, and networks to digital attack has been demonstrated. Yet the locus of U.S. information infrastructure centers of gravity remains obscure to those who must defend those centers of gravity because of the lack of efforts to map information resources and systems across different organizations, sectors of activity, and the nation as whole. Establishment of a U.S. strategic information defense must apply the limited political, financial, and human resources available to the most vulnerable and valuable centers of gravity. The NIPC, JTF-CND, and other DOD organizations recognize the need to conduct assessments of the vulnerability and value of the various U.S. information infrastructures. Their efforts need more support, however, and must be extended into the private/commercial sector.

The federal government should focus its information infrastructure assurance efforts on influencing future technological trajectories as well as reacting to problems presented by current technological processes. Given the accelerated technological change prevalent in advanced information infrastructures, the significance of today's specific security challenges will fade over time, and probably a very short time at that. Designing and implementing stronger technological foundations would reduce future problems across all sectors and centers of gravity. U.S. government agencies responsible for strategic information warfare defense should consider proactive measures to influence forums such as the Internet Engineering Task Force and the World Wide Web Consortium by identifying security concerns related to next-generation technologies, protocols, and standards. Stronger support for outreach and educational efforts, such as those currently pursued by the Software Engineering Institute, can help teach technology producers about how to effectively and efficiently engineer security and reliability features in products and processes. These efforts must strive to deal with emerging technologies, such as Java programming languages and wireless Internet protocols, recognizing that employing expertise related to such technologies will prove expensive and that some technologies will never reach widespread implementation. Despite risks of investing in efforts with uncertain payoffs, however, aggressively pursuing stronger technological foundations should offer substantial overall benefits in strengthening U.S. national capabilities for protecting information infrastructures.

U.S. strategic information warfare defenses should also emphasize improved capabilities to conduct reconstitution and recovery operations after an attack as a means of reducing vulnerability. The continuing emergence of incident response and commercial security services within the private sector should be supported. The federal government should consider providing tax subsidies or rebates and insurance for organizations that engage in such activities. Additionally, the concept of developing National Guard and reserve units with capabilities for information infrastructure testing, protection, and reconstitution should receive increased attention. These capabilities should focus on responses to protect and recover information infrastructures where constrained resources and lack of everyday threats may limit efforts toward self-protection.

Increasing the Difficulty of Adversary Assessments of U.S. Information Infrastructures

As the U.S. government endeavors to understand the nation's degree of reliance on its information infrastructures and increase awareness of threats to specific centers of gravity, it must also protect key findings about U.S. vulnerabilities from adversaries who could use such information to plan and conduct strategic information warfare campaigns. Organizations such as the National Infrastructure Protection Center or the Information Sharing and Analysis Centers would provide prime intelligence targets for adversaries facing the difficult task of discerning critical U.S. vulnerabilities and centers of gravity. Counterintelligence efforts to protect such organizations should therefore receive high priority. Concerns about the risks involved in disclosure of classified information may also impose constraints on U.S. government agencies to provide detailed information about security matters in nongovernmental and international forums. Strengthening interagency coordinating mechanisms as well as those between the public and private sectors will be required to properly weigh the difficult trade-offs involved.

National policies should also foster diversity in the evolution of information infrastructures. The federal government should provide strong support for exploring cost-effective improvements to information infrastructure robustness and redundancy, such as research into artificial software diversity conducted by DARPA, as a component of a forward-looking technology management strategy. A more controversial initiative would involve federal government efforts to add national security to the balance of equities considered in determining whether to pursue antitrust actions to limit monopolistic behavior in the information technology industry. The dominance of limited numbers of underlying technologies in U.S. information infrastructures increases the significance of their vulnerabilities, limiting the intelligence and targeting efforts required of adversaries.

Incidents such as the widespread disruption enabled by known vulnerabilities in Microsoft's Windows NT operating system in March 1998 provide a rationale for considering such a proposal. Yet a confrontational approach with key technology producers, such as Microsoft, might have a counterbalancing drawback in discouraging them from taking more responsibility for producing secure and reliable products.

U.S. national and sectoral indications and warning systems must emphasize capabilities to correlate suspicious activity to discern potentially threatening patterns of activity indicative of preparations for or the initial stages of a digital strategic attack as well as those for identifying the actors involved. Care must be taken that a focus on discerning and combating criminal activity does not overly detract from monitoring the broader range of infrastructures and activity that may be involved in strategic information warfare. The experience and capabilities of the Department of Defense and intelligence community must continue to be applied to broader national indications and warning efforts geared toward strategic digital warfare.

Establishing Credible Retaliatory/Escalatory Responses

Diffuse vulnerabilities and limited resources also require defensive efforts predicated on managing the risk of attacks rather than establishing comprehensive defenses capable of assured protection. During the Cold War, the United States did not establish strong defenses to protect itself against nuclear attack, relying instead on the threat of retaliation to counteract the nuclear threat. Committed adversaries may have the potential to inflict significant disruption against U.S. centers of gravity via digital attacks. Yet the U.S. possesses considerable military strength in a variety of realms. An additional way to manage the risk posed by strategic digital attacks is through deterrence. The U.S. should establish declaratory policy that it will use its varied sources of strength if an adversary launches a strategic information warfare attack.

The ability to retaliate in kind through digital warfare could provide the most credible threat against adversaries with significant information infrastructure–based vulnerabilities. The United States has openly acknowledged the utility of offensive strategic information operations in its military doctrine. U.S. commercial enterprises are also the world's technology leaders, and their products are globally exported and implemented in information infrastructures. If U.S. strategic information warfare forces can sustain the highest level of knowledge about globally deployed information technologies, improvements to defenses at home and ability to respond if provoked should make adversaries more wary of the consequences of launching digital attacks. Such robust U.S. digital warfare capabilities may prove a much less effective threat, however, against state and nonstate actors that have minimal reliance on information infrastructures.

Additionally, the United States should establish a declaratory deterrence policy related to strategic information warfare. The policy should clearly state U.S. willingness to respond to digital attacks with the range of military forces at its disposal against adversaries who threaten the nation's physical and economic security. Such a policy would require the United States to establish the level of provocation that would provoke retaliation. As with past deterrent threats against actors such as the Soviet Union and Iraq, a calculated ambiguity about what constitutes a transgression requiring a response would probably serve best, but setting certain specific boundaries might also prove useful. The United States may wish to declare that information attacks that cause or threaten harm to U.S. citizens or significant economic interests constitute acts of war that will justify use of all possible means in the aggressive pursuit of culprits and use of force in response. Credible deterrent threats will rely on improved capabilities to discern responsibility for digital attacks, as discussed above. Also creation of effective defenses for centers of gravity may provide significant synergies in improving the U.S. chances for success in deterrence through access denial.

Establishing international legal norms regarding the conduct of digital warfare would improve the credibility and legitimacy of retaliatory threats. An initiative to establish these norms would face important limitations, however. Efforts to prohibit the possession of digital warfare capabilities would likely prove futile due to the nature of the technologies involved. Furthermore, trade-offs would exist for the United States in terms of advocating limits on the offensive use of digital warfare capabilities. Yet if the international community believes declarations that the United States suffers from an asymmetric vulnerability because of the degree to which it relies on advanced information infrastructures, international agreements prohibiting the use of digital attacks on nonmilitary information infrastructures could enhance U.S. pursuit of its security. As with post–Cold War arms control efforts focused on WMD, such international regimes must address the potential for nonstate actors to possess and use digital warfare capabilities. For instance, as with the conventions dealing with chemical and biological weapons, agreements could contain provisions requiring state parties to criminalize activity that constitutes digital warfare by nonstate actors. An international convention dealing with strategic digital attacks should place the burden on state governments to undertake internal enforcement efforts and cooperate with international initiatives to eradicate sources of prohibited activity.

Understanding Adversaries

Finally, the United States must improve its understanding of its potential adversaries in the realm of strategic information warfare. Assumptions about the degree of U.S. information infrastructure vulnerability and the diffuse availability of digital warfare means have resulted in assessments that portray a dire situation. Official assessments of the Defense Science Board and the PCCIP have declared that numerous state and nonstate actors have the capability to conduct orchestrated digital attacks against the United States. However, these declarations do not provide judgments regarding the potential strategic utility to these various actors of using such means to wage a conflict. Without such evaluations, threat assessments provide little guidance for defensive efforts about how to gauge realistically the likelihood or scope of attacks based on the capabilities and intent of possible adversaries. U.S. national defense efforts do not involve explicit programs to counter British and French nuclear forces or the Mexican army. Government and commercial organizations based in places like Japan and Israel may prove most capable of developing the capacity to wage digital warfare. However, these possible digital attackers are not likely U.S. adversaries in terms of strategic information warfare.

The difficult question involves assessing the set of actors who may view the emergence of this new strategic warfare means as an opportunity worth the costs of developing it and the risks of retaliation if such means were employed in a conflict. Chapter 2 provided a framework for identifying actors who may find their situation encourages the development of strategic information warfare capabilities. Table 6.1 illustrates three speculative scenarios based on this framework.

Despite the availability of technological tools for digital warfare, the utility of engaging in strategic information warfare for U.S. adversaries will vary based on their political objectives, likely campaign strategies, and willingness to risk retaliation and escalation. Efforts to defend U.S. information infrastructures must understand and respond to such differences. German air defenses inflicted a heavy toll on U.S. bomber forces in World War II by conducting highly concentrated, exposed attacks against limited numbers of targets. The North Vietnamese minimized their center-of-gravity vulnerabilities to sustain a war effort

Table 6.1

Illustrative scenarios for U.S. adversaries' use of strategic information warfare

	Possible U.S. Adversaries		
	China	Iraq/Iran	Drug cartel
Potential political objective	Defend against U.S. response to forceful reunification with Taiwan	Deter U.S. intervention in Persian Gulf	Coerce U.S. into less vigorous drug interdiction
Strategic approach/ Campaign strategy	Disabling attack on military command and control and support infrastructures	Threats to military deployment and civilian targets	Protracted attacks against civilian targets
Enabling conditions			
Offensive advantage?	Depends on degree of preparation to target/disrupt key targets	Likely can access a range of possible targets for attack	Very likely able to hit targets susceptible to single attacks if sustained effect not required
Vulnerable targets?	Depends on DII and critical infrastructure defenses	Can threaten disruption; credibility of sustained damage uncertain	Depends on public reaction to attacks
Risk of response escalation by the U.S.?	In-kind—Likely, but damage likely limited Escalation—Unlikely if damage limited	In-kind—Probably difficult Escalation—likely if deterrence fails	In-kind—Near impossible Escalation may also be difficult
Ease of targeting?	Difficult to precisely disable U.S. forces	Threatening damage plausible, scope difficult to determine	Easiest to hit vulnerable targets when accessible
Ease of command and control?	Relatively easy	Depends on involvement of insiders/mercenaries	Depends on effectiveness of defensive reaction
Adversary tolerance of risks of failure and/or escalation	Low tolerance	Greatest chance for miscalculation	Probably most tolerant

in the face of attack by the world's most powerful air force. The United States developed highly sophisticated, very expensive, centrally controlled offensive deterrent forces in the Cold War to respond to the threat posed by a massive Soviet nuclear attack. Efforts to combat chemical and biological terrorism envisage much more diffuse detection and response capabilities in the hands of U.S. national security, law enforcement, and emergency response agencies.

Likewise, effective U.S. strategic information warfare defenses must also account for differences among potential adversaries. Defenses geared to warning about, defending against, and recovering from a massive cyberstrike designed to inflict maximum damage in minimum time would stress different characteristics than those geared to deal with a protracted, low-intensity strategic information warfare campaign designed to erode political will. State adversaries might be deterred by credible threats of retaliation. Digital defenses to deal with transnationally based nonstate actors might more effectively rely on keeping the level of disruption caused to a minimum through diversity and redundancy while providing for fast recovery of key systems. The thrust of U.S. efforts to develop international cooperation in managing threats posed by strategic information warfare should also involve determinations of the most likely and most threatening adversaries.

Assessing the capacity of various actors to wage strategic information warfare constitutes a mission for national foreign intelligence organizations, not law enforcement agencies. Not all adversaries will have equal abilities to turn technological tools into offensive and defensive organizational capabilities. Effective collaboration between law enforcement and intelligence agencies can help in making critical assessments regarding which actors pose the greatest threats. Efforts to make such capability assessments will likely prove difficult, however, given the widespread availability, dual-use nature, and limited observability of digital warfare tools. Unlike in efforts to characterize strategic air and nuclear warfare capabilities, highly developed U.S. imagery intelligence capabilities will prove of limited utility. Establishing orders of battle consisting of numbers of units and types of equipment will both prove very difficult and fail to describe in a useful way the disruptive or defensive capabilities of strategic information warfare forces. Instead, the U.S. intelligence community must understand how potential adversaries develop processes and human expertise to employ digital warfare tools. Intelligence gathered by spies and recruiting an adversary's insiders will prove more useful in discerning the presence of new digital warfare organizations, doctrine, and operational concepts. The intelligence community must make greater use of information not normally associated with national security concerns to track the implementation of new technologies and human expertise under development by actors of greatest concern. For example, unclassified information about the development of Chinese efforts to mandate reporting of viruses discovered on private networks and the level of expertise achieved by Iranian programmers working for U.S. corporations may prove central to useful assessments of the development of Chinese and Iranian strategic information warfare capabilities. Intelligence organizations will require analysts with new skills to understand the driving forces behind developments in information technology and infrastructures and the nature of the cyberspace environment. Finally, new methodologies will be necessary for characterizing organizational capabilities and learning capabilities of potential adversaries.

In general, U.S. defensive information warfare capabilities should endeavor to improve understanding of political objectives and digital threats posed by potential adversaries. No "digital Pearl Harbor" has yet occurred to cause a public outcry for massive resource investment or government involvement in securing the nations information infrastructures against attack. Our understanding of the value and large-scale vulnerabilities of these centers of gravity remains underdeveloped. U.S. government-led policies to implement strategic information warfare defenses face difficult trade-offs based on the possibility of such defenses impinging on individual rights and economic freedom. In the beginning of the twenty-first century, establishment of U.S. strategic information warfare capabilities should stress a balanced response involving the development of international norms for use of digital warfare and improving the credibility of U.S. responses to deter the broadest possible range of adversaries. Moreover, U.S. policy should encourage cooperative, proactive measures by the private sector to limit vulnerabilities in the technological foundations of information infrastructures to enhance the overall strength of the nation's strategic information warfare defenses.

Looking Back and Reaching Forward

The United States is entering a new century filled with opportunity and fraught with challenges. Dawning awareness of a potential new form of strategic warfare has been accompanied by bold assertions about its significance and how the United States should respond. Yet we have only begun to comprehend the underlying considerations that will shape the nature of strategic information warfare.

Development of strategic information warfare capabilities requires efforts to identify issues and evaluate uncertainties, not react to individual events and accept simple answers. The analysis of strategic information warfare requires a deeper understanding of the linkage between applying digital force and intended political effects. Past efforts to wage strategic warfare have often failed because of inadequate understanding of the ways that applying force related to the political objectives sought rather than because of the shortcomings of technological tools for inflicting pain. Those contemplating strategic information warfare must additionally address the fundamentally new challenges of a man-made cyberspace environment largely developed and operated outside the control of national governments. Given the rapid pace of technological change and organizational complexity posed by this environment, actors who sustain their capacity to learn and adapt will likely prove the most effective strategic information warfare combatants.

Notes

1.   Giulio Douhet, *Command of the Air*, trans. Dino Ferrari (New York: Coward-McCann, 1942), 265.
2.   Frederick W. Kagan, "High Tech: The Future Face of War?—A Debate," *Commentary*, January 1998, 31.

Epilogue

This book provides frameworks for analyzing a phenomenon undergoing rapid evolution. As we begin the twenty-first century, developments continue to illuminate both difficulties and progress in understanding strategic warfare in cyberspace. When I originally envisaged writing an epilogue, the idea was simply to address implications of the Year 2000 (Y2K) computer bug and what we observed during the rollover periods. However, other events have occurred in just a few short months that also deserve mention. I hope this brief section reminds readers how recent developments illustrate themes developed in the work.

The manner in which Y2K problems in computer systems evolved and were dealt with raises questions regarding the knowledge we have about complex information infrastructures. Numerous nations, organizations, and individuals undertook massive efforts to investigate and remedy problems posed by Y2K programming glitches in their software and hardware. Even those who prepared, however, knew that all possible failures could not be foreseen. Systems that had been checked and tested could still have errors in code. New software defects could have been inserted accidentally or maliciously during remediation. Most important, those concerned with avoiding Y2K problems understood that their success depended on how well others fared. Given the interconnections between computer systems and infrastructures reliant on computers, internal efforts might not prevent disaster if the data of business partners was horribly corrupted or the power grid failed. Scenarios for Y2K disruptions included blackouts and social unrest in cities, failures of transportation infrastructures that could prevent delivery of food and other supplies for weeks, and upheavals in the stock markets. Others stressed the possibility of hackers, criminals, and even states using the period of computer disruption to launch attacks and release viruses to create mayhem, steal money, or insert trojan horses for later use.

As a result, significant programs were established to monitor the situation during Year 2000–related dates and manage efforts to handle emergencies, restore service, and protect against digital attacks. The U.S. government led the establishment of an Information Coordination Center to provide global awareness and response. Within the United States, most government agencies and private sector organizations established procedures for Y2K preparations and had personnel ready to welcome the new millennium. As the media increasingly came to focus on the Y2K challenge in the fall of 1999 and into the holiday season, most individuals within the United States also became aware of the potential for disruptions. Choices about how to prepare ranged from buying extra water and stockpiling cash to changing vacation plans to avoid flying on or immediately after January 1.

In the actual event, however, the level of disruption fell far below most expectations. As the world celebrated the arrival of the New Year, those in government and business operations centers around the globe sighed in relief. Problems occurred, but most involved minor systems. For example, cash registers on U.S. military installations in Okinawa, Japan, failed to operate properly due to date-related glitches. A few relatively significant events occurred too.[1] In the United States, much attention focused on the failure of the ground processing facilities of a satellite system to process intelligence data for a period of hours after the rollover. Medical equipment failed in Sweden and Egypt. However, these computer systems (or adequate workarounds) were brought on line very quickly. Noticeably absent were the cascading effects of problems from one system or infrastructure to another. The level of disruption was arguably within the normal bounds of computer- and infrastructure-related problems. In fact, the U.S. House of Representatives held hearings in late January under the title "Year 2000 Computer Problem: Did the World Overreact? What Did We Learn?"

Why did this mismatch of expectation and reality occur? In large measure, the efforts to prepare for the problem were successful. Overall, the U.S. government and private sector spent an estimated $100 billion on Y2K preparations. U.S. federal government outlays were $8.4 billion. The *Washington Post* reported that Citigroup spent $950 million, AT&T $700 million, and General Electric $650 million on Y2K repairs.[2] However, the code remediation and testing efforts were not the only reasons for lack of problems. The nature of the Y2K problem was such that numerous dates presented potential difficulties, not just January 1, 2000. In August 1999, older Global Positioning System hardware and software faced a period of potential date-related failures. September 9, 1999 (9/9/99), and the federal government's 1999 fiscal year end on September 30 also provided rollover periods. Although few systems failed during these periods, practice during these events allowed organizations to check on remediation and code-testing efforts as well as to exercise and fine-tune consequence management procedures. The leap year rollover on 29 February 2000 went even more smoothly than the calendar year rollover, despite earlier concerns that the complexities of date problems for this period had greater potential to cause failures. Earlier Y2K rollover periods provided confidence that internal systems were well prepared and allowed year-end efforts to focus on dealing with external dependencies and linkage into higher-level consequence management networks. These dedicated consequence management efforts also afforded organizations quick recognition of problems and the ability to orchestrate technical and operational solutions before cascading effects could begin. Yet dedicated programs only existed to fix Y2K-related hardware/software vulnerabilities and manage failures during a very short time period. Without the presence of such focused efforts, the ability of the U.S. government and private organizations to deal with other similar challenges to include digital attacks may not succeed as well.

The limited knowledge of regarding interconnectivity within information infrastructures and between these infrastructures and other critical systems such as power, transportation, and emergency services caused even well-prepared nations and organizations to overestimate the potential for widespread disruption. Within the U.S. Air Force, confidence was high that systems would weather Y2K rollovers well but that other U.S. systems might have more significant problems, and it was considered likely that problems overseas would affect U.S. service people and bases.[3] Yet even Russia and China suffered few known difficulties, despite experts' predications that their Y2K preparations had been far too little and made too late. The implications of how different types of information infrastructures fared during Y2K deserve much greater scrutiny as we consider the robustness or fragility of such complex systems. Did other nations prepare better than Western experts had judged? Did less developed information infrastructures mean that lower levels of reliance and interconnection simply reduced the opportunity for significant failures? We must also consider that our limited visibility into the problems occurring around the globe may have hidden some significant weaknesses encountered during Y2K.

As 1999 came to a close, the U.S. government increasingly recognized that efforts to prepare for Y2K also could improve nascent U.S. efforts in the critical infrastructure protection realm. Of particular significance, the Government

Accounting Office issued a report in October entitled *Critical Infrastructure Protection: Comprehensive Strategy Can Draw on Y2K Experiences,* followed by Senate hearings on the same subject.[4] Calls for leveraging Y2K preparations to improve the nation's digital defenses focused on two major areas. First, the Y2K challenge required organizations to undertake an extensive review of their information systems and resources to prioritize code remediation and testing efforts. Systems were categorized as mission critical, mission essential, mission support, and administrative based on assessments of their contribution to organizational mission accomplishment. Later these same system evaluations were used to guide consequence management planning and recovery. Y2K forced organizations to develop new processes and expertise involving technology producers, network and systems operators, and information resource users to assess the value and vulnerabilities of information infrastructures. Moreover, because most assets lacked a single owner/operator, these processes cut across multiple interdependent communities in a way that was unique for most organizations. The resultant mapping of information resource value to organizations and the means to create such knowledge are both valuable in terms of critical infrastructure protection and digital defenses.

Second, the consequence management endeavors conducted across the government and private sector required investing significant resources to establish special coordination centers to fuse reporting on Y2K events. New organizations and facilities with the ability to communicate across a range of infrastructure operators and display information to enable sound decisions about response and reconstitution sprang up in a period of months. People were trained to handle infrastructure incident response and reconstitution. Yet for mapping and consequence management efforts, a sunset clause exists for almost all Y2K efforts. In the spring of 2000, people were reassigned back into their old jobs and funding stopped.

Despite the calls of the Congress and others, only limited efforts are being made transfer valuable resources developed during Y2K work to improve critical infrastructure protection. The conversion of consequence management centers to digital defense facilities has been proposed. The Air Force is considering turning the Y2K Fusion Center developed at Gunter Air Force Base into the core of an Air Force Network Operations and Security Center that will work in conjunction with its Computer Emergency Response Team to conduct its computer network defense. Although the national cyberdefense plan described below touts the important lessons learned through the Y2K experience for understanding and protecting our critical infrastructures, the federal government has dropped plans to transition the ICC personnel and facilities into its cyberdefense efforts. Less tangible resources have received minimal attention. Personnel with unique experience in assessing the value of information infrastructures and managing restoration operations are quickly moving out of Y2K offices as they close. Even more fundamentally, the processes by which organizations mapped the value to the mission of information infrastructure assets will quickly atrophy if not captured and sustained. Without such mapping, our strategic information warfare defenses will revert to a crisis management mode. Each digital attack or new threat will require a new evaluation of risk to the organization affected and debate over appropriate resources to deploy in response.

What implications did our experience with infrastructure robustness during Y2K have for efforts to prepare the United States for strategic warfare in cyberspace? On a hopeful note, the lack of both major disruptions and cascading failures offers some reassurance about the inherent robustness of information infrastructures. As seen in the case of numerous natural disasters and manmade incidents, operators and users of these systems in the United States and elsewhere demonstrated a capacity to keep impacts isolated and to recover relatively quickly. Yet great caution should be used in taking such a lesson too far. Y2K and other events did not accurately represent how a dedicated adversary with thoughtful efforts might attack key infrastructure nodes, cause cascades, and attempt to sustain disruption in the face of reactions by defenders. One point worth considering is that if cascading effects are generally not inherent in information infrastructures, the challenges of effective targeting become even more significant for those attempting to launch strategic digital attacks. Randomly disrupting information systems and networks when little is known about their connectivity and significance to the operation of the rest of the adversary's infrastructure systems may have little effect. As strategic information warriors sort through their challenges, the Y2K experience may indicate that attackers who lack well-developed intelligence and targeting capabilities will have a difficult time achieving significant impacts. More sophisticated adversaries, however, may still pose significant threats given a capacity to discern and affect key infrastructure nodes. Y2K events provide few clear lessons about defense against large-scale, well-structured strategic information warfare attacks.

A final, less publicized area where reality did not meet expectation involves the lack of disruptive digital attacks over the New Year period. For months, information warfare pundits expounded upon how Y2K disruption and possible distraction of defenders could offer opportunities for hackers and others to add to confusion by releasing viruses or conducting denial-of-service attacks. Alternatively, cybercriminals and U.S. adversaries could slip in during the noisy period to map networks and create backdoors in systems to accomplish a wide range of future objectives. The DoD CERT predicted increases in malicious code infections, probing and scanning of networks, and new types of digital attacks involving denial-of-service and e-mail tunneling techniques.[5] The National Infrastructure Protection Center (NIPC) released official warnings that government and civil sector organizations should prepare for such activity. The NIPC, the National CERT at Carnegie Mellon, the Joint Task Force-Computer Network Defense (JTF-CND), the AF Computer Emergency Response Team, and many other cyber-defenders prepared plans and conducted exercises to deal with the potential threat. Y2K planning efforts created tight contacts between U.S. cyberdefense organizations and Y2K consequence management organizations to sort out potential malicious activity from other Y2K disruptions and respond in a coordinated fashion. However, the dearth of specific threat data led most organizations to couch guidance for security preparations as simple reinforcement of generally sound practices. In the event, only limited disruptive activity occurred. The JTF-CND's review of hacker activity during 1999 found that hacking of web pages and virus releases did increase during the New Year period, but only moderately and within the bounds of normal variation in such activity. They tracked only seven viruses specifically designed to execute on December 31. Of particular significance, Department of Defense systems were affected at a much lower rate.[6] The reason for this difference is unclear. Hackers may have felt that DOD systems were better protected and presented a greater risk of discovery and legal prosecution, or they consciously avoided attacks that would degrade the ability of the department to protect its systems and the nation. Again, disconnects between expectation and reality should give us pause regarding the warning capability within U.S. information infrastructure protection, computer network defense, and commercial information security efforts. If those conducting strategic indications and warning for U.S. information infrastructures cry wolf too often, their credibility will be undermined and the attention of those who must implement defensive responses in the government and private sector will diminish.

After the United States had easily surmounted the Y2K challenges, the president issued *Defending America's Cyberspace: National Plan for Information Systems Protection, Version 1.0* in early January.[7] This plan, mandated by PDD-

63, took more than eighteen months to develop. While PDD-63 calls for a plan that addresses both physical and digital protection of U.S. infrastructures, the *Defending America's Cyberspace* plan focuses solely on defense against digital attack, stating that preexisting programs already provide capability against physical threats. Draft versions of the plan were originally intended to address Y2K challenges as well as long-term digital defenses. However, the decision was made to separate the government's preparation efforts for Y2K from the longer-term planning for critical infrastructure protection and delay issuing the plan until it was clear that Y2K had been adequately addressed.

The approach detailed in the plan implements the vision outlined in the PCCIP's *Critical Foundations* and builds on the organizational structure delineated by PDD-63. Three broad objectives are laid out in the plan:

• Prepare and prevent: Those steps necessary to minimize the possibility of a significant and successful attack on our critical information networks and to build an infrastructure that remains effective in the face of such attacks.

• Detect and respond: Those actions required to identify and assess an attack in a timely way, contain the attack, quickly recover from it, and reconstitute affected systems.

• Build strong foundations: The things we must do as a nation to create and nourish the people, organizations, laws, and traditions that will make us better able to prepare and prevent, detect and respond to attacks.

The plan delineates the activities needed to accomplish these objectives across three sectors: the Department of Defense, the rest of the federal government, and the private sector. The underlying logic for this approach was that the DOD has progressed farthest in its critical infrastructure protection efforts and could provide a model upon which to build others. In particular, the plan details how the U.S. Space Command's Joint Task Force-Computer Network Defense provides the department with an organization that can bring together an understanding of infrastructure vulnerabilities and recommendations for remediation, and orchestrate responses to attacks across the diverse set of military services and DoD agencies.[8] The plan goes on to address how the General Services Administration will develop a Federal Intrusion Detection Network (FIDNet) to ensure the digital defense of the federal government. The plan also details how the private sector Information Sharing and Analysis Centers (ISACs) called for by the PCCIP and in PDD-63 would play a similar role in the private sector for each of the major critical infrastructures. While stressing the need for partnership between the private sector and state and local governments through a

"Partnership for Critical Infrastructure Security," the plan acknowledges that these efforts have only started. Significantly, the vision in this regard deals much more with federal government interaction with the private sector than with state and local governments. The plan calls for the NIPC to bring together the efforts of all these centers across the DOD, federal government, and private sector to share incident/attack warning information and lead the U.S. response to digital attacks.

The *Defending America's Cyberspace* plan includes a number of initiatives designed to address major challenges to establishing effective defenses. This plan envisions a significant role for government research and development. The focus of these efforts would be on large-scale intrusion detection, malicious code detection, and infrastructure survivability. The plan directs creation of an Institute for Information Infrastructure Protection (I3P) able to fund information security in shortfall areas where other government or private security R&D may be lacking. The I3P would maintain only a small professional staff and not involve any new "bricks and mortar" facilities. The plan also tries to address the acute shortage of skilled IT personnel, particularly those focused on security. It proposes five programs under the rubric of a Federal Cyber Services (FCS) education and training initiative. The plan calls for the first students to enter a scholarship-for-service program in January 2001. Other programs involve a Center for IT Excellence to help maintain and improve skill levels, an information security awareness curriculum, and a high school–level work and internship initiative. As with any education and training program, the potentially substantial gains in improving the nation's strategic information warfare defenses will take a considerable time to realize.

The administration is also raising federal spending on infrastructure protection. It budgeted $1.74 billion for FY2000, and the FY 2001 budget calls for $2 billion. This almost doubles the $1.14 billion allotted in FY 1998.[9] The majority of this funding, however, goes to the national security sector (57%) and much of the remainder (26%) to R&D initiatives. Although far from fully protected, the DOD and intelligence communities have the nation's most developed cyberdefenses. The FIDNet system would receive only $10 million in FY2001 while federal R&D investments in computer security increase by 32 percent to $606 million in the same year. The heavy emphasis on R&D must also be questioned as relying too much on security tools, without properly acknowledging the fundamental role of people and processes in establishing digital defenses. It should be hoped that R&D efforts will focus on the concepts and tools to provide large-scale information infrastructure survivability as envisioned by DARPA rather than stressing enhancements of technologies such as firewalls. The I3P is slated to receive $50 million to prime the pump for the institute's startup until private sector funding begins. The willingness of the private sector to become involved, however, has yet to be proven. Efforts at improving human resources are also underfunded. The Federal Cyber Services Training and Education initiative will receive only $25 million, enough to begin the multiple programs envisaged but well shy of the resources necessary to establish the deep well of expertise needed for a large-scale infrastructure protection and defense against strategic digital attack.

Despite the broad approach detailed in *Defending America's Cyberspace*, the United States still lacks a comprehensive plan for establishing a strategic information warfare defense. Simply relying on infrastructure operators and users, organized around the sectors outlined in PDD-63, to protect their own assets remains a critical fault, as laid out here in chapter 5. The plan mostly side-steps the issues of how to adequately motivate technology producers to create secure foundations for the nation's infrastructures. Nowhere in this plan or in ongoing PDD-63 implementation efforts by the DOD or others are provisions made for identifying and addressing the critical distributed vulnerability of tech-nologies (such as signaling systems) embedded throughout the information infra-structure that no operator or user actually owns but that are relied upon by many. At best, the plan envisions that government R&D efforts and the Institute for Information Infrastructure Protection will lead to some progress in assisting the private sector in addressing these concerns. However, the recent record of government–private sector inability to cooperate and rancor over encryption con-trols should provoke healthy skepticism about the gains such limited efforts will achieve.

At an even more fundamental level, the United States has yet to step up to the challenges of strategic information warfare. As with the PCCIP and PDD-63, the *Defending America's Cyberspace* approach endeavors to address chal-lenges ranging from accidents to individual heckers to national security threats in the cyber realm. In actuality, the plans focus on establishing organizational capabilities to understand vulnerabilities, react to isolated incidents, and reme-diate limited problems. The plans do not provide a foundation for waging cam-paigns in cyberspace against organized digital attacks by a committed adversary over an extended period of time. The approach calls for a highly cooperative mode of DOD, federal government, and private sector interaction in preparing and reacting to digital attacks. However, the plan lacks necessary details of how the National Command Authorities would direct a defense of the United States against a strategic information warfare attack. Conspicuously lacking is the role of state and local governments and their relationship to federal and private sector efforts. Although it provides examples of efforts such as the New Mexico Critical Infrastructure Assurance Council, the plan lacks any details regarding incentives for state and local governments to invest in digital defenses or how these efforts would be orchestrated in a strategic information warfare campaign. The political and economic costs of preparing the nation for such a conflict remain too high and the threat remains sufficiently vague for the plan to directly address the difficult trade-offs involved in establishing defenses against large-scale, orchestrated digital attacks.

We have yet to engage in strategic information warfare, but over time the technological potential for such conflicts becomes ever more clear. A series of denial-of-service attacks against major companies in the e-commerce sector also occurred in early 2000. These attacks both reinforced the growing potential for strategic warfare in cyberspace and illuminate the challenges of establishing effective defenses against digital attacks. From February 6 to 8, a relatively new method of overloading targeted computers was used to disrupt the activities of numerous web sites. The major companies affected, dates, and downtimes are listed below:[10]

• Yahoo	6 February	3 hours
• Amazon	7 February	3 hours, 45 minutes
• Buy.com	7 February	4 hours
• Ebay	7 February	5 hours
• CNN.com	7 February	3 hours, 30 minutes
• E*Trade	8 February	2 hours, 45 minutes
• ZDNet	8 February	3 hours, 15 minutes

Numerous other companies were hit during this flurry of attacks. The attacks against e-commerce web sites stopped on February 8 and major incidents have not occurred as of this writing.

The new technique known as a distributed denial-of-service (DDOS) attack was briefly mentioned in chapter 5. The DDOS technique can be combined with other well-known tools such as Back Orfice 2000. The DDOS technique involves attackers placing variants of DDOS software tools such as TRINOO on unsecured computers connected to the Internet. This allows the attacker to access and control the machine. The attacker can then provide commands to the "zombie" computers where the tools have been placed and direct these machines to continuously send messages to a targeted site. As a result, the targeted computer is overloaded and no one can access the site. Targeted sites must discern which computer connections are causing the overload and divert or block traffic from those sites. Tracing DDOS attacks back to the source is extremely difficult because the attack orginator does not even have to be online once a command to the "zombie" computers is issued.

The National Computer Emergency Response team had issued warnings in the fall of 1999; incidents involving the DDOS technique had been occurring against Internet Relay Chat sites and universities since at least August. The NIPC eventually issued a warning about the DDOS technique in late December.[11] Protection against such denial-of-service attacks is particularly difficult. Most tools designed to stop intrusions do not work when the attack simply overloads the target system. Firewalls can help by preventing access from "zombie" computers, but the source IP address information necessary to program these defenses may only be available once the attack has occurred and is already causing disruption.

The purpose of the February attacks remains unknown. Because they do not seem to have been launched for known political objectives or as part of a sustained campaign, they should not be classified as examples of information warfare. Some have suggested that the attacks may be an instance of anti–e-commerce "hacktivism" that shades into the boundaries of strategic warfare in cyberspace as set down in chapter 1. The attackers have not acknowledged responsibility or declared objectives, however, unlike earlier instances of hacktivism in support of the Zapitistas and other causes discussed in chapter 2. Others posit that attackers may be engaged in corporate competition waged by e-commerce firms to erode consumer confidence in competitors. This scenario is highly unlikely, however, as the risks of retaliation and loss of public standing if the perpetrators were discovered would be serious, and such attacks may simply lower general confidence in e-commerce. Interestingly, the federal government (as during Y2K) remained basically untouched by this round of attacks. The most likely explanation remains that the attacks were conducted by hackers, either as individuals or in groups, for the normal sorts of motivations. Front-page headlines and responses from the president certainly would produce bragging rights for those involved as long as they remain free.

As with most digital attacks, discerning the long-term impact of these events proves difficult. Most estimates revolve around economic damage: According to Forrester Research, Amazon.com would lose $4.5 million and Yahoo $1.6 million in revenues if their web sites were shut down for twenty-four hours.[12] Another potential impact was on consumer confidence in the particular companies involved or in the e-commerce sector as a whole. Although the companies hit by the DDOS attacks did suffer minor drops in stock prices the week of the attack, the losses were as short-lived as the attacks themselves. The NASDAQ market subsequently surged to record highs in February and March. The attacks seemed to have little effect on consumer or business confidence in the information technology sector. The impact of a sustained campaign of attacks against e-commerce, however, has yet to be tested. Interesting to note, the stock prices of firms in the information security sector such as Internet Security Services and Axent rose significantly in the aftermath of these attacks.

The federal government reacted vigorously. On February 7, in the midst of the attacks, Attorney General Janet Reno pledged that the FBI was "committed in every way possible to tracking down those responsible." In the succeeding weeks, FBI agents seized computers and conducted interviews with well-known hackers. As of late May, however, the government had not positively identified any attackers. Whether the high level of attention and resources devoted to tracking down the attackers has played a role in deterring further DDOS activity is unknown. Those responsible for critical infrastructure protection used the events as an opportunity to highlight the threats to the nation's well-being and the need to invest more heavily in security measures. President Clinton declared, "We know we have to keep cyberspace open and free. We have to make, at the same time, computer networks more secure and resilient, and we have to do more to protect privacy and civil liberties."[13] The information technology security firm iDefense ran full-page "I TOLD YOU SO" ads in the *Washington Post* and *New York Times* after the February attacks, highlighting how they had warned clients of this threat during the previous fall. Most technology industry leaders remained quiet in public, however, possibly fearing that by speaking out they would highlight themselves to the unknown attackers.

The fallout from the event involved the highest levels of the administration. The White House sponsored a meeting on February 15. The president and senior officials from the Departments of Justice, Defense, and Commerce and the National Security Council met with information technology leaders from firms such as Intel, Sun Systems, MCI Worldcom, Microsoft, 3Com, EDS, E*Trade, and

Ebay, and security experts from academe and the CERT community. Although wide agreement existed that providing increased security on the Internet poses a significant problem that requires a government-industry partnership, no firm commitments by private sector representatives were made. Press accounts after the meeting made clear that fundamental tensions continue to thwart progress toward fundamental improvements in strategic digital defenses. Business leaders and heads of privacy advocacy groups stressed that security improvements to the Internet's infrastructure and management must not overly sacrifice cost, service, or personal rights. The challenge for the critical infrastructure protection community remains to devise processes and develop tools that contribute to progress on multiple fronts of increased security, reliability, and privacy.

Some key lessons for strategic information warfare can be learned. The DDOS technique provides an illustration of the difficulties of defending against digital attacks. The CERT community had provided notification of the problems and offered fix procedures months before the February attacks. Other organizations had already suffered from this type of digital attack. Yet major e-commerce firms were unprepared. Multiple possible explanations exist. Those responsible for defending these sites may have not been tied to the CERT community and NIPC/FBI warning mechanisms. If the warnings were heard, those responsible for operating these web sites may have decided that DDOS vulnerability was not important enough to warrant attention. Alternatively, the means for mitigating risks may have proved too complex for those on the front lines of protecting e-commerce sites, or the cost in time and money too burdensome. Those responsible for U.S. strategic information warfare defenses must make the effort to understand the relevant combination of these factors. As we enter the twenty-first century, most organizations reliant on advanced information infrastructures are on their own in providing security. National infrastructure protection efforts cannot address underlying dynamics that make the foundations of cyberspace weak without a complete understanding of private sector concerns, capabilities, and constraints.

As we begin the new millennium, our understanding and ability to conduct strategic information warfare will increase, but more slowly than most anticipate. The United States must continue to expand its knowledge in areas such as coupling within information infrastructures and leverage efforts related to critical infrastructure protection, notably our Y2K preparations. We continue to have conflicting indications about the significance of strategic information warfare. Y2K events seem to indicate that causing cascades in infrastructures may prove difficult, but the DDOS attacks in February demonstrated how technology continues to put disruptive means in the hands of individuals. High levels of government and media concern attended Y2K and later the DDOS attacks, but the impact of these events was emphemeral.

The federal government continues to plan for protection of the nation's information infrastructures, but resource investment remains light. Therefore effective defensive strategic information warfare capabilities remain a long way off. In FY 2001, the Clinton administration requested $2 billion for the entire nation's cyberdefense. Crucial questions remain unanswered regarding the proper level of investment and path of development for our strategic information warfare capabilities. The PCCIP was correct in stating that we do not yet face a national emergency. The level of threat remains unproven, and a crash program to build defenses against large-scale digital attack could result in counterproductive policies and poor resource allocation given our lack of understanding. We must invest intelligently and avoid a temptation to overemphasize technology relative to human expertise and organizational capacity.

As I bring this book to an end, my final recommendation must revolve around the requirement to learn and adapt quickly if we are to effectively wage strategic war in cyberspace. Dealing with change usually poses a formidable task for nations and institutions. Once more, the challenge confronts us.

Notes

1. The information regarding these and other Y2K incidents can be found in Statement of Harris N. Miller, President, U.S. House of Representatives, Joint Hearing of Subcommittee on Government Management, Information, and Technology and Subcommittee on Technology, Hearings on "Year 2000 Computer Problem: Did the World Overreact? What Did We Learn?" 106th Congress, 2nd Session, 27 January 1996; and Rajiv Chandrasekaran, "How Did It All Go Right?: Officials, Experts Happily Seek Answers to Y2K Riddle," *Washington Post*, A1 and A8, 2 January 2000.

2. All figures from Rajiv Chandrasekaran, "The Bug That Didn't Bite," *Washington Post*, A1 and 25, 1 January 2000.

3. Based on the author's role in U.S. Air Force Y2K consequence management planning. In particular, these conclusions were the consensus of more than 100 attendees at a major Air Force consequence management planning conference held in June 1999.

4. Government Accounting Office, *Critical Infrastructure Protection: Comprehensive Strategy Can Draw on Y2K Experiences* (Washington, DC: GAO/AIMD-00-D1, October 1999).

5. Elizabeth A. Siemers, "DoD Computer Security Tips for Y2K Preparation" *IAnewsletter* 3, no. 2 (Fall 1999): 22–23.

6. Assessments of Y2K Hacker Activity from Joint Task Force-Computer Network Defense Briefing, "First Generation CND Activity," January 2000.

7. White House, *Defending America's Cyberspace: National Plan for Information Systems Protection, Version 1.0*, January 2000, available at ⟨www.ciao.gov⟩, accessed January 2000.

8. The plan also addresses the National Security Incident Response Center (NSIRC) within the National Security Agency as providing assistance to the JTF-CND, FIDNet, and the NIPC in isolating, containing, and resolving attacks on national security systems. The activities of the NSIRC are addressed on p. 49.

9. Figures used are from *Defending America's Cyberspace*, Annex C, 120–127, and presentation by Guy Copeland, Vice President, Information Infrastructure Advisory Program and Special Assistant to the CEO, Computer Sciences Corporation, "Government/Industry Partnerships," at American Institute of Engineers Conference, April 2000 in Tyson's Corner, Virginia.

10. Figures from Deborah Salomon, "Electronic Hit and Run," *USA Today*, A1–2, 10 February 2000.

11. Statement of Douglas G. Perritt, Deputy Director of the National Information Protection Center, during his presentation at Jane's Information Group conference on "Information Warfare and Y2K," 11 May 2000 in Arlington, Virginia.

12. Solomon, A1.

13. John Schwartz and Ariana Cha, "Clinton Pledges to Help Industry Fight Hackers," *Washington Post*, E1, 16 February 2000.

Acronyms

AAA	anti-aircraft artillery
AAF	Army Air Force
ABC	American-British-Canadian
ABM	Anti-Ballistic Missile (ABM) treaty
ACTS	Air Corps Tactical School
AEF	American Expeditionary Forces
AFCC	Air Force Combat Command
AFCERT	Air Force Computer Emergency Response Team
AFDD	Air Force Doctrine Document
AFIWC	Air Force Information Warfare Center
ASD/C31	Assistant Secretary of Defense for Command, Control Communications, and Intelligence
ASIM	Automated Security Incident Measurement (ASIM) system
ASSIST	Automated Systems Security Incident Support Team
ATM	asynchronous transfer mode
AT&T	American Telephone and Telegraph Corporation
AWPD	Air War Plans Division (AWPD)
BNCCs	Base Network Control Centers
CAT scans	computerized axial tomography
CBO	Combined Bomber Offensive
C2	command and control
CEOs	chief executive officers
CERT/CC	Computer Emergency Response Team/Coordination Center
CERT	Computer Emergency Response Team
CIA	Central Intelligence Agency
CIAO	Critical Infrastructure Assurance Office
CICG	Critical Infrastructure Coordination Group
C4I	command, control, communications, computers, and intelligence
CIRT	computer incident response teams
CISS	Center for Information Systems Security
CITAC	Computer Investigations and Threat Assessment Center

CIWG	Critical Infrastructure Working Group
CMET	Countermeasures Engineering Team
CND	computer network defense
COA	Committee of Operations Analysts
COTS	commercial off-the-shelf
CSI/FBI	Computer Security Institute/Federal Bureau of Investigation
C2W	Command and Control Warfare
DARPA	Defense Advanced Research Projects Agency
DDOS	distributed denial of service
DIA	Defense Intelligence Agency
DII	Defense information infrastructure
DISA	Defense Information Systems Agency
DOD	Department of Defense
DOS	denial-of-service
DOT	Department of Transportation
DSB	Defense Science Board
EES	Encryption Escrow Standard
EFF	Electronic Frontier Foundation
EMP	Electromagnetic pulse
EPIC	Electronic Privacy Information Center
FAA	Federal Aviation Administration
FBI	Federal Bureau of Investigation
FCC	Federal Communications Commission
FEMA	Federal Emergency Management Agency
FERC	Federal Energy Regulatory Commission
FIDAC	Federal Intrusion Detection Analysis Center
FIDNET	Federal Intrusion Detection Network
FIRST	Forum of Incident Response Teams
FIWC	Fleet Information Warfare Center
FSTs	Field Support Teams
GAO	General Accounting Office
GCCS	Global Command and Control System
GCSS	Global Combat Support System
GDP	gross domestic product
GETS	Government Emergency Telephone System
GHQ	General Headquarters
GII	global information infrastructure
GOSC	Global Network Operations and Security Center
GPS	Global Positioning System
GSA	General Services Administration
GSSP	Generally Accepted Systems Security Practices
html	hypertext markup language

IATAC	Information Assurance Technology Analysis Center
ICBMs	intercontinental ballistic missiles
IGOs	intergovernmental organizations
IITF	Information Infrastructure Task Force
INFOSEC	information systems security
INMARSAT	International Marine Satellite Consortium
INTELSAT	International Telecommunications Satellite Consortium
IO	information operations
IPTF	Infrastructure Protection Task Force
IRA	Irish Republican Army
ISAC	information sharing and analysis centers
ISDN	integrated services digital networks
ISPs	Internet service providers
ISSG	Information Security Services Group
IT	information technology
ITU	International Telecommunications Union
IW	information warfare
IWFs	information warfare flights
IWS	Information Warfare Squadron
JC2WC	Joint Command and Control Warfare Center
JFT-CND	Joint Task Force-Computer Network Defense
JSC	Joint Security Commission
LAN	local area network
MEII	minimum essential information infrastructure
MIRV	multiple independent reentry vehicle (MIRV) systems
MLS	multilevel secure (MLS) systems
MOP	Memorandum of Policy
MRI	magnetic resonance imaging
NASA	National Air and Space Agency
NATO	North Atlantic Treaty Organization
NAVCIRT	Navy Computer Incident Response Team
NCC	National Coordinating Center
NCIC	National Crime Information Center
NCS	National Communications System
NDP	National Defense Panel
NGI	Next Generation Internet
NIAC	National Infrastructure Assurance Council
NIE	national intelligence estimate
NII	National Information Infrastructure
NIPC	National Infrastructure Protection Center
NIRC	Network Interoperability and Reliability Council
NIST	National Institute of Standards and Technology

NLETS	National Law Enforcement Telecommunications Systems
NMCI	Navy and Marine Corps Intranet
NMCI	Navy Marine Corps Intranet
NORAD	North American Air Defense Command
NOSCs	Network Operations and Security Centers
NRC	National Research Council
NSA	National Security Agency
NSC	National Security Council
NS/EP	national security and emergency preparedness
NSIE	Network Security Information Exchange
NSIRC	National Security Incident Response Center
NSTAC	National Security Telecommunications Advisory Committee
NSTISSC	National Security Telecommunications and Information Systems Security Committee
NTMS	National Telecommunications Management Structure
OASIS	Open Access Same-Time Information System
OECD	Organization for Economic Cooperation and Development
OMB	Office of Management and Budget
ONA	Open network architecture
OSI	Open systems interconnection
OSTP	Office of Science and Technology Policy
PCCIP	Presidential Commission on Critical Infrastructure Protection
PDD	Presidential Decision Directive
PGMs	precision-guided munitions
PGP	Pretty Good Privacy (PGP) algorithm
PSN	public switched network
PSTNs	public-switched telecommunications networks
PTT	post, telegraph, and telephone services
RAF	Royal Air Force
R&D	research and development
RMA	revolution in military affairs
ROSCs	Regional Security and Operations Centers
RVWG	Reliability and Vulnerability Working Group
SALT	Strategic Arms Limitation Treaty
SATAN	Security Administrator's Tool for Analyzing Networks
SCADA	supervisory control and data acquisition (SCADA) systems
SDI	Strategic Defense Initiative
SONET	synchronous optical network
SPB	Security Policy Board
START	Strategic Arms Reduction Talks
TCP/IP	transmission control protocol/Internet protocol
TTP	trusted third-party

USSBS	U.S. Strategic Bombing Survey
USSPACECOM	U.S. Space Command
USSTAF	U.S. Strategic Air Forces in Europe
VSATs	Very Small Aperture Terminals
WMD	weapons of mass destruction
Y2K	Year 2000

Index